Principles of Business: Leadership

Principles of Business: Leadership

Edited by
Frederic B. Mayo, Ph.D., M.B.A.
New York University

SALEM PRESS

A Division of EBSCO Information Services, Inc.
Ipswich, Massachusetts

GREY HOUSE PUBLISHING

Cover photo: iStock

Copyright © 2019, by Salem Press, A Division of EBSCO Information Services, Inc., and Grey House Publishing, Inc.

All rights reserved. No part of this work may be used or reproduced in any manner whatsoever or transmitted in any form or by any means, electronic or mechanical, including photocopy, recording, or any information storage and retrieval system, without written permission from the copyright owner.

For information contact Grey House Publishing/Salem Press, 4919 Route 22, PO Box 56, Amenia, NY 12501

Principles of Business: Leadership, published by Grey House Publishing, Inc., Amenia, NY, under exclusive license from EBSCO Information Services, Inc.

∞ *The paper used in these volumes conforms to the American National Standard for Permanence of Paper for Printed Library Materials, Z39.48 1992 (R2009).*

Publisher's Cataloging-In-Publication Data
(Prepared by The Donohue Group, Inc.)

Names: Mayo, Frederic B., editor.
Title: Principles of Business: Leadership / edited by Frederic B. Mayo, Ph.D., M.B.A., New York University.
Other Titles: Leadership
Description: [First edition]. | Ipswich, Massachusetts : Salem Press, a division of EBSCO Information Services, Inc. ; Amenia, NY : Grey House Publishing, [2019] | Includes bibliographical references and index.
Identifiers: ISBN 9781642652871 (hardcover)
Subjects: LCSH: Leadership.
Classification: LCC HD57.7 .P75 2019 | DDC 658.4092--dc23

PRINTED IN THE UNITED STATES OF AMERICA

Contents

Publisher's Note vii
Introduction ix
List of Contributors xiii

Authentic Leadership 1

Best Practices 5
Building Human Assets 6
Business, Ethics & Society 13
Business Strategy and Policy 19
Business Succession Planning 24

Charismatic Authority 30
Coaching 35
Collective Bargaining 37
Communications in the Workplace 42
Communications, Networking
  and Security 48
Comparative Management 53
Conflict Management 58
Corporate Communication 63
Corporate Social Responsibility 64
Corporate Strategy 71
Creativity 77
Crisis Management 81
Critical Thinking in the
  Management of Technology 88
Cross-Cultural Relations 94

Decision Making 100
Decision Making Under Uncertainty 105
Delegation 110
Directing and Managing Volunteers 114
Diversity in te Workplace 118

Emotional Intelligence 125
Employee Engagement 127
Employee Monitoring 131
Employee Retention 133
Employee Value Proposition 138
Employee Well-being and
  Organizational Support 142
Ethical Responsibilities of Business 146
Executive Compensation 152
Executive Leadership 157

Expectancy theory 163
External Business Communications 164

Flat Organizational Structure 169
Followership 173

Gender & Management 175
Glass Ceiling 181

Hierarchical Organizational Structure 184
Human Resource Economics 188
Human Resource Issues in
  High-Performing Organizations 193
Human Resources for the Emerging Firm 198

Impression Management 204
Inclusive Leadership 206
Innovation 210
Innovation Leadership 211

Job Performance 216
Job Satisfaction 217
Johari Window 219

Leader Member Exchange 221
Leadership 222
Leadership and Motivation 226

Management Competencies 233
Management of Human Resources 239
Managerial Leadership 246
Managing Conflict within
  Organizations through Negotiations 251
Managing in a Turnaround Environment 258
Managing the Process of Innovation 263
Motivation, Productivity, and
  Change Management 270

Negotiations 276
Nonprofit Leadership and Management 281

Organization Design 288
Organization Development 293
Organizational Behavior 299
Organizational Consulting 304

v

Contents

Organizational Culture................... 310
Organizational Effectiveness............. 312
Organizational Learning.................. 314
Organizational Life Cycle................ 318

Participative Leadership................. 322
People Skills............................ 324
Performance Appraisal.................... 326
Professional Ethics...................... 332
Project Management....................... 334
Public Relations......................... 339

Quality Management....................... 344

Race, Ethnicity, and Public Policy....... 346
Religious Accommodation
   in the Workplace...................... 352

Servant Leadership....................... 356
Service Operations Management............ 360
Sexual Harassment........................ 365
Shared Leadership........................ 370
Strategic Thinking....................... 371

Talent Management........................ 374
Team Management.......................... 375
Teams & Team Building.................... 381
Time Management.......................... 387
Toxic Leadership......................... 389
Training Analysis........................ 390
Trait Leadership......................... 394
Transactional Leadership................. 399
Transformational Change.................. 400
Transformational Leadership.............. 402
Types of Business Organizations.......... 406

Virtual and Traditional Teams............ 411

Women in the Workforce................... 413
Workplace Harassment..................... 415

Zero Sum Game............................ 420

Glossary................................. 425
Index.................................... 433

Publisher's Note

Leadership is the seventh volume in our *Principles of Business* series. Recently published volumes in this series include *Marketing, Management, Finance, Entrepreneurship, Economics, and Accounting. Globalization* will follow. These resources are intended to introduce students and researchers to the fundamentals of business topics using easy-to-understand language. We hope that these books will become a go-to resource for interested readers seeking understanding of these important and far-reaching business topics.

The entries in this volume are arranged in an A to Z order, from "Authentic Leadership" to "Zero Sum Game," making it easy to find the topic of interest. Each entry includes the following:

- *Abstract* giving a brief introduction to the topic;
- Clear, concise *presentation of the topic*, including a discussion of applications and issues;
- *Bibliography* of works discussed in the article;
- Helpful list of *further reading*.

Added features include numerous illustrations and helpful diagrams of relevant topics. The back matter in *Principles of Business: Leadership* contains a thorough and valuable glossary of terms as well as an index.

Salem Press extends its appreciation to all involved in the development and production of this work. The signed entries have all been written by scholars and experts in business. Without these expert contributions, a project of this nature would not be possible. A full list of contributor's names follows this Note. *Principles of Business: Leadership* is available in print and as an e-book.

Introduction

Leadership is both a fascinating concept and a continual challenge to those whose job it is to be a leader. There have been many studies conducted on leadership and shelves and shelves of books written about the topic. In addition, many successful leaders, coaches, and managers have published their personal stories with advice about how to follow their example. If you are interested in reading more about leadership, then this volume is for you. The book contains over 100 articles covering a wide range of topics in the field of leadership, and is arranged alphabetically for your convenience.

Before you begin, though, some background information might be helpful in understanding this complex and fascinating topic.

Management versus Leadership

For many years, scholars and executives have argued the similarities and differences between management and leadership. In small organizations, they are often very similar and in large organizations, leaders and C-suite executives usually carry both leadership and managerial responsibilities.

One way to distinguish between the two concepts involves recognizing that leaders set the vision and mission of the organization, create the culture, and select priorities, while managers make the organization run effectively, ensure that polices and priorities are honored, and build employee skills and talents. However, the challenges a leader faces are often similar to the challenges of managers – ensuring the effective operation of the company or organization, marketing the products and services, making sure the right people are in the right jobs, and keeping everyone focused on the larger picture of what the company or organization is trying to do. Of course, there is always the challenge of monitoring the finances and other resources needed for the effective operation of the company.

Successful leaders pay attention to establishing a vision for the company or organization and promulgating it consistently and continuously. They also establish and honor a set of values for the company or organization. Sometimes, a leader has a chance to develop the mission, vision, and values. Other times, he or she inherits them in an ongoing organization.

Forces Affecting Current Leaders

Many current trends affect the challenges that leaders face in maintaining their companies' effectiveness. Some of them have been powerful trends for some time. Others are more recent. These trends can be broadly classified into four categories.

- Cultural changes
- Generational changes
- International changes
- Technological changes

The cultural changes that the world has undergone over the past thirty years have drastically altered the function of leadership, making it more complex. The attention to civil rights, the encouragement of diversity, and the need to incorporate women and other groups of individuals into companies have provided new opportunities for leaders as they alter their tried and true methods of leading groups and organizations. Diversity now includes the consideration and celebration of a range of issues that leaders must recognize; in addition, they are responsible for ensuring that employees and followers understand and honor differences among people. Currently, the term "diversity" covers issues of race, ethnicity, gender and gender identity, sexual orientation, age, generation, religion and religious beliefs, disability, socioeconomic status, educational background, values, working style, learning style, veteran status, and life experience. Not only are these issues protected by legislation such as the Pregnancy Discrimination Act, the Americans with Disability Act, the Civil Rights Act, and the Equal Pay Act, but the contemporary culture in the United States now demands the recognition and celebration of diversity.

Generational changes have altered the ways in which leaders can engage followers in their enterprises. Whether it involves working with volunteers, leading a project team at work, managing a department, or leading a large corporation, leaders often confront members of generations that differ significantly from theirs. Millennials (people born roughly between 1980 and 1995) and members of Generation Z (those born after 1995) have different attitudes toward work, careers, and work-life balance than most baby boomers (those born between 1946 and 1964) and Generation X (born between 1965 and 1980). As the differences in generations in the workplace have changed the ways in which leaders have to operate, many authors have offered suggestions for how to lead these different generations. A recent Deloitte Touche study suggested that leaders who are baby boomers need to recognize differences among generations in the areas of communication style, patterns of communication, priorities for work-life balance, attitudes toward change, and learning methods (Buckley 2015). The suggestions for leaders included:

- Mix and match project teams
- Let newer or youngers professionals lead teams
- Work off site and break up common routines
- Customize your style to individuals

International changes involve the increasing globalization of business, in both the profit-making and nonprofit sectors. The increasing number of businesses that use vendors from other countries and sell products and services to other countries has changed the way business is conducted and brought a more international focus to leaders who have to pay attention to local issues in countries where their companies do business. This focus—in which the leader serves as both spokesperson and manager of international affairs—widens the scope for leadership in both the profit-making and nonprofit sectors.

Technological changes include the development of new hardware, software, and systems that enable the processing and analysis of massive amounts of data and the need to protect that data from hacking and other forms of interception. The prevalence of computers, tablets, and other electronic devices has changed both the method and the speed with which people communicate; the increase in social media platforms has also made information widely available, sometimes more accessible to employees than to managers and leaders. Leaders need to recognize that these changes have impacts, which include:

- Efficiency and increased productivity
- Increased collaboration
- Improved cost management
- Heightened level of security
- Better employee experiences (Dukes 2014)

BECOMING A LEADER
There have been many books on how to become a better leader. One of the most focused and useful, published in 1988, is *The Leadership Challenge* by James Kouzes and Barry Posner who conducted extensive research on practices essential to effective leadership; they found that the five most important practices included:

1. Model the way
2. Inspire a shared vision
3. Challenge the process
4. Enable others to act
5. Encourage the heart

When leaders practiced these behaviors, the authors found, they empowered their followers and made significant improvements in their organizations.

Two years later, Steven Covey published his book *The 7 Habits of Highly Effective People*, which provided leaders with personal advice on which behaviors were important to their effectiveness. These ideas—still valid today—include specific behaviors for all individuals, not just leaders. However, they have been helpful and used widely in many leadership development programs. The seven habits include:

1. Be proactive
2. Begin with the end in mind
3. Put first things first
4. Think win-win
5. Seek first to understand and then to be understood
6. Synergize
7. Sharpen the saw

More recently, the research on emotional intelligence—publicized by Daniel Goleman—has pointed out the value of introspection and the importance of interpersonal skills. Leaders who have learned to identify and master their personal values and traits are not overwhelmed by them. Another aspect of emotional intelligence involves learning to listen, understand, and empathize. According to Goleman, there are five aspects or skills involved in emotional intelligence:

1. Self-awareness
2. Self regulation

3. Internal motivation
4. Empathy
5. Social skills

Although obviously not developed exclusively with leaders in mind, these ideas are important for people who do want to become leaders or to improve their leadership skills and strategies.

Conclusion

This introduction has explained some of the more important aspects of leadership and introduced various perspectives and approaches toward leadership covered in this volume. It remains a fascinating topic and one that everyone involved in working with others can benefit from studying. These resources are here for your benefit. Dig into them and enjoy the adventure!

Bibliography

Bass, Bernard M., *A New Paradigm of Leadership: an Inquiry into Transformational Leadership.* Alexandria, VA: U.S. Army Research Institute for the Behavioral and Social Sciences, 1996.

Bass, Bernard M., *Bass & Stogdill's Handbook of Leadership: Theory, Research, and Managerial Applications.* New York: Free Press, 1990.

Beck, John D. W., *The Leader's Window: Mastering the Four Styles of Leadership to Build High-Performing Teams.* New York: Wiley, 2003.

Bennis, Warren G., *On Becoming a Leader* Reading, MA: Addison-Wesley, 1994.

Bennis, Warren G., *Beyond Leadership: Balancing Economics, Ethics, and Ecology.* Cambridge, MA: Blackwell Business, 1994.

Bennis, Warren G., *An Invented Life: Reflections on Leadership and Change.* Reading, MA: Addison-Wesley Pub. Co., 1993.

Bennis, Warren G., *Why Leaders Can't Lead: the Unconscious Conspiracy Continues.* San Francisco: Jossey-Bass Publishers, 1989.

Block, Peter, *The Empowered Manager: Positive Political Skills at Work.* San Francisco: Jossey-Bass, 1991.

Buckley, Patricia, Peter Viechnicki, and Akrur Baru. "Millennials: Generational differences reexamined Issues by the Numbers" Deloitte Touche, October 2015. https://www2.deloitte.com/insights/us/en/economy/issues-by-the-numbers/understanding-millennials-generational-differences.html

Chrislip, David D., *Collaborative Leadership: How Citizens and Civic Leaders Can Make a Difference.* San Francisco, CA: Jossey-Bass, 1994.

Clark, Kenneth E., *Choosing to Lead.* Greensboro, NC: Leadership Press Ltd., 1994.

Collins, Jim and Jerry I, Porras. *Built to Last: Successful Habits of Visionary Companies (Good to Great Book 2)* New York: HarperBusiness, 2004.

Collins, Jim. *Good to Great, Good to Great: Why Some Companies Make the Leap...And Others Don't.* HarperBusiness, 2001.

Collins, Jim. *How The Mighty Fall: And Why Some Companies Never Give In (Good to Great)* HarperCollins 2009.

Covey, Stephen R., *Principle-Centered Leadership.* New York: Simon & Schuster, 1992.

Covey, Stephen R., *Ethics, the Heart of Leadership.* Westport, CT: Praeger, 2004

Covey, Stephen R., *The Seven Habits of Highly Effective People.* New York: Simon and Schuster, 1990.

Dukes, Elizabeth. "Technology in the Workplace: 5 Ways Technology has Changed the Modern Workplace" iooffice, 2014. https://www.iofficecorp.com/blog/4-ways-technology-has-changed-the-modern-workplace

Greenleaf, Robert K., *Servant Leadership: a Journey Into the Nature of Legitimate Power and Greatness.* New York: Paulist Press, 2002.

Greenleaf, Robert K., *The Power of Servant-Leadership: Essays.* San Francisco: Berrett-Koehler Publishers, 1998.

De Pree, Max. *Leading Without Power: Finding Hope in Serving Community.* San Francisco: Jossey-Bass, 1997.

Dreher, Diane. *The Tao of Personal Leadership.* New York: Harper Business, 1996.

Fairholm, Gilbert W., *Values Leadership: Toward a New Philosophy of Leadership.* New York: Praeger, 1991.

Gardner, Howard. *Leading Minds: an Anatomy of Leadership.* New York, NY: Basic Books, 1995.

Glacel, Barbara, *Light Bulbs for Leaders: a Guide Book for Team Learning.* New York: John Wiley, 1996.

Goleman, Daniel. "Primal Leadership," Cambridge: Harvard Business School Press, 2002

Goleman, Daniel. *Working with Emotional Intelligence.* New York: Bantam Books, 1998

Hackman, Michael Z., *Leadership: a Communication Perspective.* Prospect Heights, IL: Waveland Press, 1996.

Hughes, Richard L. *The Leader's Companion: Insights on Leadership Through the Ages.* New York: Free Press, 1995.

Kouzes, James and Barry Z. Posner, *The Leadership Challenge.* New York: Wiley, 1987.

Moore. J.F., *The Death of Competition: Leadership and Strategy in the Age of Business Ecosystems.* New York: Harper Business, 1996.

Nair, Keshavan. *A Higher Standard of Leadership: Lessons From the Life of Gandhi.* San Francisco: Berrett-Koehler, 1994.

Oakley, Ed. *Enlightened Leadership: Getting to the Heart of Change.* New York: Simon & Schuster, 1994.

Roberts, Wess and Bill Ross, *Make It So: Leadership Lessons From Star Trek, the Next Generation.* New York: Simon and Schuster, 1995.

Senge, Peter M., *The Fifth Discipline: The Art and Practice of a Learning Organization.* New York: Doubleday, 1990.

Spears, Larry, *Insights on Leadership: Service, Stewardship, Spirit, and Servant-Leadership.* New York: Wiley, 1998.

Toffler, Alvin, *Powershift: Knowledge, Wealth, and Violence at the Edge of the 21st Century.* New York: Bantam Books, 1990.

Vroom, Victor, *Leadership and Decision-Making.* Pittsburgh, PA: University of Pittsburgh Press, 1973.

Frederic B. Mayo, Ph.D., M.B.A.

List of Contributors

Michael Auerbach, M.A.
New Hampshire Dental Society

Seth M. Azria, J.D.
Independent Scholar

John D. Benson, M.B.A.
Independent Scholar

Tyler Biscontini
Northeast Editing

Courtney Brogle
Independent Scholar

Josephine Campbell
Independent Scholar

Kehley Coviello
Independent Scholar

Edwin D. Davison, J.D., M.B.A.
Independent Scholar

Joseph Dewey, Ph.D.
University of Pittsburgh

Frances Duffy, M.B.A.
Independent Scholar

Mark Dziak
Independent Scholar

Marlanda English, Ph.D.
Capella University

Michael Erbschloe, M.A.
Webster University

Simone I. Flynn, Ph.D.
National Physician's Alliance

John Mark Froiland, Ph.D.
Purdue University

Julia Gilstein
New England Journal of Medicine Group

Marie Gould, Ph.D.
American Public University

Laurence Grimm
University of Illinois at Chicago

Allison Hahn, Ph.D.
Baruch College

Gavin D.J. Harper, Ph.D., M.B.A.
University of Birmingham

Steven R. Hoagland
Belmont College

Patricia Hoffman-Miller, Ph.D.
Prairie View A&M University

Douglas R. Jordan
Independent Scholar

Bill Kte'pi
Independent Scholar

Sharon M. LeMaster
Independent Scholar

Anna Lowe
Independent Scholar

Laura L. Lundin, M.A.
Independent Scholar

Michael Mazzei, J.D.
Ladder Capital

Trudy Mercadal, Ph.D.
Independent Scholar

Shari Parsons Miller
Accenture

List of Contributors

Steven Nakisher, Ph.D.
Independent Scholar

Elena Popan, Ph.D.
Texas Tech University

Elizabeth R. Purdy, Ph.D.
Independent Scholar

Lindsay Rohland
Penn Foster

Carolyn Sprague, M.L.S.
Ex Libris Group

Vanessa A. Tetteh, Ph.D.
Dexterity Consult

Richa S. Tiwary, Ph.D., M.L.S.
Independent Scholar

Ruth A. Wienclaw, Ph.D.
Independent Scholar

Jeremy Wick
Independent Scholar

Scott Zimmer, M.L.S., M.S., J.D.
Alliant University

AUTHENTIC LEADERSHIP

ABSTRACT

Authentic leadership is a concept that began to emerge in its modern form in the 1960s but its theoretical origins can be traced as far back as ancient Greece. Fundamentally, authentic leadership characterizes an individual who combines two qualities. The first is a deep level of understanding of one's own internal emotional and psychological state, an awareness of one's values, beliefs, and priorities (Bellin 2012). The second is a commitment to behaving in ways consistent with these values, beliefs, and priorities. The result is a leader able to inspire trust, projecting an image such that "what you see is what you get."

OVERVIEW

In addition to the traits of self-awareness and self-consistency, a number of different factors have been identified as contributing to the development of authentic leadership. One of these traits is the presence of frequent and effective self-monitoring. This work requires an individual to make it a personal priority to take time to reflect on his or her behavior and assess whether that behavior seems to be in line with the individual's espoused ideals. Only when a mechanism for self-monitoring exists is it possible to embody a commitment to self-consistency (Godino 2013).

Another factor that supports authentic leadership is optimism. The role of leaders is often to decide what goal an organization will pursue, from among a variety of options. Because managers of organizations do not normally plan to fail, they generally pursue goals that they believe they can attain. Determining an organizational goal requires not only that a leader have a realistic understanding of the capability of the organization and its members, but also a degree of faith in the organization—a belief that through hard work and careful planning, things will work out. This quality is at the heart of optimism, and it is essential for a leader to project such optimism, because without it there is not much chance that people in the organization will feel inspired to work to their utmost ability. After all, why should staff members do their best if they get the sense from the boss that the project has little chance of succeeding? Furthermore, optimism is difficult to fake, which is unsurprising given its connection with authentic leadership (Watson and Johnson 2013). If an organization's workers believe that leaders are only feigning optimism in order to lead them into working harder, then the long-term consequences for the organization will usually be worse than if no such deception had been attempted.

Closely related to the quality of optimism, and equally important for authentic leadership, is a leader's sense of hope. It can be difficult to determine the difference between optimism and hope because there is a large amount of overlap between the two, and in everyday language, people tend to use the words interchangeably. Organizational psychologists distinguish optimism from hope as follows: Optimism is the ability to acknowledge one's own contributions to positive events while also being able to interpret negative events as being partially caused by factors outside of one's control. Hope is defined as an outlook that allows one to develop goals and to perceive how those goals can be achieved.

Naturally, it would be difficult for leaders to function without either optimism or hope, because without optimism they would blame themselves for setbacks and attribute successes to temporary good luck, while the absence of hope would prevent them from even conceiving of goals to strive for, much less the means of achieving them. On the other hand, leaders armed with optimism and hope are prepared to embark on a journey with their organization, giving and receiving support to staff members along

A businesswoman addresses her followers (Photo Courtesy of Asamblea Nacional del Ecuador)

the way. The third major component underlying authentic leadership's practice of self-awareness and self-consistency is resiliency. Resiliency is the ability to recover one's sense of equilibrium after a stressful event (Woldeyes 2014). Examples of stressful events include a severe illness, the loss of a job, a divorce, or even a promotion that entails additional responsibility. When such events occur, a natural response is to experience stress and discomfort. Some people have difficulty moving beyond those feelings, while others adapt within a reasonable time frame to the new circumstances and return to the level of functionality they enjoyed before the stress-inducing event. Those in the latter category are said to be more resilient (Ladkin and Spiller 2013).

Resiliency is needed for authentic leadership because any organization or individual can expect to experience setbacks while working toward a goal; the only cases in which this does not happen are those in which the actor has chosen a goal so simple to achieve that it is virtually without significance. When all of these components are present, authentic leadership is possible. Resiliency, optimism, and hope are required in order for a leader to function effectively—the leader must be able to conceive of worthwhile goals and the means of achieving them, while having the internal strength to avoid being deterred by setbacks and doubts. If these qualities are in place and the leader is able to exercise self-awareness and self-consistency, then possibilities of transformation can open up at the individual and organizational levels. This is because of the power of authentic leadership to build and maintain trust throughout the organization.

Authentic leadership's main benefit is that it encourages people to have faith in one another and to bring down the protective barriers that most people surround themselves with on a daily basis. By lowering these defenses, new and more powerful connections become possible, and previously isolated members of the organization are able to share their knowledge and experience with one another.

APPLICATIONS

Some research into the nature and efficacy of authentic leadership has highlighted the fact that it tends to be highly context-dependent. In other words, authentic leadership is believed to grow out of an individual's collected life experiences; it is difficult, if not impossible, to make someone an authentic leader. Instead, authentic leadership is a quality that emerges on its own although some argue that it can be helped along the way by deliberately engaging in self-reflective activities. The root of authentic leadership is the leader's particular combination of life experiences and ethical perspectives, which together produce a set of core beliefs and values (Auerbach 2012). If the leader is able to stay in touch with those beliefs and values while continuing his or her work, then authentic leadership can be achieved. For many leaders, however, it appears that the ability to remain authentic is grounded in the context with which they are most familiar. For example, if one were to take a highly successful corporate executive who is adept at leading his or her team authentically to achieve greater profits while maintaining a high level of quality and place him in a position with a nonprofit organization that has as its mission the provision of in-home assistance to the elderly, there would likely be some difficulty experienced by all concerned. The executive would likely still be able to lead the nonprofit, but doing so in an authentic manner would present some challenges (Redmond 2009) because the executive has a fully developed set of values and priorities that pertain specifically to the profit-oriented, corporate sphere of activity. He or she is so thoroughly familiar with this realm that he or she is able to fulfill his role authentically with very little conscious effort. However, that lack of familiarity with the demands of the nonprofit leadership role may lead to struggles to understand its system of values; she may only be able to enact them authentically after she has spent sufficient time to absorb and embrace them.

Another perspective on how to develop authentic leaders puts the process in a more positive light. Instead of being discouraged by the somewhat ineffable nature of authentic leadership, authentic leadership can be seen as an emergent property that develops out of how one responds to one's life circumstances, which means that everyone has the potential to become an authentic leader. If authentic leadership were an inborn trait, then only a lucky few would have access to it (Mundahl 2013). In the same way that many scientists have come to believe that an individual's characteristics are determined by a combination of genetics and environment—nature and nurture—many in the field of authentic leadership research affirm that people from all walks of life have access to the elements necessary for developing into an authentic leader. While there is little doubt that this view tends to gloss over many of the significant obstacles people face—discrimination, poverty, physical or mental illness, and so forth—the idea everyone is equal in opportunity to develop authentic leadership is largely agrees with Western ideas of meritocracy, rugged individualism, and pulling oneself up by one's bootstraps. It is important to keep in mind that while the benefits of authentic leadership are theoretically attainable by everyone, for most people, they will remain elusive without a concerted effort being made to develop the qualities upon which authentic leadership relies.

Viewpoints
There is widespread agreement that self-awareness is the most difficult authentic leadership quality to attain, as it requires a level of honesty and introspection that most people do not have either time or courage to pursue because most people spend a large portion of their waking hours trying to fit in with groups of other people, whether at work, at home, at school, or elsewhere. Fitting in usually requires some degree of compromise on the part of each person, and over time these compromises tend to accumulate, bringing one further and further away from one's core identity. Rediscovering this core identity can be a time-consuming and even painful process, as it forces the recollection of the many compromises one has made, some unwillingly. The more challenges a person faces in her day-to-day life—financial, relational, emotional, etc.—the more difficult it will be to devote the time and energy necessary to developing the self-awareness that is required for authentic leadership (Neider and Schriesheim 2014).

Another concept frequently associated with authentic leadership is transparency, an absence of subterfuge and an affirmative effort to be as open as possible with one's team and with other actors in the environment. By definition, one cannot practice authentic leadership if one feels the need to conceal one's motives or behavior because the very act of concealment is contrary to the nature of authenticity (Heminsley 2013). When leaders strive for transparency, they make it a priority to communicate to their constituents not simply the nature of a decision and its immediate consequences but also the reasons for taking the decision, particularly if the matter at hand is a sensitive one. For example, when a company finds it necessary to lay off some of its employees in order to stay in business, the situation is extremely difficult for those who are being let go and for those who remain but fear that they might be next. The anxiety that surrounds the issue makes it easy for people to look for someone to blame and try to avoid being the target of blame. For this reason, many leaders facing the situation simply announce the cuts and terminate the discussion, hoping to put an end to unrest. Usually this approach has the opposite effect, as it increases feelings of anger, mistrust, and fear. An authentic leader would likely take a different approach, by including with the announcement an explanation of what factors contributed to the decision. To continue the example, it might be that the company's online sales have taken off while its brick-and-mortar sales have steadily declined, leading management to the conclusion that if a cut must be made, it should be from the retail locations the firm operates. This information may not make it any easier for the employees who are affected to cope with the dire news, but it does make it more difficult for people to interpret the reductions as attributable to malice or incompetence. The result is that people are more likely to have a sense that they are being dealt with fairly, even if the situation remains unpleasant.

It should be remembered, however, that transparency is not always as simple as it sounds, and sometimes it is virtually impossible to implement. Situations that involve confidential information or legal liability may sometimes prevent leaders from being as transparent as they might wish to be, although even in these situations, it may be possible to at least share a description of the constraints preventing disclosure.

BIBLIOGRAPHY

Auerbach, Susan. *School Leadership for Authentic Family and Community Parnerships: Research Perspectives for Transforming Practice*. New York: Routledge, 2012.

Bellin, Walter. *Self Mastery and Mindful Leadership: How to Maximise Your Capacity for Authentic and Effective Leadership*. Edgecliff, Australia: Jane Curry, 2012.

Godino, Pilar. *The Business Alchemist: A Road Map to Authentic and Inspirational Leadership*. Australia: Hay House, 2013.

Heminsley, Tana. *Awaken Your Authentic Leadership: Lead with Inner Clarity and Purpose*. Vancouver, Canada: Authentic Leadership Global, 2013.

Kehan, Xiong, Lin Weipeng, Jenny C. Li, and Wang Lei. "Employee Trust in Supervisors and Affective Commitment: The Moderating Role of Authentic Leadership. *Psychological Reports* 117, no. 3 (2016): 829–48. Web. 21 Dec. 2016.

Ladkin, Donna, and Chellie Spiller. *Authentic Leadership: Clashes, Convergences and Coalescences*. Cheltenham, UK: Edward Elgar, 2013.

Mundahl, Steven. *The Alchemy of Authentic Leadership*. Bloomington, IN: Balboa Press, 2013.

Neider, Linda L., and Chester A. Schriesheim. *Advances in Authentic and Ethical Leadership*. Charlotte, NC: Information Age, 2014.

Redmond, Kathleen. *Leadership Engagement: Leading Through Authentic Character to Attract, Retain, and Energize*. Newmarket, Canada: Centre for Character Leadership, 2009.

Watson, Lemuel, and Joshua M. Johnson. *Authentic Leadership: An Engaged Discussion of LGBTQ Work as Culturally Relevant*. Charlotte: Information Age, 2013.

Woldeyes, Billene S. *Transformative Spaces: Enabling Authentic Female Leadership through Self Transformation—the Case of AWiB*. Wien: Lit Verlag, 2014.

SUGGESTED READING

Baron, Louis, and Élise Parent. "Development Authentic Leadership within a Training Context: Three Phenomena Supporting the Individual Development Process." *Journal of Leadership & Organizational Studies* 22, no. 1 (2015): 37–53. Web. 22 Mar. 2015.

Berkovich, Izhak. "Between Person and Person: Dialogical Pedagogy in Authentic Leadership Development." *Academy of Management Learning & Education* 13, no. 2 (2014): 245–64. Web. 22 Mar. 2015.

Bird, James, Wang Chuang, Jim Watson, and Louise Murray. "Teacher and Principal Perceptions of Authentic Leadership: Implications for Trust, Engagement, and Intention to Return." *Journal of School Leadership* 22, no. 2 (2012): 425–61. Web. 22 March. 2015.

Braun, Susanne, and Lars Homuf. Authentic Leadership and Followers' Cheating Behavior—A Laboratory Experiment from a Self-Concept Maintenance Perspective. Palgrave Macmillan, 2017.

Duigan, Patrick A. "Authenticity in Educational Leadership: History, Ideal, Reality." *Journal of Educational Administration* 52, no. 2 (2014): 152–72. Web. 22 Mar. 2015.

Gatling, Anthony, and William F. Harrah. "The Authentic Leadership Qualities of Business Coaches and Its Impact on Coaching Performance." *International Journal of Evidence Based Coaching & Mentoring* 12, no. 1 (2014): 27–46. Web. 22 Mar. 2015.

Juanmei, Zhou, Ma Yueru, Cheng Weibo, and Xia Bing. "Mediating Role of Employee Emotions in the Relationship between Authentic Leadership and Employee Innovations." *Social Behavior & Personality: An International Journal* 42, no. 8 (2014): 1267–78. Web. 22 Mar. 2015.

Pathak, Manavi. "Authenticity: The New Leadership Standard." *Human Capital* 20, no. 5 (2016): 52–53. Web. 21 Dec. 2016.

Wilson, Michael. "Critical Reflection on Authentic Leadership and School Leader Development from a Virtue Ethical Perspective." *Educational Review* 66, no. 4 (2014): 482–96. Web. 22 Mar. 2015.

Woolley, Lydia, Arran Caza, and Lester Levy. "Authentic Leadership and Follower Development: Psychological Capital, Positive Work Climate, and Gender." *Journal of Leadership & Organizational Studies* 18, no. 4 (2011): 438–48. Web. 22 Mar. 2015.

Scott Zimmer, M.L.S., M.S., J.D.

B

BEST PRACTICES

ABSTRACT

Best practices refer to a set of methods with a proven track record of success for accomplishing certain tasks. Best practices are applied in a variety of professions, including the agricultural and farming industry, environmental management, manufacturing, business, education, government, nonprofit organizations, and teaching. They are also used in laboratory science in an effort to apply key lessons from others' successes; avoid areas prone to mistakes or inefficiencies; and to standardize processes across the field.

OVERVIEW

Best practices have been used in a variety of instances over history, arising when someone observes a technique that improves a process in one area and applies it to a process in another area, making the technique a standardized procedure. Many consulting firms capitalize on advising businesses and organizations on implementing best industry practices for their respective fields, which include, but are not limited to, health and human services, government organizations, and marketing. Additionally, consultants advise a standardized process for developing and implementing best practices. This method includes the following steps:

1. Develop realistic expectations of what needs to be achieved.
2. Analyze smart practices used in other areas to see how than can be applied.
3. Observe the best practices.
4. Describe possible vulnerabilities that can occur when implementing the new process or practices.
5. Determine if the new practice will meet the expectations and needs of the area where it will be applied.

Best practices have also been extensively used in the leadership development and managerial methodologies in the field of human resources. They provide practical examples and techniques for dealing with human capital management issues, such as writing performance appraisals, dealing with insubordinate employees, delegating responsibilities or tasks, or enhancing overall leadership style and team management. Best practices can also be applied to interview techniques and résumé-writing skills.

Best practices are also applied in the field of education, providing guidelines for standardizing classroom

Employees discuss how best to proceed (Photo courtesy of Melina Masnatta)

techniques in distance learning classrooms, online learning, and mobile learning environments. For example, common best practices used in education include: encouraging interaction between students and teachers, using active learning techniques, emphasizing task deadlines, respecting diversity of talents and ways of learning, clearly communicating task expectations and parameters, developing collaboration among students, and providing prompt feedback and evaluation through open dialogue. These best practices have been applied to all levels of educational instruction—from elementary school classrooms to higher education environments—because of direct impact they have had on creating a successful learning environment for students.

Best practices have also been applied to standardized healthcare services in doctors' offices and hospitals worldwide, with healthcare professionals routinely sharing best practices and techniques through professional conferences, research collaboration, and publication of research in academic and medical journals. Development and implementation of best practices combined with advancing technology continues to foster cutting-edge improvements in the field of medicine.

BIBLIOGRAPHY

Baber, Angela. "Using Community Colleges to Build a STEM-Skilled Workforce." *National Governors Association Center for Best Practices*. National Governors Association. Web. 19 July 2011.

Bogan, Christopher E., and Michael J. English. *Benchmarking for Best Practices: Winning through Innovative Adaptation*. New York: McGraw, 1994.

Drummond, Tom. "A Brief Summary of the Best Practices in College Teaching." University of North Carolina–Charlotte, Center for Teaching and Learning, Division of Academic Affairs. U of North Carolina–Charlotte. Web. 1995.

Frederick, Peter J. "Student Involvement: Active Learning in Large Classes." In *Teaching Large Classes Well*, edited by M. G. Weimer. San Francisco: Jossey-Bass, 1987.

Laura L. Lundin, M.A.

BUILDING HUMAN ASSETS

ABSTRACT

Since human assets account for a significant proportion of company expenditure and company value, a company's real value must incorporate the value of its human assets. Through compensation management, investments, and by appealing to the minds and hearts of employees, a company's human assets can be built to become a significant source of competitive advantage. However, this is not without risk, as there are uncertainties posed by the dynamic nature of companies, markets, and employees. Carefully planned human resource initiatives can help reduce these uncertainties.

OVERVIEW

Every company has both hard assets and soft assets. Hard assets, also known as physical or tangible assets, include items such as buildings and machinery, and soft assets include intangible assets like human beings. Business success requires a combination of hard and soft assets. Human assets consist of a company's employees and their value in terms of the quantity and quality of their knowledge, skills, abilities, competencies, talents, experience, and attitudes. Another term for human assets is human capital. The concept of human assets or human capital initially originated in the field of economics, where it was first used to explain the economic growth of countries. This concept has only in recent decades entered the field of management, thanks to the realization that a greater proportion of the added value created by corporate entities is not dependent on physical assets alone, but is increasingly dependent on other assets. In fact, the added value created by corporate entities is increasingly dependent on intangible assets.

Companies make investments in human assets. They buy human assets by hiring employees, and they make or build human assets through training, job experience, and other strategies. A company's human assets are its main sources of competencies and capabilities, and they constitute a valuable strategic asset which is necessary for creating and sustaining competitive advantage. As income generating assets, employees are a form of organizational wealth, with a potential for impacting shareholder value. The actions and professionalism of employees also have an effect on customer perceptions of a company. Given that human assets account for a significant proportion of company expenditure, it is surprising that managers tend to know less about their human assets than they do about other assets of their company.

Human Resource Accounting
Due to the vast significance of human assets, coupled with the recognition that human resources are assets with value, recommendations have been made for human assets to be incorporated into company accounts, a move which gives investors and all stakeholders a better valuation of a company. In response to these recommendations, academics and practitioners in the fields of economics, accounting, human resource management and general management, have been striving to define, evaluate and measure human assets. Their efforts have led to the creation of a subfield known as human asset accounting or human resource accounting, which is concerned with determining the value of the human resources employed in an organization, to that organization.

Apart from gaining a realistic appraisal of their corporate worth, companies that are able to place value on their human assets enjoy a myriad of additional benefits, including the measurement of the return on investments they make on their employees, and improved decision making. In addition, valuing human assets helps companies plan their future employment needs and also helps them to generate objective information for making projections for training and management development activities. Once they know the value of their human assets, human resource managers will be able to enlighten managers about the real value of lost skills, knowledge, and expertise. Both companies and investors will be able to understand the factors that drive corporate performance; and companies will be able to identify future sources of value in a competitive business environment. They will also be able to understand how investing in people creates value.

Methods for Determining Human Asset Value
There are several means of determining the value of human assets to an organization. These include the following:

- **Economic value:** This approach defines the value of human assets as the present value of that portion of the future earnings of the company, attributed to human resources. Economic value can be calculated through the use of the Discounted Cash Flow model, which tries to predict the future earnings employees will generate, by discounting these cash flows to the present.
- **Opportunity costs:** In this approach, the value of human assets is defined as their value (or worth) in their best alternative use.
- **Value to the undertaking**: When a company has several cost centers (be they plants, divisions, or departments) competing for a particular employee, the employee is assigned to the highest bidder, and the bid price denotes the value of the employee to the company and to the cost center.
- **Total contribution:** This approach measures the performance of the company, and the contribution of its human assets to this performance.
- **Historical costs:** This approach considers the costs of acquiring, developing, maintaining, and utilizing personnel. Personnel expenses are treated as investments and the costs are treated as costs of long term assets, spread over the expected useful period of the investments. If an employee leaves the company before this period is over, the balance when he or she leaves is considered to be a loss.
- **Replacement costs:** This concept involves calculating the estimated cost to the firm for replacing employees with other people of equivalent talents and experience. Like the historical cost approach, this approach also considers the costs of acquiring, developing, maintaining, and utilizing the replacement employees.

In the area of human assets, as with all other assets, value determination must be an ongoing activity, since the value of people can appreciate or depreciate due to several factors: first, people tend to move constantly within their company, as well as between companies; and second, the gain from employees is subject to change, as business conditions, technology, company conditions, and individuals undergo change.

FURTHER INSIGHTS

As they face the challenge of increasing global competition, human resource professionals must ensure that their company's human assets are adding as much value as possible to their products and services. Human resources professionals must build on their human assets by selectively hiring and attracting employees, and motivating them to stay with the company. Job satisfaction, a key factor for motivating employees to stay in a company, has five dimensions: compensation, supervision, coworkers, promotion, and the work itself.

Building Human Assets through Compensation Management

Pay satisfaction tends to decrease when employees perceive inequity or injustice of pay distribution within a company. Therefore, some employees may be more affected by pay differentials within a company than by pay differentials in the labor market. This reality creates opportunities for a company to increase job satisfaction through internal changes rather than by competing with other companies. Often, employees will not compare their pay across companies unless they encounter problems with their employers.

Companies are more likely to generate profit from their employees if they practice shared ownership initiatives such as profit sharing, group incentives, and performance-based compensation. Shared ownership helps to bind employees to their company, and it also encourages employees to align their individual goals with those of the company, since their personal rewards will be linked with company performance.

Levels of Shared Ownership

There are three levels of shared ownership, the first being at the organizational level. Shared ownership at this level can be affected through means such as stock ownership and profit sharing. The effectiveness of shared ownership at the organizational level is reduced in cases where there are low amounts of profit to be shared; where employees do not have much of a say in company matters, and; where employees can easily cash in their stock. Therefore, shared ownership at the organizational level works best when it is focused on senior, influential employees who have more of a say in decision making, and who are less likely to dispose of their stock, since any such move might affect overall stock value.

At the group level, shared ownership is appropriate in cases where production is team based rather than individual based, and it should be linked to group level performance measurement. The smaller the group, the more effective the incentive. Shared ownership incentives at the individual level work best when there is ample information in the company to justify giving individual incentives to those whose effort will greatly influence company performance. In these cases, the individual rewards must be highly valued by the recipients.

Building Human Assets through Investments

Companies typically make four types of investments in order to build their stock of human assets. These are:

1. Direct expenditures on education
2. Direct expenditures on health
3. Direct expenditures on internal migration
4. On-the-job training

Employees require ample knowledge to enable them to direct their skills appropriately; and they cannot apply those skills if they are not in good health. Poor health leads to unavailability and undesirable attitudes, causing poor job performance. Employees tend to be impacted strongly by the manner in which management satisfies their knowledge, skill and health needs. On-the-job training is an important success factor: Extensive training has been found to be a key characteristic of the most profitable companies. One may talk of two types of training: general training, whose costs are typically borne by employees and firm specific training, whose costs are borne by a company or shared between the employee and the employer The sharing of training costs is tantamount to an investment in the company on the part of an employee, and it often leads to increased job security for the employee.

Building Human Assets through the Minds & Hearts of Employees

Nonfinancial dimensions of job satisfaction can be put in place to create a congenial work climate that can be as satisfying as monetary compensation, with low need for maintenance, and low cost. Companies with the best human asset management practices share the following characteristics:

- **A belief in value for competitive advantage:** All employees try to ensure that every task adds value in achieving competitive advantage, for instance, by making sure that the work environments portray strongly shared values and as such, promote individual integration and greater employee commitment.
- **Long-term commitment to a core strategy:** Everyone in the company understands that success depends on long-term commitment to a core strategy. Any change introduced by management is considered very carefully before being implemented.
- **Strong culture:** A strong, widely shared corporate culture and company systems are closely linked and managed for consistency and efficiency in the company.
- **Constant and extensive two-way communication:** Management believes that people have the ability to deal with all types of information, both good and bad. All available media are used and all vital information—including financial and performance information—is shared with employees and other stakeholders.
- **Partnering with stakeholders:** There is recognition of the need to partner with stakeholders, both within and outside the company; and there is a need to involve them in decision making as well as in the design and implementation of new programs.
- **A high level of collaboration:** All functions and sections in the company enjoy a high level of collaboration and involvement, and they receive support to collaborate on new product development.
- **Innovation and risk:** Such companies are not afraid to take risks or innovate or even to make drastic changes—they realize that innovation and risk-taking are absolutely necessary in a volatile marketplace.
- **Commitment to continuous improvement:** Such companies have their systems and processes set up to actively encourage and gather new ideas from all sources.
- **Building human assets through other means:** There are many other means by which companies can build their human assets, such as through interpersonal relations; a team-based work environment;

the nature of the work itself, and; promotion among others. Interpersonal relationships play a large role in job satisfaction, since job satisfaction increases with employees' satisfaction with their coworkers. Companies can also decentralize to self-managed teams, thus creating a team-based work environment which can be maintained and nurtured through social activities.

Professionals, especially, have their job satisfaction closely linked to the nature of their work. Companies should therefore endeavor to motivate their professionals through creative job design. Promotion is another tool for enhancing job satisfaction. Companies can structure the career paths of individual employees, offering job assignments as rewards. Other nonfinancial sources of job satisfaction include employment security, and reduced status distinctions and barriers.

Making Human Assets a Source of Competitive Advantage

Companies cannot gain sustainable advantage simply by having talented employees. In order to have sustained competitive advantage, apart from using the typical financial, strategic, and technological means, companies must work on establishing their organizational capability, which is the ability to generate commitment from the human assets in the organization. Without commitment, there will be high employee turnover.

When companies set up systems of human resource practice that are difficult to replicate or imitate by their competitors, their employees are less likely to leave. They can seek to achieve this goal through their corporate culture, work climate, congenial interpersonal relations, and teamwork.

Creating Firm Specific Employees

Companies should equip their human assets with a stock of special skills, knowledge, routines, and/or personal relationships that are unique to their organization, thus creating firm specific employees. According to Kulkarni and Fiet (2007), a company and its specialized employees are mutually dependent on each other, and one of the ways in which a company can foster this mutual dependence, is through training. Companies that make firm specific investments in training should share training costs and benefits with their employees. Employees who have received such firm specific training would lose out if their job contracts were terminated, since their firm specific skills would be less valuable to another company. As such, employees endowed with firm specificity have less incentive to leave their employers, and likewise, companies have less incentive to let them go. This situation applies mostly to senior management: Offstein and Gnyawali (2006) proposes that the greater the capacity of the human assets in the top echelon, the greater the competitive advantage of that company.

General Human Assets
General human assets—those employees with general skills and knowledge—on the other hand, have the potential for high turnover, since their skills can be easily traded on competitive labor markets. Fortunately, though, even for general human assets, there are some means of alleviating turnover problems, such as increasing pay, making work challenging, and offering firm specific compensation. Firm specific knowledge can be enhanced by creating unique equipment, processes, teams, and/or communication. Firm specific promotion opportunities should also be put in place. Shared governance is also a valuable initiative since it increases employee participation and information sharing, thus increasing job satisfaction. Such strategies help to reduce—though not completely—the risk of employee turnover.

ISSUES

Risk & Risk Reduction
There are risks associated with building and investing in human assets. Like all other assets, their future value or future return can be uncertain. Companies, the market, and employees themselves, are all potential sources of uncertainties in the area of human assets. Through human resources practices, companies can help reduce the costs and/or reduce the uncertainties of human assets.

Uncertainty of Returns
The value of human assets can depreciate or appreciate and so too can the value they generate for the company. These types of human asset risks are termed uncertainties of returns. When faced by high levels of uncertainties of returns, companies can invest more in growth and learning opportunities, for instance; training for new skills and improved learning abilities. They can also increase selectivity when recruiting employees with broad-based skills; and they can also introduce skill-based pay. Such interventions will help lower and manage the risks of obsolete skills, as well as the demand for future skills.

Uncertainty of Human Assets
Companies can be responsible for causing uncertainties of human assets. For instance, a change in strategy can lead to changes in job responsibilities, and it can also lead to sudden demands for skills not possessed by employees. Uncertainties of combination are created by the risk of employees being wrongly matched to their job responsibilities, due to variations in demand and supply.

Uncertainty of Combination
Uncertainties of combination can be reduced through job rotation and team-based work. Through job rotation, employees develop multiple and flexible skills and behaviors by being rotated among different types of jobs. Team-based work achieves similar results by ensuring that employees move among temporary teams formed for particular projects or jobs.

Uncertainty of Cost
Uncertainties of costs are concerned with variations in the ratio of total expenditure on human assets to company revenues, caused by changes in company performance and remuneration. In such cases, variable compensation plans, performance-based incentive plans, and defined contribution pension plans, may be used to prevent and restore imbalances in the ratio of total expenditure on human assets to company revenues.

Market Changes
The market can also cause changes in business conditions, customer needs and competitor actions, which can lead to fluctuations in the supply and demand of suitable potential employees from both within and outside the company. External changes can also lead to skills obsolescence, as employees face a lack of present or future skills.

Employee Nature

Uncertainties are brought about by the nature of employees themselves, since a company does not have control over individuals. Unlike other assets, human assets have control over themselves. Individual employees make behavioral choices which are sometimes unpredictable. Employees may decrease their performance, making them less fitting for a particular job, thus causing a loss in productivity.

Uncertainty of Volume

The risk and reality of employee turnover leads to uncertainties of volume, counteracting efforts to build human assets, and any company committed to building human assets must strive to reduce turnover. This goal can be accomplished through the means discussed above, including offering highly competitive pay; employee stock options; participation programs; voice mechanisms, like grievance procedures and suggestion schemes; attractive benefits packages; and flexible work arrangements. Those companies that have very critical uncertainties of volume should endeavor to alter their operating scales and timing, so that they utilize contingent, part time and contractual employees when necessary.

Options

In order to be able to proactively manage uncertainties and respond immediately to change, companies must develop options, which are investments in assets that provide the capability to respond to unplanned future changes, and to manage uncertainty. It is important, however, that every option, program or package that is developed to build human assets must fit in with company strategy; must be affordable to the company; and must be perceived as valuable by the employees.

TERMS & CONCEPTS

- **Competitive advantage:** A gain that a firm has over its competition, causing it to generate higher sales or margins and/or retain more customers than its competition.
- **Discounted cash flow model:** A model that tries to predict the future earnings employees will generate, by discounting the future cash flows to the present.
- **Firm-specific employees:** Employees with a stock of special skills, knowledge, routines, and/or personal relationships that are unique to their company and not easily transferable to other companies.
- **General human capital:** Employees with general skills and knowledge.
- **Hard assets:** The physical or tangible assets of a company.
- **Human assets:** Also known as human capital, human assets are a company's employees and their value in terms of the quantity and quality of their knowledge, skills, abilities, competencies, talents, experience and attitudes.
- **Options:** Investments in assets that provide the capability to respond to unplanned future changes, and to manage uncertainty.
- **Organizational capability:** The ability to generate commitment from the human assets in an organization.
- **Performance-based compensation:** Comparatively high compensation dependent on organizational performance.
- **Soft assets:** The intangible assets of a company.
- **Uncertainties of combination:** Uncertainties about employees and their job responsibilities being wrongly matched due to variations in demand and supply.
- **Uncertainties of costs:** Uncertainties regarding changes in company performance and changes in remuneration, and the resultant variations in the ratio of total expenditure on human assets to company revenues.
- **Uncertainties of returns:** Human asset risks concerning depreciation or appreciation in the value of human assets, and in the value they generate for a company.
- **Uncertainties of volume:** Uncertainties regarding employee turnover.

BIBLIOGRAPHY

Ananthram, Subramaniam, Alan Nankervis, and Christopher Chan. "Strategic Human Asset Management: Evidence from North America." *Personnel Review* 42, no. 3 (2013): 281–99. Web. 15 Nov. 2013.

Ambler, Tim. "Valuing Human Assets." *Business Strategy Review* 10, no. 1 (1999): 54. Web. 23 Dec. 2007.

Becker, Gary S. "Human Capital." In *The Concise Encyclopedia of Economics.* Library of Economics and Liberty. Web. 23 Dec. 2007.

Bhattacharya, Mousumi, and Patrick Wright. "Managing Human Assets in an Uncertain World: Applying Real Options Theory to HRM." *International Journal of Human Resource Management* 16, no. 6 (2005): 929–48. Web. 23 Dec. 2007.

Brown, Ronald Jr., and Joseph O'Neill. "Appraising the Human Asset for Business Life Insurance Requirements." *Journal of the American Society of Chartered Life Underwriters* 11, no. 4 (1957): 340–52. Web. 23 Dec. 2007.

"CFOs Now Seek a More Active Role in Human Asset Management." *Human Resources Department Management Report* 3, no. 5 (2003): 1. Web. 23 Dec. 2007.

Clarke, Robert. "Investing in Human Assets." *hfm (Healthcare Financial Management* 52, no. 11 (1998): 16. Web. 23 Dec. 2007.

Coff, Russell. "Human Assets and Management Dilemmas: Coping with Hazards on the Road to Resource-Based Theory." *Academy of Management Review* 22, no. 2 (1997): 374–402. Web. 23 Dec. 2007.

De, R.N. "Renewing Human Assets in Indian Ports: Issues and Strategies for Improving Performance." *Vision* 9, no. 4 (2005): 1–13. Web. 23 Dec. 2007.

Dittman, David, Hervey Juris, and Lawrence Revsine. "On the Existence of Unrecorded Human Assets: An Economic Perspective." *Journal of Accounting Research* 14, no. 1 (1976): 49–65. Web. 23 Dec. 2007.

Elias, Juanita, and Harry Scarbrough. "Evaluating Human Capital: An Exploratory Study of Management Practice." *Human Resource Management Journal* 14, no. 4 (2004): 21–40. Web. 23 Dec. 2007.

Kor, Yasemin, and Huseyin Leblebici. "How Do Interdependencies among Human-Capital Deployment, Development, and Diversification Strategies Affect Firms' Financial Performance?" *Strategic Management Journal* 26, no. 10 (2005): 967–85. Web. 23 Dec. 2007.

Kulkarni, Surashree, and James Fiet. "A Transaction Cost Analysis of Restructuring Alternatives." *Advances in Competitiveness Research* 15, nos. 1–2 (2007): 81–102. Web. 23 Dec. 2007.

Lajili, Kaouthar. "Embedding Human Capital into Governance Design: A Conceptual Framework." *Journal of Management & Governance* 19, no. 4 (2015): 741–62. Web. 26 Jan. 2018.

McDonald, Paul, and Jeffrey Gandz. "Identification of Values Relevant to Business Research." *Human Resource Management* 30, no. 2 (1991): 217–36. Web. 23 Dec. 2007.

Meilich, Ofer. "Are Formalization and Human Asset Specificity Mutually Exclusive? A Learning Bureaucracy Perspective." *Journal of American Academy of Business, Cambridge* 6, no. 1 (2005): 161–69. Web. 23 Dec. 2007.

Morse, Wayne. "A Note on the Relationship between Human Assets and Human Capital." *Accounting Review* 48, no. 3 (1973): 589–93. Web. 23 Dec. 2007.

Myers, M. Scott, and Vincent Flowers. "A Framework for Measuring Human Assets." *California Management Review* 16, no. 4 (1974): 5–16. Web. 23 Dec. 2007.

Neumann, Seev, Eli Segev, G. Rejda, and S. Travis Pritchett. "Human Capital and Risk Management: A Proposal for a New Insurance Product." *Journal of Risk & Insurance* 45, no. 2 (1978): 344–52. Web. 23 Dec. 2007.

Offstein, Evan, and Devi Gnyawali. "A Humanistic Perspective of Firm Competitive Behavior." *Competitiveness Review* 16, nos. 3–4 (2006): 248–61. Web. 23 Dec. 2007.

Rector, R., and P. Kirby. "Human Resources—The Zero Value Asset." *Industrial Management* 24, no. 4 (1982): 30. Web. 23 Dec. 2007.

Rhode, John, Edward Lawler III, and Gary Sundem. "Human Resource Accounting: A Critical Assessment." *Industrial Relations* 15, no. 1 (1976): 13–25. Web. 23 Dec. 2007.

Savich, Richard, and Keith Ehrenreich. "Cost/Benefit Analysis of Human Resource Accounting Alternatives." *Human Resource Management* 15, no. 1 (1976): 7–18. Web. 23 Dec. 2007.

Savino, David M., K.S. McGuire, and K.M. White. "Human Asset Management: A Comparison of the Artifact-Based Approach versus Input Methods." *Journal of Management Policy & Practice* 13, no. 1 (2012): 39–45. Web. 15 Nov. 2013.

Smith, Priscilla. "The 8 Practices of Exceptional Companies: How Great Organizations Make the Most of Their Human Assets" (book review). *Human Business Source Complete* 36, no. 3 (1997): 367–69. Web. 23 Dec. 2007.

SUGGESTED READING

Cherian, Jacob, and Sherine Farouq. "A Review of Human Resource Accounting and Organizational Performance." *International Journal of Economics & Finance* 5, no. 8 (2013): 74–83. Web. 15 Nov. 2013.

Elias, Nabil. "The Effects of Human Asset Statements on the Investment Decision: An Experiment." *Journal of Accounting Research* 10, no. 3 (1972): 215–33. Web. 23 Dec. 2007.

Fitz-Enz, Jac. *The 8 Practices of Exceptional Companies: How Great Organizations Make the Most of Their Human Assets.* New York: American Management Association, 1997.

O'Reilly, Charles, and Jeffrey Pfeffer. *Hidden Value: How Great Companies Achieve Extraordinary Results with Ordinary People.* Boston: Harvard Business School Press, 2000.

Pfeffer, Jeffrey. *Competitive Advantage through People: Unleashing the Power of the Work Force.* Boston: Harvard Business School Press. 1994.

Vanessa A. Tetteh, Ph.D.

BUSINESS, ETHICS & SOCIETY

ABSTRACT

This article focuses on how corporations and the government have responded to unethical behavior by employees. It discusses the role of whistle-blowers as well as ways regulations such as the False Claims Act, Sarbanes-Oxley Act, and the Lloyd-La Follette Act, which have been implemented to encourage employees to report acts of misconduct. In addition, there will be a review of how employees use organizational justice as a factor in the whistle-blowing process.

OVERVIEW

Given the competitiveness in the world today, many people are tempted to go outside of the rules and regulations of society to get ahead. Although many would argue that traits such as honesty and credibility are valued, temptations have lured some to act irresponsibly. Actions such as cheating, stealing, lying, and bribing have become common in the workplace. Good moral values and actions are becoming the exception rather than the rule. How can the trend turn? Organizations must put policies in place that will encourage employees to do the right thing and inform the proper authorities when illegal actions and dishonesty take place.

Unfortunately, when employees step forward and alert the organization of wrongdoings, they are labeled whistle-blowers, and other negative labels are applied to them. Instead of being considered heroes for doing the right thing, they tend to be chastised, and some never fully recover from the experience. For many of these individuals, there is a loss of trust in fellow employees and the organizations in which they work:

> *For some, the earth moves when they discover that people in authority routinely lie and that those who work for them routinely cover up. Once one knows this, or rather once one feels this knowledge in one's bones, one lives in a new world. Some people remain aliens in the new world forever. Maybe they like it that way. Maybe they don't have a choice. (Alford 2001, 52).*

This knowledge can be a devastating moment for many. Everything that they have believed and trusted is turned upside down. In some cases, these employees may have been friends with the culprits outside of the workplace, which may place an additional burden on the potential whistle-blower. It is unfortunate that society has come to a point where individuals with moral values and a sense of right and wrong are treated as outside societal norms. Whistle-blowers have been ostracized, reprimanded, transferred, referred to psychiatric care, assigned to menial duties, dismissed, and blacklisted. There are reports of where they have been unable to seek employment at other companies because there is a fear that the same situation will occur. Organizations respond to whistle-blowers with hostility and fear.

The federal government and some states have passed legislation to protect employees who decide to become whistle-blowers. According to Sheeder (2006), the federal False Claims Act provides protection for:

> Any employee who is discharged, demoted, suspended, threatened, harassed, or in any other manner discriminated in the terms and conditions of employment by his or her employment because of lawful acts done by the employee on behalf of the employee or others in furtherance of an action under this section (i.e., a whistle-blower action) shall be entitled to all relief necessary to make the employee whole (39).

Many courts will provide protection when:

- An employee becomes a participant in a "protected activity" (i.e., when an employee decides to confront an employer about illegal activities such as fraud).
- The employer becomes aware of the "protected activity."
- The employee is penalized as a result of coming forth about the "protected activity" (e.g., termination, harassment).

When it has been determined that an employee is a victim of retaliation, he or she may petition for:

- Reinstatement with the same seniority that he or she would have had if the adverse action did not occur
- Two times back pay
- Interest on the back pay
- Special damages (e.g., compensation for emotional distress, recovery of litigation costs, and reasonable attorney's fees)
- Any type of relief that will assist the employee in becoming a whole person again (Sheede 2006, 39–40).

An employee is entitled to all of the relief listed above as well as any recovery obtained by the government based on the regulations of the False Claims Act. Given the financial penalties for acts of wrongdoing, employers are encouraged to monitor the activities of their organization so that these fines are not imposed.

In order to avoid the costly expenses of these types of situations, many organizations are encouraged to draft policies that will assist employees in feeling comfortable about coming forward to advise the senior management team and the outside world of fraudulent behavior occurring in companies today. Tennebaum provided four elements of a good whistle-blower policy. The four elements include:

Bill Friday speaks at an international business ethics panel discussion (photo courtesy of the State Archives of North Carolina)

1. A policy that has a clear purpose and a statement of intent to protect whistle-blowers to the fullest extent possible. The purpose may include creating an environment where the whistle-blower can feel safe.
2. Guidelines that provide a detailed explanation of how the organization will attempt to protect the whistle-blower.
3. Procedures on who, when, and how to contact the organization in order to report unethical and/or illegal behavior.
4. A statement declaring what the organization will do as a result of the whistle-blowing activity. (Associations Now 2007, 12)

In addition, employers should be proactive and see if they can determine (1) the types of behaviors or situations that encourage employees to participate in unethical behavior, and (2) the types of actions that encourage employees to step up and become whistle-blowers. Sheeder (2006) identified six common factors that have encouraged employees to become whistle-blowers. In most cases, the lack of organizational support was enough for the employee to seek external assistance in correcting improper behavior. Each of the mentioned scenarios is based on a real-life case study.

- **Expect employees to participate in fraudulent conduct.** There have been many situations where senior managers are the culprits. In an effort to improve the organization's image and financial records, some executives have encouraged and mandated employees to participate in unethical behavior. Excuses such as "it's really not hurting anyone," "we are getting what we deserve," "be a team player," and "this action offsets the system" have been used in order to justify the organization's behavior. When an employee refuses to play the game, he or she may be terminated, which forces the former employee to file a retaliation lawsuit.
- **Dismiss employee concerns or complaints.** Some employees have attempted to alert the appropriate officials only to find out their concerns have been ignored. Once they have worked through the appropriate channels within the organization, they may feel as though their only recourse is to hire an external attorney to champion their cause.
- **Forget about a professional's ethical duty to report.** Some employees may feel that they are obligated to report unethical practices in order to maintain the image of their profession. For example, a police officer may become aware of the fact that his or her partner is working with criminals. After attempting to reason with the partner, the police officer may feel a need to alert internal affairs in order to (1) maintain a positive image of police officers in the eyes of the community and (2) protect the public from criminal activities.
- **Don't give "public duty" enough respect.** There have been cases where an organization may be overbilling another entity and the employee may not be able to support the deception. For example, some hospitals have been accused of overcharging Medicare programs. There may be an employee who believes that the process is unethical, and innocent people may suffer as a result of the deceptive actions. Therefore, the employee feels obligated to turn the hospital in to the proper authorities. The employee may believe that it is his or her civic and public duty to do so.
- **Fail to take prompt and proper action correction.** Many employees have followed the company's policy on reporting fraudulent activity only to find out that their good deed has been ignored. They believe their only alternative is to expose the situation externally since the system has failed internally.
- **Underestimate the perseverance of an employee.** Some organizations wrongly assume that if they ignore the employee, the problem will go away. However, there are employees with a conscience, and they will pursue their cause until the problem has been resolved.

Organizations need to realize there are people who value their conscience over their job. The government recognized that big business may not always do the right thing. Therefore, it has introduced and implemented some regulations to level the playing field and allow employees to come forth. Examples of such legislation are:

- **False Claims Act:** A *qui tam* provision that was enacted during Abraham Lincoln's tenure as president. This legislation was aimed at preventing the sale of faulty war equipment by fraudulent suppliers to the government (during the Civil War). Revisions were made to the act in 1943 and 1986. In 1986, there was a significant expansion of the rights of whistle-blowers and their attorneys. The law allows individuals to file actions against federal contractors claiming fraud against the government. People filing under the act may receive 15–25 percent of any recovered damages.
- **Sarbanes-Oxley Act:** Legislation passed in 2002 with the purpose of encouraging employees to become effective corporate monitors and report misconduct and unethical behavior in corporations. The act has two approaches that encourage employees to become corporate whistle-blowers (Moberly 2006). The first step is a clause that provides protection to whistle-blowers from employer retaliation once they have disclosed improper behavior. The second step requires employers to provide employees with guidelines, policies, and procedures to report organizational misconduct within the organization.
- **Lloyd-La Follette Act:** This act was enacted in 1912 and was designed to protect American civil servants from retaliation. The purpose was to ensure the rights of employees when they wanted to provide the House of Congress, a committee or indi-

vidual congressman with information about fraud. The intent was to provide conferring job protection rights to federal employees.

- **No-FEAR Act:** The Notification and Federal Employee Antidiscrimination and Retaliation (No-FEAR) Act of 2002 went into effect on October 1, 2003. The law applies to federal agencies and is aimed at keeping employees informed of their rights under anti-discrimination and whistle-blower protection laws. The No-FEAR Act also protects against retaliatory actions on the part of employers and provides for the reimbursement of current and former federal employees and federal applicants for costs incurred in the course of asserting their rights under these antidiscrimination and whistle-blower protection laws.

APPLICATION

Life of a Whistle-blower

Two of the most discussed fraud cases in history have been Enron and Worldcom. Coincidentally, both of the whistle-blowers in these two cases were women who had risen to the ranks of vice president in their respective organizations. A study conducted by two professors at St. Mary's College in Indiana found that female business students value honesty and independence more than their male counterparts (Allen 2002). Women may be more prone to expose wrongdoing due to their value system.

Cynthia Cooper was a vice president at Worldcom, and Sherron Watkins was a vice president at Enron. The circumstances surrounding both cases were so shocking that it made the public acknowledge how corrupt some organizations had become. Worldcom would become known as the company that created the largest accounting fraud in history (Ripley 2002). "Enron and Worldcom have become America's twin symbols of business malfeasance, but share a different kind of similarity: In each case the public learned the extent of the scandal in large part through the actions of a brave woman who did the right thing by going over her boss' head" (Colvin 2002, 56).

Worldcom

Worldcom's headquarters were located in Clinton, Mississippi. The founder, Bernie Ebbers, went to college there and wanted to move his company to the area. Cynthia Cooper had grown up in the area as well and was proud of the organization. She became the vice president of internal auditing. Unfortunately, in June of 2002, she had to tell the audit committee of Worldcom's board that the organization was unethical in its accounting practices (Ripley 2002).

Worldcom had started out as a small company in 1983 but became a major powerhouse in the 1990s. Most of the executives were in their late thirties making millions of dollars. However, there was a glut of companies like Worldcom by early 2001. Many believe that this time was when the organization started to use creative accounting practices. Cooper was not a part of the illegal activities, but many of the people whom she had respected were a part of the scandal. Even the organization's external auditor, Arthur Andersen, was alleged to be a part of the cover-up. Many of the activities were geared toward providing fraudulent information to the Securities Exchange Commission (SEC).

Cooper stayed at Worldcom once she became a whistle-blower. Although she became physically and emotionally exhausted, she persevered because she did not want the innocent employees of the company to suffer. Even though Cooper can be credited as a major influence for the country starting to take corporate governance to heart, no one from the senior management team at Worldcom acknowledged the sacrifice that she had made. When speaking at different conferences, she has offered the following advice to corporations:

- Protect whistle-blowers so that they can continue to provide information to support their allegations.
- Set an ethical tone at the top. In the Worldcom situation, the deceitful few were members of the senior management team.
- Hold more committee meetings and consider going into executive sessions.
- Remain flexible in the course of auditing and maintain an element of surprise (Peterson 2005).

VIEWPOINT

Organizational Justice

Alford (2001) has been quoted as saying that "the whistle-blower is a political actor in a nonpolitical world" (97). This statement should be interpreted as meaning that the whistle-blower responds to his or her value system in an organization where the value system has no role. Employees may view situations in terms of right or wrong; whereas, the employer may view situations in terms of the bottom line and financial profit. In essence, the purpose of the employee is to make sure that the business makes money. The end justifies the means. What can an organization do to support employees who want to do the right thing and view the organization as a fair and ethical place to work? Organizational justice is a concept that explores an employee's perception about whether or not an organization is fair in making decisions and/or the decision-making processes within organizations and the influence of those perceptions on behavior. Research has shown that organizational performance is improved as a result of improved ethical decision making (Hatcher 2002; Swanson 1999). Many have researched this area in hope of understanding why and how ethical decisions are made. By understanding the thought process behind an employee's decision making, human resource professionals may be able to create an environment that encourages ethical actions in the organization. "According to a national business ethics survey, 40 percent of professionals in human resource management and development roles must respond to their organization's ethical situations and in 70 percent of organizations, these same professionals are viewed as their organization's experts on ethics" (Joseph and Esen 2003).

As the business community embraces a global economy, there has been a push to speed up processes in order to make more profit. As a result, some employees see taking shortcuts as the only way to stay on top in a competitive environment. In order to accomplish ambitious goals, some may be tempted to participate in unethical behavior. Thus, organizational acceptance may be a factor as to why some people make unethical decisions. Research supporting the understanding of the ethical decision-making process may assist human resource professionals in creating an environment where employees are encouraged to make ethical decisions.

"The result of justice research suggests that the effects of injustice within organizations may be much broader than previously thought" (Cropanzano, Goldman, and Folger 2003). "Not only do victims directly affected by organizational injustice consider and sometimes take retributive actions, but so do neutral observers" (Kray and Lind 2002). As a result of the recent scandals, institutions of higher education have been challenged to teach students the virtues of ethical behavior and organizations have been challenged to create an ethical environment. Those who have devoted their time to researching the importance of organizational justice may be helpful to this cause.

CONCLUSION

Given the competitiveness in the world today, many people are tempted to go outside of the rules and regulations of society in order to get ahead. Although many would argue that traits such as honesty and credibility are valued, temptations have lured some to act irresponsibly. Unfortunately, when employees step forward and alert the organization of wrongdoings, they are labeled whistle-blowers and other negative labels are applied to them. Instead of being considered heroes for doing the right thing, they tend to be chastised, and some never fully recover from the experience. Once Cynthia Cooper realized her work had been done at Worldcom, she left and formed her own consulting firm. Cynthia decided to branch out and speak at corporations, associations, and universities about ethics and leadership and how it related to her situation at Worldcom (Amer 2005.)

The federal government recognized that big business may not always do the right thing. Therefore, it has introduced and implemented some regulations to level the playing field and allowed employees to come forth. The federal government and some states have passed legislation to protect employees who decide to become whistle-blowers. In order to avoid the costly expenses of litigation, many organizations are encouraged to draft policies that will help employees feel comfortable about coming forward to advise the senior management team and the outside world of fraudulent behavior occurring in companies today.

Organizational justice is a concept that explores an employee's perception about whether or not an organization is fair in making decisions and/or the decision-making processes within organizations and the influence of those perceptions on behavior. By understanding the thought process behind an employee's decision making, human resource professionals may be able to create an environment that encourages ethical actions in the organization.

Bibliography

Alford, C. Fred. *Whistleblowers: Broken Lives and Organizational Power.* Ithaca and London: Cornell University Press, 2001. Web. 6 June 2007.

Allen, J. "Women Who Blow Whistles…" *U.S. News & World Report* 133, no. 25 (2002): 48. Web. 6 June 2007.

Amer, S. "Do the Right Thing." *Successful Meetings* 54, no. 3 (2005): 72. Web. 6 June 2007.

Baden, Denise. "Look on the Bright Side: A Comparison of Positive and Negative Role Models in Business Ethics Education." *Academy of Management Learning & Education* 13, no. 2 (2014): 154–70. Web. 10 Nov. 2014.

Colvin, Geoffrey. "Wonder Women of Whistle Blowing." *Fortune* 146, no. 3 (2002): 56. Web. 6 June 2007.

Cropanzo, Russell, Barry Goldman, and Robert Folger. "Deontic Justice: The Role of Moral Principles in Workplace Fairness." *Journal of Organizational Behavior* 24, no. 8 (2003): 1019–24.

"Elements of Whistleblower Policy." *Associations Now* 3, no. 5 (2007): 12. Web. 6 June 2007.

Floyd, Larry A., Fenu Xu, Ryan Atkins, and Cam Caldwell. "Ethical Outcomes and Business Ethics: Toward Improving Business Ethics Education." *Journal of Business Ethics* 117, no. 4 (2013): 753–76. Web. 10 Nov. 2014.

Hatcher, Tim. *Ethics and HRD: A New Approach to Leading Responsible Organizations.* Cambridge, MA: Perseus Publishers, 2002.

Joseph, J., and Evren Esen. *SHMR/Ethics Resource Center 2003 Business Ethics Survey.* Alexandria, VA: SHRM, 2003.

Joshi, Jyoti. "Ethics, Business and Society: Managing Responsibility." *South Asian Journal of Management* 19, no. 3 (2012): 148–50. Web. 15 Nov. 2013.

Kelly, J. "The Year of the Whistleblowers." *Time South Pacific* (Australia/New Zealand ed.) 51–52 (2002, Dec. 30): 10. Web. 6 June 2007.

Kray, Laura, and E. Allan Lind. "The Injustices of Others: Social Reports and the Integration of Others' Experiences in Organizational Justice Judgments." *Organizational Behavior and Human Decision Processes* 89, no. 1 (2002): 906–24. Print.

Lin-Hi, Nick, and Igor Blumberg. "Managing the Social Acceptance of Business: Three Core Competencies in Business Ethics." *Business & Professional Ethics Journal* 31, no. 2 (2012): 247–63. Web. 15 Nov. 2013.

Moberly, Richard. "Sarbanes-Oxley's Structural Model to Encourage Corporate Whistleblowers." *Brigham Young University Law Review* 2006, no. 5 (2006): 1107–75. Web. 6 June 2007.

Peterson, Ann. "Inside the WorldCom Fraud." *Credit Union Magazine* 71, no. 8 (2005): 15–20. Web. 6 June 2007.

Rakas, Smilja. "Global Business Ethics–Utopia or Reality." *Megatrend Review* 8, no. 2 (2011): 385–406. Web. 15 Nov. 2013.

Ripley, Amanda. "The Night Detective." *Time Canada* 160–161, nos. 27–1 (2002): 36. Web. 6 June 2007.

Ruud, Judith, and William M. Rudd. "Law and Ethics: Society and Corporate Social Responsibility: Is the Focus Shifting?" *Journal of Academic & Business Ethics* (2011). Web. 15 Nov. 2013.

Sheeder, Frank. "Whistleblowers Are Not Born That Way—We Create Them through Multiple System Failures." *Journal of Health Care Compliance* 8, no. 4 (2006): 39–73. Web. 6 June 2007.

Swanson, Richard. "Foundations of Performance Improvement and Implications for Practice." In *Performance Improvement Theory and Practice,* edited by R. Torraco, 1–25. San Francisco: Berrett-Koehlner, 1999.

Suggested Reading

Abend, Gabriel. "The Origins of Business Ethics in American Universities, 1902–1936." *Business Ethics Quarterly* 23, no. 2 (2013): 171–205. Web. 10 Nov. 2014.

Aguilera, Ruth, Deborah Rupp, Cynthia Williams, and Jyoti Ganapathi. "Putting the S Back in Corporate Social Responsibility: A Multilevel Theory of Social Change in Organizations." *Academy of Management Review* 32, no. 3 (2007): 836–63. Web. 6 June 2007.

Barrier, Michael, and Cynthia Cooper. "One Right Path." *Internal Auditor* 60, no. 5 (2003): 52–57. Web. 6 June 2007.

Gleeson, W., and J. Minier. "Why Companies Need to Adopt Whistleblower Policies Now." *Banking & Financial Service Policy Report* 22, no. 1 (2003): 1–6.

McNamee, Michael, and Scott Fleming. "Ethics Audits and Corporate Governance: The Case of Public Sector Sports Organizations." *Journal of Business Ethics* 73, no. 4 (2007): 425–37. Web. 6 June 2007.

Marie Gould, Ph.D.

BUSINESS STRATEGY AND POLICY

ABSTRACT

Continued business success is the result of systematic planning, the process of developing strategies to increase the organization's market share and policies to promote this goal and meet other requirements placed on the firm. The first step in strategic planning is to develop sound objectives for the organization based on a rigorous analysis of available data about the marketplace, the competition, and the resources of the organization. These goals must be specific with measurable outcomes so that success can be objectively determined. Supporting plans and budgets can then be developed to provide a practical guide for carrying out the budget strategy and meeting its objectives. Although much of corporate strategy revolves around the bottom line, not all approaches to strategy and policy are about sales and marketing. Total Quality Management (TQM) and Six Sigma strategies help better position an organization in the marketplace by emphasizing quality.

OVERVIEW

A wise person once said that if you don't know where you're going, you'll never get there. This axiom is no more true anywhere than in the business arena. Development of a successful business does not happen as a result of luck; it requires hard work. As in pathfinding, the roadmap to success in the business world is to determine where one wants to go and then how to get there most efficiently.

In business, determining the target destination for the organization is called goal setting. Goals define in practical terms what the organization would like to be within a specific period of time. Determining the best way to accomplish these goals is called strategic planning. A strategy is a plan of action to help the organization reach its goals and objectives. A good business strategy is based on the rigorous analysis of empirical data, including market needs and trends, competitor capabilities and offerings, and the organization's resources and abilities. Implementation of the plan is done through policies and practices. These guiding principles or specific procedures or courses of action help the organization meet its goals and objectives. Policies are typically developed to support business strategies or in response to government regulations. For example, an organization may have a series of customer service policies that deal with how employees are supposed to interact with customers in order to keep them loyal to the organization's brand. It may also have a series of human resource policies for how it deals with its own employees to not only encourage them to maximize their performance, but also to

Businessmen discuss their strategy (Photo courtesy of Christopher Miche

comply with various laws regarding equal treatment, minimum wage, and so forth. An organization may also have policies about social and environmental concerns or other factors that it perceives as important to its reputation and success.

Determining the organization's business goals requires an examination of several areas of the firm's functioning. To avoid falling into the trap of doing activities that appear to reach a goal but that, in fact, are only spinning the corporate wheels without making real progress, the objectives of the organization need to be expressed in concrete terms. For example, rather than stating that the goal of the company is to maximize profits and return on investment, develop new and high-quality products, or meet the corporate social responsibility, objectives need to be specific and state how success will be determined in measurable terms. For example, rather than saying that the organization is going to increase profits, a well-stated objective would state how much profit the organization is trying to make and within what time frame (e.g., increase profits to $5 million in the next fiscal year). Rather than vaguely stating that new products will be developed, a well stated objective would specify the types of products to be developed and the quality standard to which they are to be developed (e.g., develop a widget that will automatically mop the floor using a process that yields less than three defects per million). Similarly, vague goals about social responsibility would be replaced by specific objectives stating in what kinds of public service activities the organization will be involved and the extent of its involvement.

Strategic planning is the process that helps the organization determine what goals to set and how to reach them. This process allows the organization to determine and articulate its long-term goals and to develop a plan to use the company's resources—including materials, equipment, technology, and personnel—in reaching these goals. This business plan summarizes the operational and financial objectives of the organization and is supported by detailed plans and budgets to show how these objectives will be achieved. In addition to articulating organizational objectives and strategies for reaching these goals, the business plan also analyzes the risks business terms, risk can be defined as the probability that a financial investment's will be lower than expected. Higher risks mean both a possibility of greater return on investment and a greater probability of loss. Since the goal of organizations is to reduce risk by managing it, risk management is an essential part of business strategy development. This process includes analyzing projected tasks and activities, planning ways to reduce the impact if the predicted normal course of events does not occur, and implementing reporting procedures so that project problems are discovered earlier rather than later in the process.

Whether the organization is trying to maintain its market share or it is trying to remain on the leading edge of the industry through sustainable innovation, there are a number of sources of data that can be tapped in order to help make better informed strategic decisions about the direction in which the organization should go. In general, it is advisable to look at every business event—whether it was a success or a failure—as a learning opportunity that can help the organization better understand and anticipate the needs of the market or how to improve internal processes and practices. The organization can also look forward by examining incongruities between the way things currently are and how the industry or organization perceives they should be (e.g., the requirement for more complicated desktop computing capabilities required the development of more affordable computing power) and developing solutions that meet these needs. Similarly, changes to the market or industry as the result of an innovation, contributed by the organization itself or by a competitor, can help organizational management better develop strategies to stay competitive, become leaders in the field, or practice sustainable innovation. Other external changes that require attention when developing strategic plans are demographic changes (e.g., the rise in the number of people in the general population who are computer-literate), the development of new knowledge (e.g., how to develop a graphical user interface that reduces the need for specialized abilities to use a computer), or changes in perceptions (e.g., the acceptance of computers as a way to make life easier).

A number of factors need to be taken into account during the strategic planning process in order to develop a sound, achievable business plan. One of the most important of these steps is setting realistic, achievable objectives. To be useful, objectives should specify the performance that the organization wants to see as a result of meeting the objective, the activities in which the organization will engage to help meet the objective, and the measurable results that will allow the organization to know whether or not the objective has been achieved. In addition, a well-written objective should specify the time period in which the improved performance will occur. For example, rather than the nebulous objective of maximizing profits, a well-written objective might be to increase profits (objective) by 25 percent (measurable criterion) over the next year (time frame) by targeting two new metropolitan areas with media ads and six additional sales calls per salesperson (actions).

In order to develop meaningful objectives that will support the organization in reaching its goals, financial concerns should be expressed in terms of objective, measurable results, such as profits, return on investment, earnings per share, or profit-to-sales ratio. For example, financial objectives should be expressed in specific, concrete terms such as increase return on investment to 15 percent after taxes within five years or increase profits to $6 million before the end of the fiscal year. Similarly, well-written objectives should be specific about the market in which these actions will take place. For example, a statement might include the market share the organization is trying to reach (increase our share of the market to 28 percent within three years), dollar amount or unit volume of sales (sell 200,000 widgets next year), or industry niche (increase commercial sales to 95 percent and reduce military sales to 15 percent over the next two years). The business strategy might also include a discussion of the productivity necessary to reach these objectives, which might include a ratio of input to output (e.g., increase number of widgets produced to 100 per eight-hour day) or the cost per unit of production (e.g., decrease cost of production to $6 per widget).

In addition to the objectives or end goals that the organization is trying to reach, strategic planning should also include a consideration of the resources necessary to get it there. One of the considerations in this process is the financial resources of the organization such as capital structure, new issues of common stock, cash flow, working capital needed, dividend payments, and collection periods. These factors also need to be stated specifically when developing the organization's objectives. For example, statements could include such objectives as decrease the collection period to 26 days by the end of the year, decrease working capital to $5 million within three years, or reduce long-term debt to $8 million within five years.

The strategic planning process also needs to give consideration to the resources necessary to accomplish the other objectives. To increase one's market share, for example, may mean a concomitant increase in the size of the production facility, the number of production workers required, and so forth. Therefore, the business plan needs to specify the physical facilities needed, including required square feet of space for offices, storage, production facilities, etc.; fixed costs such as rent and utilities; and the number of units that can be produced within these constraints. For example, objectives might include increase production capacity to 8 million widgets per month within the next two years or increase storage capacity to 15 million barrels by the end of December. Similarly, the plan should express the organization's goals for human resources quantitatively, not only in terms of numbers of employees needed, but also in terms of employee performance and employee management. These goals may include consideration of absenteeism, tardiness, turnover, number of grievances, need for training, etc. For example, objectives might include reducing absenteeism to less than 4 percent within six months or conducting a 20-hour, in-house management training program for first-line supervisors by the end of next year at a cost not to exceed $500 per participant. In addition, strategic planning may take into account changes that need to be made to the structure or design of the organization itself in order to accomplish these goals, such as implementing a team structure, decentralizing decision making, etc.

Also specified within the strategic planning process are the research and development efforts that go into continued innovation and new product development. As with the other organizational goals, these goals need to be specific, including the associated budget for each effort. For example, an objective for research and development might be to develop an engine in the $2,000 price range with an emission rate of 5 percent within two years at a cost not to exceed $500,000.

Finally, increasingly, organizations are realizing that to be successful, their concerns need to go beyond the profit and loss statement and include statements about being a good corporate citizen of the planet. Therefore, many organizations are including social concerns within their strategies. These may be expressed in terms of types of activities, number of days of service, or financial contributions. For example, an organization may have as its goals reducing greenhouse emissions by 10 percent over the next year, establishing a scholarship fund for underprivileged students to study engineering at the local university, or hiring and successfully training 120 hard-core unemployables to be acceptable widget production specialists against existing standards within the next two years.

APPLICATIONS

Business strategy is not only about plans or even about selling. Strategy includes everything the organization intentionally does to better position itself within the marketplace and to earn a larger market share. Strategy, therefore, can include the organization's intentional attempts at improving customer satisfaction through the institution of such programs as around-the-clock customer service lines or email rebate systems; positioning itself to be perceived as environmentally or socially aware by lessening the environmental impact of a product or instituting a recycling plan; or improving quality-control methods or reducing the number of defects per group of products.

One strategy that has been widely adapted in recent years for increasing the quality of goods and services and concomitant customer satisfaction is Total Quality Management (TQM). TQM attempts to reach these goals by raising awareness of quality concerns across the organization. This management strategy emphasizes the use of teams in the workplace as a way to improve quality and meet customer demands. TQM emphasizes developing an organizational environment that supports innovation and creativity as well as taking risks to meet customer demands using such techniques as participative problem solving that includes not only managers, but employees and customers as well.

The five cornerstones of the TQM strategy are the product, the process that allows the product to be produced, the organization that provides the proper environment needed for the process to work, the leadership that guides the organization, and the commitment to excellence and quality throughout the organization. To successfully implement a TQM program, consideration needs to be given to all five of the primary emphases of product, process, organization, leadership, and commitment. To help ensure that the TQM strategy will work, it is necessary that an environment of quality be fostered within the organization which should include an emphasis on consistency, integrity, and other positive interpersonal relationship skills. The organizational culture should also foster pride in the product or service and professionalism among the all team members through all levels in the organization. To foster the teamwork necessary to bring about high quality, TQM also encourages organizations to implement a decentralized authority structure where decisions are made close to those affected, and all individuals have a chance to participate in the process. This situation helps employees feel like they are part of the system and a vital part of the organization, and not just hirelings. Other ways to improve the ownership of team members in the product is to increase the flow of communication across all levels of the organization and provide each employee the training that he or she needs to successfully add value to the product.

TQM differs from many other business strategies because it emphasizes the product, not the job. For example, if Harvey works on an assembly line attaching steering wheels to cars, TQM emphasizes making Harvey feel that he was integral to building the car, not that he just attached the steering wheel. This perception is intended to improve pride in one's work, which in turn helps increase the team spirit and enables employees to better feel that they are important parts of the outstanding process. Similarly, leadership in a TQM organization is taught to focus on the outputs rather than on the inputs that helps sharpen the focus on producing a high-quality product (the output) rather than on unimportant events that may happen on the way to producing that product. To encourage this attitude, managers are taught to reinforce productive employee behaviors and discourage nonproductive behaviors. In addition, quality is continuously monitored and employees are given timely feedback so that any corrections are made sooner rather than later in the process to enable the organization to perform at a high level.

TQM not only looks at the bottom line in terms of numbers but also helps link the concepts of value to the customer with the cost of the product. This expansion can help in market positioning and increasing market share. This strategy can be enabled by continually assessing the marketplace of the organization's product vis a vis the organization's skills and resources, which helps strategic efforts to better position the organization to excel in the marketplace.

The Six Sigma process is a spin-off of TQM and was first developed by Motorola. The term Six Sigma is a statistical term referring to how far (i.e., the number of standard deviations, symbolized by the Greek letter sigma) a data point is from the middle of the normal curve. This distance signifies the degree to which a product reaches its quality goal. At Six Sigma above normal, a product is reaching its quality goal 99.9999997 percent of the time, or has only 3.4 defects per million. Six Sigma is the goal toward which manufacturing and quality-control efforts in the organization are focused. In addition, the Six Sigma process is also targeted toward improving nonmanufacturing processes and functions within the organization.

The Six Sigma program is targeted at reducing costs by making changes before defects or problems occur. As part of the Six Sigma program, employees and managers are trained in statistical analysis, project management, and problem-solving methodology so that they can use these skills to reduce defects in their products. Most organizations that have implemented Six Sigma programs report increased profitability due to lower production costs from doing it correctly the first time in combination with reduced costs for not having to redo work previously done.

Globalization

The Internet has facilitated the internationalization of companies. By the end of the first decade of the twenty-first century, even medium-sized companies could reach markets worldwide (Bell, 2010). With globalization, however, come a number of risks including information and product piracy, as well as cyber-sabotage by competitors and mischievous hackers. Patent protection is especially problematic (Kim and Kim 2011). Improvements in the transportation of goods have made possible the globalization of the supply chain, allowing manufacturers in high-wage countries to take advantage of labor in low-wage countries. Consumer perception of worker exploitation may backfire, even on popularly esteemed companies such as Apple. Company negligence in supply-chain management, however, is particularly observable in low-cost producers (Hoejmose, Brammer, and Millington 2013).

BIBLIOGRAPHY

Bell, James, and Sharon Loane. "'New-Wave' Global Firms: Web 2.0 and SME Internationalization." *Journal of Marketing Management* 26, nos. 3–4 (2010): 213–29. Web. 27 Oct. 2013.

Creech, Bill. *The Five Pillars of TQM: How to Make Total Quality Management Work for You*. New York: Truman Talley Books/Dutton, 1994.

Hoejmose, Brammer, Stephen, and Andrew Millington. "An Empirical Examination of the Relationship between Business Strategy and Socially Responsible Supply Chain Management." *International Journal of Operations & Production Management* 33, no. 5 (2013): 589–621. Web. 27 Oct. 2013.

Kim, Taeha, and Beomsoo Kim. "Regulatory Policies and Business Strategies on Patent Protection: A General Model and Cases for the East Asian Economy." *Global Economic Review* 4 (2011): 463–81. Web. 27 Oct. 2013.

Landy, Frank J., and Jeffrey M. Conte. *Work in the 21st Century: An Introduction to Industrial and Organizational Psychology*. Boston: McGraw Hill, 2004.

SUGGESTED READING

Boyd, Brian. "Strategic Planning and Financial Performance: A Meta-Analytic Review." *Journal of Management Studies* 28, no. 4 (1991): 353–74. Web. 26 Apr. 2007.

Dean, James W., and Mark P. Sharfman. "Does Decision Process Matter? A Study of Strategic Decision Making Effectiveness." *Academy of Management Journal* 39, no. 2 (1996): 368–96. Web. 26 Apr. 2007.

Fredrickson, James W., and Terence R. Mitchell. "Strategic Decision Processes: Comprehensivess and Performance in an Industry with an Unstable Environment." *Academy of Management Journal* 27, no. 2 (1984): 399–423. Web. 26 Apr. 2007.

Papadakis, Vassilis M., Spyros Lioukas, and David Chambers. "Strategic Decision-Making Processes: The Role of Management and Content." *Strategic Management Journal* 19, no. 2 (1998): 115–47. Web. Apr. 26 2007.

Talavera, Gloria V. "Development and Validation of TQM Constructs." *Gadjah Mada International Journal of Business* 6, no. 3 (2004): 355–81. Web. 26 Apr. 2007.

Ruth A. Wienclaw, Ph.D.

BUSINESS SUCCESSION PLANNING

ABSTRACT

The succession of a closely held family-owned business to the next generation presents a complex challenge. Historically, family-owned businesses have not fared well through the generations, a fact that underscores the need for careful and comprehensive business succession planning. To maximize the effectiveness of a succession plan, attention should be given to both the financial and nonfinancial aspects. Financial aspects include considerations of tax, finance, and law. The nonfinancial aspects are concerned with the relationships, expectations, and desires of the family members. This article provides an overview of some major points in the area of business succession planning.

OVERVIEW

Family-owned businesses are important to the United States' economy as well as the growth of the nation, as measured by the contribution to the gross national product (GNP) of family-owned business. They are also significant creators of new jobs, generating an estimated nine out of every ten new jobs (White, Krinke, and Geller 2004). The entrepreneurs that own and operate these businesses are often fully engaged in the daily operations of their enterprises. They must increase revenue, limit costs, secure adequate staff, and meet financial obligations; these activities leave little time to consider the future of their businesses. Only about one-third of the businesses survive until the second generation, and only ten to twenty percent make it until the third generation. This difficulty can be largely attributed to the lack of trained and capable successors to run a business. That problem can largely be overcome by a clear and well-designed business succession plan (White, Krinke, and Geller 2004).

Business succession planning is the process of creating and implementing a strategy to turn over control and ownership of a family business as a going concern. It is the owner's exit strategy that seeks to achieve the owner's financial and family objectives. Ownership of a business typically represents a substantial portion of the owner's overall estate and warrants careful consideration. Unlike other parts of a person's estate, which can be handled with the familiar estate planning tools including wills and trusts, a business succession plan presents a separate challenge that typically involves more complex issues, related to the difficulty of maintaining successful operations.

Accordingly, the primary object of a business succession plan is the closely held family business. A closely held business refers to a business, usually a corporation, whose stock is not freely traded and which is held by a few shareholders. The succession of the business can be to either family members or nonfamily members, depending on the owner's goals and particular family situation. Either way, the process involves complex legal, tax, financial, and management planning issues that can extend over a lengthy period of time. The planning process must also involve many people, including family members, professional advisors, shareholders, partners, and key employees. To ensure the maximum result, it is preferable to begin succession planning earlier rather than later. An unexpected death of a business owner can cause extreme emotional and financial problems for a family. Without proper planning, the sudden lack of leadership and management can cause a business to suffer and ultimately contribute to the failure of the business. Moreover, unmitigated tax consequences of an unexpected death can be disastrous and can cripple the financial condition of the business and the family member(s) who inherit(s) it.

Separating Ownership from Control
A common initial step before a specific technique is employed to transfer the ownership of a business is to separate the ownership from control. Typically, in a closely held business, stock or units (in the case of an LLC) have voting rights and therefore ownership of a majority of the stock results in control of the business. Ownership and control are unified. Ownership and control can be separated by

A businessman poses with his protegé (Photo courtesy of beachanchor)

recapitalizing the company into voting and nonvoting shares. Recapitalizing means to alter the way in which the financial interests of a company are held. For a simple example, a company with one class of shares would be said to recapitalize if an additional class of nonvoting stock were created in addition to voting stock.

As a general matter, a corporate structure vests the authority to manage a company in a board of directors and the board of directors appoints officers to manage the daily operations of a company. The shareholders, by voting their shares, elect the board of directors. By use of votes, the shareholders in the corporate structure ultimately control the company, despite being a couple steps removed from the daily operations. In the case of a closely held family corporation, a single person or a few people tend to have multiple roles and the loss of control can manifest more quickly and directly than in a large publically held corporation. An owner may be the chair of the board of directors, the president, and a significant stockholder. With a single class of voting stock, transfer of the stock would also cause the loss of control by the owner. By separating the stock into voting and nonvoting stock, the owner can retain control over operations during life and begin to transfer ownership of the company to others in the form of nonvoting shares.

Alternatively, a family-limited partnership could be set up with control settled in the general partnership interest and only ownership settled in the limited partner interests. This method is the same concept as in the case of a corporation. As a general matter, a limited partnership is a partnership between a general partner and any number of limited partners. Similar to the owner of voting shares in a corporation, the general partner has control over operations, and like nonvoting shares in the corporation, the limited partners have only a financial interest in the business. The limited partners have limited legal liability and limited involvement in the business. The general partner has unlimited liability and ultimate control and responsibility for the management of the business. Under either method, after the restructuring, the primary owners will have both controlling and noncontrolling interests in the business and can begin to transfer the business by giving away the noncontrolling interests to family members (White, Krinke, and Geller 2004).

Transferring Interest to Family Members

There are several options for a business owner who wishes to transfer an interest in a business to family members. As a general matter, there are four ways to transfer ownership: by gift during life, by gift at death, by sale during life, and by sale at death. Gifts of stock during life can be made tax free to the extent provided by the IRS ($12,000 per year per recipient at the time of writing). Each gift reduces the size of the owner's estate and reduces the potential for estate tax liability at death. However, to qualify for tax free treatment, the gifts must be complete and the owner loses control of the stock once gifted. Gifting is a method that can be effectively employed over time and is a relatively simple transaction. However, a critical part of the choice for a vehicle to transfer a business is tax planning, and tax planning is a highly specialized field of endeavor. Tax professionals, including accountants and lawyers, may use several particular measures according to current state of the appropriate tax law. The important point to remember is that tax considerations are very important to the process and should be considered carefully by a competent professional.

Buy-Sell Agreements
The buy-sell agreement is a very important succession planning tool that transfers ownership to another generation and may often be combined with gifting to accomplish the desired transfer. A buy-sell agreement is an arrangement between owners of a business to buy or sell interests in the business at a determinate price when a particular event occurs. These agreements are useful to restrict the transfer of a business interests to unwanted third parties; to provide for the method of funding a buy-out of a withdrawing or deceased owner's interest; to prevent delay of the administration of a deceased shareholder's estate because details of the transfer had been addressed in advance; and to prevent the disputes between a surviving spouse and children of a deceased owner and remaining owners. Some of the common events that trigger buy-sell agreements are death, divorce, third-party purchase offers, retirement, and bankruptcy. Key issues addressed in a buy-sell agreement are the types of events that trigger the agreement, the method for establishing the value of the business, the guarantee of adequate funding for purchase of the stock or interests when a triggering event occurs, and the tax implications of the transaction.

Types of Buy-Sell Agreements
Generally, there are three main types of buy-sell agreements: cross-purchase, stock redemption, and hybrid (Birch 2006). In the cross-purchase agreement, each remaining business owner becomes personally responsible for buying the departing owner's interest upon the happening of a specified event. In the case of death as a triggering event, each owner would be beneficiary of a life insurance policy taken on each of the other owners. For example, a company with four owners would have twelve insurance policies; each owner would own three policies, one for each of the other owners. The stock redemption plan obligates the business to repurchase an owner's interest in the business upon the happening of a specified event. If insurance is used to fund the purchase obligation, the business would be the beneficiary of a policy taken on each owner. Once an obligation under a buy-sell agreement has been triggered, it may be funded from a number of sources. However, as indicated, life insurance is a particularly important option because it removes the difficulty inherent in generating large amounts of cash at a single time. In the event that a cross-purchase agreement is in place, each owner will own a policy on each of the other owners so that in the event of death, the proceeds of the life insurance policies will be available fund the obligations under the buy-sell agreement. If a stock redemption plan is in place, the business will own the insurance policy on each owner to fund the corresponding obligation. As the name suggests, the hybrid plan may have features of both plans and other mechanisms appropriate to the situation.

A Business' Continued Success
In addition to the specific plan for transferring ownership, presumably the majority owner wishes the business to continue to be a success. Often, a business's continued success depends not only upon the family members that assume control, but also upon the key employees. The owner should be sure to identify the important employees that serve critical and perhaps unique functions vital to the ongoing operations. Identifying and understanding their position on certain issues is important to continued success and to provide options for its transfer. Whether and how long a key employee will remain with the company under new ownership is a critical question. Does a particular employee have the expertise to run the business? Are the employees willing and able to run or buy the company? Answers to these questions can help prepare the business for the eventual change in ownership by ensuring that proper personnel are available. Moreover, depending on the answers to these questions, a majority owner can consider the sale of the business or accommodate heirs that do not wish to be involved in management.

APPLICATION

Business, Financial, & Tax Related Matters vs. Emotional Matters

In reality, a business succession plan has two components: the business, financial and tax related matters and the emotional or people matters. Beyond the legal, financial, and tax implications and considerations of a business succession plan are serious family and relational issues. Traditional succession plans tend to focus on legal strategies that seek to avoid taxes and transfer control to the next generation. While those considerations are important, an overwhelming majority of second and third generation family businesses fail, leading some to argue that more strategies are required to effectively transfer a business. Values, morals, and matters of the heart may be a vital and often overlooked component of the business succession planning process. For businesses that do thrive, either intentionally or inadvertently, younger generations have embraced family traits that lead the family to business success in the first place (Harris 2007).

Closely held family business succession plans involve parties with longstanding relationships, and interests that can complicate the process of a management turnover to a younger generation. Families can reach an impasse in the process of drafting a buy-sell agreement and otherwise making plans to pass a family business to the next generation unless emotional and relational issues are addressed. Problems can arise from the emotional impact of the sale of a business interest and the perceived impact the transfer could have on family members' lives. To avoid potentially bitter conflicts during the planning and drafting process, the goals of the majority owner should be clearly defined.

The majority owner should carefully consider questions and develop a clear vision of the future of the business. The majority owner may consider whether the proportion of ownership will differ between children. An owner may consider differing interests for children involved in the business and those not employed by the business. Whether the owner wants the children to have outright ownership or ownership through an entity, like a trust, is another important question that includes a host of situation specific facts. The owner may also want to develop a clear idea as to whether ownership in the business should be exclusively for family members or whether it may pass to outsiders. A related question is the projected role of future owners in the business and ways they will deal with co-owners. Another consideration is whether or not the majority owners wish to use the business as a device to keep the family connected to one another. Finally, the owner should make clear any wishes regarding the sale of the business. These questions are typically answered by the majority owner with reference to personal and family beliefs and values. The decisions, usually reached after several rounds of conversations, should be made as family decisions, and not simply business decisions. Accordingly, the majority owner should include family members in the process as appropriate (White 2007).

The owner's spouse is a particularly important family member to consider in an effort to avoid potential problems. If the spouse's interests in the family unit are ignored, there may be significant difficulty forging an agreement acceptable to all parties. Spouses often have different goals for a buy-sell agreement than the owner and are often more concerned with fairness among children and harmony within the family. Likewise, the interests of the next generation should be considered. Often majority owners assume that a child wants to continue a business when many children may prefer to receive monetary benefits and the freedom to pursue their own career direction. There is also pressure for a succeeding family member to honor the wishes of the parents or grandparents and maintain the company to support other family members who have a financial stake but who are not involved in management. Moreover, when a larger benefit is provided for managing children, nonmanaging children may perceive favoritism or inequality. These potential issues and others should be investigated and addressed to ensure that a business succession plan goes smoothly (White 2007).

CONCLUSION

In comparison to large publically traded companies, the succession of closely held family-owned business presents a far more complex challenge, due to the close family relationships, and the mixture of ownership and management. Historically, family-owned businesses have not fared well through the generations. This fact underscores the need for careful and comprehensive succession planning. To maximize the effectiveness of a succession plan, attention should be given to both the business aspects and the relational aspects. The business aspects include considerations of tax, finance, and law. The tax consequences of a business transfer can be great and, if not adequately planned for, can cause a significant financial burden. Improper financing of an agreement to buy or sell a business can also generate such hardship. The need to generate significant amounts of cash to meet those obligations can jeopardize the business itself as a viable entity. The relational aspects deal with the relationships, expectations, and desires of the family members and are critically important to the continued success of a family business.

This article has merely touched upon some major points in the area of business succession planning and is only intended to provide a basic foundation from which to begin acquiring other information. The issues are complex and any person seeking to transfer a business should engage the appropriate professionals, including lawyers, accountants, insurance professionals, and appropriate business consultants.

IRS Circular 230 Notice: To guarantee compliance with requirements established by the IRS, we advise you that any U.S. tax information provided within this article is not intended to be used, and cannot be used, for the purpose of (i) avoiding penalties under the Internal Revenue Code or (ii) promoting, marketing, or recommending to another party any transaction or matter addressed herein.

TERMS & CONCEPTS

- **Business succession planning:** The process of creating and implementing a strategy to turn over control and ownership of a family business as a going concern.
- **Buy-sell agreement:** An arrangement between owners of a business to buy or sell interests in the business at a determinate price when a specific event occurs.
- **Cross-purchase:** A type of buy-sell agreement whereby each remaining business owner becomes personally responsible for buying the departing owner's interest upon the happening of a specified event.
- **Stock redemption plan:** A type of buy-sell agreement that obligates a business to repurchase an owners interest in the business upon the happening of a specified event.

BIBLIOGRAPHY

Berg, D. "SMB Succession Planning." *SaskBusiness* 31 (2010): 43. Web. 15 Nov. 2013.

Butler, John, Phillip Phan, Borje Saxberg, and Soon Hoon Lee. "Entrepreneurial Succession, Firm Growth and Performance." *Journal of Enterprising Culture* 9 (2001): 407. Web. 2 May 2007.

Daley, Jason. "Family Affair." *Entrepreneur* 39 (2011): 97–105. Web. 15 Nov. 2013.

Eddleston, Kimberly A., Franz W. Kellermans, Steven Floyd, et al. "Planning for Growth: Life Stage Difference in Family Firms." *Entrepreneurship: Theory & Practice* 37 (2013): 1177–1202. Web. 15 Nov. 2013.

Harris, J. "Business Succession Strategies That Work." *Practical Accountant* 40 (2007): 20–21. Web. 2 May 2007.

White, Paul. "Hidden Dragons: Handling Family Conflicts in Buy-Sell Agreements for Business Succession." *Journal of Financial Planning* 20 (2007): 70–76. Web. 2 May 2007.

White, William, Timothy Krinke, and David Geller. "Family Business Succession Planning: Devising an Overall Strategy." *Journal of Financial Service Professionals* 58 (2004): 67–86. Web. 2 May 2007.

SUGGESTED READING

Birch, R. "Preparing for the Handover: Getting Business Succession Planning Right." *Pennsylvania CPA Journal* 77 (2006): 1–4. Web. 2 May 2007.

"Family Business Succession Checklist." *Journal of Accountancy* 174 (1992): 24. Web. 2 May 2007.

Giarmarco, Julius. "Life Insurance in Business Succession." *Advisor Today* 102 (2007): 20–22. Web. 2 May 2007.

Morrow, Edwin. "Your Business Succession Plan: Are You Going Barefoot?" *Journal of Financial Planning* 14 (2001): 52–54. Web. 2 May 2007.

Powell, Larry, and John Venturella. "Succession Planning Two Ways: Business Items and Emotional Items." *Production Machining* 6 (2006): 22–24. Web. 2 May 2007.

Radloff, Peter. "Now's the Time to Discuss Business Succession Planning with Clients." *National Underwriter / Life & Health Financial Services* 111 (2007): 22–29. Web. 2 May 2007.

Rearson, Dennis. "Life Insurance Funding Strategies for Buy-Sell Agreements. *Journal of Financial Service Professionals* 59 (2005): 10–12. Web. 8 May 2007.

Widland, James. "Small Business Succession Planning: Making the Most of the Family's Golden Goose." *New Mexico Business Journal* 30 (2006). Web. 2 May 2007.

Seth M. Azria, J.D.

Charismatic Authority

ABSTRACT

Charismatic authority is one of the three types of legitimate authority identified by Max Weber. Weber's theory of legitimate authority can be traced back to the dramatic political changes Germany underwent during the late nineteenth and early twentieth centuries. The charismatic leader gains power and authority solely on the basis of his or her "larger than life" personal appeal and charm. All three of Weber's forms of legitimate authority are theoretical or ideal concepts, meaning that, in reality, it is rare for an authority to be purely one type. Ayatollah Ruhollah Khomeini and Fidel Castro offer good examples of charismatic authority.

OVERVIEW

British television host Sir David Frost has the distinction of having interviewed some of the most powerful and influential individuals in the world, including six British prime ministers, seven US presidents, and countless celebrities. However, when asked who was the most charismatic individual he had ever interviewed, Frost chose a man whose name can be literally interpreted as troublemaker—Nelson Rolihlahla Mandela. In particular, he commented on Mandela's 28 years of wrongful captivity on Robben Island and how he famously emerged with no signs of bitterness. When Frost asked Mandela about this unusual degree of patience, the future president of South Africa replied, "David, I would like to be bitter, but there is no time to be bitter. There is work to do" (Human spirit 2008).

Mandela's desire to reemerge into the public arena and lead South Africa beyond the shackles of the apartheid era is a testament to both his professional capabilities and his personal appeal as a unique, dynamic individual. His example makes an important point about authority and leadership: political leadership relies on a myriad of personal and professional qualifications and particularly, the ability to garner the support of the people. Political leaders must be able to speak to the public in such a way that they convey they understand the issues and are capable of addressing them. In short, leaders need to have charisma.

It is no surprise, therefore, that the eminent German sociologist Max Weber viewed charismatic leadership as one of his ideal forms of authority. To be sure, Weber did not view this form of leadership with a great esteem, having lived in the shadow of multiple charismatic leaders in his lifetime. Nevertheless, despite his personal attitudes concerning such concepts, Weber could not claim that charismatic authority was irrelevant or ineffectual.

Max Weber & Charisma

Max Weber was no stranger to charisma. Growing up in the Germany constructed by Otto von Bismarck, the "Iron Chancellor," and headed by the outspoken emperor Kaiser Wilhelm II, Weber had firsthand experience of these leaders' impacts on German society. It was leaders like them who inspired Weber to develop a profile of the ideal forms of authority. His three types of legitimate authority provide not a set of guidelines for others to follow but rather a commentary on the aspects of effective leadership and the shortcomings of ineffectual rulers.

Weber's Germany was anything but a placid political environment. When Bismarck unified the country's war-torn regions in the middle of the nineteenth century, he did so by centralizing the German bureaucracy around him. When he and another powerful German ruler, the Kaiser, began to clash over the question of rule, he left office out of respect for him. However, the nation's administrative system was ill-equipped to address the Germans' needs when its central authority, Bismarck, no longer operated it. Germany, in Weber's eyes, was well-positioned to prosper under the administrative hand of Bismarck's bureaucracy but, ironically, fell into disrepair under the charismatic authority of the very same man.

Unfortunately, the Kaiser's move to push out Bismarck did little to strengthen his own regime. In fact, subsequent chancellors proved at best ineffectual, in part due to Wilhelm's desire to avoid another Iron Chancellor. The sparring continued among the German leadership until the early twentieth century, when the Kaiser's disastrous militaristic campaign in the First World War prompted a revolution of sorts, forcing Wilhelm II to abdicate his throne. Socialists quickly filled the void, led by Kurt Eisner. Eisner, rather than asserting his group's dominance, reached out to potential rivals and peasants alike to form a "United States of Germany" (Rempel 2008).

Like his predecessors, however, Eisner fell into a trap of his own design. His vanity and sense of moral superiority altered his reputation and eventually undermined his brief stint as prime minister of Bavaria (Mitchell 2003). Weber, who at one time spoke quite highly of Eisner, changed his opinion of the socialist "revolutionary" as he saw Eisner begin to embrace his eccentricities and personal appeal rather than build a long-lasting political infrastructure (Hopkins 2007).

In light of his experiences, it comes as no surprise that Weber would seek to understand the forms of legitimate authority in the modern world. It is also understandable that part of these observations would center on the charismatic leader.

Weber's Three Types of Legitimate Authority

Max Weber was first and foremost a sociologist. An unabashed adherent to the concept of natural justice and fairness, he possessed a firm grasp of the legal world and was called upon in other arenas of social study, including economics and, of course, political science. However, his views on the latter subject would reveal a sense of cynicism toward political leadership.

Based on this ingrained concern for leadership, Weber offered his notion of three types of legitimate authority: rational-legal rule, traditional authority, and charismatic authority. Each of these forms of authority, as presented by Weber, was considered "legitimate"; in other words, they were not put in place through a violent coup or illegal activities. Rather, society accepted these authorities and their regimes. In many cases, the leader was reelected, the leader's political party experienced growth and success, and the regime was endorsed by the body politic.

The first of these manifestations of leadership—the rational-legal rule—was the one preferred by Weber: Within this type, authority is legitimized via the rule of law in a system that features a strong bureaucracy. No single leader stands out, at least in the sense that he or she dominated the administrative activities of that bureaucracy. The second of Weber's types was traditional authority. Within this type, ruling authority was legitimized on the basis of traditions such as religious rites or cultural histories. Leaders achieved their power simply because it had always been done this way. Monarchies and religious governments both demonstrate this form of leadership. The third of Weber's ideals of authority—charismatic—derived his or her legitimacy on the basis of his or her extraordinary personal characteristics, not qualification or legal precedent. His or her supporters offered their devotion to the individual,

Max Weber in 1894

not his or her regime or administration, through volunteerism, honorary gifts, and donations (Joosse 2006).

Charismatic leaders were, in Weber's construct, often received by their followers in a more heroic light than other rulers. They might be called prophets, visionaries, or warriors rather than mere people. Rather than advocate, the charismatic leader fights for the people and his or her cause. Even the cause appears more spiritual than mundane: the charismatic leader might refer to his or her work as a "mission" or "spiritual duty" rather than a mere policy response or initiative (Boje 2008).

Since the charismatic leader's authority was not based on legal precedent, society did not legitimize the authority of such a leader on the basis of a constitutional provision, administrative organ, or set of governmental or infrastructural rules. Rather, the charismatic leader gained power and authority solely on the basis of his or her larger-than-life personal appeal and charm. This view suggests that the charismatic figure did not usually embrace existing governmental or administrative institutions and systems; he or she was likely to be a radical or revolutionary who spoke out against the status quo. By defying the rational legal form of government, the charismatic leader clearly distanced himself or herself from the bureaucracy and the economy and instead embraced a radical shift that is based on little more than rhetoric (Boje 2008).

The annals of human history do not lack examples of the Weberian charismatic ruler. Cleopatra, Napoleon Bonaparte, Adolf Hitler, and Mao Zedong all qualify as individuals who did not achieve their power or authority as a result of the democratic process, bureaucratic institution, or traditional rites or beliefs. Rather, these individuals inspired their followers with calls for a new world order through the upheaval of the cumbersome systems they felt were bringing down society.

FURTHER INSIGHTS

An expert on organized religion, Max Weber saw a bit of the divine in the charismatic ruler. In fact, charisma itself, Weber asserted, is a superhuman trait or a sign of extraordinary powers. Like the traditional ruler, who is legitimized on the basis of religious, cultural, or hereditary rites, the charismatic ruler is given legitimacy on the basis of his or her extraordinary personal characteristics, not qualification or legal precedent. His or her supporters offer their devotion to the individual, not his or her regime or administration, through volunteerism, honorary gifts, and donations (Joosse 2006).

Charismatic authority remains present even in the post-industrial international community. This paper will next turn to some examples of charismatic rule in the modern world.

Iran & the Islamic Revolution

Between 1941 and 1979, Iran underwent a period of modernization the likes of which its people had never before seen. Unfortunately, the efforts at modernization made by the monarchist regime of Shah Reza Pahlavi did more to divide Iran than to bring the people into a collective economic boom. A relative few technocrats did reap the fruits of Iran's technological advances, but a much larger percentage of the population remained locked in poverty. Adding to the tumult was the fact that the new classes, while enjoying advances toward modernity, also had very little political autonomy in the Shah's government. Meanwhile, the increasing power of the Islamic leadership, particularly of Ayatollah Ruhollah Khomeini, empowered both the lower classes and the modernized but isolated technocrat class.

By offering them a sense of value and solidarity they failed to experience under the Shah, Khomeini carried a strong appeal for these groups. While Khomeini did seem to espouse modernization, his true gift lay in proliferating the central tenets of Islamic fundamentalism among the increasingly disgruntled masses. Even if these tenets seemed contrary to modernization, Iranians welcomed Khomeini's ideals and ousted Pahlavi in 1979 in favor of creating an Islamic state (Amineh and Eisenstadt 2007).

To be sure, Iran does have a parliamentary system as well as an executive. However, the heavy infiltration of Shi'a ideology into government, as well as the legitimacy bestowed upon the Ayatollah over the years, has largely turned Iran's government, like most other parts of life in this Middle Eastern nation, into a theocracy with the Ayatollah at the helm. The charisma of Ayatollah Ali Khameini, as the chief religious figure in the country and a representative of the system that ousted a stumbling Shah's regime, continues to provide Iranians with little substance in terms of social, economic, or political policy. Then again, Khameini, like Khomeini in 1979, has succeeded in providing ideological sentiment and rhetoric to Iranians who continue to look to their faith for a political anchor.

The Castros & Cuba
In the case of Cuba, revolution was not a response to economic stagnation or even a class struggle. Rather, it was in response to a coup that led to the installation of a dictator. In 1933, Fulgencio Batista y Zaldivar seized power over the country during a military officer uprising. Interestingly, he was elected president in 1940, only to be voted out of office in 1944. In 1952 he ran again for president, but three months before the election, he staged another coup and again took control as a dictator.

In 1953, a young Fidel Castro led an attack on a military barracks and was summarily arrested. Authorities sent him into exile, but he returned in 1956 to initiate a guerilla-style rebellion that would ultimately lead to the defeat and expulsion of the Batista regime in 1959. Castro's revolution sent the nation's former leaders and countless others across the short spit of ocean that separated Cuba from the United States, and relations quickly deteriorated as a result. The United States imposed an embargo on Cuban imports and, in 1961, attempted to invade the country at the Bay of Pigs. Cuba then turned to the Soviet Union for protection and trade. Matters became still worse in 1962 when the Soviet Union attempted to install nuclear missiles in Cuba (Recent Political Developments 2008).

Over the course of his nearly 50-year rule of Cuba, Castro largely maintained his power through his personal appeal. He has described himself as a "spiritual influence, a mentor" to Cuba and led the country "by inspiring an almost cultish mix of love and fear" among the people (A Hard Act to Follow 1996). His polished oratorical skills and virulent anti-American rhetoric have also kept the country united against a national enemy. Castro retired in 2008 and his brother, Raul, assumed control.

CONCLUSIONS

This paper has provided some examples of charismatic leaders of varying legacies. Some charismatic leaders, like Hitler, used their authority to establish totalitarian or authoritarian regimes. Others, like Mandela, used their dynamic personalities to bring their countries together under the banners of peace, freedom, or equality.

Charisma is appealing, especially to societies in search of inspiration after many years of stagnation, war, or poverty. However, any social group that relies solely on a charismatic leader is likely to flounder unless the leader's rhetoric is supported by visible gains. Mao Zedong, for example, successfully overthrew the ineffectual and elitist Kuomintang of China and activated millions of rural and impoverished Chinese citizens to rebuild the country's infrastructure. Likewise, Fidel Castro also survived government repression to lead a revolution that overthrew an entrenched dictator.

Then again, Weber spoke of legitimized authority: the power that is given to the ruler by the people. A populace may endorse a charismatic figure, especially one who overthrew an oppressive regime, but it may also withdraw that support if the figure in question fails to move the nation forward. Mandela, for example, had great staying power because of his initiative to return South Africa to the international community via trade and cultural exchanges and his work to build an exceptional economy. Wilhelm, on the other hand, forced out Bismarck, his most effective chancellor, and, despite his attempts to connect with the German populace, was unable to maintain the essential German bureaucracy. As a result, he failed to stay in power very long after Bismarck's departure.

In the two examples of modern charismatic rulers provided above, Iran's ayatollahs and Cuba's Fidel Castro, their regimes have been legitimized by a deep-seated national distrust of the United States and the West. That the United States has consistently sided against Iran and continues to maintain strict sanctions against Cuba has inadvertently galvanized the populaces of those nations to legitimize their charismatic leaders. Nevertheless, each of these two regimes has felt the need to appease the populace through substantive policy reforms

The typical charismatic ruler, under the Weber paradigm, is legitimized via what the populace sees as his or her apparently supernatural ability to connect with the people. However, unless external elements continue to foster legitimacy in singularly charismatic leaders, as is the case in Iran and Cuba, rhetoric and posturing can only take a nation so far. Similarly, bureaucracy and the rational-legal system of governance may keep a nation running smoothly, but they do not tend to excite or inspire a society the way a fiery campaign speech can. Additionally, an individual's charisma may inspire loyalty and support, but a royal family or a religious icon in the traditional sense can inspire sentiments of grace and faith.

It is important to reiterate that each form of authority within this context is an ideal, pure, and uncontaminated by the other forms. In light of this fact, the definition of a charismatic leader is extreme and fails to recognize a leader's other personal and professional qualifications. Taking this point into consideration, it is likely that each pure ideal may not be able to stand on its own without incorporating at least some elements from the other ideals. In this light, charisma alone may not effectively rule a nation, though it can help inspire effective government.

TERMS & CONCEPTS

- **Charismatic authority:** One of Weber's three forms of legitimate authority, in which an individual's ruling power is legitimated on the basis of his or her personal appeal.
- **Legitimate authority:** Leadership that is accepted by the people.
- **Max Weber:** A late nineteenth- and early twentieth-century German sociologist, economist, and political scientist. Author of *The Three Types of Legitimate Rule*.
- **Rational-legal:** One of Weber's three forms of legitimate authority, in which leadership is legitimated by legal precedent and carried through a bureaucracy.
- **Traditional rule:** One of Weber's three forms of legitimate authority, in which leadership is legitimated by cultural or religious rites or beliefs.

BIBLIOGRAPHY

Amineh, M.P., and S.N. Eisenstadt. "The Iranian Revolution." *Perspective on Global Development and Technology* 6 (2007): 129–57. Web. 24 Apr. 2008.

Boje, David M. "Max Weber." Web. 24 Apr. 2008.

Chryssides, George D. "Unrecognized Charisma? A Study and Comparison of Five Charismatic Leaders: Charles Taze Russell, Joseph Smith, L. Ron Hubbard, Swami Prabhupada and Sun Myung Moon." *Max Weber Studies* 12 (2012): 185–204. Web. 28 Oct. 2013.

"A Hard Act to Follow." *Macleans* 109 (1996): 19. Web. 9 May 2008.

Hathazy, Paul. "Enchanting Bureaucracy: Symbolic Violence and the (Re)production of Charismatic Authority in a Police Apparatus." *International Sociology* 27 (2012): 745–67. Web. 28 Oct. 2013. Hopkins, Nicholas. "Charisma and Responsibility." *Max Weber Studies* 7 (2007): 185–211. Web. 22 Apr. 2008.

"Human Spirit." (2008). Web. 21 Apr. 2008.

Josse, Paul. "Silence, Charisma and Power." *Journal of Contemporary Religion* 21 (2006): 355–71. Web. 24 Apr. 2008.

Mitchell, Allan. "Kurt Eisner 1867–1919." *Central European History* 36 (2003). Web. 22 Apr. 2008.

"Recent Political Developments." (2008). Country Profile: Cuba. Web. 24 Apr. 2008.

Rempel, Gerhard. "The German Revolution of 1918." Web. 22 Apr. 2008.

Sommer, Michael. "Empire of Glory: Weberian Paradigms and the Complexities of Authority in Imperial Rome." *Max Weber Studies* 11 (2011): 155–91. Web. 28 Oct. 2013.

Whimster, Sam. "Editorial." *Max Weber Studies* 4 (2004). Web. 22 Apr. 2008.

SUGGESTED READING

Andreas, Joel. "The Structure of Charismatic Mobilization: A Case Study of the Chinese Cultural Revolution." *American Sociological Review* 72 (2007): 434–58. Web. 25 Apr. 2008.

Breuilly, John. "Max Weber, Charisma and Nationalist Leadership." *Nations & Nationalism* 17 (2011): 477–99. Web. 28 Oct. 2013.

Kallis, Aristotle A. "Fascism 'Charisma' and 'Charismatisation'." *Totalitarian Movements and Political Religions* 7 (2006): 25–43. Web. 25 Apr. 2008.

Lepsius, M. Rainer. "The Model of Charismatic Leadership and Its Applicability to the Rule of Adolph Hitler." *Totalitarian Movements and Political Religions* 7 (2006): 175–90. Web. 25 Apr. 2008.

Mitchell, Karen. The Extraordinary Woman: Engendering Max Weber's Theory of Charisma. (2007). Conference Papers–Midwestern Political Science Association. Web. 25 Apr. 2008.

Pombeni, Paolo. "Charismatic Leadership between Ideal Type and Ideology." *Journal of Political Ideologies* 13 (2008): 37–54. Web. 25 Apr. 2008.

Michael P. Auerbach, M.A.

Coaching

ABSTRACT

Coaching is a strategy, most commonly used in business-related organizations, to help executives increase their personal effectiveness and manage their careers. There are several models of coaching including personal coaching, co-coaching, and executive coaching. In businesses, executive coaching has become a prevalent strategy to provide developmental support for managers and leaders.

OVERVIEW

Executives in most organizations, regardless of their levels of responsibility, are challenged with the impact of technology, competitive markets, consumer demands, the expectations of a diverse workforce, and the problems associated with leadership. The practice of executive coaching, as an intervention, has been used in business settings since the 1970s. During this period, executives were enrolled in short-term programs to learn skills such as business etiquette and employee relations. In the 1980s, more sophisticated programs were developed that also focused on personal effectiveness. By the late 1990s, executive coaching became one of the fastest growing areas in consulting, with the number of coaches estimated in the tens of thousands.

The increased popularity of coaching is linked to its efficiency and cost-effectiveness. It is intended to be a goal-focused, personally organized strategy to help managers understand and improve their performance, enhance a career, or work through organizational issues. The one-on-one, targeted, and confidential approach of coaching adds to its appeal.

Models of Coaching

Coaching can be categorized into three areas: feedback coaching, developmental coaching, and content coaching. Each is delivered differently, and variations are based on company needs. However, all types of coaching are designed to help managers enhance their skills or improve in a specific area. Feedback coaching involves helping managers create a plan that addresses a particular need and gives them support while implementing it. An assessment instrument is used to identify strengths and areas needing improvement. Coaching usually occurs through several in-person conversations over a one- to six-month period. It begins with a planning meeting and is followed by subsequent sessions that assess progress and challenges and provide encouragement. The final meeting is used to conduct a mini assessment and update the development plan. At this point, there also may be an option to continue coaching.

In-depth coaching generally lasts between six months and one year. This type of coaching is characterized as a close, intimate relationship between the executive and the coach. The information collection and analysis phases are extensive, and they typically involve interviews with the executive's staff, colleagues, and, in some instances, clients, vendors, and family members. Multiple assessment tools are used to measure competencies, interests, and strengths. The coach may even observe the executive at work.

These data are reviewed during an intensive feedback session, which may last up to two days and results in the creation of a development plan. The coach continues to be involved during the implementation phase of the plan to determine progress, discuss roadblocks, and offer support. This work continues until the development plan has been completely implemented and the executive has made noticeable improvements.

A business executive applies the lessons he has acquired from his coach (Photo courtesy of Natonal Assembly for Wales)

Content coaching distinguishes itself from the other types of coaching because its goal is to help managers learn about specific areas of knowledge or develop a certain skill. For example, a manager may need to know more about global marketing or how to improve presentation skills. Content coaches, as experts in specialized fields, may require managers to read books to increase their content knowledge about a topic and participate in follow-up discussions. Other forms of coaching may involve analyzing videotaped role-playing or demonstrations and attending seminars or one-on-one meetings. The manager's goals, skill level, and the desired outcomes determine the duration of the coaching.

External Versus Internal Coaches

The cornerstones of the coaching relationship are trust and confidentiality. The degree of a coach's involvement with the organization whose members are being coached is the source of debate, especially regarding whether a coach should be external or internal. External coaches offer a safe place for the coaching process since they have no personal involvement in the company and no appearance of a conflict of interest. Since they have no company-related interest in the outcome, the managers can speak freely without fear of reprisal.

Internal coaches have the dual role of serving both the company and the employee. An advantage is that the internal coach knows the organization's policies and people. This knowledge can serve to benefit the overall organizational and individual goals. However, the sense of anonymity is lost, which could result in a compromise of the coaching relationship. In either instance, the confidentiality and integrity of the coaching relationship remains essential to its success.

The Future of Coaching

Although coaching is characterized by the individual nature of the relationship between the executive and the coach, it occurs within the context of an organization. Many coaches believe that merely helping executives to change is insufficient, because these executives have created organizations that reflect their own personalities and inadequacies. Therefore, the responsibilities of the coach often broaden to encourage the executive to implement changes in a way that will benefit the entire organization. The notion of coaching can then be extended to that of coaching organizations. In this way, team building and performance-support techniques enable employees to manage themselves and their own behavior with increasing competence.

Bibliography

Cook, Marshall. *Effective Coaching.* New York: McGraw, 1999.

Flaherty, James. *Coaching: Evoking Excellence in Others.* Boston: Butterworth, 2005.

Gilley, Jerry W., and Nathaniel W. Boughton. *Stop Managing, Start Coaching: How Performance Coaching Can Enhance Commitment and Improve Productivity.* New York: McGraw, 1997.

Goldsmith, Marshall, Laurence Lyons, and Alyssa Freas, eds. *Coaching for Leadership: How the World's Greatest Coaches Help Leaders Learn.* San Francisco: Jossey-Bass, 2000.

Markle, Garold L. *Catalytic Coaching: The End of the Performance Review.* Westport: Quorum, 2000.

McCarthy, Grace, and Julia Milner. "Managerial Coaching: Challenges, Opportunities, and Training." *Journal of Management Development* 32.7 (2013): 768–79. Print.

O'Neill, Mary Beth. *Executive Coaching with Backbone and Heart: A Systems Approach to Engaging Leaders with Their Challenges.* 2nd ed. San Francisco: Jossey-Bass, 2007.

Passmore, Jonathan, David B. Peterson, and Tereza Freire. *The Wiley-Blackwell Handbook of the Psychology of Coaching and Mentoring.* Hoboken, NJ: Wiley, 2013.

Reilly, Edward T. *AMA Business Boot Camp: Management and Leadership Fundamentals That Will See You Successfully through Your Career.* Toronto: American Management Assn., 2013.

Rostron, Sunny Stout, Daniel Marques Sampaio, and Marti Janse Van Rensburg. *Business Coaching International: Transforming Individuals and Organizations.* 2nd ed. London: Karnac, 2014.

Whitworth, Laura, Karen Kimsey-House, Henry Kimsey-House, and Phillip Sandahl. *Co-active Coaching: New Skills for Coaching People toward Success in Work and Life.* 2nd ed. Mountain View, CA: Davies-Black, 2007.

Anna Lowe

Collective Bargaining

ABSTRACT

For centuries, guilds and unions have fought for worker rights and benefits while managers have fought back to protect the company from going out of business. These parties have worked to find common ground via the collective bargaining process, where both sides meet to establish an agreement on how the work will be conducted. This article examines collective bargaining, reviewing the process and ways it has evolved over the last several centuries. The essay also reviews some of the issues that commonly present themselves during such negotiations.

OVERVIEW

In 1969, the Western film *Death of a Gunfighter* opened in theaters across the country. Starring Richard Widmark and Lena Horne, the film was well received by critics, including one of the most well-known, Roger Ebert. Ebert hailed the film and its director, Alan Smithee, of whom he said "a name I'm not familiar with." Smithee would direct more than a dozen other films from that point forward, and would appear in the credits for a number of television shows and even music videos.

Ebert's comment on Smithee's seeming anonymity was telling—no one had previously seen Alan Smithee's work, because in fact, Alan Smithee was not real. According to many accounts, Widmark strongly disagreed with the direction of Robert Totten, having him replaced with director Don Siegel. Siegel felt that Totten did most of the work, and did not wish to have his name on the film. The Directors Guild of America, which set the rules for film directors and worked to protect them within the industry, allowed Siegel to change his name in the film's credits. Over the following decades, the use of Alan Smithee's name by directors would be known as an act of defiance against interfering studio management.

For centuries, workers and business managers have often coexisted in an adversarial relationship. Guilds and unions have fought for worker rights and benefits while managers have fought back to protect the company from going out of business. These parties have worked to find common ground via the collective bargaining process, where both sides meet to establish an agreement on how the work will be conducted.

A Brief History of Unions & Bargaining

The labor movement began during the Industrial Revolution in the eighteenth century. As industrialized nations began to further their evolution, building a wide range of industries, the workforce expanded with them. Increased demand meant harder work and longer hours, often under dangerous and or unsanitary conditions. Many workers were kept on factory assembly lines for twelve- and fourteen-hour shifts in unventilated, poorly lit factories. In Great Britain, after such conditions became well publicized, Parliament enacted a set of Factory Acts in the early nineteenth century (Montagna 1981). While the implementation of these measures in England did call attention to the issue, such conditions continued in other environments. Workers began to see the value in joining together in solidarity to change those conditions, since government

Senator Robert F. Wagner who gave his name to the National Labor Relations Act of 1935 (painting by Steven Polson)

did not seem interested in comprehensive reforms, believing that heavy regulation would stymie industrial growth.

The United States would also undergo this growth, both in terms of populations in urban centers and in the industrial workforce. The first US unions jelled in New York and Philadelphia in the late 18th century. Over the following century, labor organizations grew in size and quantity, diversifying with industrial diversification. Their success rate was minimal, however, in light of the political and economic power industrial leaders held at the time (Teasley 2009). Their plight was worsened by the Great Depression, with only the craft unions surviving that economic period.

However, the Great Depression would also help labor find a resurgence. The fact that more than a third of Americans were put out of work helped give the working individual a sympathetic ear from the government. The federal government, led by new President Franklin Delano Roosevelt, enacted a number of laws designed to place greater restrictions on antiunion policies. The first of these acts was the 1932 Norris-La Guardia Act, which rendered unenforceable so-called yellow-dog contracts, agreements in which the employee agreed to not join a union in order to keep his or her job. That law also limited the ability of courts to intervene in strikes and other labor protests (The Great Depression and Labor, 2009). In 1935, the National Labor Relations Act, also known as the Wagner Act gave workers the right to form unions. This law also gave unions the ability to enter into negotiations with their employers. These negotiations would become known as collective bargaining.

In addition to strict restrictions on the intervention of external elements into labor disputes, the National Labor Relations Act (NLRA) stated "to bargain collectively is the performance of the mutual obligation of the employer and the representative of the employees to meet at reasonable times and confer in good faith with respect to" such matters of pay and benefits, hours and other aspects of employment (National Labor Relations Act 1935, Sec. 8 (d)). Collective bargaining, therefore, would entail the periodic negotiations between employers and employees (as represented by a union and/or union representatives). These negotiations would result in a legally binding contract, which could not be terminated unless both sides agreed.

In modern times, unions and collective bargaining are found worldwide, although they tend to be more active in areas where industrialization and subsequent economic growth are increasing. While unions have suffered membership declines in recent years, the passions that have long been part of their unifying philosophies have remained. In fact, there are those who believe that unionization and collective bargaining are fundamental privileges not dissimilar from human rights; these advocates assert that if the sentiments of the International Labor Organization (the intergovernmental organization charged with advocating for both human and labor rights) were adopted in specific countries, the laws protecting collective bargaining would provide greater protection (Adams 2005).

FURTHER INSIGHTS

Understanding Collective Bargaining

At its most basic, collective bargaining entails the negotiation of terms and conditions of employment between management and workers. Under ideal conditions, the key to this concept involves the two sides meeting to establish common ground under set rules and equitable conditions. In the same vein as individual bargaining in employment, the assumption is that both sides are expected to make compromises in order to reach a mutually beneficial agreement.

Collective bargaining owes its roots to a perceived unpredictability in how industry earnings may be split between employers and employees. In 1867, British statistician Jacob Waley argued that the distribution of business returns would be in a constantly fluctuating environment and as such, no clear standards could be established. Therefore, he suggested, "the precise place at which the line is drawn will to a very considerable extent be determined by circumstances which may fairly be called fortuitous, and may be greatly influenced by a bargain between the employer and the employed" (cited in Hutt 1954, 82–83).

Collective bargaining does not entail two individuals; the negotiations occur between representatives of the respective parties. The employer is represented by human resource managers, legal counsel and managers of the areas in which the work will be performed. On the other side, the workers are represented by the unions, which are member supported labor organizations whose purpose is to advocate for and protect the workers benefits. Unions place the collective good of the entire workforce over the individual which is an important distinction about collective bargaining in comparison to individual employment negotiations.

Since the resurgence of labor and unions after the Great Depression, collective bargaining in the United States has generated considerable controversy, as few legislative or regulatory attempts to reform or modify collective bargaining have avoided intense lobbying and political polarization. Advocates for collective bargaining assert that the process gives a voice to those who might otherwise have no input into employment conditions. While collective bargaining negotiations may last a long period of time (sometimes weeks and even months), advocates stress that such lengthy periods are well worth the time and expense if it means improvements in the workers' lives. The arduous process, proponents say, may in fact be wrought with inefficiencies, but such issues are again negated by the fact that the best interests of the workers are being met as a result of the negotiations (Block and Berg 2003).

Some employers seek to limit or modify collective bargaining. They assert that collective bargaining is an imperfect process, inflexible to the needs of an ever-changing economy and business environment. To some critics of collective bargaining, a conflict of interest exists: unions rely on the monetary dues of members—the more workers earn, the more they are able to pay to the unions. As such, unions will seek the maximum revenues possible from higher wages negotiated by the unions. Regarding this issue, one expert says that the "union is thought of as a profit-maximizing entity rather than a wage-fixing agency for labor" (McConnell 1955, 14).

In light of the often adversarial relationship between employers and employees (or, more specifically, between employers and unions), governments have stood as intermediaries in formulating the methods by which collective bargaining units may proceed with their negotiations. In the United States, The NLRA remains the fundamental basis for governing collective bargaining; although states have implemented their own laws on unions and collective bargaining, the Constitution states that any federal laws pertaining thereto, such as NLRA, supersede those state laws (Collective Bargaining 2009). Although collective bargaining has evolved considerably and has generated significant controversy during that development, the practice of this employer-employee negotiation remains common.

The Art of Negotiation
At the genesis of collective bargaining is the formation of the union. Permissible under the NLRA in the United States, unions may be formed in a private, for profit business, nonprofit organization or a public (government) agency. Unions are typically formed when a majority of workers within a business vote by secret ballot to be represented by such organizations. Once this vote has been conducted, the National Labor Relations Board (NLRB), the federal agency charged with union oversight, certifies the vote and validates the union. Meanwhile, management of the business must also accept the vote and recognize the union as the agent representing employees at the collective bargaining unit.

The goal of the collective bargaining unit is a contract under which the required work will be performed. Many such negotiations focus on single worksites and single employee organizations. However, many larger employers may have multiple sites in other regions. They may conduct single contract negotiations with the unions on behalf of the entire breadth of the organization's operations or negotiate contracts that are site specific.

Traditional Bargaining
There are two general styles of negotiating employed during collective bargaining units. The first of these is the more traditional form, in which both sides act solely on behalf of their respective interests. Employers will proceed from the perspective of the business, the union from the perspective of the workers. It is an adversarial and occasionally extremely bitter form of bargaining, often involving sacrifices from both parties, resulting in a contract in which a sizable percentage of the provisions are considered negative by each party. Despite the confrontational nature of this approach, the traditional view of collective bargaining remains a long-standing preference among negotiators.

Partnership Approach
The partnership style is a more congenial and conciliatory approach. Employers are given an ability to

see and appreciate the interests of the employees and vice versa. From this mutually beneficial perspective, it is believed that an agreement can be more quickly completed. Because both sides understand the needs and concerns of their counterparts, it is believed that this approach is less controversial and more efficient than the traditional approach, resulting in a contract with which both parties can find accord.

Strikes

Of course, given the inherently adversarial relationship that exists between employers and unions, there are occasions in which collective bargaining reaches an impasse. As negotiations extend longer than expected or break off altogether, both sides may employ a range of tactics designed to hamper the other. Unions may call for a strike, taking workers out of their jobs until employers return to the table or agree to their demands. In the event of such an incident, employers may retaliate by hiring nonunion employees to replace the striking workers. When collective bargaining reaches this point, it may be further intensified by charged rhetoric, public battles on the media and intervening political figures.

Arbitration

In the event that such an impasse occurs, both parties may agree to seek arbitration. As an alternative to litigation, arbitration offers a solution to an extended and increasingly combative standoff. A neutral third-party arbitrator is called in by both parties to review the unresolved issues and render a decision that is legally binding. The decision may not be fully agreeable to either party, but arbitration offers an end to lengthy disputes.

ISSUES

Unions & Legislation

Unionization and collective bargaining have long been the subjects of controversy in political circles as well as business operations. Proposed changes to state and national laws pertaining to these issues have been introduced in great quantities for decades. Most recently, for example, a significant push in the United States has been initiated by unions to increase membership by eliminating the secret ballot vote and replacing it with more open card check process, whereby employees vote for or against unionization simply by signing their names to the process. Part of a larger bill known as the Employee Free Choice Act, the measure is seen by proponents as a way to expedite unionization and minimize employer interference, while opponents see it as a vehicle by which unionization will be imposed upon workers who might not otherwise vote for it.

In Canada, relevant legislation has been introduced on a number of fronts. In the late 1990s, bills were introduced to lessen the impact of contentious collective bargaining negotiations by restricting strike declarations and regulating when non union workers could be used while employees were on strike (Cramton, Gunderson and Tracy 1999). The consistently integrating European Union is exploring ways by which collective bargaining in transnational and multinational business may be made uniform, a concept opposed by employers and advocated by unions (Gennard 2008).

Collective bargaining continues to adapt to a constantly evolving business environment. Although it remains largely adversarial, collective bargaining in a general sense is likely to continue to be the primary vehicle for employer-employee labor negotiations.

In 1981, over 12,000 members of the Professional Air Traffic Controllers (PATCO), who were mired in a bitter collective bargaining unit with the Federal Aviation Administration (FAA), walked off the job over a lack of amenable pay raises. Although the law allowed for replacement workers to be hired to replace striking workers, few employers had until then acted on that ability to hire them. President Ronald Reagan issued a simple but harsh warning to Professional Air Traffic Controllers: return to work within forty-eight hours or their jobs would be terminated. Professional Air Traffic Controllers called Reagan's bluff, but he did not flinch. Reagan terminated all of the employees' jobs, replacing them with nonunion personnel. Reagan's heavy-handed approach had two results. In the short term, he effectively ended an arduous collective bargaining unit with one bold, swift move. In the long term, he set a fearful precedent for would-be strikers: in the decades before the Professional Air Traffic Controllers incident, there were about three hundred major strikes per year—since then, there have only been an average of thirty per year in the United States (Schalch 2006).

CONCLUSION

The example of the Professional Air Traffic Controllers underscores the typically adversarial and often contentious relationship between labor and employers during collective bargaining. In a general sense, the nature of both parties' respective perspectives has not changed since the Industrial Revolution, nor have the issues (such as hours, wages, safety and job requirements) that widen the gulf between employer and employee during negotiations. Collective bargaining continues to evolve as the business environment itself changes. Despite the oft-bitter and at times politcally charged conflicts that arise through collective bargaining, it remains an important tool in helping employers and employees seek and establish common ground.

BIBLIOGRAPHY

Adams, Roy. "Collective Bargaining as a Human Rights and Labor Relations Issues in Canada." [Transcript]. National Union of Public and General Employees. (2005, 24 Mar.). Web. 25 Oct. 2009.

Alan Smithee. Internet Movie Database. (2009). Web. 24 Oct. 2009.

Block, Richard, and Peter Berg. "Collective Bargaining in Context: Comparing the United States and Europe." In *Bargaining for Competitiveness: Law, Research and Case Studies*. Kalamazoo, MI: W.E. Upjohn Institute for Employment Research, 2003. Web. 26 Oct. 2009.

Caverly, Natasha, Bart Cunningham, and Lari Mitchell. "Reflections on Public Sector-Based Integrative Collective Bargaining." *Employee Relations* 28 (2006): 62–75.

Chamberlain, Neil. "The Nature and Scope of Collective Bargaining." *Quarterly Journal of Economics* 58 (1944): 359–387. Web. 28 Oct. 2009.

"Collective Bargaining." In *Wex—LLI's Collaboratively Built Law Dictionary and Encyclopedia*. (2009). Web. 27 Oct. 2009.

Cloutier, Julie, Pascale L. Denis, and Henrietta Bilodeau. "Collective Bargaining and Perceived Fairness: Validating the Conceptual Structure." *Relations Industrielles / Industrial Relations* 67 (2012): 398–425. Web. 24 Nov. 2013.

Cramton, Peter, Morley Gunderson, and Joseph Tracy. "The Effect of Collective Bargaining Lesiglation on Strikes and Wages." *Review of Economics and Statistics* 81 (1999): 475–87. Web. 28 Oct. 2009.

Gennard, John. "Negotiations at Multinational Company Level?" *Employee Relations* 30 (2008): 100–03. Print.

The Great Depression and Labor. Adapted from Christopher Conte and Al Karr. *Outline of the U.S. Economy*. (2009). Washington, DC: U.S. Department of State. Web. 25 Oct. 2009.

Hutt, William H. *The Theory of Collective Bargaining*. Glencoe, IL: The Free Press, 1954. Web. 27 Oct. 2009.

Javits, Joshua M. "Better Process, Better Results: Integrating Mediation and Arbitration to Resolve Collective Bargaining Disputes." *ABA Journal of Labor & Employment Law* 32, no. 2 (2017): 167–187. Web. 4 Jan. 2018.

McConnell, Campbell. "Trouble Spots in Collective Bargaining Theory." *American Journal of Economics and Sociology* 15 (1955): 13–30. Web. 26 Oct. 2009.

Montagna, Joseph. "The Industrial Revolution." *An Interdisciplinary Approach to British Studies*, Vol. II, 1981. Web. 24 Oct. 2009.

National Labor Relations Act. National Labor Relations Board, 1935. Web. 25 Oct. 2009. Sachs, Benjamin. "The Unbundled Union: Politicals without Collective Bargaining." *Yale Law Journal* 123 (2013): 148–207 Web. 24 Nov. 2013.

Schlach, Kathleen. 1981 Strike Leaves Legacy for American Workers [Transcript]. *Morning Edition*, NPR. Web. 28 Oct. 2009.

Teasley, C. "The Rise of Labor Unions during the Industrial Revolution." Helium.com, 2009. Web. 24 Oct. 2009.

SUGGESTED READING

Hassel, Anke, Thorsten Schulten. "Globalization and the Future of Central Collective Bargaining: The Example of the German Metal Industry. *Economy and Society* 27 (1998). Web. 28 Oct. 2009.

Jensen, Vernon. "The Process of Collective Bargaining and the Question of Its Obsolescence." *Industrial & Labor Relations Review* 16 (1963): 546–56. Web. 28 Oct. 2009.

Kochan, Thomas, and Hoyt Wheeler. "Municipal Collective Bargaining: A Model and Analysis of Bargaining Outcomes." *Industrial & Labor Relations Review* 29 (1975): 46–66. Web. 28 Oct. 2009.

Lewin, David, Jeffrey H., and Thomas A. Kochan. "The New Great Debate about Unionism and Collective Bargaining in U.S. State and Local Governments." *Industrial & Labor Relations Review* 65 (2012): 749–78. Web. 24 Nov. 2013.

Murray III, H.F. "Federal Appeals Court Sanctions National labor Relations Board in Ongoing Battle Over Management Rights Provisions in Collective Bargaining Agreements." *Employee Relations Law Journal* 42, no. 4 (2017): 64–67. Web. 4 Jan. 2018.

Michael P. Auerbach, M.A.

Communications in the Workplace

ABSTRACT

Good communication skills are essential for success in virtually any organization. No matter how good one's technical skills or how innovative one's ideas, if not communicated clearly to others, they are irrelevant. Employees today need to be able to effectively communicate within the organization to each other, their bosses, and their subordinates as well as outside the organization to customers or clients and vendors. Clear communication that unambiguously conveys one's meaning, however, is not a simple task and can be hampered by numerous barriers including different perceptions of a situation, filtering, language, jargon, and ambiguity. In addition, cultural and gender differences can compound the process, making communication even more difficult. However, through such techniques as active listening, disclosure, and feedback, employees can learn to become better communicators and improve their own effectiveness and that of the organization.

OVERVIEW

I once worked on a project that required me to use a technical manual written for Japanese fax repair technicians that had been translated very literally (and badly) into English. "Imagine," it started, "two giants standing on opposite mountaintops in the fog." The illustration went on to describe a scenario in which the giants wished to communicate, but were having difficulty because the mountaintops were too far away to allow them to be heard by each other and the fog obscured their view so they could not signal each other. Eventually, the two giants threw boulders through the fog in an attempt to attract each other's attention. The story sounds strange and unprofessional to Western ears, but the point is that communication can be a complex process between sender and receiver, and requires that each party is paying attention and that the "fog" of distortion is cleared away no matter where in the world occurs. Even the very strangeness of the story illustrates how cultural expectations can color what we anticipate to hear.

Communication is the process of transmitting information between two or more parties. Although communication is often thought of as a verbal process, transmissions can also be written or even nonverbal with our actions or body language communicating our message. Communication can be intentional (the interoffice memo describing a new implementation policy) or unintentional (the boss receives the message—correct or not—that the employee is not a hard worker when he or she never gets assignments in on time). Good communication

A businesswoman conducts a telephone meeting (Photo courtesy of Rhoda Baer)

skills are essential for success in business. No matter how innovative one's idea is, no matter how skilled the service one offers, no matter how much the marketplace needs the product or service, if the business cannot articulate what it can do for potential customers or clients, it will not be successful.

Good communication skills, however, are not only necessary for successful marketing. Employees must be able to communicate with each other and management must be able to communicate with employees. A boss who expects employees to be mind readers will not be a boss for long. A team whose members cannot communicate their ideas to each other will not be able to achieve the synergy that is the goal of such work groups. The technical expert who cannot communicate his or her flash of insight will not be able to use it to help the organization. In short, communication is the key to success not only on an organizational level, but on a personal level as well.

A study of entry-level job requirements listed in the job advertisements from newspapers in 10 large metropolitan areas found that "interpersonal skills" were mentioned most frequently. Even for jobs such as accounting where it would be reasonable to assume that mathematical ability was more important than communication skills, it has been found that up to 80 percent of work time is actually spent in communication rather than in working with numbers. Despite the importance of good communication skills in the workplace, research has found that employees often do not possess adequate communication skills for success. As a result, 89 percent of US companies give communication training to employees in areas such as team building; public speaking and presentation skills; interviewing skills; and business and technical writing.

At its simplest, communication starts when the sender decides to transmit a message to the receiver. He or she decides what message to communicate and how best to express this message (words, gestures, body language, intonation). This message is then sent to the receiver. This person then decodes the message and forms the appropriate feedback, be it a nod of the head, a smile, or other body language; an action such as doing what the sender requested; or forming another verbal or nonverbal reply to show that the message was understood or not understood. This message is then transmitted to the original sender who, in turn, receives and decodes the response, and forms a return message (see figure 1).

This simple process, however involves more than the sender transmitting a message and the receiver responding. There are numerous places during the process where barriers to communication can keep the receiver from correctly understanding the message sent in the way that the sender intended it. When this confusion happens, miscommunication can occur. There are a number of different types of barriers to communication that can lead to miscommunication by hindering the unambiguous transmission and reception of a message between parties trying to communicate: different perceptions of a situation, filtering, language, jargon, and ambiguity. Other sources of miscommunication include the degree to which the vocabulary (professional, technical, or general) of the two persons is shared, differences in their assumptions and expectations, and their relative skill at forming and decoding messages.

For example, Harvey may wish to tell George that the budget report that he had turned in was acceptable. So, Harvey forms a message: "Good job." However, George may consider the budget report to have been his best work to date or a significant improvement over his previous attempts, and is looking for more effusive praise. The terse "good job" may not carry with it sufficient information to supply George with the feedback he is seeking. As a result, George may think that Harvey did not appreciate his work or that Harvey did not think that George had done an outstanding job. Therefore, even though Harvey may have been trying to praise George, the message that George receives is that the work was neither extraordinary nor noteworthy. Such a situation can result in resentment or discouragement and may damage the relationship between the two coworkers.

Everyone comes to a situation with his/her own unique perspective, including assumptions and expectations. This perspective helps determine how an individual will react to what the other person says or does. For example, in the illustration of Harvey and George above, if George has entered the situation with the perception that Harvey is less than pleased with his previous work, then the offhand "good work" could make him doubt his competence in other areas or lower his self-esteem. On the other hand, if his perception is that Harvey is pleased with his work in general, then the offhand "good work" could be a confirmation even if Harvey was condemning the report with faint praise. On a small scale, this confusion could cause needless friction in the workplace. However, if the miscommunication is between George and a customer, it could potentially lead to lost contracts or hours spent focusing on the wrong thing because an off-hand remark was misunderstood.

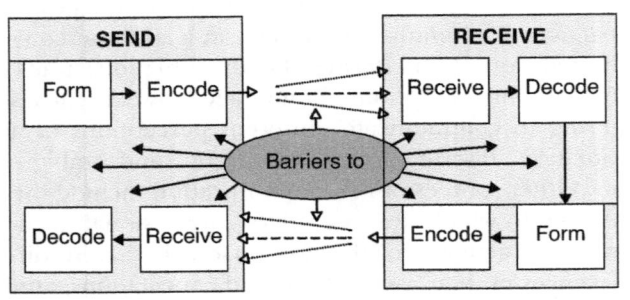

Figure 1: The Communication Process Model (adapted from McShane and Von Glinow 2003, 324)

Different perceptions, however, are not the only reason for miscommunication in the workplace. Because the nature of workplace communication is often more formal than social, communications are often filtered to remove unwanted messages. For example, the culture in some organizations rewards good news but punishes bad news. In such cases, employees may tell only the good news ("we can put on a demonstration for the customer next week") but filters out the bad news ("but only if we get needed input from a vendor on time"). Similarly, when delivering performance feedback, supervisors may try to phrase negative feedback in a positive manner in the hope that it will be encouraging ("you may want to try to make your reports a little longer in the future") rather than giving the employee the entire message ("this report had none of the needed information in it and is totally unacceptable"). In the first example, if the needed input does not come from the vendor, not only does the employee look bad for not having delivered what was promised, but also the supervisor looks bad to the customer or executives because the needed demonstration was a failure. In the second example, the employee's feelings were not hurt in the short term. However, in the long term, he or she will be left confused and bitter because raises, promotions,

or other rewards that were reasonably expected on the basis of a perceived positive performance appraisal did not materialize.

To communicate effectively, both parties need to speak the same language and use words that clearly say what is meant. This requirement does not just mean the difference between English and German, but the words chosen within the same language. One such language barrier is the use of jargon, any technical language, acronyms, specialized language, or other words or phrases that are unique—or uniquely interpreted—to a given group or organization but that are not in wide acceptance outside of that group. For example, the following message might not make sense to many people:

I've kluged a POC for the demo next week, but I need to stay down in the weeds so you'll have to pretty it up for the big boys.

However, to an engineer, it means that the sender has pulled together ("kluged") a proof-of-concept ("POC") to demonstrate that a theory will work. However, the sender of the message needs to work on other details ("stay down in the weeds") so the receiver will have to fine-tune it so that it looks viable ("pretty it up") when shown to the company executives ("big boys"). Although such short hand may enable communication between parties who both understand the jargon, it prevents communication when one or more parties do not.

Similarly, text messaging and other byproducts of today's high tech society have brought with them a language all their own. For example, the message "c u here @ 445 on 4/5" may mean to meet the sender at 4:45 on the 5th of April at his/her office. However, unless the organizational culture supports the use of such abbreviations, they are best left for less formal, social occasions. Using established rules of communication and grammar, however, apply not only to the abbreviations one might use in emails, but also to any written—or oral—communication. One's professionalism is judged in part by the way that he or she expresses himself or herself. The inability to write a coherent sentence using the established rules of English can prevent one from advancement within the organization or in one's career. There are social boundaries to language and its use. What is an acceptable way to speak or write to one's friend or in a social situation is not necessarily acceptable in a business setting.

Another language barrier to communication regarding the use of language is ambiguity. For example, Harvey asks George if he would like to redo the report, it could be taken in several ways: (1) a polite response to George's concern that the report might not be acceptable, but which is assumed George will not do, (2) an option that can be taken at George's discretion, or (3) a polite way of telling George that the report needs to be redone. If Harvey is merely making a polite response but George interprets it as a mandate to redo the report, much time is wasted. If Harvey is demanding that the report be redone but George interprets it as a polite response not requiring action, the miscommunication can lead to a strained working relationship.

APPLICATIONS

The current trend toward cultural diversity in the workplace makes communication an interesting proposition. Each individual comes with his or her own set of values, assumptions, and communication styles, yet needs to be able to communicate with others who have an entirely different set of communication rules. Further, the communication pattern that is effective in one work group may actually hamper communication between groups because of differing jargon or other barriers to communication. However, good communication skills are not only necessary but also essential to the success of the organization. Fortunately, there are methods to improve communication skills both within the organization and between the organization and other parties so that work gets done more efficiently.

Cross-Cultural & Gender Communications

Culture is defined as the basic shared assumptions, beliefs, norms, and values held consciously or unconsciously by a group of people. In today's diverse workplaces, cultures often collide, causing miscommunications as a result of differing assumptions or differing ways of expressing oneself. For example, in Japan it is considered important that neither party in a transaction "lose face." As a result, communication tends to be much more formal and even ritualistic than is usually the case in the West. Telling a Japanese businessperson negative information in a blunt way would be considered a terrible breach of etiquette because it would cause him/her to lose face. Similarly, a Japanese businessperson would be considerate of the other person's feelings even when delivering bad news. Therefore, he or she might say that serious consideration would be given to the other person's idea but use body language that—to the knowledgeable observer—indicates just the opposite. One does not have to travel halfway around the world to encounter different communication styles.

Even within a culture, men and women frequently (although not universally) have different communication styles. While men, for example, tend to feel comfortable communicating in larger groups; women often prefer one-on-one communication or small group communication. Men also tend to multitask (doing two or more things at once such as looking for or even reading a report while talking), while women tend to make eye contact and focus on only the conversation at hand. Men often jump from topic to topic in their conversations, while most women prefer to talk about one topic at length. Although these may seem like little differences, they can cause significant problems. For example, a woman in conversation with a man might interpret his multitasking as a lack of concern or that he is not taking her seriously. If differences in communication style are not understood, such misunderstandings can lead to serious problems in the workplace.

To help employees become better communicators and better understand the text and subtext of the communications between people from different cultures, many organizations offer diversity training. This type of training is designed to help employees deal with persons from different cultures more effectively by helping them gain an understanding of the assumptions, values, and communication styles of the people that they may encounter in the workplace. With this understanding, employees are better prepared to be effective communicators in the workplace and both understand the message of others and get their own message across.

Improving Communication

Although good communication can be a complex process with many potential barriers that can distort the message that one is trying to send, it is also a skill that can be learned and improved. In addition to diversity training, many organizations offer training courses that help employees learn how to improve their communication skills with each other as well as with customers and clients in order to improve their effectiveness and the organization's success. Such skills relate not only to being a better sender of messages, but also to being a better receiver. There are many techniques that can help improve communication. Two of these are active listening—a way to improve one's skills as a receiver of messages and communication—and the Johari Window—a model used to explain techniques for improving communication effectiveness.

Active listening is an approach to improving communication through techniques to help better decode the message received from the sender, clarify the message, and respond appropriately. To listen actively, one must receive and process all the signals being transmitted by the sender. This activity includes not only the actual words that are said, but also the body language and other nonverbal cues that accompany the verbal message. For example, if Harvey smiles and pats George on the back while telling him that his report shows that he is ready for a promotion, the message is quite different than if Harvey says that same thing with his arms crossed and in a sarcastic tone. Active listening skills include receiving and processing all the signals that the sender receives. This approach means that the receiver needs to postpone evaluation of what the sender is saying until all the information has been received. To further this process, the receiver should avoid interrupting, postpone evaluating what the sender says until he or she is finished and maintains interest. These skills help the receiver obtain sufficient data to accurately decode the message and form appropriate feedback.

After the information has been received, the receiver needs to evaluate the information he or she has received, organize it, and form an appropriate response. Part of this process includes showing the receiver that he or she has been understood and that his or her thoughts and feelings have been taken into account. Such displays of empathy are critical to showing the sender that both verbal and nonverbal cues have been received and understood. In addition, the receiver needs to organize the information that he or she has received. Human beings tend to process what they hear three times faster than the average rate of speech. The active listener uses this opportunity to organize the information received into key points rather than becoming distracted while the sender completes transmission of the message. In complicated communications, it can also be helpful to summarize this information when the sender is finished to make sure that both parties understand the message in the same way. Similarly, active listeners take the opportunity to clarify any ambiguity in the transmission to avoid misunderstandings.

In most communication, each party is both a sender and receiver and each needs to be aware of the potential barriers to communication and how these can be avoided. One approach to helping people improve their communication through mutual understanding is called the Johari Window (see figure 2). In this model, it is posited that true communication occurs in the "arena"; that area where both the sender and receiver strive for open, honest communication. This area can be increased through disclosure and feedback. Disclosure in the workplace would include making sure that all parties to the communication understand the assumptions and preconceptions of each other. For example, when trying to communicate on a technical matter, it is helpful to know at what level to talk to the other person. Two engineers talking to each other, for example, would share many assumptions and knowledge in common, so could use professional jargon and talk at a higher level than if one person did not have a technical background. Disclosure can also apply to other areas in the person's life, too.

Feedback is when one party gives the other party information about how the communication is received. As in active listening, this activity could include information about how well the message was received by paraphrasing or summarizing it to make sure that it was correctly received. Feedback could also include information about the nonverbal portion of the communication: "When you say that in that way, I am not sure if you are kidding or not." Such comments—when considerately and empathetically expressed—can help both parties better understand both the text and subtext of the conversation.

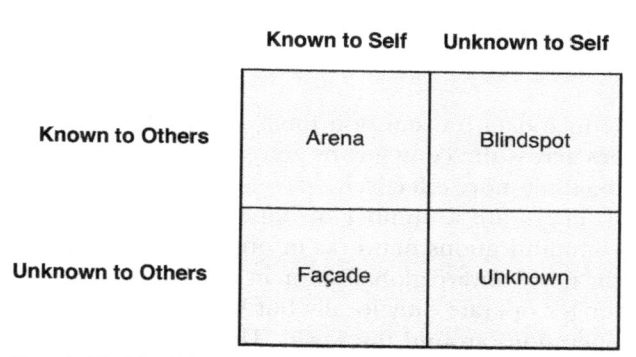

	Known to Self	Unknown to Self
Known to Others	Arena	Blindspot
Unknown to Others	Façade	Unknown

Figure 2: The Johari Window (based on Hall, J. "Communication Revisited." *California Management Review* 15 (1973, Spring): 56–57)

When disclosure and feedback are not used to increase the openness of communication, miscommunication is more likely to arise. Sometimes this confusion is intentional: the hidden area or façade that everyone uses from time to time to keep the communication on a profession level by not revealing likes and dislikes, personal experiences, or other attitudes that are not appropriate or relevant to the situation. Increasing the area of the arena through feedback also improves communication effectiveness by helping the person understand things that he or she does not know about himself or herself (Harvey frequently says "um" while giving a presentation, which is distracting to the listener). The combination of disclosure and feedback can also help the person discover more of his or her hidden potential; that unknown area that neither party understands in isolation.

Information and Communication Technologies

A strong social network has been shown to improve employee performance since a worker who is able to seek timely advice from colleagues will benefit from a broad knowledge pool. One's reputation within such a network motivates a worker to defend perceptions of his or her competence, and feedback stimulates innovative problem solving. These dynamics have transferred to online social networking. Much face-to-face interaction has given way to technology-based modes of communication. The office memo has been almost entirely replaced by email, and employees can access forms and policy statements from the company website rather than encounter someone from human resources. Internal "ticketing" systems allow queries to find those best able to respond without the query poster having to personally track down the right parties. Online communications provide documentation of conversations, which is more reliable than memory or note taking. Such documentation, however, has also been problematic for employees who regard their conversations as private and do not practice discretion. Companies in litigation may have their email records subpoenaed.

BIBLIOGRAPHY

Chaffee, John. *Thinking Critically*. 6th ed. Boston: Houghton Mifflin, 2000. Web. 31 Oct. 2013.

Gil, Barry. "E-Mail: Not Dead, Evolving." *Harvard Business Review* 91, no. 6 (2013): 32–33. Web. 31 Oct. 2013.

Keyton, Joann, Jennifer Caputo, Emily Ford, et al. "Investigating Verbal Workplace Communication Behaviors." *Journal of Business Communication* 50, no. 2 (2013): 152–69. Web. 31 Oct. 2013.

Kinnick, Katherine, and Sabrena R. Parton. "Workplace Communication." *Business Communication* 68, no. 4 (2005): 429–56. Web. 5 Apr. 2007.

Landy, Frank L., and Jeffrey M. Conte. *Work in the 21st Century: An Introduction to Industrial and Organizational Psychology*. Boston: McGraw Hill, 2004.

McShane, Steven L., and Mary Ann Von Glinow. *Organization Behavior: Emerging Realities for the Workplace Revolution*. 2nd ed. Boston: McGraw-Hill/Irwin, 2003.

Xiaojun, Zhang, and Viswanath Venkatesh. "Explaining Employee Job Performance: The Role of Online and Offline Workplace Communication Networks." *MIS Quarterly* 37, no. 3 (2013): 695–A3. Web. 31 Oct. 2013.

SUGGESTED READING

Couzins, Martin, and Scott Beagrie. "How to…Produce Powerful Business Writing." *Personnel Today* 12 (2004, Nov. 30). Web. 5 Apr. 2007.

Dulye, Linda. "De-functionalizing" Communication." *Strategic Communication Management* 8, no. 2 (2004): 6–7. Web. 5 Apr. 2007.

Gorman, Bob. "Communicating to Engage, Not Just to Inform." *Strategic HR Review* 2, no. 2 (2003): 14–17. *Strategic HR Review*. Web. 5 Apr. 2007.

Nicoll. David C. "Acknowledge and Use Your Grapevine." *Management Decision* 32, no. 6 (1994): 25–30. Web. 5 Apr. 2007.

Schonfeld, Erick. "Communication Goes Flat." *Fortune* 130, no. 5 (1994): 16. Web. 5 Apr. 2007.

Ruth A. Wienclaw, Ph.D.

Communications, Networking and Security

ABSTRACT

One of the keys to success in most twenty-first-century businesses is the ability to exchange data and information quickly and accurately. Networks of computers enable organizations to better perform their tasks and meet the needs of their customers. Networks are particularly useful for enabling the fast transmission of messages, information, and documents and for allowing virtual meetings over long distances. Such technologies are not without their drawbacks, however. Networks are at risk from numerous threats both internally and externally. Although network threats continue to evolve, a number of general precautions and specific technologies can be used to reduce network security risks.

OVERVIEW

Most organizations need to be able to access data and communicate within the organization and with outside agencies. For example, a dry cleaner needs to be able to quickly locate the customer's contact information as well as the customer's clothes. The mom-and-pop grocery store needs to know what items it has in stock and what items it needs to order; it also needs to communicate with suppliers to continue to serve its customers. Banks need access to multiple types of sensitive personal and financial information about their customers and must be able to account for every cent in a customer's account. Engineering firms need to be able to share and coordinate information between employees and work teams, order supplies and equipment, and communicate with customers and government agencies. No matter the type of organization, information management and communication are vital to success in the twenty-first century. Modern technology offers organizations better ways to communicate, manage, and exchange information than ever before. The ability to network, or electronically link computers together, further enhances an organization's ability to optimize these technologies to enhance performance and improve viability in the marketplace. In the Information Age, communications networks have become a necessity for most businesses to facilitate information flow, reduce data transmission time, and enable employees across the company or across the globe to work together more effectively.

There are a number of impetuses to the use of communications networks in organizations, such as the trend toward globalization in which businesses no longer operate only locally but have customers and operations around the world. This trend creates an interconnected, global marketplace operating outside the constraints of time zones or national boundaries. To be successful in the global marketplace, businesses also need to be able to communicate and exchange information outside of these constraints.

In addition, the increasing use of high-speed communication technologies for information exchange has changed the expectations of many industries. Businesses are no longer willing to wait for information to be delivered via the mail but need and expect immediate access to keep their processes going. This better and faster communication has also helped businesses become more aware of what is going on in other departments and form strategic alliances with other businesses for their mutual benefit. This trend extends to suppliers and agencies that have an impact on the business's operation.

Communications networks can be used for a number of purposes. They are commonly used to transmit messages and documents. These include email, voicemail, electronic document exchange, electronic funds transfer, and internet access. In addition, communications networks can be used for purposes of e-commerce to buy and sell goods or services, including products and information retrieval services, electronically rather than through conventional means. Networks also support group activities such as the ability to hold meetings with participants at geographically dispersed sites. Audio and videoconferencing capabilities combined with electronic document exchange capabilities can obviate the need for extensive travel to meetings.

Although data communications and networking bring capabilities to businesses that enhance performance and allow them to perform tasks that were previously more laborious and time-consuming, the use of this technology is not without its risks and complications. Without adequate safeguards in place,

Photo courtesy of Jeff Attaway

networked computers are open to both external and internal attacks. Such attacks can affect the validity of data and the reliability of network processes. They can harm not only the organization's reputation and ability to do business but the customer's security and safety as well. The impact of security breaches on the customer can range from false charges to the theft of sensitive information or even identity theft of the individuals whose data are contained in compromised databases. Therefore, it is essential that a business protect its information technology assets. The destruction or sabotage of information technology hardware, software, or data can be expensive for the organization.

Threats to the enterprise's network security can come from both external hackers who gain access to the system illegally and from the business's own employees. The enterprise must protect its data and processes from both sources of threat. Computer systems and networks are also vulnerable to computer viruses and worms. These are malicious programs or pieces of code, which are loaded onto a computer without the user's knowledge and against the user's wishes. They alter the way the computer operates or modify the data or programs that are stored on the computer. Simple viruses can be self-replicating and use up a computer's memory or otherwise slow down or disable a computer; more complex viruses can transmit themselves across networks and bypass security systems to infect other computers or systems, corrupting or erasing programs or data. Computer viruses can be loaded onto the computer intentionally by internal or external hackers, but also through the receipt of infected email attachments.

There are a number of categories of computer crimes to which an enterprise may become susceptible if sufficient security measures are not in place. One such category involves the unauthorized entry of criminal hackers into the enterprise's computer system. Piggybacking falls into this category. When piggybacking, the criminal uses the codes or passwords of an authorized user to gain illegal access to the system. Piggybacking also refers to the unauthorized use of a terminal in the system. Another type of computer crime involving illegal access is entry through a trapdoor, an unknown entry point in a program or network that allows criminals to gain access to and control the system.

A second category of computer crime involves intentionally damaging the system's data. Data diddling involves the changing of data and information before they enter the system. As opposed to honest mistakes or keyboarding errors, data diddling is intentionally done to damage the enterprise's ability to conduct business. Similarly, data leakage is the intentional erasure or removal of files or even entire databases from a system without leaving any trace that they have been removed or even that they existed. Data leakage can result in cost to the enterprise in the recovery or replacement of the lost data as well as from loss of customers' confidence due to errors resulting from the data loss. Customers can also be harmed from data leakage if the leakage results in receipts or credits not being posted correctly or at all. Another way in which the enterprise's communications networks can be harmed is through zapping, the process of damaging or erasing data and information. Scavenging is another type of crime in this category. It involves searching through the physical trash can in the computer center or the electronic trash can in the computer to find discarded data or other information about the system's programs or processes. Zapping typically occurs as a result of the criminal bypassing the enterprise's security systems.

Another category of computer crime revolves around the attempt to steal or capture data in the enterprise's systems. Eavesdropping is the use of electronic surveillance devices to either listen to or capture the content of electronic transmissions. Similarly, wiretapping is the use of any device to electronically capture data during transmission or to listen to conversations that take place over the network. Both wireless transmissions and those that occur over copper wire are susceptible to wiretapping. In addition, small amounts of the enterprise's data can be captured or rerouted through salami or data slicing. This crime involves the development or modification of software to capture small amounts of financial transactions and redirect them to a hidden account. Because the amounts ("slices") are so small, they typically go unnoticed. However, over time, a large volume of small losses can yield significant amount of stolen money.

Sometimes, however, computer criminals are not out to steal data or money from a business but aim to sabotage its computer systems. Logic bombs are programs that are designed to sabotage data, programs, or processes. Logic bombs are set to execute when certain conditions exist in the system. Similarly, time bombs are programs that monitor the computer's internal calendar and execute on a specific date. Trojan horses are programs that look as if they perform one function but actually do something else. Although Trojan horses appear to be harmless applications, once they are loaded into the computer, they wreak damage.

Because of the potential for external and internal attacks, information technology systems need to address several levels of security issues. In general, a business needs to protect its information technology resources from both intrusions by forced, unauthorized entry into the system as well as interception and capture of data by unauthorized personnel. The security of the computer centers and other rooms where information technology processing activities take place and data and other resources are stored must be ensured. These locations include the security of equipment and facilities. Unauthorized users need to be denied access through the use of security protocols and procedures. Similarly, the security of both the data and application software needs to be taken into account. The enterprise needs to put into place security procedures to limit access to data and processes by those who do not need to access them. In addition, the communications networks, access to the internet, and any intranets or extranets must be carefully controlled to limit the potential for viruses and other opportunities for hackers.

APPLICATIONS

There are a number of general measures can be taken to help protect the enterprise and its communications networks from security breaches. An obvious first step is to hire trustworthy, reliable employees who will not sabotage the system or steal data and who will safeguard the system from possible intruders. To assist employees in this task, a number of other general policies and procedures can be put into place to help reduce the risk of computer crime. The enterprise's computer networks should only be accessible using a code word and password. Employees should keep these confidential and not allow any unauthorized access to their terminal. Employees should be encouraged to report any suspected security breaches immediately. In addition, it is often helpful to set up the system so that it requires users to change their access passwords frequently. For situations where sensitive, classified, or otherwise restricted data are stored, used, and processed, in some cases it is cost effective to use biometric devices such as retinal, fingerprint, or palm scanners. Such devices are extremely difficult to access without authorization. Similarly, many organizations set up security procedures to control who is allowed to gain access to the system and the data. Employees should be educated on the importance of data and system security, the ways that computer criminals gain access to systems, and guidelines on how to respond when unauthorized access is suspected.

Other ways to keep data secure include not allowing users unlimited access to the system. Users should only be able to access those data and functions they need to use for their jobs. For those functions that are critical in terms of value or risk, procedures can be set in place so that more than one authorized employee is necessary to gain access to those functions or data. In addition, data can be scrambled, coded, or otherwise encrypted to make it more difficult for potential hackers to use them. Similarly, network and database administrators should be given separate responsibilities for controlling system access. In some situations, it can also be helpful to keep a record of all transactions and user activities and the person responsible for each. From time to time, the system should also be audited by an independent party. In an audit, the transactions and processing should be analyzed to determine if there were any unauthorized activities and what impact they had on the system.

In addition, an enterprise can take some specific measures to reduce the possibility of experiencing a security breach. Virus protection software comprises special application programs that scan the computer to detect or intercept viruses before they gain access to the computer. There are two types of virus protection software. Scanning programs search the computer's memory for viruses, typically notifying the user if any are found. The user can then use the software to destroy the virus and repair any damage if possible. Detection or interception programs monitor the computer's processing and stop viruses from accessing and infecting the computer. Another way to prevent damage from viruses is through the use of digital signature encryption. This technology transmits a mathematically encoded signature that can be used to authenticate the identity of the individual sending a message.

Another application of encryption technology is to code data transmissions so that they cannot be easily intercepted by hackers or other computer criminals. One way to encrypt data is through the use of a public key infrastructure. This technology uses an algorithm to create a public and a private key. The private key is given only to the requesting enterprise, whereas the public key is a searchable directory. To transmit a message, the sender searches a digital certificate directory to find the recipient's public key and uses it to encrypt the message. The message is decoded by the recipient using the private key. Security credentials and public keys are issued and managed by an independent certificate authority. Messages can also be encrypted through the use of a "pretty good privacy" (PGP) program. This program is available as freeware or shareware and works with most popular email programs. The public key is part of the program and is registered with a pretty good privacy server. A third option for data encryption is through the use of a virtual private network. This technology uses a public telecommunications infrastructure to provide secure communications between individual users or the enterprise and remote locations.

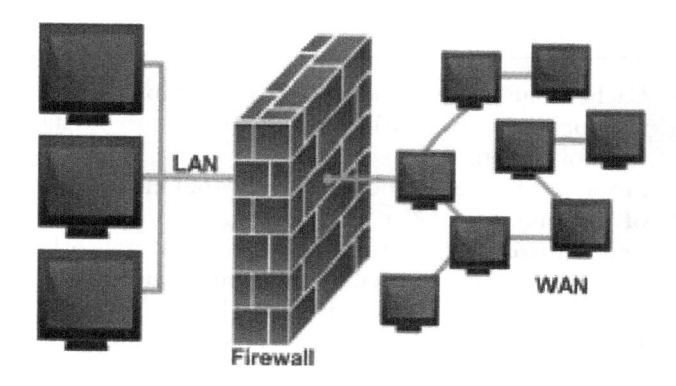

Figure 1: An Illustration of where a firewall would be located in a network. (Courtesy of Bruno Pedrozo via Wikimedia Commons)

Firewalls are another security measure employed by many enterprises. A firewall is a special purpose software program or piece of computer hardware that is designed to prevent authorized access to or from a private network. Firewalls are often used to prevent unauthorized access to a private network from the internet. The firewall is located at the network gateway server and examines incoming messages to determine their origin, destination, purpose, contents, and attachments before making the decision whether to forward the message to the intended recipient. Although firewalls are useful for protecting against intruders, they often filter out executable programs or attachments of excessive length on the assumption that they may contain harmful contents. Historically, firewalls have been separate application programs that were loaded onto a system. Increasingly, however, they are being built into operative systems and communication devices.

Another information technology security device is the proxy server. These devices are used as an intermediary between a personal computer and the internet. They separate the enterprise network from the internet or other outside networks. Proxy servers are often used in tandem with firewalls.

When they receive a request to access the internet, they determine whether the user is allowed to make the request and then look to see if a copy of the requested web page is stored in cache. If the web page is stored in cache, it is sent to the user; otherwise, the server requests the page from the internet.

TERMS & CONCEPTS

Cache memory: Special high-speed random access memory that temporarily holds frequently used data or information.

Firewall: A special-purpose software program or piece of computer hardware that is designed to prevent unauthorized access to or from a private network. Firewalls are often used to prevent unauthorized access to a private network from the internet.

Hacker: Although the term is used by some to refer to any clever programmer, it is used specifically to refer to an individual who attempts to break into a computer system without authorization.

Information technology: The use of computers, communications networks, and knowledge in the creation, storage, and dispersal of data and information. Information technology comprises a wide range of items and abilities for use in the creation, storage, and distribution of information.

Local area network (LAN): Multiple computers that are located near each other and linked into a network that allows the users to share files and peripheral devices such as printers, fax machines, and storage devices.

Metropolitan area network (MAN): Computer networks that transmit data and information citywide and at greater speeds than a local area network.

Network: A set of computers that are electronically linked together.

Security: The process of safeguarding and protecting the data, hardware, software, and processes of a business's information technology assets.

Virus: In computer science, a virus is a program or piece of code that is loaded onto the computer without the user's knowledge and against the user's wishes that alters the way that the computer operates or modifies the data or programs that are stored on the computer. Simple viruses can be self-replicating and use up a computer's memory or otherwise disable a computer; more complex viruses can transmit themselves across networks and bypass security systems to infect other computers or systems.

Wide area network (WAN): Multiple computers that are widely dispersed and linked into a network. Wide area networks typically use high-speed, long-distance communications networks or satellites to connect the computers within the network.

BIBLIOGRAPHY

Dey, Debabrata, Atanu Lahiri, and Zhang, Guoying. "Hacker Behavior, Network Effects, and the Security Software Market." *Journal of Management Information Systems* 29 (2012): 77–108. Print.

Gupta, Alok, and Dmitry Zhdanov. "Growth and Sustainability of Managed Security Services Networks: An Economic Perspective." *MIS Quarterly* 36 (2012): 1109–A7. Print.

Juels, Ari, and Alina Oprea. "New Approaches to Security and Availability for Cloud Data." *Communications of the ACM* 56 (2013): 64–73. Print.

Lucas, Henry C., Jr. *Information Technology: Strategic Decision Making for Managers.* New York: John Wiley and Sons, 2005.

Mangili, Michele, Fabio Martignon, and Stefano Paraboschi. "A Cache-Aware Mechanism to Enforce Confidentiality, Trackability, and Access Policy Evolution in Content-Central Networks." *Computer Networks*, 76126–145. Web. 2015.

Prince, Brian. "Cybersecurity." *Forbes* 194 (2014): 136–42.

"Security of the Internet and the Known Unknowns." *Communications of the ACM* 55 2012): 35–37. Print.

Senn, James A. *Information Technology: Principles, Practices, Opportunities.* 3rd ed. Upper Saddle River, NJ: Pearson/Prentice Hall, 2004.

Strauss, Karsten. "How Small Businesses Can Improve Their Cyber Security." *Forbes.com*, 8. Web. 2015.

SUGGESTED READING

Engebretson, David. "The Beginnings: Beyond the PC." *Distributing & Marketing* 34 (2004): 74–76. Print.

Hui, Kai-Lung, Hui, Wendy, and Yue, Wei T. "Information Security Outsourcing with System Interdependency and Mandatory Security Requirement." *Journal of Management Information Systems* 29 (2012): 117–56. Print.

Kamens, Michael. "Making User Access Policies Work for You." *Network World* 24 (2007): 33. Print.

McPherson, Danny. "IP Network Security: Progress, Not Perfection." *Business Communications Review* 37 (2007): 54–58. Print.

"The Practice of Network Security Monitoring." *Network Security* (2014): 4. Print.

Sax, David. "State-of-the-Art Safeguards." Bloomberg Businessweek, 4467. Web. (2016): 51–52.

Stallings, William, and Tom Case. *Business Data Communications: Infrastructure, Networking and Security*. 7th ed. Boston: Pearson, 2013.

Essay by Ruth A. Wienclaw, Ph.D.

COMPARATIVE MANAGEMENT

ABSTRACT

Many theorists believe that management style loses its effectiveness when applied in a different culture. With the increasing trend toward globalization in many organizations, there is a concomitant increase in the study of management practices in different countries and the ways they relate to organizational effectiveness. Cultural norms, assumptions, and values need to be understood by a manager who desires to be effective in cross-cultural situations. This understanding can be helped through cross-cultural training for expatriate managers as well as by ensuring that the management team in an offshore operation includes members who understand the local culture and its implications.

OVERVIEW

Practitioners and theorists alike spend significant time examining organizations to determine what differentiates those organizations that succeed from those organizations that fail. Significant time and energy is expended to determine the best practices and how these practices can be generalized or extrapolated to become universal truths that help other organizations succeed. This impetus led to the Industrial Revolution and to the development of novel ways to mass produce goods. As a result, contemporary businesses are able to produce goods more effectively and efficiently than ever before. This impetus also led to the Technological Revolution with its burst of new technologies and their application to both the home and workplace. As a result, many tiresome or routine tasks have been eliminated, and employees are better supported in the design and development of even more and better goods and services. What such technological innovations cannot change, however, is the human factor.

No matter how high tech or automated a contemporary organization is, it still remains dependent on the input and work of human beings. Human beings are necessary not only to run the machines upon which a business relies, but to design, develop, and repair them. Wherever there are human beings in an organization, their activities need to be coordinated and supervised to optimize their performance and increase the success of the organization. Management is the process of efficiently and effectively accomplishing work through the coordination and supervision of others.

When management first became a recognized field of study, the goal was to reduce the empirical observations of successful practices in isolated cases to simple lists of practices a manager should or should not do in order to be effective. When these practices were unsuccessfully applied in another organization, a new list was promulgated. Leadership theories were developed that described the difference between successful leaders and unsuccessful leaders and posited the characteristics or practices that differentiated between the two. However, human behavior is a complex and multifaceted thing, and it was found that such universal truths were apt to be neither universal nor truths.

Eventually, this discrepancy was recognized and the study of management became a multidisciplinary effort drawing on the insights from scientific research rather than isolated or casual observation and incorporating the insights and practices of other fields of study including psychology, sociology, and anthropology. Insights gained from empirical research eventually led to the conclusion that there is not one best way to lead. Rather, effective management requires the consideration of numerous factors including the nature of the job to be done (routine, mechanized vs. creative, artistic), the readiness of the workers to do their jobs (experience, degree of training), personality and work style of the workers, as well as the ability and personality of the manager. Further, it was found that as some of these variables changed (the workers became more experienced as they learned on the job), the most appropriate management style also changed (experienced workers require less close supervision than those who are new to the job).

The effectiveness of a management style is also based on the type of organization in which it is used. The large organizations that came into being following the Industrial Revolution were often production facilities where a military command and control model was effective at the time. Many contemporary organizations, on the other hand, do not follow this model. Today, more organizations offer services rather than goods and the educational levels of employees are rising in many fields. Each type of organization and its concomitant workers requires a different type of management in order to be effective. An engineering organization, for example, where workers are hired to develop new ideas or products, cannot be managed on a piecework philosophy, which can be done in some production facilities. Rather, different types of organizations require different styles of management in order to be effective.

The changing landscape of organizations is made even more complex by the increasing globalization in many industries. In particular, the practice of offshoring—relocating part of an organization's business to another country with lower labor costs or less taxes—can present significant challenges to an organization as it works in a foreign culture with different assumptions, practices, and laws. In particular, culture can play a significant role in the expectations on managers and the effectiveness of management practices. Cultural differences also can affect how people communicate, what assumptions they make, and how they perceive the world in general. For example, many cultures—including both Germany and Japan—tend to be more formal than US culture. If a manager acts without sensitivity to this fact, she or he can appear to local workers as rude, and can quickly lose effectiveness.

Comparative management is the study of management practices in different countries and how they relate to organizational effectiveness. To do this, comparative management theorists look at how managerial practices are similar and how they differ in order to accommodate the needs of the local culture. By looking at management styles and techniques that work well in different venues, it is possible to gain insight into which management issues are universal and how local culture and conditions require adaptation of management practices. Specifically, the field of comparative management seeks to help organizations and their managers to better understand the impact of local culture—the consciously or unconsciously held shared assumptions, beliefs, norms, and values held by a group of people—on the way that people and processes need to be managed.

There are several different theoretical approaches to studying comparative management. The socioeconomic approach primarily examines variations in economic development between two or more countries and ways these variations affect what constitutes effective managerial practice. Unfortunately, this approach is not easy to test empirically. In addition, this approach cannot account for differences in management style or effectiveness within a given country because it rests in part on the assumption that organizations operating at the same level of industrialization would have similar management practices. This assumption, however, is not borne out in fact.

Another approach to the study of comparative management is the environmental approach. This approach emphasizes the external factors—environmental factors and constraints—under which the organization must operate. As with the socioeconomic approach, however, the environmental approach cannot explain differences between organizations operating within the same environment. This inability is due in part because both approaches fail to take into account the internal factors that can affect managerial effectiveness.

On the other end of the spectrum is the behavioral approach, which focuses on the psychological factors (beliefs, values, attitudes, assumptions) that affect individual and group behavior within organizations. Although this approach rectifies the major shortcoming of the socioeconomic and environmental approaches, it fails to consider the external factors that can also affect organizational and managerial effectiveness.

To make up for these shortcomings, various eclectic models have been proposed that take into consideration both the broad societal issues that affect organizational effectiveness as well as the organizational factors. Some of these models also consider the possible interaction between the two sets of variables.

APPLICATIONS

The comparison of international differences in effective management is of more than heuristic interest. The trend toward globalization spurred on by the search for lower personnel and production costs means that increasing numbers of organizations are offshoring parts of their operations. To be able to do this successfully, both executives and managers need to understand the differences in culture and how these differences affect organizational structures and management styles.

Cross-Cultural Comparisons

Comparative management is an emerging field, and models for predicting the success of managers in foreign operations are works in progress. However, theorists and practitioners have been observing the cultural differences and concomitant managerial imperatives associated with different cultures for years. These observations are not only helping to form newer and better models of comparative management, but they are also providing clues for how to manage more effectively in a foreign culture.

One of the reasons that it is important for the manager to understand the culture in which he or she works is to better understand what motivates the employees. This understanding can help a manager achieve the objectives of the organization by being better able to reward the employee for desired behavior. Workers tend to be motivated by rewards that support their cultural patterns. For example, in sub-Saharan Africa, cultural values include respect for elders and for authority, family orientation (including the extended family), and collectivism. These traits have significant implications for how sub-Saharan Africans can most effectively be managed. Although African cultures tend to support absolute obedience to authority, the manager cannot count on this factor alone to force local employees into a foreign way of thinking. The collectivist nature of the sub-Saharan African culture means that local employees tend to be more comfortable working in a group than working alone. Consequently, the incentive of a private office as a reward for high performance may not have the effect expected by a Western manager. The family orientation of these cultures may help bond work groups together, but it may also mean that it is difficult to reach agreement between teams or work groups. Further, motivating employees to work overtime or to not take time off for family obligations may be difficult in these cultures. Such considerations tend to be more important to African workers than meeting organizational goals. It is perhaps for this reason that sub-Saharan African organizations rarely implement formal performance appraisal systems.

Another cultural pattern affecting sub-Saharan African organizations is resistance to change and aversion to risk taking. As a result of these patterns, managerial insistences on new techniques such as reengineering, just-in-time practices, or total quality management that are successful in Western organizations are unlikely to be met with enthusiasm or success. In fact, the respect for tradition prevalent in African cultures may result in a workforce that is neither flexible nor easily adaptable. Although workers ascribing to these cultural patterns can be managed effectively, they are unlikely to respond well to American concepts of independence or rugged individuality. To be effective, managers need to understand these cultural values and reward and encourage employees within those parameters.

East Asia also has cultural patterns that vary widely from those in the West. Chinese culture, for example, is also collectivistic in nature and emphasizes social interests and downplays personal goals and accomplishments. In fact, in China there tends to be an emphasis on harmony and conformity that governs all interpersonal relations. These cultural patterns can result in disagreement with Western management styles where conflict is taken as a matter of course. In Japan, the organization's goals are widely shared throughout the company, leaving top executives free from day-to-day management while middle managers carry out both operational and strategic activities. Although to the Japanese mind this management approach is a tribute to the competence of the middle managers, to the American mind it is indecisive and incompetent. This structure also means that the Japanese organizational chart is often little more than a listing of job titles rather than a formal definition of roles and responsibilities. As in the other cultures described above, Japanese management style also relies heavily on consensus resulting from extensive verbal consultation, a concept foreign in most US businesses. In addition, cultural norms in Japan do not accept the unpleasant face-to-face confrontations that Americans frequently think are a normal part of any interpersonal relationship; the face of the organization as a "happy family" is important in Japan. As a result, communication patterns rely much more heavily on nonverbal messages so that the façade can be maintained. Since an organization is dependent upon good communication for success, it is essential that this fact be recognized for a Western manager working in the Japanese culture.

Practical Concerns for Expatriates
Understanding the cross-cultural considerations associated with management in foreign countries arises from two sources: the intellectual knowledge of cultural and managerial differences and the practical knowledge of these things that can only be acquired through immersion in the culture. There are a number of things that an organization can do on a micro level to help make the transition for expatriates—employees who are not citizens of the country in which they are working—easier. Language training alone is insufficient: expatriates also need to be sensitive to the culture in which they work so that they can interpret situations and events in the same way as persons native to the culture in which they take place. This knowledge will prepare them to make better and more effective management decisions.

Fortunately, intercultural sensitivity is a learned process. Therefore, it is important that the organization provide cross-cultural training to help orient the prospective expatriate manager to the conditions that will be encountered as a manager in the foreign operation as well as more general orientation to the assumptions, values, and norms of the local population in general. Cross-cultural training programs are designed to help employees deal effectively with persons from a different culture by familiarizing them with various cultural differences including values, assumptions, and communication styles. In this way, cross-cultural training attempts to reduce potential misunderstandings that might arise. For example, the unacceptability of direct confrontation in Japan could be inadvertently breached by an American not used to this norm. Similarly, ignorance of the comparatively high level of formality in communication (using formal pronouns and titles for those one does not know well, particularly when higher in the organizational hierarchy) that one encounters in Germany could lead not only to misunderstandings, but to an inability to be effective in one's job.

There are several general objectives to most cross-cultural training programs. First, potential expatriates are taught about the reality of cultural differences and how these differences can impact managerial effectiveness or other business outcomes. Trainees are also familiarized with the process by which attitudes and stereotypes—both positive and negative—are formed and how such assumptions can unconsciously influence how a person interacts with those from a different culture. In addition, cross-cultural training usually provides specific information about the country in which the person will work, including any skills needed for business success. Cross-cultural training may also include intensive or advanced language skills training or other cultural adjustment skills.

In addition to helping expatriate managers acquire an intellectual appreciation for and empathy with both the general culture and the managerial culture in which they work, comparative management theorists have also noted a number of practical actions that can be taken on an organizational level to help increase the managerial effectiveness of expatriates working in offshore operations. Many of the problems that arise in cross-cultural management situations can be resolved simply and do not require changes in corporate policy. For example, although it may be tempting to put a person from the home country in charge of the foreign subsidiary, it is more important that the foreign subsidiary be run by someone who understands the needs and assumptions of the local culture. This structure will not only enable the subsidiary to better deal with any cultural clashes that may occur but also will help prevent them from occurring in the first place. In addition, because of the relatively smaller size of offshore operations in relation to corporate headquarters, the person in charge of a foreign subsidiary will more than likely need to run the entire local operation and will not have the same infrastructure available as when running a part of a larger operation. Top management in foreign operations, therefore, also needs to have an entrepreneurial spirit and the psychological ability to adapt to the new culture.

There are other practical steps that can be taken to help ensure the effectiveness of expatriates. Due to the prevalence of culture shock for expatriate employees and their families, many find themselves living in enclaves within the larger culture. Although this housing plan may seem like a good idea, it does not help one to understand the new culture better and also tends to reinforce an "us-them" attitude that is counterproductive to being a good manager. In addition, performance appraisal of the expatriate should be done by the local supervisor rather than by the corporate supervisor because the local supervisor will be better able to understand how effective the expatriate manager is in working within the norms of the new culture and whether or not his/her outcomes are within the expected outcomes for that locality.

BIBLIOGRAPHY

Beugré, Constant, and O. Felix Offodile. "Managing for Organizational Effectiveness in sub-Saharan Africa: A Culture Fit Model." *International Journal of Human Resources Management* 12, no. 4 (2001): 535–550. Web. 5 Apr. 2007.

Campbell, John P., Marvin D. Dunnette, Edward E. Lawler III, and Karl E. Weick. *Managerial Behavior, Performance, and Effectiveness*. New York: McGraw-Hill Book Company, 1970.

Dessler, Gary. *Human Resource Management*. 10th ed. Upper Saddle River, NJ: Pearson/Prentice Hall, 2005.

Endenich, Christoph, Michael Brandau, and Andreas Hoffjan. "Two Decades of Research on Comparative Management Accounting—Achievements and Future Directions." *Australian Accounting Review* 21, no. 4 (2011): 365–82. Web 31 Oct. 2013.

Landy, Frank J., and Jeffrey M. Conte. *Work in the 21st Century: An Introduction to Industrial and Organizational Psychology*. Boston: McGraw Hill, 2004.

McShane, Steven L., and Mary Ann Von Glinow. *Organizational Behavior: Emerging Realities for the Workplace Revolution*. 2nd ed. Boston: McGraw-Hill/Irwin, 2003.

Neelankavil, James P., and Anil Mathur. "Determinants of Managerial Performace: A Cross-Cultural Comparison of the Perceptions of Middle-Level Managers in Four Countries." *Journal of International Studies* 31, no. 1 (2001): 121–40. Web 5 Apr. 2007.

Newman, William H. "Comparative Management: A Resource for Improving Managerial Adaptability." *Columbia Journal of World Business* 13, no. 2 (1978): 5–6. Web. 5 Apr. 2007.

Tsurumi, Yoshi. "The Best of Times and the Worst of Times: Japanese Management in America." *Columbia Journal of World Business* 13, no. 2 (1978): 56–61. Web. 11 Apr. 2007.

Tung, Rosalie L. "The Use of the Organizational Climate Construct in Comparative Management Models." *Academy of Management Proceedings*. 292296. 1978. Web. 5 Apr. 2007.

SUGGESTED READING

Hattori, Iohiro. "A Proposition on Efficient Decision-Making in the Japanese Corporation." *Columbia Journal of World Business* 13, no. 2 (1978): 7–15. Web. 5 Apr. 2007.

Jackson, Gregory, and Andreas Moerke. "Continuity and Change in Corporate Governance: Comparing Germany and Japan. *Corporate Governance* 13, no. 3 (2005): 351–61. Web. 5 Apr. 2007.

Teagarden, Mary B., and Mary Ann Von Glinow. "Toward a Theory of Comparative Management Research: An Idiographic Case Study of the Best International Human Resources Management Project." *Academy of Management Journal*, 39, no. 5 (1995): 261–87. Web. 5 Apr. 2007.

Thomson, Andrew. "The Case for Management History." *Accounting, Business & Financial History* 11, no. 2 (July 2001): 99–115. Web. 5 Apr. 2007.

Ruth A. Wienclaw, Ph.D.

Conflict Management

ABSTRACT

Conflict frequently arises in the workplace. Goal incompatibility between groups or individuals, differentiation, task interdependence, scarce resources, ambiguity, and communication problems can all lead to a situation that promotes conflict. There are a number of conflict management styles that can be used to effectively resolve such conflicts: competing, collaborating, compromising, avoiding, and accommodating. However, although each individual has his or her own preferred conflict management style, not every style is optimally effective in every conflict situation. To maximize the effectiveness of conflict management efforts, management and parties to the conflict need to be aware of their short- and long-term goals and strategies for both the task and the people involved. They also need to monitor their personal involvement and emotions in the conflict, their personal conflict management style, and the knowledge of which styles work best in which situations.

OVERVIEW

It often seems as if whenever two or more parties attempt to work together, there are at least three opinions. Although sometimes this situation can lead to synergy and a more creative final product, in many cases it leads to conflict. Although the most common view of conflict is that it is by its very nature dysfunctional and needs to be resolved, in many cases—if it is properly managed—it can be both functional and help the conflicting parties work together better or produce a better product than if the conflict had not arisen in the first place. Conflict between groups may also improve team dynamics, cohesiveness, and task orientation. However, if the conflict becomes too emotionally charged, a win-lose mentality can arise, with negative results such as groupthink, frustration, job dissatisfaction, and stress.

Very few people have the option to work in complete isolation of others. Even those who telecommute or work independently frequently find themselves in a position in which they need to interact with other persons such as clients, suppliers, editors, etc. In virtually any situation in which there is more than one party with interests in the outcome, conflicts are likely to arise. In this context, conflict refers to any situation "in which one party perceives that its interests are being opposed or negatively affected by" the interests or actions of another party (McShane and Von Glinow 2003). Conflict can manifest in any number of ways ranging from a mild disagreement between individuals to an all out war between nations. In the workplace, conflict typically begins with a situation that is conducive to conflict, such as the need to share a single piece of equipment or other scarce resource. For example, Group A needs the copier to reproduce a proposal for a tight deadline for a potential client and Group B needs to use the copier to produce a deliverable to an equally tight—and incompatible—deadline for a current client. As the parties realize that conflict exists, the situation usually manifests itself in actions that outwardly demonstrate that an underlying conflict exists (e.g., a member of Group A tries to monopolize the copier so that it cannot be used by Group B).

Conflict need not lead to a dysfunctional workplace, however. Through appropriate conflict management techniques—either actions taken by one or more parties to the conflict or by an objective outside party in the attempt to deescalate the conflict—the severity and form of the conflict can be altered to maximize its benefits and minimize its negative consequences.

Types of Workplace Conflict – Goal Incompatibility & Differentiation

As shown in figure 1, conflict can arise from any one or more general sources in the workplace (McShane and Von Glinow 2003). First, conflict can arise in the workplace due to incompatible goals between individuals or groups. For example, if two individuals are competing for the same promotion, it is likely that conflict will arise unless more than one position is available. Goal incompatibility becomes an even stronger source for potential conflict in situations in which there are financial rewards for achieving one's goals since, in such situations, employees tend to be more motivated to achieve their own goals at the expense of others. A second source of conflict in organizations is differentiation. This occurs when individuals or groups of employees hold divergent beliefs and attitudes as a result of their different backgrounds, experiences, or training. For example, differentiation often leads to conflict situations following business mergers and acquisitions. In such situations, the cultures, practices, and shared experiences of the formerly separate entities lead to an "us vs. them" situation.

Interdependence
A third source of potential conflict in organizations is task interdependence, the degree to which individuals or groups must share common inputs, interact during the course of performing their separate tasks, or receive outcomes that are partly determined by the mutual performance of both parties. There are three basic types of task independence:

- Pooled interdependence
- Sequential interdependence
- Reciprocal interdependence

The lowest level of interdependence is pooled interdependence. Under this condition, individuals or teams work independently of each other except for their common reliance on a resource or authority. An example of pooled interdependence is the common reliance on a single copy machine, cited above. Sequential interdependence is a situation in which the output of one person or group becomes the direct input for another person or group. This situation frequently arises in assembly line situations where the output of one process becomes the input to another process (McShane and Von Glinow 2003). For example, the packing department cannot complete its task unless the department that makes the boxes or packing materials first completes its task. The third type of interdependence in organizations is reciprocal interdependence. This highest level of interdependence occurs in situations in which work outputs are exchanged back and forth among individuals or groups. An example of this type of interdependence would be the relationship between bus drivers and maintenance crews. The drivers cannot drive the buses unless the maintenance crews maintain them, and the maintenance crews cannot maintain the buses unless the drivers bring them into the depot.

Scarce Resources, Ambiguity, Communication
A fourth type of situation that can lead to conflict in the workplace occurs when there are scarce resources. For example, if multiple technicians need the same laboratory equipment and there is insufficient equipment for each to have his or her own, conflict is likely to arise. Ambiguity in the workplace can also lead to conflict because such a situation increases the risk that one party may interfere with the achievement of the other party's goals. Situations of ambiguity in the workplace often lead to increased office politics. Another problem that can lead to conflict in the workplace is the lack of opportunity, ability, or motivation to communicate effectively.

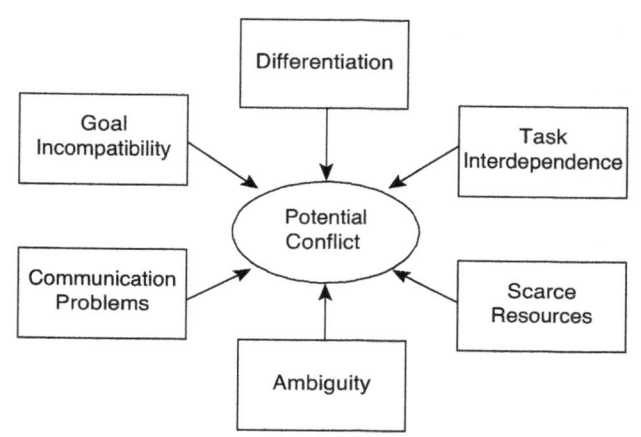

Figure 1: Sources of Conflict in Organizations (adapted from McShane and Von Glinow 2003)

When effective communication does not exist, the likelihood that stereotypes will develop increases and conflict escalates. Good interpersonal skills are necessary in order to communicate with other parties in a diplomatic, nonconfrontational manner. The lack of necessary skills for diplomatic communication can escalate a conflict situation and result in less motivation for effective communication in the future. Lack of communication skills is a common problem that occurs in cross-cultural conflicts.

APPLICATIONS

Resolving Conflict
As shown in figure 2, there are a number of ways to deal with conflict (Ruble and Thomas 1976).

Although sometimes it is assumed that there is only one best way to manage conflict, research has show that one conflict management style is best modified to fit the needs of the specific situation. These approaches to conflict management vary on the degree to which the party is cooperative—or motivated to satisfy the interests of the other party in the conflict (e.g., allow the other group to use the copier)—and assertive—or motivated to satisfy its own interests (e.g., make sure that it is able to use the copier whenever it needs it).

Collaboration
In collaboration, the parties attempt to resolve their conflict by finding a mutually beneficial solution through problem solving. Collaborative solutions are high in both cooperativeness and assertiveness. In the collaborative style of conflict management, information is shared among the parties to the conflict so that all parties can help identify solutions that will potentially satisfy the needs or interests of all parties. Collaboration is the preferred method for conflict management when the parties do not have perfectly opposing interests and when there is sufficient trust and openness between the parties so that information can be shared.

Avoidance
On the opposite side of the conflict management style grid is avoidance, an approach that is low in both assertiveness and cooperativeness. Avoidance is an approach to conflict management in which the parties attempt to manage their differences by smoothing them over or avoiding or minimizing the situations in which conflict might arise. Although avoidance is not a functional long term solution to conflict situations, it can be useful in the short term as a way to temporarily cool down heated disputes or for situations where the issue causing conflict is trivial. For example, sometimes it is better to leave the room and cool off rather than to continue to unproductively try to resolve conflict. In such situations, avoidance can not only prevent a conflict situation from escalating but also may actually help it de-escalate.

Competition
A third approach to conflict management is competition. In this approach to conflict management, one party attempts to "win" at the other party's expense. Competition tends to be a win-lose situation characterized by high assertiveness and low cooperativeness. The underlying assumption in such an approach is that there is a fixed pool of resources from which to draw (e.g., hours during which the copier can be used) and that a gain on one side means a loss on the other side. Competitive solutions to conflict situations can be appropriate if the party knows that its solution is correct and a quick solution is needed or where the other party would take advantage of a more cooperative approach.

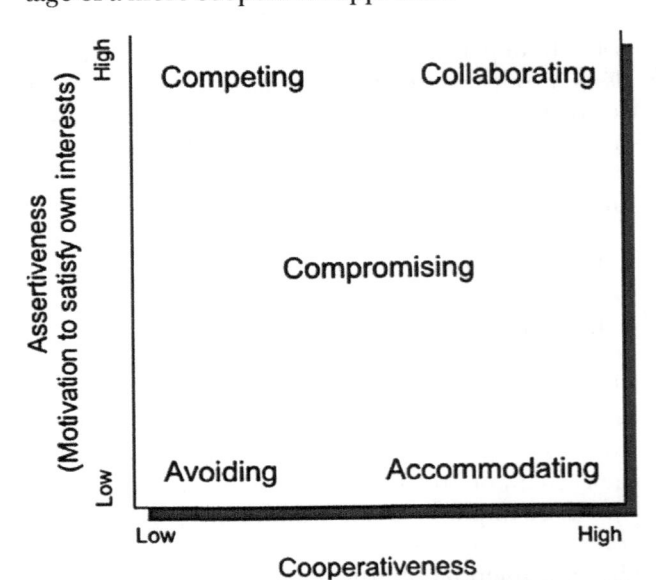

Figure 2: Interpersonal Conflict Management Styles (Ruble and Thomas 1976)

Accommodation
On the opposite side of the grid is the accommodation style of conflict management, which is low on assertiveness and high on cooperativeness. In this approach, one party completely gives in to the position of the other party or acts with little or no attention to its own interests. Accommodation can be a functional conflict management approach if the opposing party has substantially more power or if the issue is not as important to the first party as it is to the opposing party.

Compromise
Finally, compromise is an approach to conflict management in which one party attempts to reach a

middle ground with the opposing party. Compromise positions tend to have moderate levels of assertiveness and cooperativeness. When attempting to compromise, parties typically look for solutions in which losses are offset by equally valued gains. Compromise tends to work best in situations in which there is little possibility of mutual gain through problem solving, both parties have equal power, and there are time pressures to settle the conflict (Ruble and Thomas 1976).

Issue—Adapting Styles for Optimal Outcome
Although most people have a preferred conflict management style, it can be useful to apply a different approach to managing conflict to better meet the needs of each situation. Shetach (2009) expanded on the two-dimensional model of interpersonal conflict management styles and developed a four dimensions model (see figure 3).

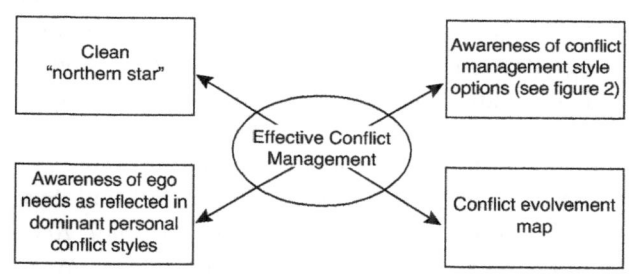

Figure 3: The Four Dimensions Model (adapted from Shetach 2009)

The model considers four critical factors that need to be taken into account in managerial attempts to increase the effectiveness of their conflict management skills:

1. "Northern star"
2. "Conflict evolvement map"
3. Awareness of available response options (see figure 2)
4. Awareness of one's preferred personal conflict management style from among these options.

"Northern star" is Shetach's metaphor for a strategy approach or long-term goal. This term is used to articulate that a manager must be aware of both the main goal for communication in the current situation as well as the long term, future objectives regarding the working relationship. By being aware of both the task at hand and the people involved, Shetach posits that it is possible to increase the likelihood that conflict can be constructively managed in order not only to meet a specific goal, but also to better manage the situation to advance one's long-term strategy. Further, by defining clear goals both for the task at hand and the people involved in the situation, one can better prioritize the variables, leading to a more constructive outcome. In addition to understanding the desired outcome for the situation, the four dimensions model also aims to help managers recognize their level of personal involvement in the conflict as well as any emotional responses so that these may be controlled and the conflict management approach can be kept on a professional, not personal, level. The four dimensions model also takes into account the various conflict management strategies discussed above and shown in figure 2.

Effective conflict management is often situational, and a manager needs to be aware of what options are available for resolving issues. In addition, it is helpful to know one's preferred personal conflict management style from among the five available options. Each approach to conflict management can lead to either a constructive or destructive conclusion, depending on the specifics of the situation. In order to maximize the effectiveness of conflict management efforts and help arrive at a win-win resolution, managers and others involved in conflict situations need to be aware of the specifics of the situation and their own personal styles, and be flexible enough to change their preferred style in order to resolve the conflict.

CONCLUSION

Wherever two or more people need to work together, share resources, or compete for scarce rewards, conflict will assuredly arise. There are a number of ways to deal with conflict, varying from concern about one's own needs to concern about the needs of the other party. Frequently, the desired outcome is a win-win situation in which the interests of both parties are met. However, depending on the circumstances, the best approach to conflict management my involve striving for a different outcome. No matter the approach used, however, it is important to realize that conflict situations can easily become personalized, and the original source of conflict forgotten. To avoid this possibility, it is important not only to know the various conflict management options available and where they are best applied but also to be aware of personal emotions and involvement, as well as short-term and long-term goals in resolving the conflict.

BIBLIOGRAPHY

Carlson, Julie. "Rockpaper Scissors: Strategies in Conflict Situations." *Baylor Business Review* 31, no. 2 (2013): 48–49. Web. 27 Nov. 2013.

Coleman, Peter T., and Katharina Kugler. "Tracking Managerial Conflict Adaptivity: Introducing a Dynamic Measure of Adaptive Conflict Management in Organizations." *Journal of Organizational Behavior* 35, no. 7 (2014): 945–68. Web. 14 Nov. 2014.

McShane, Steven L., and Mary Anne Von Glinow. *Organizational Behavior*. 2nd ed. Boston: McGrawHill/Irwin, 2007.

Ruble, Thomas L., and Kenneth W. Thomas. "Support for a Two-Dimensonal Model of Conflict Behavior." *Organizational Behavior and Human Performance* 16, no. 1 (1976): 143–55. Print.

Sadri, Golnaz, et al. "Choosing Conflict Resolution by Culture." *Industrial Management* 55, no. 5 (2013): 10–15. Web. 27 Nov. 2013.

Saeed, Tahir, et al. "Leadership Styles: Relationship with Conflict Management Styles." *International Journal of Conflict Management* 25, no. 3 (2014): 214–25. Web. 14 Nov. 2014.

Sinha, Akinchan. "Conflict Management: Making Life Easier." *IUP Journal of Soft Skills* 5, no. 4 (2011): 31–42. Web. 27 Nov. 2013.

Shetach, Ana. "The Four Dimension Model: A Tool for the Effective Conflict Management." *International Studies of Management and Organization* 39, no. 3 (2009): 82–106. Web. 27 Apr. 2010.

SUGGESTED READING

Atteya, Nermine M. "The Conflict Management Grid: A Selection and Development Tool to Resolve the Conflict between the Marketing and Sales Organizations." *International Journal of Business & Management* 7, no. 13 (2013): 28–39. Web. 27 Nov. 2013.

Busby, Dean M., and Thomas B. Holman. "Perceived Match or Mismatch on the Gottman Conflict Styles: Associations with Relationship Outcome Variables." *Family Process* 48, no. 4 (2009, Dec.): 531–45. Web. 27 Apr. 2010.

Ergeneli, Azize, Selin Camgoz, and Pinar B. Karapinar. "The Relationship between Self-Efficacy and Conflict Handling Styles in Terms of Relative Authority Positions of the Two Parties." *Social Behavior and Personality* 38, no. 1 (2010): 13–28. Web. 27 Apr. 2010.

Eunson, Baden. *Conflict Management*. Hoboken, NJ: John Wiley & Sons, 2012. Web. 27 Nov. 2013.

Furumo, Kimberly A. "The Impact of Conflict and Conflict Management Style on Deadbeats and Deserters in Virtual Teams." *Journal of Computer Information Systems* 49, no. 4 (2009): 66–73. Web. 27 Apr. 2010.

Godse, Anand S., and Nutankumar S. Thingujam. "Perceived Emotional Intelligence and Conflict Resolution Styles among Information Technology Professionals: Testing the Mediating Role of Personality." *Singapore Management Review* 32, no. 1 (2010): 69–83. Web. 27 Apr. 2010.

Liberman, Erry, Yael F. Levy, and Peretz Segal. "Designing and Internal Organizational System for Conflict Management." *Dispute Resolution Journal* 64, no. 2 (2009): 62–74. Web. 27 Apr. 2010.

Salami, Samuel O. "Conflict Resolution Strategies and Organizational Citizenship Behavior: The Moderating Role of Trait Emotional Intelligence." *Social Behavior and Personality* 38, no. 1 (2010): 75–86. Web. 27 Apr. 2010.

Somech, Anit, Helena S. Desivilya, and Helena Lidogoster. "Team Conflict Management and Team Effectiveness: The Effects of Task Interdependence and Team Identification." *Journal of Organizational Behavior* 30, no. 3 (2009): 359–78. Web. 27 Apr. 2010.

Way, Kristen A., Nerina L. Jimmieson, and Prashant Bordia. "Supervisor Conflict Management, Justice, and Strain: Multilevel Relationships." *Journal of Managerial Psychology* 29, no. 8 (2014): 1044–63. Web. 14 Nov. 2014.

Ruth A. Wienclaw, Ph.D.

Corporate Communication

Corporate communication refers to the exchange of ideas and information used by businesses and organizations. It can refer to internal communication among employees and executives or external communication with groups such as shareholders, the media, and the general public. Corporate communication is typically undertaken in order to share positive messages and information about the organization, and it is closely managed with a consideration of marketing, branding, and public image. It can also take the form of advertising, speeches, events, and publications. Corporate communication is a subset of organizational communication.

OVERVIEW

The field of communication studies examines the processes of human communication in terms of the creation, mode, delivery, and intent of the communication. As a discipline, it is most closely related to social studies and sociology, rhetoric, and psychology. The subfield of corporate communication involves written and spoken communications, both inside and outside of the organization. Corporate communications are generally targeted, well planned, and intended to send specific messages.

On an organizational level, corporate communication deals with the transmission of information to people operating outside of the company itself, such as messages to investors and shareholders. Corporate communication often includes public relations, media relations, or publicity, fields that are often represented by a dedicated group or department within an organization. Internally, corporate communication can include communication between management and employees, often related to business objectives and mission statements, goals, and values as well as policies and practices.

Corporate communication can take a variety of forms. Often, publications such as magazines, memos, and newsletters are distributed in order to share information. Email has also become an increasingly common way for organizations to communicate to employees and outsiders. As the use of digital communication becomes more widespread, organizations may also use alternative means of sending messages, including text messages, blogs, and social networking sites such as Facebook and Twitter.

Corporate communication is closely linked to advertising and marketing. The goal of corporate communication focuses on crafting and maintaining the organization's image in order to carefully brand the company. To do so, the organization must take its audience into account and determine the best methods of delivery to reach all the relevant audiences. The methods can include company websites and mailing lists, direct mailings, and even the use of sponsorships and spokespersons. External communication can also relay important information about corporate social responsibility.

A key component of all forms of corporate communication is the consistency of image and brand, all with the goal of maintaining and projecting the organization's identity. This focus can be as literal as incorporating logos and catchphrases, or it can simply mean adhering to predetermined qualities and attributes. The overarching goal is to link the company's perceived and projected identities through carefully monitored communication to best mold the organization's reputation.

Executives address their company's shareholders (Photo courtesy of MCCTransport)

BIBLIOGRAPHY

Allori, Paola Evangelisti, and Giuliana Garzone, eds. *Discourse, Identities and Genres in Corporate Communication: Sponsorship, Advertising and Organizational Communication.* Bern, Switzerland: Lang, 2011.

Crescenzo, Steve. "Ready for Change." *Communication World* Jan.–Feb. 2011: 10–12. Print.

Eppler, Martin J. "Manage the Message." *Communication World* Mar.–Apr. 2012: 14–20. Print.

Guillamón-Saorín, Encarna, and Francisco J. Martínez-López. "Corporate Financial Communication and the Internet: Manipulating Investor Audiences?" *Online Information Review* 37.4 (2013): 518–37. Print.

Liu, Brooke Fisher, J. Suzanne Horsley, and Abbey Blake Levenshus. "Government and Corporate Communication Practices: Do the Differences Matter?" *Journal of Applied Communication Research* 38.2 (2010): 189–213. Print.

Mathur, Meera, and Jyoti Jain. "Green Advertising: A Corporate Communication Approach towards Sustainable Future." *Researchers World* 4.1 (2013): 130–34. Print.

Meng, Juan, and Po-Lin Pan. "Using a Balanced Set of Measures to Focus on Long-Term Competency in Internal Communication." *Public Relations Review* 38.3 (2012): 484–90. Print.

Schielke, Thomas. "Light and Corporate Identity: Using Lighting for Corporate Communication." *Lighting Research & Technology* 42.3 (2010): 285–95. Print.

Kehley Coviello

CORPORATE SOCIAL RESPONSIBILITY

ABSTRACT

This article examines the evolution of corporate social responsibility. The driving forces behind the corporate shift toward responsibility are examined including regulatory issues, social and political activism, marketing, and consumer pressure. The role and activities of several organizations that focus on corporate social responsibility are reviewed. The process of shareholder activism in pushing for corporate social responsibility is explained along with how the shareholder processes work. Reasons for failure in corporate social responsibility campaigns are also reviewed and issues with global efforts clashing with local efforts are explained.

OVERVIEW

Corporate Social Responsibility (CSR) is a subject of much interest within the managerial world. Corporate social responsibility is also frequently described as social responsibility or community relations. Corporate social responsibility has been under discussion for several decades. Even Peter Drucker has commented in the past that corporate management has three tasks (cited in Phillips 2006, 69):

1. Increase economic performance.
2. Make the worker productive and efficient.
3. Manage social impacts and responsibilities.

Phillips (2006) defines corporate social responsibility as "both the philosophy and practice of for-profit organizations voluntarily acting to positively assist society in ways beyond that required to obtain profit objectives" (69).

Corporate social responsibility has the attention of the business community, investors, customers, and the business media. The *Harvard Business Review*, the *Economist*, and the *Wall Street Journal* have all run a significant number of articles focused on corporate social responsibility (Bernstein 2005). Over the years, corporations have voluntary contributed billion of dollars to various social endeavors. In 1999, only 35 percent of the 250 largest companies in the world reported on corporate responsibility, but in 2011, 95 percent did, an indication of the importance that major companies and their leaders place on the issue of corporate social responsibility (KPMG 2011).

Corporate social responsibility, like ethics, has no universal definition. Approaches include "a manager's duty or obligation to make decisions that nurture, protect, enhance and promote the welfare and well-being of stakeholders and society as a whole" (Jones, George, and Hill 2000, cited in Phillips 2006, 69). But corporate social responsibility efforts are often global, and in 2010, the International Standards Organization (ISO) launched an ISO standard for corporate social responsibility: ISO 26000. The ISO Bulletin states that "ISO 26000 provides guidance on how businesses and organizations can operate in a socially responsible way. This means acting in an ethical and transparent way that contributes to the health and welfare of society "(ISO n.d.). In addition, there is a growing acceptance of corporate social responsibility principles among intergovernmental organizations. One international organization, the UN Global Compact, is a corporate citizenship project has had more than 7,000 companies from 145 countries participate in the program since its inception in 2000. The International Finance Corporation (IFC), which is the World Bank's private lending division has not only accepted corporate social responsibility principles but is working to perpetuate corporate social responsibility in general. The International Finance Corporation has implemented a comprehensive set of labor and environmental standards for all of its loan recipients in order to be eligible for loans (Senser 2007).

Corporate Social Responsibility & Civil Society Engagement

Civil society participation in evolving corporate social responsibility issues has grown immensely over the last several decades. There are numerous nongovernmental organizations (NGOs) and networks of cooperating organizations spread around the world now deeply involved in corporate social responsibility. There is also a long list of consumer groups and trade unions that are also mobilized, mostly focusing on the elimination of child labor and sweatshops. Other groups have focused their attention on issues such as fair trade and the rights of indigenous peoples.

The nongovernmental organizations sector is still growing, and for nongovernmental organizations to succeed they need two things: money to finance their mission and enough people who believe that the mission is worthwhile in order to successfully solicit contributions. Many of those contributors feel that government programs have been a massive failure when it comes to addressing social issues and the needs of people. Those people that feel this way have been ready to support an alternative, and nongovernmental organizations have stepped into fill the gap.

The diversity in the nature of nongovernmental organizations is also rather broad. Some focus on human issues while others may focus on environmental issues, which have contributed to the growth of watchdog activism, a process where an organization becomes specialized in an issue and then takes political as well as social positions about that issue. This focus appeals to many contributors because it provides an opportunity to support a cause that they believe in and on which they would like to see action and change (Utting 2005).

Corporate social responsibility also constitutes a development of a new element in corporations' advertising strategy; a new signifier. Corporations make big news out of their ethical actions and socially responsible policies. They issue press releases and prominently display their activities and accolades on their websites. Many feel this publicity contributes to high levels of affinity with their customer base who strongly desire to do right by doing business with companies that do right (Manokha 2004).

APPLICATIONS

Corporate Social Responsibility via Stockholder Action

When there is a strong business case for corporate social responsibility, both the sponsoring company of a program or initiative and society as a whole can benefit. If socially responsible actions can lead to higher profits, the company is more financially viable and shareholders as well as all stakeholders in the company benefit. In many cases, however, a direct profit or benefit may not be realized. However, the secondary benefits such as building goodwill and gaining from positive media coverage also have value.

Another force in the corporate social responsibility movement has been the rise of the activist investor. Corporate social responsibility activist investors often see corporations as a tool or a means of achieving social change. There have been many such activists who are willing to sacrifice financial gains in order to achieve social goals. These activists have an arsenal of strategies to use in their attempts to influence the actions of corporations even if some of them may not be stockholders. For example, People for the Ethical Treatment of Animals (PETA) actively utilizes publicity-seeking tactics including advertising, public outreach campaigns, and even public demonstrations to call attention to their cause. Other activists have become stockholders in companies which they would like to see change and use the shareholder proposal (or

A PETA protest in White Plains, NY (photo courtesy of SVTCobra)

a shareholder-sponsored resolution) to push for change and to raise awareness of the importance of their proposed changes.

The shareholder-sponsored resolution can be viewed as an effort to lobby corporate management to implement corporate social responsibility reforms which range from improving environmental controls to instituting antidiscrimination policies (Tkac 2006). Shareholder activism has also been taking the form of ethical investing where mutual funds, retirement funds, or individuals purchase shares in a company and use the Annual General Meeting of shareholders to propose changes to corporate policy (Utting 2005).

Shareholder-Sponsored Resolution

Securities and Exchange Commission (SEC) Rule 14a-8 established the process for submitting a shareholder proposal to be included on a proxy statement. Basically a shareholder is eligible to submit one proposal providing they have continuously held shares in a company for one year that were worth at least $2,000, or 1 percent of firm value. The proposal needs to be 500 words or less and is submitted at the annual stockholders meeting.

Corporate managers are also allowed to petition the Securities and Exchange Commission to exclude a proposal and will likely have their request granted if the proposal reflects a personal grievance or requires the firm to violate laws. The exclusionary rights are often granted to deter repetitive frivolous proposals that can cost the company unnecessary money without any reasonable outcome being possible. In addition, the proposals submitted by shareholder activists are typically nonbinding on corporate management.

Types of Shareholders

On average, about 250 different proposals are submitted each year. The shareholder activists that have sponsored corporate social responsibility resolutions generally fall into one of several different types of groups:

- Individuals—Investors who meet the ownership requirements with their individual stockholdings in a particular firm and that pursue agendas based on personal preferences.
- Pension funds and endowments—Mostly public pension funds that are often seeking greater financial returns for their beneficiaries.
- Unions—Labor unions that manage multiemployer defined benefit pension funds which also may be seeking economic benefits for their members.
- Religious organizations—Organizations that are pursing changes based on religious values.
- Social organizations—Organizations that are pursuing specific changes such as improvements to environmental
- Socially responsible mutual funds—Funds that are pursuing the performance and social criteria that their investors are seeking.

Shareholder Targets

The success that shareholder activists have may influence their choice of target companies. If a firm already has a high profile, then a shareholder proposal may attract more media attention, which in turn may further an activist's causes even if the proposal at the annual meeting is a failure. In addition, if a corporation already has a track record of being a good corporate citizen, upper management may be more interested and willing to act on the concerns of social activist investors to further the company's reputation as a good citizen. The most common themes of shareholder proposals involve some form of international conduct, addressing environmental issues, and those related to antidiscrimination (Tkac 2006).

ISSUES

Opponents to Corporate Social Responsibility

Not everyone agrees that corporate social responsibility agendas benefits society. A notable example of this viewpoint is Milton Friedman who argued that it is not the role of corporations to provide such services. Those opposed to corporate social responsibility often argue that human services should only be supported by individual, not corporations, and those services should only be offered through charities and churches. They also contend that private companies should focus on making profits or increasing shareholder wealth (Tkac 2006). Regardless of the arguments for or against corporate social responsibility, it has become a viable industry. Sponsorships or contributions made by corporations can create very positive and highly visible press coverage and help establish the company as a good corporate citizen (Ingham 2006).

When CSR Efforts Fail

When corporations want to create a positive corporate image and be on a list of favorite companies of consumers, they often engage in corporate social responsibility activities. When corporate scandals become more popular than soap operas on day-time television, it is increasingly important for corporations to maintain a positive image. Even those companies that are in less than socially respectable activities, such as the tobacco and oil companies, are attempting to change their negative images by implementing a socially appealing corporate social responsibility campaigns.

For the most part, research into corporate social responsibility and the results of corporate social responsibility programs for sponsoring corporations still only provides a theory-based examination into the circumstances in which corporate social responsibility activities may improve a corporation's image. Many analysts feel that corporate social responsibility activities are based on a rather naïve business theory that has a root assumption that customers and consumers in general will accept the activity as legitimate and feel that the sponsoring company is doing good and is worthy of business.

This proposition is rather consistent with a far-reaching body of research and published articles in various media on attribution. Further, it demonstrates a pervasive positive bias in the articles and the research. In general, there is an underlying assumption that consumers view those companies that do bad things as bad companies and that they perceive those companies that do good things as good companies.

Many people are skeptical by nature and have learned over time not to trust advertising, political statements, or the motivations of people that may claim that they are doing good things. Trust in society is basically down. Thus most consumers may be generally skeptical of a corporation's actions unless they have more in-depth knowledge of those actions or unless those actions are very consistent with their personal beliefs and desires about social change. For example, when Philip Morris started to support a youth smoking prevention campaign, both critics and consumers criticized its corporate social responsibility campaign. This result is certainly contrary to what the company had hoped to achieve (Yoon, Gürhan-Canli, and Schwarz 2006).

Accountability

The concept of accountability has become a mainstream issue within international development policy and research with a focus on a lack of accountability of government agencies in various countries. The issue that arises again and again is how poorly government programs are managed and how economic development money may be spent, which often results in maldevelopment (Bendell 2005). Examples of poorly managed economic policy and negative outcomes include extractive industries which often take more from a developing country than they give back. Political and bureaucratic leaders in many countries that need money either do not know how to manage extractive industries or do not care what they do. However, there remains a strong trend in the corporate social responsibility movement to hold companies responsible for the outcomes of their extractive business models regardless of where they are doing business (Frame 2005).

Nongovernmental organizations have played a role in bringing maldevelopment problems to the discussion table for over a decade. As a result many companies have worked with the nongovernmental organizations to develop policies and processes to address their impact on local societies. These efforts have spawned a long list of partnerships and collaborative efforts between nongovernmental organizations and private companies as well as local governments. The creation of these multistakeholders initiatives has become a mainstay in many international development efforts.

Worldwide Responsible Apparel Production
A good example of a multistakeholder initiative is the Worldwide Responsible Apparel Production (WRAP), a project of the American Apparel Manufacturers Association (AAMA). The apparel industry had received considerable bad press and negative publicity about sweatshop manufacturing and child labor. In response, the AAMA developed the Worldwide Responsible Apparel Production (WRAP) principles.

Worldwide Responsible Apparel Production seemed to help the industry's image in the United States, but it did not please everybody in the southern hemisphere. For one thing most of the board members of the organizations were US citizens. The American Apparel Manufacturers Association put together the principles without much input from the workers in the south and without coordinating with activist organizations located in countries were clothing was being manufactured.

When Worldwide Responsible Apparel Production started working in El Salvador, it ended up competing directly with a local initiative headed by a nonprofit Salvadoran group working to protect workers' rights. The Salvadoran Independent Monitoring Group (GMIES), established in 1996, was the first group to launch a program of external monitoring and assessment of labor conditions perpetuated by contractors that produced apparel for companies based in the United States and Europe. While Worldwide Responsible Apparel Production was taking a distant and soft approach to protecting workers, the Salvadoran Independent Monitoring Group wanted more everyday involvement and monitoring and to advocate for workers. Apparel manufacturers of course much preferred the Worldwide Responsible Apparel Production approach and were reluctant to cooperate, if not totally uncooperative, with the Salvadoran Independent Monitoring Group (Bendell 2005).

CSR Concerns for NGOs
There are several concerns about the participation of nongovernmental organizations that participate in voluntary multistakeholder initiatives for corporate social responsibility. Foremost is that nongovernmental organizations need to recognize the strong possibilities of co-optation. If a nongovernmental organization becomes dependent on funding or comes under the influence of a contributing industry, for example, the objectivity of the nongovernmental organization may be diminished as it courts funding sources by modifying its agenda and principles of corporate social responsibility. Even though collaboration with industry or even individual companies may end up being very beneficial, it is important to bear in mind that corporate social responsibility can be a tool used by corporations to leverage their position in a community or even a country.

On the other hand, corporate executives should also be concerned about involvement with nongovernmental organizations which often have very limited accountability for the actions and the outcomes of their corporate social responsibility initiatives. As corporations work to improve their image they do not want a public relations disaster on their hands because of mismanagement of a nongovernmental organizations or if a multistakeholder initiative ends up doing more harm than good. The same issues can impact socially responsible investment funds. There are also questions of corruption. When multistakeholder initiatives involve local governments there is a chance that corruption at the local level can turn multistakeholder initiatives into public relations nightmares (Bendell 2005).

CONCLUSION

There has been a growing acceptance of corporate social responsibility principles among intergovernmental organizations. The United Nations and the World Bank are both involved with corporate social responsibility initiatives as well as other nongovernmental organizations around the world (Senser 2007).

However, there is not a universal consensus on corporate social responsibility or the role of corporations in social change and some people still feel that a corporate social responsibility agenda does not necessarily benefit society. Those opposed to corporate social responsibility often argue that any human services should only be supported by individuals, not corporations, and those services should only be offered through charities and churches. They also contend that private companies should focus on making profits or increasing shareholder wealth (Tkac 2006).

Many analysts feel that corporate social responsibility activities are based in a rather naïve business theory that has a root assumption that customers and consumers in general will accept the activity as legitimate and feel that the sponsoring company is doing good and is worthy of business. Even without the consensus, corporate social responsibility has become a viable industry. Sponsorships or contributions made by corporations can create very positive and highly visible press coverage and help establish the company as a good corporate citizen (Ingham 2006).

Corporate social responsibility has become part of a corporations' arsenal of public relations and advertising strategies. Many corporations make big news out of their ethical actions and socially responsible policies. They issue press releases and prominently display their activities and accolades on their websites. Many feel this contributes to high levels of affinity with their customer base who strongly desire to do right by doing business with those companies that do right (Manokha 2004).

Bibliography

Bendell, Jem. "In Whose Name? The Accountability of Corporate Social Responsibility." *Development in Practice* 15, nos. 3–4 (2005): 362–74. Web. 29 Nov. 2007.

Cohen, Jeffrey, Lori Holder-Webb, and Samer Khalil. "A Further Examination of the Impact of Corporate Social Responsibility and Governance on Investment Decisions." *Journal of Business Ethics* 146, no. 1 (2017): 203–18. Web. 29 Nov. 2007.

"Corporate Social Responsibility Reports a Danger to Sustainable Future." *Ecologist* 36 (2006): 9. Web. 29 Nov. 2007.

Frame, Bob. "Corporate Social Responsibility: A Challenge for the Donor Community." *Development in Practice* 15, nos. 3–4 (2005): 422–32. Web. 29 Nov. 2007.

Flammer, Caroline. "Corporate Social Responsibility and Shareholder Reaction: The Environmental Awareness of Investors." *Academy of Management Journal* 56 (2013): 758–81. Web. 22 Nov. 2013.

Ingham, Bernard. "CSR: The Worf in Sheep's Clothing." *Journal of Public Affairs* 6 (2006): 283–85. Web. 29 Nov. 2007.

International Standards Organization. (n.d.). *ISO 26000—Social Responsibility*. Web. 22 Nov. 2013.

KPMG. *KPMG International Survey of Corporate Responsibility Reporting 2011*. (2011, Nov.). Web. 22 Nov. 2013.

Manokha, Ivan. "Corporate Social Responsibility: A New Signifier? An Analysis of Business Ethics and Good Business Practice." *Politics* 24 (2004): 56–64. Web. 29 Nov. 2007.

Phillips, Edwin. "Corporate Social Responsibility in Aviation." *Journal of Air Transportation* 11 (2006): 65–87. Web. 29 Nov. 2007.

Senser, Robert. "Corporate Social Responsibility." *Dissent* 54 (2007): 77–82. Web. 29 Nov. 2007.

Tkac, Paula. "One Proxy at a Time: Pursuing Social Change through Shareholder Proposals." *Economic Review* (07321813). 91 (2006): 1–20. Web. 29 Nov. 2007.

Utting, Peter. "Corporate Responsibility and the Movement of Business." *Development in Practice* 15, nos. 3–4 (2005): 375–88. Web. 29 Nov. 2007.

Yoon, Yeosun, Zeynep Gürhan-Canli, and Norbert Schwarz. "The Effect of Corporate Social Responsibility (CSR) Activities on Companies with Bad Reputations." *Journal of Consumer Psychology* 16 (2006): 377–90. Web. 29 Nov. 2007.

Suggested Reading

Barry, Max. "Corporate Social Responsibility-Unworkable Paradox or Sustainable Paradigm?" *Engineering Sustainability* 156, 156 (2003): 129–30. Web. 29 Nov. 2007.

Beal, Brent D. *Corporate Social Responsibility: Definition, Core Issues, and Recent Developments*. Thousand Oaks, CA: Sage Publications, 2014.

Black, Leeora, and Charmaine Hartel. "The Five Capabilities of Socially Responsible Companies." *Journal of Public Affairs* (14723891) 4 (2004): 125–44. Web. 29 Nov. 2007.

Chanin, Joshua. "The Regulatory Grass Is Greener: A Comparative Analysis of the Alien Tort Claims Act and the European Union's Green Paper on Corporate Social Responsibility." *Indiana Journal of Global Legal Studies* 12 (2005): 745–78. Web. 29 Nov. 2007.

Delmas, Magali A., Dror Etzion, and Nicholas Nairn-Birch. "Triangulating Environmental Performance: What Do Corporate Social Responsibility Ratings Really Capture?" *Academy of Management Learning & Education* 12 (2013): 255–67. Web. 22 Nov. 2013.

Diener, Keith. "The Charitable Responsibilities Model of Corporate of Social Responsibility." *Journal of Academic & Business Ethics* 71 (2013): 13. Web. 22 Nov. 2013.

Hale, Angela, and Jane Wills. "Women Working Worldwide: Transnational Networks, Corporate Social Responsibility and Action Research." *Global Networks* 7 (2007): 453–76. Web. 29 Nov. 2007.

Harjula, Liisa. "Tensions between Venture Capitalists' and Business-Social Entrepreneurs' Goals." *Greener Management International* (2006): 79–87. Web. 29 Nov. 2007.

Hatcher, Mark. "New Corporate Agendas." *Journal of Public Affairs* (14723891). 3 (2003): 32. Web. 29 Nov. 2007.

Henderson, David. "The Case Against 'Corporate Social Responsibility'." *Policy* 17 (2001): 78. Web. 29 Nov. 2007.

Hill, Marquita, Thomas Saviello, and Stephen Groves. "The Greening of a Pulp and Paper Mill: International Paper's Androscoggin Mill, Jay, Maine." *Journal of Industrial Ecology* 6 (2002): 107–20. Web. 29 Nov. 2007.

Homburg, Christian, Marcel Stierl, and Torsten Bornemann. "Corporate Social Responsibility in Business-to-Business Markets: How Organizational Customers Account for Supplier Corporate Social Responsibility Engagement." *Journal of Marketing* 77 (2013): 54–72. Web. 22 Nov. 2013.

Jenkins, Rhys. "Globalization, Corporate Social Responsibility and Poverty." *International Affairs* 81 (2005): 525–40. Web. 29 Nov. 2007.

Joseph, Ella. "Promoting Corporate Social Responsibility: Is Market-Based Regulation Sufficient?" *New Economy* 9 (2002): 96. Web. 29 Nov. 2007.

Joseph, Ella. "Corporate Social Responsibility: Delivering the New Agenda." *New Economy* 8 (2001): 121. Web. 29 Nov. 2007.

Khanna, Arun. "Pharmaceutical Industry's Corporate Social Responsibility towards HIV/AIDS." *Journal of Postgraduate Medicine* 52 (2006): 194–96. Web. 29 Nov. 2007.

Lee, Ki-Hoon, and Robert Ball. "Achieving Sustainable Corporate Competitiveness." *Greener Management International* (2003): 89–104. Web. 21 Nov. 2007.

Menon, Satya, and Barbara Kahn. "Corporate Sponsorships of Philanthropic Activities: When Do They Impact Perception of Sponsor Brand?" *Journal of Consumer Psychology* 13 (2003): 315. Web. 29 Nov. 2007.

Mikkelsen, Bent E. "Declining Role of Governments in Promoting Healthy Eating: Time to Rethink the Role of the Food Industry?" *Scandinavian Journal of Nutrition* 49 (2005): 127–30. Web. 29 Nov. 2007.

Mohr, Lois, Deborah Webb, and Katherine Harris. "Do Consumers Expect Companies to Be Socially Responsible? The Impact of Corporate Social Responsibility on Buying Behavior." *Journal of Consumer Affairs* 35 (2001): 45. Web. 29 Nov. 2007.

Newell, Peter. "Citizenship, Accountability and Community: The Limits of the CSR Agenda." *International Affairs* 81 (2005): 541–57. Web. 29 Nov. 2007.

Payne, Adrian. "Corporate Social Responsibility and Sustainable Development." *Journal of Public Affairs* (14723891). 6, nos. 3–4 (2006): 286–97. Web. 29 Nov. 2007.

Sharma, Manoj. "Corporate Social Responsibility and Alcohol: The Need and Potential for Partnership." *Journal of Alcohol & Drug Education* 49 (2005): 85–88. Web. 29 Nov. 2007.

Siegele, Linda, and Halina Ward. "Corporate Social Responsibity: A Step towards Stronger Involvement of Business in MEA Implementation?" *Review of European Community & International Environmental Law* 16 (2007): 135–44. Web. 29 Nov. 2007.

Sullivan, Rory. "NGO Expectations of Companies and Human Rights." *Non-State Actors & International Law* 3 nos. 2–3 (2003): 303–22. Web. 29 Nov. 2007.

Michael Erbschloe, M.A.

Corporate Strategy

ABSTRACT

This article explores the topic of corporate strategy and ways it fits within the strategic management process. Specifically, it examines the various types of corporate strategy, providing a framework to recognize when a given strategy is most appropriate. Also, it includes real-life examples of corporate strategy in action, along with an overview of corporate portfolio tools used in corporate strategy formulation.

OVERVIEW

Strategy is defined as "the art of devising or employing plans or stratagems toward a goal" (Merriam Webster online 2007). Within a broad business context, strategy is an integrated set of plans for achieving long-term organizational goals. Multiunit corporations have three levels of organizational strategy: corporate strategy, business strategy, and functional strategy. "Corporate strategy concerns two different questions: what businesses should the company be in and how the corporate office should manage the array of business units" (Porter 1987). In a broad sense, corporate strategy establishes the overall direction of the firm. Also, corporate strategy is a smaller part of a larger and distinct process known as the strategic management process, consisting of several interrelated stages, of which corporate strategy development falls within the strategy formulation stage. (There are five fundamental stages of strategic management: environmental scanning, strategy formulation, strategy implementation, evaluation, and control.) Strategy formulation exists on a three-level hierarchy (see Figure 1 below). Typically, the strategy formulation process is an interactive top-down process beginning with corporate-level strategy developed by top management, followed by the business and functional levels of strategy. Depending on the organization, managers at the functional and business levels provide varying degrees of input throughout the entire strategy formulation process.

Business Strategy—Once corporate strategies are developed, the focus is upon formulating business-level strategies. Business strategy is sometimes referred to as competitive strategy (Porter 1980), a strategy that gives the firm a competitive advantage. Business strategy development occurs within a multiunit firm's divisions and subsidiaries, sometimes referred to as strategic business units or SBUs. A firm's internal strengths are sources of competitive advantage and are collectively defined as a firm's core competency. Porter (1985) outlines a set of generic business strategies, such as a cost leadership strategy, emphasizing low-cost production or distribution of products or a differentiation strategy, which distinguishes company products and services on the basis of superior service, quality, unique features, etc. Either strategy may opt to target a broad market or focus on a narrow market segment. Functional strategy flows out of an organization's functional departmental areas, developed to advance the aforementioned corporate and business level strategies. Functional area strategies include:

- Operations strategy—Designing production processes that meet customer product/service requirements.
- Financial strategy—Preparing budgets and securing needed financial resources.
- Marketing strategy—Identifying customers, customer requirements, pricing strategies, promotional methods, and distribution channels.

A wall of PepsiCo products at a North Carolina rest station (photo courtesy of Washuotaku)

- Human resource strategy—Recruiting, selecting, training, compensating, and organizing employees.
- Research & design strategy—Creating new products or updating existing products and services.

APPLICATIONS

Corporate strategy responds to a number of questions related to how a firm intends to compete on a broad scale. How will the corporation grow? What businesses will the firm compete with? Is growth strategy an appropriate option to choose from? If so, does the firm possess the financial capability to grow? Is the firm's target market attractive enough to allow for growth in their current industry? Must the firm look outside of its current industry for growth opportunities, and if so, which industries? These questions are the ones a corporate strategy addresses. Depending on the answers to these questions, corporate-level strategy is addressed through a growth strategy or a defensive strategy. Note that growth strategies may be pursued by internal or external means. For example, when choosing internal growth mechanisms, a firm develops and markets new products, improves upon existing products, or sells existing products to new markets. Alternatively, when a firm implements external growth strategies, the firm acquires growth assets outside of the organization.

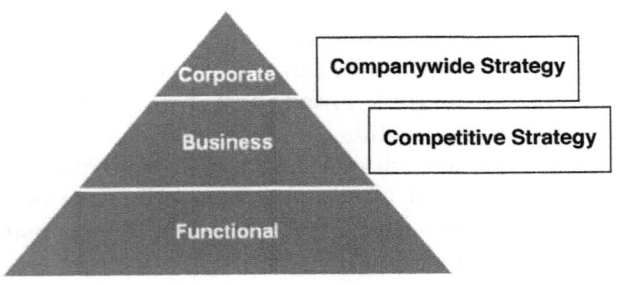

Figure 1

Growth Strategy

Growth strategy is that strategy employed to grow a firm's profits and lies within two broad categories: diversification and concentration. Diversification strategy adds products/services somewhat related or unrelated to the firm's core business. Concentration strategies are those growth strategies whereby a firm maintains a competitive focus within its particular industry. The two types of concentration strategies are vertical integration and horizontal integration.

Concentration Strategies

With vertical integration strategy, a firm takes over the supply function and/or distribution function that was previously handled by outsiders. There are several types of vertical integration strategies: forward vertical integration, backward vertical integration, and full integration. Forward vertical integration strategy involves a manufacturer assuming the distribution function for its products or services. A failed attempt at forward vertical integration is personal computer maker Gateway's attempt to distribute personal computers (PCs) through company-owned retail stores. This strategy was a failure due to the high overhead costs associated with their bricks-and-mortar retail stores. Gateway switched to marketing PCs exclusively through their website and over the phone. More successful examples of companies taking over the distribution function are found in the factory outlet shopping mall phenomenon. In effect, various manufacturers sell their products directly to consumers through company-owned stores—companies such as Nike, Tommy Hilfiger, Sketchers, Pepperidge Farms, Samsonite, etc. However, unlike Gateway, these companies do not rely on forward vertical integration entirely since they also rely on third-party retailers for the bulk of their sales. Backward vertical integration is when a firm assumes the supply function for their respective value chain. With increasing global competition and the rising costs of commodities, (e.g., copper, rubber, aluminum, iron, and oil, etc.), a trend shows an increased amount of backward vertical integration activity. In order to ensure reliable supply and to control costs, manufacturers have been acquiring suppliers of critical inputs to their production processes. Examples include: Japan tire manufacturer Bridgestone's purchase of an Indonesian rubber plantation, and Toyota' acquisition of a controlling interest in its main supplier of batteries for its hybrid vehicles (Gross 2006). On the other hand, Bob Evans Farms Inc. has always relied on a backward vertical integration strategy. Best known for offering pork sausage products to the retail grocery market, Bob Evans controls the supply function of their business by raising and slaughtering hogs on company-owned farms, then preparing and packaging their park sausage products for sale.

Full integration occurs when a firm takes over the entire value chain of supplying the inputs of production (i.e., raw materials or component parts), manufacturing the product, and distribution of the product to the ultimate consumer. Examples of complete vertical integration are oil and gas companies such as ExxonMobil, BP, and Royal Dutch Shell PLC, etc. These fully integrated companies engage in oil exploration, extract crude oil with their own drilling operations, refine oil into gasoline at company owned refineries, and then distribute gasoline products through company-owned gas stations. Note that vertical integration exists in varying degrees along the value chain. The ranges of vertical integration are: nonintegration, quasi-integration, taper integration, and full integration (Harrigan 1984).

Full Integration is when a manufacturer retains in-house responsibility for its supplies and is the sole distributor of its products. Taper Integration occurs when a firm is forward or backward vertically integrated, yet relies on outside firms for supplying only a portion of production inputs or a portion of distribution needs. Quasi-integration is an arrangement whereby a company does not make any supplies or distribute any of its products, but owns a partial interest in a supplier or distributor to guarantee access to supplies and distribution channels. For example, in a forward quasi-integration arrangement, PepsiCo could purchase a partial equity interest in Kroger supermarket chain in order to ensure access to Kroger's distribution network. Or in a backward quasi-integration arrangement, GM could conceivably acquire a minority equity interest in a supplier of automotive electrical components. Non-integration involves the use of contractual arrangements, i.e., long-term agreements between the firm and its suppliers and/or distributors to provide services over a specified time period. With this type of arrangement, no ownership transfer or exchange of assets occurs. The automotive industry commonly makes use of such nonintegration arrangements. Horizontal Integration is when a firm acquires a competitor in the same industry. Also, horizontal integration tends to be the most preferred growth strategy for many industries. Mergers and acquisitions are the typical method by which horizontal integration is achieved (David 1996). For example, the personal computer industry has undergone a number of horizontally integrated transactions with Gateway Computer's acquisition of low-cost rival e-Machines, and HP's merger with rival PC maker Compaq. Likewise, in the telecommunications sector, SBC Communications merged with AT&T. Automotive industry examples of horizontal integration include Ford Motor's acquisition of Volvo, Jaguar, Aston Martin, and Land Rover, as a way of quickly moving into a high-end automotive segment. Other examples include GM's acquisition of Swedish carmaker Saab, and Germany's DaimlerBenz' acquisition of US-based Chrysler Corp.

Diversification Strategies
Diversification strategies are of two varieties: concentric diversification and conglomerate diversification. Concentric diversification is an assortment of related products in the firm's portfolio. As one of the world's largest food and beverage companies, PepsiCo Inc. practices concentric diversification (http://pepsico.com/PEP%5fCompany/BrandsCompanies/index.cfm). The company's related business units include:

- Frito-Lay snacks
- Pepsi-Cola beverages
- Gatorade sports drinks
- Tropicana juices
- Quaker Foods

On the other hand, conglomerate diversification is a collection of unrelated lines of business in the corporate portfolio. For example, when many people think of General Electric (GE), they automatically think of lightbulbs or appliances; yet the GE of today is a truly diversified conglomerate, made up of six business units:

1. GE Infrastructure consists of aircraft engines, energy, oil and gas, rail and water process technologies, and more.
2. GE Commercial Finance provides loans, operating leases, financing programs, commercial insurance, and reinsurance products.
3. GE Health offers medical imaging and information technologies, medical diagnostics, patient monitoring systems, performance

4. GE Industrial includes appliances, lighting and inducts, factory automation systems, etc.
5. GE Money offers financial products such as credit cards, personal loans, mortgage, and motor solutions.
6. NBC Universal is a media and entertainment business consisting of news production, movies, theme parks etc. (http://www.ge.com/en/company/businesses/ge_nbc_universal.htm)

Defensive Strategy

Defensive strategies are those strategies used when experiencing financial trouble, indicated by declining sales and profits. The need for retrenchment strategy may be due to an industry-wide problem (e.g., an unattractive industry such as a typewriter company) or a firm-specific problem (e.g., poor management, lack of financial resources). There are four types of defensive strategies that firms employ: retrenchment, divestiture, joint venture, and liquidation (David 1996). Retrenchment strategy (also known as turnaround strategy) involves the imposition of cost reductions, with an emphasis on improving the operational efficiency of the firm. An example of a successful turnaround effort is Nissan Motors Ltd. In 1999, after seven straight years of record unprofitability, Nissan named as its new chief executive officer (CEO), Carlos Ghosn, an executive vice president from Renault. As part of his retrenchment strategy, Ghosn closed manufacturing plants in Japan, reduced employee headcount by 21,000, cut in half the number of suppliers to around 600, and reduced parts costs by 20 percent. Under Ghosn's leadership, Nissan went from a $5.5 billion loss in fiscal 2000 to a $2.7 billion profit in 2001—far exceeding expectations (http://www.gsb.stanford.edu/news/headlines/vftt%5fghosn.shtml).

Divestiture involves the spin-off of a firm's business units that are unprofitable or do not represent a good strategic fit with the firm's core business. IBM's former desktop personal computer business is a prime example. In 2004, IBM sold its personal computer business to Chinese computer maker Lenovo Group for $1.75 billion. IBM's rationale for the deal was a continuation of IBM's strategy shift from selling low margin hardware products to selling higher margin consulting services, software, and high-end computers. Likewise, IBM viewed the deal as an inroad to the vast, fast growing Chinese market for servers and technical services (Spooner and Kanellos 2004).

Joint ventures are temporary partnerships between two firms, typically utilized when both firms wish to capitalize on a mutually beneficial opportunity. Technically speaking, the IBM/Lenovo deal is a divesture transaction, yet it also contains elements of a joint venture between the two companies, with IBM maintaining an 18 percent equity investment in Lenovo. For example, Lenovo has been the preferred supplier of PCs to IBM and was allowed to use the IBM brand for five years. Also, IBM has provided marketing support to Lenovo via the IBM corporate sales force. From a benefits perspective, the deal rid IBM of its personal computer business, while gaining an entry point into China for other IBM products and services. On the other hand, Lenovo gained access to IBM's extensive corporate customer base, the IBM name, and IBM's marketing expertise (Spooner and Kanellos 2004).

Liquidation involves selling off a company's assets for their tangible net worth and signals the end of the firm's existence. This strategy is employed when a firm is losing significant amounts of money with no prospect of recovery; all other retrenchment strategies have been tried, yet were either inappropriate, or ended in failure. Generally, liquidation occurs as part of a court-ordered bankruptcy sale under Chapter 7 bankruptcy. However, a firm may undertake a voluntary path to liquidation outside of bankruptcy, yet this route is less common. Examples of firms forced to liquidate are passenger airline carriers Trans World Airlines (TWA) and Pan American Airways. Note that Chapter 7 liquidation is not to be confused with a Chapter 11 bankruptcy in which a firm is allowed to reorganize its financial affairs in the hopes of remaining an ongoing firm. (For more information on the types of corporate bankruptcies, visit the US Security and Exchange Commission website at: http://www.sec.gov/investor/pubs/bankrupt.htm.)

Factors Influencing Corporate Strategy Choice

There are a number of factors influencing the choice of corporate strategy (David 1996):

Forward Integration

Used when a firm's present distributors are too expensive or incapable of meeting distribution needs and the availability of quality distributors is limited in number. This strategy works best when competing in an industry experiencing high market growth or when the organization has the capital and capability to manage the distribution function.

Backward Integration

Used when present suppliers are too expensive, unreliable or incapable of meeting the firm's needs; This strategy works best when the number of suppliers is limited, with many existing competitors; when the industry is experiencing rapid growth; resources are needed quickly; or when the organization has the capital and capability to manage the business of supplying its own parts.

Horizontal Integration

Used when the industry is a growth industry. This strategy works best when increased economies of scale provide competitive advantage; when the organization has the capital and capability to manage an expanded business; or when competitors are failing due to a lack of managerial expertise that they firm possesses.

Concentric Diversification

Used when the industry faces poor growth prospects. This strategy works best when new or related products or services would enhance the sale of existing products; when related products can be offered for sale at competitive prices; when new products offer a seasonal counterbalance against the seasonality of existing products; or when current products are in a decline stage of their life cycle.

Conglomerate Diversification

Used when the industry is declining in sales and profits. This strategy works best when the organization has the capital and capability to manage a diversified business line; when existing markets are saturated; when an attractive investment exists in an unrelated business; or when antitrust concerns prevent pursuing companies in the same industry.

Also, Porter (1987) identified three tests for making diversification choices that are most likely to create shareholder value.

1. Attractiveness test—Is the industry attractive or capable of being made attractive?
2. Cost-of-entry test—Is the cost of entry reasonable enough so as not to jeopardize future profits?
3. Better-off test—Does the parent corporation offer competitive advantage to the new unit or will the new unit bring a competitive advantage? In other words, are meaningful synergies likely to result between the new unit and the corporation?

Joint Venture

Used when the distinctive competencies of the two firms complement one another. This strategy works best when there is a reduction in risks resulting from an alliance; when smaller firms are having trouble competing against larger firms; or when there is a need to get a new technology to market quickly.

Retrenchment

Used when the firm has a weak competitive position. This strategy works best when the firm is plagued by inefficiency, low profits, or stockholder pressure to improve performance; when the organization has grown so large that an internal reorganization needs to take place; or when a distinctive competency exists, yet the firm has failed to capitalize on it.

Divestiture

Used when the retrenchment strategy was a failure. This strategy works best when a product line or division needs more resources in order to compete and survive; when a division is performing poorly; when a division is a poor strategic fit with the firm's overall corporate vision; or when an infusion of cash is needed but can't be obtained elsewhere.

Liquidation

Used when divestiture and retrenchment have failed. This strategy works best when bankruptcy is the only alternative; when liquidation allows for the orderly sale of assets; or when liquidation allows the firm's stockholders to minimize their losses.

Corporate Portfolio Approaches

"Corporate strategy concerns two different questions: what businesses should the company be in and how the corporate office should manage the array of business units" (Porter 1987). In managing the array of business units, there are several corporate portfolio approaches. One of the first portfolio approaches developed is the BCG (Boston Consulting Group) matrix. The BCG matrix is a two-dimensional analysis of a business unit's strength, determined by relative market growth rate and relative market share. Market growth rate is the annual growth rate in which the firm competes, with market share being the firm's market shares relative to all other direct competitors. Companies are divided into various categories based on their placement on the matrix:

1. Cash cows are profitable business units with a low market share and high growth rate. They should be milked for cash, with the cash flow being deployed elsewhere.
2. Dogs possess a low market share and low growth rate and should be liquidated or divested.
3. Question marks are typically found within new product areas and have a low market share with a high growth rate. Given their high growth rates, question marks should be infused with cash to develop them into stars. 4.
4. Successful question marks become stars; stars have a high growth rate and high market shares, hence a growth strategy of integration would be employed here (Thompson and Martin 2005).

The BCG matrix's simplicity—a recognized strength—is also one of its weaknesses. The market growth rate dimension (one indication of industry attractiveness) and relative market share (one determinant of competitive advantage) overlook other important determinants of profitability. In response to this limitation, consulting firm McKinsey and Co. derived a more comprehensive model from the BCG Matrix, i.e., the GE Business Screen Matrix. The GE matrix, developed for GE by McKinsey, considers a three-dimensional analysis of high, medium, and low industry attractiveness and competitive position. Industry attractiveness is substituted for BCG's market growth rate, and is comprised of external factors such as entry barriers, market growth, industry profitability, market size, pricing trends, etc. Competitive position replaces BCG's market share measure, and includes internal strengths and weakness factors including market share, relative brand strength, management strength, profitability, size, etc. (Thompson and Martin 2005).

CONCLUSION

Corporate strategy does not exist in a vacuum—it is a smaller, yet integral part of a larger and distinct process known as the strategic management process, interrelating with the formulation of a firm's business strategy, as well as its functional strategy. Is there one best corporate strategy? The answer is an unequivocal no—there is no single best corporate strategy. Likewise, the process of developing corporate strategy has become a more daunting task in light of the global competitive forces firms must confront. Corporate strategy is dependent on numerous factors as outlined with respect to industry attractiveness and the relative competitive strengths of the respective company. Once again, the fact that corporations operate in a global environment greatly complicates the formulation and coordination of corporate strategy. Hence, the formulation of corporate strategy is a dynamic, interactive, iterative process, sometimes requiring midstream adjustments as a result of unexpected changes in the firm's competitive environment. Therefore, the wrong corporate strategy choices, in addition to improper implementation, can mean the difference between success and failure.

BIBLIOGRAPHY

Bharadwaj, Anandhi, Omar A. El Sawy, P.A. Pavlou, and Nirmala Venkatraman. "Digital Business Strategy: Toward a Next Generation of Insights." *MIS Quarterly* 37, no. 2 (2013): 471–82. Web. 20 Nov. 2013.

Caescu, Stefan, and Maia Ploesteanu. "Corporate Strategies of Integrated Marketing." *Romanian Journal of Marketing* 6, no. 3 (2011): 22–29. Web. 20 Nov. 2013.

David, Fred R. *Strategic Management.* Upper Saddle River, NJ: Prentice Hall, 1996.

Gobble, MaryAnne, Irene Petrick, and H. Wright. "Innovation and Strategy." *Research Technology Management* 55, no. 3 (2012): 63–67.

Gross, D. "Disintegration?" Slate.com. (2006, 17 Aug.). Web 30 Apr. 2007.

Harrigan, Kathryn. "Formulating Vertical Integration Strategies." *Academy of Management Review* 9, no. 4 (1984): 638. Web. 2 May 2007.
Porter, Michael E. *Competitive Strategy.* New York: Free Press, 1980.
Porter, Michael E. *Competitive Advantage: Creating and Sustaining Superior Performance.* New York: Free Press, 1985.
Porter, Michael E. "From Competitive Advantage to Corporate Strategy." *Harvard Business Review* 65, no. 3 (1987): 43–59. Web. 1 May 2007.
Spooner, John G., and Michael Kanellos. "IBM Sells PC Group to Lenovo." (2004, 8 Dec.). Web. 30 Mar. 2007.
Stanford Graduate School of Business. "Nissan Motor CEO Carlos Ghosn Is Turnaround Hero." (2000, 11 Nov.). Web. 30 Mar. 2007.
Thompson, John L., and Frank Martin. *Strategic Management—Awareness and Change.* 5th ed. London: Thomson Learning, 2005.

SUGGESTED READING

Ansoff, H. Igor. "Strategies for Diversification." *Harvard Business Review* 35, no. 5 (1957): 113–24. Web. 7 May 2007.
Campbell, Andrew, Michael Goold, and Marcus Alexander. "Corporate Strategy: The Quest for Parenting Advantage." *Harvard Business Review* 73, no. 2 (1995): 120–32. Web. 1 May 2007.
Farid, Mamdouh, and David Flynn. "The Strategic Choice of Chapter 11: An Examination of the Critical Factors." *Review of Business* 13, no. 4 (1992): 32. Web. 2 May 2007.
Harridan, Kathryn, and Michael Porter. "End-Game Strategies for Declining Industries." *Harvard Business Review* no 61, no. 4 (1983): 111. Web. 2 May 2007.
Henderson, Vicky, and David Hobson. "Optical Liquidation of Derivative Portfolios." *Mathematical Finance* 21, no. 3 (2011): 365–82. Web. 20 Nov. 2013.

Edwin D. Davison, M.B.A., J.D.

CREATIVITY

ABSTRACT

Creativity is a crucial factor in the sustainability of businesses. Every aspect of business offers opportunities to be creative, and innovation—the product of creativity—is the engine of success for most firms. Creativity is considered a rare and an elusive quality. Research, however, suggests that creativity and innovation can be fostered in successful companies by creating an organizational culture appropriate for the development of creativity and innovation.

OVERVIEW

Generally speaking, the term creativity refers to the generation of new ideas by way of the imagination, as well as inventiveness. Although most often used in the arena of the arts, experts argue that creativity—and its accompanying phenomenon, innovation—are crucial elements to the sort of thinking that leads to the development of technology, all types of commercial products and strategies, and processes required in the daily management of firms.

In the area of management, creativity is understood as the development and expression of new ideas within the framework of a company's objectives and goals. Properly managed, it should lead to financial success by involving the participation of all members of the firm and, in the process, generating a positive organizational culture and high rates of employee satisfaction and loyalty (Usheva 2015).

To understand how creativity functions in the organization and how it leads to innovation, it is important to understand what creativity is. Psychologists have explained it as a phenomenon linked to the human psyche or personality, which may be determined by an admixture of personality and situational factors. Sometimes, creativity is viewed as an element naturally belonging in individuals or groups who are viewed as having a predisposition toward thinking creatively, such as artists or people in the fields of arts and design.

Creativity at work (Photo Courtesy of Drew Coffman)

There is, however, nothing in creativity that implies it should be limited to specific fields of production. In other words, creativity is not the province of one sole organizational field. In fact, creativity can be and is used on a daily basis by individuals in all sorts of occupations. For example, one of the most commonly used definitions for the purposes of modern business management was offered by Dorothy Leonard (1999), who describes it as a process of development and expression of new ideas that can be useful.

Edward De Bono (2008) describes creativity as the merging of ideas that have never been combined before or combining them in a novel way. This action may be accidental or purposeful, and generally responds to an incentive or a provocation, that is, the search for a solution to a problem. Experts recommend specific strategies for building and maintaining a creative environment in the organization, including hiring creative staff, designing a controlled environment geared toward fostering creative thinking, inviting the expression of new ideas by a diversity of people, and applying, in a practical way, creative ideas (Usheva 2015).

Devoting Resources for Innovative Thinking

All organizations need to solve problems and require insightful thinking to find the best solution possible. The application of these solutions in new ways is what many refer to as innovation. Creativity is, therefore, the ability to generate new ideas, and innovation is the implementation of those ideas. This concept applies to all sorts of business activities, including production, processes, sales, and management.

For creativity to flow, it is necessary to allow for different perspectives and freedom of expression. In an environment constrained by an excess of written and unwritten rules, it is difficult for new ideas to flow. Organizations, then, must find ways to create spaces of trust and flexibility so that staff can contribute their ideas without fear.

Successful companies understand the importance of creativity and innovation for the company's success. By encouraging creativity, members may explore unknown territory—or what is popularly known as thinking outside the box—that leads to the innovative strategies, new ideas, and cost-effective solutions that are so important to a well-run organization. For this situation to occur, it is not sufficient for an organization to encourage employees to think creatively. It is necessary to provide space, resources, and time for creative thinking to occur.

Moreover, creative solutions and ideas may come from a wide array of sources both inside and outside the firm. It is important to seek feedback—ideas on how to do better—from customers and clients, providers, partners, and other stakeholders or interested parties. Such a diversity of perspectives is sure to provide fresh ideas, and business managers must make sure that they listen with an open mind. Making sure that the exchange of ideas is supported and respected in the company is an important step toward making the company an arena of creativity.

Managers often believe they have to seek out particularly creative individuals. However, good ideas can come from the unlikeliest sources. Experts in creativity insist that everybody has the ability to think creatively. That is why they encourage the teaching of creative thinking from earliest infancy throughout elementary and high school, all the way to adulthood. These educational strategies—which can also be practiced in the organization—include creating an environment of trust, in which self-censure and fear of difference is discouraged. In fact, these are qualities that not only lead to creative thinking, but are also often sought in modern leadership.

Strategies

The creative process benefits from a controlled system that, while allowing for the free flow of ideas, also provides a roadmap to reach its objective successfully. Among the most popular strategies for encouraging a creative process developed by experts are the four steps of the creative process proposed by Byttebier and Vullings (2015):

- Ask the right questions.
- Generate abundant ideas.
- Select the appropriate ones.
- Implement them.

A possible difficulty lies in the fact that individuals vary in their creative processes. Golen (1983) has established a more detailed five-step process, which is considered by many as successful in teaching and stimulating creativity across different types of personalities:

1. Preparation/saturation—becoming steeped in or very familiar with a problem;
2. Deliberation/frustration—analyzing and challenging ideas, considering them from different angles;
3. Incubation—relaxing, turning off conscious and goal-oriented thinking;
4. Illumination—hitting upon a new, different approach, an idea that gives all the feeling of being on the right track; and
5. Elaboration/accommodation—the moment to clarify ideas, re-considering the needs and requirements, adapting it, and getting other people's feedback.

Both these strategies can be combined or merged; for example, Golen's five steps can be incorporated into the four phases of the creative process for a more organized approach.

FURTHER INSIGHTS

Organizational culture is a double-edged sword. It can affect an organization's ambiance and performance in positive and negative ways. Organizational culture is of paramount importance to fostering an environment suitable for creativity and innovation. In a positive organizational culture, the exchange of ideas is encouraged and supported. Firms strong in creativity and innovation are characterized by qualities such as trust, tolerance to risk, solid team work, open communication, transfer of knowledge, autonomy, and resources that nurture creativity and innovation.

The role of managers is crucial in such an organization. Managers are responsible for organizing, implementing, and controlling the creative process among employees (and other stakeholders when appropriate). They must ensure that everything is suitable to the creative process: the distribution of groups and tasks, access to opportunities, the work environment, as well as the resources and tools necessary to stimulate and guide the creative process (Lukić, Džamić, Knežević, et al. 2014).

Employees must feel comfortable in expressing their opinions, even when they may run against approved company policy. If employees cannot trust that their ideas will not get them into trouble or be met with disapproval, the free flow of communication might be stifled. The fear of embarrassment, of being perceived as foolish, is also stifling to many. Therefore, management must make employees feel safe, providing a nurturing space for ideas. It is also important that employees have access to opportunities in which their ideas, if suitable, may be applied and that they are not made to feel inadequate if their ideas are not suitable.

Innovation does not generate spontaneously or out of thin air. Companies, who intend to be sustainable—that is, survive long term—must constantly adapt to changing conditions. To remain competitive and to grow, they must constantly develop new strategies, products, and processes. Furthermore, companies must be proactive—responding rapidly to challenges—and open to some level of risk. The acceptance of risk is crucial to the kind of thinking that leads to useful and creative ideas, particularly for organizations of an entrepreneurial bent.

Finally, change is a crucial factor for creativity and innovation. Innovation is itself a response to change. By definition, implementation involves changes to existing systems, organizations, or practices, which may range from mild to drastic. Innovation can be applied gradually, in an incremental fashion, or may involve large-scale or radical changes. In practice, however, incremental changes are often combined with elements of disruptive change, as appropriate to the purposes of the organization (Robinson and Stubberud 2015).

Issues

Creativity in the business field is desirable and even necessary, yet it faces some potential obstacles.

These, however, are usually situations that, managed properly, may even turn into positive experiences. Among the problems that firms may have to deal with in ensuring a creative environment is diversity, rewards, and having adequate resources.

One of the most useful strategies or techniques in a creative process is brainstorming.

Brainstorming
Brainstorming implies the participation of all members of a group or team who contribute ideas—even those that may at first glance appear outlandish or inadequate. These ideas should be encouraged; however, since they may later be adopted, adapted, and improved upon. Great ideas often come from brainstorming sessions. Moreover, brainstorming is inexpensive and uncomplicated to organize, which makes it popular with management.

Brainstorming requires time, effort, and sincerity; that is, managers must intend to take into account the contributions of participants if they prove adequate. Time is required, as well, because brainstorming takes much longer than an executive order from above. Particularly in diverse societies, people from different backgrounds may contribute a great many ideas that may appear contradictory to the norms or expectations of others. It is precisely this diversity, however, that makes brainstorming a valuable strategy to acquire valuable fresh ideas. Creativity thrives in diverse groups (Robinson and Stubberud 2015).

Moreover, because creativity also thrives from seemingly unrelated ideas merging together in novel ways, including a variety of people, it provides opportunities for individuals from different cultural backgrounds or kinds of expertise to contribute their ideas and create fruitful synergy. Teams formed of diverse groups—also known as blended or mixed groups—aggregate the number of fresh ideas and perspectives. Brainstorming is often more effective with groups that are not homogeneous which is why innovative organizations increasingly search for the type of employee mix that will help foster creativity in an organization.

Motivation and Reward
Another issue that has concerned firms is the proper motivation of employees. Some behavioral theories suggest that rewarding individuals for their behavior is an effective motivator for them to repeat the action. Rewarding people for their creative ideas with monetary compensation beyond their salaries has obvious drawbacks, such as feelings of resentment among other group members who might feel that their ideas were worthier than the one selected and rewarded. Research shows, however, that a positive organizational culture and intangible rewards are crucial to motivation.

Individuals feel motivated when the firm leads them to feel that their work and contributions are meaningful and appreciated. A strong organizational culture fosters a feeling of belonging and identity with the firm, which leads to higher levels of personal satisfaction, increased productivity, and higher rates of creativity and innovation.

Determinants for Success
Experts recognize four key determinants that an organization must provide in order to support creativity and innovation:

- Adequate organizational structure
- Strategies for fostering creativity
- Organizational culture that supports creativity and innovation
- Support resources and mechanisms

Research also shows that transformational organizational leadership is a key factor that can contribute to greater creativity and innovation in an organization.

A potential obstacle to the successful development of such an environment, however, is lack of investment—in time, in training, or in financial resources. Moreover, large companies, with more people to collaborate in developing projects, are better able to implement these strategies than smaller ones, yet have been shown to be less likely to complete innovation projects than smaller businesses. Successful innovation, then, is not limited to companies with abundant resources, although it does place the burden on smaller companies to be more resourceful at developing their own creative processes.

Contemporary business takes place in a world of a constantly changing economic and social landscape. This places great pressure on firms, which must function in a state of perpetual change. Innovation has become crucial because for some firms, processes must be updated or renewed as a matter of maintenance. The rapid pace of technological advance, competition, and accelerated social and financial global movements, has made companies less secure and stable in their position. In such an environment, some experts argue, the main goal of the firm has become adaptation and re-adaptation to change. Without the capacity for innovation, and therefore the fostering of creativity, the company will eventually fail.

BIBLIOGRAPHY

Byttebier, Igor, and Ramon Vullings. *Creativity in Business: The Basic Guide for Generating and Selecting Ideas*. Amsterdam, Netherlands: BIS Publishers, 2015.

De Bono, Edward. *Six Frames for Thinking about Information*. London: Vermillion, 2008.

Egri, Carolyn P. "Introduction: Enhancing Business Education through Creativity, Mindfulness, and Accreditation. *Academy of Management Learning & Education* 11 (2012): 703. Web. 23 Oct. 2016.

Golen, Steven, Jack Eure, M. Agnes Titkemeyer, et al. "How to Teach Students to Improve Their Creativity in a Basic Business Communication Class." *Journal of Business Communication* 20, no. 3 (1983): 47–57. Web. 23 Oct. 2016.

Kaikati, Andrew M., and Jack G. Kaikati. "Doing Business Without Exchanging Money: The Scale and Creativity of Modern Barter." *California Management Review* 55, no. 2 (2013): 46–71. Web. 23 Oct. 2016.

Leonard, Dorothy, and W. Swap. *When Sparks Fly: Igniting Creativing in Groups*. Brighton, MA: Harvard Business Review Press, 1999.

Lukić, Tamara, Vladimir Džamić´, Goranka Knežević, et al. "The Influence of Organization Culture on Business Creativity, Innovation and Satisfaction." *Management* (1820–0222). 73 (2014): 49–57. Web. 23 Oct. 2016.

Robinson, Sherry, and Hans Stubberud. "A Comparison of Methods of Creativity in Small and Large European Businesses. *International Journal of Entrepreneurship* 19 (2015): 140–51. Web. 23 Oct. 2016.

Usheva, Mariana. "Creativity, Creations, and Innovations in the Management of Small and Medium Sized Business." *Economic Processes Management* 2 (2015): 14–28. Web. 23 Oct. 2016.

SUGGESTED READING

De Brabandere, Luc. Thinking in New Boxes: A New Paradigm for Business Creativity. New York: Randon House, 2013.

"Innovation Revelations." Independent Banker 66, no. 3 (2016): 46–49. Web. 23 Oct. 2016.

Meinel, Martin, and Kai-Ingo Voigt. "The Application and Impact of Creativity Techniques in Innovation Management." Proceedings Of ISPIM Conferences (2016): 1–11. Web. 23 Oct. 2016.

Montgomery, Angus. "What Can Design and Creativity Bring to Business?" Design Week (online ed.) 5 (2015). Web. 23 Oct. 2016.

Moreau, C. Page, and Marit G. Engeset. "The Downstream Consequences of Problem-Solving Mindsets: How Playing with LEGO Influences Creativity. Journal of Marketing Research 53, no. 1 (2016): 18–30. Web. 23 Oct. 2016.

Safian, Robert. "15 Lessons of Creativity for 2016." Fast Company (2016): 20–22. Web. 23 Oct. 2016.

Trudy Mercadal, Ph.D.

CRISIS MANAGEMENT

ABSTRACT

This article examines the factors that influence a manager's determination of an event or situation as a crisis. Various strategies of responding to a crisis are explained along with factors that may influence the strategy chosen to ameliorate a crisis situation. The methods that companies use to prepare for future crises are also reviewed. Several past business crises and the scope of those crises are reviewed. The selection and execution of crisis response strategies to a recall prompted by Salmonella typhimurium are examined along with specific actions that several companies in the food industry took in response to the situation. The role of US government agencies in the recall process is also explained.

OVERVIEW

The term "crisis" is used to describe a wide variety of events and circumstances. However, what comprises a crisis, or when a company decides that they are experiencing a crisis, is dependent on a number of variables. First, to what extent are there internal capabilities in place to deal with an event or situation that is disrupting business? Second, what is the magnitude of the event and what are the consequences of not successfully handling the crisis? Third, to what extent does the event affect other businesses, the surrounding community, or even the country where the company is located?

In an ideal world a company would be able to predict and be prepared for every possible event and thus minimize the perception that the event had turned into a crisis (Klein 2007). The larger the company and the more experience that corporate staff has in handling a specific type of event, the less likely it is that the event will be considered a crisis. In a situation involving a product recall, for example, some companies have considerable experience and have staff in place to deal with the recall. This situation is true for the automobile industry, where products are recalled frequently. On the other hand, in a small company with limited staff, or in one that has never faced a recall of its products, the event may become a crisis.

Identifying & Predicting Crisis Situations

If the magnitude of the event is small and limited to one location or one product, or if that event has little if any impact on day-to-day operations, it is likely the event will not be viewed as a crisis. If the event is wide in scope and devastates operational capability, the event may be viewed as a crisis. In addition, if the negative consequences of not successfully handling the crisis are minimal, then the event will not turn into a crisis. But if the consequences of failing to properly handle an event are extensive, it will likely be treated as a crisis (Top managers lack confidence 2009). The geographical scope of an event or the economic scope of an event may also influence whether or not managers in a particular company will consider the event a crisis. A natural disaster that affects several counties or states, for example, may be seen as a disruption but not particularly as a crisis. In such events, federal, state, or local responses deal with many of the consequences of the event. There is also most likely some sort of insurance coverage in place to aid in the recovery.

If the event affects only one company, or the supply chain in which the company operates, managers may consider the event a crisis. In other words, the more the consequences of the event fall singularly on a specific company or industry, the more likely it is that the event will be viewed as a crisis (Freda, Arn, and Gatlin-Watts 1999). In case of the 2008 economic downturn, the collapse of the mortgage industry was viewed as a crisis, which in turn affected the banking industry in general and many corporations that were dependent on the availability of affected monies (Verma 2009). However, it could be argued that the media and politicians who continuously emphasized the events as a crisis contributed to the effects of the downturn (Levinson 2009). In this vein, the identification of the downturn as a crisis could be seen as strategic, since it allowed Congress to be persuaded into action and also presented certain opportunities to savvy businesses (Garmhausen 2009; Maddock and Vitn 2009).

Strategy Creation & Execution

Once a company has decided that an event is a crisis, a strategy must be executed to minimize the effect of the crisis. One of the first desires that corporate managers have is to control the damage to company operations, reputation, business relationships, and, in some cases, stock prices. This focus requires the ability to rapidly organize efforts and mobilize the right people for the job (Miller 2006). Above all, speed is of the essence and the chief executive officer (CEO) should play a key role (Kimes 2009). If operations are disrupted, it is important to restore normal functioning as quickly as possible and remedy any defects that may be related to the current crisis. But the work is not finished there. During this time, a focus on reputation management, also known as image repair, may have more overall importance and value than an organization's functions. The CEO, with support from the crisis management team, is a key player in this part of the crisis drama. Much of the world outside the walls of the company views the CEO as the chief communicator for a company. In addition, the CEO's reputation is also on the line (Gaines-Ross 2009).

Corporate Crisis Examples

There have been long lists of companies that have each faced rather severe crises. In 1984, in Bhopal, India, a Union Carbide chemical plant spewed pollution into the local community and caused a disaster for which the company has suffered consequences ever since (Haseley 2004). In 1980, Proctor and Gamble introduced the Rely Super-Absorbent Tampon, which was later linked to hundreds of cases of toxic shock syndrome and numerous lawsuits (Weinberger and Romeo 1989). The Ford Motor Company suffered embarrassment as well as a class-action lawsuit over the Ford Pinto, a small compact car introduced in the 1970s that had a tendency to burst into flames if hit from the rear (Weinberger and Romeo 1989). In the late 1970s, the Firestone 500 series tires were blowing out and coming apart as people drove in their cars, which resulted in deaths and lawsuits (Gatewood and Carroll 1981). One of the most dramatic crises to ever befall an organization was the Space Shuttle *Challenger* explosion, which happened on January 28, 1986, just after liftoff. It was also televised around the world and especially in the classrooms of public schools in the United States. Among its crew was a schoolteacher, to be the first teacher in space. As *Challenger* exploded, millions of children were traumatized, the education community was outraged, parents were horrified, and politicians held their banners of anger high. NASA (National Aeronautics and Space Administration) managers were tried and then convicted (Watson 2006). Another major crisis for a corporation, and the environment, was the 2010 Gulf of Mexico oil spill involving British Petroleum (Valvi and Fragkos 2013). In response to the spill, BP set up a $20 billion trust to settle claims against the company (King 2010).

Application Crisis Management in Product Recall Situations

During the Industrial Revolution, innovation and business soared at a rapid rate, and there was little government intervention as to the quality and safety of the products that manufacturers were sending to market. After World War II this situation started to change. Federal authority to ensure the safety of consumer products, food and drugs, and transportation products was expanded. New laws were passed, federal agencies were created, and the age of product recalls began. The expansion of regulations and the growth of government oversight have certainly benefited the consumer. From a business perspective, this oversight and resulting recalls have caused a long list of dramatic organizational crises.

GOVERNMENT AGENCIES EXECUTING RECALLS

The US Consumer Product Safety Commission

The US Consumer Product Safety Commission (CPSC) is the federal agency responsible for ensuring the safety of consumer products, including toys, baby accessories, electrical tools and appliances, household chemicals, and over 15,000 other products (CPSC 2009). The CPSC was created in 1972 when the Consumer Product Safety Act became law. The CPSC issues hundreds of recalls every year and has prevented and removed hundreds of millions of items from the market in the United States (CPSC 2003).

The US Food and Drug Administration

The US Food and Drug Administration (FDA) has jurisdiction over most food products, human and animal drugs, therapeutic agents of biological origin, medical devices, radiation-emitting products, cosmetics, and animal feed. The scope of the FDA's monitoring activities is huge; covering over $1 trillion worth of products annually and involving not only manufacturing but also import, transport, and storage. The agency traces its roots back to 1862 as a division of the United States Department of Agriculture. In 1980, the FDA was moved to the newly formed United States Department of Health and Human Services where it took on its current role and structure (FDA 1998). The FDA has executed over 3,200 food product recalls since 1980, of which about twenty five percent were Class I recalls (recalls on products that pose a reasonable probability of causing serious adverse health consequences or death if eaten). There have also been hundreds of drug recalls resulting in some drugs being removed from the market permanently (US Government Accountability Office 2000). In some cases, when the FDA does not feel that companies with recalled products are responding appropriately or with due urgency, it will send US Marshals to confiscate products (Weise 2008).

The National Highway Traffic Safety Administration

The National Highway Traffic Safety Administration (NHTSA) manages safety recalls involving motor vehicles and motor vehicle equipment. Manufacturers can execute a voluntary recall or a recall can be ordered by the NHTSA. There have been thousands of recalls in the last several decades; while some recalls were very serious, the majority involved relatively non-life-threatening defects. The manufacturer is required to file a public report describing the safety-related defect or noncompliance with a federal motor vehicle safety standard. NHTSA monitors every safety recall, and the law requires that manufacturers provide safe, free, and effective remedies. Manufacturers are also required to attempt to notify owners of recalled products (NHTSA 2009).

Product Recalls & Business Crisis Management

A product recall can be a serious crisis for many businesses, especially smaller to mid-sized companies without in-house legal counsel or other staff that have experience in dealing with recalls. Many advisers suggest immediate and straightforward action and note that an off-the-shelf response plan may not be the answer to the crisis (Dezenhall 2009). There are numerous strategies that a company can take. They can be defensive or they can have a problem-solving orientation. They can communicate openly or they can communicate very little or not at all to the public and their customers (Falkheimer and Heide 2006; Huang and Su 2009).

The Peanut Corporation of America Salmonella Scare

The recalls of the last several years created rather serious business crises involving food products. In terms of analyzing a business crisis, these recalls are interesting because the products involved were part of a complex and lengthy supply chain. Fortunately, the supply chain management systems were useful in helping to mitigate damage. Much to the surprise of many, an American staple, peanut butter, was at the center of one of the largest, most widespread food recalls in history. Because of its use in the production of numerous other food products, the complexity and costs of the recall were multiplied across the industry. Over 2,500 products were recalled and the tainted products resulted in hundreds of illnesses and perhaps several deaths. The products all had ingredients manufactured by the Peanut Corporation of America (PCA) and were tainted with Salmonella typhimurium (Cook 2009; Schmit and Weise 2009). PCA voluntarily ceased operations in February and soon filed for bankruptcy. A criminal investigation by the United States Justice Department had been filed on January 30. Four years later, in February 2013, four former company officials were indicted on 75 counts including obstruction of justice and introduction of adulterated food into interstate commerce (Tavernise 2013). One of the PCA products, peanut paste, is commonly found in cookies, crackers, cereal, candy, ice cream, and pet treats, among hundreds of other types of food products (Cook 2009). On February 20, 2009, PCA issued a statement indicating it had filed for Chapter 7 bankruptcy and that it was no longer able to communicate with customers regarding recalled products (FDA 2009).

Not only was the PCA in a business crisis, but other manufacturers that used PCA products were also thrown into the crisis. In addition, restaurants, school districts, nursing homes, and probably even the military had to deal with examining over 2,500 products and dispose of any that had hit the recall list. Thus the PCA crisis spilled out of the corporation and into the supply chain, into the wholesalers and retailers selling any of the 2,500 products, and down to the home and the mouth of the food consumer. While the occurrence of situations that pose a threat to a business are somewhat inevitable, the way the situation is handled can mean the difference between a career-ending crisis and future success. As the Salmonella outbreak unfolded, there was a congressional hearing about the contamination and the conduct of PCA. The House subcommittee wanted the president of PCA, Stewart Parnell, and the Blakely, Georgia, plant manager to testify. By refusing to do so, the PCA set a tone of noncompliance and portrayed a lack of concern for the situation. This, in addition to internal emails deemed unfavorable to the PCA, placed the association in a bad position (Schmit 2009, Feb. 12). The companies that used peanut products in their manufacturing process started weighing in publicly and quickly. Perry's Ice Cream initiated a voluntary recall of select products containing peanut butter that could have been contaminated with Salmonella. Dreyer's Grand Ice Cream announced that neither the company nor its suppliers bought ingredients from PCA (Processors respond 2009). Unilever publicly stated that it did not use PCA products to make Skippy Peanut Butter, Slim-Fast shakes or bars, or its ice-cream products: Breyers, Good Humor, Klondike, Popsicle, and Ben & Jerry's (Angrisani 2009). Kellogg's made public that it recalled several snack products that ended up costing the company between $65 and $75 million (Schmit 2009, Feb. 6). Kellogg's was strongly criticized during the House subcommittee hearings but has stated that it will now do its own audits on those suppliers making products most vulnerable to bacterial contamination. Nestle officials contended that they had chosen not to use PCA products (Weise and Schmit 2009). Retailers Dorothy Lane Market and Costco made public that they had removed products from their stores and notified their customers using personal phone calls, letters, and automated calls (Gallagher 2009). Wegmans Food Markets made public that it had contacted each of its suppliers to determine where ingredients came from and examined its private-label products, removing from shelves those products that were potentially contaminated. United Supermarkets published an online list of food products it removed from shelves (Angrisani 2009). Food Lion and Walmart moved quickly and publicly discussed their quality control programs and the requirements they set for suppliers for food safety and testing (Garry 2009). This sole crisis example illustrates the wide range of responses that companies can assume during a product recall crisis. Retailers were quick to execute a plan and hope that the plan would be viewed positively by their customers. Food producers that used PCA products also moved quickly, but not all of them will escape further scrutiny for not have better quality control procedures in place. PCA, on the other hand, chose to be silent and to fold the company.

Issue Can a Company Really Be Prepared for a Business Crisis?

There are three obvious paths that companies can take to plan for a potential business crisis. Each has its benefits and each has its drawbacks. Business managers sometimes consciously choose their path while others sort of muddle through. Some companies do nothing and survive, others do nothing and perish.

Plan Making
Some companies plan and plan. They make plans. Then they make more plans. There are strategic plans, growth plans, marketing plans, business continuity plans, disaster recovery plans, general emergency plans, succession plans, and dozens of others. In many instances those plans serve companies very well—especially when these plans have a strong communication aspect built into them (Cagle 2006). One clear criticism of the process of making plans is that once plans are designed, documented, and bound, they often are put upon a shelf, where they age and become outdated. Staff come and go, and many new staff members do not even know the plans exist or where they are kept (Greek 1998). The old plans may have misinformation and may not address updated legal requirements.

Team Making
Instead of making plans, some companies train and develop staff that can respond to a variety of situations with a consistent corporate philosophy and a coordinated course of action. This structure requires developing individuals as well as teams. It also requires staff knowledge of the company, the industry in which it exists, and the potential threats within the industry environment. In the PCA contamination case, it was clear that some of the proactive businesses had dealt with recalls and health issues in the past and knew how to mobilize their resources (Angrisani 2009; Gallagher 2009; Garry 2009).

Risk Analysis
One method of selecting crisis action guidelines is to perform a sound risk analysis which requires good research, thorough analysis, and above all, realistic and clear thinking. As research is best accomplished when bias is minimized and analysis is best accomplished when the researcher has not yet decided the answer they are seeking, realistic and clear thinking are the elements most necessary in conducting a sound risk analysis (McConnell and Drennan 2006). Many of the companies in the supply chain in the PCA case were realistic. They came to grips with the fact that Salmonella was indeed a risk in the food business. The staff in the companies may even have had to respond to contamination situations in the past. The evidence was there for viewing; there had been numerous contamination cases since the early

2000s. In 2005 and 2006, for example, there were four large multistate outbreaks of Salmonella infections resulting from the consumption of raw tomatoes, mostly in restaurants (Bidol et al. 2007). Cases span the last decade with some being localized and others being rather widespread (Salmonella outbreak 1999)

CONCLUSION

What type of event or circumstance constitutes a crisis will vary from company to company. What may be routine business operations for some companies may be a serious crisis for others. Both the perception of events and experience in dealing with events influence the evolution of a crisis. If a crisis is in fact recognized, it is important to mobilize resources promptly in order to effectively control the damage. Necessary resources include experienced staff as well as outside assistance, if necessary. The CEO should be the leading spokesperson for the company when dealing with the media and the public. This role shows that the company is serious about its efforts to address the crisis and can remedy any problems that may have caused the crisis.

As the government started regulating industries more strictly and setting standards for products and processes, more companies found themselves in the public spotlight because of product recalls for defects or safety issues. Regulations and standards now cover virtually every consumer product on the market in the United States. The government also works to keep unsafe products from entering ports in the United States, and officials confiscate and destroy millions of pounds of items every year. The process of planning and preparing for future crisis can be complex and expensive. Planning certainly helps some companies, but plans are often shelved and become outdated and ineffective. Having well-trained staff with experience in crisis management and effective communication skills can help minimize the impact of a wide range of crisis situations.

Bibliography

Angrisani, Carol. "Recall Keeps Retailers on Alert." *SN: Supermarket News* 57, no. 6 (2009): 28–30. Web. 9 Apr. 2009.

Bidol, S., Elizabeth Daly, Robert Rickert, et al. "Multistate Outbreaks of Salmonella Infections Associated with Raw Tomatoes Eaten in Restaurants—United States, 2005–2006." *MMWR: Morbidity & Mortality Weekly Report* 56, no. 35 (2007): 909–11.

Cagle, Jimmy. "Internal Communication during a Crisis Pay Dividends." *Communication World* 23, no. 2 (2006): 22–23. Web. 10 Apr. 2009.

Cook, G. "Peanut Recall Causes Concern for Schools." *American School Board Journal* 196, no. 4 (2009): 6–7. Web. 8 Apr. 2009.

Dezenhall, Eric. "What to Do in a Product Safety Crisis." *Business Week Online* (2009, Mar. 9): 23. Web. 7 Apr. 7 2009.

Falkheimer, Jesper, and Mats Heide. "Multicultural Crisis Communications: Towards a Social Constructionist Perspective." *Journal of Contingencies & Crisis Management* 14, no. 4 (2006): 180–89. Web. 7 Apr. 2009.

Fletcher, M., and J. Casale. "Peanut Firm's GL Insurer Seeks Coverage Ruling." *Business Insurance* 43, no. 6 (2009): 3–21. Web. 9 Apr. 2009.

Freda, G., J. Arn, and R. Gatlin-Watts. "Adapting to the Speed of Change." *Industrial Management* 41, no. 6 (1999): 31. Web. 8 Apr. 2009.

Gaines-Ross, Leslie. "Damage Control." *Leadership Excellence* 26, no. 3 (2009): 8. Web. 8 Apr. 2009.

Gallagher, Julie. "Retailers Limit Tainted Peanut Butter's Spread." *SN: Supermarket News* 57, no. 5 (2009): 12. Web. 9 Apr. 2009.

Garmhausen, Steve. "In Turmoil, Bankers See a Chance to Woo Advisers." *American Banker* 174, no. 31 (2009): 8–9. Web. 8 Apr. 2009.

Garry, Michael. "Vetting the Food Supply." *SN: Supermarket News* 57, no. 8 (2009): 24–27. Web. 9 Apr. 2009.

Gatewood, Elizabeth, and Archie Carroll. "The Proctor and Gamble Rely Case: A Social Response Pattern for the 1980s?" *Academy of Management Proceedings* (1981): 369–73. Web. 8 Apr. 2009.

Greek, D. "Taking the Drama Out of a Crisis." *Professional Engineering* 11, no. 14 (1998): 17. Web. 10 Apr. 2009.

Haseley, K. "Twenty tears after Bhopal: What You Need to Know about Managing Today's Crises." *Chemical Market Reporter* 266, no. 18 (2004): 21–22.

Huang, Yi-Hui, and Shih-Hsin Su. "Public Relations Autonomy, Legal Dominance, and Strategic

Orientation as Predictors of Crisis Communicative Strategies." *Journal of Business Ethics* 86, no. 1 (2009): 29–41. Web. 7 Apr. 2009.

Kimes, Mina. "How Do I Keep My Company's Reputation Intact When Our Industry Has Been Tainted by Bad News?" *Fortune* 159, no. 5 (2009): 30. Web. 8 Apr. 2009.

Ki, Eyun-Jung, and Kenon A. Brown. "The Effects of Crisis Response Strategies on Relationship Quality Outcomes." *Journal of Business Communication* 50, no. 4 (2013): 403–20. Web. 15 Nov. 2013.

King, Neil. "Feinberg Ramps Up $20 Billion Compensation Fund." *Wall Street Journal* (2010, June 22): A6. Print.

Klein, Karen. "Planning Ahead for Crisis Management." *Business Week Online* (2007, Oct. 18): 21. Web. 7 Apr. 2009.

Levinson, Mark. "The Economic Collapse." *Dissent* (00123846). 56, no. 1 (2009): 61–66. Web. 8 Apr. 2009.

Linsley, Philip, and Richard Slack. "Crisis Management and an Ethic of Care: The Case of Northern Rock Bank." *Journal of Business Ethics* 113, no. 2 (2013): 285–95. Web. 15 Nov. 2013.

Maddock, G. Michael, and Raphael Vitn. "Don't Let a Good Crisis Go to Waste." *Business Week Online* (2009): 10. Web. 7 Apr. 2009.

McConnell, Allan, and Lynn Drennan. "Mission Impossible? Planning and Preparing for Crisis." *Journal of Contingencies & Crisis Management* 14, no. 2 (2006): 59–70. Web. 10 Apr. 2009.

Miller, J. "Damage Control." *Inside Counsel* 16, no. 181 (2006): 42–44. Web. 7 Apr. 2009.

"Processors Respond to Peanut Recall." *Dairy Foods* 110, no. 2 (2009): 10. Web. 9 Apr. 2009.

Salmonella Outbreak Hits More Than 120 Students at California's Pomona College." *Nation's Restaurant News* 33, no. 31 (1999): 21. Web. 8 Apr. 2009.

Schmit, Julie. "Peanut Plant's Practices Not 'Rampant'." *USA Today* (2009, Feb. 6): 4B. Print.

Schmit, Julie. "Peanut President Refuses to Testify." *USA Today* (2009, Feb. 12): 1B. Print.

Schmit, Julie, and Elizabeth Weise. "Peanut Butter Recall Grows." *USA Today* (2009, Jan. 29): 1B. Print.

Tavernise, Sabrina. "Charges Filed in Peanut Salmonella Case." *New York Times* (2013, Feb. 22): B5.

"Top Managers Lack Confidence in Corporate Leadership's Plans to Counter Economic Crisis." *Corporate Board* 30, no. 175 (2009): 28–29. Web. 7 Apr. 2009.

US Consumer Product Safety Commission. *2003 Annual Report.* Bethesda, MD: The US Consumer Product Safety Commission, 2003. Web. 8 Apr. 2009.

US Consumer Product Safety Commission. *CPSC Overview.* Bethesda, MD: The US Consumer Product Safety Commission, 2009. Web. 8 Apr. 2009.

US Food and Drug Administration. *History of the FDA.* Silver Spring, MD: US Food and Drug Administration, 2009. Web. 8 Apr. 2009.

US Food and Drug Administration. *Peanut product recalls: Salmonella typhimurium.* Silver Spring, MD: US Food and Drug Administration, 2009. Web. 9 Apr. 2009.

US Government Accountability Office. *Food Safety: Actions Needed by USDA and FDA to Ensure That Companies Promptly Carry Out Recalls.* Washington, DC: US Government Accountability Office, 2000. Web. 8 Apr. 2009.

Valvi, Alkateini C., and Konstantinos C. Fragkos. "Crisis Communication Strategies: A Case of British Petroleum." *Industrial & Commercial Training* 45, no. 7 (2013): 383–91. Web. 14 Nov. 2013.

Verma, A. "Navigating the Financial Crisis." *Communication World* 26, no. 1 (2009): 4–7. Web. 8 Apr. 2009.

Watson, T. "Teacher's Space Goal Delayed 21 Years." *USA Today* (2006, Nov.): 6A. Print.

Weinberger, Marc, and Jean Romeo. "The Impact of Negative Product News." *Business Horizons* 32, no. 1 (1989): 44. Web. 8 Apr. 2009.

Weise, Elizabeth. "FDA Sends in Federal Marshal to Seize Tainted Heparin." *USA Today* (2008, Nov. 7): 10B. Print.

Weise, Elizabeth, and Julie Schmidt. "Nestle Did Its Own Peanut Inspection." *USA Today* (2009, Mar. 20): 1B. Print.

"What Is a Safety Recall?" The National Highway Traffic Safety Administration (NHTSA), Office of Defects Investigation (ODI). Washington, DC: The National Highway Traffic Safety Administration, 2009.

Suggested Reading

Ethelberg, Steen, M. Lisby, Mia Torpdahl, et al. "Prolonged Restaurant-Associated Outbreak of Multidrug-Associated Outbreak of Multidrug-Resistant Salmonella Typhimurium among

Patients from Several European Countries." *Clinical Microbiology & Infection* 10, no. 10 (2004): 904–10. Web. 8 Apr. 2009.

Haohua, Yuhang. "Finding Opportunities in the Crisis." *China Chemical Reporter* 20, no. 9 (2009): 22. Web. 10 Apr. 2009.

Harugeri, Anand, Gurumuthy Parthasarathi, Madhan Ramesh, et al. "Story of Heparin Recall: What India Can Do?" *Journal of Postgraduate Medicine* 54, no. 3 (2008, July): 222–24. Web. 8 Apr. 2009.

Kallenberg, Kristian. "The Role of Risk in Corporate Value: A Case Study of the ABB Asbestos Litigation." *Journal of Risk Research* 10, no. 8 (2007): 1007–25. Web. 7 Apr. 2009.

Larson, Gerry. "Two Courses in Crisis Management." *Business & Commercial Aviation* 101, no. 5 (2007): 54–57. Web. 7 Apr. 2009.

Michael Erbschloe, M.A.

CRITICAL THINKING IN THE MANAGEMENT OF TECHNOLOGY

ABSTRACT

Managing technology requires the ability to think critically. Besides managing technological assets and human resources, managers of technology must guide organizations and staff in identifying problems, designing solutions, evaluating solutions and solution providers, implementing selected solutions, and closely monitoring results at each juncture. Technology managers can augment technical skills by implementing critical-thinking strategies. Critical thinking supports solving complex and unstructured problems.

Critical-thinking strategies are characterized by taking an active approach to planning and executing problem solving. Using critical thinking helps technology managers adapt to the changing demands of the technology itself and the environment that must support it. Critical thinking can be developed and is often developed through experience. Meanwhile, there have been changes in the existing standards for technology education to place emphasis on teaching critical-thinking skills. Educational institutions have come to the realization that technology management no longer depends primarily on technical skills but requires other skills that extend beyond simple knowledge. The inability to apply knowledge in a critical and timely fashion can lead to undesirable results in the real world. In other disciplines, there is disagreement as to whether or not critical thinking has a common definition or can be effectively taught.

OVERVIEW

Critical thinking is a way of conducting mental processes in order to "decide what to believe or do" (Schafersman 1991). Technology managers are likely to have many inputs into decision making. Technical staff, business oriented operational staff and peer managers are just a few of the internal sources of input. Technology vendors, competitors, government regulators and customers are other groups influencing and providing input to technology decisions made by managers. Skillful technology managers must balance competing and critical inputs to decision making. At times there will be the luxury of making decisions and having ample time, resources and information to do so. In other cases, technology management decisions are based on unforeseen problems; products, service or system failures; and other undesirable events.

The focus of critical thinking is on evaluating successful alternatives for action. Thinking critically is also an automatic filter that can prioritize activity in a changing environment. Critical thinking allows professionals to manage daily challenges by methodically yet creatively solving problems. Pennsylvania State University (2004) considers critical thinking an essential competency for students. Pennsylvania State's curricular guide defines critical thinking as:

> a term used to refer to those kinds of mental activity that are clear, precise, and purposeful. It is typically associated with solving complex real world problems, generating

multiple (or creative) solutions to a problem, drawing inferences, synthesizing and integrating information, distinguishing between fact and opinion, or estimating potential outcomes, but it can also refer to the process of evaluating the quality of one's own thinking.

Technology managers must check their own thinking because of the risk of bias or personal preference influencing decisions. Riddell (2001, 121) suggests that critical thinking requires getting away from "programmed ways of thinking." Programmed thinking can come from personal beliefs, experiences, stereotypical thoughts, and even assumptions made about the way decisions will be received within an organization or by other key decision makers. The management of technology may require creative and multiple solutions because outcomes may be difficult or impossible to predict yet return on investment must be assured. Some technology implementations are based on unrealistic timelines or costs due to the problems with predicting results. The world of technology is fraught with the constant trend toward obsolescence with the advent of many new technologies every day that threaten the stability of any current technology infrastructure. Decision making regarding technology standards may be challenging to managers because there are no guarantees the standards will infinitely support organizational goals. It is also a possibility that staying with standards too long will limit the migration path to new or required technology. Decisions that are not in the best interests of an organization may not manifest themselves until later when it is discovered that the decision can become more costly over time.

Many managers and professionals may possess a large amount of knowledge and skill, but the application of that skill within the context of a specific problem or scenario is not necessarily automatic. If problems are simple, concise and unchanging, a manager may have little trouble handling the issue or even handing it off to other less experienced personnel. However, in the real world, problems are seldom of limited scope or nature where simple knowledge alone will facilitate coordination of a solution. In technology, it is quite likely that the problems a manager will face may be beyond the experience of the manager or technical staff no matter the level of experience or training. One such problem is that of interoperability. Managing technology calls for managing different products and solutions from various vendors that may or may not easily operate together without some or even significant customization or adjustment. Once customization patching is done, it may have to be done and updated on a continual basis. Managing these updates may make the solution more costly than the organization can afford.

Technology tends to change quite often for many different reasons. Some technological change is the result of new capabilities being available such as higher capacity storage devices or greater functionality in software. Technology changes can also be due to vendors adopting new standards, merging technologies with other vendors or otherwise changing the direction of research and development. Neither the speed of change nor the direction of change in technology is easy to predict. It is very possible that managers of technology may have to manage technology change without having access to internal resources to support these efforts. In this case, managers have to consider how to complete projects using external resources such as consultants and systems integrators or outsourced staff, assets, networks, or facilities.

The management of technology involves bringing technical leadership to the mission and purpose of an organization. Managing technology also requires what Hargrove (2001, 222) calls "block and tackle" managers who remove obstacles and barriers to staff achievement. Technical staff can exhibit creativity but can be thwarted by management's need to adhere to a set agenda, program, direction, or timeline.

The technical aspects of managing technology can include project planning and can require an understanding of the systems development life cycle. Technical managers also have to understand typical information technology tasks, what makes up these tasks, and how long tasks take in order to estimate and allocate project resources.

How to Solve Technology Problems
Management of technology can range from managing information to applying technology to solve a problem or to meet a user or customer need. The process of solving the problems that management of technology indicates may not be a straight line because of the complex nature of most problems.

Laudon and Laudon (2007, 18) suggest a four-step problem-solving methodology that starts with problem identification and is followed by solution design, solution evaluation and choice, and ends with implementation of the solution.

When managers examine how technology should be managed, careful consideration has to be given to the needs of users and various stakeholder groups while balancing the features and functionality of technology. Because of competing needs and a requirement to balance technology needs versus organizational needs, the ability to conceive different paths and alternatives becomes a necessity. Hence, the opportunities for critical thinking abound. Management problems in technology often include dealing with technical staff. One important technical staff issue is ensuring that internal skills are up to date and useful in meeting organizational needs.

Technology training for technical staff is expensive and time consuming. Many technical professionals spend a considerable amount of personal time and money getting up to speed on new technology. The problem of technology training is not just reserved for technical staff. Increasingly, end users have to upgrade technology skills to be productive and contribute to organizational success. Managers of technology have to grapple with the most efficient and effective means of training end users given that most are at varying levels of initial knowledge. Sometimes, vendors offer training at no cost when major solutions are implemented. Vendor training is often standardized and may exceed the effectiveness of internally developed training as it is deployed more often in many different situations.

Leadership for the Front Lines (1999) recognized that increasingly nontechnical managers may be responsible for using, recommending and managing technology. Technology consultant Barbara E. Miller has several recommendations, including requiring managers to assess their personal technology competence. Managers can be hampered by what is unknown but overwhelmed when trying to determine how much depth of knowledge is really necessary. Another recommendation is to ask important questions about the use of technology and what benefits are provided at a personal, team, or departmental level. A critical question involves the use of technology and whether or not staff people use technology to its greatest benefit. Miller believes that managers need to "understand the dynamics of change" noting that a small percentage of people are able to adapt easily to change while half have some difficulties and a third or more resist change.

Managing technology can also mean that managers foster a certain type of environment that fosters the type of responses needed. Managers can encourage users and technology professionals to engage in continuous learning for personal and organizational benefit (Leadership for the front lines, 1999 6).

Managers of technology may have to deliver news that is not well received by some in an organization. Some unpopular decisions may include a requirement that all users have to participate in training, make changes to certain practices, and honor limits on certain resources. Other decisions, such as outsourcing, may affect whether or not technology employees will have a job in the future. While these decisions may be very popular with senior managers if they reduce costs significantly, they may cause a work slowdown or quick defection by affected employees. Miller also found that new technology requires new standards to inform employees on the effective use of new technology.

A great deal of planning is necessary to visualize the impact and to communicate standards. While some issues may arise in attempting to buy in on standards from users, other problems may be avoided by establishing standards as early as possible. Managing technology may deal with the problem of managing and qualifying information for use as business intelligence to manage operations and solve problems. A recent experience of service problems plagued JetBlue Airlines when passengers were stranded for hours on a runway was blamed by JetBlue's chief executive officer (CEO) on faulty business intelligence. Technology allows access to large amounts of data but cannot always guarantee that the right data is available at the right time or that the data is accurate. JetBlue felt that the problem could have been avoided by using accurate business intelligence that would have informed the airline about previous patterns and decisions.

Difficulties in Incorporating Critical Thinking
Critical thinking is defined as "an ability to evaluate information and opinions in a systematic, purposeful, efficient manner" (Cunningham, Cunningham,

and Saigo 2002). While it may sound great to include critical thinking in the arsenal of technology managers, facilitating critical thinking is not a sure science. Riddell (2007, 124) suggests that critical thinking may be nice to have but the ability to teach it is not supported by research. The author cites a 28-year study of nursing education that did not show a correlation between increased education and an increased ability to utilize critical-thinking skills.

Riddell (2007) notes that there is no single agreed upon definition of critical thinking and discussion of the topic in theoretical terms is much easier and more prevalent than application to the practice of a discipline. Riddell (2007, 122) also cites the commonalities in definitions given over 25 years by experts in the field of critical thinking to include:

- Reflection
- Identification and appraisal of assumptions
- Inquiry, interpretation, and analysis
- Consideration of context.

Reflection provides the manager of technology with an opportunity to step away from assumptions about technology that may be long-held. However, although a manager may be able to address personal long-term beliefs, convincing others to also release assumptions is another critical task. Reflection tends to expose limitations, and many in the technology profession enjoy being thought of as very knowledgeable about technology. Reflection may also take time and the cycle of technology delivery is already long for most end users given design issues, compatibility issues, vendor delays, rollout phases and decision making about budgets.

Identification and appraisal of assumptions is somewhat like reflection in that it takes time; however, traversing assumptions can provide valuable input prior to launching a technology project. Knowing whether or not assumptions are valid can be helpful in reducing the cost and time associated with a technology project. Organizational influences can affect the objective appraisal of assumptions because most organizations still have a hierarchy, and groups and factions can form that hold onto appraisal methods that prefer a specific school of thought. Vendors can be helpful in the identification and appraisal of assumptions by providing a view of what others are doing. Managers need to balance the views of vendors since providing information can be quickly transformed into a sales pitch.

Inquiry, interpretation, and analysis can include research and pilot testing. These valuable activities can be limited by a lack of willingness by managers to be thorough or to consider unfamiliar technology alternatives. Managers are often cognizant of staying with safe solutions offered by large and familiar companies to avoid trouble should an explanation be needed to justify a decision. In this case, time is again a factor in the level of rigor applied to research and testing. The prevalence of information can lead to almost limitless searching and evaluation of products and approaches. The beginning of the inquiry phase must include guidelines so managers can tailor the search for information and guide the testing without limiting the evaluation.

Managers of technology must always consider the context of the situation in which decisions are made. Context may end up dictating whether or how a decision is made. If the purse strings are controlled by an end user group that values speed over functionality, the best solution in the technology manager's mind may not be selected. End user managers, for example, may value cost over technology standards. A solution may be appropriate because it is inexpensive even if it doesn't fit into existing information technology standards. A solution may be selected because it is the best available for the money and allows an end user group to perform specific functions that are needed today. Selecting a slightly inferior solution now may be a preferred course of action when weighed against the cost of not having functionality and waiting for it to appear in a more stable technology at an unknown later date.

Management of technology can benefit if managers possess critical-thinking skills; however, most technology decisions are not made in a vacuum and exist in the context of other organizational decisions, opinions and assumptions. Along with critical thinking, managers may need to polish persuasive skills to influence and convince others when decision making is shared.

VIEWPOINT

Who controls technology management decisions? In previous years, some may have assumed that the management of technology was best left to technical wizards who excelled in understanding how technology works. As a result, the more technical personnel were obvious choices to consult about or to control technology management decisions. As technology implementation has matured, organizations have realized that a myriad of skills are needed to truly manage the proliferation and implementation of technology solutions. Just what skills are needed is often up for debate. The level of skill in terms of depth and breadth is often challenging and expensive to acquire. A high level of technical skill may not be a guarantee that decisions are also based on business strategy and organizational goals. Dubie and Duffy (2005, 41) feel both technology details and business acumen must be emphasized to be successful in today's organizations. The authors state "Even those pursuing the executive ranks should become conversant in technology."

In some circles, technology managers are required to have significant technical backgrounds in order for technical managers to gain and maintain the respect of technical staff. In other scenarios, technical managers may experience management difficulties due to a lack of business, operational, or managerial skills. Critical-thinking skills can help managers who are weak in a particular area, technical or business, by allowing identification of barriers to decision making.

The ability to think critically may come naturally to some individuals but can also be incorporated into the education that students receive in a variety of disciplines. Greifner (2007) notes that in 2007 the International Society for Technology in Education revised its National Educational Technology Standards to include what students "should know about technology." The Society has six categories of educational standards including: "creativity and innovation; communication and collaboration; research and information retrieval; critical thinking, problem solving, and decision making; digital citizenship; and technology operations and concepts."

The management of technology requires a creative approach to problem solving. Robbins (2001, 134) described a three-component model of creativity that merges expertise, creativity skills, and task motivation. Success as a manager of technology is found in a balance of these three components. Some may argue that technology skills are most difficult to acquire for those without technology backgrounds; however, managers who excel at talent selection can surround themselves with technical individuals with specific attributes. Task motivation can dictate the skills technology professionals must have. Technical professionals are needed who can easily summarize technology issues and alternatives and who understand how technology meets business objectives. Translating business objectives into technology requirements is also a key skill. Organizations will determine whether or not the background of the individual is valued by the manner in which professionals are promoted or allowed to participate in technology decision making. Promoting from within sends a signal that whether an individual has a technology, business or industry background, the perception is that the skills necessary are available from within. Organizations can also bolster skills by providing ongoing training in management and technology skills for key employees.

Another battleground is departmental control of information technology. An information technology department may select and deploy various solutions or technology assets. But, once those assets are owned by a business unit and technology knowledge begins to proliferate, information technology departments may find that users want to exert greater control over how technology dollars are spent. Creative application of critical-thinking skills can help managers navigate or control these conflicts.

Creativity in Managing Technology
For most managers of technology, the management of technology incorporates the ability to manage multiple competing objectives, a high tolerance for controlling and explaining ambiguity, and discovery of creative solutions to complex problems as needed. Creativity is "the ability to produce novel and useful ideas" (Robbins 2001, 133-35).

Creativity is needed because managers have to operate at a "speed of light pace" (Leadership for the Front Lines 1999). Some of this pressure is due to the fact that users of technology have become used to an instantaneous response from computer systems and expect 100 percent uptime and immediate recovery from failures. Spangler (2006) reported on a 2005 Deloitte and Touche survey of information technology professionals, which indicated that 12.1 percent of those polled had "zero tolerance" for downtime or computer outages. Only 7.8 percent stated that their businesses could operate for 72 hours without technology. Creativity may also mean dealing with situations that have not occurred before.

As the ability to collect data and analyze has expanded with the speed and power of computing, technology has developed to capture opportunities for using and monetizing it. Technology managers need to remain current on program updates and available alternatives and be able to integrate new applications and systems as part of a continual upgrading process. The very structure of an industry can change rapidly with introduced technologies, necessitating organizational changes that will depend on the critical thinking and visionary capabilities of technology managers and their subordinates (Drnevich and Croson 2013).

One of the most important areas in which creativity is needed is in managing relationships. Both internal and external relationships have an impact on the ability to assess technology needs, acquire appropriate solutions, and effectively implement and manage technology. Managers of technology must purchase talent and technology and establish relationships with vendors to have resources available to provide assistance and information when needed. Relationships in the industry can help managers become aware of the availability of scarce talent resources and competitive trends. Strong internal relationships can ensure that support is available for decisions and projects. Some organizations are trending towards using cross-functional teams for technology project implementations meaning that a technology department employee may not be the normal makeup of a project team member. Creative management of individuals who are not direct reports requires developing solid relationships with peer-level managers as well as subordinates and superiors.

Creativity in managing technology and technology problems will likely find managers looking for new ways to apply criticalthinking skills to save time and money. Zhen (2005) defines five steps to the process of managing problems including:

- Detection
- Identification
- Determination
- Resolution
- Reflection.

Zhen suggests that new technology is needed to help determine the root cause of information technology problems. According to Zhen, existing UNIX-based tools provide volumes of data that is difficult to search quickly and that do not have the capability to recognize time-stamped data. So while time data is available, the tools cannot incorporate that information automatically into the research process causing manual and slower processing of information. In addition, programming of complex UNIX commands may be required to create a search argument that adequately addresses the information needed. Zhen suggests that the concepts learned and devised in online search engines are the next step to making information technology problem solving more creative and effective. Technology management requires applying all available skills including creative and critical thinking to ensure productivity increases and costs are contained and reduced where possible.

Guillemette and Paré (2012) suggest that business objectives must be "constantly renewed and adjusted" and that the function of information technology (IT) departments must be aligned with these objectives. This requires clarification on the part of top management as to what exactly is expected from the company's technology assets. How IT can support the strategic mission is a primary challenge for technology managers. A company's agility in the marketplace in the twenty-first century is directly tied to strategic investment in and use of technology (Lu and Ramamurthy 2011).

BIBLIOGRAPHY

Cunningham, William, Mary Ann Cunningham, and Barbara W. Saigo. *Environmental Science: A Global Concern.* [Glossary]. McGraw Hill Online Learning Center. Web. 6 Apr. 2007.

Drnevich, Paul L., and David C. Croson. "Information Technology and Business-Level Strategy: Toward an Integrated Theoretical Perspective." *MIS Quarterly* 37, no. 2 (2013): 483–509. Web. 31 Oct. 2013.

Dubie, Denise and Jim Duffy. "The Best Advice I Ever Got. *Network World* 22, no. 47 (2005): 40–42. Print.

Greifner, Laura. "Technology Standards." *Education Week* [In the News Report Roundup] 26, no. 25 (2007). Print.

Guillemette, Manon G., and Guy Paré. "Toward a New Theory of the Contribution of the IT Function in

Organizations." *MIS Quarterly* 36, no. 2 (2012): 529–51. Web. 31 Oct. 2013.

Hargrove, Robert. *E-Leader: Reinventing Leadership in a Connected Economy.* New York: Perseus Books Group, 2001.

Laudon, Kenneth, and Jane P. Laudon. *Essentials of Business Information Systems.* 7th ed. Upper Saddle River, NJ: Pearson Education, Inc., 2007.

Leadership for the Front Lines, 7. (15 July 1999). Web. 25 Mar. 2007.

Lu, Ying, and K. Ramamurthy. "Understanding the Link between Information Technology Credibility and Organizational Agility: An Empirical Examination." *MIS Quarterly* 35, no. 4 (2011): 931–54. Web. 31 Oct. 2013.

Penn State University. *Guide to Curricular Procedures* [Glossary]. 2004. Web. 24 Mar. 2004.

Riddell, Thomas. "Critical Assumptions: Thinking Critically about Critical Thinking." *Journal of Nursing Education* 46, no. 3 (2007): 121–25. Print.

Robbins, Stephen P. *Organizational Behavior.* 9th ed. Upper Saddle River, NJ: Prentice Hall, Inc., 2001.

Schafersman, Steven D. "An Introduction to Critical Thinking." [Paper]. Web. 24 Mar. 2007.

Spangler, Todd. "Out of Scope: Tales from the Tech Front." *Baseline* 57 (2006): 88. Web. Apr. 6 2007. This eWeek. *eWeek* 24, no. 7 (2007): 5. Web. 6 Apr. 2007.

Zhen, Jian. "Searching for a Root Cause." *Computerworld* 39, no. 45 (2005): 35. Print.

SUGGESTED READING

Brookfield, Stephen. Developing Critical Thinkers: Challenging Adults to Explore Alternative Ways of Thinking and Acting. San Francisco: Jossey-Bass, 1987.

Mezirow, Jack. Transformative Dimensions of Adult Learning. San Francisco: Jossey-Bass, 1991.

Paul, Richard. "A Draft Statement of Principles." National Council for Excellence in Critical Thinking Web Site. 2004. Web.

Marlanda English, Ph.D.

CROSS-CULTURAL RELATIONS

ABSTRACT

Above all else, cross-cultural relations foment understanding among varying groups and societies. As this paper will demonstrate, this comprehension can prove pivotal in the establishment of other forms of interstate and intrastate relationships, which can bring enormous benefits to both contributors.

OVERVIEW

In a world comprised of a multitude of languages, religions, political ideologies, ethnicities and races, it is a critical necessity for nations to establish relations between one another in order to better understand each other. The exchange of ideas, knowledge, and value systems rest at the core of cross-cultural relations. Cultural relationships, however, are different in many ways from political and economic relations, but form the foundation of these two arenas.

Of course, cross-cultural relations are not entirely established on an interstate basis. After all, nations and states are developed from the beliefs that preceded them—the people that comprise the country. Many of these individuals and groups come from distinct cultures, the aggregate of which form the populace of that country. The histories and value systems that gave rise to these cultures permeate all levels of a country's society. Therefore, cross-cultural relations are often intrastate as well.

The Culture & the State

There is a common misconception that the term cultural relations refers to the interaction between two foreign countries. This view is not entirely accurate. While interstate relations do entail a bridging (or in some cases, a clash) of cultural gulfs, one does not necessarily need to move beyond borders in order to experience a cross-cultural situation.

The United States, for example, has sewn into the fabric of its society a myriad of subcultures. Many of them are carried over via immigration, others are based on religious tradition. While each of these

The 3M Headquarters in Maplewood, Minnesota (photo courtesy of Acroterion)

subgroups of the American way of life are proud to be considered Americans, their cultural upbringing remains an important, if not unconscious and/or repressed, determinant of their beliefs, views, and actions.

In many ways, an individual's cultural heritage is a major contributor to the nation's identity. The Pilgrims, for example, sought freedom to express their religious heritage (which had both spiritual and mundane permutations), and sailed across the Atlantic. One of the most popular foods in Great Britain is of Indian origin, tracing its way back to the days of British rule in the subcontinent. In Japan, a country rich in its own historical development, one of the three forms of written language is not Japanese in origin, but Chinese. Meanwhile, in China, there are literally hundreds (if not thousands) of individual spoken dialects, each of which traces itself back to some cultural subgroup.

There are also countless indigenous cultural groups that, while often seen as a minority, play a significant role in a country's historical and modern society. In the United States, there are a multitude of Native American tribes. In Australia, the people to welcome the British Empire's exiled criminal element were the Aboriginal tribes. In South Africa, the indigenous people have long been the *majority*—millions of black South Africans, many of whom trace their lineage to Zulu and other indigenous tribes have, since the days of the British Empire's reign, lived under the rule of non-native, white-skinned Afrikaaners. As one observer puts it succinctly, "Without an indigenous modality we are in danger of losing a unified worldview of reality" (Marais and Marais 2007).

While intrastate multiculturalism ideally works to the benefit of the state, it can also cause inadvertent tumult. There was a significant backlash against Irish immigrants in the United States at the turn of the twentieth century, and throughout American history, African Americans have been treated with at best mixed levels of respect in integrated, white dominated society. In twenty-first century America, the rate of acceptance for various cultural groups has not completely changed.

The events of September 11, 2001, for example, represented a sea change in the way Arab Americans were treated. The unexpected manner by which radical Islamic terrorists entered the country and surreptitiously enacted an elaborate scheme to kill thousands of Americans was only exacerbated in the public's eyes by the fact that they did so exploiting the country's stated heritage of serving as a melting pot of cultures. In the aftermath of that inhuman act, Americans began to show signs of distrust toward Arabs and Muslims (Mahajan 2007).

This situation is not localized in the United States, either. In the European Union, some questions have arisen regarding citizenship issues in an era in which state legitimacy is becoming somewhat clouded. The specter of international terrorism in Europe, in light of this concern, adds intensified feelings of insecurity among residents and political leaders alike. Increased policing in areas particularly populated by those of Middle Eastern descent may be doing more to fan the flames of xenophobia than help it, as many in these areas of greater police scrutiny, according to one observer, "see themselves as mere objects or targets of propaganda. They do not feel like informed or active citizens. Muslim people especially feel the embrace of state authorities as menacing" (Hintjens 2007).

Laying the Groundwork for Political Accord
One cannot discount the significance of the Peace Corps, particularly when one considers the era in which it was introduced. After all, the late 1950s and early 1960s were years in which international mistrust abounded, with two dominant political forces (democracy and communism) building their assets in direct competition with each other. The development and strategic placement of nuclear weapons

added fuel to the fire, as smaller, unaffiliated countries lived under an umbrella of fear of an impending third world war.

In 1961, President John F. Kennedy established the Peace Corps, a program in which college graduates would be sent abroad to apply their professional skills in impoverished and undeveloped countries. The stated purpose of the Peace Corps was threefold. The first of these mission statements was to help countries develop their own workforces through training, infrastructure-building, and consultative services. The latter two focused on more intangible goals. One was the projection of American culture abroad so that the values and principles on which this country is based are truly understood by other nations. The other was that the other cultures can be better understood by American society (Peace Corps 2007). Since that day, the Peace Corps has sent more than 200,000 American men and women to almost 140 countries around the globe, and is actively recruiting more at the invitation of newly established and stabilizing nations.

This ideological competition gave rise to seemingly apolitical missionary style cultural exchanges. Doctors, engineers, social workers, and others traveled to the developing world to help build roads, address public health issues, deliver food, reconstruct water supplies, train workers, and even foster political infrastructure-building. President Kennedy saw the Soviet Union implementing such philanthropic programs, and recognized that these thousands of emissaries were aiding in the development of these countries in the name of communism. The Peace Corps, despite its altruistic mission statement, was borne of this competitive endeavor to win the hearts and minds of neutral societies before the Russians could extend their influence in a similar vein.

One of the mitigating factors in the development of the cultural exchange programs offered by the Peace Corps may have been an ideological rivalry, but this element does not diminish the contributions to cross-cultural relations that this program has offered in its decades of existence. Rather, the fact that multiple political entities embraced cross-cultural relations as their vehicle of choice underscores the invaluable nature of creating understanding of differing cultures.

In fact, the prevailing view of the international community during the 1950s and 1960s was that the way to avoid war and put in its place peaceful relationships was to exchange cultural values. In Asia, Africa, and even the volatile Middle East, Peace Corps volunteers were building the grounds for long-term peaceful relationships as well as trading cultures (Young 2005). The United States was not the only Western country to implement cross-cultural development programs in the face of the Cold War. During a seven-year period, seventeen other countries, including the tiny nation of Liechtenstein, enacted so-called "goodwill" volunteer programs (Cobbs 1996).

Employing a realist perspective, cross-cultural relations does not just help developing countries build the wherewithal to become an international player. Such activities also help foster alliances. During the Cold War, such allies were pivotal in the ongoing Western effort to fortify defenses against the forces of the USSR, and vice versa. In the early twenty-first century, the view remains the same.

Bringing Security to Chaotic Environments
In Iraq, in the years immediately following the fall of Saddam Hussein, the tight relationship between the US government and the interim Iraqi coalition government did relatively little to counteract the foreign-based anti American insurgency outside of Baghdad. However, this statement in no way suggests that such solidarity was counterproductive—it was important for the US and Iraqi leadership to work together to ensure long-term development of that war-torn country. Still, the real war was a conflict for the approval (or at least noninterference) of the countless nongovernmental entities that still hold power beyond the city limits of Baghdad. Among these are the Kurdish and Sunni minorities, but also involved are innumerable clans and tribes, each of which holds some degree of power in their respective regions of post-Saddam Iraq.

The American effort was helped by addressing these cultural groups. Rather than unilaterally entering strongholds loyal to these tribes and clans and enforcing the American military will on residents, military personnel engaged these individuals in a spirit of cross-cultural exchange and understanding. American personnel met with leaders, speaking in Arabic and demonstrating the utmost respect for these senior individuals and groups. In exchange, the American military garnered important information about the activities of foreign-born insurgents. One commander observed that this tactic created a sense of mutual respect and forged long-term friendships that proved invaluable to fighting against al-Qaeda and other terrorist organizations:

> Tribal engagement has played a particularly prominent role in [Operation Iraqi Freedom]. This reflects the enduring strength of the tribes in many of Iraq's rural areas and some of its urban neighborhoods. And tribal engagement has been key to recent efforts to drive a wedge between tribally based Sunni Arab insurgents and Al-Qaeda in Iraq ... as well as efforts to undermine popular support for the Mahdi Army in largely Shi'ite neighborhoods and regions of the country. (Eisenstadt 2007).

As the example above illustrates, the employment of cross-cultural relations has even found a home in military and security operations. Of course, political stability and military security are not the only elements of society that stand to benefit from cross-cultural relationships.

Building Economic Relationships
Culture is often seen as a separate concept from business. Businesses, after all, tend to create their own individual cultures in terms of policy, protocols and even corporate philosophies. Ethnicity, religious affiliation, race, or the heritage that stems from such elements are usually expected to be overlooked in the face of individual productivity, personal conduct, and contributions to corporate performance and the bottom line.

However, in this era of globalization, where multinational corporations are prominent in every corner of the world, culture plays a significant role in business. Individual philosophies, as an afterthought to business productivity, may hold true when the company in question is based within the culture from whence it was developed. If, however, a company seeks to expand into a foreign country, where values, philosophies, and other cultural traits are considerably different than those with which it is familiar, culture becomes a central factor in that business's growth.

In this vein, therefore, cross-cultural relationship building is an element that cannot be underestimated. After all, most of the individuals that that company will hire to do work in the foreign country in question claim a local culture that may be significantly different from American or European culture. Without an understanding of the culture in which a company is about to be immersed, the corporation may not see much success. However, with an appreciation of the way of life from which their employees hail, strong business relationships may pave the way to strong productivity.

3M, the Minnesota-based diversified technology corporation, took this point to heart. When expanding operations into the newly capitalist economy of Russia, the company performed careful analysis of that country's cultural traits and customs. They did so primarily out of concern regarding Russia's increasingly unfavorable reputation as a place where corruption abounds and business is unconcerned with long-term investments (preferring instead the quick return). However, 3M saw double-digit sales growth in Russia, in large part due to the adoption of its employees' cultural attributes. Tapping into the people's attitude that favors a group mentality rather than individual practice, for example, 3M developed a cooperative team dynamic that plays on this cultural notion. Additionally, the Russian practice of local philanthropy has also become a 3M activity, and the company has donated reflective badges to schoolchildren and contributed heavily to the repair and reconstruction of local churches. The company has become a beacon of inspiration for many Russians, due in no small part to its careful examination and practice of Russian cultural practices (Gratchev 2001).

Indeed, in this era of globalization, it is likely that multinational corporations will need to understand, more fully, the cultures from which they draw their international workforces. As the example of 3M demonstrates, cross-cultural relationship building can be an invaluable tool for twenty-first-century corporate success.

CONCLUSIONS

Since international political relations are vital to maintaining connectivity between governmental entities, cross-cultural relations are important to establishing better lines of communication and understanding between the peoples who comprise those nations.

President Kennedy made this point clear when, in 1961, he challenged an audience at the University of Michigan to join his Peace Corps. This program has, since its inception, sent hundreds of thousands of Americans to developing countries for two purposes. The first of these goals is to help those nations build (or rebuild) a modern infrastructure capable of joining the international community. The second is to promote bilateral cultural understanding. The Peace Corps's overwhelming success underscores the point that cross-cultural relations are essential in a global community. The vision of the leaders, who, even before Kennedy's program, sent volunteers to engage other societies, reflects their recognition of the enormous potential benefits of such relationships.

The most interesting aspect of cross-cultural relations is the fact that such activities do not necessarily cross borders. Rather, they are the connections between the individual ideologies and groups that, in part or in full, comprise the populations of those states. In multicultural societies, such as the tapestry of cultures contained within the United States, the relationships that result from such endeavors are not always the same in scope. They are as myriad as the varying groups they involve.

However, this specificity is all the more beneficial to the pursuit of connectivity. As the case in Iraq demonstrates, engagement with the plethora of tribes, clans, minorities, and disenfranchised subgroups of the post-Saddam regime has proven useful for American military personnel seeking to establish order and repel al-Qaeda-affiliated foreign insurgents in areas outside of Baghdad.

The benefits of cross-cultural relationship building are plentiful. First, cross-cultural relationships can help foment long-term alliances. The case of the Peace Corps, for example is illustrative of the correctly perceived belief that such development and assistance programs can foster positive relationships that can lead to national level political, security, trade, and economic partnerships. Kennedy pointed out that the Soviet Union's goal in such endeavors gave Russia inroads to reap these benefits; the Peace Corps, however noble in substance, was also an offshoot of Cold War competition over the minds and hearts of potential allies to counter the communist threat.

Outside of the political arena, economics and business also stands to gain from the employment of cross-cultural relations. As shown in this essay, one multinational corporation took what many perceived as a risk—investment in a Russian environment that, while steeped in potential as a large and newly liberalized economy, was still mired in business corruption, organized crime, a poorly trained workforce, and unstable infrastructure. 3M, however, took account of the attitudes of the Russian worker and used what it knew of the workforce's system of beliefs to modify its way of doing business. As shown by the marked profit margin during that short time, cross-cultural networking can pay off for multinational corporations.

Cross-cultural relationships operate within as well as beyond borders. In a way, such practices mirror a world in which borders are dissipating in the face of multinational economic and political networks. Cultures continuously evolve and, as such, are not easily quantified. Still, the very notion of linking cultures bilaterally (or multilaterally) can create strong potentials for profitability, stability, and peace in the twenty-first century.

BIBLIOGRAPHY

Cobbs, Elizabeth A. "Decolonization, the Cold War, and the Foreign Policy of the Peace Corps." *Diplomatic History* 20 (1996): 79. Web. 17 Dec. 2007.

Eisenstadt, Michael. "Iraq." *Military Review* 87 (2007): 13–31. Web. 17 Dec. 2007.

Gratchey, Mikhail. "Making the Most of Cultural Differences." *Harvard Business Review* 79 (2001): 28–31. Web. 18 Dec. 2007.

Hintjens, Helen M. "Citizenship Under Siege in the Brave New Europe." *European Journal of Cultural Studies* 10 (2007): 409–14. Web. 16 Dec. 2007.

Lo, Kevin D. "Chinese Guanxi and Anglo-American Networking: A Comparative Investigation of Cross-Cultural Interpersonal Business Relationships." *Journal of International Management Studies* (1993–1034), 7 (2012): 216–23. Web. 26 Nov. 2013.

Mahajan, Gurpeet. "Multiculturalism in the Age of Terror." *Political Studies Review* 5 (2007): 317–36. Print.

Marais, Lorraine, and Lizelle Marais. "Walking between Worlds." *International Social Work* 50 (2007): 809–20. Web 16 Dec. 2007.

Nini, Yang. "Cross-Cultural Industrial Relations in the Context of Socioeconomic Changes: The West, the East, and the Emerging Markets." *Journal of International Business Research* 12 (2013): 93–112. Web. 26 Nov. 2013.

Peace Corps. 2007. Web. 16 Dec. 2007.

Young, Yun Kim. "Inquiry in Intercultural and Development Communication." *Journal of Communication* 55 (2005): 554–57. Print.

Zofi, Yael. "Why Cross-Cultural Communication Is Critical to Virtual Teams and How to Overcome the Intercultural Disconnect." *People & Strategy* 35 (2012): 7–8. Web. 26 Nov. 2013.

SUGGESTED READING

Frase, Martha. "Show All Employees a Wider World." *HRMagazine* 52 (2007): 98–102. Web. 20 Dec. 2007.

Friedman, Harris, Gerald Glover, Ed Sims, et al. "Cross-Cultural Competence: Performance-Based Assessment and Training." *Organization Development Journal* 31 (2013): 18–30. Web. 26 Nov. 2013.

Ragotte, J. "International Flair." *Direct* 19 (2007): 22. Web. 20 Dec. 2007.

Scholtens, Bert, and Lammertjan Dam. "Cultural Values and International Differences in Business Ethics." *Journal of Business Ethics* 75 (2007): 273–84. Web. 20 Dec. 2007.

Wofford, Harris. "The New Work Begins at Home." *Nation* 241 (1985): 577–79. Web. 17 Dec. 2007.

Michael P. Auerbach

D

Decision Making

ABSTRACT

This article discusses decision making in a business environment. While leaders are ultimately responsible for business decisions, problem solving is a shared responsibility among top managers who make strategic decisions, middle managers who make tactical decisions, and lower-level managers who make operational decisions. By having accurate information, decisions are more likely to be based on facts, sound reasoning and intelligence. This article provides an overview of decision making and includes a discussion of factors that lead to good business decisions.

OVERVIEW

Leadership & Decision Making

One of the earmarks of an effective leader is someone who makes decisions while motivating people to implement them. He or she must learn to communicate and deal with high and low-performing workers and bring out the best in both employees and managers while demonstrating authority and creativity. While leaders have different decision-making styles, a leader needs to choose the right people to participate in the decision-making process, and there are some basics steps they must follow.

Leaders need to spot and solve problems while seeking opportunities to move the company forward. In order to do so, accurate information needs to be obtained, and a number of alternatives need to be developed and evaluated for strengths and weaknesses. Decisions are made after developing a number of ideas, debating a variety of options and encouraging an exchange of opinions in order to find the best course of action (Garvin and Roberto 2001).

While leaders are ultimately responsible for making business decisions, problem solving is a shared responsibility among people at different levels in a company. Further, there are different types of decision-making responsibilities and these include strategic decisions, tactical decisions, and operational decisions.

Strategic Decisions

Top managers are often responsible for making strategic decisions or decisions that concern the long-term goals of the company. For example, a company might decide to develop new products or focus its efforts on increasing the volume of an existing product. Strategic decisions establish company policy and these decisions are often complicated because the future is uncertain and accurate information is often limited. In these cases, managers must rely on their past experiences as well as their instincts (Janczak 2005).

There are four techniques available to senior managers:

1. They must be able to generate conflict that needs to be resolved.
2. Employees should be encouraged to question existing assumptions.
3. The work environment should be one that encourages learning.
4. Managers need to be able to distinguish between available resources and services and customer needs. (Young 2005)

Tactical Decisions

Once a company's goals and policies are established by senior management, tactical decisions aimed at achieving a company's goals and implementing company policy need to be made. Such decisions are

Management-level employees try to reach a decision (Photo courtesy of Anupriya19)

usually made by middle managers and require managers to focus on specific actions that will bring about the company's objectives. For example, a mid-level manager might devise a plan to provide employees with incentives in order to increase production. This activity requires mangers to have accurate information so that their decisions are based on facts.

Operational Decisions
Lastly, decisions regarding the day-to-day functions of a business also need to be made. These decisions are considered operational decisions and they are subordinate to strategic and tactical decisions. While these decisions are the responsibility of low-level managers, good decision making is crucial here since such decisions focus on productivity, quality control, and employee performance. Moreover, operational decisions can be broken down into:

- Short-term planning needs like ordering supplies, establishing work priorities, and enlisting temporary help.
- Medium-term planning like hiring and firing personnel, purchasing equipment, training individuals, and modifying procedures.
- Long-term planning like replacing subcontractors, redesigning production facilities, and modifying capacity. (Copeland and Globerson 1986)

Importance of Debate & Open Exchange of Ideas
Although decision making and problem solving occur at different levels of a company, leaders are ultimately responsible for every business decision and this fact requires a leader to have an understanding of strategic, tactical and operational decisions. Further, decision making rests not only on what decisions are made, but also who makes them, and how they are made. Business decisions often require an inquiry process, developing and debating a number of ideas in order to find the best course of action. This approach to decision making is a test of strength among competing ideas (Garvinand Roberto 2001).

In order to encourage debate and a free exchange of ideas, a leader needs to have a high level of emotional intelligence so that he or she can manage conflict that invariably arises in such an environment. Some leaders have a tendency to make decisions that are not based on sound reasoning while other decision makers can be rigid in their dealings with other people. However, leaders that exercise emotional intelligence can motivate people to be creative and to realize a vision (Batool 2013). In the end, a decision-making process that relies on debating a number of ideas should strive for a balance and a number of factors.

Successful leaders are flexible and open to the ideas of others, but also they adhere to a set of core values—essentially an internal determination regarding what a company's goals and aspirations are and how they plan to achieve them. At the same time, decisions must be made with an awareness of the outside world; leaders and managers must be capable of knowing what the truth is outside of the organization. This task means understanding what factors are affecting the market and understanding how these factors will allow for good strategic decisions. Further, decision makers need to understand how the markets are changing and to what extent the business can contribute to those changes. Such an understanding will lend itself to good tactical decisions. Finally, everyone involved in the decision-making process must understand what the company needs to do in order to be successful in its markets since it will result in effective operational decisions (Unseem 2005).

In the end, all levels of decision making—strategic, tactical, and operational—require access to accurate information. By having accurate information, leaders and managers will be better equipped to make decisions based on facts, sound reasoning and intelligence. This information can also be thought of as business intelligence. Effectively employing business intelligence will enable leaders to provide managers with the right information at the right time. Having the right information will ensure that decisions will be based on facts and allow for decisions to be made more quickly. Moreover, because business intelligence relies on factual information, it encourages a rational approach to management.

APPLICATIONS

Importance of Business Intelligence

Most businesses exist to provide goods and services to their customers and this reality requires decisions on how to deliver those goods, pricing, the handling of unsatisfied customers, and how to treat repeat or high volume customers (Rhode 2005). Such decisions require "mission critical business intelligence" and there are technologies that enable businesses to understand "customer buying behaviors and preferences," "product pricing and promotion" and "product assortment." (Ross 2007, 25). By evaluating this information, a business is better able to make operational decisions

Information Gathering

Not only is having access to business intelligence critical for operational decisions, such information also plays a role in strategic and tactical decisions. Supporting such decisions means "gathering actionable information on the competitive environment" (Heath 1996, 52). This type of information has been termed "competitive intelligence" of which there are basically two sources—traditional and nontraditional. Traditional sources of intelligence refer to published material such as newspapers, magazines, government and court documents and company reports, while nontraditional sources include interviews with employees, suppliers, distributors and customers. Having access to this kind of business intelligence will prove valuable as a company makes strategic decisions like whether to enter into a new market. Competitive intelligence will also facilitate tactical decisions regarding how to enter a new market—such as by forming an alliance or merging with a company that already exists in a particular business sector (Heath 1996).

Manager Instinct

Armed with this information, a successful leader will encourage managers to participate in the decision-making process by debating ideas; however, he or she must also exercise leadership by making the final decision and ensuring that decision is fully understood by employees. Moreover, the final decision must be implemented promptly. Some managers stress intuition and believe they can rely on 'gut instincts' when faced with the necessity for a speedy decision. Some business consultants agree, saying that decision making is really all about trusting one's intuition (Drury and Kitsopoulos 2005). Others emphasize the value of facts and data.

While wisdom may stem from experience, there are many who believe that innovation and invention require a person to be highly intelligent, both intellectually and emotionally, and these abilities are not necessarily a matter of experience. Further, decisions are sometimes required in the face of incomplete information. Many managers are able to rely on a minimum amount of information when making decisions in a timely manner. A leader is one who can sense and articulate the aspirations of people and empower them to take action. Even though there are technologies that allow for more timely data analysis, a leader's gut instinct might require a decision that relies on his or her vision more than any technical analysis (Drury and Kitsopoulos 2005).

Technology Use

In contrast, evaluating more options in less time requires decisions to be based on reason, and relying on gut instincts may lead to unsuccessful outcomes. As situations become more complex, relying on intuition does not lend itself to good decision making since individuals really base their decisions on preconceived notions about past events. Technological advances have increased the amount of accessible information and decreased the amount of time available in the decision-making process. At the same time, technology also provides the means to process information more quickly. Today, computer programs enhance preexisting decision-making tools, such as system dynamics and decision trees, which have been utilized by business people (Bonabeau 2003).

System dynamics is a way of studying and managing complex feedback systems. This method identifies a problem, explains the cause of the problem, builds a computer model that reproduces those causes, considers alternative ways to solve the problem, and finally implements a solution. A decision tree is a tool used when there are choices between several courses of action. Decision trees consider a variety of options and the possible outcomes of choosing those options. They also form a balanced picture of the risks and rewards associated with each possible course of action. In short, these analytical methods assist business people with quickly processing large amounts of information so that the facts about a given situation can be accurately determined. With these facts at their disposal, and after the issues have been thoroughly debated, managers and leaders are in a better position to make good decisions (Bonabeau 2003).

While there are numerous methods and technologies for analyzing information and a myriad of solutions that can be applied to strategic planning, good decisions ultimately rest on a leader's emotional intelligence and vision. A leader must also be able to make rational decisions and communicate his or her vision and the reason for decisions to all levels of management. In some organizations, however, senior managers often make decisions themselves and then try to persuade people to buy into those decisions. According to Unseem, that approach precludes options and ideas that managers may not have even considered. At the same time, all participants need to take responsibility for their involvement in the process. While a leader needs to choose the right people to fulfill managerial roles, it is the leader's job to communicate effectively with the managers. In the end, the role of all employees in a business organization is to represent the company as well as to work together to ensure the business' success. Having the right people engage in an exchange of ideas creates an environment where information flows freely and success is more likely (Unseem 2005).

VIEWPOINTS

Technological Advancements & Decision Making
The amount of information that people can access has expanded dramatically because of technological advances. In light of these developments, managers and leaders have more choices and data at their disposal, but less time to make decisions.

Communication
As the internet evolved, many businesses developed their own internal internets, known as intranets, and these innovations have enabled employees to become more involved in the decision-making process. Moreover, other Internet-based technologies are being deployed on Intranet systems. Currently, the development of social software like web logs (blogs) and podcasting enables people to communicate and exchange information easily. A blog is a web-based journal written by one or more people. For example, chief executive officers (CEOs) are using blogs to communicate with the rank and file as well as for different groups in the organization to share their accomplishments. A podcast is an audio file that can be used for broadcasting executive speeches throughout the company. Finally, most businesses today have internal email and instant messaging capabilities that allow people to readily share information (Holtz 2005). Businesses are also utilizing popular social media portals such as YouTube, Facebook, and Twitter to enhance workplace communications (Koster 2012).

Further, having alternative means of communication can lend itself to creating a constructive environment for engaging in critical debate. But the use of email, intranets, and social media creates a whole other layer of policies as to their proper use. A wrongly placed or used word in an email can lead to misunderstandings and even legal action and companies must be aware of those implications at all times (Lieber 2011).

Use of Consultants
Although technological advances can enable people to process and analyze more information quickly, people—not machines or software programs—ultimately make decisions. There are many factors beyond the technical analysis of data—such as the managerial and decision-making style of a leader, the interpersonal skills of the staff, and the corporate culture—that affect these decisions. According to Sargeant, since technology does not allow a company to make determinations about the group dynamics, objective opinions of managerial consultants are needed. To be effective, consultants need to understand the business and be comfortable addressing a variety of issues such as leadership, finance and organization. Further, consultants can

be useful if they are called upon to make assessments in a short time period and assist managers and leaders with communicating the goals of the company to those involved in the decision-making process, thereby getting those individuals to cooperate and also enlisting the cooperation of other divisions within the company (Sargeant 2005).

The fact that leaders are ultimately responsible for making decisions means that they must often make strategic decisions and then delegate tactical and operational decisions to the right managers. Further, leaders must ensure that middle and low-level managers have access to sufficient information as well as the technological assets to analyze that information. In the final analysis, a successful business consists of successful people; therefore, it is reasonable to expect them to work towards implementing a leader's final decision. However, emotions often become a factor in decision making. To be successful, a leader must be able to manage his or her emotions and also recognize the emotions of others. This skill allows a leader to encourage people to work towards implementing strategic decisions. A leader also needs to be an effective communicator and remain open to new ideas and different views, especially concerning tactical and operational decisions. One way to accomplish this goal is by asking questions, pushing employees for more in depth explanations and in the end, explaining the rationale for the final decision (Garvin 2004).

There are a number of ways a business can improve its decision-making processes. Whether they rely on advanced technology or the advice of independent consultants, successful decisions really require businesses to establish a set of core values. Doing so will allow an organization to attract employees and customers who are aligned with those values.

BIBLIOGRAPHY

Batool, Bano. "Emotional Intelligence and Effective Leadership." *Journal of Business Studies Quarterly* 4, no. 3 (2013): 84–94. Web. 13 Nov. 2013.

Bonaneau, Eric. "Don't Trust Your Gut." *Harvard Business Review* 81, no. 5 (2003): 116–23. Web. 29 Jan. 2007.

Copeland, R., and S. Globerson. "Improving Operational Performance in Service Industries." *Industrial Management* 28, no. 4 (1986): 23. Web. 10 Apr. 2007.

Cryer, Bruce. "Listen to the Heart." *Leadership Excellence* 22, no. 9 (2005): 20. Web. 29 Jan. 2007.

Drury, Meghann, and S.C. Kotsopoulos. "Do You Believe in the Seven Deadly Myths?" *Consulting to Management* 16, no. 1 (2005): 28–31. Web. 1 Feb. 2007.

Garvin, David, and Michael A. Roberto. "What You Don't Know about Making Decisions." *Harvard Business Review* 79, no. 8 (2001): 108–16. Web. 29 Jan. 2007.

Heath, R.P. "Competitive Intelligence." *Marketing Tools* 3, no. 5 (1996): 52–59. Web. 10 Apr. 2007.

Holtz, Shel. "The Impact of New Technologies on Internal Communication." *Strategic Communication Management* 10, no. 1 (2005): 22–25. Web. 29 Jan. 2007.

Janczak, Sergio. "The Strategic Decision-Making Process in Organizations." *Problems & Perspectives in Management* (2005, Jan.): 58–70. Web. 10 Apr. 2007.

Koster, Kathleen. "Social Media Tools Gain Acceptance." *Employee Benefit News* 26, no. 12 (2012): 14. Web. 13 Nov. 2013.

Lieber, Lynn D. "Social Media in the Workplace: Proactive Protections for Employers." *Employment Relations Today* 38, no. 3 (2011): 93–101. Web. 13 Nov. 2013.

Rhode, Frank. "Little Decisions Add Up." *Harvard Business Review* 83, no. 6 (2005): 24–26. Web. 28 Feb. 2007.

Ross, D. "What Is BI and What Do We Do with It?" *Retail Merchandiser* 47, no. 3 (2007): 25. Web. 10 Apr. 2007.

Sargeant, J.R. "Saving Troubled Companies." *Consulting to Management* 16, no. 1 (2005): 21–24. Web. 1 Feb. 2007.

Unseem, Jerry. "Jim Collins on Tough Calls." *Fortune* 151, no. 13 (2005): 89–94. Web. 29 Jan. 2007.

Young, David. "Strategic Decision Making: It's Time for Healthcare Organizations to Get Serious." *Healthcare Financial Management* 59, no. 11 (2005): 86–92. Web. Apr. 10 2007.

SUGGESTED READING

Connelly, Shane, Whitney Helton-Faith, and Michael D. Mumford. "A Managerial In-Basket Study of the Impact of Trait Emotions on Ethical Choice." *Journal of Business Ethics* 51, no. 3 (2004): 245–67. Web. 29 Jan. 2007.

Pech, Richard, and Geoffrey Durden. "When the Decision Makers Went Wrong: From Capitalism to Cannibalism." *Corporate Governance: The International Journal of Effective Board Performance* 4, no. 1 (2004): 65–75. Web. 29 Jan. 2007.

Sayegha, Lisa, William Anthony, and Pamela Perrewe. "Managerial Decision Making under Crisis: The Role of Emotion in an Intuitive Decision Process." *Human Resource Management Review* 14, no. 2 (2004): 179–200.

Richa S. Tiwary, Ph.D., M.L.S.

DECISION MAKING UNDER UNCERTAINTY

ABSTRACT

Every day, managers make decisions that affect the profitability, effectiveness, and viability of the organization. Sometimes the factors affecting the predictability of events can be determined. However, not all variables affecting outcomes are neatly predictable. Decisions made under uncertainty are decisions for which there is no meaningful probability distribution underlying the various outcomes. In these situations, the decision maker simply does not know what will happen for the various decision alternatives. There are several approaches to decision making under conditions of uncertainty, including application of the Bayes' Decision Rule, Markov processes, and gaming. In the end, however, virtually every decision requires judgment. Knowledge of stochastic processes alone is insufficient to guide decision making.

OVERVIEW

Every day, managers make decisions that affect the profitability, effectiveness, and viability of the organization. Although in some of these cases the parameters are known (e.g., if Harvey gives a raise to the production workers, there will not be enough money left over to buy parts to make widgets), in other cases they are not known (e.g., if Harvey does not give the production workers a raise, he does not know whether or not they will stay and continue to make widgets). Similarly, many of the decisions facing managers are complex (e.g., Harvey can ask the workers to postpone getting a raise and continue to make widgets while the company tries a new marketing strategy; if the workers do not continue to make widgets, the company cannot afford the new marketing campaign. However, there is no way to predict with 100 percent accuracy whether or not the campaign will be successful enough to bring in the added revenue to enable the company to give the workers a raise).

FACTORS AFFECTING THE PREDICTABILITY OF EVENTS

Trends, Business Cycles & Seasonal Fluctuations
Sometimes the factors affecting the predictability of events can be determined. These deterministic variables are those for which there are specific causes or determiners and include trends, business cycles, and seasonal fluctuations. Trends are persistent, underlying directions in which a factor or characteristic is moving in either the short, intermediate, or long term. In most cases, trends are linear rather than cyclic; growing or shrinking steadily over a period of years. For example, the increasing tendency for business to outsource and offshore technical support and customer service in many high tech companies over the past few years is a trend. However, not all trends are linear. Trends in new industries tend to be curvilinear as the demand for the new product or service grows after its introduction and then declines after the product or service becomes integrated into the economy.

Another type of deterministic factor is business cycles which are continually recurring variations in total economic activity. Business cycles usually occur across most sectors of the economy at the same time. For example, it has been noted that several years of a boom economy with expansion of economic activity (e.g., more jobs, higher sales) are often followed by slower growth or even contraction of economic activity. Business cycles may occur across one

105

industry, a business sector, or even the economy in general.

A third type of deterministic factor is seasonal fluctuations. These changes in economic activity occur in a fairly regular annual pattern and are related to seasons of the year, the calendar, or holidays. For example, office supply stores typically experience an upsurge in business in August as children receive their school supply lists for the coming year. Similarly, the demand for heating oil is typically greater during the cool months than it is in the warm months.

Stochastic Variables

However, not all variables affecting outcomes are so neatly predictable. Stochastic variables are caused by randomness or include an element of chance or probability. These variables include both irregular and random fluctuations in the economy that occur due to unpredictable factors. For example—a natural disaster such as an earthquake or flood, political disturbance such as war or flu epidemic—that causes high absenteeism is often unpredictable and can affect a business' profitability. In conditions of uncertainty, there is no meaningful probability distribution for the various outcomes. In these situations, the decision maker does not know what will happen for the various decision alternatives.

Conflicting Interests in Decision Making

Another factor complicating real-world decision-making processes is the fact that there is often more than one party to the decision and the parties may have conflicting interests. In fact, systems theory posits that the organization includes multiple sub-systems and that the functioning of each affects both the functioning of the others and the organization as a whole. For example, in the illustration above concerning giving raises to the workers during a time of flux, there are at least two major parties to the decision. From the workers' point-of-view, getting a raise now is better than maybe getting a raise later. Their raise or lack thereof, in turn, affects other parties not directly in the discussion such as their families (e.g., if there is no raise, the family cannot pay for Johnny's tuition) and their creditors (e.g., if there is no raise, the family cannot meet the increased payment on their adjustable rate mortgage). Management, of course, has a different point-of-view. If it gives the workers a raise now, there will not be sufficient funds available for the new marketing campaign that will bring in more revenue. Without the additional revenue, the management may have to lay off some of the workers, which means that they will not be able to meet an increased demand for widgets even if they do launch the new marketing campaign. Management could take money to pay the production workers from the monies set aside for raises for new product development, but then the company would not be able to gain a competitive edge over the companies offering similar items in the marketplace. In addition, management needs to report to its stockholders, and increased wages may mean decreased profits.

Categories of Decisions to be Made Certainty & Uncertainty

The decisions facing managers in the business world can be classified into several categories: decisions made under certainty or uncertainty, under risk, or under conflict. A decision made under certainty occurs when all the facts of the situation are known and the model provides the decision maker with the exact consequences of choosing each alternative. This knowledge, however, does not mean that the decision is either obvious or trivial. There may be many possible courses of actions that can be taken, each with different consequences, and the decision maker needs to consider the advantages and disadvantages of each and weigh them against each other. Decisions made under uncertainty, on the other hand, are decisions for which there is no meaningful probability distribution underlying the various outcomes. In these situations, the decision maker simply does not know what will happen for the various decision alternatives.

Multiple Criteria Decision Making

Multiple criteria decision making is a discipline that deals with the problem of making decisions in complex situations where there are conflicting objectives. Multiple criteria decision making is founded on two interrelated, key concepts. Satisficing is the attempt to find solutions that satisfy all the constraints rather than optimizing them. For example, the workers may be given a raise, but only in six months after the new marketing campaign goes into effect. This decision would still give them a raise, but it would also give the company an opportunity to get back on its feet. From the workers' point-of-view, the optimal situation would be to get the raises now. From management's point-of-view, the optimal situation would be to keep wages low so that there are more profits. Neither one of these situations is optimized in this solution, but the constraints of both are satisfied. The second key concept of multiple criteria decision making is bounded rationality. This process involves setting the constraints of the situation and then attempting to find solutions that satisfy the constraints. This iterative process involves adjusting the constraints as necessary and continuing the search for solutions until a satisfactory solution is found. For example, the workers at Widget Corporation may be willing to postpone getting a raise only if the raise that they get in six months is greater than the one that they would accept today.

Methods for Solving Multiple Criteria Decision-Making Problems
As shown in table 1, there are a number of methods available for solving multiple criteria decision making problems. Deterministic decision analysis is used to find the most preferred alternative in the decision space using value functions. Stochastic decision analysis does the same thing, but it uses utility functions and stochastic outcomes. In the stochastic approach, both the utility function and the probability of the various outcomes are estimated by the decision maker. The multiobjective mathematical programming approach includes both multiobjective linear programming and multiobjective integer programming.

Decision Theory
Decision theory is a body of knowledge and related analytical techniques designed to give decision makers information about a situation or system and the consequences of alternative actions in order to help him or her choose among the set of alternatives. One tool often useful in decision making is modeling building. Models are representations of a situation, system, or subsystem. Conceptual models are mental images that describe the situation or system. This type of model is the first step in creating mathematical or computer models that represent the situation or system using one or a series of mathematical equations. The development of models that accurately represents the real world is typically an iterative process. Models must usually be tested and refined until they represent the real world to the degree desired by the analyst or decision maker. Initially, conceptual models tend to be broad or general representations without much detail but which span the range of variables to be considered. However, the initial model helps the analyst better understand the situation or system under consideration and to refine the representation of the real world. As the model is analyzed and the situation is better understood, the model can be refined to better reflect the underlying reality.

Decision Outcomes	Decision Space	
	Explicit	Implicit
Deterministic	Deterministic multiattribute decision analysis	Deterministic multiobjective mathematical programming
Stochastic	Stochastic multiattribute decision analysis	Stochastic multiobjective mathematical programming

Table 1: Taxonomy of multiple criteria decision-making approaches (from Ramesh and Zionts, 539)

APPLICATIONS

Approaches for Decision Making Under Uncertainty
Bayes' Decision Rule

There are several approaches to decision making under conditions of uncertainty. One of these is the application of Bayes' Decision Rule. This decision-making strategy involves choosing the option with the largest expected payoff determined by multiplying the consequences of each act by the probability of the several occurrences and then adding the products together. Decision models in these situations are characterized by several basic elements. First, there is a set of options from which the decision maker may choose as well as a set of consequences that may occur as a result of a given decision. In addition, Bayes' Decision Rule assumes that there is an underlying probability distribution that can be used to quantify the decision maker's beliefs about the relationship between the various choices and resultant consequences. Further, this approach involves a utility function that quantifies the decision-maker's preferences among the various consequences.

Markov Processes

Another frequently used approach in this type of situation is the application of Markov processes. These are stochastic processes in which the probabilities of future events are completely determined by the current state of the process. So, for example, if one knows the current state of the process, no additional insight can be gained from previous states of the process. A Markov chain is a random process comprising discrete events in which the future development of each event is either independent of past events or dependent only on the immediately preceding event. Markov chains are often used in marketing, for example, to model subsequent purchases of products (i.e., the probability of the customer making a purchase from a particular business or brand is dependent only on his or her last purchase of that brand or independent of the brand).

Gaming

A third approach to decision making under uncertainty is the application of gaming to real world problems. Gaming is an activity in which two or more independent parties attempt to achieve objectives within a limiting context. In business, gaming involves the use of mathematics in determining optimal strategies and making the best possible decisions in context. Gaming, however, is a controversial approach to decision making, and is typically more art than science. However, it is possible to gain insights into a real world situation by designing, playing, or analyzing a game. Game design is a multistage process. First, one sets the objectives for the game and defines the parameters in which the game will be played. Once these constraints are articulated, a conceptual model is developed and decisions are made as to how best to represent it. The game is then constructed and refined. As opposed to other methods for making decisions under conditions of uncertainty, gaming is not a solution method nor does it lead to a forecast, solution, or prediction. However, a game does help the decision maker to better understand the situation about which a decision needs to be made, including its constraints, consequences, and greater ramifications.

Compromises in Decision Making

From a scientific point of view, it would be comforting to be able to collect data, build a mathematical model or perform a statistical analysis, and be given a number that could be looked up in a table to tell one whether to choose Option A or Option B. Unfortunately, real-world decisions are not so simple. As discussed above, real world decisions often are made in situations where it is impossible to predict or even know all the parameters that affect the decision. Further, real world decisions are more complicated than decisions made in a laboratory setting because even in those few situations where there is only one decision maker in a business setting, a decision can ripple throughout the organization and its stakeholders. A decision that results in an optimal situation for one stakeholder may be disastrous for another stakeholder. Frequently, there is no best answer and the decision must be made as a series of compromises. In addition, it must be remembered that the interpretation of data analysis and the very data themselves are subject to the skill and qualitative assessment of the decision maker or analyst. It has been argued that the probabilistic and value-related factors of Bayesian methods imply a degree of precision that is impossible to obtain in the real world.

As a result, the conclusions drawn on this methodology are too precise to be given much credence. Others have argued against the presumption of normalcy underlying Bayes' rule.

Forecasting for Business Decisions
Opinion about the best way to forecast for business decisions can be sharply divided between those that rely on statistical methodology and those that prefer to use their gut to determine where the industry, supply chain, or market is going. Both approaches have advantages and disadvantages, however. Statistical methods can be less prone to bias than judgments. In addition, statistical methods tend to be more reliable and can more efficiently make use of historical data. On the other hand, statistical techniques can only work with the data given. Judgmental decision making can be useful particularly when there are recent events about which the decision maker is aware but which have not yet had sufficient time to result in observable data for analysis. There are, however, risks inherent in decisions that are made purely on subjective criteria. Human error can make the analyst or manager more optimistic (or pessimistic) than actually warranted, trends or factors may be read into the data that are not actually there, or the effects of correlated variables may not be taken into account.

The Importance of Judgment
In the end, virtually every decision requires judgment. First, judgment is key to determining which data are relevant to the model or game or that is considered in the analysis. Potential variables affecting decisions in the real world are virtually limitless. However, no statistical model or analysis can take all variables into account. Even if it could, spurious positive results would be seen due to the effects of probability alone. Therefore, it is essential that expert judgments be used to reduce the inputs into the process. Judgment is also important in decision making because different analytic techniques can yield different results. It is the judgment of the analyst that determines which technique is most appropriate to analyze the data. The value of the end result of the analysis depends heavily on correctly choosing the most appropriate analytical method. Finally, expert judgments can be essential to help the analyst understand the situation and give insight into the parameters through which the data and subsequent analysis

should be interpreted. Statistical processes alone are insufficient to guide decision making.

BIBLIOGRAPHY

Armstrong, J. Scott. "Forecasting." In *Encyclopedia of Operations Research and Management Science*, edited by Saul I. Gass and Carl M. Harris, 304–10. New York: Wiley, 2001. Web. 18 July 2007.

Armstrong J. Scott, and Fred Collopy. "Integration of Statistical Methods and Judgment for Times Series Forecasting: Principles from Empirical Research." In *Forecasting with Judgment*, edited by George Wright and Paul Goodwin. New York: John Wiley & Sons, 1998.

Armstrong, J. Scott, and Kesten C. Green. "Select a Forecasting Method (Selection Tree)." (2006, Sept.). Web. 19 July 2007.

Delage, Eric, and Shie Mannor. "Percentile Optimization for Markov Decision Processes with Parameter Uncertainty." *Operations Research* 58, no. 1 (2010): 203–13. Web. 15 Nov. 2013.

Eggers, Jamie P. "Falling Flat: Failed Technologies and Investment Under Uncertainty." *Administrative Science Quarterly* 57, no. 1 (2012): 47–80. Web. 15 Nov. 2013.

Laskey, Kathryn B. "Bayesian Decision Theory, Subjective Probability and Utility." In *Encyclopedia of Operations Research and Management Science*, edited by Saul I. Gass and Carl M. Harris, 57–59. New York: Wiley, 2001. Web. 9 Aug. 2007.

Lee, Yen Yu, and Ross Baldick. "A Frequency-Constrained Stochastic Economic Dispatch Model." *IEEE Transactions on Power Systems* 28, no. 3 (2013): 2301–12. Web. 15 Nov. 2013.

Miller, Douglas R. "Markov Processes." In *Encyclopedia of Operations Research and Management Science*, edited by Saul I. Gass and Carl M. Harris, 486–90. New York: Wiley, 2001. Web. 10 Aug. 2007.

Ramesh, RamaSwamy, and Stanley Zionts. "Multiple Criteria Decision Making." In *Encyclopedia of Operations Research and Management Science*, edited by Saul I. Gass and Carl M. Harris, 538–43. New York: Wiley, 2001. Web. 9 Aug. 2007.

Schum, D.A. "Decision Analysis." In *Encyclopedia of Operations Research and Management Science*, edited by Saul I. Gass and Carl M. Harris, 194–98. New York: Wiley, 2001. Web. 9 Aug. 2007.

Schwabe, William. "Gaming." In *Encyclopedia of Operations Research and Management Science*, edited by

Saul I. Gass and Carl M. Harris, 321–23. New York: Wiley, 2001. Web. 11 Aug. 2007.

Wang, Ying. "A Fuzzy-Normalisation-Based Group Decision-Making Approach for Prioritising Engineering Design Requirements in QFD Under Certainty." *International Journal of Production Research* 50, no. 23 (2012): 6963–77. Web. 15 Nov. 2013.

SUGGESTED READING

Borgonovo, Emanuele. "Measuring Uncertainty Importance: Investigation and Comparison of Alternative Approaches." *Risk Analysis: An International Journal* 26, no. 5 (2006): 1349–61. Web. 9 Aug. 2007.

Courtney, Hugh, Jane Kirkland, and Patrick Viguerie. "Strategy Under Certainty." *Harvard Business Review* 75, no. 6 (1997): 67–79. Web. 31 July 2007.

Eichberger, Jurgen, Ian R. Harper, Christian Pfeil, and Florian Scheid. "Decision-Making Under Certainty." In *Solutions Manual for Financial Economics*, edited by Ian R. Harper, Christian Pfeil, and Florian Scheid, 1–19. New York: Oxford University Press, 2002. Web. 9 Aug. 2007.

Foss, Nicolai, Volker Mahnke, and Ron Sanchez. "Demand Uncertainty and Asset Flexibility: Incorporating Strategic Options in the Theory of the Firm." In *Competence, Governance & Entrepreneurship*, edited by Nicolai Foss, Volker Mahnke, and Ron Sanchez, 318–32. Web. 9 Aug. 2007.

Gottleib, Daniel A., Talia Weiss, and Gretchen B. Chapman. "The Format in Which Uncertainty Information Is Presented Affects Decision Biases." *Psychological Science* 18, no. 3 (2007): 240–46. Web. 98 Aug. 2007.

Goyal, Manu, and Serguei Netessine. "Strategic Technology Choice and Capacity Investment under Demand Uncertainty." *Management Science* 53, no. 2 (2007): 192–207. Web. 9 Aug. 2007.

Hitch, Gunter. "Am Empirical Model of Optimal Dynamic Product Launch and Exit under Demand Uncertainty." *Marketing Science* 25, no. 1 (2006): 25–50. Web. 31 July 2007.

Ruth A. Wienclaw, Ph.D.

DELEGATION

ABSTRACT

Delegation is the practice of assigning duties to another person. Delegation is widely viewed as an important component of leadership. An effective leader trusts followers to be able to perform tasks delegated to them, making it possible to divide up the labor among a group or team. Those who fail to delegate properly are often seen as having an excessive need for control or perfection, both of which are qualities that most people deem undesirable in a leader or colleague.

OVERVIEW

One of the most prized skills in the modern business environment is the ability to delegate effectively. Many reasons have been given to explain the major role that delegation plays in the workplace. Some point out that while on its surface delegation might seem like increasing a subordinate's workload; this situation is not true with effective delegation.

When one delegates meaningful work to another, an opportunity for growth and achievement is created for the person to whom the task has been assigned. In a very real sense, the person delegating is extending an offer to another person based on trust that the work will get done in a timely and satisfactory manner. Trust, more than any other commodity, is what an enterprise runs on, because it is not possible for people to work well together if they do not trust one another. Delegation, seen through this lens, is similar to an exercise that members of an optimally functioning organization regularly perform because it is necessary and because it increases the overall level of trust between members of the organization.

In addition to benefitting the person to whom work is delegated, the organization itself experiences a number of other positive outcomes beyond enhanced trust. One benefit is that delegation facilitates the dissemination of knowledge throughout the organization. When delegation is not encouraged, knowledge—in the form of procedures, best practices, past experience, and so on—tends to become concentrated in a few key members of the organization. These people know how to do everything and they immediately understand how an event will impact the organization and who needs to be informed of it. However, when those in possession of this organizational knowledge are not available, either because they are physically absent or because they are no longer members of the organization, then work may grind to a halt while others attempt to fill in the gap by locating the person with the required knowledge or by acquiring it themselves, which can take a considerable amount of time. A better approach is for the organization to encourage knowledge sharing practices such as cross-training and delegation.

Delegation creates a situation where the person delegating a task (the delegator) must explain how the task is done to the person to whom it is being delegated (the delegate). Thereafter, even once the task has been completed, the delegate retains the knowledge gained and can apply it in the future, if the need should arise. These actions make the organization better equipped to respond to unexpected events. Delegation is also beneficial through its ability to help members of an organization reduce their levels of stress, by sharing their workload with others. Instead of a single person struggling to meet deadlines on numerous projects, that person can delegate some of the work to others.

It is important to bear in mind that not everyone understands the subtleties of delegation. It is common for people to confuse the act of assigning tasks to others with real delegation. The assignment of tasks does not really require any special consideration; there is an assumption that the person who will be doing the work already knows what to do; therefore, training and guidance are not necessary. True delegation is a very different matter. When one delegates a task, one does not completely sever all ties to the work, nor does one give up responsibility for the products that result. The delegator retains responsibility for the quality of the output, and therefore remains emotionally, intellectually, and professionally invested in assuring that all necessary tasks are performed well and completely.

In the ideal delegatory relationship, the delegator remains engaged to the extent that he or she is available to provide support and advice to the delegate, but not so engaged that the delegator winds up micromanaging the work. Micromanaging is not simply ineffective and inefficient; it actively undermines the development of trust that is vital to the function of an organization. When a delegator micromanages, he or she is sending a clear message to the delegate that the delegator does not trust him or her to do a good job.

Assigning a task is much easier than delegating, because when a task is assigned, the person to whom it is assigned carries all of the responsibility for performing it. When a task is delegated, on the other hand, the responsibility is shared between the delegate and the delegator, meaning that they must work together to negotiate how the task will be done, since they are both responsible for its completion.

With all of the benefits that delegation provides, one could be forgiven for assuming that everyone would delegate whenever the opportunity arose. Unfortunately, many people resist the notion of delegation, either consciously or subconsciously. They are adept at coming up with reasons why delegation is not possible or not appropriate in a given situation. Some say that they are too busy to delegate, because it would mean taking time out of their schedules to show the delegate what to do. Others say the delegator is wary of losing control by delegating tasks.

In most cases, showing someone else how to perform a task takes less time than actually performing the task oneself. Furthermore, showing the delegate what to do saves time in the long run, because the next time a similar situation arises, the delegate will remember the training previously received and will be able to take on the task without additional instruction. Another objection sometimes raised is that the person feels that the need to perform the task himself or herself because it is the person's duty or because it has been entrusted to the individual. This situation also tends to be inaccurate, because in most situations an employee is only responsible for making sure that the final output of a task is accomplished—how the task was completed or by whom is typically not relevant.

FURTHER INSIGHTS

An issue that often arises when work is delegated is the distinction between authority and responsibility because, all too often, delegates are given the responsibility to perform a task but they are not given the authority that the task requires. This recipe for disaster creates frustration on the part of the delegate. Responsibility is a straightforward enough concept; it means that one has a duty to do something, and that failing to do it may carry negative consequences, such as being penalized, reprimanded, overlooked for promotion, or even terminated.

Authority is more complex, but in this context it basically means that one has the power—even if only temporarily—to marshal the resources necessary to perform the task. These resources can be tangible, such as computers and photocopiers, or can be intangible, as when a manager requires staff from other departments to rearrange what they are doing and help out on an urgent project. The manager in such a situation uses his or her authority to set new priorities for other employees. This situation can become necessary when a delegate has been asked to perform a task that requires the cooperation of other offices or departments in the organization.

If the delegate has been given only the responsibility to ensure that the task is completed but not the authority to compel others to cooperate, then the person may simply refuse to help, or only help at a time that suits them, rather than when the task needs to be done. Avoiding this kind of situation is why one must always delegate both the necessary authority and responsibility.

Delegation requires preparation to succeed either because many delegators delegate on the spur of the moment and thus poorly, or because it occurs behind the scenes, out of sight of the delegate and others in the organization. The would-be delegator must think carefully about what work will be delegated and why. For larger projects, there is often a question of whether to delegate the entire project, or only a portion of it. Either way, the boundaries of the delegated work must be clear to everyone involved, so that every part of the work is accounted for and assigned to someone.

It is also important to think about the outcome one wants to achieve through delegation, in terms of both the work and the development of the delegate. This task means having a clear idea of what needs to be delivered at the end of the delegated task—for example, a research report or a new sales contact—and what skills the delegate will have an opportunity to either develop or practice during the project.

Finally, the delegator must carefully consider to whom to delegate a given project. The person must have the necessary skills or have the ability to acquire them during the performance of the task, but just as important, the delegate must have the right temperament for the particular task. If a project requires great concentration and technical skill, then it would not be appropriate to delegate it to someone who does not possess those qualities.

Issues

Much of the theoretical literature regarding delegation focuses on the situation in which a single delegator delegates a task to a single delegate. While this explanation makes it easier to understand the concepts associated with delegation, it does not necessarily reflect in an accurate way the types of delegation that workers are most likely to encounter.

Workgroups

Often, work is delegated not to a single individual, but to a group of coworkers who possess skill sets similar to one another, but none of whom has authority over the others. This situation can be very difficult to navigate, since it places additional constraints on the delegation process. This approach tends to be used when the task being delegated is too large for a single individual to keep track of. Groups often need a leader to make sure that their work gets done, but it is not always clear who that person should be.

Members of the group may feel a sense of urgency about completing their tasks, but still feel reluctant to push the group in a particular direction. For these reasons, delegation to a workgroup rather than an individual requires some forethought in addition to that needed under ordinary circumstances. If the group is to meet its deadline, some method of organization is required. The delegator may impose a method—for example, by designating a temporary group leader—or the delegator may leave this task for the group itself, perhaps as part of a broader team building strategy.

The group will have to have some means of dividing up the different parts of the work among its members, since it would not make sense to delegate a task to a group and then have only one person in the group do all of the work. Team-based delegation creates other types of complications, particularly with projects that cannot be accomplished in a short period of time. The longer the timeline of a delegated project, the higher the need for meetings to coordinate activities and update members on various individuals' progress. Scheduling these meetings is made more difficult with each additional person added to the mix. Strategies such as the use of virtual delegation and teleconferencing help but do not solve every problem.

Complications

Ultimately, delegation solves many problems but it also creates its own complications. It is not too dissimilar from other practices that have become part and parcel of the modern, interconnected workplace. While delegation and other strategies save time, share expertise, and encourage new forms of employee development, they do not happen without careful planning and effort. Delegation, when practiced most effectively, represents the skillful cultivation of an organization's human resources and the mindful application of these resources to the task of solving the organization's challenges.

It can take many years of practice for employees to learn how to appropriately delegate to others and how to accept delegation from others. Perhaps unsurprisingly, one of the most effective, and most common, ways of learning delegation is by going through one or more episodes of poor delegation, when things are not handled in the way that they should be. Because of delegation's complexity, this experience happens far more often than is desirable, but it does provide clear guidance for what not to do, and in many cases living through these unsuccessful experiences helps employees do a better job of delegating when they find themselves in a position that requires it.

Bibliography

Banford, Christopher G., M. Ronald Buckley, and Foster Robers. "Delegation Revisited: How Delegation Can Benefit Globally-Minded Managers." *International Journal of Physical Distribution & Logistics Management* 44, no. 8–9 (2014): 646. Web. 23 Oct. 2016.

Bar-Gill, Oren, and Cass R. Sunstein. "Regulation as Delegation." *Journal of Legal Analysis* 7, no. 1 (2015): 1–36. Print.

Bryant, Eileen. "Delegation in Practice." *Practice Nurse* 45, no. 8 (2015): 22–25. Print.

De Varo, Jed, and Suraj Prasad. "The Relationship between Delegation and Incentives across Occupations: Evidence and Theory." *Journal of Industrial Economics* 63, no. 2 (2015): 279–312. Web. 23 Oct. 2016.

Dobrajska, Magdalena, Stephan Billinger, and Samina Karim. "Delegation within Hierarchies: How Information Processing and Knowledge Characteristics Influence the Allocation of Formal and Real Decision Authority." *Organizational Science* 3 (2015): 687–704. Web. 23 Oct. 2016.

Ellis, Peter. "Leadership and Management: Delegating for Success." *Wounds UK* 11, no. 2 (2015): 70–71. Print.

Jansen, Thijs, Arie van Lier, and Arjen van Witteloostuijn. "Managerial Delegation and Welfare Effects of Cost Reductions." *Journal of Economics* 116, no. 1 (2015): 1–23. Web. 23 Oct. 2016.

Kayis, Enis, Feryal Erhun, and Erica Plambeck. "Delegation vs. Control of Component Procurement under Asymmetric Cost Information and Simple Contracts." *Manufacturing & Service Operations Management* 15, no. 1 (2013): 45–56. Web. 23 Oct. 2016.

Stonehouse, David. "The Art and Science of Delegation." *British Journal of Health Care Assistants* 9, no. 3 (2015): 150–53. Print.

Terry, Mark. "The Power of Delegation." *Podiatry Management* 35, no. 5 (2016): 119–22. Print.

Suggested Reading

Callander, Steven, and Keith Krehbiel. "Gridlock and Delegation in a Changing World." *American Journal of Political Science* 58, no. 4 (2014): 819–34. Web. 23 Oct. 2016.

Fanti, Luciano, and Nicola Meccheri. "Managerial Delegation under Alternative Unionization Structures." *LABOUR: Review of Labour Economics & Industrial Relations* 27, no. 1 (2013): 38–57. Web. 23 Oct. 2016.

Hagel, Jack. "From CGMA Magazine: How to Be a Better Delegator." *Journal of Accountancy* 216, no. 6 (2013): 1–3. Web. 23 Oct. 2016.

Martin, W. Michael, Alexander McKelvie, and G. Tom Lumpkin. "Centralization and Delegation Practices in Family Versus Non-family SMEs: A Rasch Analysis." *Small Business Economics* 47, no. 3 (2016): 755–69. Web. 23 Oct. 2016.

Matsudaira, Kate. "Delegation as Art." *Communications of the ACM* 59, no. 5 (2016): 58–60. Web. 23 Oct. 2016.

Mukherjee, Arjit, and Yingyi Tsai. "Managerial Delegation, Cost Asymmetry and Social Efficiency of Entry." *Economic Record* 90, no. 288 (2014): 90–97. Web. 23 Oct. 2016.

Scott Zimmer, J.D.

DIRECTING AND MANAGING VOLUNTEERS

ABSTRACT

This article focuses on the steps an organization can take when developing a quality volunteer management system. Such a system is necessary in order to effectively direct and manage the activities of volunteers. Various models will be introduced and the role of recruitment, training, retention, and recognition of volunteers is discussed.

OVERVIEW

There are many activities that rely on the assistance of volunteers who are crucial to some organizations—especially nonprofit organizations—since they have the ability to administer programs for their targeted audience. "Existing research has almost exclusively focused on the human resource management of employees working in large for-profit organizations, with non-profit organizations and volunteer dependent organizations receiving scant attention (Cuskelly, Taylor, Hoye, and Darcy 2006, 142). This article attempts to present some of the techniques that may be helpful in managing and directing volunteers in a variety of organizations. Volunteers do not receive a salary. Therefore, it is important to determine how an organization can recruit and retain loyal and hard working volunteers.

Before recruiting volunteers, it may be beneficial to have an effective internal system for identifying, recruiting, educating, coordinating, training, thanking, evaluating, and encouraging volunteers. Those managing the volunteers must establish processes, policies and procedures that will provide the volunteers with information about how the organization and programs are run. Some of the best practices can be documented based on the systems in place at a variety of organizations.

Three Step Volunteer Management System

In 2005, the American College of Healthcare Executives (ACHE) established an effective volunteer management system that was based on three easy steps.

Step 1: Prepare for volunteers

Organizations can work on promotional opportunities concerning their organization prior to recruiting. One of the advantages for taking this approach is that it is possible to develop a network of potential volunteer candidates prior to the official recruiting campaign. Many people want to learn about an organization prior to volunteering their time. In addition, people want to know that their time is valued. Given the fact that the average person is juggling multiple and competing priorities, it is important to know that an organization is well organized and structured prior to making a commitment to give time, no matter how important the cause may be. Therefore, some of the following efforts should be in place prior to the recruitment of volunteers.

- Establish policies, procedures, and record-keeping systems, and document them in a volunteer handbook.
- Resolve legal and liability issues pertaining to volunteer involvement.
- Create systems for evaluating the performance of volunteers and the outcome of volunteer initiatives.

- Train volunteer recruiters to speak knowledgeably and enthusiastically about the organization's goals and programs.
- Review the organization's upcoming initiatives to identify volunteer needs. Every organization should make sure that there is a place for the volunteers.
- Create brief position descriptions for each volunteer role, including the pros and cons of volunteering.

Step 2: Recruit volunteers
Once the foundation has been laid in the first step, the organization may turn its attention to recruiting volunteers. Recruiting the right volunteers involves more than asking people to help out. Before recruiting individuals, it is best to look at what the organization's needs are. When conducting the needs assessment, some of the questions that should be asked include:

- Who is qualified for and interested in the position?
- Who is able to meet the time requirement of the position?
- Where can the organization find these people?
- What is the best way to approach potential recruits?

The type of recruiting strategy (i.e., targeted or broad based) is dependent on the outcomes of the needs assessment. Targeted recruitment is the preferred approach when the organization is attempting to find potential candidates with a specific set of skills, interests, and availability needed for a particular position. On the other hand, a broad-based recruitment approach may be more appropriate when the projects require many volunteers, and they only need a minimum amount of training.

Step 3: Recognize volunteers
It is only human nature for people to want to receive appreciation and recognition for the work that they have done on a project. Therefore, it is important for organizations to develop a reward and recognition system to honor the volunteers once projects have been completed. Recognition can take many forms, and it would be wise to poll the volunteers to see what is important to them. Examples of recognition efforts include:

- Make an announcement at organization/departmental meetings.
- Include a statement of recognition in the organization's newsletter and/or website.
- Send personal thank you notes from the top leader of the organization (i.e., the president).
- Hold an annual dinner (or other meal) celebration for all volunteers.
- Offer complimentary benefits to volunteers.
- Present awards and inexpensive gifts for exceptional contributions.

APPLICATION

The Layered Approach
By following the three steps mentioned in the overview section, an organization has established a successful volunteer management system from the beginning to the end. Kent (1992) developed a manual that covered many of the same points. However, her concept had five crucial elements of a successful volunteer management program. The five elements were:

1. **Assessment of needs:** Ask questions such as,: How many volunteers does the organization need; what tasks need to be done; and what skill should volunteers have. Basically, it is consistent with what was listed above.
2. **Recruitment:** Devise a plan to identify, recruit, and acquire the volunteers that are needed.
3. **Risk management audit, interviewing, and screening:** interview potential volunteers to assess their match with the culture of the organization. Create job descriptions for volunteer positions. Assess the risk involved with volunteer positions. Ensure appropriate screening techniques because there may be some candidates that you do not need or want.
4. **Orientation, training, and monitoring:** Design an orientation process that will help the volunteers understand their roles. Provide a training program for volunteers to develop their skills. Initiate a continuous feedback and evaluation mechanism.
5. **Retention and recognition:** Develop techniques, events, and programs that acknowledge volunteers' contributions. (Woods 2006, 20)

Although Kent's model includes some of the approaches of the first model that was presented, there is a special focus on ensuring a holistic approach when utilizing the services of volunteers. Her position is that a successful volunteer management program requires a layered approach that considers risks, resources, and rewards (Forsyth 1999). Balancing these considerations could be difficult given the type of organization and volunteers expressing interest. Although it's important to take the volunteers' wishes into consideration, those managing the volunteer function must ensure that the different types of risks are evaluated as well. Based on the assessment, the manager should assign each volunteer position a risk category of low, medium, or high.

Levels of the Layered Approach
According to Forsyth (1999), there are three levels— or types of volunteer involvement—in the layered approach:

- **Layer 1** Includes short-term volunteer opportunities such as one-time events, annual fund-raising activities, or short-term program assistance ranging from a few hours to a few months. These volunteer positions are usually very low risk, with no access to vulnerable populations.
- **Layer 2** Involves longer commitments, usually two to twelve months. Volunteer positions involved directly with programs and services and ad hoc board committees, which are often directed to a specific task and disbanded when the task is completed, fall into this category.
- **Layer 3** Tends to be the most intensive. It accommodates nonprofits' needs for long term volunteer commitments. Organizations that provide services to vulnerable populations usually require at least a one-year commitment which is particularly important when the volunteer works directly with clients. The long-term volunteer position usually involves extensive screening, supervision, and evaluation. Board positions also fall into this layer since they usually require at least a one-year term and often a longer commitment. (Forsyth 1999, p. 41)

When deciding on which layer to select, one should consider time, resources, impact, and risk. Time and resources takes into consideration the length of the volunteer's task and the human recourses and materials needed to complete it. Impact and risk involves evaluating the impact the volunteer task has on the organization and the degree to which loss, injury or harm might occur during its completion.

VIEWPOINT

Management Perspective
The first step that every leader considering a volunteer management system should take is to analyze and evaluate why there is a need for such a system and what does it seek to create, expand, and/or improve. Unfortunately, most leaders provide answers that are one sided. Many organizations do not consider the needs and desires of the volunteers. Rather, the focus is on how the volunteers can lift some of the burden from full-time staff members, especially when there isn't a budget to hire additional personnel. This type of perspective is what Ellis (1986) labeled as "second choice" versus "first choice" explanations for implementing a quality volunteer management system.

Instead of looking at the project of recruiting and using volunteers as a reactionary task, many organizations would benefit from taking a proactive approach and creating a system that is cutting edge and futuristic. Tedrick and Henderson (1989) provided a list of the many benefits for taking the positive approach. Some of the advantages include:

- Volunteers offer credibility because they are not salaried. As a result, volunteers tend not to be motivated by personal financial gain. Rather, there is a desire to help others. In addition, volunteers can be objective evaluators when salary is not an issue. Volunteers can be direct and blunt without fearing retaliation, which is a concern of full-time employees.
- Volunteers tend to feel less pressure about performing tasks since they are the ones that have control when determining their schedule for activities.
- Volunteers are free to experiment and try new approaches versus playing it safe. Full-time

Campaign volunteers create material to distribute to potential voters (Photo courtesy of Quadell)

employees tend to shy away from risks because they are unsure how their initiatives will affect their future employment and promotion opportunities.
- Volunteers are representative of the community in which they serve so they are excellent public spokespersons for an organization.
- Volunteers typically donate financial support as well as their time to organizations where they volunteer.

CONCLUSION

Before recruiting volunteers, it is beneficial to have an effective internal system in place. Those managing the volunteers must establish processes, policies and procedures that will provide the volunteers with information about how the organization and programs are run. Some of the best practices can be documented based on the systems in place at a variety of organizations.

By following the three steps mentioned in the overview section, an organization can establish a successful volunteer management system from beginning to end. Kent (1992) developed a manual which covered many of the same points. In addition, her concept had five crucial elements of a successful volunteer management program. Although Kent's model includes some of the approaches of the first model that was presented, there is a special focus on ensuring that a holistic approach is taken when utilizing the services of volunteers. She found that a successful volunteer management program required a layered approach that took risks, resources, and rewards into consideration (Forsyth 1999). Balancing these considerations could be difficult given the type of organization and volunteers expressing interest. Although it's important to take the volunteers' wishes into consideration, those managing the volunteer function must ensure that the different types of risks are evaluated as well. Based on the assessment, the manager should assign each volunteer position a risk category of low, medium, or high.

The first step that every leader considering a volunteer management system should take is to analyze and evaluate why there is a need for such a system and what does it seek to create, expand, and/or improve. Unfortunately, most leaders provide answers that are one sided. Many organizations do not consider the needs and desires of the volunteers. Rather, the focus is on how the volunteers can lift some of the burden off of full-time staff members, especially when there isn't a budget to hire additional personnel. This type of perspective is what Ellis (1986) labeled as "second choice" versus "first choice" explanations for implementing a quality volunteer management system.

BIBLIOGRAPHY

Bowers, Kristen M., and William L. Hamby Jr. "An Analysis of Volunteer Leader Behavior: Self-Reported Measures." *Academy of Business Research Journal* (2013). Web. 15 Nov. 2013.

Cuskelly, Graham, Tracy Taylor, Russell Hoye, and Simon Darcy. "Volunteer Management Practices and Volunteer Retention: A Human Resource Management Approach." *Sports Management Review* 9, no. 2 (2006): 141–63. Web. 4 Dec. 2007.

Ellis, Susan. "Budgeting for a Volunteer Program." *Nonprofit World* 4, no. 1 (1986). Print.

Forsyth, Janice. "Volunteer Management Strategies: Balancing Risk and Reward." *Nonprofit World* 17, no. 3 (1999, May): 40–43. Web. 4 Dec. 2007.

Kent, Judy. *Effective Organizations: A Consultant's Resource.* Ottawa, ON, Canada: Skills Program for Management Volunteers, 1992.

Rafe, Stephen C. "Motivating Volunteers to Perform." *Nonprofit World* 31, no. 5 (2013): 18–19. Web. 15 Nov. 2013.

Rodell, Jessica B. "Finding Meaning through Volunteering: Why Do Employees Volunteer and What Does It Mean for Their Jobs?" *Academy of Management Journal* 56, no. 5 (2013): 1274–94. Web. 15 Nov. 2013.

Tedrick, Ted, and Karla A. Henderson. *Volunteers in Leisure: A Management perspective*. Reston, VA: AAHPERD, 1989.

"Three Steps to Effective Volunteer Management." *Healthcare Executive* 20, no. 1 (2005): 68. Web. 4 Dec. 2007.

Woods, Terry B. "Rhetoric of Volunteerism: Strategies to Recruit and Retain Volunteers in Nonprofit Organizations." Georgia State University. Web. 4 Dec. 2007.

SUGGESTED READING

Mirsky, Julia, Amos Avgar, and Roni Kaufman. "A Brigade Model for the Management of Service Volunteers: Lessons from the Former Soviet Union." *International Journal of Nonprofit & Voluntary Sector Marketing* 9, no. 1 (2004): 57–68. Web. 4 Dec. 2007.

"New Fundraiser Volunteer Module Eases Management Tasks." *GUI* Program News 16, no. 4 (2005, Apr.). Web. 4 Dec. 2007.

Marie Gould

DIVERSITY IN THE WORKPLACE

ABSTRACT

Diversity in the workforce is an offshoot of antidiscrimination legislation, which seeks to bring workplace harmony, growth, productivity, creativity and profitability to organizations, through the acceptance and harnessing of individual and group differences for the corporate good. There is no single method of implementing and managing diversity that works for all organizations, but there are certain factors that are essential for the creation of an environment that may engender success with diversity strategies.

OVERVIEW

In most Western nations, the corporate workforce has historically been dominated by white males. In other parts of the world, the story is similar; one group or a few groups of people tend to be the majority in the workplace. In the 1960s, President Lyndon Johnson introduced the concept of affirmative action with the aim of correcting the wrongs caused by hundreds of years of slavery and segregation. The civil rights cause was then taken up by women and other minority groups, who also felt that they had been discriminated against.

Legislation such as Title VII of the Civil Rights Act of 1964, the Age Discrimination in Employment Act of 1967, and Americans with Disabilities Act of 1990, helped to reduce discrimination among minority groups in the United States, and gave organizations the mandate to maintain diverse workforces. US companies responded to legislation in the late 1960s by making formal efforts to eliminate discrimination. In Europe, cooperation through the European Union led to the removal of barriers and increased freedoms, such as the freedom of movement between member states, and the right to be treated equally. These developments gave rise to legislation such as the EU Article 13 Race and Employment Directives, the Racial Equality Directive 2000/43/EC, and the Employment Equality Directive 2000/78/EC, prohibiting discrimination on the grounds of religion or belief, disability, age or sexual orientation.

A narrow definition of diversity concentrates on race and gender, but diversity in the workplace can be broadly defined as differences, similarities, and related tensions among people in the workplace based on visible dimensions, secondary influences, and work diversities. All of these differences affect the manner in which people function within an organization. Visible dimensions include age, race/ethnic heritage, gender, physical ability and qualities (including obesity), mental ability and qualities, and sexual or affectional orientation. Secondary influences include religious beliefs, socioeconomic class, background, and education. Work diversities include differences like management versus union; functional level; classification; and proximity or distance to the corporate headquarters. Other differences include personality and work style.

In sum, diversity concerns the differences, similarities and related tensions between the characteristics and experiences of every individual in the workplace. There are also other, lesser recognized forms of diversity related to the workplace, such as customer, product, function, acquisition/merger, family, or community diversity. The increase in workplace diversity has led to increasing challenges for organizations seeking to have and maintain a diverse workforce. Even in the twenty-first century there is still much to learn about how to minimize the negative outcomes of diversity (e.g., stereotyping, confusion, and discomfort); and how to maximize the positive outcomes.

Equal Employment Opportunity and Affirmative Action

Diversity is different from equal employment opportunity (EEO), affirmative action, or quota systems. With equal employment opportunity, every candidate has an equal chance at employment regardless of race, gender, religion, or any other characteristic. Emphasis is placed on avoiding discrimination and unfairness, and on increasing the proportion of minority groups—mainly women, ethnic minorities and people with disabilities—in the workplace. EEO is more to do with positive action than corporate vision. Affirmative action is a means of achieving EEO. It requires employers to pay heed to demographic factors like race/ethnicity, gender, and so on, when making employment decisions, either to meet government guidelines or to meet the goals an organization sets for itself. Affirmative action has been alleged to discriminate against one group to help another.

Compliance with legislation, through initiatives such as affirmative action and equal employment opportunity, still has its place; however, there is more to diversity than mere compliance or recruiting and retaining disenfranchised groups of people. So serious is the issue of diversity that some scholars believe that the management of diversity is the single biggest factor that will determine the survival of firms in the twenty-first century.

Management of Diversity

Diversity management involves making good quality decisions in the midst of a diverse workforce in order to eliminate the negative outcomes of interactions between individuals. Basically, diversity management involves enhancing an organization's effectiveness by developing suitable organizational structures, systematic strategies and processes, and by creating an equitable and fair work environment for all kinds of employees.

Diversity management involves a three-stage process: the identification stage, where the diversity mixture is recognized and the necessary action determined; the implementation stage, where appropriate actions are selected and used; and the maintenance stage. Diversity management differs from affirmative action and EEO, in that it is based on scholarship and practice rather than law; and it includes organizational activities that are meant to enhance information sharing and acceptance—even celebration—of cultural differences.

Many companies have experienced success with diversity programs. For example, diversity is touted as the untold reason for the successful turnaround of firms such as IBM in the mid-1990s. When IBM dramatically altered its already diverse composition, the company created millions of dollars in new business through expanding its minority markets. Proctor & Gamble also created a diversity strategy; Wisconsin Power and Light has made employee diversity one of its key goals; and Chevron Corporation has incorporated diversity programs into all levels of their business planning because of their multinational activities and changing demographics. Boeing Co. has been advertising throughout the United States to attract women and ethnic minorities who do not feel properly utilized in their current jobs.

Ensuring diversity in the workplace is a process which takes time, often years. First, organizations must introduce the necessary changes in systems and processes; and second, they have to review their organizational culture. Real changes in organizational culture take place when the group with the most power (which is often the senior management team) considers its behavior and makes any necessary changes, both on a personal level and on an organizational level.

Before preparing a diversity management program, an organization must undertake a diversity audit, otherwise known as a cultural assessment, where current diversity levels and issues are assessed. The diversity audit is conducted through interviews, focus groups, surveys, and the collection of both archival and systems data.

A diversity management program should also be based on a policy document which must include a clear definition of diversity. The role of diversity in the organization should be clarified, as should leadership roles and the organization's expectations for its diversity initiatives. The advantages of diversity should also be stated, and in particular, the business case (the fact that diversity can lead to better organizational performance) should be highlighted. Furthermore, the diversity policy should include a plea for all employees to lend their support to the diversity program. The policy and all related documents should be widely published and circulated within the organization.

Managing diversity involves the implementation of creative strategies for diversity recruitment, selection, retention and training, among others. To help in their moves towards greater diversity, organizations may choose to hire a diversity consultant, who can help design a diversity strategy tailored to the organization's unique culture and circumstances, which will be valued and supported in the organization's systems and processes. Diversity consultants can also steer leadership in the direction it needs to move. Diversity consultants can be brought in at any stage of the diversity management process, and they can also assist in areas such as education and training, conflict mediation, and team building.

A Changing Labor Force

As of 2014, in the United States, women represent 47 percent of total employment; according to the US Department of Labor, that number is predicted to decline slightly by 2022. Already, in Australia, women outnumber men in the nation's population. With these demographic shifts, creative recruitment efforts will ensure that organizations have access to a large pool of recruits, and since the best employment candidates are not found in only one particular group of people, organizations would do well to recruit from the widest possible range of recruitment sources, making sure they have access to all groups and communities.

To this end, many organizations are now targeting minority colleges for their recruitment efforts, advertising to minority groups, and offering scholarships and awards to minority students. The very fact that an organization has—and implements—a diversity policy, also serves as an attraction to diverse people, making the organization a likely employer of choice. Selection procedures must also be perceived as valid, reliable, and fair; and when these conditions are in place, they encourage improved performance from employees. Once new hires are in place, organizations must implement a range of long-term strategies to retain them.

Initiatives and workplace programs that help retain diverse employees in the workplace include the following:

- Talent management, which involves the identification and nurturing of talent, as well as the rewarding and promotion of talent by fair appraisal, treatment and management.
- Flexible working, telecommuting, and adoption support, which appeal to certain groups such as working mothers and single parents.
- Mentoring, career development and succession planning.
- Lifelong learning to help employees meet their career goals without having to leave the organization.
- Enrichment programs.
- Listening forums, which allow the organization to acknowledge the different needs of different groups of employees.
- Network support groups, which can be enhanced through online discussion on corporate intranets.
- Flexible health and dependent care spending accounts.
- Seniority pay, part-time work, and phased retirement, which are essential for retaining those workers from the baby boom generation who have reached retirement age.
- Elder care.

- Domestic partner benefits, which would particularly be appreciated by employees with same sex partners.

Diversity Training
It is said that practically every employee claims to be diverse, and that everyone has biases, although they may not admit it. When diverse, biased people come together in the workplace, people tend to be uncomfortable with cultural differences because of their limited knowledge and resistance to change. Organizations lose productivity and revenue due to the negative effects of diversity like high turnover, absenteeism, recruiting and retraining, miscommunication, and conflict.

The growing field of diversity training can help employees understand diversity and be receptive to change, both of which will, in turn, lead to the retention of talent. Diversity training helps promote harmony in the workplace, by affording all employees the opportunity to learn more about cultural diversity, the values of others, and their own responses to people who are different. Diversity training also helps employees improve their cross-cultural communication skills and develop leadership skills, thus promoting healthy information flows and good interpersonal relations.

Organizations differ greatly in their diversity training goals and methods, and therefore, training interventions do differ, but in order to ensure the effectiveness of training, diversity must be linked to business success, and must be defined to encompass all groups, including historically predominant groups such as white men. Diversity training must be well-thought-out and introduced to employees, to avoid negative reactions from participants. Generally, attendance should be voluntary, and therefore, care should be taken so that employees are not forced into diversity training programs. However, senior and line managers must attend the diversity training courses. In addition, all staff must be briefed on discriminatory attitudes and behavior, disciplinary consequences, and ways to raise a grievance.

Diversity training can be carried out formally or informally. Formally, it may be conducted through dedicated training programs or as a component of other programs. There are several forms of formal diversity training, including awareness training, skill-based diversity training, and aspects of leadership development, team building and mentoring programs. In particular, a diversity training program is likely to comprise one or more of the following components:

- Introduction to diversity;
- Ethnic, black, or feminist studies;
- Skill building;
- Cultural awareness;
- Sexual or other forms of harassment;
- Psychotherapeutic approaches, which may involve group therapy for groups experiencing conflict;
- Sensitivity training;
- Dissonance creation, where dissonance is purposely created with the hope that the target audience will change their attitudes and behaviors;
- Legal awareness, where discrimination laws and illegal practices are explained;
- Focused awareness, with emphasis placed on understanding the nature, functions, and prevalence of various stereotypes through individual and small group interactions;
- Integrated diversity training, where appropriate diversity issues are integrated into the course of preexisting and new training efforts that target specific functional skills or business goals.

Advantages of Diversity
Those who are not in favor of diversity tend to blame it for an increase in poor working relationships, and they deem it wasteful and unnecessary. However, the converse is true; the advantages of diversity are numerous. For example, greater creativity and innovation ensue when different cultures, ideas and perspectives come together under one organizational umbrella. Therefore, diversity has been heralded as a means of improving organizational performance through greater adaptability and flexibility in today's rapidly changing marketplace. Due to their partnerships with external stakeholders such as minority communities and suppliers, organizations with diverse workforces gain reputations as employers of choice. Furthermore, employee loyalty increases as employees gain pride in their organization for its corporate social responsibility (of which diversity is a part) and good community relations.

When diversity is well managed, organizations gain competitive advantage through positive improvements in corporate culture, employee morale, retention and recruitment; and they also experience a reduction in costs associated with turnover, absenteeism, low productivity and discrimination litigation. Return on investment increases, and organizations experience sustained growth in market share through an expanded diverse customer base.

A diverse workforce will promote access to minority sales and profits. Countries whose populations are becoming increasingly diverse are experiencing shifts in purchasing power, with minority groups growing in purchasing power. For instance, it has been projected that in the United States, the most diverse nation in the world, the purchasing power of minorities will soon overtake that of Caucasians. To be able to reach the minority groups, organizations must make use of the knowledge of minority employees who can relate to different groups in the marketplace. Likewise, when minority employees can relate to customers in the global marketplace, organizations will enhance their capacity to capture, retain and serve their international customers.

Success with Diversity
Every organization will manage its diversity differently, depending on their unique business needs, workforce issues, and situational factors. However, there are certain factors that scholars and practitioners recognize as factors which help to engender success with diversity in the workplace. These factors include accountability, strong support and commitment from an organization's leaders; total buy-in from all employees; the expertise of strong diversity professionals; integration of management practices with diversity efforts; links between diversity and performance evaluation; and extended definitions of effective performance.

Success with diversity also requires operating philosophies that state that all employees are different but equal. In addition, it requires the development of a diversity scorecard which is capable of providing financial and nonfinancial recognition of diversity return on investment initiatives, as well as relevant feedback.

The Role of Human Resources
Human resources professionals, who are best placed to engender an organizational culture that promotes successful diversity, have experience in areas such as team building, change management, conflict resolution, and cross-cultural communication. In order to enhance an organization's competitive advantage through diversity management, human resources experts must continually assess and improve all their company policies, programs and diversity initiatives, in order to eliminate any biases that may create potential challenges for diverse employees. Human resources professionals must also identify individuals within the organization who can champion the diversity cause and help bring about the necessary change. They must also network with human resources professionals outside of the organization, to discover different styles of diversity management, challenges encountered and recommended best practice.

Diversity places many challenges on the leaders of organizations, as they attempt to encourage teamwork and cooperation between increasingly diverse work groups. Conflict increases as teams become more diverse, and in order to bring out the best from teamwork, the teams must view conflict as a necessary part of the creative process, in order to get the best results. Managers must be trained to find the good in conflict and diversity, and turn it around, knowing that the culture of the company is most important. To carry out their work effectively, an organization's leaders will need to develop additional skills, not only in the area of conflict management, but also in the areas of interpersonal communication, feedback gathering, and role modeling.

Human resources professionals must constantly remind the chief executive officer (CEO) and top management team that diversity is a business strategy. In order for diversity in the workplace to be successful, the organization's leaders must be accountable; they must have a passion for diversity; and they must have sustained involvement in all diversity initiatives. Their commitment must be visible to all employees. As often as possible, diversity should be on the agenda at executive meetings and organizational conferences, and where possible, diversity candidates should be appointed to top positions. Clear roles and responsibilities should be assigned to the senior management team regarding diversity management, and participation in diversity councils should be recommended as a development path for senior leaders.

CONCLUSION

The field of diversity management is still a young one, and much remains to be learned in terms of the specific applications of diversity to different groups of people in the workforce; measuring diversity's success; and many other issues that require clarification. One thing is clear, though—diversity is here to stay.

Bibliography

Adams, Marc. "Building a Rainbow, One Stripe at a Time." *HR Magazine* 43, no. 9 (1998): 72.

Alverson, Marchel. "The Call to Manage Diversity." *Women in Business* 50, no. 4 (1998): 34. Web. 18 Dec. 2007.

Arai, Marguerite, Maryanne Wanca-Thibault, and Pamela Shockley-Zalabak. "Communications Theory and Training Approaches for Multiculturally Diverse Organizations: Have Academics and Practitioners Missed the Connection?" *Public Personnel Management* 30, no. 4 (2001): 445. Web. 18 Dec. 2007.

Barrille, Sergio. "Managing Successfully…Managing Diversity." *Businessdate* 121, no. 2 (2003): 5. Web. 18 Dec. 2007.

"Building on the Promise of Diversity." *HR Managing* 51, no. 3 (2006): 137–38. Web. 18 Dec. 2007.

Bunton, Wilett, and A. Reaves. "Diversity in the Workplace." *Armed Forces Comptroller* 45, no. 3 (2000): 30. Web. 18 Dec. 2007.

Dick, Penny, and Catherine Cassell. "Barriers to Managing Diversity in a UK Constabulary: The Role of Discourse." *Journal of Management Studies* 39, no. 7 (2002): 953–76. Web. 18 Dec. 2007.

Dijk, Hans van, M.K. van Engen, and Jaap Paauwe. "Reframing the Business Case for Diversity: A Values and Virtues Perspective. *Journal of Business Ethics* 111, no. 1 (2012): 73–84. Web. 22 Nov. 2013.

Doke, Deedee, and Scott Beagrie. "How to…Manage a Diversity Programme." *Personnel Today* (2003, Feb. 4): 31. Web. 18 Dec. 2007.

Forseter, M. "Retailing in an Age of Diversity." *Chain Store Age* 81, no. 6 (2005): 12. Web. 18 Dec. 2007.

Hewlett, Sylvia A., Melinda Marshall, and Laura Sherbin. "How Diversity Can Drive Innovation." *Harvard Business Review* 91, no. 12 (2013): 30. Web. 11 Nov. 2014.

Hon, Linda, and Brigitta Brunner. "Diversity Issues and Public Relations." *Journal of Public Relations Research* 12, no. 4 (2000): 309–40. Web. 18 Dec. 2007.

"How Does Workplace Diversity Affect Productivity?" *Point for Credit Union Research & Advice* (2003, Apr. 14). Web. 18 Dec. 2007.

Ivancevich, John, and Jacqueline Gilbert. "Diversity Management." *Public Personnel Management* 29, no. 1 (2000): 75. Web. 18 Dec. 2007.

Kandola, Baljinder. "The Value of Reflection." *Personnel Today* (2005, Aug. 23): 17. Web. 18 Dec. 2007.

Lockwood, Nancy. "Workplace Diversity: Leveraging the Power of Difference for Competitive Advantage." *HRMagazine* 50, no. 6 (2005): 1–10. Web. 18 Dec. 2007.

"Making Diversity Work: Seven Steps for Defeating Bias in the Workplace." *Journal for Quality & Participation* 27, no. 4 (2004): 53. Web. 18 Dec. 2007.

Martin, A. "Affirmative Action Must Remain Part of the American System." *PA Times* 23, no. 2 (2000): 6. Web. 18 Dec. 2007.

Miller, Sandra K., and J.J. Tucker III. "Diversity Trends, Practices, and Challenges in the Financial Services Industry." *Journal of Financial Service Professionals* 67, no. 6 (2013): 46–57. Web. 22 Nov. 2013.

Nielsen, Bernard B., and Sabine Nielsen. "Top Management Team National Diversity and Firm Performance: A Multilevel Study." *Strategic Management Journal* 34, no. 3 (2013): 373–82. Web. 11 Nov. 2014.

Outtz, James. "The Psychology and Management of Workplace Diversity." *Personnel Psychology* 57, no. 4 (2004): 1041–44. Web. 18 Dec. 2007.

Overell, S. "Ouseley in Assual on Diversity." *People Management* 2, no. 9 (1995): 7. Web. 18 Dec. 2007.

Ragins, Belle, Jorge A. Gonzalez, Kyle Ehrhardt, and Romalia Singh. "Crossing the Threshold: The Spillover of Community Racial Diversity and Diversity Climate to the Workplace." *Personnel Psychology* 65, no. 4 (2012): 755–87. Web. 22 Nov. 2013.

Soni, V. "A Twenty-First-Century Reception for Diversity in the Public Sector: A Case Study." *Public Administration Review* 60, no. 5 (2000): 395–408. Web. 18 Dec. 2007.

Thomas, David. "Diversity as Strategy." *Harvard Business Review* 82, no. 9 (2004): 98–108. Web. 18 Dec. 2007.

Van Eron, Ann. "How to Work with a Diversity Consultant." *Training & Development* 50, no. 4 (1996): 41. Web. 18 Dec. 2007.

SUGGESTED READING

Caleb, P. "How Diversity Works." *Scientific American* 311, no. 4 (2014): 43–47. Web. 11 Nov. 2014.

Fisher, Anne. "Could Bonuses Lead to More Diversity at the Top? *Fortune.com* (2013): 1. Web. 22 Nov. 2013.

Gardenswartz, Lee, Anita Rowe, Patricia Digh, and Martin Bennett. *The Global Diversity Desk Reference: Managing an International Workforce*. San Francisco: John Wiley & Sons, Inc., 2003.

Hubbard, Edward. *The Diversity Scorecard: Evaluating the Impact of Diversity on Organizational Performance*. Burlington, MA: Elsevier Butterworth-Heinemann, 2004.

Jayne, Michael, and Robert Dipboye. "Leveraging Diversity to Improve Business Performance: Research Findings and Recommendations for Organizations." *Human Resource Management* 43, no. 4 (2004): 409–24. Web. 18 Dec. 2007.

Judy, Richard, and Carol D'Amico. *Workforce 2020: Work and Workers in the 21st Century*. Indianapolis, IN: Hudson Institute, 1997.

Matton, Janine, and Christine Hernandez. "A New Study Identifies that 'Make and Breaks' of Diversity Initiatives." *Journal of Organizational Excellence* 23, no. 4 (2004): 47–58. Web. 18 Dec. 2007.

McCann, Jack, and Suhanya Aravamudhan. "Employee Perceptions of Workplace Diversity in the Manufacturing Industry." *International Journal of Human Resources Development & Management* 13, no. 2 (2013): 224–239. Web. 22 Nov. 2013.

Richard, Orlando, and Nancy Johnson. "Understanding the Impact of Human Resource Diversity Practices on Firm Performance." *Journal of Managerial Issues* 13, no. 2 (2001): 177–96. Web. 18 Dec. 2007.

Thiederman, Sondra. *Making Diversity Work: Seven Steps for Defeating Bias in the Workplace*. Chicago: Dearborn Trade Publishing, 2003.

Thomas, R. Roosevelt Jr. *Building on the Promise of Diversity: How We Can Move to the Next Level in Our Workplaces, Our Communities, and Our Society*. New York: AMACOM, 2006.

Vanessa A. Tetteh, Ph.D.

Emotional Intelligence

ABSTRACT

Emotional intelligence is often referred to as a skill, ability, competency, and even a personality trait. Its definition, therefore, is constantly changing and somewhat controversial. It was first coined as a term by Peter Salovey and John Mayer in 1990 and popularized by Daniel Goleman in 1995. It has become an important concept in the evaluation of any leader's competency and effectiveness.

INTRODUCTION

The concept of emotional intelligence is relatively new to the field of psychology. The ideas and concepts that are now referred to as emotional intelligence first came to be in the 1980s, when Howard E. Gardner first proposed his theory of multiple intelligences. The term "emotional intelligence" was introduced by Peter Salovey and John Mayer in a 1990 research paper. In 1995, the publication of Daniel Goleman's *Emotional Intelligence: Why It Can Matter More Than IQ* popularized the concept. Three common models of emotional intelligence have been developed: the ability-based model (Mayer and Salovey's four-branch model based on emotional skills and abilities); the mixed model (Goleman's model based on skills and competencies); and the trait model (based on personality traits). Because of the differences that exist among the three models and because the field is growing at such a rapid pace, a standardized definition of emotional intelligence has yet to emerge. Although not agreed on by researchers in the field, two common definitions of emotional intelligence are one, the ability to monitor the feelings and emotions of the self and of others and to use this information to guide one's behaviors, and two, the ability to identify and control emotions in oneself and in others.

Measurement and Assessment

Several tools have been developed to assess emotional intelligence. The two most prominent tools are the Mayer-Salovey-Caruso Emotional Intelligence Test (MSCEIT) and the Emotional Competence Inventory (ECI). The MSCEIT is a self-report test, consisting of 141 items based on the four-branch abilities model of emotional intelligence. It measures abilities on each of the four branches, and then computes a separate score for each branch and an overall emotional intelligence score. The test includes eight tasks that measure the four branches of emotional intelligence—perceive emotions, use of emotions to facilitate thought, understanding emotions, and managing emotions—as defined by Mayer, Salovey, and David R. Caruso. The ECI is based on Goleman's mixed model of emotional intelligence. The instrument is a 360-degree survey that assesses emotional intelligence by asking the person and multiple raters to answer questions about the person's behavior. The test measures eighteen competencies that fall under the four dimensions of emotional intelligence as identified by the mixed model approach: self-awareness, self-management, social awareness, and relationship management. The competencies measured in the ECI are said to be learned capabilities, which enables individuals to improve and develop each of the four emotional intelligence dimensions.

Training and Application

Since its inception, the concept of emotional intelligence has been used in a wide variety of contexts to help people perform on their jobs and live more successfully. Although some of the first contexts in which emotional intelligence was used focused on worker productivity and satisfaction, the concept has since been applied successfully in a broad range of areas.

One of the areas in which emotional intelligence has proven to be very helpful is in relationship

Daniel Goleman (photo courtesy of anonimoa)

training. Emotional intelligence, by its nature, has a strong focus on empathy and on understanding the ways in which emotions influence people. When people are able to combine a sense of how their own emotions can guide or derail them with a developed awareness of how others feel, they are equipped to navigate the complexities of relationships across many situations. Emotional intelligence has also been applied in structuring educational settings for students, teachers, and parents. Curricula have been designed that incorporate appropriate emotional modeling, helping children regulate their emotions and connecting emotional experience to activities and events.

Training children in the classroom in social and emotional skills has been shown to increase academic performance by 11 percentile points and to reduce conduct problems and aggression by 9 percent. Emotional intelligence has also been widely used in skills training for supervisors and managers. In one randomized, controlled study with corporate executives, people who received training in emotional intelligence competencies were superior to the no-intervention control group in measures of social awareness, relationship management, self-management, and self-awareness, as reported by bosses, peers, and employees.

CONCLUSION

In fact, emotional intelligence and the possession of certain traits have become as important as intellect in the hiring process. Emotional intelligence in the workplace not only promotes better work habits, but it can also help create an environment conducive to productivity.

BIBLIOGRAPHY

Asli, Arash. "Emotional Intelligence: The Key Trait to Reducing Stress and Improving Quality of Life." *The Huffington Post*, 30 Nov. 2016. Web. 19 Dec. 2016.

Chamorro-Premuzic, Tomas. "Why Being a Great Second in Command Requires Emotional Intelligence." *Forbes*, 10 Dec. 2016. Web. 15 Dec. 2016.

Cherniss, Cary, and Mitchel Adler. *Promoting Emotional Intelligence in Organizations*. Alexandria, VA: American Society and Training and Development, 2000.

Deleon, Mariah. "The Importance of Emotional Intelligence at Work." *Entrepreneur*. Entrepreneur Media, 8 May 2015. Web. 5 Oct. 2016.

Goleman, Daniel, Zenobia Barlow, and Lisa Bennett. *Ecoliterate: How Educators are Cultivating Emotional, Social, and Ecological Intelligence*. San Francisco: Jossey-Bass, 2012.

Goleman, Daniel. *Emotional Intelligence: Why It Can Matter More than IQ*. New York: Bantam, 1995.

Goleman, Daniel, Richard E. Boyatzis, and Annie McKee. *Primal Leadership: Unleashing the Power of Emotional Intelligence*. 10th ed. Boston: Harvard Business Review, 2013.

Grant, Adam. "The Dark Side of Emotional Intelligence." *Atlantic*. Atlantic Monthly Group, 2 Jan. 2014. Web. 29 Jan. 2016

Kahn, Jennifer. "Can Emotional Intelligence Be Taught?" *New York Times*. New York Times, 11 Sept. 2013. Web. 29. Jan. 2016.

Llopis, Glenn. "5 Ways to Lead with Emotional Intelligence—and Boost Productivity." *Forbes*. Forbes Media, 24 Sept. 2012. Web. 5 Oct. 2016.

Matthews, Gerald, Moshe Zeidner, and Richard D. Roberts. *Emotional Intelligence 101*. New York: Springer, 2012.

Mayer, John D., Peter Salovey, and Marc A. Brackett. *Emotional Intelligence: Key Reading on the Mayer and Salovey Model*. Port Chester, NY: Dude, 2004.

Murphy, Kevin R., ed. *A Critique of Emotional Intelligence: What Are the Problems and How Can They Be Fixed?* Mahwah, NJ: Erlbaum, 2006.

Ovans. Andrea. "How Emotional Intelligence Became a Key Leadership Skill." *Harvard Business Review*. Harvard Business School, 28 Apr. 2015. Web. 5 Oct. 2016.

"Strengthen Your Manufacturing Line with Good Emotional Intelligence." *The Manufacturer*, 19 Dec. 2016. Web. 19 Dec. 2016.

Zeidner, Moshe, Gerald Matthews, and Richard D. Roberts. *What We Know About Emotional Intelligence: How It Affects Learning, Work, Relationships, and Our Mental Health*. Cambridge, MA: MIT Press, 2009.

Jeremy Wicks, Steven Nakisher, and Laurence Grimm

Employee Engagement

ABSTRACT

Companies all over the world wrestle with how to better engage their employees in the workplace. Engagement is necessary for companies to promote long-term productivity and well-being. Companies that fail to promote engagement lose money because employees are absent more and invested less in their work when they are present. All too often employers fail to create an environment that supports employees' intrinsic motivation for work. Furthermore, many companies fail to invest in enhancing leadership communication styles, which are important for promoting motivation, engagement, and happiness in the workplace.

OVERVIEW

Many organizations struggle to adequately engage their employees at work. In fact, companies across the world collectively waste billions of dollars a year by not adequately engaging employees with daily work and training opportunities. Engagement is much more than employees merely showing up for work and logging in a certain number of hours, which is called "presenteeism." Many disengaged employees are present most days, but are doing the bare minimum to earn their salary. Others are performing fairly well, but still below their potential, thereby squandering talent.

Engagement entails concentrating on work-related tasks, investing one's energy in meaningful behavior at work, actively participating in meetings, and having productive conversations with colleagues and clients, as well as other behaviors that serve the organization's goals and mission. Highly engaged employees generally produce higher quality work than other employees, have fewer accidents, and make better use of their time. When engagement is a manifestation of employees' intrinsic motivation for work (a love for what they do), they are more likely to be happy and are at a lower risk of being anxious or depressed. This situation, in turn, leads to less mental and physical illness, thereby reducing insurance claims and minimizing lost productivity due to absences. Furthermore, highly engaged employees that also enjoy their work are likely to spread a positive attitude to their coworkers, helping to create better morale and greater collective productivity.

FURTHER INSIGHTS

Burnout

No employee can be expected to be fully engaged 100 percent of the time. However, the hyperbolic notion of giving 110 percent, which is commonly encouraged in workplaces that value engagement, can lead to unnecessary stress, anxiety, depression, frustration, and burnout. Burnout is a type of disengagement that has a large impact on productivity. Workers that are burned out no longer enjoy work, take extra days of sick leave, function poorly on the job, and may eventually leave their field altogether.

The latter is an economic problem for society in many fields that serve society such as teaching, nursing, or social work, where highly qualified professionals leave the field after years of training. Abandonment of the field represents a loss of personal as well as institutional investment, because professional training has been undertaken at a cost, often with the aid of student grants and loans and staff development programs. Companies, hospitals,

A burned-out employee

schools, and other organizations face disruption, loss of productivity, increased costs, and loss of revenue when employees they have trained leave because of burnout. Furthermore, burned out employees may model negative attitudes and behavior for fellow employees before they actually resign or are fired.

To prevent employee burnout, it is important for employers to hold and convey realistic notions of employee engagement. Employees that take brief breaks to stretch out, get water, look out the window at beautiful scenery, or take a brief walk may return to tasks invigorated, such that they end up being more productive than those who do not take restorative breaks (Csikszentmihalyi 2000). Such breaks can also reduce job stress and promote long-term physical health. Likewise, eating a healthy lunch most days will support employees' concentration, energy, and physical health. Unfortunately, some employees feel pressured to skip lunch in order to impress employers or get more done, but such practices are believed to lead to decreased productivity and increased health issues.

Work "Flow"
Flow entails peak levels of performance, enjoyment of the task, and engrossment during periods of time at work. People that experience periods of flow demonstrate high levels of engagement and may later report that they felt like time flew by. When an employee is in a period of flow for just two to three hours, he or she may produce a better quality and greater quantity of work than he or she normally would in a whole day. Thus, employers interested in employee engagement would be wise to promote flow in the workplace.

Flow is especially likely to happen when there is an optimal match between the employee's skill level and the challenge provided. Thus, organizations that wish to create the conditions for this high level of engagement would be wise to assign employees to tasks that they will find neither too easy nor too difficult. This situation means that adequate training must be provided for employees who are expected to take on tasks beyond their current skill level, and employees should not be given many tasks for which they are highly overqualified. In other words, ongoing sound assessment of employee skills and abilities is required in order to enhance the likelihood of an optimal match.

However, a skill and challenge match does not guarantee flow. Certain people are more likely to experience flow at work than others. For instance, employees who have developed and maintained a high level of intrinsic motivation for what they do are more likely to experience flow. Intrinsic motivation entails seeing the beauty, purpose, or meaning in what one does (Froiland 2014). This attitude leads to happiness (Froiland 2013), fewer depressive symptoms, less work-related anxiety (Froiland 2011), greater creativity, a deeper engagement in general, and a greater proclivity to experience flow. It also means that companies that want to see their employees have higher levels of engagement and want to foster flow need to support the development of employees' intrinsic motivation.

Incentives and Motivation
Money is a powerful incentive and can activate an employee's extrinsic motivation, which is one's desire to work in order to obtain a reward. Research on entrepreneurs finds that extrinsic motivation can be crucial for helping someone to keep working hard when they are dealing with certain phases of their project that they find less inspiring, such as writing a grant or seeking a patent, whereas intrinsic motivation is especially crucial when creating a new product or adapting an intervention or program to a new environment. Other research indicates that intrinsic motivation leads to greater depth of understanding of what one reads and better developed problem-solving abilities, whereas extrinsic motivation leads to greater speed on relatively easy tasks.

The most dominant theory of intrinsic motivation in the workplace is self-determination theory, which posits that people across the world have a need for autonomy, relatedness, and competence (Deci and Ryan 2008). Self-determination theory indicates that extrinsic motivation is the fourth motive. When the three universal intrinsic needs are supported at work and home, people will be more intrinsically motivated and have deeper levels of engagement. Research in numerous countries in every region of the world supports self-determination theory.

Research based upon the sixteen basic desires theory indicates that there are a greater variety of intrinsic motives to consider when supporting engagement (Reiss 2012). The sixteen basic desires theory indicates that there are sixteen motives, such as desires for physical activity, romance, social contact, independence, order, helping others, curiosity, acceptance, eating, tranquility, power, savings, honor, competition, prestige, and family, all germane to engaging employees (Reiss 2012). In fact, knowing an employee's top three or four motives can lead to a greater match between the employee and the assigned task or project, which promotes greater enjoyment at work, more engagement, and superior performance. Furthermore, when managers become aware of how their own personality profile may clash with certain employees, misunderstandings and ineffective communication can be prevented, leading to more productive relationships between management and employees. Employers can also use such personality profiles to better select the right employees for specific positions. Although the sixteen basic desires theory leads to very individualized task assignments, self-determination theory has generated a much greater abundance of related research for companies to consider.

Communication

Research from a self-determination theory perspective indicates that employees thrive when their managers or supervisors communicate with them in a manner that supports their autonomy (Deci and Ryan 2008). Autonomy supportive communication meets the universal needs for relatedness and autonomy by acknowledging employees' feelings, explaining the underlying purpose for assignments or tasks, clarifying how tasks contribute to an inspiring vision, providing employees with opportunities to help develop innovative practices, highlighting the interesting aspects of tasks, and using noncontrolling language (Froiland 2014).

Authoritarian bosses employ controlling language, often without realizing that it has a negative effect on motivation, morale, and engagement. Despite poor results, supervisors sometimes resort to an authoritarian style because they themselves feel pressure to perform. Furthermore, some aspects of controlling communication are subtle and hard to identify. Many leaders don't realize, for example, that not taking time to listen to an employee's concerns or ignoring employees' feelings has a controlling effect. Busy managers may not believe they have time to listen to employees and get to know them, but it is an investment of time that will reap dividends in engagement and perhaps loyalty in the long run (Mishra, Boynton, and Mishra 2014).

Yelling at employees is a common communication technique. A manager who raises his or her voice angrily toward a subordinate may be met with acquiescence and therefore believe that the mode of communication was clear and effective. The employee, however, may in future be more hesitant to share ideas, thereby exhibiting less engagement. Fear of a negative performance evaluation (an extrinsic motive) may become a more prominent concern for the employee than any intrinsic motivation to think deeply about or discuss important issues related to the company's mission. The employee who is now less engaged may be thinking of finding a better work environment. A byproduct of this management style is a tendency toward "group think," in which teams with diverse expertise agree on decisions that are actually bad for the company because they fear the manager.

It is much more healthy for a team to welcome divergent views and what David W. Johnson refers to as "constructive controversy," the view that some of the most innovative ideas and rich discussion happen when people respectfully share their insights and points of view rather than disengaging and rushing toward an uninformed unanimous decision. Creating an atmosphere for constructive controversy and cooperative learning versus mindless group think is important for teams that wish to nourish and help their company and clients to do the same.

Viewpoints

Organizations often rely too heavily on the carrot-and-stick method of motivating engagement, which entails providing extrinsic incentives for showing up to work regularly (especially, a paycheck) and for excellent performance (for example, employee of the month awards or bonuses). Likewise, consequences are usually provided for unsatisfactory performance such as poor performance reviews, verbal reprimands, withholding promotions, and the threat of being fired.

People are complex and can be operating with extrinsic ("I want to be promoted so that I can make more money") and intrinsic ("I want to help my clients be healthier") motives at the same time. Unfortunately, many managers and administrators have been trained within a behavioral paradigm that relies almost exclusively on incentives and consequences to influence engagement-related behaviors. These managers are often unaware of the importance of cultivating intrinsic motivation. Alternatively, some managers believe that intrinsic and extrinsic motivations are diametrically opposed. This model precludes practices that promote the development of a motivational synergy in which both intrinsic and extrinsic motivations are supported. In either case, employee engagement will not be optimized without actively supporting both types of motivation, because motivation fuels engagement.

Many companies will need leadership interventions that help leaders better communicate with employees if they want to promote deeper engagement (Biggs, Brough, and Barbour 2014). One such emphasis lately has been on developing servant leaders who demonstrate their passion for serving others (Carter and Baghurst 2014), making it more likely that others will follow their example and become more passionately engaged in their work (Froiland 2014).

Bibliography

Biggs, Amanda, Paula Brough, and Jennifer P. Barbour. "Enhancing Work-Related Attitudes and Work Engagement: A Quasi-Experimental Study of the Impact of an Organizational Intervention." *International Journal of Stress Management* 21 (2014): 43–68. Web. 25 Nov. 2014.

Carter Danon, and Timothy Baghurst. "The Influence of Servant Leadership on Restaurant Employee Engagement." *Journal of Business Ethics* 124 (2014): 453–64. Web. 25 Nov. 2014.

Csikszentmihalyi, Mihaly. *Beyond Boredom and Anxiety*. Hoboken, NJ: Jossey-Bass, 2000.

Deci, Edward, and Richard M. Ryan. "Self-Determination Theory: A Macrotheory of Human Motivation, Development, and Health." *Canadian Psychology* 49 (2008): 182–85. Web. 25 Mar. 2015.

Froiland, John M. "Parental Autonomy Support and Student Learning Goals: A Preliminary Examination of an Intrinsic Motivation Intervention." *Child & Youth Care Forum* 40 (2011): 135–49. Web. 22 Mar. 2015.

Froiland, John M. "Parents' Weekly Descriptions of Autonomy Supportive Communication: Promoting Children's Motivation to Learn and Positive Emotions." *Journal of Child and Family Studies* 24 (2013): 117–26. Web. 22 Mar. 2015.

Froiland, John M. *Inspired Childhood: Parents Raising Motivated, Happy, and Successful Students from Preschool to College*. Seattle: Amazon, 2014.

Mishra, Karen, Lois Boynton, and Aneil Mishra. "Driving Employee Engagement: The Expanded Role of Internal Communications." *Journal of Business Communication* 51 (2014): 183–202. Web. 25 Nov. 2014.

Reiss, Steven. "Intrinsic and Extrinsic Motivation." *Teaching of Psychology* 39 (2012): 152–56. Web. 22 Mar. 2015.

Suggested Reading

Baker, Arnold. "Daily Fluctuations in Work Engagement: An Overview and Current Directions." *European Psychologist* 19 (2014): 227–36.

Chaudhary, Rioha. "A Multilevel Investigation of the Factors Influencing Work Engagement." *The Psychologist-Manager Journal* 17 (2014): 128–58.

Courtright, Stephen H., Amy Colbert, and Daejeong Choi. "Fired Up or Burned Out? How Developmental Challenge Differentially Impacts Leader Behavior." *Journal of Applied Psycholgy* 99 (2014): 681–96. Web. 25 Nov. 2014.

Forck, Matt. "7 Keys to Worker Engagement." *Professional Safety* 59 (2014): 31–33. Web. 25 Nov. 2014.

Handa, Meenakshi, and Aastha Gulati. "Employee Engagement." *Journal of Management Research* 14 (2014): 57–67. 09725814. Web. 25 Nov. 2014.

He, Hongwei, Weichun Zhu, and Xiaoming Zheng. "Procedural Justice and Employee Engagement:

Roles of Organizational Identification and Moral Identity Centrality." *Journal of Business Ethics* 122 (2014): 681–95. Web. 25 Nov. 2014.

Landes, Les. "Great Managers Boost Employee Engagement." *Journal of Financial Planning* 27 (2014): 10. Web. 25 Nov. 2014.

Lu, Xiaojun, and Mary E. Guy. "How Emotional Labor and Ethical Leadership Affect Job Engagement for Chinese Public Servants." *Public Personnel Management* 43 (2014): 3–24. Web. 25 Nov. 2014.

Sharif, Monica M., and Terri A. Scandura. "Do Perceptions of Ethical Conduct Matter during Organizational Change? Ethical Leadership and Employee Involvement." *Journal of Business Ethics* 124 (2014): 185–96. Web. 25 Nov. 2014.

John Mark Froiland, Ph.D.

Employee Monitoring

ABSTRACT

Employee monitoring, or employee surveillance, is a way for employers to supervise their employees. Employers conduct monitoring in order to increase employee productivity, to prevent the theft of proprietary information and other intellectual property, and to avoid liability related to copyright infringement or the creation of a hostile work environment. Employee monitoring techniques include email scanning, keystroke logging, global positioning system (GPS) tracking, telephone and voicemail tapping, video surveillance, and the remote viewing of employees' computers in real time. Some employers have used devices that look like ordinary employee identification (ID) badges to collect biometric data such as voice patterns and stress levels. Employee monitoring raises important legal and ethical questions about employees' right to privacy, and case law on the subject continues to evolve.

OVERVIEW

In the United States, an individual's right to privacy is based on a "reasonable expectation of privacy," which sets limitations on individuals' rights to privacy in public places. In US workplaces, expectations of privacy are minimal and may be reduced further through notices, employee handbooks, and end user policies that make explicit that company networks are monitored. In contrast, European

A user's privacy is breached

courts make it difficult for employers to defend their employee monitoring practices based on such notices, and European workers are more likely to win privacy based lawsuits than their American counterparts.

In the United States, the right to privacy has been inferred from the Fourth Amendment to the Constitution, which guarantees protection against unreasonable searches and seizures by the government. However, in terms of employee monitoring, this protection applies only to public sector employees. Employees in the private sector must rely on state laws, which tend to be limited and to favor employers. US Supreme Court cases such as *O'Connor v. Ortega* (1987) and *City of Ontario, California v. Quon* (2010) have recognized the privacy rights of government employees but have upheld the right of government employers to monitor employees as long as there is a reasonable, work-related justification for the surveillance and the scope of the surveillance is limited to the original work-related justification.

Employers are motivated to monitor their employees for a number of reasons: to prevent the theft of company data or property, to increase employee productivity and compliance, to remove illegal software or malware that could compromise network security, and to avoid liability related to copyright infringement or harassment by employees. The Supreme Court cases *Burlington Industries, Inc. v. Ellerth* (1998) and *Faragher v. City of Boca Raton* (1998) established that employers can be held liable for a hostile work environment created by an employee. In order to defend against such liability, employers must demonstrate that they took reasonable care to prevent and address hostile or harassing behavior by employees. Monitoring internal employee communications offers employers a means to track and document any harassment. Other benefits of employee monitoring include the ability to learn how employees work best; to keep employees safe, and to help train and evaluate employees.

Although there are many benefits to employee monitoring, studies also show that monitoring activities can negatively affect employee morale and motivation. Several surveys have found that employees subjected to invasive monitoring techniques report her levels of company loyalty and higher levels of stress and anger, which could negatively affect productivity. As a company's monitoring program becomes more extensive, the associated policies and guidelines must become more specific and detailed, which may deter new candidates from joining the company, thereby driving away talent. Another unintended consequence of employee monitoring is that highly supervised employees tend to take fewer risks, choosing to closely follow company polices, and they are therefore less likely to develop leadership and decision-making skills.

A 2005 survey by the Society for Human Resource Management found that more than one-third of employees surveyed believed that monitoring demonstrated a company's lack of trust in its employees, whereas only 2 percent of managers cited lack of trust as a reason for adopting monitoring systems; managers were more likely to cite the need to protect company assets and to avoid liability. However, several studies have suggested that employees are more willing to accept employee monitoring tactics when the company's policy allows for small but realistic amounts of computer time for personal use during the workday.

BIBLIOGRAPHY

Alder, G. Stoney, et al. "Employee Reactions to Internet Monitoring: The Moderating Role of Ethical Orientation." *Journal of Business Ethics* 80.3 (2008): 481–98. Print.

Bolderdijk, Jan W., Linda Steg, and Tom Postmes. "Fostering Support for Work-Floor Energy Conservation Policies: Accounting for Privacy Concerns." *Journal of Organizational Behavior* 34.2 (2013): 195–210. Print.

Campbell, Dennis, Marc J. Epstein, and F. Asis Martinez-Jerez. "The Learning Effects of Monitoring." *Accounting Review* 86.6 (2011): 1909–34. Print.

Ciocchetti, Corey A. "The Eavesdropping Employer: A Twenty-First Century Framework for Employee Monitoring." *American Business Law Journal* 48.2 (2011): 285–369. Print.

Determann, Lothar, and Robert Sprague. "Intrusive Monitoring: Employee Privacy Expectations Are Reasonable in Europe, Destroyed in the United States." *Berkeley Technology Law Journal* 26.2 (2011): 979–1036. Print.

Farlee, Mitchell A. "Disclosure and Secrecy in Employee Monitoring." *Journal of Management Accounting Research* 22 (2010): 187–208. Print.

Friedman, Barry, and Lisa Reed. "Workplace Privacy: Employee Relations and Legal Implications of Monitoring Employee E-mail Use." *Employee Responsibilities and Rights Journal* 19.2 (2007): 75–83. Print.

Hazelhurst, Jeremy. "Surveillance: How Much Is Too Much?" *People Management* (2014): 36–39. *Business Source Complete.* Web. 18 June 2015.

Katz, Lee Michael. "Big Employer Is Watching." *HR Magazine* 60.5 (2015): 66–74. *Business Source Complete.* Web. 18 June 2015.

Kaupins, Gundars, et al. "Human Resource Professional Ethical Perceptions of Organizational Online Monitoring." *International Journal of Business and Public Administration* 9.3 (2012): 1–14. Print.

"Workplace Monitoring Laws." *Society for Human Resource Management.* SHRM, n.d. Web. 26 Sept. 2013.

Employee Retention

ABSTRACT

Employee retention is influenced by myriad factors, such as the leadership style of management, individual employees' intrinsic motivation and engagement, burnout, collective morale of staff, the influence of the family, salary, and the desirability of the job's location. Employees who view their corporation or organization as ethically sound are also more likely to be committed to staying there. Transformative leadership and servant leadership are both receiving increasing worldwide research attention as ways of promoting employee engagement, commitment, and retention.

OVERVIEW

Leadership style is increasingly becoming recognized as one of the key alterable factors that influence employee engagement and retention. Leaders are crucial because they influence the motivation and morale of employees. Good leaders can also help prevent burnout by creating a healthy and happy work environment, while making sure not to overwork employees. According to self-determination theory, rich engagement (actively participating in meetings, deeply concentrating at work, and putting forth one's best effort much of the time) is a manifestation of one's motivation for work and learning at work (Froiland, Oros, Smith, and Hircert 2012; Ryan and Deci 2000). Intrinsic motivation (seeing the purpose, joy, and value in one's work) is especially likely to lead to long-term deep engagement, whereas extrinsic motivation (working primarily to gain money or recognition) is more likely to lead shorter-term or superficial levels of engagement (Froiland et al. 2012; Ryan and Deci 2000).

Extrinsic motivation of employees is usually much better for a company than no motivation at all, but purely extrinsically motivated workers (focused primarily on financial success) are more likely to have lower levels of psychological health and make selfish decisions that may be harmful to coworkers or clients (McHoskey 1999; Ryan and Deci 2000). Thus, when leaders focus on elevating engagement and retention by focusing exclusively or heavily on financial incentives (e.g., bonuses for high sales) and consequences (e.g., the imminent threat of being fired for not meeting sales goals), they are risking orienting employees toward lower-quality engagement, more anxiety, and potential Machiavellianism (use of power in a way that benefits the one wielding the power while harming others). In order to promote long-term high-quality engagement and retention, it is important for leaders of companies, schools, and hospitals to promote intrinsic motivation for work, which will, in turn, make it more likely that employees will adopt the vision and values of the company, enjoy working there, and intend to stay with the company for a long time (Eyal and Roth 2011).

FURTHER INSIGHTS

Leadership Styles
There are three leadership styles, all somewhat interconnected, that show promise for increasing intrinsic motivation for work, engagement, and retention. The first is autonomy supportive leadership. Autonomy supportive leaders practice numerous high-quality communication techniques, such as: acknowledging the feelings of employees, taking time to listen to employee perspectives, helping employees to see the underlying purpose in company policies and new initiatives, expressing warmth, focusing on personal growth of each employee rather than comparing them to peers, and conveying a strong appreciation for intrinsic life goals such as helping others rather than aiming exclusively for financial gain (Froiland 2014; Graves and Luciano 2013; Kasser and Ahuvia 2002). Autonomy supportive leaders also refrain from using controlling techniques, such as focusing exclusively on financial rewards or recognition to motivate employees, providing excessive use of pressure, and using unnecessary imperatives such as, "You should have," "You'd better," or controlling questions, such as "Don't you think you should start making more sales?" (Froiland 2014). Autonomy supportive leaders promote intrinsic motivation for work by preparing for fruitful and respectful exchanges with employees, which in turn promotes employees' job satisfaction, sense of vitality, and emotional attachment to the organization (Graves and Luciano 2013).

Servant leaders are also likely to inspire employees toward long-term engagement and retention. Servant leaders model the very characteristics they want employees to internalize, such as a strong desire to help clients, a passion for the organization's vision, deep levels of engagement in pursuing the organization's mission, and a genuine desire to see employees thrive. This palpable desire to help employees and clients thrive sets servant leaders apart from other leaders and is positively associated with employees perceiving that their organizations are ethically sound (Jaramillo, Grisaffe, Chonko, and Roberts 2009).

Servant leadership is both directly and indirectly (via employees perceiving that their companies are ethical) positively related to organizational commitment, which correlates with less turnover intention (Jaramillo et al. 2009). Servant leaders generally promote excellent engagement and retention outcomes, but servant leaders are not always easy to find, because many people attracted to leadership positions in organizations have a stronger desire for financial success than for helping others.

Transformative leaders aim to inspire their employees to catch the vision for their company's mission. Transformative leadership is the opposite of transactional leadership, which focuses on the careful use of rewards and consequences to motivate hard work (Ruggieri 2009). Transactional leadership may be perceived of as controlling by employees and thereby cause decreased intrinsic motivation and inspiration for work, which eventually leads to reduced retention. However, a notable strength of the transactional style is leadership's ability to make expectations and roles very clear, which can actually support autonomous motivation (Graves and Luciano, 2013). However, one can convey clear expectations along with an autonomy supportive, servant, or transformative leadership style.

Transformative leaders have the following key qualities: charisma; a reliance on inspirational motivation; a focus on stimulating the intellect of employees; and willingness to take time to individually consider each employee's development (Ruggieri 2009). The latter three transformative leadership keys are in accordance with the tenets of autonomy supportive leadership. People perceive transformative leaders as being creative, nurturing, embracing change, and full of endurance, whereas transactional leaders are perceived of as having a high need for order, seeking to establish dominance, and lower on originality. People also find tasks more satisfying when working for transformative leaders (Ruggieri 2009).

Personal Employee Considerations
Although leadership style and the individual motivation of employees are crucial factors affecting engagement and retention, there are some factors that are often beyond the control of the company. For instance, mothers in the United States often leave the workforce or quit their full-time job for a few years after having a baby; these decisions to leave the workforce are often exacerbated by family unfriendly policies, such as the lack of paid parental leave, flex time,

and affordable high quality childcare. Furthermore, 16 percent of parents with young children in the United States report that they work excessively and allow their children to watch more television than other parents (Froiland and Davison 2014).

This excessive work and lack of time for supporting their children's development can put them at risk for burnout and affect job turnover. Autonomy supportive and transformational leaders often recognize how much time and effort needs to go into parent involvement and parent-child communication and convey understanding about their employees' perspectives on balancing work and home life (Froiland 2014; Powell, Son, File, and Froiland 2012). Companies can adopt family-friendly policies such as flexible scheduling and providing free or subsidized childcare, but these types of adaptations do not guarantee the prevention of work-family conflict. Work-family conflict occurs when a person feels that his or her motives for meeting family needs and work needs clash.

Neighborhood conditions, such as socioeconomic well-being (safety, percentage of occupied homes, and percentage of neighbors with a college education) and neighborhood social networks can also influence whether workers and their families experience stress at night or support and revitalization (Froiland, Powell, Diamond, and Son 2013; Froiland, Powell, and Diamond 2014). Furthermore, for social service workers and other employees who work in low-socioeconomic-status neighborhoods, the safety of the neighborhoods in which they work affects job satisfaction and thereby retention (e.g., Bell, Mock, and Slutkin 2002). Companies that are in low-socioeconomic-status neighborhoods or know that their employees often live in less affluent neighborhoods would be wise to consider collaborating with community leaders and residents in order to increase safety and social support. In fact, many cities and cutting-edge companies are quite aware that in order to attract and retain highly educated and talented employees, the cities must have dependable and easily accessible public transportation as well as safe and aesthetically pleasant neighborhoods, vibrant arts, beautiful urban green space or access to nearby nature, very good publication education, and well-planned places for recreation (Florida 2010).

Viewpoints

Program evaluators and organizational consultants for companies often focus on either individual or collective job satisfaction when examining risk for nonretention. However, job satisfaction can differ significantly by occupation within a company or unit. For instance, psychiatrists, psychologists, and social workers are more likely than nurses and administrative staff to view their work as a calling, whereas nurses and administrative staff are more likely to view work as a means to obtaining financial resources that help with other areas of life (Baruch, et al. 2013).

The case in which many obstetricians who are often fairly altruistic have been pressured by hospital administrators to perform unnecessary caesarean sections (Gibbons, et al. 2010) is another example in which the motivation of the employees may be stronger or more salubrious than that of the leaders. This difference poses an interesting challenge for companies that wish to inspire their employees to catch a passionate vision for serving patients or customers, because certain positions within companies are more likely to attract employees with a greater passion for their work.

Furthermore, there is the possibility that leading administrators are more motivated by financial gain than the employees who tend to focus on serving or helping others, which may be discouraging to altruistic employees and hinder responsiveness to leadership interventions aimed at developing transformative or servant leaders. If organizational consultants and chief executive officers (CEOs) are aware of this possibility, they may be better equipped to recruit leaders who are inspirational or invest in the rigorous training it would take to help controlling leaders truly become servant, autonomy supportive, or transformational leaders.

Terms & Concepts

Autonomy supportive communication: A way of speaking to others that involves acknowledging their perspective, helping them to see the purpose in what they are doing, and avoiding controlling language.

Burnout: A combination of exhaustion and indifference toward work that employees may experience after long periods of overexertion without enough time, psychological resources, or social support to revitalize.

Incentive: Reward for good behavior, visible engagement, or productivity.

Intrinsic Motivation: Doing something because one enjoys it, sees it as purposeful, or finds that it otherwise meets core psychological needs.

Organizational commitment: An employee's attachment and dedication toward the company, university, hospital, or school.

Servant leadership: A style of leadership marked by beneficence, in which leaders make it clear that they are serving both employees and consumers, in order to make their lives better. As with transformational leadership, there is a focus on empowering employees to become more effective.

Transactional leadership: A common leadership style in which employees are seen as lacking internal motivation, thereby requiring the careful use of rewards and consequences to motivate hard work. Transactional leaders are often skilled in creating clear expectations and roles.

Transformative leadership: A leadership style that focuses on inspiring and empowering employees to reach their potential. It may also focus more on partnering with employees rather than making them feel bossed around.

Turnover intention: An employee's plan to leave a job.

BIBLIOGRAPHY

Baruch, Yehuda, Marnina Swartz, S. Sirkis, et al. "Staff Happiness and Work Satisfaction in a Tertiary Psychiatric Centre." *Occupational Medicine* 63 (2013): 442–44. Web. 22 Mar. 2015.

Bell, Carl C., Lynne Mock, and Gary Slutkin. "The Prevalence of Victimization and Perceptions of Job Neighborhood Safety in a Social Service Agency and the Need for Screening." *Journal of the National Medical Association* 94 (2002): 602. Print.

Eisler, Riane, and Susan Carter. "Transformative Leadership: From Domination to Partnership." *ReVision* 30 (2010): 98–106. Print.

Eyal, Ori, and Guy Roth. "Principals' Leadership and Teachers' Motivation: Self-Determination Theory Analysis." *Journal of Educational Administration* 49 (2011): 256–75. Print.

Florida, Richard. *Who's Your City?: How the Creative Economy Is Making Where to Live the Most Important Decision of Your Life.* New York: Random House.

Froiland, John M. *Inspired Childhood: Parents Raising Motivated, Happy, and Successful Students from Preschool to College.* Seattle, Washington: Amazon.

Froiland, John M., and Mark L. Davison. "Home Literacy, Television Viewing, Fidgeting and ADHD in Young Children." *Educational Psychology.* (2014). Advance online publication.

Froiland, John M., Emily Oros, Liana Smith, and Tyrell Hirchert. "Intrinsic Motivation to Learn: The Nexus between Psychological Health and Academic Success." *Contemporary School Psychology* 16 (2012): 91–100. Print.

Froiland, John M., Douglas R. Powell, and Karen E. Diamon.d. "Relations among Neighborhood Social Networks, Home Literacy Environments, and Children's Expressive Vocabulary in Suburban At-Risk Families." *School Psychology International* 35 (2014): 429–44. Print.

Froiland, John M., Douglas R. Powell, Karen E. Diamond, and Seung-Hee Claire Son. "Neighborhood Socioeconomic Wellbeing, Home Literacy, ad Early Literacy Skills of At-Risk Preschoolers." *Psychology in the Schools* 50 (2013): 755–69. Print.

Gibbons, Luz, Jose M. Belizán, Jeremy Lauer, et al. "The Global Numbers and Costs of Additionally Needed and Unnecessary Caesarean Sections Performed Per Year: Overuse as a Barrier to Universal Coverage." *World Health Report* 30 (2010): 1–31.

Graves, Laura M., Margaret M. Luciano. "Self-Determination at Work: Understanding the Role of Leader-Member Exchange." *Motivation and Emotion* 37 (2013): 518–36. Print.

Jaramillo, Fernando, Douglas B. Grisaffe, Lawrence B. Chonko, and James A. Roberts. "Exaining the Impact of Servant Leadership on Salesperson's Turnover Intention." *Journal of Personal Selling Sales Management* 29 (2009): 351–66. Print.

Powell, Douglas R., Seung-Hee Claire Son, Nancy File, and John M. Froidland. "Changes in Parental Involvement across the Transition from Public School Prekindergarten to First Grade and Children's Academic Outcomes." *The Elementary School Journal* 113 (2012): 276–300. Print.

Ruggieri, Stefano. "Leadership in Virtual Teams: A Comparison of Transformation and Transactional Leaders." *Social Behavior and Personality: An International Journal* 37 (2009): 1017–21. Print.

Ryan, Richard M., and Edward L. Deci. "Self-Determination Theory and the Facilitation of

Intrinsic Motivation, Social Development, and Well-Being." *American Psychologist* 55 (2000): 68–78. Print.

SUGGESTED READING

Arthur, Winfred Jr., Suzanne T. Vallado, Anton J. Vallado, and Dennis Doverspike. "The Use of Person-Organization Fit in Employment Decision Making: An Assessment of Its Criterion-Related Validity." *Journal of Applied Psychology* 91, no. 4 (2006): 786–801. Print.

Austen, Siobhan, Clinton McMurray, Gil Lewin, and Rachel Ong. "Retaining Workers in an Ageing Population: Insights from a Representative Aged and Community Care Organisation." *Australasian Journal on Ageing* 32 (2013): 41–46. Web. 2 Dec. 2014.

Autor, David H., and David Scarborough. "Does Job Testing Harm Minority Workers? Evidence from Retail Establishments." *Quarterly Journal of Economics* 123, no. 1 (2008): 219–77. Print.

Balakrishnan, Lata. "A Study on Retention Strategy's Followed by Education Institutions in Retaining Qualified Employees." *SIES Journal of Management* 10 (2014): 69–80. Print.

Brunetto, Yvonne, and Stephen Teo. "Retention, Burnout and the Future of Nursing." *Journal of Advanced Nursing* 69 (2013): 2772–73. Web. 2 Dec. 2014.

Campbell, Dennis. "Employee Selection as a Control System." *Journal of Accounting Research* 50, no. 4 (2012): 931–66. Print.

Delmestri, Giuseppe, and Peter Walgenbach. "Interference among Conflicting Institutions and Technical-Economic Conditions: The Adoption of the Assessment Center in French, German, Italian, UK, and U.S. Multinational Firms." *International Journal of Human Resource Management* 20, no. 4 (2009): 885–911. Print.

Dessler, Gary. *Human Resource Management.* 10th ed. Upper Saddle River, NJ: Prentice Hall, 2005.

Dwivedi, Sulakshna and Sanjay Kaushik. "Impact of Organizational Culture on Commitment of Employees: An Empirical Study of BPO Section in India." *Vikalpa: The Journal for Decision Makers* 39 (2014): 77–92. Web. 2 Dec. 2014.

Dwoskin, Linda B., Mellissa Squire, and Jane E. Patullo. "Welcome Aboard! How to Hire the Right Way." *Employee Relations Law Journal* 38, no. 4 (2013): 28–63. Print.

Ekuma, Kelechi. "The Importance of Predictive and Face Validity in Employee Selection and Ways of Maximizing Them: An Assessment of Three Selection Methods." *International Journal of Business & Management* 7, no. 22 (2012): 115–22. Print.

Garcia, Maria F., Richard A. Posthuma, and Adrienne Colella. "Fit Perceptions in the Employment Interview: The Role of Similarity, Liking, and Expectations." *Journal of Occupational and Organizational Psychology* 81, no. 2 (2008): 173–89. Print.

Gardiner, Maria, Hugh Kearns, and Marika Tiggemann. "Effectiveness of Cognitive Behavioural Coaching in Improving the Wellbeing and Retention of Rural General Practitioners." *The Australian Journal of Rural Health* 21 (2013): 183–89. Web. 2 Dec. 2014.

Hariharan, Selena. "Physician Recruitment and Retention: A Physician's Perspective." *Physician Executive* 40 (2014): 44–48. Web. 2 Dec. 2014.

Hunt, Eleanor. "An HR Conundrum: Talent Attraction and Retention Abroad." *Baylor Business Revieww* 32 (2014): 38–43. Web. 2 Dec. 2014.

Idris, Aida. "Flexible Working as an Employee Retention Strategy in Developing Countries." *Journal of Management Research* 14 (2014): 71–86. Web. 2 Dec. 2014.

Ito, Aki. "Hiring in the Age of Big Data." *Bloomberg Businessweek* (2013): 40–41. Print.

Landy, Frank J., and Jeffrey M. Conte. *Work in the 21st Century: An Introduction to Industrial and Organizational Psychology.* Boston: McGraw-Hill, 2004.

Luminta, Popa. "The Assessment Center, a New 'Fashion' in Personal Selection." *Annals of the University of Oradea, Economic Science Series* 18, no. 4 (2009): 439–441. Print.

Malakate, Ann, Constantine Andriopoulos, and Manto Gotsi. "Assessing Job Candidates' Creativity: Propositions and Future Research Directions." *Creativity and Innovation Management* 17, no. 3 (2007): 307–16. Print.

Mignonac, Karim, and Nathalie Richebé. "No Strings Attached? How Attribution of Disinterested Support Affects Employee Retention." *Human Resource Management Journal* 23 (2013): 72–90. Web. 2 Dec. 2014.

Munchinsky, Paul M. *Psychology Applied to Work: An Introduction to Industrial and Organizational Psychology.* 7th ed. Belmont, CA: Wadsworth/Thomson Learning, 2003.

Oliphant, Gary C., Katherine Hansen, and Becky J. Oliphant. "A Review of a Telephone-Administered Behavior-Based Interview Technique." *Business Communication Quarterly* 71, no. 3 (2008): 383–86. Print.

Paillé, Pascale. "Organizational Citizenship Behaviour and Employee Retention: How Important Are Turnover Cognitions? *International Journal of Human Resource Management* 24 (2013): 768–90. Web. 2 Dec. 2014.

Piotrowski, Chris, and T. Armstrong. "Current Recruitment and Selection Practices: A National Survey of Fortune 1000 Firms." *North American Journal of Psychology* 8, no. 3 (2006): 489–96. Print.

Samson, S.M. "Attrition Issues and Retention Challenges of Employees." *Asia Pacific Journal of Research in Business Management* 4 (2013): 1. Web. 2 Dec. 2014.

Scroggins, Wesley A., Steven L. Thomas, and Jerry A. Morris. "Psychology Testing in Personnel Selection, Part I: A Century of Psychological Testing." *Public Personnel Management* 37, no. 1 (2008): 99–109. Print.

Scroggins, Wesley A., Steven L. Thomas, and Jerry A. Morris. "Psychology Testing in Personnel Selection, Part III: A Century of Psychological Testing." *Public Personnel Management* 38, no. 1 (2009): 67–77. Print.

Singh, B., and T.T. Selvarajan. "Is It Spillover or Compensation? Effects of Community and Organizatinoal Diversity Climates on Race Differentiated Employee Intent to Stay." *Journal of Business Ethics* 115 (2013): 259–69. Web. 2 Dec. 2014.

Tamir, Eran, and Sally A. Lesik. "Jewish Day School Teachers: Career Commitments in the 21st Century." *Journal of Jewish Education* 79 (2013): 131–56. Web. 2 Dec. 2014.

Thornton, George C., and Diana E. Krause. "Selection versus Development Assessment Centers: An International Survey of Design, Execution, and Evaluation." *International Journal of Human Resource Management* 20, no. 2 (2009): 478–98. Print.

Tillott, Sarah J., Ken Walsh, and Lorna Moxham. "Encouraging Engagement at Work to Improve Retention." *Nursing Management-UK* 19 (2013): 27–31. Web. 2 Dec. 2014.

Topor, David, Stephen Colarelli, and Kyunghee Han. Influences of Traits and Assessment Methods on Human Resource Practitioners' Evaluations of Job Applicants." *Journal of Business and Psychology* 21, no. 3 (2007): 361–76. Print.

Van Iddekinge, Chad H., and Robert E. Ployhart. "Developments in the Criterion-Related Validation of Selection Procedures: A Critical Review and Recommendation for Practice." *Personnel Psychology* 61, no. 4 (2008): 871–925. Print.

Wermeling, Linda, Vanessa Hunn, and Tara McLendon. "Social Work Education's Effect on Retention." *Journal of Social Work Education* 49 (2013): 222–34. Web. 2 Dec. 2014.

Wilson, J. "Time to Recruit Talent." *Journal of Accountancy* 215 (2013): 20. Web. 2 Dec. 2014.

John Mark Froiland, Ph.D.

Employee Value Proposition

ABSTRACT

The employee value proposition includes all of the benefits, both tangible and intangible, that an organization's employees receive in exchange for offering the employer their time, effort, and expertise. The employee value proposition includes traditional forms of compensation, such as employee salaries, but it also extends much further to include any kind of programs or policies in place at the organization that tend to improve the experience of those who work there.

OVERVIEW

In most sectors of the economy, the competition for jobs is fierce. Job seekers who are able to find employment are happy just to receive a salary, and most other benefits derived from the position are not major considerations. In some fields, however, profits are high and employers are anxious to attract the most talented individuals in order to benefit from their expertise and acquire an advantage over their competition; examples include the pharmaceutical industry, technology firms, doctors, and lawyers. In these settings, it takes more than just a high salary to entice the best and brightest. Employers find that instead they must consider the whole employee value proposition (EVP), a concept that encompasses everything that employees find valuable about working at an organization, from healthcare benefits and retirement plans to perquisites such as on site dry cleaning and open bars. Employee value propositions even include the organizational and office cultures, with many employees preferring more open and less hierarchical structures (Verbeke 2008).

Organizations that put effort into their employee value proposition often attract attention because building an employee value proposition is employee-centric, while most companies in the modern world are employer-centric. Employer-centric organizations are ones in which the leadership places the needs of the organization first, and the needs and wants of customers and employees second. An example would be a company that lays off part of its workforce in order to reduce the liabilities on its balance sheet, making the company appear more profitable and thereby pleasing shareholders and potential investors, which in turn increases the company's value (Storey 2005). In contrast, an employee-centric company would put its efforts into creating the most attractive work experience possible, in order to lure top talent to the organization; these talented individuals would then give their utmost to the organization in the form of creativity, hard work, and dedication, ultimately improving the quality of the organization and its products and services, and thereby benefiting the entire organization and those whose lives it touches. Both approaches seek to accomplish the same overall goals of growth and improvement, but they differ in how they think this goal can best be accomplished (Ellwood 2014).

Viewpoints
Employers who want to take control of their employee value proposition, as opposed to simply living with the "default" employee value proposition that an organization develops unintentionally and which may not present the image of the organization that the employer desires, typically find that their first step is to conduct research. Just as a company would not begin producing a product before finding out if the market has any demand for that product, smart companies develop their employee value propositions by first asking a few basic questions to find out what current employees like and dislike about the company, what the company's competitors are doing to build their own employee value proposition, and what types of elements are valued by the people in the company's talent pool, that is, what is important to the people the company wants to hire (Sison 2015).

This information is gathered in a variety of ways. Some of it can be collected by reviewing the literature on human resource development within the relevant field, but more detailed and more current data usually is obtained by distributing surveys to current and prospective employees, holding focus groups with internal and external constituents in order to ask open-ended questions about their likes, dislikes, and priorities, and then coding and organizing all of this data for later analysis. Once the information has been reviewed, the organization can then begin to construct a draft employee value proposition based on the preferences revealed in the data collection phase of the project.

For example, if surveys had indicated that a high percentage of the talent pool targeted by the company were pet owners, then the company likely would have used this information in its focus groups to find out more about how the respondents feel about their pets; in the employee value proposition drafting stage, this information could then be used to include services designed to appeal to pet owners, such as having a pet-sitting service and pet grooming facility located in the workplace for the convenience of employees.

It is important to keep in mind that the ultimate reason that employers go through this process is to benefit the organization (Pellet 2009). Benefitting the employees by offering them services they value is essentially a means to the larger end of recruiting and retaining top talent, who will then help the organization to perform at a higher level than its competitors, increasing profitability and market share.

As some observers have noted, the drive to expand services for employees can occasionally result in an "employee value proposition arms race." This situation where a relatively small number of employers are intensely competing with one another for a few brilliant hires has occurred in Silicon Valley during the so-called Dot Com Boom of the late 1990s. As each firm implemented a new service to build its employee value proposition, its competitors immediately matched that service with their own, while adding still more services. If one company installed a coffee bar (free for employees) in its offices, then its competitors could be relied upon to do the same before too much time passed, and go them one better by adding a frozen yogurt station as well (Wilson 2015).

One objection to the idea of employee value proposition that is often raised is that the premise upon which it is established is faulty, namely, that employees care about anything other than how much they earn. These critics assert that salary is paramount, it always has been, and it always will be, for the simple reason that if an employee is paid enough, then that employee will simply be able to purchase whatever goods and services might be offered through an employee value proposition program. In the example above, they suggest, it would be much more cost effective to simply pay the company's top performers enough so that they could buy their own coffee and frozen yogurt, rather than the company having to supply it for everyone at the firm.

Employee value proposition critics suggest that rather than having a meaningful impact on employee recruitment and retention, employee value propositions should be seen as part marketing gimmick (for prospective hires) and part brainwashing tool (for current employees). They also suggest that employee value proposition perquisites have more to do with corporate showmanship than with employee satisfaction, because they sometimes appear to be little more than means by which large companies can show the rest of the world how successful they are. The reality of the modern economy, critics say, is such that the bottom line of salary is all that anyone really considers when deciding to accept a position or remain in one, because salary is what everything else in a person's life depends on—home, family, car, recreation, travel, and so forth (Trost 2014).

Employee value proposition skeptics point to environments such as San Francisco, where housing is so expensive that thousands of employees are forced to commute for hours each day because they cannot afford to live closer to work; for people in this situation, the employee value proposition is little more than a theoretical concept, because if the salary is not adequate for them to afford a place to live within driving distance, then no amount of gourmet lunches will make it possible for them to work there.

Employee value proposition supporters respond to such critiques in a variety of ways. It is true that an employee value proposition has the greatest effect among employees for whom salary is not the prevailing concern. Typically these are highly skilled professionals who possess talents that are rare or even unique, and who are in such demand that they have multiple job offers to consider at any point in time, any one of which would provide a salary more than adequate for their needs. Naturally, for a person in this situation, factors other than salary would take on additional importance, and could conceivably become decisive in a person's employment decisions. One would select a position with an employer providing the greatest number of value enhancing programs based on one's own preferences, and salary would have less influence on the final determination. These options can include flexible work schedules, on-site lifestyle services, and intangible benefits such as a relaxed and collaborative office culture (Schwartz et al. 2011)

Employee value proposition proponents assert that these benefits are not solely of value to the elite—they also contribute to the quality of life of every other employee and, over the long term, tend to encourage people to join the company and stay there. Seen in this way, the employee value proposition is not always a feature-rich benefits package that is the make or break item in every employee's compensation package (or "people deal"); instead, it is a subtle but substantial part of the organization's atmosphere that makes employees feel that they are valued as members of a community of shared values, rather than just another number in the payroll system. The best way to build this sense of community, according to human resources experts, is to begin by asking questions that reveal the organization's fundamental character and priorities. A key question of this sort is to hypothesize what qualities the organization has that would attract and retain talented people, if the organization was for some reason not able to pay salaries on par with the market. Asking this question forces members of the organization to think about the kind of workplace they have collectively brought into being, whether intentionally or unintentionally, and then to consider whether it is a place that people want to come to every day. Whatever the answer to this question, the organization can benefit from the inquiry. If the organization is a place that people are happy, then the inquiry will produce a list of reasons why that is the case, and these can then be compiled into a formal employee value proposition that may be used to recruit new employees. If the answers to the question reveal that people in the organization do not find a great deal to value apart from their paychecks, then ideally this would spur the organization's leaders to reconsider the direction the firm is heading in (Heneman, Judge, and Kammeyer-Mueller 2012).

Indeed, one of the less often discussed benefits of developing an intentional employee value propositions has nothing to do with recruiting new employees. The organizational self-study that employee value proposition development requires can also lead to a reinvigoration of the commitment of existing employees to the group. This excitement happens because in order to develop an employee value proposition, an organization must be able to succinctly state its real purpose for existing, and the kind of place the organization is to work in. Organizations need to go through this type of self-reflection periodically due partially to the natural turnover that causes some people to depart the organization and others to join it. Those who leave take some of the organization's collective knowledge with them, and those who arrive need to learn the history of the organization, even as they bring in fresh ideas and experience.

Organizations do not exist in a vacuum—their environment is continuously changing, and over time this dynamic requires the organization to realign itself with its surroundings. Going through the process of developing an employee value proposition can be an excellent way of adapting. The most challenging aspect can be to find and retain leaders for the organization who have the proper understanding of the nature of the employee value proposition and its importance to an employee-centric organization.

All too often, leaders either fail to appreciate the potential of an employee-centric attitude, or they reject this attitude in favor of a more pragmatic, and/or cynical, marketing orientation. When this thinking happens, the employee value proposition loses its real power and can become little more than an elaborate effort at corporate communications. This short-term view concentrates on improving the organization's situation within a time frame of months or years, rather than the multiyear outlook that is the focus of an authentic employee value proposition undertaking. Ironically, such is the volatility of the contemporary economy that those organizations that do not choose to aim for the long term will more than likely not be around long enough to eventually see the error of their ways (Benz 2014).

BIBLIOGRAPHY

Benz, Jennifer. "Will Purpose Rebalance the Employee Value Proposition?" *People & Strategy* 37, no. 2 (2014): 10–11. Web. 3 Jan. 2016.

Coleman, Alison. "Anatomy of a Present-Day Employee Value Proposition." *Employee Benefits* 1 (2014)> Web. 3 Jan. 2016.

Ellwood, Iain. *Marketing for Growth: The Role of Marketers in Driving Revenues and Profits.* New York: PublicAffairs, 2014.

Heneman, Herbert G., Timothy Judge, and John D. Kammeyer-Mueller. *Staffing Organizations.* Middleton, WI: Mendota House, 2012.

Mandal, Akhilesh, and Sandeep K. Krishnan." Creating a Compelling Employee Value Proposition." *Human Capital* (2013): 38–42. Web. 3 Jan. 2016.

McLean-Conner, Penni. "Employee Value Propositions: A Foundation in Building a Competitive Work Force." *Electric Light & Power* 93, no. 1 (2015): 18–19. Web. 3 Jan. 2016.

Pellet, L. (2009). The cultural fit factor: Creating an employment brand that attracts, retains, and repels the right employees. Alexandria, Va: Society for Human Resource Management.

Pellet, Lizz. *The Cultural Fit Factor: Creating an Employment Brand That Attracts, Retains, and Repels the Right Employees.* Alexandria, VA: Society for Human Resource Management, 2009.

Schwartz, Tony, Jean Gomes, and Catherine McCarthy[o1]. *Be Excellent at Anything: The Four Keys to Transforming the Way We Work and Live.* New York: Free Press, 2011.

Sison, Alejo José. *Happiness and Virtue Ethics in Business: The Ultimate Value Proposition.* Cambridge, UK: Cambridge University Press, 2015.

Storey, John. *Adding Value through Information and Consultation.* Basingstoke, UK: Palgrave Macmillan, 2005.
Trost, Armin. *Talent Relationship Management: Competitive Recruiting Strategies in Times of Talent Shortage.* New York: Springer, 2014.
Verbeke, Alain. *Growing the Virtual Workplace: The Integrative Value Proposition for Telework.* Cheltenham, UK: Edward Elgar, 2008.
Wilson, Clive. *Designing the Purposeful Organization: How to Inspire Business Performance Beyond Boundaries.* Philadelphia: Kogan Page, 2015.

SUGGESTED READING
Barton, Tynan. "Creating an Employee Value Proposition to Win the War for Talent." *Employee Benefits* 10 (2014). Web. 3 Jan. 2016.
Barton, Tynan. "Capital One Builds Enticing Employee Value Proposition." *Employee Benefits* 8 (2014). Web. 3 Jan. 2016.
"We've Condensed Our Values into Something We Can Really Use." *People Management* (2015). Web. 3 Jan. 2016.

Scott Zimmer, J.D.

EMPLOYEE WELL-BEING AND ORGANIZATIONAL SUPPORT

ABSTRACT

Growing numbers of organizations believe that implementing well-being programs increases their productivity and public image. A firm's success is not based solely on its profits and productivity, but also on its capacity to attract, motivate, develop, and retain its workers. Therefore, programs designed to increase well-being in the workplace have steadily expanded and gained popularity, and, in many corporations, have become an established part of its corporate social responsibility (CSR) program. An important, but often neglected part of organizational well-being, is its social well-being component.

OVERVIEW

Well-being refers to a series of conscious efforts to make intelligent health decisions, meant to benefit an individual–or a community's—mental, physical, and social needs. Organizational well-being, then, are programs and practices implemented by firms to ensure that the organization provides employees with a workplace that leads to a safe, healthy, and happy environment.

Modern organizations, both public and private, find it important to have a healthy and satisfied workforce. Performance and the delivery of a high-quality product or service have been proven to correlate directly with employee well-being. It also correlates with behaviors that affect morale in the organization, such as commitment and absenteeism. In fact, according to a wide variety of studies, healthy sense of employee well-being in the organization is related to a wide variety of positive outcomes, such as satisfaction, feelings of happiness, and productivity. When factors exist that lower employee well-being and morale, workers report feelings of stress, work overload, and burnout. It is not surprising, then, that workers would be more prone to falling sick and being absent.

As organizations became aware of these facts, many have included policies of workplace well-being under their corporate social responsibility programs. Corporate social responsibility refers to a firm's strategies of taking responsibility for its impact on the public good, that is, the environment and communities that surround them. The idea behind corporate social responsibility is involving businesses in going beyond what is expected or required of them by law and government regulations. Corporate social responsibility also transcends merely ameliorating or reducing any negative impact it may have on the world around it.

The concept of corporate social responsibility first appeared in the United States in the late 1950s, as an organizational trend aimed at making firms, internally and externally, more sound and sustainable. This implied a vision of an organization as an entity that lived not only as a self-sustained profit-making firm, but also as an entity that lived socially and environmentally. In the years after World War II, Asian business experts began to implement practices that included the development of their workers.

A workstation with ergonomic keyboards (photo courtesy of Mikael Altemark)

As Japanese firms became internationally successful, organizations worldwide began to take note of the inclusive workplace practices.

In time, American firms discovered that to implement successful corporate social responsibility programs, they needed to consider the firm's relationship with its employees. Since corporate social responsibility includes extending beyond the requirements of regulations and norms, it includes relationships with employees. Corporate social responsibility includes, then, efforts to advance employees' health and personal and career development beyond what is required of work contracts between organizations and its workers. In other words, corporations started focusing on engaging in actions that made people feel a valued part of the firm.

Organizations that invest in the development of their workers, not only for workplace skills but also their physical and psychological health, have been shown to significantly increase their productivity. A firm oriented toward its workers offers quality of life improvements, including not only the employees' workplace environment, but also their life beyond the workplace, especially their family life. For example, individuals may face conflict in their family life or situations that impact their family life, such as addiction or mental health problems. When employees suffer personal strife outside of the workplace, it may affect their workplace performance in negative ways, such as increasing absenteeism, lowering motivation and performance, and ultimately termination. Therefore, many firms offer psychology or counseling services for workers and their families, not only to help them cope, but also to ensure that valuable employees stay with the firm.

Another issue that may impact the workplace negatively is intolerance, and its attendant behaviors of harassment and bullying. Harassment and bullying refers to any uninvited and unwanted behavior that creates feelings of hostility in the workplace, and makes others feel offended, intimidated, humiliated or persecuted. Such behaviors may be single or group behaviors, overt or covert. In fact, it may even occur without management's awareness and include a wide variety of actions, such as spreading rumors, unwanted physical contact, undermining behaviors, and unwarranted exclusion.

According to the U.S. Equal Employment Opportunity Commission, harassment becomes unlawful under several conditions, such as when it is severe or constant enough that people find it hostile, intimidating, or abusive. Discrimination and harassment are hostile or aggressive behaviors based on race or ethnicity, religion, gender, age, disability, and genetic information. Harassment is naturally unwelcome and disruptive and may take the form of gestures, words, or actions. Further, harassers may be supervisors, coworkers, and even clients.

Discriminatory behavior is inherently hostile in that it is uninvited and causes personal discomfort, although it may take the form of seemingly friendly actions. In this case, it is called "microaggression." Microaggressions may be unintentionally hurtful or insulting and generally result from stereotypical assumptions, violations of personal boundaries, and exploitation of social or workplace power dynamics. A hostile work environment not only impacts its victims negatively but also lowers overall workplace morale. Therefore, it is important for a firm to ensure that it informs and educates all employees on all elements that may be considered workplace discrimination, harassment, and bullying.

Workplace intolerance and discriminatory behaviors lead to unhappiness in the workplace and, in consequence, affect company morale and performance. Furthermore, these behaviors are illicit and should be dealt with as soon as they occur. Leading organizational experts suggest that in order to prevent these behaviors before they occur, firms should have in place a set of policies and procedures that help identify intolerance; pertinent strategies, which may include training workshops on tolerance,

143

awareness, and antidiscriminatory legislation; and action plans to deal with these events as they arise. The latter should include a confidential channel of communication in which employees feel safe in filing discrimination or bullying complaints without becoming a target of retaliation.

Finally, a company health and well-being promotion program may prove very beneficial to the firm and its employees. In 2017, The World Health Organization (WHO) defined workplace health promotion as the shared efforts of a firm with its employees to improve the health and well-being of people in the workplace. This area includes encouraging the development of personal and professional skills. Health promotion in the workplace should include elements that are not covered in legislation, such as workplace safety. Health promotion should include family well-being and practices that lead to a healthy lifestyle.

In short, a firm reaps the benefits of having healthy and happy employees. A thoughtful and inclusive well-being program decreases stress and absenteeism, while increasing workers' morale and productivity. Making workers feel valued and safe leads them—and the firm—to make intelligent decisions. Moreover, most well-being programs are relatively inexpensive to implement, whereas the negative outcomes from stress, hostility, discomfort, and fatigue in the workplace are likely to generate long-term difficulties and high costs. Problems stemming from low levels of well-being may lead a firm to gain a negative reputation, which, in turn, may affect its brand reputation and ability to attract and retain quality talent.

APPLICATIONS

Firms implement well-being programs to improve the physical and mental health of their workers. These programs may include training workshops or educational seminars, counseling, clinics, childcare, healthy lifestyle education, recreation, and many others. Some firms offer well-being programs on company premises, while others may hire third party companies to provide them. They may cover the full costs as part of a benefits package or, in some cases, employees cover part of the cost.

Experts offer some basic recommendations for implementing company well-being programs to ensure that workers feel valued by the firm and develop feelings of ownership and loyalty. According to *Business Insider's* 2016 ranking of the best 50 companies to work for in the United States, the companies that report the highest level of worker satisfaction are precisely those that most invest in their workers' well-being. Companies with the highest reported level of employee well-being include American Express, Google, and Facebook, all organizations where company leaders realized that workers' creativity and innovation increased proportionally with their rate of workplace satisfaction.

Other recommendations provided by firms with high rates of employee satisfaction include the following:

- **Maternity and paternity leave.** Google famously offers five months parental leave with a full salary for new mothers and fathers.
- **Ergonomic workstations and furniture.** Poor posture may cause strain to back, neck and wrists, leading to chronic health problems and decreased productivity. Ergonomic design optimizes products and spaces for best workplace use.
- **Healthy snacks.** Many clinical studies have shown that what people eat affects their well-being and productivity. Healthy snacks may increase nutrition and provide a hungry worker with a clearer mind and more long-term energy. Firms that provide healthy snacks for employees help them improve their performance and health.
- **Employees' ability to work from home.** Some corporations allow 30 to 50 percent of their employees to work from home if they prefer to do so.
- **Meaningful work.** Beyond earning a salary, employees work best when they believe they are engaged in meaningful work that somehow contributes to society.
- **Pets on site.** More and more companies worldwide are adopting pet-friendly policies. The presence of animals reduces stress in a variety of organizations.
- **Decent pay.** People who earn competitive salaries feel rewarded and are unlikely to want to leave.
- **Pampering.** Companies such as Facebook offer employees the services of doctors and chiropractors as well as generous vacations. Others offer playrooms and other recreational opportunities.
- **Workplace nurseries and daycare.** More companies are providing workers with diverse forms of

on-site childcare. Workplace daycare is correlated with a marked decrease in workplace absenteeism by parents facing childcare challenges.

Not all firms are able to follow these suggestions or need to do so. However, all workplaces may come up with workable ideas of their own. The final purpose is to work toward providing a happy and healthy environment for workers as a way of keeping them motivated and of incentivizing their productivity.

Moreover, in addition to treating employees well, intelligent management invests in ensuring that a worker is a good fit for the job. Many studies have found that the fit between worker and work impacts performance and outcomes. An organization's well-being strategy, then, should include ways to provide an appropriate environment and matching work tasks with an employee's personal skills and inclinations. Employees who feel out of place or unproductive will soon become frustrated and discontent.

Issues

Organizations often focus on employees' physical well-being by investing in occupational safety, an ergonomic environment, and promoting healthy lifestyles programs. These may include allowing spaces and time for exercise, healthy food options and pleasant eating areas, sports programs, gym memberships, and clinics and plans for specific health problems. However, while all the former are good organizational practices, firms often neglect the social aspect of well-being.

Social well-being is an important factor of organizational well-being and can have a profound impact on the general sense of well-being in a workplace. To a large extent, social well-being involves a healthy balance between work life and personal life, as well as positive interactions in the workplace and outside of it. Firms frequently underestimate the impact that social interactions have on an employee's sense of self and satisfaction with life.

Studies amply demonstrate that workers that are ranked as the highest producers tend to be those who also report an excellent sense of social well-being. Therefore, it behooves firms to create environments that promote social interactions in ways that also stimulate productivity. These may include the creation of environments appropriate to interaction—open spaces, spaces for informal interaction, playrooms—or events that promote these interactions, such as potlucks, friendly intraoffice competitions, and yoga classes.

Social well-being includes emotional and psychological well-being. Individuals need to feel that, as chaotic as the world may be, they are in control of their own life and goals which includes developing a sense of acceptance and belonging to his or her different environments, including their workplace. People may be extraordinarily healthy in body, but if they do not enjoy emotional well-being, they tend to report low levels of well-being in general. Moreover, experts stress the importance of workers feeling a sense of belonging, so that firms should promote a positive organizational culture and optimal social conditions for employees. For this, it is important to bear in mind that workers who feel excluded or harassed will develop negative feelings in the workplace, likely to impact directly their psyche and their work.

CONCLUSION

Organizational wellness impacts firms positively, by improving creativity and productivity. Thus, employee well-being programs also make good business sense. The best wellness program is one in which workers actively choose to participate in a healthier lifestyle, rather than feel compelled to it, and in which its positive effects transcend the workplace. It is important to remember that different things motivate people, so that an appropriate wellness program is that which offers a variety of options for collaboration and participation.

BIBLIOGRAPHY

Ahmed, Ezas, Peter Reaburn, Ataus Samad, and Heather Davis. "Towards an Understanding of the Effect of Leadership on Employee Wellbeing and Organizational Outcomes in Australian Universities." *Journal of Developing Areas* 49, no. 6 (2015): 441–48. Print.

Avci, Nilgün. "The Relationship between Coworker Supports, Quality of Work Life and Wellbeing: An Empirical Study of Hotel Employees." *International Journal of Management Economics & Business / Uluslararasi Yönetim Iktisat Ve Isletme Dergisi*, 13, no. 3 (2017): 577–89. Print.

"Eyecare Enhances Employees' Wellbeing and Productivity." *Management Services* 60, no. 1 (2016): 15. Print.

Kaye, John. "Take a Bespoke Approach to Employee Wellbeing." *Occupational Health* 69, no. 5 (2017). Print.

Krainz, K. Dezmar. "Enhancing Wellbeing of Employees through Corporate Social Responsibility Context." *Megatrend Review* 12, no. 2 (2015): 137–54. Print.

Shahid, Ahmad U., Rizwan Q. Danish, Afzal A. Humayon, et al. "The Impact of High Quality Relationship on Innovative Work Behavior of Employees through Psychological Wellbeing: A Case of Pharmaceutical Sector in Pakistan." *Journal of Comparative International Management* 19, no. 1 (2016): 95–119. Print.

Tuisku, Katinka, L. Pulkki-Råback, and Marianna Virtanen. "Cultural Events Provided by Employer and Occupational Wellbeing of Employees: A Cross-Sectional Study among Hospital Nurses." *Work* 55, no. 1 (2016): 93–100. Print.

van Loon, Nina M., Wouter Vandenabeele, and Peter Leisink. "On the Bright and Dark Side of Public Service Motivation: The Relationship between PSM and Employee Wellbeing." *Public Money & Management* 35, no. 5 (2015): 349–56. Print.

SUGGESTED READING

Barrett, Richard. *The Values-Driven Organization: Cultural Health and Employee Well-Being as a Pathway to Sustainable Performance.* London, UK: Routledge, 2017.

Botezat, Alina. "Austerity Plan Announcements and the Impact on the Employees' Wellbeing." *Journal of Economic Psychology* 63 (2017): 1–16. Print.

Boyd, Neil M., and Branda Nowell. "Testing a Theory of Sense of Community and Community Responsibility in Organizations: An Empirical Assessment of Predictive Capacity on Employee Well-Being and Organizational Citizenship." *Journal of Community Psychology* 45, no. 2 (2017): 210–29. Web. 1 Jan. 2018.

Caesens, Gaetane, Florence Stinglhamber, Stephanie Demoulin, and Matthias De Wilde. "Perceived Organizational Support and Employees' Well-Being: The Mediating Role of Organizational Dehumanization." *European Journal of Work & Organizational Psychology* 26, no. 4 (2017): 527–40. Web. 1 Jan. 2018.

Moen, Phyllis, Erin L. Kelly, Wen Lee, et al. "Does a Flexibility/Support Organizational Initiative Improve High-Tech Employees' Well-Being? Evidence from the Work, Family, and Health Network." *American Sociological Review* 81, no. 1 (2016): 134–64. Web. 1 Jan. 2018.

Trudy M. Mercadal, Ph.D.

ETHICAL RESPONSIBILITIES OF BUSINESS

ABSTRACT

This article explores the ethical responsibilities of business. Business ethics became a hot-button issue in the wake of the corporate scandals that were exposed in the late 1990s through the early 2000s. Businesses do not exist in a vacuum; they play a vital role in sustaining economic growth, providing jobs, giving employees access to health care, and more—businesses can and do exist for the betterment of our society. However, people run businesses, and human nature sometimes manifests itself in unethical conduct. The way toward maintaining ethical business standards is by adhering to the basic moral codes of trustworthiness, respect, responsibility, fairness, caring, and citizenship and examining the moral character of business people, employees, and consumers and. In short, the ethical responsibility of business is to be a good corporate citizen, and adhering to moral codes is a responsibility that we all share.

OVERVIEW

Whether it was fraudulent accounting practices of publicly traded companies, front running stocks and investments by mutual funds, raiding pension funds by businesses heading for bankruptcy, manipulative sales and lending practices by multinational banks, or the predatory lending practices of consumer finance companies, recent decades have seen an

Sen. Paul Sarbanes, left, and Rep. Michael G. Oxley, co-sponsors of the Sarbanes-Oxley Act

increase in the exposure of corporate malfeasance. These episodes are not limited to a particular industry, and a similar strain runs through all of these events: a lack of business ethics. However, there is a growing business ethics movement that has ushered in increased regulatory scrutiny by state and federal government agencies, class action lawsuits, and the initiatives of consumer advocates and not-for-profit organizations dedicated to the social responsibility of business.

Business ethics may seem like an ambiguous or even counterintuitive term. After all, the primary objective and responsibility of any business is to make and maximize profits. There are times, however, when the means employed to make profits conflict with a society's moral and legal codes. Essentially, business ethics are rules geared toward establishing and maintaining trustworthiness in a business or commercial setting. While it may be hard to identify, there is a growing business ethics movement in the wake of the recent business scandals. Moreover, state and federal regulatory agencies have stepped up their monitoring activities across multiple lines of business.

Increasing Regulations and Legal Action

For example, the accounting scandals that ultimately led to the much-publicized demise of Enron (and the loss of thousands of jobs as well as the retirement funds of many former employees) and the prosecution of Tyco's former chief executive eventually prompted the US Congress to enact the 2002 Sarbanes-Oxley Act. In 2004, the Financial Services Agency of Japan ordered a multinational bank to close one of its foreign private banking divisions after an investigation revealed manipulative sales and lending practices. Later, a major New York–based commercial banking institution was fined for laundering billions of dollars for criminal enterprises emanating from Russia, and this punishment to the bank's eventual acquisition by a larger banking entity. At the state level, following the subprime mortgage crisis of 2007 and 2008, a number of regulatory agencies responsible for overseeing consumer loans and mortgage lending were empowered by state legislatures to crack down on predatory lending practices. Quite a few consumer finance companies and multistate mortgage banks were held accountable for charging excessive points and fees for unsecured consumer loans as well as loans collateralized by residential dwellings.

Not only have the actions by regulatory agencies affected business practices but also regulatory scrutiny has opened the door to class action lawsuits. Whether these were brought by firms representing shareholders who claim they were defrauded by accounting practices that did not truly represent the value of a company, or other actions on behalf of consumers who were harmed by so-called predatory lending practices of consumer finance companies, such lawsuits have resulted in multi-million-dollar settlements and these, in turn, have had a significant impact on profits. However, in a controversial practice, several businesses adopted arbitration clauses in the 2010s that forced customers to settle disputes with the company though arbitration, preventing customers from joining others in a class action lawsuit. In some cases, regulatory oversight and legal actions were prompted by the initiatives of consumer advocates and not-for-profit organizations. In short, concerned citizens at the grassroots level are paying close attention to how companies operate and holding them accountable for their actions.

Corporate Ethics and Social Responsibility

While the Enron and Tyco scandals were front-page news, these prosecutions have not been the norm. At times, the potential financial benefit from behavior that is short of ethical may seem to be worth the risk for some decision makers. However, in the long run, good ethics is good for business, as a company's professional reputation can have a positive impact on its relationships with customers and vendors and enable it to develop strategic alliances with other similar businesses. Professional reputation is a matter of perception, and society's perceptions closely link business performance to a company's social, environmental, and ethical conduct. Consumers have become increasingly concerned that businesses should be responsible not only for ensuring that they provide quality products but also for treating employees fairly. In light of the increased regulatory scrutiny, legal actions, and consumer advocacy, corporate social responsibility has become a growing concern for many business entities.

Compliance Procedures
To enhance corporate social responsibility, companies are increasingly concerned that they have efficient and effective compliance procedures to ensure that their business practices adhere to the regulatory guidelines of their particular industry. Having a clearly defined compliance program enables a company to integrate compliance into its business model. By doing so, the company has awareness of the potential regulatory issues that can arise in the event of an audit by a regulatory agency. This knowledge can empower an organization to take proactive corrective steps prior to the commencement of an adverse regulatory action. Moreover, having effective compliance systems in place will create positive working relationships with regulatory agencies.

The goal of regulatory agencies is not to be an impediment to business. After all, if their goal were merely to put companies out of business, there would be no business to regulate and no need for regulatory agencies. Thus, companies and governmental agencies must have a symbiotic relationship. By recognizing the nature of this relationship, business people understand both that there is no need for an adversarial posture with the agency that regulates an industry and that establishing harmonious relationships with regulators will be good for business in the long run.

Enforcing an Ethical Culture and Compliance
The challenge for many business enterprises goes beyond legal and compliance initiatives. Business owners and executives need to raise the bar and consider whether their business decisions are ethical. This reality requires decision makers to develop and encourage a culture of ethics and compliance, and this task can be daunting. There are numerous pressures confronting business in addition to increasing sales, maintaining competitive advantage and market shares, and being profitable. Mergers and acquisitions, downsizing, and outsourcing have dramatically changed the shape of corporations. In many cases, they do not have the luxury of time to develop a "corporate culture" as their personnel goes through greater turnover today than in previous eras.

Despite these pressures and considerations, there is still a need for companies to develop a code of ethics that is communicated to all their employees. While ethical behavior should start at the top—with owners, executives, and managers adhering to moral standards—developing an ethical culture also requires having ethical employees. As we have seen, in order to adhere to regulatory guidelines and maintain its professional reputation, a company needs to have effective compliance procedures and internal controls. The goal is to create a code of ethics. In many instances, a corporate code of conduct is a written policy and is sometimes incorporated into a company's mission statement.

The Mission Statement
A mission statement defines the purpose of an organization, its reason for existing, and the goals of employees who work for the organization. If the goal of the organization is to provide quality products and adhere to a code of ethics, there are standard moral principles that should be incorporated into its code of ethics. These may be lofty notions to some, but ethics are essential virtues that many people learn from their families. Some of these virtues include integrity, justice, competence, and utility.

- Integrity means to be open, honest, and sincere.
- Justice relates to being impartial, having sound reasoning, and being conscientious.
- Competence is being capable, qualified, and reliable.
- Utility means being practical and useful.

Not only should a code of conduct be based on the foregoing virtues, the code should incorporate the following basic values of moral conduct: trustworthiness, respect, responsibility, fairness, caring, and citizenship.

These are not merely theoretical notions, but rather virtues and ethical standards that will be reflected in the way a company conducts its business, the practices of treating its employees, and the organization's relationship with its customers and vendors. Simply put, an ethical business enterprise is one that pays its bills expediently, treats its employees fairly, and provides quality products and service to its customers. Unethical behavior such as not paying vendors for their services, subjecting employees to hostile work environments, or not having reliable customer service will undo an organization in the end.

Financial Reporting and the Sarbanes-Oxley Act

Further, because of the Sarbanes-Oxley Act (SOX), publicly traded entities must have higher standards of ethical conduct as they relate to their financial reporting requirements. Essentially, a company's income statements and balance sheets must accurately reflect the company's financial standing. This requirement means that their revenues, liabilities, and net worth must be accurate and true, and executive officers are now required to attest to the accuracy of those statements.

In this regard, there have been numerous violations discovered where financial reports contained deficiencies. These deficiencies are usually related to the timing of revenue recognition as well as contracting practices. The timing of revenue recognition and contracting practices are directly related to relatively straightforward, if not mundane, matters such as accurately tracking accounts receivable and inventory accounts.

Essentially, certain companies were found to have practices deemed to improperly recognize revenues. One of these practices concerns the treatment of accounts receivable. Certain companies were found to have been backdating invoices in an attempt to lower their outstanding or uncollected receivables for a particular quarter that gave the appearance of greater cash flows at the close of a quarter. Another deficient practice has been termed "channel stuffing." Here, a company attempts to boost sales results by shipping more products to subsidiaries or vendors prior to the end of a reporting quarter. This activity gives the appearance of higher sales figures and reduced inventory, and thus greater revenue for that quarter.

Manipulating financial statements in such a manner is a violation of the SOX. Not only have companies and the responsible individuals been convicted of fraud under this law, but also investors have suffered undue hardship as the value of the companies' stock price fell dramatically in these cases. This situation opened the door to class action lawsuits. Defending against these suits can be quite expensive and can have a material adverse effect on a company's profits, its reputation, and its viability as a business entity. In short, not having ethical standards can have serious implications as they relate to financial reporting requirements. Causing financial losses to its investors is not a theoretical matter; it is an endeavor that can stain a business's reputation and eventually cause its demise.

Hostile Work Environments

An ethical organization is one that also treats its employees well. Many companies meet this standard simply by providing jobs, giving employees access to healthcare, and creating professional work environments. However, there have been many instances of unethical conduct as it relates to work environments. For example, sexual harassment lawsuits have been brought when employees were subjected to a hostile work environment. A hostile work environment can be one where a superior makes outright and unwanted sexual advances on a subordinate, or even where inappropriate comments by people running the mailroom take on a sexual tone. Most organizations have clearly defined policies regarding these matters and policies and procedures to ensure that hostile environments are not sustained.

Allegations of sexual harassment are not the only situations that indicate a hostile work environment. Such an environment also includes the use of obscene language, verbal abuse and intimidation, and derogatory comments about a person's ethnic or racial background, religious affiliation, gender, or sexual orientation.

How does a hostile work environment relate to the virtues and moral values mentioned above? If a company adheres to the basic moral values of caring and citizenship, hostile work environments would not exist. A business that aspires to fairness and trustworthiness is one that expediently pays it vendors for services provided. By not treating its vendors fairly, a company can jeopardize its professional reputation and undermine its professional relationships. An organization that believes in responsibility will ensure that its people are held accountable for their performance. The persons can be the controller, who is responsible for maintaining books and records and financial reporting; the human resource manager, who is responsible for implementing the company's policies and procedures as they relate to the treatment of employees; or the compliance officer, who is responsible for developing and implementing policies and procedures that adhere to regulatory guidelines.

The overriding moral value is respect. In fact, respect is the foundation of any relationship. Respect is not an abstract notion. To be respectful is to recognize the value of other people. At the end of the day, business organizations are not "brick-and-mortar" entities. Companies are not automated enterprises that run on their own. Business enterprises are made up of people. How people relate to one another within an organization is directly related to the ethical values of the business. Therefore, it is the shared responsibility of all the people in an organization to treat one another (the internal customer), as well as its customers, with respect. Customers who perceive a business is not treating them with respect will find another business to provide them with the goods or services they desire. Employees who feel that their coworkers or superiors are disrespectful will find another job. In the final analysis, though, the first relationship any individual has is with oneself. If people have self-respect, they will treat others respectfully, and they will respect the organizations that they work for, shop at, or invest in.

Viewpoints

Business enterprises do not exist in a vacuum; they are integral to society. A company that seeks to maintain ethical standards will better serve society. Being a good corporate citizen is not much different from being a good citizen. The moral values required for each are the same. Further, under the law, businesses are considered persons in many cases, and there are legal ramifications that go with that distinction. Beyond the legal ramifications that we are well familiar with by now, there is a difference between the letter of the law and the spirit of law, and the latter really speaks to ethics.

While many instances of unethical corporate behavior have created harm, it is a reasonable proposition that an unethical business will not survive in the long run. At the same time, one might wonder why such instances of unethical conduct occurred in the first place. If unethical business practices can trigger regulatory scrutiny that might cause a business's demise, then it seems prudent for businesses to implement and maintain ethical practices.

Although government agencies and attorneys general have far reaching abilities and ample resources, their regulatory enforcement actions are limited in scope and usually aimed at large organizations with so-called deep pockets; that is, businesses with financial resources that make it worthwhile to commence a regulatory action or a legal proceeding. While it may be of little value for an organization to spend needless amounts of time, resources, and money defending itself against regulatory enforcement actions or litigation, businesses that have ample financial resources are often successful in mitigating the damage of such proceedings. It is possible, therefore, that certain business decisions that might not appear ethical are made with the inherent regulatory or legal risks carefully considered. At times, the potential for financial gain may exceed the risk of financial losses that might occur in the event of an enforcement action or lawsuit. Moreover, in light of the fact that enforcement actions and class action lawsuits are more likely to be aimed at companies that have ample financial resources, smaller companies that engage in unethical practices are less likely to be detected.

However, the energies and effort of a business enterprise are better focused when they are generating profits. To paraphrase the late economist Milton Friedman, the business of business is business. Friedman believed that the social responsibility of business is to generate profits. In many ways,

Friedman is, to some extent, right. A business that believes its social responsibility is to generate profits will conduct itself in a manner that will prove to be successful. In so doing, a business's success will contribute to the economic growth of a society, and it will provide people with jobs and opportunities for growth.

Considering the importance of business ethics, then it is self-evident that to sustain itself, a business enterprise needs to attract and retain qualified and competent people. This practice reinforces one of the four virtues mentioned earlier. In addition to competence, the other virtues include integrity, justice, and utility. With respect to the last of these, the simple question is whether the goods or services a company provides are useful. Of course, that is a matter of debate; after all, in a consumer-driven society, there are many goods sold to and purchased by the public that are of dubious utility. An organization that is delivering valuable and useful goods, services, or commodities is acting for the betterment of society. One can look to the technological innovations of recent years and see that national economies have become more efficient.

In the final analysis, the social responsibility of a business is to be profitable, since the company will contribute to sustaining economic growth. A business that incorporates a code of ethics into its business practices will protect itself from regulatory and legal actions and will enhance its relationships with its employees, customers, and vendors. In so doing, a business can ensure its viability, which is also an ethical responsibility.

Terms & Concepts

Accounts receivable: Money owed to a business entity for goods, services, and merchandise purchased on a credit basis.

Business ethics: Rules geared toward establishing and maintaining trustworthiness in a business or commercial setting.

Business model: The means by which a company generates revenue and profits, how it serves its customers, and the strategy and implementation of procedures to achieve this end.

Compliance procedures: Business practices and procedures that adhere to federal, state, and regional laws, rules, and guidelines.

Corporate culture: The beliefs, attitudes, and behaviors of an organization and its employees that determine a corporation's character.

Financial services agency: The government organization in Japan responsible for overseeing the banking, securities and exchange, and insurance sectors.

Inventory accounts: The name given to an asset of a business relating to merchandise or supplies on hand or in transit at a particular point in time.

Mission statement: A statement that explains the core purpose of an organization, including why it exists, how it intends to conduct its business, and what the expectations of the employees in achieving these aims are.

Moral conduct: A rule or habit of behavior that is right or wrong according to socially accepted norms.

Predatory lending practices: Lending practices aimed at minority groups or senior citizens who have weaker credit ratings and financial resources than other demographic groups. Government investigations that began in the late 1990s have revealed that senior citizens and minority groups are ultimately charged more fees or offered higher interest rates for consumer loans.

Regulatory agencies: Federal, state, and regional government agencies that are responsible for enforcing laws, rules, and guidelines.

Sarbanes-Oxley Act (SOX): Federal law in the United States enacted in 2002 that requires executives of publicly traded companies to attest to the accuracy of their financial statements and requires the organization to establish extensive internal procedures and controls to ensure compliance with the act.

Social responsibility: The obligation of a business to conduct its business in a manner that is socially, environmentally, and ethically responsible.

Bibliography

Ahmad, Noor H., and T.T. Ramayah. "Does the Notion of 'Doing Well by Doing Good' Prevail among Entrepreneurial Ventures in a Developing Nation?" *Journal of Business Ethics* 106 (2012): 479–90. Print.

Alzola, Miguel. "Virtuous Persons and Virtuous Actions in Business Ethics and Organization Research." *Business Ethics Quarterly* 25, no. 3 (2015): 287–318. Print.

Atkinson, Joe, and Susan Leandri. "Best Practices: Organizational Structure That Supports Compliance." *Financial Executive* 21 (2005): 36–40. Print.

Banyard, Paul. "Banking Ethics: Some Surprises Along the Way." *Credit Management* (2006, June): 22–23. Print.

Cant, Michael C., and Claudette van Niekerk. "Survival or Ethically Correct? Small Business Owners' Attitude Towards Ethical Concerns." *Annual International Conference on Business Strategy & Organizational Behaviour* (BizStrategy). (2013): 1–7. Print.

Millman, Gregory J. "Black and White Fever: The State of Business Ethics." *Financial Executive* 22 (2006): 26–28. Print.

Okoro, Ephraim. "Ethical and Social Responsibility in Global Marketing: An Evaluation of Corporate Commitment to Stakeholders." *International Business & Economics Research Journal* 11 (2012): 863–70. Print.

Preuss, Lutz, Ralf Barkemeyer, and Ante Glavas. "Corporate Social Responsibility in Developing Country Multinationals: Identifying Company and Country-Level Influence." *Business Ethics Quarterly* 26, no. 3 (2016): 347–78. Print.

Schrempf-Stirling, Judith, Guido Palazzo, and Robert A. Phillips. "Historic Corporate Social Responsibility." *Academy of Management Review* 41, no. 4 (2016): 700–19. Print.

Williams, C.E., and Jonathan T. Scott. *Concise Handbook of Management: A Practitioner's Approach*. London: Hawthorn Press, 2005.

SUGGESTED READING

Crossman, Joanna, and Vijayta Doshi. "What Not Knowing Is a Virtue: A Business Ethics Perspective." *Journal of Business Ethics* 131, no. 1 (2015): 1–8. Print.

Francis Ronald D., and Guy Murfey. *Global Business Ethics: Responsible Decision Making in an International Context*. London: Kogan Page, 2016.

Jackson, Kevin T. "Towards Authenticity: A Sartrean Perspective Business Ethics." *Journal of Business Ethics* 58 (2005): 307–25. Print.

Knox, Simon, Stan Maklan, and Paul French. "Corporate Social Responsibility: Exploring Stakeholder Relationships and Programme Recording across Leading FTSE Organizations." *Journal of Business Ethics* Part 3, no. 61 (2005): 7–28. Print.

Maclagan, Patrick. "Conflicting Obligations, Moral Dilemmas and the Development of Judgment through Business Ethics Education." *Business Ethics: A European Review* 21 (2012): 183–97. Print.

Stango, Marty. "Ethics, Morals and Integrity: Focus at the Top." *Healthcare Financial Management* 60 (2006): 50–54. Print.

Wempe, Johan. "Ethical Entrepreneurship and Fair Trade." *Journal of Business Ethics* 60 (2005): 211–20. Print.

Richa S. Tiwary, Ph.D., M.L.S.

EXECUTIVE COMPENSATION

ABSTRACT

The subject of executive compensation has been much discussed since the financial collapse of 2008. The manner in which corporations and other businesses pay their top leaders for their services is popularly believed to be out of touch with the economic realities faced by ordinary people on a daily basis. Certainly the issue is a complex one, with cogent arguments on both sides, not least because there are so many different forms that executive compensation can take.

OVERVIEW

The best-known form of compensation for executives is salary. Just as with the salary paid for any other type of position, it consists of cash payments made to the executive at specified intervals or pay periods. The advantage to cash compensation is that it is one of the more flexible forms of payment. It can be used immediately and for virtually anything. The disadvantage to salary payments tends to be their tax implications. In the United States, federal income taxes are paid by wage earners for their income during each

Brendan Kennedy, CEO of Tilray, whose total 2018 compensation was $256 million (photo courtesy of SAM_3980)

calendar year. Those who earn a high salary tend to have larger tax burdens. US executives tend to be in the highest income bracket, according to federal income tax rules. This fact is one of the main reasons that many executives prefer other forms of compensation, or a mix of different types.

Benefits as Compensation
Another type of compensation for executives, and one that is often overlooked, is benefits. Benefits include health insurance (physical and mental health) and vision and dental coverage and may include employee wellness programs that offer auxiliary benefits such as basic legal counseling, retirement planning, and so forth. For most employees, the cost of these benefits is partially subsidized by the employer, so the employee pays only a percentage of the cost of the benefits (Rahman 2016).

This payment structure allows for employees to benefit from group pricing, but does not place the entire entire financial burden on the employer. For most employees, the choice of benefits is the same regardless of one's position in the organization. For executives, there is somewhat more room for negotiation, since executive compensation packages are not normally standardized, but tailored to the particular employment agreement of an executive. Therefore, some executives do not have part of their salary taken to pay for benefits; the benefits are provided without any employee contribution. Nevertheless, the value of the benefits the executive receives is still counted as part of his or her total compensation (Schneider 2013).

Closely related to benefits is the option to offer compensation to executives in the form of low cost or free insurance, whether life, auto, home, accidental death and disability, or all of the above. Companies may choose to offer executives some of these plans as a relatively inexpensive way of sweetening the pot by increasing the total value of the company's compensation package. In most cases the full value of the policies will never be paid out, but they do provide added peace of mind, and this support can sometimes be important in and of itself. In this sense, insurance as a form of executive compensation is similar to another category of benefits known as perquisites. They are part of the compensation package because they make it more attractive, but on their own they very likely would not be the deciding factor in an executive's deliberations about whether or not to accept a job offer.

In other situations, executives are provided with housing subsidies, automobiles, club membership, and other perquisites appropriate to their responsibilities.

Perquisites as Compensation
Perquisites, also known as paid expenses or perks, are amenities such as a company car or even a company jet at one's disposal, an expense account or stipend for incidental expenses, memberships in exclusive clubs and societies, and so forth. While many of these perquisites might seem like somewhat frivolous luxuries, they can play an important role if they are connected with something personally significant to the executive, such as membership in a golf club for an avid golfer or critical to the ability to accomplish

the work expected of executives (Wong, Gygax, and Wang 2015).

Short-Term Incentives
Some types of benefits are virtually unique to executives; these are broadly described as incentives. Because executives hold top leadership positions in the organizations in which they are employed, it would not be sensible for them to put in only the minimum amount of effort required to keep the organization running. Executives are hired for their creativity and initiative, so they can find bold new directions for the company, and devise innovative ways of getting there. Encouraging executives to excel at a portfolio that includes these broad responsibilities requires extraordinary forms of motivation; therefore, companies usually use a combination of short- and long-term incentives (Boudreaux 2015).

Short-term incentives are usually those whose value can be realized within a year or less. Examples of short-term incentives include quarterly or annual bonuses. These cash payments are typically contingent upon the achievement of some personal or organizational goal, such as a 10-percent increase in sales or a 10 percent reduction in expenses. Bonuses like these are awarded after the event that justifies them and usually are at the discretion of the executive's superiors.

Other short-term incentives may be agreed upon before the event that triggers them, such as an increase in salary if a project goal is achieved on schedule; these incentives are usually attached to a formula of some kind. For example, an executive might be promised that for every day before the deadline she completes a project, her salary will be increased by 1 percent. Incentives like this one, which are agreed upon before performance, begin to resemble contracts, so they ordinarily are not subject to discretion. This structure means that if the executive performs according to the agreement, then the incentive must be awarded (Ntim, Lindop, Osei, and Thomas 2015).

Long-Term Incentives
While short-term incentives can be very effective at encouraging top level performance, their brief duration does not permit them to provide executives with a compelling reason to stay with their employer over an extended period. Companies wish to retain high-performing executives, so they can continue to benefit from the executives' skills. Additionally, it is desirable to prevent competitors from luring away valued executives and making it more difficult to remain competitive. For these reasons, companies also offer their executives long-term incentives, which are typically defined as incentives that take longer than a single year to become available.

The best known example of long-term incentives is company shares or options to buy shares at a future time and price. Shares are partial ownership interests in the company, and for companies that perform well, the price of shares increases over time as investors compete to acquire the limited number of shares the company issues. The person receiving shares can either hang onto them and continue to allow their value to increase or sell them at a profit.

What makes options and shares long-term incentives is a restriction known as vesting. Vesting imposes a time period on a grant of shares or options, before which they may not be sold or transferred. Only after the grant has vested—typically this occurs anywhere from three to five years after the shares or options are granted—may the recipient receive value from them.

Shares and stock options have tax advantages for the recipient in many cases. These long-term incentives encourage the recipient to think about the future of the company and to act in its best interest not only for the present but also for the years to come (Ims, Pedersen, and Zsolnai 2014). For example, if an executive receives shares in the company that will vest in three years, it would be in the executive's best interests to spend those years doing everything possible to improve the company, because this will increase the value of the company and thus make the shares more valuable.

FURTHER INSIGHTS

Executive compensation has trended upward for several decades and has now reached the point, in the United States, that large numbers of people consider it to be symptomatic of inequalities embedded deeply within society. This situation occurs because executive compensation has not simply increased over the years along with inflation; it has also increased dramatically in relation to the salaries of average workers. Not so long ago, it was typical for a corporate executive to earn in one year twenty times the annual salary earned by a worker on the company's production line. Now, some executives are earning forty times or more as much as their frontline employees.

Many critics point to the rise in executive compensation as the reason for the concentration of wealth that has occurred, observing that globally the richest 1 percent control about half the world's resources. In the United States, 1 percent of the population now controls more wealth than the other 99 percent. These observations were responsible for much of the anger and resentment expressed in the wake of the economic crash of 2008, especially in the United States (Pittinsky and DiPrete 2013). At that time there emerged a general feeling that well-paid executives were responsible for crashing the economy, yet they themselves were not severely impacted by the consequences.

In response to this type of sentiment, some companies have begun to reevaluate their executive compensation practices, with the goal of either making them more equitable, making them appear less egregious, or both. As part of this effort, there have been several stories in the media about chief executive officers (CEOs) choosing to limit their own compensation to amounts smaller than that which might otherwise be authorized by their boards of directors (Kim Kogut, and Yang 2015).

Issues
Some scholars working in the field of business and finance have begun to question the soundness of traditional approaches to executive compensation. In particular, they point to the curious prevalence of the practice of using performance-based metrics to determine how much executives will be paid.

As discussed above, many executive positions are designed so that compensation is dependent upon performance, meaning that if performance does not meet the standards that have been established, then compensation will be reduced. Often, the reverse is also true: If performance exceeds the required levels, then compensation may scale upwards along with it. To many executives, this type of compensation system matches their worldview—that is, if one works harder, then one should be paid more, without any upper limit being imposed to limit the ascent.

Critics, however, note that in many ways it is nonsensical to rely on performance-based measures to motivate executives. One reason they cite is that executives and candidates for executive positions are, by their very nature, already highly motivated individuals for whom the pursuit of personal and professional excellence are intrinsically rewarding. To put it more simply, executives are, for the most part, people who are driven to do and be their best, regardless of the circumstances they find themselves in. Therefore, they do not require bonuses, stock options, or other rewards to motivate them to achieve their utmost performance (Pepper and Gore 2015).

Further, it has been suggested that in some sectors of the economy, there can be dire consequences for society traceable to the use of performance-based compensation for executives. The concern is that a performance-based compensation system is essentially one that operates without regard for morality and without regard for scope. Thus, if the performance that is being incentivized by compensation has negative implications for others, then there will need to be some type of regulation on that performance that is imposed from outside.

The foremost example raised to illustrate this situation comes from the mortgage crisis that started in the United States around the year 2008. According to the critics of performance-based compensation, the mortgage crisis arose because mortgage company executives were receiving performance-based compensation incentives, where they received more compensation as they created more mortgages. This situation became a problem when the industry began to have difficulty locating enough well-qualified mortgage applicants. To continue their high levels of performance (and the increased compensation that came with it) they began selling mortgages to applicants who were less qualified and at greater risk for default.

This trend continued without significant government intervention, and eventually many of these borrowers defaulted, triggering an economic crisis (Johnson, Sheka, & Weeden, 2015). While a disaster of this scope is not the inevitable outcome of executive compensation that is based on performance, the experiences of recent years are certainly providing food for thought throughout the business world. It remains to be seen if these arguments will eventually produce an industrywide change in executive compensation practices.

BIBLIOGRAPHY

Boudreaux, Donald J. "Thomas Piketty's Flawed Analyses of Public Debt and Executive Compensation." *Independent Review* 20, no. 2 (2015): 285–89. Web. 23 Oct. 2016.

Ims, Knut, Lars Pedersen, and Laszlo Zsolnai. "How Economic Incentives May Destroy Social, Ecological and Existential Values: The Case of Executive Compensation." *Journal of Business Ethics* 123, no. 2 (2014): 353–60. Web. 23 Oct. 2016.

Johnson, Kyle, Kate Sheka, and Jennifer Weeden. "Give to Get: Magnifying the Impact of Executive Compensation through Charitable Giving." *Journal of Financial Service Professionals* 69, no. 1 (2015): 63–72. Web. 23 Oct. 2016.

Kim, Jerry W. Bruce Kogut, and Jae-Suk Yang. "Executive Compensation, Fat Cats, and Best Athletes." *American Sociological Review* 80, no. 2 (2015): 299–328. Web. 23 Oct. 2016.

Ntim, Collins G., Sarah Lindop, Kofi A. Osei, and Dennis A. Thomas. "Executive Compensation, Corporate Governance and Corporate Performance: A Simultaneous Equation Approach." *Managerial & Decision Economics* 36, no. 2 (2015): 67–96. Web. 23 Oct. 2016.

Pepper, Alexander, and Julie Gore. "Behavioral Agency Theory: New Foundations for Theorizing about Executive Compensation." *Journal of Management* 41, no. 5 (2015): 1045–68. Web. 23 Oct. 2016.

Pittinsky, Matthew, and Thomas A. DiPrete. "Peer Group Ties and Executive Compensation Network." *Social Science Research* 42, no. 6 (2013): 1675–92. Print.

Rahman, Dewan M. "Investor Sentiment, Executive Compensation, and Investment—Some International Evidence: A Pitch." *Accounting & Management Information Systems /Contabilitate Si Informatica De Gestiune* 15, no. 2 (2016): 428–33. Web. 23 Oct. 2016.

Schneider, Paul J. "The Managerial Power Theory of Executive Compensation." *Journal of Financial Service Professionals* 67, no. 3 (2013): 17–22. Web. 23 Oct. 2016.

Wong, Ling H., Andre Gygax, and Peng Wang. "Board Interlocking Network and the Design of Executive Compensation Packages." *Social Network* 41 (2015): 85–100. Print.

SUGGESTED READING

Balsam, Steven, Jeff Boone, H. Liu, and J. Yin. "The Impact of Say-on-Pay on Executive Compensation." *Journal of Accounting & Public Policy* 35, no. 2 (2016): 162–91. Web. 23 Oct. 2016.

DeYoung, Robert, Emma Y. Peng, and Meng Yan. "Executive Compensation and Business Policy Choices at U.S. Commercial Banks." *Journal of Financial & Quantitative Analysis* 48, no. 1 (2013): 165–96. Web. 23 Oct. 2016.

Ding, Shujun, Chunxin Wilson, and Zhenyu Wu. "Political Connections and Agency Conflicts: The Roles of Owner and Manager Political Influence on Executive Compensation." *Review of Quantitative Finance & Accounting* 45, no. 2 (2015): 407–34. Web. 23 Oct. 2016.

Dye, Ronald A., and Sri S. Sridhar. "Hedging Executive Compensation Risk through Investment Banks." *Accounting Review* 91, no. 4 (2016): 1109–38. Web. 23 Oct. 2016.

El-Sayed, Nader, and Hany Elbardan. "Executive Compensation, Corporate Governance and Corporate Performance: Evidence from the UK." *Journal of Organizational Studies & Innovation* 3, no. 2 (2016): 31–49. Web. 23 Oct. 2016.

Focke, Florens. "The Impact of Firm Prestige on Executive Compensation." *Journal of Financial Economics* 123, no. 2 (2017, July 28). Print.

Hong, Bryan, Zhichuan Li, and Dylan Minor. "Corporate Governance and Executive Compensation for Corporate Social Responsibility." *Journal of Business Ethics* 136, no. 1 (2016): 199–213. Web. 23 Oct. 2016.

Laschever, Ron A. "Keeping Up with CEO Jones: Benchmarking and Executive Compensation." *Journal of Economic Behavior & Organization* 93 (2013): 78–100. Web. 23 Oct. 2016.

Madsen, Peter M., and John B. Bingham. "A Stakeholder Human Capital Perspective on the Link between Social Performance and Executive Compensation." *Business Ethics Quarterly* 24, no. 1 (2014): 1–30. Web. 23 Oct. 2016.

Scott Zimmer, J.D.

Executive Leadership

ABSTRACT

Leadership is slightly more obvious than it is valuable. One can exemplify leadership in a variety of ways. Maintaining an awareness of the bodies of knowledge on the topic is one way. With an ability to draw from various sources and perspectives in a timely manner, an effective leader demonstrates preparation and readiness to articulate ideas, specify recommendations, and convince others of decisions and actions. This essay explains some of the major points in transactional leadership, transformational leadership, and servant leadership. In addition, it summarizes leadership thought from a historical viewpoint. About 80 years ago, most experts believed that leaders were individuals born possessing specific characteristics. Those older approaches gave way to some seeking to find the one best way to lead. More recent thinking suggests executive leadership effectiveness depends on the degree to which there is a match between style and organization of situations. The main focal points of executive leadership include mission accomplishment, resource acquisition, and external affairs. A recent shift in thinking holds the potential for emphasizing service over results. It is likely that service to others will gain importance given the expected growth of jobs and leadership opportunities in the non profit sector. In brief, this essay aims to help readers recognize some requirements of leadership, so prospective leaders may prepare to act on them.

OVERVIEW

Leadership is both valuable and obvious. Most people would probably define leadership according to their observations of people with whom they interact daily. In terms of the workplace, some would agree that managers, supervisors, and executives are leaders in a formal sense though they may fall short of the leadership we expect to see in them. Fortunately, some coworkers and associates with informal relationships fit the leadership role better than others who occupy authoritative positions. The need for leadership is present at every level within and between organizations; this essay tends to focus on the top level and makes frequent references to the nonprofit sector.

Aside from job growth projections, significant differences exist between nonprofit organizations and governmental or for-profit entities. "To measure its effectiveness, a nonprofit must ask itself, 'Are we really delivering on our mission, not just meeting budget, and are we getting maximum impact from our expenditures?'" (Epstein and McFarlan 2011). Leaders of nonprofit organizations should hold or acquire skills that allow them to fulfill missions, acquire resources, develop strategies, and navigate external and political environments. In short supply, some publications on the topic of nonprofit executive leadership tend to focus attention on interactions between presidents of the organization and their boards of directors. It takes time to rise to the top of the organizational ladder, yet prospective leaders begin developing their skills early in their careers rather than later, for the benefits become more evident with the passage of time and through service in diverse settings.

The current state of knowledge on the topic asserts that leadership has more to do with influencing others than it does with exercising authority over others through title or position. Moreover, the literature suggests that leaders influence followers and vice versa while formal authority often fades away into the background. In other words, some scholars and practitioners assert that a leader usually gains authority because his or her followers are willing to lend it. In essence, leaders exist only if they have followers and, some leaders function by serving their followers. Indeed, some studies have shown that to improve service quality and maintain customers, organizations must ensure their employees' job satisfaction (Pan-soo and Jang-Hyup 2013).

APPLICATIONS

Through what approaches can one become an exemplary leader? A countless number of today's college students and high school students are satisfying graduation requirements by earning credits for service learning projects, community service tasks, experiential learning arrangements, and the like. This fact alone may serve to demonstrate the immediate and future needs to pursue effective leadership through various means. Another fact of interest is that the literature on this topic contains a lot of material debating whether experience or instruction is the most effective approach for learning about leadership.

Corporate governance is related to corporate performance (Chun-Yao, Zong-Jhe, and Chun-Yi 2013). Corporations and management consultants argue that leadership is essentially self-taught. In contrast, business schools claim those corporate entities offer programs primarily geared toward issues facing a specific firm and industry, concluding that they fall short of exposing participants to larger environmental contexts in which leaders truly operate. In brief, it is important to assert that personal traits are ineffective and leadership styles are irrelevant in the absence of skillful communications. Some combination of them will keep workers and organizations moving toward their futures. In the broadest sense, an organization is by definition a group of individuals who come together to share responsibility for achieving three general goals common across the universe of organizations: growth, stability, and survival.

One of the challenges an executive faces is how to channel individual energy and group activities toward goal achievement and how to maximize performance levels and improve output and service qualities. In essence, organizational results are a function of leadership skill development and its perpetual application to challenging situations. There are a variety of approaches and perspectives on how executives and their subordinates can pursue and meet those challenges. A good place to begin is with an overview of various perspectives on leadership. By understanding those perspectives, readers will find themselves prepared and ready to handle a variety of situations they might encounter during the course of their personal or professional livelihoods.

Leadership Foundations & Perspectives

Able to borrow from various perspectives in a timely manner, an executive leader must be ready to articulate ideas, specify recommendations, and convince others that the underlying rationale is sound. Those analytical and communication skills also arise, in part, due to the leader's exposure to opportunities for interactions with other highly respected leaders. In addition, the number of interactions and those abilities are a result of the passage of time because individuals accumulate experiences and encounter a variety of settings as they tend to their personal and professional lives. In the process, leadership learning occurs as they sharpen their self-awareness and recognize the influences they have on others.

According to Chester Barnard, leadership is the ability of a superior to influence the behavior of a subordinate or group and persuade them to follow a particular course of action. In addressing the topic of executive leadership, it is necessary to introduce readers to the primary responsibilities or functions of executives. In his classic book *Functions of the Executive* (1968), Barnard outlines those responsibilities. Many recognize them in abbreviated form as POS-D-CORB, which is a device by which to remember respectively the following list of functions: Planning; organizing; staffing; directing; coordinating (drops one letter); and, budgeting. It may serve students of executive leadership well to gain some experience in each in addition to memorizing them.

Efficiency & Effectiveness

Barnard also drew attention to the efficacy of organizations at a time when there was a mechanistic fixation on efficiency. Long before the organic and systems perspectives on organizations came into existence, some problems arose as subunits attempted to maximize their own efficiencies in isolation from each other. In effect, subunits would look inward, thereby creating some operating distance between them and other subunits and between the organization and those on the outside whom it serves. Obviously, it takes multiple subunits to deliver a good or service to a customer, but the fixation on departmental efficiencies virtually disrupted the focus on deliveries to clients, customers, and the like. In sum, the organization became highly efficient at the expense of becoming highly ineffective. That is, it began to lose sight of external demands and was able to do so at minimal cost, a serious problem.

Management scholars and organization theorists during the 1970s asked questions, such as, "Does it matter if organizations do the right thing when there is a prevailing emphasis on doing whatever they do at the lowest average cost?" Certainly, making more of an unwanted item will enhance efficiency as will cutting the costs of producing that item. An inward-looking focus on efficiency will only last until another set of problems arises. Consequently, an ongoing challenge for executive leadership is to provide the right bundles of goods and services at an acceptable level of cost.

Cost cutting while ignoring market situations may lead the organization to produce the wrong bundles at the lowest cost, which is probably a situation most organizations should avoid. Acquisition of additional resources is far more challenging than keeping an eye toward the reduction of existing expenses. Organization survival requires providing, offering, and selling bundles that members of society value, want, and demand. This goal means executives should opt for effectiveness over efficiency whenever given a choice between them, especially when the cost-effectiveness point remains uncharted and unproven. Efficiency and effectiveness are two concepts integral to advancing Barnard's notion of cooperative systems. A systems perspective takes into account characteristics of the internal operation and highlights the need to pay attention to the external environment in which the organization operates. In brief, a cooperative system of efficiency and effectiveness is required, according to Barnard. In addition, he asserted that purpose is the unifying and coordinating principle. Basic leadership requires individuals who know with precision an organization's purpose, whether it is generating financial returns at the pleasure of stockholders, covering social services at the pleasure of stakeholders, or fulfilling other needs and desires.

Values, Mission, & Vision
Values, mission, and vision are elements that frequently define an organization's purpose. Warren Bennis, a leadership scholar and a former university president, pointed out in the late 1990s that the foremost responsibility of a leader is defining a vision for the organization and then building the capacity to realize the vision. Around the same timeframe, as a temporary point of departure, the shared leadership view emerged independently of Bennis and from within the context of quality improvement. It suggests a durable vision is one that a relevant community crafts in concert with a formal leader or authority figure. Whatever the method, a vision may unite the masses and its fruition is the result of bringing people together as they go about their work internalizing the vision. In his book On *Becoming a Leader*, Bennis elaborates on the distinction between managers and leaders.

Three Forms of Leadership
That distinction between managers and leaders serves as an introduction to two traditional and one emergent form of leadership. On one hand, transactional leadership takes a short-term view in which managers keep an eye on profitability and focus on doing things right. Managers typically use existing systems, maintain controls, and create anguish while striving to answer questions of how and when. In contrast, leaders create trust, facilitate innovation, and use inspiration as they strive to answer questions of what and why. On the other hand, transformative leadership takes a long-term view in which leaders keep an eye toward the future and focus on doing the right things.

Leadership thinking has come a long way since the 1920s and 1930s when most experts held the view that some individuals are born with specific traits and innate characteristics that made them natural leaders. That trait approach gave way to a style approach, which represented the continuous attempt to define the best way to lead. More recent thinking is much broader in scope and focuses on leader effectiveness as a quality that depends on the degree to which a leadership style matches current and future organization situations.

Transactional Leadership
In the political realm, Burns (1978) introduced transactional leadership and transformative leadership as a dichotomy into which leaders are classified as one or the other. That seminal work generated a lot of studies and empirical results. Some of those scholars, including Bass (1985) and others, converted Burns's original classification into a continuum. Drawing from those works, researchers (Bass 1985; Bass and Avilio 1990) constructed four behaviors typically exhibited through transactional leadership. The first is contingent reward, which refers to a focus on resource exchanges. Followers receive various types of support and resources in exchange for their efforts and performance. The second two are variants of management by exception (MBE), which may be active or passive in nature. With a focus on setting standards, active management

by exception leaders intervene by taking corrective action when it is required whereas passive management by exception leaders intervene only when problems become serious. The last is laissez-faire which refers to leaders who adopt a hands-off approach, allowing followers to find their own way to meet organizational goals; in this approach, leaders sometimes avoiding leadership responsibilities altogether.

Executive Leadership
In contrast to the routine-oriented, transactions view of the workplace, executive leadership highlights behaviors that create and communicate clear direction for the organization's future, for implementing changes in structures and processes, and for evaluating critical success factors. It is obvious that leaders of effective organizations focus on doing the right things, which involve strategies that extend leadership beyond an organization's boundaries and into the external environment. Herman and Heimovics (2005) advance the executive leadership concept by noting that strategies often cross organization boundaries and require political acumen. In short, executive leadership focuses on the relevance of accomplishing missions and acquiring resources and strikes a close resemblance to transformational leadership theory.

Transformational Leadership
Drawing from the works of Burns and others, Judge and Piccolo (2004) constructed four behaviors that delineate genuine transformational leadership.

- The first is idealized influence, which refers to leaders who form high standards for conducting business in a moral and an ethical manner, who gain respect by doing so, and who receive loyalty from followers.
- The second is inspirational motivation, which refers to leaders who articulate a strong vision based on ideals and values, thereby generating enthusiasm, instilling confidence, and producing inspiration among followers. Frequently, they employ symbolic actions and persuasive speeches. When these first two behaviors congeal, the result is charisma.
- The third is intellectual stimulation, which refers to leaders who challenge the status quo by encouraging divergent perspectives and innovative strategies.
- The last is individual consideration, which refers to leader behaviors that involve developing, coaching, and consulting followers.

Servant Leadership
It is noteworthy that the year before Burns published *Leadership*, Robert K. Greenleaf (1977) introduced the notion that a servant leader places the interests of followers ahead of his or her own. From a historical perspective, servant leadership received attention from a few researchers who proclaim it is a sound theory worthy of further study and application. Unfortunately, academic journal references to Greenleaf's works are scant in comparison to those of Burns. Nonetheless, the research that is available shows that servant leaders exhibit the following the characteristics: listening; empathy; healing; awareness; persuasion; conceptualization; foresight; stewardship; commitment as mentors; and, community building. It is rather odd that a servant leader's motivation prompts him or her to serve followers as opposed to leading them. Until recently, its popularity appears to be greater as a topic more suitable for professional workshop and seminar settings than for academic settings and college classrooms.

Servant leadership theory is ripe for empirical support and especially more so now and into the distant future. Contemporary thinking is emphasizing the importance of servant leadership as evident in the fact that service learning is becoming an integral part of secondary and postsecondary education. Washington (2007) points out that servant leadership theory is a subject of growing interest in the leadership literature. Her research examines relationships of servant leadership theory to transformational and transactional theories of leadership.

Some key findings from that original research indicate that servant leadership compares with transformative leadership, contingent rewards, and active management by exception. Conversely, it contrasts with passive management by exception and laissez-faire. These findings hold promise for future leaders as they seek to uncover which leadership styles are most appropriate for them and in what situations. Washington (2007) concludes that servant leaders and transformative leaders share a common orientation to people, but the focal point of the former is organizational service; whereas the focal point of latter is organizational results. These findings are both timely and informative.

Service to others will gain importance given the growth of jobs and leadership opportunities in the nonprofit sector. Executive leadership is likely to evolve naturally through those who choose to serve a nonprofit's need for mission fulfillment and resource acquisition and those who want to develop skills enabling them to span boundaries and navigate political environments. Until additional results from studies on servant leadership become available, the body of knowledge on transformative leadership seems to be an appropriate source for individuals aspiring to become tomorrow's leaders.

Leadership for the Future

The state of the art in leadership remains divided over whether practice or instruction is the best teacher. Academicians assert that the ideal environment for leadership development is one that teaches students technical business and communication skills and helps them gain a better understanding of ethics, self-awareness, and values. In contrast, practitioners assert that development occurs primarily through on-the-job training. This paradox begs the question, "How, then, do the inexperienced become leaders?" In actuality, leadership instruction in college classrooms and in corporate workplaces has occurred for the past 50 years, but recent research is beginning to illuminate similarities and differences among the various perspectives.

A wide array of sources on leadership is available; they focus on developing skills in the following areas: intrapersonal, interpersonal, intercultural, organizational, and nonverbal communications; listening; feedback; small group interactions; persuasion; public speaking; interviewing; question formation and articulation. It is obvious that communication skills play a vital role not only in type but also in transmission medium. The three major communication media are oral, written, and electronic. Those media and skills often determine leadership effectiveness.

It takes much more than courses, seminars, and books to master leadership skills. A scan of documents or a search on the internet will produce a significant amount of information in a short period. An initial pass through some of the course offerings suggest approaches by which someone aspiring to be an executive leader can realize his or her goal. In general, the nature of executive leadership involves the ability to serve as a change agent and to communicate effectively. More specifically, it involves crafting visions and anticipating their consequences on an organization. Usually, linkages between organization performance and executive leadership appear on a daily or quarterly basis, which illustrates the need for preparation and readiness.

Developing a personal leadership plan may provide benefits to an organization, other leaders, and subordinates. Other points include how to garner trust while attempting to implement change while avoiding as many pitfalls as possible during those processes. Still others mention the importance of acquiring, interpreting, and using information whether it originates from inside or outside the organization. Embedded with all those suggestions, recommendations, and anecdotes are strands of theory intertwined with strands of reality. In essence, leaders will likely serve themselves and others well by combining the best that theory and practice have to offer. Obviously, this work will take a considerable amount of time to navigate the work, readings, and conversations. However, an acceleration of those processes often begins with some initial guidance that theoretical frameworks afford.

Whether experience or education is the best teacher, a need for outcomes assessment seems to exist. Assessment may take the form of using three basic steps and asking specific questions.

- First, there is a need for direct observation that compares learning outcomes and objectives as stated on paper to the contents of seminars and assignments. Did teaching occur?
- Second, examinations of participant portfolios over time will allow the teacher and the learner to see progress and enhance self-awareness. Did feedback occur?
- Lastly, follow-up via open-ended questions may reveal individual outcomes providing at the least some anecdotal evidence of learning. Did teaching and learning occur? Some leadership scholars contend that leaders reach their pinnacle by acting in accordance with their values and intuitions.

CONCLUSION

A large portion of leadership is a function of the specific time in which the person lives and the opportunities that present themselves. Prospective leaders need to:

- Gain an understanding of personal strengths and weaknesses
- Assure the possession of various traits and qualities; build the capacity to become whatever type of leader and to use any type of style that an organization needs at a given time
- Hold an interest in honing communication and other essential skills
- Develop a dual desire to locate a mentor and become a protégé
- Invoke a constant search for opportunities to practice leadership

In closing, readers who want to improve their leadership abilities will most likely need to enroll in a variety of courses, workshops, and seminars and work toward convening their own as an instructor.

Bibliography

Barnard, Chester I. *The Functions of the Executive.* Cambridge, MA: Harvard University Press, 1968.

Bass, Bernard M. *Leadership and Performance beyond Expectations.* New York: Free Press, 1985.

Bass, Bernard M. and Bruce J. Avolio. *The Multifactor Leadership Questionnaire.* Palo Alto, CA: Consulting Psychologists Press, 1990.

Burns, James M. *Leadership.* New York: Harper & Row, 1978.

Chun-Yao, Tseng, Wu Zong-Jhe, and Lin Chun-Yi. "Corporate Governance and Innovation Ability." *International Business Research* 6, no. 7 (2013): 70–78. Web. 22 Nov. 2013.

Greenleaf, Robert K. *Servant Leadership.* Mahway, NJ: Paulist Press, 1977.

Herman, Robert D., and Richard D. Heimovics. "Executive Leadership." In *The Jossey-Bass Handbook of Nonprofit Leadership & Management,* edited by Robert D. Herman & Associates, 153–70. San Francisco: John Wiley & Sons, Inc., 2005.

Judge, Timothy A., and Ronald F. Piccolo. "Transformational and Transactional Leadership: A Meto-Analytic Test of Their Relative Validity." *Journal of Applied Psychology* 89 (2004): 755–68. Print.

Pansoo, Kim, and Han Jang-Hyup. "Effects of Job Satisfaction on Service Quality, Customer Satisfaction, and Customer Loyalty: The Case of a Local State-Owned Enterprise." *WSEAS Transactions on Business & Economics* 10, no. 1 (2013): 49–68. Web. 22 Nov. 2013.

McClesky, Jim A. "Situational, Transformation, and Transactional Leadership and Leadership Development." *Journal of Business Studies Quarterly* 5, no. 4 (2014): 117–30. Web. 17 Nov. 2014.

Rao, M.S. "Transformational Leadership: An Academic Case Study." *Industrial and Commercial Training* 46, no. 3 (2014): 150–54. Web. 17 Nov. 2014. Washington, Rynetta R. "Empirical Relationships between Theories of Servant, Transformation, and Transactional Leadership." *Academy of Management Proceedings* (2007): 1–6. Web. 21 Nov. 2007.

Suggested Reading

Allio, Robert. "Band Leaders: How They Get That Way and What to Do about It." *Strategy & Leadership* 35, no. 3 (2007): 12–17. Web. 18 Nov. 2007.

Antonakis, John, and Robert J. House. "Instrumental Leadership: Measurement and Extension of the Transformational-Transactional Leadership Theory." *Leadership Quarterly* 25, no. 4 (2014): 746–71. Web. 17 Nov. 2014.

Burke, Ronald. "Why Leaders Fail: Exploring the Darkside." *International Journal of Manpower* 27, no. 1 (2006): 91–100. Web. 18 Nov. 2007.

Chandran, Jay P. "The Relevance of Chester Barnard for Today's Manager." (n.d.). Web. 14 Nov. 2007.

Choi, Jaepil, and Heli Wang. "The Promise of a Managerial Values Approach to Corporate Philanthropy." *Journal of Business Ethics* 75, no. 4 (2007): 345–59. Web. 12 Nov. 2007.

Day, David V., and Robert G. Lord. "Executive Leadership and Organization Performance: Suggestions for a New Theory and Methodology." *Journal of Management* 14 (1988): 453–64.

Epstein, Marc J., and F. Warren McFarlan. "Measuring the Efficiency and Effectiveness of a Nonprofit's Performance." *Strategic Finance* 93, no. 4 (2011): 27–34. Web. 26 Nov. 2013.

Hackman, J. Richard, and Ruth Wageman. "Asking the Right Questions about Leadership." *American Psychologist* 62, no. 1 (2007): 43–47. Web. 18 Nov. 2007.

Jones, Stephanie, and Riham Moawad. "The Effective Executive Leadership in Crisis Times." *Hyderbad* 19, no. 4 (2016). Web. 28 July 2017.

Lakshman, C. "Top Executive Knowledge Leadership: Managing Knowledge to Lead Change at General Electric." *Journal of Change Management* 5, no. 4 (2005): 429–46. Web. 12 Nov. 2007.

Maak, Thomas. "Responsible Leadership, Stakeholder Engagement, and the Emergence of Social Capital." *Journal of Business Ethics* 74, no. 4 (2007): 329–43.

Tonidandel, Scott, Derek Avery, and McKensy Phillips. "Maximizing Returns on Mentoring: Factors Affecting Subsequent Protégé Performance." *Journal of Organizational Behavior* 28, no. 1 (2007): 89–110. Web. 12 Nov. 2007.

Steven R. Hoagland, Ph.D.

Expectancy Theory

ABSTRACT

Expectancy theory is a theory of motivation focusing on how and why people become motivated. Business expert Victor Vroom identified the attributes of expectancy theory in 1964, although some researchers believe the original theory dates back to Edward Tolman's work in the 1930s. Tolman, an American psychologist, suggested that human behavior is directly affected more by expectation than by any direct stimuli. Vroom's work, however, greatly impacted the understanding of how cognitive processes affect an employee's motivation to perform.

OVERVIEW

Expectancy theory consists of three basic components: (1) the employee's expectation that working hard will lead to his or her desired level of performance; (2) the employee's expectation that working hard will thus ensure that rewards will follow; and (3) the employee's perception that the outcome of working hard is worth the effort or value associated with hard work. Vroom's expectancy theory is often formulated using the equation:

MF (motivational forces) = V (valence) x I (instrumentality) x E (expectancy).

The effort exerted by an employee is directly influenced by the expectation (E) that by trying hard, the task can be successfully performed. If, however, the employee believes that trying hard will not generate successful performance (I), the effort exerted by the employee will decline due to a lack of anticipated rewards (V).

In the application of this formula, motivational forces (MF) directly relate to those internal and external variables affecting an individual's performance and effort. Employees consistently leverage the results of their efforts with the expectation that hard work will lead to intrinsic or extrinsic rewards. The perception of acquiring potential rewards based on their individual effort must then be measured in terms of value: is my effort worth the reward expected?

Expectancy (E), therefore, is directly associated with the belief that successful performance will lead to rewards. In an organizational context, individuals maximize their instrumentality through the achievement of high performance goals with the understanding that successful performance will be followed by rewards. When employees perceive that rewards are not congruent with performance, the value (V) of their effort decreases due to the perception that the efforts gained as a result of hard work are not worth the effort expended. The influence of instrumentality and value subsequently affects the effort to which an employee will persist in hard work.

The theoretical implications of expectancy theory are complex and depend upon numerous factors that may possibly influence employee motivation. The degree to which individual employees assigns a value to his or her instrumentality will determine the level of effort devoted to a particular task.

Numerous factors must be taken into consideration when measuring the perceived rewards and consequences of effort as postulated by Vroom's expectancy theory. Despite the complexities of expectancy theory, there are numerous applications in education, business, social sciences, and government.

CONCLUSION

Expectancy theory has been widespread and used to understand an important aspect of employee motivation—the notion that rewards are connected to effort and commitment. In Vroom's theory, employees who consider that their work quality is excellent and that excellent work is recognized by the company work hard in anticipation of recognition and rewards. However, if they do not see a possible and probably connection between their work and some recognition or rewards, employees lose their motivation and work less hard and with less passion and enthusiasm.

BIBLIOGRAPHY

Baker-Eveleth, L., and Robert Stone. "Expectancy Theory and Behavioral Intentions to Use Computer Applications." *Interdisciplinary Journal of Information* 3 (2008): 135–46. Print.

Cassar, Gavin, and Henry Friedman. "Does Self-Efficacy Affect Entrepreneurial Investment?" *Strategic Entrepreneurial Journal* 3.3 (2009): 241–60. Print.

Estes, Brent. "Predicting Productivity in a Complex Labor Market: A Sabermetric Assessment of Free Agency on Major League Baseball Performance." *Business Studies Journal* 3.1 (2011): 23–58. Print.

Estes, Brent, and Barbara Polnick. "Examining Motivation Theory in Higher Education: An Expectancy Theory Analysis of Tenured Faculty Productivity." *International Journal of Management, Business and Administration* 15.1 (2012): n.p. Print.

Jex, Steve M., and Thomas W. Britt. *Organizational Psychology: A Scientist-Practitioner Approach.* 3rd ed. Malden, MA: Wiley, 2014.

Lunenberg, Fred C. "Expectancy Theory of Motivation: Motivating by Altering Expectations." *International Journal of Management, Business and Administration* 15.1 (2011): n.p. Print.

Miles, Jeffrey A., ed. *New Directions in Management and Organizations Theory.* Newcastle upon Tyne, UK: Cambridge Scholars, 2014.

Nasri, Wadie, and Lanouar Charfeddine. "Motivating Salespeople to Contribute to Marketing Intelligence Activities: An Expectancy Theory Approach." *International Journal of Marketing Studies* 4.1 (2012): 168. Print.

Renko, Maija, K. Galen Kroeck, and Amanda Bullough. "Expectancy Theory and Nascent Entrepreneurship." *Small Business Economics* 39.3 (2012): 667–84. Print.

Shweiki, Ehyal, et al. "Applying Expectancy Theory to Residency Training: Proposing Opportunities to Understand Resident Motivation and Enhance Residency Training." *Advances in Medical Education and Practice* 6 (2015): 339–46. Print.

Ugah, Akobundu, and Uche Arua. "Expectancy Theory, Maslow's Hierarchy of Needs, and Cataloguing Departments." *Library Philosophy and Practice* 1 (2011): 51. Print.

Patricia Hoffman-Miller, M.P.A, Ph.D.

EXTERNAL BUSINESS COMMUNICATIONS

ABSTRACT

External business communications are the activities through which a company transmits information generated within the company to one or more constituencies outside of the company. Information can be transmitted in this way to a wide variety of constituencies, from customers and shareholders to industry regulators and even business competitors. Some communications are made deliberately, but some become external inadvertently, such as confidential information that is leaked to outside sources. Most information, however, is distributed with the purpose of improving the company's position in some way.

OVERVIEW

Business communication is often categorized based on what parts of the company the communication concerns, and the most important factor in making this determination is the boundary between what goes on inside the company and what occurs outside

Commuters walk past an advertisement in a New York subway station (photo courtesy of the Metropolitan Transit Authority of the State of New York)

of company control. "Internal communication" is the term used to describe all the information exchanges that occur within the firm, and includes types of communication such as employee training, interoffice memos and presentations, and office coordination activities—ordering office supplies, requesting help from the information technology department, and so on. Because these types of information transfer occur inside the company, the company can exercise more control over them, setting rules or establishing official procedures, ensuring that these policies are followed by everyone, and imposing consequences if they are not followed.

External communication is much less under the company's control, because it involves all the ways in which information is communicated by the company to the outside world. Although the company can try to control what information is sent out, it cannot do much to regulate what happens to that information once it is outside the company or how it is interpreted by others. The most that a company can do with regard to external communications is to try to exert influence over information that is released by selecting what information can be released and then phrasing that information in a way that is most beneficial to the company (Rollins and Lewis 2014).

External business communication is not monolithic—there are many different types and forms that it can take, just as there are numerous audiences at which it may be directed. The different groups that have an interest in learning about a company are known as stakeholders—they have a stake in what happens to the company, either because they own shares of the company, the value of which they would like to see increase, or because they or their friends and relatives work at the company or do business with it (Stoykov 2007). Even customers and potential customers are stakeholders. A person who is considering the purchase of an expensive product, for example, would be very interested to hear about whether or not the company that manufactures it is expected to remain in business for the next few years, because this reality will affect the type of support the purchaser could expect to receive in the event that the product malfunctions.

Corporations are aware of the differing interests of their stakeholders, and when they prepare external communications, they craft them to better fit the needs of the group or groups they are targeted at. Advertising messages emphasize the company's products and the ways they enhance people's lives, financial reports focus on how the company is positioning itself in order to take advantage of expected conditions in the marketplace, and so on (Waldeck, Durante, Helmuth, and Marcia 2012).

Press Kits
One of the most important external groups that a company can communicate with is made up of representatives of the media. These can include journalists working for newspapers, television stations, or internet news sites. Some journalists may regularly monitor companies as part of their business and finance coverage, while others will inquire only about unusual events such as a product recall or the release of a much-anticipated product. Still others may be hostile to the corporation due to a conflict between their personal beliefs and the corporation's real or perceived activities—these journalists may conduct investigative reports intended to reveal information that the company might prefer to keep obscure.

Whatever the motivation of members of the media, corporations seek to manage their communication with them accordingly in an effort to encourage them to provide favorable or at least neutral coverage of the company. One way this is done is by preparing and distributing press kits, which are sets of pre-packaged background information about the company and its products (Miletic & Đurovic 2015). The purpose of a press kit is to make it easier for a journalist to prepare a story about the company by gathering together basic facts about the firm. Since companies create the press kits themselves, they invariably include the information that will improve their corporate image. When the average person picks up a newspaper or tunes in to a television segment, he or she is often unaware that a significant part of the report is taken directly from the press kit—that is, the company's own public relations department.

Advertising
Another major component of external business communication is advertising, which involves the company informing customers and potential customers about its products and services to encourage them to purchase those products and services or improve their opinion about the company. Advertising is vital to the success of most businesses because people cannot support the company by buying its products if they do not know that those products exist.

Even when consumers are aware of a product, there may be other products that have been developed by competing firms with which the product must vie for favor—in these situations, advertising is used to explain to consumers why they should choose one product over others. Because the livelihood of a business largely depends on encouraging people to buy what it is selling and because advertisers have time to carefully craft their advertising to influence customers, advertising is the form of external business communication in which companies invest the most time and attention, spending large portions of their budgets to develop marketing plans and advertising campaigns (Patrutiu-Baltes 2016).

Financial Reports
In addition to the forms of external communication that a company produces more or less voluntarily, there are some types of information that companies may be required to reveal to the outside world. Often this information includes the financial state of the company, as government regulations require that certain kinds of data be released periodically, so that investors and those who are considering making an investment can base their decisions on current performance figures.

In some cases providing this information does not present a problem, apart from the company's need to expend sufficient resources to collect and organize the information in preparation for its release; this work may require hiring accountants and financial analysts to pore over the firm's balance sheets and create quarterly and annual earnings reports, for example. This situation is usually the case when the company is performing well, and the news that is to be shared with the public is good. When the news is bad, however, this information can have a severe impact on the company and its employees, because it may cause investors to decide to pull their money out of the company by selling their shares or avoid purchasing shares in the first place, placing the company in an even more precarious situation (Gerdewal & Seçim 2014).

Websites
Regardless of the type of information being externally communicated or its intended audience, a company's website is one of the main tools used to distribute it. In the days before the internet, company information was primarily distributed in annual reports printed and mailed to investors and in financial statistics gathered and published by business news outlets and later collected in reference sources that compiled such information from many different firms. The internet has revolutionized external business communications in the same way that it has affected so many other aspects of modern life.

Instead of having to publish hard-copy reports in huge numbers, company information and annual reports can easily be made available online and delivered worldwide in a matter of seconds instead of days or weeks. There is virtually no limit to the types of company information that a corporation may choose to place on its website, from directories of its officers and staff to detailed research data used to help develop and test its products; for example, a drug manufacturer might use its website to link to copies of the scientific research that establishes that its medicines are safe and effective in the hope that doing so will increase consumer confidence in the medication and result in higher sales (Shrivastava 2012).

Lobbying
Some types of external communication are controversial by their very nature, and prominent among these is the practice of lobbying. Lobbying is the practice of meeting with elected representatives and other government officials in an attempt to influence public policies and legislation to favor the interests of the person or organization doing the lobbying.

Many companies, especially large corporations, spend large sums on lobbying each year. Critics of lobbyists argue that corporations' use of lobbyists and campaign donations results in these entities having an unfair amount of influence, since average citizens lack the resources to lobby for protection of their interests. Lobbyists and the corporations that employ them respond that all they are really doing is communicating their needs to legislators and anyone can do the same.

Lobbyists explain to government officials the challenges that a company is facing and the government actions that would be most helpful in allowing the corporation to overcome them. Typically, these actions involve the modification or elimination of regulations that restrict how the company can operate, or the provision of tax incentives for the corporation that will make it less costly to conduct its business (Bruyer, Jacobs, and Vandendaele 2016).

FURTHER INSIGHTS

In part because businesses must manage their communications with so many different external interest groups, some types of external communication can interfere with each other. The overall goal of external business communication is always to portray the company in a favorable light, but this focus means different things to different groups. The company might wish to communicate with environmental groups about how safe its products are for the environment and how much research and development has gone into making sure they do not contaminate the natural world. However, when investors hear about this message, they may become concerned that too much time and money is being spent on unnecessary, ecofriendly activities. This situation could have the unintended consequence of causing investors to reconsider their support of the company.

Similarly, lobbying often has negative effects on the public's perception of the company, because some people feel that companies unfairly use their political connections and financial resources to convince legislators to protect them from unfriendly laws and regulations. Companies must therefore be extremely cautious in developing their external communication strategy, so they can attempt to compartmentalize each communication to the greatest degree possible, by using media channels specific to each target audience (Gramatnikovski, Stoilkovska, and Serafimovic 2015).

Since the early part of the twenty-first century, social media networks have proliferated and are now many people's primary source for news and information. Most people in the developed world belong to multiple social networks, and membership in at least one or two is common even in less developed regions. This presents a dilemma for companies seeking to manage their external communications, on at least two levels. First, most companies feel the need to have a presence on the larger social media networks, so that users of those networks can find out about the company, contact the company's support staff, and stay up to date on new developments.

Just as with any other form of external communication, corporate social media accounts must be carefully managed and integrated into the firm's overall communication plan. At the same time, employees of the company all belong to their own social networks, and the "inside information" that they have access to by working at the company can therefore be put at risk by even the most innocent of social media posts. This situation has led corporations to implement strict policies about what may and may not be shared on social media by employees.

At the same time, some companies have realized that their own employees can use social media to help support the company's activities by posting information about the company's products and helping to spread enthusiasm about them. Still, even this type of activity must be well-thought-out, lest it be perceived as contrived or even manipulative; there have been a number of cases where a company tried to get its employees to spread the word about a product while concealing the fact that the company was pressuring them to do so. If and when consumers find out this masquerade has occurred, there is often a backlash against so-called astroturfing. The name is derived from the observation that the company is trying to fake a grassroots community (Beckers & Bsat, 2014).

BIBLIOGRAPHY

Beckers, Astrid M., and Mohammed Z. Bsat. "An Analysis of Intercultural Business Communication." *Journal of Business & Behavioral Sciences* 26, no. 3 (2014): 143. Print.

Bruyer, Tom, Geert Jacobs, and Astrid Vandeldaele. "Good Pharma? How Business Communication

Research Can Help Bridge the Gap between Students and Practitioners." *Business & Professional Communication Quarterly* 79, no. 2 (2016): 141. Web. 23 Oct. 2016.

Gerdewal, M. Tarek,, and Haberleri Seçim. "A Business Communication Design for Information Technlogy (IT) Organizations Based on Information Technology Infrastructure Library (ITIL)." *Business Management Dynamics* 4, no. 5 (2014): 12. Web. 23 Oct. 2016.

Gramatnikovski, Sasho, Aleksandra Stoilkovska, and Gordana Serafimovic. "Business Communication in Function of Improving the Organizational Culture of the Company." *UTMS Journal of Economics* 6, no. 2 (2014): 267. Print.

Miletic, Slavomir, and Djuro Djurovic. "Improving Enterprise Interests Through the Process of Business Communication." *Ekonomika* 61, no. 1 (2015): 43. Web. 23 Oct. 2016.

Patrutiu-Baltes, Loredana. "The Impact of Digitalization on Business Communication." *SEA: Practical Application of Science* 4, no. 2 (2016): 319. Print.

Rollins, Wayne, and Stephen Lewis. "A Comparison of Processes Used by Business Executives and University Business Communication Teachers to Evaluate Selected Business Documents." *Journal of Organizational Culture, Communications, and Conflict* 1 (2014): 139. Web. 23 Oct. 2016.

Shrivastava, Sanjay. "Identifying the Major Components of Business Communication and Their Relevance: A Conceptual Framework." *IUP Journal of Soft Skills* 64, no. 4 (2012): 51–66. Web. 23 Oct. 2016.

Stoykov, Lubomir. "Nature and Definitions of Business Communication." *Language in India* 7, no. 2 (2007): 2–37. Print.

Waldeck, Jennifer, Cathryn Durante, Briana Helmuth, and Brandon Marcia. "Communication in a Changing World." *Journal of Education for Business* 87, no. 4 (2012): 230–40.

SUGGESTED READING

Chernobaeva, Gulnara. "Importance of Integration of Marketing Communications in the Project Activity." Proceedings of the International Conference on Management, Leadership & Governance. (2013): 372–78. Web. 23 Oct. 2016.

Conrad, David, and Robert Newberry. "24 Business Communication Skills: Attitudes of Human Resource Managers Versus Business Educators." *American Communication Journal* 13, no. 1 (2011): 4–23,

Sinha, Akinchan B. "Business Communication: The Mainstay of an Efficient Business." *IUP Journal of Soft Skills* 6, no. 1 (2012): 7–15. Web. 23 Oct. 2016.

Turpen, Richard, and Haley Dyer. "Working with External Auditors." *Internal Auditor* 72, no. 1 (2015): 17–19. Web. 23 Oct. 2016.

Scott Zimmer, J.D.

FLAT ORGANIZATIONAL STRUCTURE

ABSTRACT

A flat organization, also known as a horizontal organization, is a system of governance and administration with few to no layers of management between managers and employees. In some cases, flat organizations are called—often incorrectly—leaderless organizations. The purpose of a flat organization is to have more productive workers since workers in a flat organization are allowed greater participation in decisionmaking, implementation, workplace roles, and idea generation than in traditional corporations. There are different kinds of flat organizations, all of which have important pros and cons; however, it is often said that it is the most democratic of all organizational structures.

OVERVIEW

"Flat," or "horizontal" structure, refers to a type of organization characterized by having few or no levels or stages of management between the head of the organization and the rest of the staff. It tends to be a decentralized structure, compared to more traditional organizational models. The theoretical framework of the flatter structures is based on democratic models and on a large body of research that shows that workers are more productive when they are directly involved in decision making and are not closely supervised by managers above them. Although flat structures are increasingly popular, its detractors argue that this type of structure is possible only in middle sized and small firms, or when a corporation's smaller units are integrated into a larger control structure. Furthermore, others explain that as companies grow, they may be able to maintain simplified structures, although not as flat as in the beginning. Flat structures are most popular among firms focused on productivity and constant innovation.

Flat organizations promote the involvement and participation of workers in decision-making processes. It also makes it easier for workers to be noticed when they promote ideas or contribute in any other way to productivity. Many consider it the most democratic organizational structure. Rather than give orders, team leaders foster the generation of ideas and help team members to make decisions. In many ways, then, managers are facilitators rather than bosses in the traditional sense. Flat systems offer further advantages: communications flow better, it is less costly, there is less bureaucracy, and decisions and outcomes occur faster. One of the characteristics of flat organizations is the ability to adapt to changes more easily than is possible for centralized and hierarchical organizations.

However, some companies do not find flat structures convenient. For these organizational structures to function well managers must share all the information and research with workers; this structure might not work with companies that prefer to guard information closely. Among the disadvantages of flat organizations is the difficulty of maintaining them as a company grows. Furthermore, work descriptions for fluid job positions may be too fuzzy, sowing confusion among workers. Some departments, such as accounting, often require conventional structures. A flat structure, then, may need more time to create and implement than traditional models. Experts raise concerns about managers or supervisors with too much work, scant control, and less expertise.

Advocates of flat organizations counter skepticism by emphasizing that for a horizontal structure to function, workers must be well trained. Skilled workers are the most productive and are in a position to contribute expertise and practical knowledge to decision making, especially when decision makers do not have to navigate multiple management layers. When workers are

A table is set up for the managers of a company to address reporters (Photo courtesy of Annika Haas)

given more responsibility in a flat organization, ideas and suggestions reach all pertinent staff and decisions are taken faster. Feedback is also faster than in a traditional organization, whether it comes from workers, managers, or even customers and venders.

Given that the interactions between workers are frequent, flat organizations depend upon and foster more personal relations between workers and management, allowing for higher rates of productivity. Moreover, as mentioned before, there are better opportunities for workers to excel. This system requires a nonauthoritarian attitude from management. Besides sharing information often and forthrightly with workers, managers must be open, tolerant, and even, according to some advocates, allow themselves to be more vulnerable.

It is important to bear in mind, however, that in flat organizations, given that there are fewer managers and a greater number of workers reporting to each manager, there is a risk that supervisors may become overburdened and exhausted and, in consequence, workers may become confused and frustrated. With too many people taking ideas and information to a single manager, a project may become difficult to achieve. However, these are issues that can be resolved by developing and implementing appropriate protocols and better practices. In the end, most flat organization advocates stress that when individuals work together, they obtain better results than when they work autonomously or under too many supervisors and directives.

To change an organization from hierarchical to flat may prove difficult, because people do not like change. It can take a large investment in time and effort to transform a conventional organization into a flat one. Changing how a company functions involves changing how people relate to work. Moreover, it requires that individuals develop high levels of self-motivation, greater team work, and even more selflessness. Workers must also become efficient managers of their time and resources. Nevertheless, employees tend to find that the benefits outweigh the negatives and that it improves their skills, standing with the company, workplace relations, and self-esteem.

Although young and innovative companies are the most likely to adopt a flat structure, or begin as one, older and larger corporations have begun to adopt flat organizational structures, too. Two of the main reasons they cite for this step is the ability to cut costs, by reducing bureaucracy and other expenses, and shorten processes and the time for decisions significantly. Some corporations that have adopted flatter models are internet-based music provider Pandora and established corporations such as Cisco and Whirlpool.

APPLICATIONS

Some flat organizations are flatter than others. Typical hierarchical structures see power, control, and communication as flowing top to bottom through many layers of managerial control. A flat structure, however, fosters opens lines of communication and control, as well as more democratic and collaborative ways. There are fewer layers of control between top and bottom. Very large organizations find it hard to be completely flat, but they can decrease managerial layers throughout the firm, making it much flatter than a traditional hierarchy. Becoming flatter results in higher efficiency and productivity. To date, many companies, large and small, are increasingly adopting this organizational model.

A degree of hierarchy remains in some flat (or flatter) firms, even as they foster trends such as greater collaboration, communication, employee participation, less dominant managerial models, better resource allocation, and so on. Moreover, for large firms to implement this model successfully, it is important that they have the appropriate technologies for communication to flow rapidly and as unimpeded as possible. Further, the implementation of technology may do away with the requirement that all work needs to happen at the workplace; allowing workers to work remotely be able to substantially reduce overhead costs but it does assume that workers can be trusted to work without close personal supervision.

Managers Roles
A flat organization theory of management views managers as facilitators rather than bosses, meant to support and listen to employees, rather than the other way around. In short, managers share authority and responsibilities with the employees and teams. People who work in a flat organization must be comfortable with flexibility, nontraditional work arrangements, and autonomous ways of working. This shift in managerial roles takes place in various ways among different companies. In some, employees have complete freedom and flexibility about where and when they work. They may also eschew traditional work titles and expectations. Some companies, such as Pandora, went as far as to implement a team solely focused on the workplace experience of employees, taking into consideration their values, personalities, workspace, and so on, in order to ensure employee satisfaction and, in consequence, higher productivity.

Some organizations are truly flat. They lack job titles and roles, seniority, and other common workplace items and trappings of traditional organizations. In such companies, all employees are equal and most, if not all, are self-directed. That is, no one in the firm is in charge of telling others what to do, how, and when. In fact, any employee is free to start his or her own project and must organize all factors necessary to make it work, from securing funds to recruiting a team. This extremely flat model may work well for smaller or medium companies or very innovative companies, but, on the other hand, it may appear impossible for corporations with thousands of employees. Some companies that start flat gradually implement some structure as they expand.

Some companies are admixtures of both hierarchical and flat organizational models. A conventional hierarchical company, for example, may have an internal unit, department, or program that operates flatly. In this situation, employees within that flat space are allowed to propose and implement new ideas and to organize teams to work on them. Among companies with this model are Lockheed Martin, 3M, and internet-based companies such as Google and LinkedIn. The goal is to have innovative teams organize and work more autonomously and with less bureaucracy. A smaller flat unit within a larger traditional system is easier to implement in a large company and can be done in specific departments, such as the research and development department, while allowing the rest of the company to operate, as needed, under more layers of control.

Other companies are experimenting with a newer version of flat organization called holacracy. A holacracy refers to a management system in which teams form systems—or circles—that are both independent yet symbiotic; that is, they operate autonomously yet have a mutually beneficial or interdependent relationship to one another. This relationship can form to accomplish specific tasks or projects. A holacracy typically operates in a flat organizational structure in which all workers or members have an equal say while, at the same time, they must follow the guidance or direction of a shared authority.

In a traditional organization, for instance, a person is assigned to a leadership role, usually written in a job description, and provided with a specific amount of power. In a holacracy, however, individuals select a role—or several—as needed; they may move between teams depending upon the skills needed in each team, at different points in time. The objective is to operate with the maximum flexibility and productivity possible. This system is a favorite with innovative and cutting-edge companies, such as Medium, an online publishing company; Valve, a popular video games platform; and Zappos, an online shoe retailer known for its embrace of change and innovation.

At the end of the day, however, a holacracy is still a hierarchical structure, even though it provides spaces for consensual and democratic decision making. Some experts have said that it is best described as a "hierarchy of circles" in which the circles operate within a hierarchy. This novel system has not yet spread far and wide, and critics have argued that while it works well for many employees, it is also a difficult work environment for others who feel more productive and comfortable in a more structured, directed workplace.

Issues

Critics argue that no flat organization can remain completely flat forever; hierarchies will eventually grow among people, organically or naturally, arising from seniority, knowledge, skill, personality, or a combination of these. Experts indicate that some people are natural leaders and that groups will eventually identify one. Research shows that even in flat organizations, people tend to naturally consider those with more seniority as more senior hierarchically, for instance, even if the hierarchy is informal. Moreover, without much formal direction, it is hard to recruit teams, as some people prefer to work alone, and others in a team may want to pull in different directions and do things in different ways. Lack of consensus might delay rather than speed up a project.

Another problem with a flat organizational structure is that, for a large organization to implement it, the process can take years and require huge amounts of resources. It is also a challenging process for companies with thousands of employees around the world. Although most companies that have implemented this structure have done well, it is not realistic for all companies. It works best, for most large organizations, to implement a flatter structure that is scalable and adaptable.

Holacracy lacks a space for customer feedback. The holacracy's system is basically internal and exists in a traditionally vertical system. Since this situation might be problematic and, according to some, a holacratic system of circles seems rather like high school cliques, in which each clique exists in a flat system—no one has any real authority over the others and leaderships arise organically—but remain within the authoritarian hierarchy of the school.

Finally, other critics have called flat organizations anarchic, that is, headless. In a truly flat organization, all employees seek to be the ones making decisions or seeking power. However, advocates argue that this is not how it tends to operate, because in a flat organization, employees must use persuasive skills to convince others of the soundness of their ideas, rather than act through coercion or authoritarianism, which is likelier in a hierarchical organization and which runs the risk of silencing great ideas. In a flat organization, when a problem arises, employees must act as a jury and arrive at decisions by argumentation, persuasion, and consensus. In other words, it is hardly a chaotic and anarchical situation. As with all situations dependent upon human beings, flat organizations can be healthy and functional, or else, dysfunctional and prone to unhealthy power plays. This why it is important for a flat organization to promote a corporate culture of best practices, good choices, team work, and the pursuit of respect for differences and consensus.

BIBLIOGRAPHY

Augusto, S.L. "Structuring the 'Structureless' and Leading the 'Leaderless': Organization, Autonomy and Accountability in the UC Movement." *Conference Papers—American Sociological Association* (2016): 1–34. Print.

Chakraborty Saha, S. "Going Beyond Designations." *Human Capital* (2013): 48–52. Print.

Claus, L. "Attracting the Next Generation of Workers." *American Fastener Journal* 34, no. 4 (2018): 52–54. Web. 1 Jan. 2019.

Holderness, J. Kip, Kari J. Olsen, and Todd A. Thornock. "Who Are You to Tell Me That?! The Moderating Effect of Performance Feedback Source and Psychological Entitlement on Individual Performance." *Journal of Management Accounting Research* 29, no. 2 (2017): 33–46. Web. 1 Jan. 2019.

Lehman, Brooke. "The Wisdom of Democracy." *OD Practitioner* 48, no. 1 (2016): 52–53. Web. 1 Jan. 2019.

Ruscio, Kenneth P. "Organized Anarchies: The Role of the President in Today's University." *Change* 49, no. 2 (2017): 26–29. Print.

Safari, Ali, Reza Salehzadeh, and Elham Ghaziasgar. "Exploring the Antecedents and Consequences of Organizational Democracy." *TQM Journal* 30, no. 1 (2018): 74–96. Web. 1 Jan. 2019.

Stark, Jordan, and Katie S. Milway. "You Don't Need a Promotion to Grow at Work." *Harvard Business Review Digital Articles* (2015): 2–4. Web. 1 Jan. 2019.

Swayze, Susan, and James R. Calvin. "Nine Months of Transformation: From Leader Development to Leadership Development." *NAAAS & Affiliates Conference Monographs* (2013): 611–624. Print.

Wadlington, Laura, Kara Stooksbury, Christine Dalton, and Jeremy Bruckner. "The Chair's Changing Role after University Reorganization: Is a Flat Organizational Structure Viable at a Small University?" *Department Chair* 25, no. 3 (2015): 13–14. Print.

Suggested Reading

Altman, Roy. "HR Organizational Structure—Past, Present, and Future." *Workforce Solutions Review* 7, no. 4 (2016): 13–15. Web. 1 Jan. 2019.

Knowledge Partner for SAP S/4HANA Transition. (2016). *Siliconindia* 19, no. 10 (2016): 97. Web. 1 Jan. 2019.

Šindelář, Jiri, and Petr Budinský. "Evaluating the Relationship between IFA Remuneration and Advice Quality: An Empirical Study." *Financial Services Review* 26, no. 4 (2017): 367–86. Web. 1 Jan. 2019.

Trudy M. Mercadal, Ph.D.

Followership

ABSTRACT

Followership is a concept that involves the ability of an individual to follow a leader. An individual who practices followership is called a follower. Followership often applies to particular roles in an organization or on a team. An organization or team has both followers and leaders. Followership can be thought of as the opposite of leadership. However, followership and leadership go hand in hand; the success of an organization or team depends on both followers and leaders. Five basic types of followers exist—alienated, conformist, courageous, passive, and pragmatic—although one of these is generally considered the ideal type. Additionally, both followers and leaders need to possess certain qualities for followership to work and to ensure the success of the organization or team.

Significance of Followership

People often emphasize leadership over followership. Nevertheless, followership is just as important as leadership when it comes to the success of an organization or team. Leadership would not exist without followership. In other words, a leader cannot lead without followers.

Followership affects performance. Good followership allows followers to feel like an integral part of the organization or team, which helps them perform effectively. Good followership, therefore, breeds good performance. Good followership also leads to high morale among followers. Additionally, successful followership allows followers to focus on the goals at hand. If followership is lacking, then performance will suffer and the organization or team will not be successful.

Types of Followers

Followers generally fall into one of five categories: alienated, conformist, passive, pragmatic, or courageous. Alienated followers are individuals who are independent, but are also negative and skeptical. They generally do not like the leaders of the organization or team and sometimes have confrontations with the leaders. Conformist followers, or "yes" people, are individuals who do exactly what they are told. They passionately support the leader and are completely dependent on the leader. They typically do not offer personal opinions. Courageous followers are individuals who are self-starters, independent, and take initiative. They are also skilled problem solvers. Like conformist followers, courageous followers support the leader. However, in keeping the best interest of the organization or team in mind, they also offer their opinions and even question the leader from time to time.

Passive followers, or sheep, prefer to blend into the background. They usually do not think for themselves. Although they perform the duties asked of them, they do not go beyond those duties. Pragmatic followers are practical in the workplace. They generally do whatever it takes to benefit themselves, sometimes manipulating others. They also try to limit conflict with people in powerful positions.

While leaders must determine which type of follower best suits their organization or team, courageous followers are typically the ideal type. Leaders should strive to hire mostly courageous followers.

Qualities of a Good Follower

Good followers should exhibit certain qualities or traits. Individuals who practice good followership have a solid work ethic, meaning they are motivated, attentive, and committed to their jobs. Successful followers should also be competent, which means that they should have the skills to perform the tasks the leader assigns. If a follower is incompetent, the leader is typically to blame. The leader should have assessed the follower's competence before assigning the task and then shown confidence in the person's performance.

Followers practicing good followership possess loyalty to the organization or team and its goals. Generally, it is more important for a follower to be loyal to the organization or team as a whole than to be loyal to a specific leader. Successful followers also possess good judgment, which allows them to determine whether directives given by a leader are right or wrong. Followers should follow the leader's directives only if they believe these directives are ethical and will benefit the organization or team.

Honesty is another quality of good followers. Followers should strive to give the leader their honest opinions and constructive feedback. Successful followers also need to have the courage to confront a leader and voice their ideas or concerns. Similarly, followers need to be courageous in situations that require them to go above the leader. Still, good followers should also have discretion, meaning they avoid saying or doing anything that would embarrass or offend their organization or team. Indiscretion among followers can harm an organization or team. Last, successful followers should be humble and not allow their egos to get in the way. Good followers are team players and do not focus solely on themselves. These qualities can help ensure successful followership in an organization or on a team.

Followership and Leaders

Just as good followers must possess certain qualities, good leaders must exhibit specific traits as well. Good leaders are trustworthy. They must show their followers that they can be trusted and that they are always honest. Successful leaders also possess optimism, meaning that they fully believe in the organization or team's product or service. They should believe that the product or service will truly make a difference in the world. Compassion is another important quality of successful leaders. Leaders should care about their followers and empathize with them during difficult times. Lastly, good leaders possess stability. They must remain composed and confident when faced with adversity. Leaders who possess these traits will be more likely to attract followers.

BIBLIOGRAPHY

Kelley, Robert E. "Followership." In *Encyclopedia of Leadership*. Vol. 2, edited by George R. Goethals, Georgia J. Sorenson, and James MacGregor Burns. Thousand Oaks, CA: SAGE Reference, 2004, 504–13.

McCallum, John S. "Followership: The Other Side of Leadership." *Ivey Business Journal*. Ivey Business School. Sep./Oct. 2013. Web. 26 Jan. 2015.

Peterson, Gary. "Leadership 310: The Four Principles of 'Followership.'" *Forbes*. Forbes.com LLC. 23 Apr. 2013. Web. 26 Jan. 2015.

Van Rooy, David. "How Followers Add Value to a Company." *Inc.* Mansueto Ventures. 8 Oct. 2014. Web. 26 Jan. 2015.

Michael Mazzei, J.D.

G

GENDER & MANAGEMENT

ABSTRACT

This article examines the impact of gender in the workplace. The impact of gender on the composition of the management team is analyzed and current trends of women in management are reviewed. Changes in the workplace over the last three decades as the number of women in the workplace has increased are explained including the emergence of the family-friendly workplace. The types of benefits offered by family-friendly companies are reviewed. Employment statistics on women in the workplace, the occupations in which women work, and the salary differentials between women and men are presented.

OVERVIEW

Gender presents at least two primary challenges to managers. One is the impact of gender on management staffing and the composition of the management team. This issue has most often been discussed in terms of women moving into management positions which have been, and still are, in parts of the world, positions traditionally held by men. The second area of impact involves human resource management, which has changed how management deals with a mixed gender nonmanagement workforce who is now often split evenly between men and women.

Women in Management

As the society and the economy changes, many companies have had to reexamine their workforce composition and their hiring practices. One shift that has been significant is that more companies have become interested in recruiting and promoting women into senior management positions. This shift provides women the opportunity to work their way to the executive levels of many corporations. Women are succeeding in a wide variety of positions and industries traditionally considered inappropriate for women. They are also beginning to succeed in areas that have historically been male-dominated including manufacturing, engineering, and financial services.

Companies are seeking women for senior management roles for several reasons. One of the most significant reasons is that women represent a very large untapped pool of talent, especially true for senior-level positions. Companies that desire to strengthen management teams want to remain competitive in a rapidly changing marketplace. They recognize that including women in the upper echelons of management can add new sources of talent and expand the perspectives of the management team.

The expanded perspective of the management group is achieved because of inherent differences between men and women. Many organizations believe that women bring alternative perspectives to the table. The ultimate goal, of course, is to gain and sustain a competitive advantage for the company. As the management team becomes more diverse, customers and clients of the company tend to view the diversity as positive. It should also be noted that women account for over 80 percent of all consumer spending in the United States. Women now routinely buy cars and invest in stocks. They also make the majority of the family buying is. Therefore, the input of women at the executive level of a company becomes more valuable as well.

Women are on the management team signals to current and potential employees that the organization is changing with the times and is embracing gender diversity. Furthermore, the presence of women on the management team can expand the perceptions of the market place and ensure that existing as well as new business opportunities are not overlooked since women constitute a large and rapidly growing consumer base.

Safra Catz, co-CEO of Oracle, the highest paid woman executive in the world (photo courtesy of Ilan Costica)

Organizations with a relatively high percentage of women executives have come to understand and capitalize on gender differences in leadership style and management behavior. These companies are also considered more likely to address actual and perceived inequalities in the workplace and have accomplished that in part by not leaving gender diversity to chance (Gender and organizational performance 2002).

Overcoming Obstacles to Female Advancement
Even though the composition of the management workforce is changing, there still are some issues that impede the progress of women. One major obstacle for women working at senior executive levels is overcoming the inherent difficulties of balancing career and family. Many things in society have changed, but it is clear that women remain the primary caregivers in most societies and probably will continue those roles. It is also likely that women who become senior managers will also be raising a family and may even be caring for their aging parents.

Many companies recognize the dual social role of women, and there have been many programs implemented to accommodate their needs such as flextime schedules and generous maternity leave packages. Women know, however, that utilizing many of these opportunities can stifle or even derail a career. To improve their return on investment for making these opportunities available, many companies have limited their generosity only to women who have proven track records of success within the company. There is also a pattern in recruiting executive women from outside which shows that recruiters and managers do not actively consider female candidates that are likely to make use of these programs.

Many corporate chief executive officers (CEOs) are white, male, and 60 years of age. Some of these men still find it difficult to picture women like their wives and daughters in senior-level positions. There could be many reasons for this blind spot, even including a lack of confidence in their wives and daughters. In some industries, competition is heavy and business is not always neat and clean. The aging CEO may feel that women cannot play aggressively enough to win the market. Thus, many older CEOs let their personal bias guide the recruiting process. Many of these CEOs had mothers who stayed at home, and many still have wives who stay at home and attend to family and social matters.

Another not so subtle discrimination in the executive corps is that male executives may exclude women managers from informal activities outside the office. These activities tend to strengthen business relationships. Season tickets to sporting events, for example, may not be offered to female vice presidents. This discrimination results in women losing important opportunities to build relationships outside the structure of the office environment (Landon 1996).

At lower management levels, women are typically placed in nonstrategic sectors, in personnel and administrative positions, rather than in professional and line management jobs leading to the top. Thus, women are cut off from networks (both formal and informal) essential for advancement within enterprises. Unfortunately, in some large companies and organizations women in high-level managerial positions such as human resources and administration are often considered less vital to the organization. This situation may be because managers tend to work long hours in order to gain recognition and even gain promotions while women have not historically made this commitment or been invited to participate in long hours (Women in management 1998).

Forces that may be underlying explanations of women's inequality in the workplace are the result of structural barriers, stereotypical assumptions, individual choice, and work-family conflict. These issues are broad, power-implicated, ideological forces (Gazso 2004). The "think manager-think male" attitude still dominates many organizations. Research shows that managerial and executive-level positions are still male sex-typed. Many executives perceive that women do not fit in these positions as well as men. Thus one conclusion that the research supports is that women are considered to be less effective managers than men (Bergeron, Block, and Echtenkamp 2006).

Programs for Advancement
Many governments, enterprises, and organizations, through policy as well as practice, have committed to programs to advance women. Some of these programs have met with limited success while others may have gained a higher profile. Generally, they are having a positive effect, especially in influencing younger generations of men and women.

The development of detailed training, promotion, and career plans in organizations has been shown to be an impetus for promoting equal opportunities in career progression. These programs may require specific support through networks, coaching, or mentoring. In addition, these must be continued even during downsizing, decentralization, and delayering. (Women in management 1998).

FURTHER INSIGHTS

Analyzing the Workforce Participation of Women
The workplace faces several challenges in the new millennium, among them that employers face a fairly serious labor shortage. There will not be enough younger people to fill jobs left vacant by retiring baby boomers. Estimates on the labor shortage in the United States range from three million to ten million workers by 2010.

The demographics of the American workforce have also changed in the last forty years. In 2012 motherhood accounted for over 70 percent of working women, and 40 percent of working wives out-earned their husbands. In 2013 it was reported that 74 percent of American women were in the workforce, and they represented approximately 47 percent of the total labor force.

The modern working woman generally enters into the workforce after completing her education, and moves in and out of the workforce several times until retirement. About three fourths of women work in administrative support or as executives, administrators, and managers. Women are obtaining the majority of bachelor's degrees and are receiving a high percentage of medical, law, and MBA degrees. According to the 2000 Census Bureau, there were about 36 million "Generation X" women in the United States and over 15 million were mothers. The Gen-X woman has achieved the greatest one-generation leap in social and gender equality in American history. They were the first to enter the legal, medical, and business professions in large numbers and percentages.

In 2006 Gen-X women comprised just over 50 percent of all workers in executive, administrative, and managerial occupations, and that number has continued to rise through 2013. At the time, this number was over 25 percent higher than it was for that age group in 1983. Gen-X women work longer hours than their elders did and have sought graduate degrees, pushing hard for their futures. In 2006 the breakdown of gender participation in the workforce by race was as follows:

- White women: 59.0%
- White men: 74.3%
- Black women: 61.7%
- Black men: 67.0%
- Hispanic women: 56.1%
- Hispanic men: 80.7%
- Asian women: 58.3%
- Asian men: 75.0% (Employment & earnings 2006).

In 2006, for women who worked full-time, wage and salary workers, the ten most prevalent occupations and number of women workers in each occupation were:

- Secretaries and administrative assistants (3,348,000)
- Registered nurses (2,309,000)
- Cashiers (2,291,000)
- Elementary and middle school teachers (2,220,000)
- Retail salespersons (1,740,000)
- Nursing, psychiatric, and home health aides (1,694,000)
- First-line supervisors/managers of retail sales workers (1,436,000)
- Waiters and waitresses (1,401,000)
- Bookkeeping, accounting, and auditing clerks (1,364,000)
- Customer service representatives (1,349,000) (Employment & earnings 2006).

Women accounted for 51 percent of all workers in the high-paying management, professional, and related occupations. They outnumbered men in such occupations as financial managers; human resource managers; education administrators; medical and health services managers; accountants and auditors; budget analysts; property, real estate, and social and community service managers; preschool, kindergarten, elementary, middle, and secondary school teachers; and registered nurses. Ten of the occupations with the highest median weekly earnings in the 2000s are pharmacists, CEOs, attorneys, information systems managers, medical doctors, software engineers, physical therapists, management analysts, health service managers and computer systems analysts.

There is a disparity in salaries between women and men; in 2012 women earned approximately 81 percent of what men earned. Women also leave their jobs more frequently than men, and in scientific or engineering jobs, women leave their jobs at about twice the rate as men (Jesse 2006).

Issues Establishing the Family Friendly Workplace
The management challenge of dealing with a mixed gender nonmanagment workforce, often split evenly between men and women, has attracted considerable attention during the last decade. This challenge is not just to deal with increased numbers of women in the workplace but to also address the needs of men who are married to women who have jobs and families; or, the dual-income household which totals over 33 million families.

Much of the human resource development efforts over the last decade have focused on women. Currently the age of working women spans multiple generations. They may be married. They may be single. They may or may not have children. The array of potential characteristics is important because it means that there is not a one-size fits all recruitment strategy or benefits package that will meet the needs of all working women. Women of baby boomer age face the challenges of eldercare more than child care. Some, however, take on the care of their grandchildren if their children are divorced or live in two-income households. When companies or nonprofit organizations recruit women, they need to bear in mind that a woman's family responsibilities may reach far beyond their own household.

Single mothers can have difficulties in keeping home and work balanced. For instance if there is a problem with a child at school, a single mother will need to attend to the problem unless they have support from grandparents or nannies. However, many single mothers would still prefer to be at a child's doctor appointment or a parent-teacher conference. This situation means that they need a flexible work schedule so they can take time off from work for these important appointments. Many single mothers do not have the support of parents or family and will need to take time off work as needed to address domestic issues. This may jeopardize their career advancement or even the stability of their jobs. Still, the middle-class single mother is basically far better off than her predecessors of previous generations (Piscione 2004).

As business conditions changed and competition stiffened, one of the easy ways for a company to expand their market share was through a merger or acquisition. The ever changing landscape of leadership that these developments created, along with postacquisitions or merger layoffs, substantially altered the employee loyalty that many companies spent decades building. As the most recently hired or the less essential employees, women have often borne the brunt of many of these changes. The need for corporate family-friendly benefits and nontraditional employment approaches has suffered through the corporate consolidations of the last two decades. In attempts to avoid high turnover rates, which in turn cause an increase in hiring and training costs, employers needed to devise new strategies to recruit and retain quality employees.

Benefits of a Family-Friendly Workplace
The term "family-friendly" encompasses a wide range of workplace benefits and practice, designed to help reduced life's stress and contribute to a sense of comfort and security, which help to support the well-being of an employee and his or her family. Such benefits often include options that enable employees to have more control of their lives. They could include flexibility in working hours or assistance with financial issues. The benefits that an employer gains by establishing a family friendly workplace include:

- Being known for practices that contribute to the support a family needs, which actually produce real economic results, such as higher profits, higher productivity, and lower attrition.
- Establishing a strong correlation between a company's culture of family support that is recognized among employees, among customers that are looking to do business with socially responsible companies, and among communities in which the company has facilities.
- An image of corporate social responsibility that can attract potential investors and new customers.
- An increase in the quality of life and job satisfaction of employees as well as upper management.

Benefits Offered
Since the turn of the century, the most common family-friendly benefits that employers have rolled out include dependent care spending accounts, job-sharing, child care, flexible work schedules and compensatory time off. Other benefits include liberal family leave options that go beyond the legal requirements for such leave. There has also been an increase in part-time telecommuting working arrangements and compressed workweeks which allow employees to work forty hours in less than five days.

Many organizations are becoming creative about the types of benefits they include in their family friendly benefit portfolios. These may include wellness programs, employee assistance programs and home buying assistance. There have also been several education related benefits thrown into the mix, such as scholarship programs for children of employees and tuition reimbursement programs. Community building benefits have included volunteer release time and even concierge services (Clark and Reed 2004).

Worker's Unions & Women
Another way that a workplace can be transformed to be more worker-friendly is through unionization of workers. Women are becoming union members at a faster rate than men, which means that unions need to focus on issues that concern women. They also need to make these changes to stem the tide of declining memberships. It may take some unions a while to shift their emphasis because many unions have been traditionally male dominated and most of the officers are men.

In terms of benefits, unions could win more women members if they would shift their benefit packages to serve women better than they have in the past. Unions may need to have more women as organizers and as leaders in order to convince potential women members that the unions are actually changing. Some unions may be able to make the shift while others may need to wait for a new generation of leadership.

Unions may also need to shift their organization targets and start forming more union groups in places where women traditionally work. If unions offer a good package of benefits to women, they may very well succeed in organizing in places that they have failed in the past. It may take decades to happen but unions will grow if they appeal to the growing number of women in the workforce (Yates 2006).

CONCLUSIONS

Organizations face several challenges in dealing with gender in the workplace. In basic terms, men and women are different in their perceptions of work, success, and life in general. Both men and women want to rise within their organization and to make more money. While they share this similarity, there are other issues and goals that are completely different for men and women.

Women have far greater social pressure than men to be both successful in their careers and to be mothers and daughters. The mother role is fairly clear and demanding both physically and emotionally. Many women are also daughters and in current times, they are often cast into the role of primary care takers for their aging parents. Although the role of men in the family setting has certainly changed over the last few decades, men still experience less of this pressure in their roles of father and son.

Given that women are both increasing their presence in the workplace and their power in the consumer market, organizations need to come embrace women on both fronts. First they must provide a workplace and benefits package that is appropriate to meet the needs of working women and their roles as mothers and daughters. Secondly, companies need to address how they position themselves as a producer, seller, or service provider to women as consumers. To make these changes, they need to understand the marketplace and the ways women view their products and services. It is not likely that men will be able to accomplish that without the help of women in management positions.

BIBLIOGRAPHY

Bergeron, Diane, Caryn Block, and B. Alan Echtenkamp. "Disabling the Able: Stereotype Threat and Women's Work Performance. *Human Performance*. 19, no. 2 (2006): 133–58. Web. 15 Dec. 2007.

Clark, Shirley, and Patricia Reed. "Win-Win Workplace Practices: Improved Organizational Results and Improved Quality of Life." 2004. U.S. Department of Labor. Women's Quality of Life, 2007.

Conti, Maurizio, and Enrico Sette. "Type of Employer and Fertility of Working Women: Does Working in the Public Sector or in a Large Private Firm Matter?" *Cambridge Journal of Economics* 37, no. 6 (2013): 1303–33. Web. 22 Nov. 2013.

Devillard, Sandrine, Sandra Sancier-Sultan, and Charlotte Werner. "Why Gender Diversity at the Top Remains a Challenge." *Mckinsey Quarterly* 2 (2014): 23–25. Web. 17 Nov. 2014.

Duberley, Joanne, and Marylynn Carrigan. "The Career Identities of 'Mumpreneurs': Women's Experiences of Combining Enterprise and Motherhood." *International Small Business Journal* 31, no. 6 (2013): 629–51. Web. 22 Nov. 2013.

Eisner, Susan. "Leadership: Gender and Executive Style." *SAM Advanced Management Journal* 78, no. 1 (2013): 26–41. Web. 17 Nov. 2014.

Employment and Earnings. (2006, Jan.). U.S. Department of Labor, Bureau of Labor Statistics. Web. 15 Dec. 2007.

Gazso, Amber. "Women's Inequality in the Workplace as Framed in News Discourse: Refracting from Gender Ideology." *Canadian Review of Sociology & Anthropology* 41, no. 4 (2004): 449–73. Web. 11 Dec. 2007.

Gender and organizational performance. (2000). *Worklife Report* 12, no. 4 (2000): 10. Web. 11 Dec. 2007.

Goudreau, Jenna. "A Golden Age for Working Women." *Forbes* 190, no. 11 (2012): 56. Web. 22 Nov. 2013.

Jesse, Jolene. "Redesigning Science: Recent Scholarship on Cultural Change, Gender, and Diversity." *Bioscience* 56, no. 10 (2006): 831–38. Web. 15 Dec. 2007.

Landon, S. "Women in the Workplace: Making Progress in Corporate America." *USA Today Magazine* 125, no. 2618 (1996): 66. Web. 11 Dec. 2007.

Piscione, Deborah. (2004, Sept.). The Many Faces of 21st Century Working Women. A Report to the Women's Bureau of the U.S. Department of Labor.

"Women in Management: It's Still Lonely at the Top." *Women's International Network News* 24, no. 4 (1998): 78. Web. 11 Dec. 2007.

Yates, Charlotte. "Challenging Misconceptions about Organizing Women into Unions." *Gender, Work & Organization* 13, no. 6 (2006): 565–84. Web. 11 Dec. 2007.

SUGGESTED READING

Bajdo, Linda, and Marcus Dickson. "Perceptions of Organizational Culture and Women's Advancement in Organizations: A Cross-Cultural Examination." *Sex Roles* 45, nos. 5-6 (2001): 399–414. Web. 11 Dec. 2007.

Bernstein, Aaron. "Women's Pay: Why the Gap Remains a Chasm." *Business Week* 3887 (2004, June 14): 58–59. Web. 15 Dec. 2007.

Browne, Beverly. "Gender and Beliefs about Work Force Discrimination in the United States and Australia." *Journal of Social Psychology* 137, no. 1 (1997): 107–16. Web. 11 Dec. 2007.

Cohen, Lisa E., and Joseph P. Broschak. "Whose Jobs Are These? The Impact of the Proportion of Female Managers on the Number of New Management Jobs Filled by Women Versus Men." *Administrative Science Quarterly* 58, no. 4 (2013): 509–41. Web. 17 Nov. 2014.

Fournier, Valerie, and Mihaela Kelemen. "The Crafting of Community: Recoupling Discourses of Management and Womanhood." *Gender, Work & Organization* 8, no. 3 (2001): 267. Web. 11 Dec. 2007.

Ganey, Jayme, Ashley Battle, and Wendy Wilson. "The Black Women's Workplace Survival Guide." *Essence* 37, no. 12 (2007): 160–86. Web. 13 Dec. 2007.

Gatenby, Bev, and Maria Humphries. "Exploring Gender, Management Education and Careers: Speaking in the Silences." *Gender & Education* 11, no. 3 (1999): 281–94. Web. 11 Dec. 2007.

Hymowitz, Kay. "Think Again: Working Women." *Foreign Policy* 201 (2013): 59–64. Web. 22 Nov. 2013.

Moore, Carole. "Climbing the Ladder to Success." *Career World* 35, no. 2 (2006): 16–19. Web. 15 Dec. 2007.

Perriton, Linda. "The Provocative and Evocative Gaze upon Women in Management Development." *Gender & Education* 11, no. 3 (1999): 295–307. Web. 11 Dec. 2007.

Prichard, Craig, and Rosemary Deem. "Wo-managing Further Education: Gender and the Construction of the Manager in the Corporate Colleges in England." *Gender & Education* 11, no. 3 (1999): 323. Web. 11 Dec. 2007.

Ribbens, Barbara. "Women in Management: Current Research Issues." *Journal of Occupational & Organizational Psychology* 72, no. 1 (1999): 121–22. Web. 11 Dec. 2007.

Rotolo, Thomas, and John Wilson. "Work Histories and Voluntary Association Memberships." *Sociological Forum* 18, no. 4 (2003): 603–19. Web. 15 Dec. 2007.

Smith, Catherine. "Notes from the Field: Gender Issues in the Management Curriculum: A Survey of Student Experiences." *Gender, Work & Organization* 7, no. 3 (2000): 158–67. Web. 11 Dec. 2007.

Solomon, Charlene. "Cracks in the Glass Ceiling." *Workforce* 79, no. 9 (2000): 86. Web. 11 Dec. 2007.

Teasdale, Nina. "Fragmented Sisters? The Implication of Flexible Working Policies for Professional Women's Workplace Relationships." *Gender, Work & Organization* 20, no. 4 (2013): 397–412.

Whitehead, Stephen. "Women as Manager: A Seductive Ontology." *Gender, Work & Organization* 8, no. 1 (2001): 84.

Wyn, Johanna, Sandra Acker, and Elisabeth Richards. "Making a Difference: Women in Management in Austrlian and Canadian Faculties of Education." *Gender & Education* 12, no. 4 (2000): 435–47. Web. 11 Dec. 2007.

Michael Erbschloe, M.A.

Glass Ceiling

ABSTRACT

Two articles written during the 1980s have been credited with coining the phrase "glass ceiling" in reference to barriers for women in the workforce. The first instance of the term appeared in a 1984 *Adweek* article about magazine editor Gay Bryant. The second article was from the March 24, 1986, issue of the *Wall Street Journal* and was written by Carol Hymowitz and Timothy Schellhardt. The term evolved to include all minorities, with the word "ceiling" describing a barrier that women experience as they try to advance within a company or organization. The glass metaphor describes the transparent quality of the ceiling, because it is not immediately recognized or acknowledged.

Workplace Issues for Women

Issues contributing to women's experience of a workplace glass ceiling include work-life balance, a lack of access to informal networks, a lack of effective mentors and role models, and stereotypes and prejudice based on traditional gender roles. A 2009 US Census Bureau study showed that women worked an average of thirty-seven hours per week, while men worked an average of forty-two hours per week. The Department of Labor concluded that women are often unable to attain seniority equal to that of men because of the time they spent away from work. Women are often the primary caregivers for children or elderly family members, and working women must often balance family life with their career.

A protestor in Seattle invokes the glass ceiling (photo courtesy of David Lee)

Women historically lack access to informal networks to develop relationships within organizations. These networks are perceived to include male activities, which tend to be sporting events such as golf where bonding and informal mentoring occur. Despite the fact that mentoring is considered a significant factor in leadership development, women have fewer opportunities to cultivate mentor relationships, especially at crucial points in their careers. Debora Spar, president of New York's all-women's Barnard College, reported that while 46 percent of graduating lawyers were women in 1994, in only about 15 percent of the partners in US law firms were women by 2013, and male partners were making salaries approximately $90,000 higher per year in 2013 than their female counterparts (Spar, 2013). Judith Smith Kaye, retired Chief Judge of New York, elaborated that a lack of mentoring within law firms and within the legal profession as a whole is a primary reason for this discrepancy.

Although obvious and explicit bias and stereotypes have diminished significantly over the years, there remains a subtle bias that women operate on more of an emotional than on an intellectual level. Other sexist attitudes include the beliefs that women are not aggressive enough to be effective leaders, that they cannot be effective in a business setting, and that they are inherently too easy-going and nurturing to be effective managers. If a female executive behaves in a warm and caring manner, she runs the risk as being perceived as weak. On the other hand, if a woman appears to be tough, logical, and unemotional—characteristics typically expected of a male leader—she may be viewed in a negative manner.

Other subtle but systematic factors preventing women's advancement in the workplace include initial placement in dead-end jobs with little to no opportunity for advancement, lack of training opportunities within a company, and sexual harassment. While breaking a glass ceiling involves the cooperation and advocacy of multiple organizational tiers, from governmental policies and legislation to proactive employers and businesses, many experts believe that women should also adopt methods and strategies of their own to move into higher level, higher paying positions. Suggested strategies include becoming comfortable taking risks by pursuing more difficult and visible assignments, gaining the support and guidance from a mentor, developing a style with which male managers feel more comfortable, and accepting the need to outperform male colleagues.

Organizational Strategies
Breaking the glass ceiling is possible as more and more agencies, organizations, and corporations address the issue. Analysts agree that a significant step toward toppling barriers to career advancement involves comprehensive organizational programs that track progress made toward breaking down cultural and gender based barriers. Recommended strategies to create more opportunities for women to reach higher-level positions include voluntary targets for representation on boards and committees, promoting flexible work hours or telecommuting in order to support a balance between work and home life, and creating mentoring programs within organizations. Other suggestions include rewarding employees based on the amount and quality of work or tasks completed rather than on the number of hours spent at the workplace. Finally, corporations have had success when policies and practices are designed to increase opportunities for upward mobility, that establish pay equity for work of comparable value, that eliminate gender, race, and ethnic-based stereotyping, that create family-friendly or parent-track workplace policies, and that collect data to track the advancement progress of women.

Impact
Although there have been attempts in the past to promote workplace equality among both men and women, such as in the 1960s with US President John F. Kennedy's Commission on the Status of Women,

it was not until the early 1990s that any formal legislation was put in place. Title II of the Civil Rights Act of 1991 established the Glass Ceiling Commission to study artificial barriers to the advancement of women and other qualified individuals in the American workplace and to make recommendations for overcoming such barriers. The commission was composed of twenty-one members, with the Secretary of Labor serving as chair. The intent of this legislation was to ensure that all workers would receive equal treatment in employment.

Bibliography

Adams, Renée B., and Patricia Funk. "Beyond the Glass Ceiling: Does Gender Matter" *Management Science* 58.2 (2012): 219–35. Print.

Aguilar, Luis A. "Merely Cracking the Glass Ceiling Is Not Enough: Corporate America Needs More Than Just a Few Women in Leadership." *US Securities and Exchange Commission.* SEC, 22 May 2013. Web. 8 Oct. 2014.

Eagly, Alice H., and Linda L. Carli. "Women and the Labyrinth of Leadership." *Harvard Business Review.* Harvard Business Publishing, 1 Sept. 2001. Web. 8 Oct. 2014.

Frenkiel, Nora. "The Up-and-Comers: Bryant Takes Aim at the Settlers-In." *Adweek* (Mar. 1984): 8. Print.

"Glass Ceiling Commission Issues Report: Discrimination Still Deprives Women and Minorities of Opportunities." *Civil Rights Monitor* 8.1 (1995): n.p. Web. 8 Oct. 2014.

Hymowitz, Carol, and Timothy Schellhardt. "The Corporate Woman: The Glass Ceiling—Why Women Can't Seem to Break the Invisible Barrier That Blocks Them from Top Jobs." *Wall Street Journal* 24 Mar. 1986: 1, 4–5. Print.

Johns, Merida L. "Breaking the Glass Ceiling: Structural, Cultural, and Organizational Barriers Preventing Women from Achieving Senior and Executive Positions." *Perspectives in Health Information Management.* (2013): 1–11. Print.

Kanter, Rosabeth. *Men and Women in the Corporation.* New York: Basic Books, 1993.

Meyerson, Debra E., and Joyce K. Fletcher. "A Modest Manifesto for Shattering the Glass Ceiling." *Harvard Business Review.* (2000): 126–36. Web. 8 Oct. 2014.

Spar, Debora L. "Lean In? Here's Why the Glass Ceiling Still Exists." *Salon.* Salon Media, 15 Sept. 2013. Web. 8 Oct. 2014.

Stith, Anthony. *Breaking the Glass Ceiling: Racism and Sexism in Corporate America—The Myths, the Realities, and the Solutions.* Orange, NJ: Bryant & Dillon, 1996.

Weiss, Ann E. *The Glass Ceiling: A Look at Women in the Workforce.* Brookfield, CT: Twenty-First Century Books, 1999.

Sharon M. LeMaster

Hierarchical Organizational Structure

ABSTRACT

A hierarchical organizational structure is a type of organization established with a series of specific hierarchies. They are one of the oldest and most long-standing types of organizations, based on deeply rooted authoritarianism. In latter centuries, hierarchical structures have experienced many types of modifications and innovations, in order to increase efficiency and production rates. As they modernized, hierarchical structures became highly specialized and bureaucratic. In the twenty-first century, there are myriad different hybridizations and versions, increasingly moving toward hierarchical structures that allow for flatter and more decentralized business models, more team work, self-directed workers, and more open managerial styles.

OVERVIEW

There are many types of organizational structures, the most common of which are a hierarchy or vertical structure and a flat or horizontal structure. From these evolve other types of hybrid organizations, such as matrix, holacracy, anarchic, and so on. In contemporary society, a hierarchical organizational structure—also known as a vertical structure—is a structure in which each entity of the organization is subordinated to a sole entity located at the top of the system. A hierarchical structure is commonly represented by a pyramid, with the most powerful at the top, the middle and lower managers in the center tiers, and the base operatives at the bottom, which is the wider part of the pyramid. The top of the pyramid is smaller because power and status, as they increase, accrue to fewer and fewer members of the organization. At the bottom, there may be thousands of operatives or workers, but each has very little to no power. In consequence, the higher the level, the more power and status is centralized in the hands of a few

The term hierarchy comes from the Greek *hierarkhia*, which means "sacred ruler" and, as its name indicates, in its inception centuries ago, it referred to a sacred organizational order. Being sacred, such a ruling system was also inviolable and indisputable. In other words, a hierarchy was a structure of power from which submission to authority and unquestioned obedience was expected from its members. Many organizations, such as established religious institutions, the military, and team sports still conform to this structure to some degree. The hierarchical structure has endured through centuries; for this reason, some scholars argue that it is the most common human organization system of all. Traditionally, the monarch was at the head of the system—the state—and in feudal times, the system provided a formal and authoritarian network based on hierarchy at all levels of society, with the monarch at the top. It is important to remember that monarchs were considered divinely appointed and thus, their power was largely unimpeachable.

There is no monarch ruling modern businesses and corporations; instead, power is closely and linearly distributed among a collective power of a parent company, a board of directors and a cadre of high executives which delegate, in turn, the management of the organization to their immediate subordinates. The high-level executives that serve immediately under the board of directors are usually known as "officers," beginning with the general director or chief executive officer (CEO) of the company. The CEO is the executive in charge of operations, and he or she reports to the board of directors and is empowered to appoint and control other managers that will report to him or her, such as a chief operations officer, chief financial officer, president and vice presidents, and other executives. A hierarchical organization, then, is

A set of nesting dolls (Photo Courtesy of Fanghong)

a regimented and dominant mode of operation common among most large organizations, corporations, governments, and religions, and each tier has its own levels of management, power and authority.

One of the most important objectives of an organizational structure is to manage the flow of communication and knowledge. In hierarchical organizations, members communicate with those in the immediate tiers above and below, that is, with their immediate superiors and subordinates. Information and instructions are imparted from above and distributed through the vertical channels of management below each level. This structure maintains a limited and orderly flow of information, reducing excess and disorder.

As all systems do, however, hierarchical structures have advantages and disadvantages. Among its advantages are simplicity and clarity of application, less friction and interference by parallel entities, direct flow of communication, and easy to maintain discipline. A hierarchical structure establishes a clear chain of command in which subaltern executives know well the parameters within which they may take decisions autonomously or in the absence of their immediate superiors. The disadvantages are also myriad, especially overburdening people with responsibilities and obligations, excessive rigidity and inflexibility, and a multi-level system that does not allow the rapid implementation of new processes and innovation.

In general, in hierarchical structures, most acts requiring creativity and innovation occur in the higher or executive levels, and the lower the levels, the more routine operations become with the most routine-oriented work set at the base of the pyramid. One of the problems inherent in such a system, then, is that workers at the lower operative level feel stifled, and their ideas are not taken into consideration. On the other hand, there are many ways in which a hierarchical structure may be organized, even though it is always vertical. One of the most common ways to divide is according to functions, such as direction and leadership, marketing, production, finances, and human resources.

In a chart, direction and leadership would be at the top (commonly responding to a board of directors), while the departments that follow, below direction and leadership (marketing, production, finances, and human resources), are all equal in hierarchical status with one another and represented horizontally. Each of these departments would respond to the top tier, not to each other.

Another way to understand a hierarchical structure in a corporate organization is to view the top levels as those where strategic activities occur, such as planning and leadership. The middle level executives are the tacticians who plan and implement the leadership directives through the corporate subsystems below them. The operatives are those in charge of performing the daily routine operations that make production possible. The power to autonomously make unplanned decisions increases with each level flowing upward, with very little to no decision making allowed to operatives at the bottom of the vertical structure.

Finally, there are different kinds of pyramids. While some may be pointed, others may be flat-topped. That means that at the top, the power is more balanced, there is greater equality between managers and the levels below; moreover, it also indicates that there are fewer people at the managerial level in relation to subordinates in general, than in the pointy-top pyramid.

APPLICATIONS

In a hierarchical structure, daily communication takes place along a vertical chain of command in which information flows between the managers and their immediate subordinates. Therefore, a supervisor or manager is responsible for his or her subordinates. Since the orders or directives originate above, a supervisor is usually relaying orders. Some hierarchical structures allow for some autonomy so that in specific situations, managers and workers have leeway as to how information and functions are communicated, designed, and implemented. Nevertheless, directives are still relayed from top to bottom, so that information flows down the chain of command in an orderly manner. Each organization differs in its level of centralization, that is, how dependent its functions are to a center of power, as well as how it allocates authority and its distribution of responsibilities and functions.

In general, theoretical approaches to organizational structures are either based on, or take into consideration, sociologist Max Weber's ideas of principles of management, bureaucracies, and organizations. For Weber, who wrote in the late nineteenth century, bureaucracy was a mark of modernity and much more efficient than the traditional structures known until then. A bureaucracy represented the official tasks and duties of management, and management had the authority to implement its structures through rules. This system ensured efficiency and economic productivity. Weber's ideal organization was meant to divide all tasks into simple and routine operations, with each department tasked with specific and well-delineated functions. Although it emphasized rules and impersonal work relations, it had the advantages of every employee knowing his or her place in the organization and the expectations that the jobs entailed.

Weber's theories fueled a wide array of organizational studies and theories. In the 1960s, business experts from the Aston University in Birmingham, UK, developed a list of factors by which to measure an organizational structure, along the lines of specialization, formalization, standardization, centralization, and layout. Of these, the most commonly used to assess an organization were:

1. Specialization or functional specialization of the organization—that is, the ways in which organizations specialize their activities along functional lines
2. Level of formalization—that is, the ways in which an organization defines roles and distributes duties and functions and the extent to which these are documented
3. Autonomy (or lack of autonomy)—that is, the extent to which decision making occurs in all levels and, in particular, above and below the chief executive officer (CEO).

Organizational context is also important to assess an organization and gauge the extent to which it is vertical and flexible; context includes organization size, whether it has a parent company, number of employees, workflow integration, technological complexity, and level of autonomy from other organizations (e.g., sister companies, parent company, etc.). Upon analyzing a hierarchical structure, it is also important to study the organizational climate—also known as corporate climate—an important term in organizational studies, based on the values, perceptions, environment, and culture promoted in the organization.

Research studies that assess all these factors in organizations find that hierarchical organizational structures are more centralized and bureaucratic; they score lower than other types of organization in management concern for employee participation and involvement; they also score lower in openness, flexibility, intellectual orientation, sociability, industriousness, and innovation or predisposition to innovate. On other hand, hierarchical organizations score higher on scientific or technological orientation, task orientation, respect for rules, protocols and procedures, and administrative efficiency. Many of these studies, however, focus on conventional hierarchical organizations, even though corporations and the business world in general, are moving toward less conventional management models. Organizations in the late twentieth century began to veer away from the most authoritarian hierarchical models and, in the twenty-first century, have increasingly adopted innovative structures and management styles.

There are different types of hybrid organizations. Some are more vertically structured, while others are flatter. In traditional hierarchical structures, power, control, communication, and information flow top-to-bottom, through many layers of managerial control. A flat structure, on the other hand, presents less managerial layers, fosters opens lines of communication, and collaborative ways of sharing information and authority. There are fewer layers of control between top and bottom, and less centralization. Large organizations would find it too challenging, if not impossible, to be completely flat. They can, however, innovate by reducing managerial layers throughout the structure, making it flatter than a traditional hierarchy. By turning flatter, hierarchical structures often report increases in efficiency and productivity.

However, even flatter organizational structures are hierarchical in some ways; adapting some horizontal systems is convenient, because it fosters greater collaboration, communication, employee participation, better resource allocation, and so on. For large corporations to implement this model successfully, it is important that they have the appropriate technologies for communication to flow speedily and freely. The problem with the implementation of cutting-edge communication technology is that it comes with a fragmentation of the workplace; that is, in a global market, work can take place anywhere in the world which challenges traditional structures of organizational hierarchy.

A useful example of a hierarchical structure is the US government. In fact, while operating as a traditional hierarchy, the US government is so vast that it really operates as a structure made of structures. At the top of the pyramid is not a person but the Constitution of the United States. The Constitution protects the rights of all citizens and as such, is the ideal that rules and guides all branches of government. Below the Constitution are the three branches of government: the executive (president), the judicial (Supreme Court), and the legislative (Senate and House of Representatives). Even though many erroneously believe that the executive, or president, is more powerful than the rest, these three branches are equal in power and all three must abide by the Constitution. None of these branches can unilaterally act in ways that go against what is stated in the Constitution. In other words, they would be represented horizontally and at the same level in a pyramid. Directly below each of the three main branches, are all sub-branches that would be represented more horizontally, or flatly, in a chart, layer after layer; for example, the departments, offices, and agencies of the executive branch, or the lower federal courts of the judicial branch.

Discourse
There are many adaptations of flat organizational models into hierarchical structures, a trend that keeps growing. One example is that of a conventional hierarchical company that has an internal unit, department, or program that operates flatly. Employees in that open space are free to share and implement new ideas and to organize teams to work on them. The final aim is to create innovative teams that work more autonomously and with less bureaucracy than the rest of the company. An example of such a hybrid or "flatter" organization is known as a holacracy. In a holacracy, teams form systems—or circles—that are both independent yet symbiotic, that is, they operate independently yet, in some aspects, they are interdependent.

A holacracy operates in an organizational structure and provides spaces where all workers have an equal say while, at the same time, they must follow the direction of a shared authority. A holacracy remains a hierarchical structure, even though it provides spaces for consensual and autonomous decision-making. Some experts describe it as a hierarchy of circles, in which the circles—flat structures internally—operate within a hierarchy.

Most companies are moving toward hybrid hierarchical structures, though it may not be a viable model for all companies. Most large organizations move slower than smaller ones and may prefer to implement a flatter structure that is gradual, scalable, and adaptable. These innovative managerial models may take years and require vast amounts of resources to implement, especially if the organization's structure was deeply hierarchical from its inception.

BIBLIOGRAPHY
Breunig, Karl. "An Exploration of the Knowledge Dynamics between Stable and Temporal Organizational Structures." *Proceedings of the International Conference on Intellectual Capital, Knowledge Management & Organizational Learning*, 34–41. Web. 26 Nov. 2018.

Dunst, Carl, Mary Beth Bruder, Deborah W. Hamby, et al. "Meta-Analysis of the Relationships between Different Leadership Practies and Organizational, Teaming, Leader, and Employee Outcomes." *Journal of International Education & Leadership* 8, no. 2 (2018): 1–45. Web. 26 Nov. 2018.

Erhardt, Niclas, and Jason Harkins. "Knowledge Transfer across Hierarchical Lines: The Important of Organizational Structure and Type of Knowledge." *Academy of Management Annual Meeting Proceedings* 2013, no. 1 (2013): 823–28. Web. 26 Nov. 2018.

Frederiksen, Anders, and Odile Poulsen. "Income Inequality: The Consequences of Skill-Upgrading When Firms Have Hierarchical Organizational Structures." *Economic Inquiry* 54, no. 2 (2016): 1224–39. Web. 26 Nov. 2018.

Friedman, Hershey H., and Linda W. Friedman. "Does Growing the Number of Academic Departments Improve the Quality of Higher Education?" *Psychosociological Issues in Human Resource Management* 6, no. 1 (2018): 96–114. Web. 26 Nov. 2018.

Mont, Simon. "Autopsy of a Failed Holacracy: Lessons in Justice, Equity, and Self-Management." *Nonprofit Quarterly* 24, no. 4 (2017): 25–33. Web. 26 Nov. 2018.

Pooler, James A. *Hierarchical Organization in Society.* London: Routledge, 2018.

Roelofsen, Erik, Tao Jue, Peter Van Mierlo, and Ben Noteboom. "Case Study: Is Holocracy for Us?" *Harvard Business Review* 95, no. 2 (2017): 151–55. Web. 26 Nov. 2018.

Wyganowska, Malgorzata. "Establishing the Optimal Number of Priority Communication Levels in an Organizational Structure Based on Mining Companies." *Proceedings of the International Multidisciplinary Scientific GeoConference SGEM* 18 (2018): 389–95. Print.

SUGGESTED READING

Diefenbach, Thomas. *Hierarchy and Organization: Toward a General Theory of Hierarchical Systems.* London: Routledge, 2013.

Kofjač, Davorin, Blaž Bavec, and Andrej Škraba. "Web Application for Hierarchical Organizational Structure Optimization—Human Resource Management Case Study." *Organizacija* 48, no. 3 (2015): 177–86.

Korzun, Dmitry, and Andrei Gurtov. *Structured Peer-to-Peer Systems: Fundamentals of Hierarchical Organization.* Cham, Switzerland: Springer, 2012.

Pellinen, Jukka, Henri Teittinen, and Marko Järvenpää. "Performance Measurement System in the Situation of Simultaneous Vertical and Horizontal Integration." *International Journal of Operations & Production Management* 36, no. 10 (2016): 1182–1200.

Trudy M. Mercadal, Ph.D.

HUMAN RESOURCE ECONOMICS

ABSTRACT

When firms hire workers they are, knowingly or unknowingly, acquiring human capital. The idea is far from new but only recently has it acquired enough stature to be considered a factor of production in its own right. Human capital theory and the resource-based view of the firm maintain that to prosper, a business must create value in ways that rivals cannot. This wellspring of innovative thinking requires the acceptance of the knowledgeable worker capable of "learning by doing." This current economic thinking drives the more traditional human resource function of screening, selecting, training, evaluating, promoting, and developing employees.

OVERVIEW

In the post-Industrial age, individual and collective prosperity increasingly depends on how well or ill organizations acclimate to the "knowledge" economy. But in order to succeed at this change, employees and managers need to see themselves as more than just hardworking members of the labor force. High wages and steady employment will increasingly go to those persons who think of themselves as an investment in "human" capital.

Employees must, in a word, build a sophisticated skills-set that adds value to prospective employers' products and services. The alternative is to become a casualty of the onward rush of technology and globalization and eke out an uncertain living at a succession of low-paying jobs. It's a grim choice with a decidedly contemporary edge to it. Actually, though, the idea of people as human capital was discussed in 1776 by the father of classical economics, Adam Smith, in *An Inquiry into the Nature and Causes of the Wealth of Nations*. Any worker who invests time and effort into mastering a skill, Smith maintained, has a right to a wage over and above a common laborer. To Smith, this higher wage was just compensation not only for the years of grueling apprenticeship the worker endured to become a tradesman but also for the immediate gratification of other needs that he willingly postponed (Wößmann 2003). Over the next two centuries, then, economists considered learning a form of consumption driven by a particular individual's utility function—the sum of goods, services, and activities afforded by working that each of us finds uniquely satisfying. To this day, ambitious people forgo income and leisure time to undertake years of demanding academic training to maximize their long term utility. But today, pivotally, this investment in human capital is seen as an organizational issue rather than a household purchase decision.

Human Capital

What exactly is human capital? The formal concept arose in the 1960s out of the work of two American economists, Theodore Schultz and Gary Becker. Schultz had observed how parents in rural households willingly chose to sacrifice their own material comfort in order to finance their children's college educations, so convinced were they about the improved earning powers a degree would bestow on their offspring. Both Schultz and Becker were struck by how their decisions were no different than a firm's forward-looking decision to reinvest profits in a new plant and equipment. The two, in fact, were so similar, they further concluded, that intangible knowledge and concrete physical capital actually mirrored each other in key respects. That very idea was the centerpiece of Becker's groundbreaking 1962 book, *Investment in Human Capital: a Theoretical Analysis*. It was a timely introduction, for the traditional factors of production—land, labor, and physical capital—added together no longer accounted for all the yearly growth in gross domestic product recorded for the US economy in the 1950s. Initially at a loss to explain the growing discrepancy, economists assigned it the nondescript label, the 'residual' factor.

Human capital proved a far more satisfying theoretical explanation (Nafukho, Hairston, and Brooks 2004) and one that, in hindsight, correctly assessed the pivotal importance technology would assume in production, service delivery, and information processing in the future (Iacob and Andrei 2011).

Human Capital Theory

Crucially, though, human capital theory, as it became known, was applied only to the household and the nation as a whole. The firm, the source of all the productive capacity and most of the employment in a national economy, was yet to be incorporated. Still, as originally formulated, it did bridge the labor-capital divide prevalent in previous economic thinking on the subject. Education and training no longer necessarily belonged in the broader definition of labor, which stemmed from the axiom that work could be both mental and or manual. Knowledge gleaned from a firm's direct experience with production processes, alternatively, no longer had to necessarily be considered a form of physical capital.

Amendment to the Theory of Production

Before the construct could be applied to the firm, though, one of the most basic models in all of microeconomics—the theory of production—was amended. It conceives the firm strictly as a production function where profits are maximized by turning raw materials, labor, and fixed capital goods (its inputs) into goods and services (its outputs). Whether a business succeeds or fails depends on its ability to simultaneously minimize short run costs and maximize both short and long term profits. To accomplish this goal, the business first has to decide the price it will charge and how much to produce. These decisions, in turn, are heavily influenced by the rents, wages, and interest it must pay out and the quantities of each productive factor it will require to meet its output quota.

The Resource-Based View

It took another twenty years for a successor model, the resource-based view of the firm, to be developed. In this model, a firm is the sum of the strategic resources available to it. And, significantly, many of these are decidedly less tangible forms of assets than the usual plant, equipment, financial capital, etc. Resources like organizational processes, knowledge, and technical expertise, in fact, contribute more toward building a sustainable competitive advantage, provided they are rare, inimitable, and not substitutable. The change of the traditional personnel department into its modern human resources reincarnation is more than just cosmetic. Fundamentally, the processes, knowledge, technical expertise, and other strategic resources vital to the survival of today's firm are the product of its human capital (Crook et al., 2011). A company has to either make or buy it and retain and encourage it thereafter. And therein lays the reason for the name change.

FURTHER INSIGHTS

Compared to human capital theory, marginal analysis, the prevailing neoclassical construct of its day, comes across as mechanistic and one-dimensional considering how simple the basic idea behind it is: The amount of output created by one additional unit of input of labor or capital is a very useful measure. And that's because all a firm has to do to maximize its profits is ensure its marginal costs equal its marginal revenues. Formulated at the turn of the twentieth century, this model bears all the hallmarks of the era of mass industrialization when most of the labor employed in manufacturing was unskilled and, therefore, homogeneous. The labor force since then, of course, has grown ever more heterogeneous and the attendant wage differentials among workers more pronounced (Teixeira 2002). Although not as quantitative perhaps, human capital theory acknowledges this changed reality. Firms that embrace it, moreover, do so because by investing in human capital, a firm is better able to increase its productivity while keeping its wages relatively constant, a sure route to profitability in the twenty-first century.

The Valuation Problem

Still, human capital is an intangible product of the mind and, therefore, cannot be quantified as easily as rents, wages, or investments in plants and equipment even though it is a full-fledged factor of production. As its supporters contend, it must have monetary value, like land, labor, and physical capital. Economists have been grappling with the challenges of determining the intrinsic net worth of the individual since 1694, but at the national not the firm or department level. For centuries, the preferred method relied on calculating the net present value of an individual's lifetime earnings net his living expenses. Applied across an entire population, income-based valuation assays the monetary worth of a nation's stock of human capital. One such exercise conducted in 1914 estimated the stock of human capital in the United States was six to eight times that of conventional capital (Kiker 1966). An alternate, cost-based method of valuation first proposed in the nineteenth century simply tallied up the expenses incurred in raising a child from birth to age 25. Subsequent refinements have veered from this original formula only in so far as drawing a distinction between the costs of someone's physical maturation on the one hand and the enhancement of the quality or productivity of his or her labor on the other. This latter category, it must be said, is rather expansive: Besides education and training, outlays for health, transportation, and other so called social costs are included. More recently, attention has turned to the more focused valuation of a country's educational stock: The aggregate sum of all the costs of every citizen's formal schooling and vocational training. Included is taxpayer spending on public education, tuition paid to private academic and trade schools, company outlays for in-house training programs, etc. Although individual or national in scope, each valuation method can also be applied more narrowly to the firm. So, for example, a firm's aggregate spending on training is one measure of its investment in human capital. However, spending on finding qualified new hires or its total expenditures on human resources also counts as a measure of investment in human capital. A separate set of income measures might include productivity per employee, return on investments in new products, licensing fees earned from patents held by the company, etc. It's fair to say, though, that no one figure completely captures the total value of a firm's human capital. Nor will there likely be one until accounting practices standardized the requisite balance sheet line items.

Human Capital in Perspective

Should knowledge in all its form be considered an asset or just some specialized subset germane to the firm's business or its industry? As far as Becker was concerned, the terms education and human capital were more or less interchangeable. He did, however, draw a distinction between "general" and "specific" education—the former being traditional schooling, and the latter on-the-job training—yet he considered each a part of a greater whole. Firms, needless to say, have long relied upon academic performance to gauge the innate cognitive abilities of prospective employees. Moreover, the reasoning, writing, numeracy, and problem-solving skills honed during the most general of liberal arts educations is thereafter at the firm's disposal. This kind of screening, though, ignores other forms of human capital—mechanical, technical, artistic, interpersonal, and leadership aptitudes—that firms can readily use to their advantage.

Theorists since Becker have thought long and hard about how best to properly weigh the economic importance of different levels of knowledge and skill. One widely accepted pyramidal hierarchy parses knowledge and skill according to whether it's specific to an individual, an industry, or a firm. The more generic the knowledge and skill, the less it contributes directly to a firm's competitive advantage. Companies always benefit from hiring people with a good academic grounding in a particular vocational field like accounting or electronics and or prior managerial or entrepreneurial experience. Although specialized to a degree, academic and vocational knowledge or functional skills of this sort can be put to use across a wide spectrum of industries. More importantly from a benefit cost perspective, new entry level hires generally have already acquired the requisite knowledge and skills at their own or others expense, not the company's. Still, successful careers in any line of business are predicated on a lifetime's worth of learning about its evolving technology platforms, manufacturing processes, product benefits, customer needs, etc. As rational economic agents, employees have a vested interest in industry specific knowledge since the more one knows about these relatively arcane subjects, the greater an asset one becomes to any firm competing in a particular market space. Too specialized for the general public yet not proprietary in nature like the firm-specific variety, industry specific knowledge lies halfway between the two (Dakhli and De Clercq 2004). Sometimes, though, the boundary lines become blurred: companies occasionally exchange firm specific knowledge when unsolved problems with enabling technologies stand in the way of developing a new class of product. At other times, the enthusiasm of most technical specialists for their work fosters informal, intermittent communication among colleagues at rival firms.

Firm-Specific Human Capital
At the pinnacle of the pyramid sits the nontransferable, firm specific knowledge. Few would dispute that the highly specialized knowledge instrumental to creating competitive advantage is much more of an asset to a firm than the general knowledge individuals use every day or industry specific knowledge: enough of an asset in fact to be the centerpiece of the resource-based view of the firm that puts a premium on rare, hard-to-imitate core competencies a firm develops internally. Purists further argue that the costs directly related to their development constitute the sum-total of a firm's human capital. If other firms have access to the same knowledge and skill sets, they do not in and of themselves create competitive advantage (Lin and Wang 2005). Perhaps not the firm's sole form of human capital, it nonetheless may well be its single most important, ongoing investment. To prosper, a firm has to be better at providing customers with a unique benefit and or reducing production costs. Over time, more conventional bulwarks—branding, market share, capitalization, and the like—are less unassailable; competitors can and will respond in kind. Be it product design, manufacturing processes, marketing plans, etc., the only durable defense is to continually innovate—something talented, knowledgeable, and technically skilled employees excel at accomplishing (Youndt and Snell 2004). Indeed, it has become almost an article of faith that a firm can successfully fend off any competitor by leveraging knowledge it alone possesses.

The resource-based view of the firm stresses the value of human capital for a reason. Innovation comes about through complex social interactions involving the informal exchange of tacit knowledge between coworkers on an ongoing basis (Hatch and Dyer 2004). Value is created via these undocumented, often spontaneous, knowledge transfers even though the evidence to support this claim is still largely qualitative and anecdotal. In the workplace, as in the rest of the real world, learning and creative collaboration takes many forms and flows through many channels; some obvious, others not. Existing cost accounting practices, simply put, do not and perhaps cannot itemize such subrosa exchanges since how exactly does a business assess the amount of a firm's profits flowing directly from something so ephemeral and episodic? That's not the same as saying human capital plays little or no role in creating value; it is very difficult to isolate and quantify (Gallié and Legros 2012).

CONCLUSION

Individuals continue to invest time and money today to acquire marketable skills on their own, much like the artisan of Adam Smith's day. Spurred on by the prospect of mutual gain, moreover, high tech firms and knowledge workers seek each other out in much the same way as buyers and sellers in any marketplace have done for centuries. What's changed is the extent to which a firm's success today, tomorrow and five years from now increasingly hinges on the organizational processes that supply the knowledge and skills it needs to carve out a defensible competitive position. Screening, selection, training and development of the firm's human resources are strategically vital tasks. Without the complimentary funding of extensive in-house training and compensation packages commensurate with the value an individual creates, and the indirect costs of structuring and perpetuating an organization where information flows freely and workers learn by doing, these efforts will be for naught. Human capital is fast becoming as important as physical capital, and any firm that fails to adjust accordingly does so at its peril.

BIBLIOGRAPHY

Basdevant, Oliver. "Some Perspectives on Human Capital and Innovations in Growth Models." *Compare: A Journal of Comparative Education* 34 (2004): 15–31. Print.

Crook, T., et al. "Does Human Capital Matter? A Meta-Analysis of the Relationship between Human Capital and Firm Performance." *Journal of Applied Psychology* 96 (2011): 443–56. Print.

Dakhli, Mourad, and Dirk De Clercq. "Human Capital, Social Capital, and Innovation: A Multi-Country Study." *Entrepreneurship & Regional Development* 16 (2004): 107–28. Print.

Gallié, Emilie-Pauline, and Diego Legros. "Firms' Human Capital, R&D and Innovation: A Study on French Firms." *Empirical Economics* 43 (2012): 581–96. Print.

Hatch, Nile, and Jeffrey Dyer. "Human Capital and Learning as a Source of Sustainable Competitive Advantage." *Strategic Management Journal* 25 (2004): 1155–78. Print.

Iacob, Amalasunta, and Andreia Andrei. "Human Capital and Organizational Performance." *Managerial Challenges of the Contemporary Society* (2011): 130–36. Print.

Kiker, B. "The Historical Roots of the Concept of Human Capital." *Journal of Political Economy* 74 (1966): 481. Print.

Le, Trinh, John Gibson, and Les Oxley. "Cost- and Income-Based Measures of Human Capital." *Journal of Economic Surveys* 17 (2003): 271–307. Print.

Lin, Kujun, and Meilan Wang. "The Classification of Human Capital according to the Strategic Goals of Firms: An Analysis." *International Journal of Management* 22 (2005): 62–70. Print.

Nafukho, Frederick, Nancy Hairston, and Kit Brooks. "Human Capital Theory: Implications for Human Resource Development". *Human Resource Development International* 7 (2004): 545–51. Print.

Teixeira, Aurora. "On the Link between Human Capital and Firm Performance: A Theoretical and Empirical Survey." *Working Papers (FEP)*—Universidade do Porto (2002): 1–38. Print.

Wößmann, Ludger. "Specifying Human Capital." *Journal of Economic Surveys* 17 (2003): 239–70. Print.

Youndt, Mark, and Scott Snell. "Human Resource Configurations, Intellectual Capital, and Organizational Performance." *Journal of Managerial Issues* 16 (2004): 337–60. Print.

SUGGESTED READING

Henderson, Daniel, and Robert Russell. "Human Capital and Convergence: A Production-Frontier Approach." *International Economic Review* 46 (2005): 1167–1205. Print.

Hitt, Michael, Leonard Bierman, Katsuhiko Shimizu, and Rahul Kochkar. "Direct and Moderating Effects of Human Capital on Strategy and Performance in Professional Service Firms: A Resource-Based Perspective." *Academy of Management Journal* 44 (2001): 13–28. Print.

Monteils, Marielle. "The Analysis of the Relation between Education and Economic Growth." *Compare: A Journal of Comparative Education* 34 (2004): 103–15. Print.

Francis Duffy, M.B.A.

Human Resource Issues in High-Performing Organizations

ABSTRACT

High-performing organizations are companies that consistently outperform their competitors. Although high levels of performance are due to a number of factors, human resource policies and procedures are a significant contributor to ongoing success in these organizations. One of the foundations of human resource management success in high-performing organizations is the objective understanding and definition of the nature of the jobs within the company, based on empirical evidence, and the establishment of hiring, performance appraisal, and other functions on that basis. In addition, high-performing organizations support and empower their workers through continued training to help them acquire even more job-related skills, involvement in organizational decision making, and financial rewards for contributing to the success of the organization.

OVERVIEW

In recent years, significant attention has been given to high-performing organizations—those companies that consistently outperform their competitors—in an attempt to determine what factors contribute to their success. In organizations that produce goods, it is tempting to point to the efficiency of the production line or automation as a factor in performance. However, the outputs of many companies today are not quite so tangible. Even in traditional production facilities, there are many more factors to performance efficiency than having the newest or best equipment. Organizations are made up of people, and human resources are the most important resource in any organization. Therefore, one of the areas that need to be analyzed in determining the factors that contribute to success in high-performance organizations is human resource management.

Although the fundamental functions of human resource management—recruitment and placement, training and development, compensation, and employee relations—are the same in every organization, research has found that there are significant differences between human resource functionality in low-performing organizations and high-performing organizations. In high-performing organizations, human resource departments tend to operate at a higher level: generating more candidates for job openings and screening them more effectively, offering more and better training opportunities for employees, linking pay and other incentives directly with employee performance, and providing a safer working environment for employees at all levels within the organization.

Not only do the processes and outcomes of human resource activities differ in high-performing organizations but also do their goals. In general, in high-performing organizations, human resource activities are at the heart of the organization's functioning rather than on the periphery, with the goal of maximizing the potential, utilization, and commitment of all employees at all levels in the organization. As modern organizations were beginning to take shape after the Industrial Revolution, there was a great distinction between the various types of workers in an organization. Business owners and managers were viewed as the driving force behind the organization, with production workers, clerks, secretaries, and others often viewed as easily replaceable entities. To run an organization under this philosophy, the command-and-control model was adopted from the military. However, in the twenty-first century, this paradigm has changed. In the Information Age, it is recognized that virtually all employees within organizations are highly skilled and can contribute to the effectiveness and performance of the organization. In current thinking among human resource managers, employees are not easily replaceable entities but rather human capital. This view regarding an organization's employees takes into account an employee's potential within the scope of his or her current tasks, as well as the employee's overall expertise, including his or her knowledge, skills, abilities, training, and education.

Employees are no longer viewed merely as bodies needed to fill positions; they are a type of corporate wealth that can be used to further the objectives of the organization in much the same way as financial capital is used. Therefore, employees need to be

The employees of Goyo Cashmere LLC (photo courtesy of Goyo Cashmere LLC)

nurtured and helped to realize their potential. In addition, their contributions need to be recognized and rewarded and their inputs considered in order to help the organization perform at a consistently high level. Under this philosophy, human resource departments need to set up policies and procedures that promote a high-performance work system. Just as performance and success in the rest of the organization needs to be objectively measurable and evaluated against objective standards, so too must the performance of the activities within the human resource department itself.

Dessler (2005) describes the results of research published in 2001 that compared the human resource practices in high performing versus low-performing organizations. A significant difference found between the two types of organizations was the emphasis placed on various functions that encourage high performance. For example, when hiring new employees, high-performing companies were more likely to promote from within (61.46 percent) than were their low-performing counterparts (34.90 percent). This difference is due in part to the fact that high-performing organizations tend to groom their employees for advancement. High-performing companies also tend to be systematic about their approach to hiring new employees. Significantly more high-performing organizations based hiring decisions in part on validated selection tests (29.67 percent) than did low-performing companies (4.26 percent). High-performing companies were more likely to attract applicants to the job, whether because of their reputation or their recruiting efforts: 36.55 applicants on average in high-performing companies versus 8.24 applicants on average in low-performing companies. On a practical level, high-performing companies have a greater applicant pool from which to fill their open jobs and, as a result, are typically more likely to find the best available person for the job (Dessler 2005).

The impact of human resource policies on organizational effectiveness and performance does not stop with hiring practices, however. Even when one has hired from within and the person in the new job is familiar with the general practices and culture of the organization, he or she will still need to learn how to perform the tasks required on the new job. Therefore, one of the functions of the human resource department is to provide training for employees. According to Dessler (2005), high-performing companies gave new employees an average of 116.87 hours of training their first year, while low- performing organizations gave new employees an average of 35.02 hours of training within their first year. Experienced employees were given an average of 72.0 hours of training in high-performing companies but only 13.4 hours of training in low-performing companies. Although training costs can have a significant impact on an organization's budget, it is very important to train employees. Initial training is necessary to teach new employees how to successfully do their new jobs. However, additional training throughout the employee's tenure is also important. Continued training enables employees to acquire the additional skills that will help them grow and make them better able to contribute to the performance of the organization.

Human resource practices and procedures are important in other aspects of the organization's functioning. In high-performing companies, for example, 95.17 percent of the employees received a regular performance evaluation, as opposed to only 41.31 percent in low-performing companies. In addition, in the high-performing companies, 51.67 percent of the employees received performance feedback from multiple sources, compared to only 3.9 percent in low-performing companies (Dessler 2005). Such feedback gives employees a better overall picture of how they are doing on the job which means that employees in high-performing companies have more information about the quality of their performance so that they know how and when to improve. Encouraging high performance within organizations is not just a matter of prodding the employees to use their knowledge, skills, and abilities in furtherance of the organization's goals. The high-performing organization also recognizes that employees will be motivated to greater performance if they are rewarded for their efforts with something of value. For example, in the high-performing companies, pay increases and incentive pay were tied to performance for 87.27 percent of the employees; in contrast, only 23.6 percent of such remuneration was tied to performance in low-performing companies. The employees in the high-performing companies not only know how they are doing against organizational standards and how they can improve, they are also given tangible monetary incentives to improve their performance and, by extension, the performance of the organization. This reality is demonstrated by the fact that 83.56 percent of employees in high-performing organizations were eligible for incentive pay, while only 27.83 percent of employees in low-performing organizations were eligible (Dessler 2005).

In addition to monetary incentives, high-performing organizations typically try to offer employees other incentives that will meet their individual needs, such as prestige, opportunities to socialize, or job security. Such differences play themselves out in the performance of the organization. According to Dessler (2005), high-performing organizations had lower turnover (20.87 percent) than low-performing organizations (34.09 percent). Reducing turnover helps not only because of the continuity of having high-skilled workers who know the job but also because it reduces the costs associated with hiring and training replacement workers. The U.S. General Accounting Office (GAO) has been very involved in analyzing high-performing organizations in an attempt to determine what practices differentiate them from other companies. The GAO has found that leadership at the highest levels in high-performing organizations is committed to doing whatever is necessary for success including envisioning what changes are necessary, implementing those changes, and communicating openly with employees. Another discovery was that high-performing organizations tend to work effectively with labor unions to resolve issues quickly. They also make sure that their employees receive the training that they need to better contribute to the organization's goals. In addition, high-performing organizations encourage the use and development of teams as a way to advance the goals of the organization. In high-performing organizations, employees are encouraged to get involved, particularly in planning and sharing performance information and helping design strategic plans.

APPLICATION

In the early twentieth century, many organizations were looking for ways to improve organizational performance by taking work from human beings and automating it. In some ways, companies still try this strategy, using computers instead of manual typewriters and PDAs instead of calendars, for example. However, because of the intellectual nature of work in many modern organizations, human capital is recognized as an invaluable asset that needs to be nurtured and utilized. To this end, high-performing organizations recognize that the organization's performance is dependent on the employees' performance, and they develop and implement policies and practices that will support high performance. At its most basic, high-performance organizations find employees who have the potential to excel, set objective performance standards that give them the criteria to know what kind of performance the organization is seeking, and link performance to rewards in order to encourage high performance.

Defining & Assessing Success

The desire to become a high-performing organization is easy to understand. However, without an objective definition of what it means, it will be difficult, if not impossible, to reach this goal. On the organizational level, achieving high performance means that the organization must perform strategic planning and set clear goals and objectives. The organization also needs to define in objective terms what high performance looks like in order to encourage employees to become high-performing workers in furtherance of these goals. The definition of what high performance entails is aided by the development of a solid job description based on an objective, thorough job analysis.

A well-written job description delineates not only the tasks and responsibilities of a job but also the knowledge, skills, and abilities necessary to do these things. In addition, a good job description sets standards for satisfactory and unsatisfactory behavior on the job. Good job descriptions are competency based, describing the job in terms of measurable, observable, behavioral competencies that the employee must demonstrate in order to perform well. The development of an objective, empirically based job description helps the organization better determine what knowledge, skills, and abilities are needed for employees in each job. Good job descriptions and their concomitant performance standards also help employees know what kind of behavior will be rewarded (or not rewarded) by the organization.

It is not sufficient, however, to merely set standards for job performance. It is also necessary to give the employee feedback on how well he or she is at meeting the set standards in order to encourage high performance. The traditional way to do this work is through performance appraisal. This process of objectively assessing the employee's current performance or performance over the past appraisal period involves determining how well the employee meets predetermined standards. Performance appraisals may describe the performance strengths and weaknesses both of the individual worker and between two or more workers. They may be based on objective data (e.g., average number of widgets produced per day; number of sales made per quarter), personnel data (e.g., number of days late to work), judgmental data (e.g., rating scales), or some combination of the three. Judgmental data in particular can be very subjective and victim to a host of rating errors or bias on the part of the person doing the rating. Therefore, in high-performing organizations, human resource policies or procedures are developed and implemented to help increase the objectiveness of the appraisal feedback or give the employee feedback from multiple sources. It is important to give feedback on an employee's performance by measuring it against a predetermined standard or set of specific goals to be achieved for the appraisal period.

One way to accomplish these tasks is through a method called management by objectives (MBO). In MBO, the manager, often in concert with the employee, sets objectives for the employee to meet during the coming appraisal period. At the next performance appraisal, the employee is evaluated in terms of how well he or she has met these goals. Although this evaluation can be done on an informal level, MBO is frequently instituted across the organization. MBO instituted at this level starts first with the organization setting enterprisewide goals and objectives based on its strategic plan (e.g., increase company profits from a particular product line by $500,000 over the next year). Using this information, each department then sets its own goals and objectives for how it will support and help reach the organization's goals (e.g., increase sales of the product in the eastern region by 10 percent over the next year). Departmental goals are then discussed with the employees in each department to help them understand what the organization is trying to achieve and to encourage them to think about how they as individuals can contribute to those goals. Individual employees and their supervisors then discuss the goals and possible contributions that can be made by the individual and set specific, short-term goals (e.g., obtain 10 more customers per quarter; call on 5 more potential customers per week; include 2 more cities in the region). The performance or progress toward these goals is periodically assessed at predetermined times, and the employee is given feedback on his or her progress.

Although MBO can be a step in the right direction in the attempt to link individual performance with organizational performance goals, it is not without its drawbacks. The most frequently encountered problem with MBO is the setting of unclear or unmeasurable objectives. For example, the objective to "come up with a better widget design in the next quarter" may be valid in principle (if the current design is unsatisfactory), but it is difficult to objectively define (how, exactly, does one define "better"?) and challenging to measure. In addition, it is not a reasonable goal: it is futile to put a time limit on creativity. Further, the process of managing by objectives is time-consuming and requires involvement at all levels of the organization to make it work. Although one can define objectives for the individual, if these are not tied in to organizational-level objectives, they probably will not meaningfully or intentionally improve the performance of the organization. Also, it can be difficult to achieve agreement between management and employees on what is a reasonable objective. Supervisors have a tendency to set the bar too high when writing objectives, while many employees tend to set the bar too low so that they can be sure to meet their objectives, particularly if their pay raises are tied to performance. For example, although a manager may want to give a programmer the objective of writing 50 pages of code a week, the programmer may know that this task is both unreasonable and impossible.

To increase the effectiveness of performance appraisal goals and feedback, it is important that the employee's goals be reasonable, objective, measurable, and based on the performance goals of the organization. Even when reasonable, objective, measurable goals are set, receiving feedback from one source is often not sufficient to encourage the type of high performance that many organizations are looking for in their employees. A technique called 360-degree feedback can help improve the feedback the employee receives by increasing the amount of feedback and the sources from which it comes. This technique is called 360-degree feedback because the feedback comes from people who work all around the employee, not just from one person working above him or her. Employees receive feedback on their job performance from representatives of the major groups with whom they interact on the job, both inside and outside the organization. For example, employees may receive feedback not only from their supervisors, as in the traditional performance appraisal paradigm, but also from their subordinates, coworkers, customers, and other groups with whom they interact. This technique gives the employee more feedback than he or she would receive from one person alone. It also gives the employee better feedback by involving those who work directly with him or her. In addition, this approach to feedback can help neutralize a biased opinion from one person by giving the employee and the supervisor a range of reactions to look at, allowing them to examine the preponderance of evidence rather than one person's reactions. The increased level of feedback received from techniques such as 360-degree feedback gives the employee a better idea of how he or she can improve performance.

Linking Performance to Rewards

Although it is important to specify what kind of behavior is expected in the organization and to encourage employees to meet or exceed these standards by providing feedback, in most cases employees need more from the organization than to know that they are helping it succeed. Even in a nonprofit or volunteer organization, workers need to get something out of the situation, whether it is a monetary reward, a feeling of accomplishment, or personal growth. To motivate employees to perform at a consistently high level, the organization must give them what they want or need. The process of determining what these things are and giving them to the employee in return for excellent performance is called motivation. One of the things that high-performing organizations do to motivate employees to contribute to the company's high performance is to link the desired performance to rewards.

Many theories have been advanced about motivation. Some theorists have tried to reduce motivation to an equation that connects the probability of increased performance with such things as the employee's perceived expectancy of obtaining a reward for doing so. Other theorists have stated that different people are motivated by different things, from having one's physical needs met (e.g., food on the table and a roof over one's head) to earning the esteem of others or some other internal incentive. No matter the theory, most motivation theorists recognize that people working in organizations both need and expect remuneration. Sometimes the reward is required to meet basic physical needs or to have the security of knowing that those needs will continue to be met for the foreseeable future. In other cases, pay incentives in the form of bonuses, raises, or promotions fill a need for recognition from others. No matter what motivators an employee has—and high-performing organizations typically seek to meet those needs within the constraints of the organization—pay is always a basic consideration.

One of the approaches to motivating desired behavior in high-performing organizations is an approach frequently referred to as pay for performance. In this approach, the employee is rewarded financially for high performance and their contribution to the organization's goals. This situation is true not only for workers at the bottom of the organizational structure, such as production workers, but for all employees, all the way up to the chief executive officer (CEO). The GAO has researched pay-for-performance systems and has found a number of factors that make them successful. First, such systems must use objective competencies to assess the quality of the employee's performance. As stated earlier, these should be based on empirical research and directly related to the goals of the organization. Second, employee performance ratings should be translated into pay increases or awards so that employees can see a direct, positive consequence of their actions. Third, when making decisions about compensation, both the employee's current salary and his or her contribution to the organization should be considered so that rewards for similar contributions are equitable. Finally, to be successful and to prevent possible abuse, pay-for-performance systems should be clear and well publicized so that employees know the basis on which decisions are made and what kinds of awards are given across the organization. There are many ways that human resource functions can aid the organization's goal for high performance. These include recognizing that employees are valuable assets to the organization (i.e., human capital) and increasing the objectiveness of standards, feedback, and the grounds on which rewards are given. By encouraging high performance in individual employees, the organization as a whole can become high performing, too.

BIBLIOGRAPHY

Dessler, Gary. *Human Resource Management*. 10th ed. Upper Saddle River, NJ: Pearson/Prentice Hall, 2005.

Kim, Hyondong, and Sung-Choon Kang. "Strategic HR Functions and Firm Performance: The Moderating Effects of High-Involvement Work Practices." *Asia Pacific Journal of Management* 10, no. 1 (2013): 91–113. Web. 21 Nov. 2013.

Kroon, Brigitte, Karina van de Voorde, and Jules Timmers. "High Performance Work Practices in Small Firms: A Resource-Poverty and Strategic Decision-Making Perspective." *Small Business Economics* 41, no. 1 (2013): 71–91. Web. 21 Nov. 2013.

McShane, Steven L., and Mary Ann Von Glinow. *Organizational Behavior: Emerging Realities for the Workplace Revolution*. 2nd ed. Boston: McGraw-Hill/Irwin, 2003.

Ming-Chu, Y. "The Influence of High-Performance Human Resource Practices on Entrepreneurial Performance: The Perspective of Entrepreneurial Theory." *International Journal of Organizational Innovation* 6, no. 1 (2013): 15–33. Web. 21 Nov. 2013.

Sun, Lin-Yun, and Wen Pan. "Differentiation Strategy, High-Performance Human Resource Practices, and Firm Performance: Moderation by Employee Commitment." *International Journal of Human Resource Management* 22, no. 15 (2011): 3068–79. Web. 21 Nov. 2013.

U.S. General Accounting Office. Human Capital: Practices That Empowered and Involved Employees. (GAO-01-1070). Washington, DC: U.S. Government Printing Office, 2001. Web. 27 Mar. 2007.

U.S. General Accounting Office. Human Capital: Implementing Pay for Performance at Selected Personnel Demonstration Projects. (GAO-04-83). Washington, DC: U.S. Government Printing Office, 2004. .Web. 27 Mar. 2007.

SUGGESTED READING

Chang, Young K., Wen-Yong Oh, and Jake G. Messersmith. "Translating Corporate Social Performance into Financial Performance: Exploring the Moderating Role of High-Performance Work Practices." *International Journal of Human Resource Management* 24, no. 19 (2013): 3738–56.

Thor, Carl G. *The Measures of Success: Creating a High Performing Organization*. New York: John Wiley & Sons, 1994.

Urwin, Peter, E. Michielsens, R. Murphy, and J. Waters. "Think Outside the Black Box: How Employee Relations Links to Performance." *People Management* 12, no. 18 (2006, Sept. 14): 52. Web. 27 Mar. 2007.

U.S. General Accounting Office. Results Oriented Cultures: Creating a Clear Linkage between Individual Performance and Organizational Success, (GAO-03-488). Washington, DC: U.S. Government Printing Office, 2003. Web. 27 Mar. 2007.

Walker, D.M. Comptroller's General Forum—High-Performing Organization: Metrics, Means, and Mechanisms for Achieving High Performance in the 21st Century Public Management Environment. (GAO-04-3434SP). Washington, DC: U.S. Government Printing Office, 2004. Web. 27 Mar. 2007.

Ruth A. Wienclaw, Ph.D.

HUMAN RESOURCES FOR THE EMERGING FIRM

ABSTRACT

It is the goal of most new business ventures to become viable operations that are successful over the long term. In some cases, the firm remains small, consisting of the individual or team that started the business venture. However, the owners of many new ventures desire to grow beyond this point and hire employees to support continuing organizational success and growth. When this desire arises, it is necessary to put a human resources system into place so that employees are treated equitably and personnel decisions are made objectively, based on empirical data. Good human resources systems also encourage high performance and reward employees for contributing to the success of the organization. Although designing and implementing a good human resources system can be intimidating, many aids are available to the small business owner to help in this endeavor.

OVERVIEW

Starting a new business is by definition an adventure. The entrepreneur or team develops a new idea or product that fills a need in the real world. Sufficient funding is obtained and the initial marketing effort is effective. If this trend continues and the client or customer list continues to grow and orders increase, the entrepreneur realizes that it is time to expand. Since in most cases the development of a viable, growing business was the goal from the beginning, this status is a good thing. However, once the business expands beyond the entrepreneur or the original team, it begins the transition from being a free form group of innovators who do things their own way to being a business with employees (who probably will not have the same vision and enthusiasm as the original team). When this change happens, the organization must develop and implement a human resources system.

Human resources management is an essential function in any business. It is the human resources system of an organization that determines what types of people need to be hired in order to support the organization's goals and processes and sets the standards for hiring the desired personnel. The human resources system provides the training that helps employees meet the organization's goals and mission and the human resources system evaluates employees' performance and rewards them for supporting the success of the organization. Without productive employees, the organization would cease to function. Without a well-structured human resources system, employees will not be enabled to do their jobs well and will have difficulty supporting the organization's mission.

As important as human resources are for the success of an organization, the emerging firm may find it difficult to develop and implement a strong human resources system. One reason is that when there is no human resources system already in place, it is difficult to know where to start. Some human resources functions are obvious: hiring employees, paying wages, providing training, and managing benefits. Other functions, however, may be less obvious: developing solid job descriptions, setting fair performance appraisal practices, and determining ways to reward employees' performance in a way that promotes the goals of the organization. Setting up a new human resources system in an emerging business is different from refining one that is already functioning. As opposed to established organizations with existing human resources systems, an emerging organization must determine what functions are needed and develop and implement the appropriate policies and practices. This shift not only requires a different skill set than is needed to start the technical side of a new venture, but also requires a different skill set from the running of an established human resources system.

It may be tempting for the emerging organization to skimp when designing its first human resources system. The decision makers may not know all the functions that human resources should fulfill in an organization, or they may think that some of the functions are not important for a small business. Such thinking may be compounded by the fact that emerging organizations tend to have a very limited budget for expenses perceived as not directly contributing to the bottom line. Without understanding the importance of the human resources system and its contributions to organizational success, therefore, it might be tempting to cut back on that portion of the budget. However, research has shown that an effective human resources system can be a significant contributor to the performance and success of organizations. It is the human resources system that develops and implements the policies and practices that determine who is hired or even who applies for a job at the company in the first place. Once employees are hired, it is the human resources system that sets the tone for how the organization values and treats them. This treatment can significantly impact how vested employees are in the success of the company and whether or not they feel motivated to perform, not only in ways that meet the minimum requirements of their jobs, but that enhance the performance of the organization as a whole.

Not only does good human resources functionality in an organization contribute to its success: Lack of appropriate policies and procedures can open the organization to a host of unwanted consequences. For example, the U.S. government has established numerous laws that regulate how one can do business from a human resources perspective. The Americans with Disabilities Act (ADA) prohibits organizations from discriminating against either applicants or employees on the basis of a disability and requires them to make reasonable accommodations for people who could otherwise do the job. (For example, a person in a wheelchair who could not reach the top shelf in the stock room could not be rejected from employment based on this fact if it was possible to provide him or her with a tool that would allow items on the top shelf to be reached.) Similarly, the Age Discrimination in Employment Act (ADEA) makes it illegal to discriminate against applicants or employees over the age of forty on the basis of their age. (For example, if a twenty-five-year old and a fifty-year-old both applied for the same job, it would be illegal to not hire the older person merely on the basis of age if all other qualifications, salary requirements, etc., of the two applicants were the same.) Title VII of the 1964 Civil Rights Act makes it illegal for employers to discriminate against persons on the basis of race, color, religion, gender, or national origin. This law covers human resources policies and practices related to hiring, compensation, terms or conditions, and privileges. Without defensible human resources policies and practices in place, the emerging firm could find itself in a position where it could be challenged in court over its human resources actions.

APPLICATION

Human Resources Essentials for Emerging Organizations

One of the foundations of a successful organization is strategic planning. The need for strategic planning is no less important in the human resources arena than it is in other areas of the organization. If, for example, a company producing computer software decides that it wants to increase its share of the business application software market, analysis, and planning may show that the best way to is to offer a new product line. As part of the planning process, the human resources system must determine how it will provide the necessary talent to turn this vision into a reality and how the organization will compensate the new employees for their performance. Planning for human resources comprises many activities, including objectively examining the goals and plans of the organization, as well as the talents of the people within it, to determine what employee knowledge, skills, and abilities will be needed in the future. Analysis and planning allow the development of action plans for how to change the makeup of the current employee talent pool in order to meet the company's needs for the future. This change can be facilitated through the hiring of new employees to meet the needs of new or expanded product lines or projects, or the training of current employees so that they can meet the future demands of the growing company. Human resources planning also involves a consideration of the other functions of human resources, including what characteristics new employees need to possess to best support the organizational mission, how it can be fairly determined whether or not potential employees have the necessary characteristics for this purpose, what fair compensation is for the new jobs and how that fits within the budget, and how and when employees should be evaluated in order to most effectively encourage them to maximize their performance. Once the organization determines what type of human resources environment it needs, the next step is to recruit, hire, and place qualified individuals in these positions. This function of the human resources system includes performing the necessary empirical research and developing objective tools (e.g., job descriptions, assessment tests, structured interview questions) to perform these actions not only fairly, but also in a way that will maximize the fit between the resources of the employee and the needs of the organization. The human resources system is also responsible for training and developing new and current employees in an effort to increase their skill sets, levels of performance, and the contributions they make to the organization. In high-performing organizations, the contributions of the individual employee are rewarded fairly with wages, compensation, perquisites ("perks"), and other rewards for performance given on an equitable basis directly attributable to performance rather than non-job-related characteristics. A good human resources system is also concerned with the fair and equitable treatment of all employees and in improving their interactions with each other and the organization as a whole.

Practical Considerations for Implementing a Human Resources System
One can, of course, implement human resources policies and procedures with a minimum of effort. Considering the fact that most emerging businesses have a limited budget, it may initially seem like a good idea. Books, software, and websites abound that tell one how to write a personnel manual in a few easy steps. Model job descriptions or generic performance rating forms are available at low cost. However, each organization is different from its competitors, and each employee is different from the person with whom he or she shares an office space, so the personnel policies and procedures of each company must take these differences into account and cater to the needs and goals of the particular organization. Although looking at the way another organization implements its human resources system can give one ideas to help form one's own plans, policies, and procedures, the importance of human resources management in supporting organizational efforts for high performance is too important to be based on someone else's organization. Part of developing and implementing the best human resources plans for an organization is to start with the strategic plan of the organization. Using this information as a starting point, one can then empirically determine the human resources needs of the organization.

A cornerstone of gathering this information is to have detailed, empirically based job analyses. A job analysis is the systematic study of a job and all its various components. A good job analysis should be behavior-centered; describing the type of behavior the employee is expected to display. (For example, rather than saying a sales clerk needs to have a "nice personality," a job analysis would collect information about the specific behaviors that define what a "nice personality" is, such as "is courteous to customers," "solves customer problems without becoming angry," etc.) A good job analysis also breaks down the tasks of the job to determine what knowledge skills, abilities, or other characteristics an employee needs in order to do it well. Breaking down information about the job to this level is important because job analysis data is used to show the job-relatedness of personnel decisions. If a hiring, firing, compensation, or any other personnel decision is made on nonobjective opinion that cannot be traced back to the specific requirements of the job, the decision can be challenged through formal or even legal means. The results of a behavior-based job analysis provide the organization with the logical, empirical information necessary to support personnel decisions by providing a structure for determining the job-relatedness of these decisions. Job analysis seeks to discover the exact nature of the job, including its features, the employee behaviors demanded by the job, and how these behaviors can be observed and measured. Job analysis uses a systematic approach to data collection, primarily using data collected from observation. This information results in a record stating what tasks the employee does, how the employee does these tasks, and why the employee does them. This information helps to demonstrate the job-relatedness of various job activities. Based on this data, human resources personnel can develop a valid and reliable selection of tests to be used in making job-related decisions regarding the hiring and placement of new employees and job-related promotion and transfer decisions, developing performance appraisal instruments that are related to both the employee's performance and its relation to the goals of the organization, fairly and equitably performing wage and salary administration, and linking rewards with employee performance.

One of the reasons it is important to do a thorough and objective job analysis is to help ensure that human resources policies and procedures are fair. This issue has both legal implications as well as ethical ones. As discussed above, a number of federal laws are in place that require employers not to discriminate on the basis of various non-job-related characteristics such as race, color, religion, sex, or national origin (Title VII), age when one is over forty (ADEA), or disability (ADA). Similarly, the Equal Pay Act of 1963 requires that equal pay be given for equal work regardless of gender. Other laws require that various types of businesses take steps to hire various types of people who may be underrepresented in the workplace (for affirmative action) as well as making sexual harassment in the workplace—actions taken on the basis of sex that significantly interfere with an employee's performance or create a hostile, intimidating, or offensive work environment—both illegal and actionable. These and other laws affecting human resources policies and procedures need to be taken into account when setting up a human resources system. The reason for these and similar laws governing workplace human resources policies is to encourage an ethical workplace where employees are treated fairly and valued according to the job they do rather than on irrelevant characteristics. Good human resources policies and practices encourage and support employees in becoming all they can become within the context of the workplace and reward them for contributing to the goals of the organization. Good human resources policies and practices are also fair, giving equal treatment to all employees in the organization. Such practices help make an organization a good place to work and encourage employees to become high performers who contribute to the success of the organization.

Human Resources Help for Emerging Organizations
Established organizations typically have at least one human resources person on staff to take care of the company's human resource system. However, emerging businesses—whether they are in the startup or growth phase—often do not have the budget or the need for a full-time person to perform these tasks. As with the design of the system itself, the solution to the problem of how to implement an affordable human resources system that meets the needs of the organization will differ from company to company. However, small businesses that need to set up a human resources system have a number of resources available to help them. The choice of which resources to invest in will depend on the needs of the organization and the quality of the resources.

Emerging businesses that are just beginning to set up a human resources system should consider two issues. First, the organization needs to gather the empirical data necessary to form the basis of objective standards that can be used in the development of performance-based job descriptions, valid and reliable selection tests for use in hiring, and performance appraisal instruments. These tools can be developed in-house, but they require training and skill in order to be developed in a way that allows human resources decisions to be made fairly and equitably and to meet the legal standards for such instruments. Frequently, small or emerging businesses do not have the necessary financial resources to hire someone to do this on a full-time basis.

To solve this problem, some small firms delegate human resources activities to someone already working in the firm. For example, the company accountant may be delegated to the human resources tasks because they involve questions of payroll and compensation, and the accountant is familiar with financial matters. However, this is an unwise approach. The creation of a human resources system from scratch requires training in such activities as how to perform an empirically based job analysis and how to develop valid and reliable assessment tools. Good human resources experts also need to be educated in the application of personnel law and how to deal with employee relations issues. Such activities require special training and cannot be delegated to someone untrained in these areas or who is already fully employed with another job in the company.

Software packages are available that will help one through the process of developing some of the tools mentioned above. However, such software packages can only address general issues in the development of such instruments. Generic software packages simply cannot provide the same quality of expertise as a trained expert who is educated and experienced in human resources issues and who can observe and analyze the jobs within the organization firsthand. As discussed above, before developing a job analysis, performance appraisal system, or other instrument to be used as a part of the human resources system, a thorough, empirically based job analysis needs to be performed. It is unlikely that a software package will be able to provide the type of expertise necessary to accomplish this task. Another option available to the emerging firm is to hire a consultant to develop the tools and set up the human resources system. Consultants are available who can perform rigorous job analyses and develop empirically based job descriptions, validate assessment tests to be used in the hiring process, and create performance appraisal instruments based on objective, measurable standards of success. Typically, the consultants who do such work for a company can also provide the training necessary for managers to use the tools effectively. Consultants can also be hired to develop and implement fair and equitable compensation packages, set up payroll software, or write personnel manuals delineating human resources policies and practices for the company.

Once this initial analytical and developmental work is done, the emerging firm may be able to handle the ongoing human resources functions itself. Human resources information system (HRIS) software can then help automate repetitive or quantitative functions and manage human resources data. These software packages are available in affordable versions for small businesses. In addition, companies are available that will consult on human resources issues for a retainer at a much lower rate than it would take to hire a full-time human resources person. The development and implementation of a valid and fair human resources system goes a long way to helping an organization—whether it is emerging or established—to thrive. Although human resources systems are just as necessary in small, emerging businesses as they are in large, established businesses, they do not necessarily require the outlay of a great deal of capital or the hiring of a full-time staff. As the company continues to grow, the human resources system can grow along with it in a way that continues to support its success.

BIBLIOGRAPHY

Dessler, Gary. *Human Resource Management*. 13th ed. Boston: Pearson/Prentice Hall, 2013.

McShane, Steven L., and Mary Ann Von Glinow. *Organizational behavior: Emerging Realities for the Workplace Revolution*. 4th ed. Boston: McGraw-Hill/Irwin, 2008.

Messersmith, Jake G., and William J. Wales. "Entrepreneurial Orientation and Performance in Young Firms: The Role of Human Resource Management." *International Small Business Journal* 31, no. 2 (2013): 115–36. Web. 20 Nov. 2013.

Ming-Chu, Y. "The Influence of High-Performance Human Resource Practices on Entrepreneurial Performance: The Perspective of Entrepreneurial Theory." *International Journal of Organizational Innovation* 6, no. 1 (2013): 15–33. Web. 20 Nov. 2013.

Savitz, Eric. "The Three Things Startup Founders Need to Know about HR." Forbes.com (2012, Apr. 9): 40. Web. 20 Nov. 2013.

Stillman, Richard J. *Small Business Management: How to Start and Stay in Business*. Boston: Little, Brown and Company, 1983.

SUGGESTED READING

Flamholtz, Eric G. *How to Make the Transition from an Entrepreneurship to a Professionally Managed Firm*. San Francisco: Jossey-Bass Publishers, 1986.

Gangemi, R.A., and D. Fenn. "FMLA? ADA? OSHA? Help!" *Inc.* 17, no. 5 (1995, Apr.): 112. Web. 29 Mar. 2007.

Paskin, Janet. "Programmers Making Sex Jokes and Other Reasons Startups Need HR Departments." Businessweek.com. (2013, Mar. 22). Web. 20 Nov. 2013.

Young, G. "How to…Implement a New HR System." *People Management* 10, no. 12 (2004, June 17): 40–41. Web. 29 Mar. 2007.

Ruth A. Wienclaw, Ph.D.

Impression Management

ABSTRACT

In the social sciences, impression management refers to the processes through which people attempt to influence the way other people perceive them. It is sometimes used more broadly to refer to the ways people attempt to influence other peoples' perceptions in general, whether of themselves, other people, an object, or an idea. However, it is in the first sense—how people influence the ways they are perceived—that the term was formulated, and that most sociological and psychological work on impression management continues to focus on.

Many of the most interesting aspects of impression management are the subconscious processes, but it also includes conscious behaviors such as simply suppressing overt emotional responses in inappropriate environments (e.g., not laughing in church or crying in business meetings) as well as consciously manipulating others' perceptions. In the 2010s, much work has focused on the way impression management occurs online and on social media.

BACKGROUND

The concept of impression management was introduced in sociologist Erving Goffman's *The Presentation of Self in Everyday Life*, first published in Scotland in 1956, but it did not reach a wide audience (even in the field) until its American publication in 1959. It has since been recognized as one of the most influential books in the social sciences. In his initial explanation of impression management, Goffman (1922–82) used an extended analogy of social interactions between individuals as a theatrical performance in which each actor is making decisions about the aspects of their persona to highlight through their performance, based on their self-conception and the impression they want to make on others.

Beyond the idea that people try to influence the way others see them, Goffman's initial formulation has two other important ideas. First, that the presentation of self is—again, consciously or unconsciously—a mutually cooperative effort, in that most social interactions include a mutually agreed-upon "definition of the situation," in Goffman's terminology. This situation leads to the actors assisting each other in maintaining their respective personae. One of the examples Goffman gives is the way that people at a formal event may pretend not to notice when a fellow attendee trips or spills a drink, just as the attendee attempts to quickly recover and pretend it didn't happen. In everyday life, people may think of these actions as simply part of etiquette or manners, as the way things are done, or, in Chinese social life, as saving face. Goffman's analysis focuses on the motivation underlying such systems of etiquette, which leads to his second idea: that the core motive driving impression management is to avoid embarrassment.

Goffman extended his work in 1967's *Interaction Ritual*, which borrowed the Chinese idea of face and turned it into a Western sociological term meaning positive social value. According to *Interaction Ritual*, etiquette can be understood as a set of ceremonial rules of conduct that act as constraints in actors' behavior during social interactions. Both of Goffman's books continue to be widely referenced in the social sciences.

OVERVIEW

Impression management is no longer solely the purview of sociology, however. It has become an area of study in psychology, business and management studies, and communication studies, including studies

A drawing of Erving Goffman (image courtesy of キヨンネ)

of social media and other computer-mediated communications. Social psychologist Edward Jones and others introduced Goffman's work to the field of psychology in the 1960s, and it helped to inform the concept of social identity—the version or construct of an individual that other people perceive in social interactions. From a social psychological perspective, impression management is a system of processes aimed at influencing one's own social identity.

Impression management begins in childhood—just how early is not something psychologists agree on, but by an early age children are able to demonstrate that they can foresee the effect that their behavior and words will have on other people's attitudes toward them and will even express concerns about this unprompted. (Impression management at very young ages depends on theory of mind—the ability to understand that other people have states of mind different from one's own. One of the major debates in child psychology is whether or not this exists in children under the age of three or four.)

Concepts of impression management have been taught in several industries in order to facilitate professional communication. For instance, impression management theory has been taught in the healthcare field as a way to explain to healthcare providers the importance of balancing the needs of professionalism with the emotional needs of patients and their loved ones. Businesses have also used impression management theory as a way to discuss cross-cultural communication and the ways that interactions can have different meanings in different cultures, or that ceremonial rules of conduct governing such interactions vary from culture to culture.

Impression management theory has found new importance with the rise of the internet and social media. Goffman's work, and most impression management work until the 1990s, focused on face-to-face interactions. Much of that work is still applicable to online interactions. But just as mentions of body language or tone of voice would be inapplicable to most online interactions, online interactions also involve previously unexplored considerations. Sociolinguists have explored the ways that spelling words out or using abbreviations and using punctuation online conveys different tones to different demographic groups—ways that have changed over the lifespan of the internet. Further, the lack of a physical presence has not only led to greater possibilities of conscious deception—from slight exaggerations to catfishing, the use of a made-up persona on online dating sites, for example—but to the phenomena of cyberbullying and trolling, with sociological studies confirming that online users feel free to be crueler in their social interactions online than they would be in face-to-face interactions.

Impression management, however, involves much more than intentional deception or manipulation. A subtler social media example would be a Facebook or Instagram user untagging themselves from a photo that they find unflattering. (Sociologists call this a subtractive strategy.) The user may give little thought to this choice, and it would be a stretch to call this action deceptive; it amounts simply to selecting the photos that are easily identified as positive depictions of the user, and thus subtly changing the online presentation of their identity.

BIBLIOGRAPHY
Bertino, Elisa, and Kenji Takahashi. *Identity Management: Concepts, Technologies, and Systems.* Norwood, MA: Artech, 2011.

Collins, Randall. *Interaction Ritual Chains.* Princeton, NJ: Princeton University Press, 2005.

Cunningham, Carolyn, ed. *Social Networking and Impression Management: Self-Presentation in the Digital Age.* Lanham, MD: Lexington, 2013.

DuBrin, Andrew. *Impression Management in the Workplace.* New York: Routledge, 2010.

Goffman, Erving. *Interaction Ritual: Essays in Face to Face Behavior.* Piscataway, NJ: Aldine, 2005.

Goffman, Erving. *The Presentation of Self in Everyday Life.* New York: Anchor, 2014.

Laurent, Maryline, and Samia Bouzefrane. *Digital Identity Management.* London: Elsevier, 2015.

Leary, Mark R., and Robin M. Kowalski. "Impression Management: A Literature Review and Two-Component Model." *Psychological Bulletin* 107.1 (1990): 34–47. Digital file.

Mose, Tamara R. *The Playdate: Parents, Children, and the New Expectations of Play.* New York: New York University Press, 2016.

Bill Kte'pi, M.A.

INCLUSIVE LEADERSHIP

ABSTRACT

Inclusive leadership is a style of management that has risen to prominence in recent years and is widely seen as a significant improvement over the relatively uninspiring transactional leadership styles common in previous generations of leaders. While it has several different interpretations, most of these agree that the inclusive leader is one who is available to subordinates, who cares about their ideas and motivations, and who is willing to hear input from all levels of the organization.

OVERVIEW

Inclusive leadership is closely related to transformational leadership, a style that seeks to inspire the members of an organization to work together in order to create a system that is greater than the sum of its parts. In the literature of the fields of business and management, the idea of inclusive leadership generally has two possible interpretations. The first interpretation revolves around an understanding of the value of diversity in organizations (Naudé, Stanley, and Ratcliffe 2015). The traditional approach to management and organizational staffing was to hire people who fit into the corporate mold, the so called "organization man" discussed in studies of the American and Japanese business worlds. The goal was to hire the "right kind" of people who would see the world in the same way that the organization's leadership did so that there would be a harmonious and productive working environment. The problem that arose with this approach was that it led to tunnel vision, because people tended to see things only from their own perspective, and if everyone in an organization has more or less the same perspective, then problems that require analysis through a different type of lens may be difficult or impossible for that organization to notice, much less solve. This situation is the reason there is a need for leadership that recognizes the importance of including many different kinds of people, each with his or her own background and beliefs (Hafford-Letchfield, Lambley, Spolander, and Cocker 2014; Ashikali and Groeneveld 2015).

The origins of this appreciation for diversity in organizations can be traced back to the 1960s and the beginnings of the Civil Rights movement, which encouraged members of many different racial and ethnic groups to advocate for their communities' needs. This work helped the struggle for women's rights and rights for lesbian, gay, bisexual, and transgendered (LGBT) persons. Companies have realized that building diverse teams is not only the right thing to do morally, ethically, and legally; it also makes good business sense. Companies develop and market products and services to all different kinds of people, so hiring only one type of person (such as white males) and expecting that group to be able to understand the needs and desires of every other group would be a recipe for disaster. Inclusive leadership understands this, and draws upon a rich variety of people and experiences in order to form a better connection with its diverse customer base (Mitchell and Conference Board 2010).

The second interpretation of inclusive leadership found in management texts refers to a leader's interpersonal style rather than to the leader's attitude toward diversity. In the past, a leader was expected to have all the answers because the assumption was that the person who best understands how things should be done is the person who should be in charge, telling everyone else what to do. Sometimes this approach made sense, especially during periods of history prior to the start of public education because leaders back then might very well be the only ones in the group with the relevant experience and education to see how a problem should be approached.

FURTHER INSIGHTS

In the modern period, it has gradually become clear that it is not very common for only the leader to understand the situation an organization faces. More often, leaders are faced with problems that arise from many different areas, and it is not uncommon for leaders to be unfamiliar with these. A factor that has contributed to this trend is the increasing specialization of the modern economy. People do jobs that are more and more detailed, requiring ever greater amounts of specialized training, so that it is beyond the capacity of a single individual to understand every task that is carried out on a day-to-day basis within the organization (Burrello, Sailor, and Kleinhammer-Tramill 2013).

One hundred years ago, the leader of a company might very well have experienced doing every single job in the firm, such that he—it would almost certainly have been a man—could walk along the factory line, giving the workers advice about their tasks. If one imagines trying to do something similar at one of Silicon Valley's giant technology firms, the need for new leadership styles suddenly becomes clear. Because it is no longer possible for one person to have all the answers, leaders are realizing that the most useful approach they can adopt is one of inclusion, where they get employees at the organization to commit their time, energy, and expertise to helping the company succeed (Hollander 2012). Modern leadership theories rely heavily on ideas around social exchange, the idea being that people follow their leaders because the leaders provide them with something in exchange for their cooperation.

Employee work engagement is a measurement of an employee's level of interest in the work he or she has been assigned to complete. Generally, employee work engagement is higher when employees are assigned tasks they know how to do and have the proper authority to perform them. Inclusive leadership strives to ensure that employee work engagement remains high by aligning workers with tasks to which they are best suited. Further, inclusive leaders are seen as workers' allies, addressing workplace issues fairly and helping solve problems. Social exchange theory states that if one person performs a task for another, then the person who benefitted will be more likely to reciprocate.

Viewpoints

Much of the discussion about inclusive leadership focuses not on whether it is a good idea—few dispute this reality—but on how it should be practiced. These conversations are of two broad types: things that a leader should do in order to be inclusive and ways that a leader should behave as part of being inclusive.

Availability. Availability is the foremost quality that should be in an inclusive leader's toolkit. This means that the leader needs to be willing to sit down with his or her staff whenever they need to discuss an issue related to their work or which might have an effect on their work. Some leaders, especially those with introverted tendencies, find it difficult to cope with this much personal contact, so they devise ways to distance themselves from staff in order to avoid it, such as closing the office door, choosing an office farther away from the rest of the department, or requiring everyone to work with a secretary or an administrative assistant to schedule a meeting instead of simply answering their own phone. Those leaders who understand the importance of inclusion, however, make themselves available to their staff, because they feel that part of a leader's role is to listen and interact with everyone on the team. After all, before everyone can be included, everyone has to be able to be heard (Rumsey 2013).

Accessibility. A quality closely related to availability is accessibility. At first the two might seem almost synonymous, but there is a distinction because it is possible for a leader to be "technically" available yet remain not very accessible. In a hypothetical call center, thirty technical support people are supervised by a manager. The manager has an open-door policy that is much spoken of, and all employees are reminded on a regular basis that they can go and see the manager any time they have an issue to discuss. This manager can say that she makes every effort to be available for her staff whenever they might need her. However, it turns out that the call center also keeps very strict metrics about how much time staff spend away from their phones. Any time spent away must have a documented explanation, and the paperwork required to document a conference with the manager is considerable. The effect of this policy would be that very few people would take the time to go and speak to the manager, unless there was a very compelling reason to do so. The manager is available (the door is always open) but not very accessible (because the call center policy acts as an obstacle to meeting with the manager). A more inclusive approach in this scenario might be for the manager to schedule fifteen minutes with each employee each week, so they all feel that they have access to someone who will hear their ideas or can help them, should the need arise (Couto 2010).

Openness. Along with availability and accessibility, the quality most often seen in inclusive leaders is openness. Openness refers to the leader's ability to be honest and authentic with followers, instead of refusing to share information with them or help them to understand how their work fits into the larger picture of the work being carried on by the organization. Some transactional leaders feel that in order to maintain a position of superiority above those around them, they need to limit others' access to information about the organization's operations. These leaders will typically give orders to others but will refuse to clarify why the orders are being given or what the ultimate use for the work being requested will be.

To continue with the call center example above, the manager of the call center might inform all employees that they must reduce their average call times to less than one minute per call. Employees who have a higher level of organizational commitment will immediately want to know more about this directive (Wuffli 2015)—whose idea is it, and what is the reason for it? It could be an attempt to reduce costs by using the phones less, or it could be an effort to make customers happier by resolving their problems more quickly. Knowing the answers to questions like these will help the employees understand how they should act: should they rush people off the phones at all costs, because the head of the company is adamant that this change happen immediately, or should they just make a mild effort to be more terse, as might be indicated if the project were just a low-stakes experiment being conducted by the office leader for a few days?

Whatever the answers to these questions might be, it is how the manager responds to them that shows the extent to which the office embraces an inclusive leadership model. A person following the traditional model of leadership would be very likely to refuse to share any additional information, making clear that the only information the employees needed was that which had been given (Brennan 2014). This type of response is frustrating for employees and can cause some to feel that there actually is no useful purpose to the orders they have been given other than to harass people and raise their levels of anxiety.

An inclusive response, on the other hand, would be one in which the leader openly shared why the change in procedure is needed. Possibly, the supervisor does not know either and is just following orders from her superiors, in which case she may empathize with the potential issues that the change might cause. Responding in this way removes barriers between leaders and followers, instead of reinforcing them. Followers who receive an inclusive response feel that they and their leader are working together, both trying to help each other get the work done even if they do not have as complete an understanding of the big picture as they might wish (Esposito and Normore 2015).

While some advocates of more charismatic leadership argue that using an inclusive style in this way could erode the authority traditionally associated with a leadership role—allowing staff to feel that they are on a par with the leader in terms of expertise and knowledge—this situation is not what usually happens. Instead, those who are exposed to an inclusive style tend to feel more committed to the organization and more willing to use their own creativity and initiative to develop improved products and processes. This willingness is known as affective organizational commitment. Katz and Miller (2014) argue that inclusive leadership is no longer optional in the rapidly evolving business environment in which agility is key to survival. Inclusive leadership's benefits include higher levels of optimism among employees, attributable to the fact that being able to share their views with their leaders gives them the feeling that ideas that they share with the management will actually be heard, considered, and possibly even implemented (Ruaire, Ottesen, and Precey 2013).

BIBLIOGRAPHY

Ashkali, Tanachia, and Sandra Groeneveld. "Diversity Management in Public Organizations and Its Effect on Employees' Affective Commitment: The Role of Transformational Leadership and the Inclusiveness of the Organizational Culture." *Review of Public Personnel Administration* 35, no. 2 (2015): 146–68. Web. 3 Jan. 2016.

Brennan, Dennis. *As a Leader: 15 Points to Consider for More Inclusive Leadership*. Mustang, OK: Tate Publishing, 2014.

Burrello, Leonard C., Wayne Sailor, and Jeannie Kleinhammer-Tramill. *Unifying Educational Systems: Leadership and Policy Perspectives*. New York: Routledge, 2013.

Choi, Suk Bong, et al. "Inclusive Leadership and Employee Well-Being: The Mediating Role of a Person-Job Fit." *Journal of Happiness Studies* (2016). Web. 28 July 2017.

Cuoto, Richard A. *Political and Civic Leadership: A Reference Handbook*. Los Angeles: SAGE Reference, 2010.

Esposito, M.C. Kate, and Anthony Normore. *Inclusive Practices and Social Justice Leadership for Special Populations in Urban Settings: A Moral Imperative*. Charlotte, NC: Information Age Publishing, 2015.

Hafford-Letchfield, Trish, Sharon Lambley, Gary Spolander, and Christine Cocker. *Inclusive Leadership in Social Work and Social Care*. Bristol, UK: Policy Press, 2014.

Hollander, Edwin P. *Inclusive Leadership: The Essential Leader-Follower Relationship*. New York: Routledge, 2012.

Katz, Judith H., and Frederick A. Miller. "Leaders Getting Different." *OD Practitioner* 46, no. 3 (2014): 40–45. Web. 3 Jan. 2016.

Mitchell, Charles, and Conference Board. *Mind the Gap: Overcoming Organizational Barriers to Develop Inclusive Leaders*. New York: Conference Board, 2010.

Naudé, Sarah, Matt Stanley, and Verify Ratcliffe. "Inclusive Leadership Matters to Performance." *Human Resources Magazine* 20, no. 4 (2015): 16–17. Web. 3 Jan. 2016.

Ruaire, G. Mac., Eli Otteson, and R. Precey. *Leadership for Inclusive Education: Values, Vision and Voices*. Boston: Sense Publishers, 2010.

Rumsey, Michael G. *The Oxford Handbook of Leadership*. New York: Oxford University Press, 2013.

Wuffli, Peter A. *Inclusive Leadership*. New York: Springer, 2015.

SUGGESTED READING

Booysen, Lize. "The Development of Inclusive Leadership Practice and Processes." In *Diversity at Work: The Practice of Inclusion*, edited by Bernardo M. Ferdman and Barbara R. Deane. San Francisco: Jossey-Bass, 2014.

Choi, Suk B., Thi H. Tran, and Byung I. Park. "Inclusive Leadership and Work Engagement: Mediating Roles of Affective Organizational Commitment and Creativity." *Social Behavior and Personality* 43, no. 6 (2015): 931–44.

Edmunds, Alan L., and Robert B. Macmillan. *Leadership for Inclusion: A Practical Guide*. Rotterdam: Sense Publishers, 2010.

Fierke, Kerry K., K.W. Lui, Gardner A. Lepp, and A.J. Baldwin. "Teaching Inclusive Leadership through Student-Centered Practices." *Journey of the Academy of Business Education* 15 (2014): 51–65. Web. 3 Jan. 2016.

"Inclusive Leadership Still Thin on the Ground." *Coaching at Work* 10, no. 1 (2015): 8. Web. 3 Jan. 2016.

Prime, Jeanine, Mike Otterman, and Elizabeth R. Salib. "Engaging Men through Inclusive Leadership." In *Gender in Organizations: Are Men Allies of Adversaries to Women's Career Advancement?*, edited by Ronald J. Burke and Debra A. Major. Northampton, MA: Edward Elgar Publishing.

Scott Zimmer, J.D.

Innovation

ABSTRACT

Innovation is the process of developing and bringing to market new products, services, ideas, or solutions to problems. This concept differs from invention, which is the development of new devices, methods, or techniques. Inventions are not necessarily innovations. For an invention to be an innovation, it must be introduced into the marketplace and become generally accepted.

Technology is intricately linked to the state of society and quality of life. Understanding innovation is not just a question of understanding business and technology, but it is also how society responds to technological change and the nature of sociotechnical systems.

OVERVIEW

Developing innovative products can be expensive, and success is far from guaranteed; as many as 75 percent of new products introduced into the marketplace fail. However, the cost of not being innovative can be just as high; many companies fail as a result of being overtaken in the marketplace by competitors with more innovative products and services. Thus, understanding innovation is important to ensure business success.

The earliest literature described the process of innovation as linear. Invention led to innovation, which then led to diffusion (the process of the innovation spreading through the marketplace). Linear models of innovation are open to many critiques because they are so basic, yet some believe this simplicity is an asset. One of the earliest models of innovation was that of "technology push," whereby a manufacturer developed a product with capabilities not then available in the marketplace. This innovation would arise from improvements in basic science and technology, which in turn led to developing, manufacturing, and selling a new design. A later but still simple linear model of innovation was that of "market pull." Here, the innovator responded to an existing need in the marketplace. By researching this need, new products were developed, manufactured, and sold into the market. From this early base, many more sophisticated models of innovation have been developed.

The "S curve," also known as a diffusion curve, is a concept that explains the life cycle of an innovation. Innovations have a life cycle that runs from their debut on the market to their replacement by newer innovations. Scholars of innovation are interested in how innovations are adopted and what sort of consumers will use the technology at each stage of its life cycle. Understanding these market segments is imperative to successfully marketing innovations. The technology adoption life cycle model, developed by Everett Rogers, is a bell-shaped curve, divided into five segments labeled innovators, early adopters, early majority, late majority, and laggards. Each segment has its own profile.

Geoffrey Moore, a well-known Silicon Valley technology consultant, advanced a variation of this model. He suggested that one of the biggest challenges is transitioning an innovation from the early adopters to the early majority; he calls this leap "the chasm."

While innovation can be physical—a new device or invention is successfully introduced to the marketplace, for example—it can also be "soft," that is, delivering enhanced outputs by reconfiguring the way companies do business. Such innovations are sometimes called business model innovations, as opposed to the more conventional technological innovations.

Silicon Valley, California, innovation epicenter

Bibliography

Betz, Frederick. *Managing Technological Innovation: Competitive Advantage from Change.* 3rd ed. Hoboken, NJ: Wiley, 2011.

Christenson, Clayton M. *The Innovator's Dilemma: The Revolutionary Book That Will Change the Way You Do Business.* New York: HarperBusiness, 2011.

Godin, Benoit. "The Linear Model of Innovation: The Historical Construction of an Analytical Framework." *Science, Technology & Human Values* 31 (2006): 639–67. Print.

Keeley, Larry, Helen Walters, Ryan Pikkel, and Brian Quinn. *Ten Types of Innovation: The Discipline of Building Breakthroughs.* Hoboken, NJ: Wiley, 2013.

Moore, Geoffrey A. *Crossing the Chasm: Marketing and Selling Disruptive Products to Mainstream Customers.* Rev. ed. New York: HarperBusiness, 2002.

Osterwalder, Alexander, and Yves Pigneur. *Business Model Generation: A Handbook for Visionaries, Game Changers, and Challengers.* Hoboken, NJ: Wiley, 2010.

Rogers, Everett M. *Diffusion of Innovations.* 5th ed. New York: Free Press, 2003.

Teece, David J. "Business Models, Business Strategy and Innovation." *Long Range Planning* 43.2–3 (2010): 172–94. Print.

Tidd, Joe, and John Bessant. *Managing Innovation: Integrating Technological, Market and Organizational Change.* 5th ed. Hoboken: Wiley, 2013.

von Hippel, Eric. "Democratizing Innovation: The Evolving Phenomenon of User Innovation." *Innovation* 1.1 (2009): 29–40. Print.

Gavin D. J. Harper, Ph.D., M.B.A.

Innovation Leadership

Abstract

Innovation leadership is a relatively new concept in the study of leadership. Its purpose is to create an organizational environment that is conducive to innovation, and the method it uses to achieve this goal is to combine elements of various leadership styles into a coordinated approach that encourages the creative development of new ideas, experimentation with and evaluation of those ideas, and implementation of the ideas where appropriate. Innovation leadership is a style that supports members of an organization in taking the risks necessary to explore novel approaches and to adapt them to practical applications.

Overview

Innovation is the production of a new idea, process, or manner of using an existing idea or process. Innovation implies an awareness of the practical applications of the idea or process. It is not enough simply to think of something new; there must also be some pathway to implementation (Kohanov 2013). This need for practicality has given rise to a conceptual distinction between two different types of innovation. Exploratory innovation involves having a breakthrough idea, while exploitative innovation takes this one step farther and finds an application for the idea.

Innovation leadership developed out of the confluence of two separate theories regarding how organizations can encourage creativity and original thinking. One of these theories is known as "path-goal theory." Path-goal theory influenced the development of innovation leadership because path-goal theory advises leaders to concentrate not on developing a single leadership style, but on becoming proficient at several different styles so that the leader may choose the style most helpful to a particular situation or work group (Hemlin et al. 2013). This approach recognizes that the creative forces needed for an organization to develop the capacity to innovate cannot be predicted or prescribed. Each person's creative process is different and is triggered in a variety of ways or under different circumstances. Within the path-goal frame of reference, a leader's role is to support the efforts of employees and work with them collaboratively to understand the leadership style that will be most conducive to releasing their own creative forces (Vasan and Przybylo 2013).

The other theory that innovation leadership grew out of can be seen as an evolutionary step forward from path-goal theory and is called "leader-member exchange theory." Leader-member exchange theory takes from path-goal theory the idea that a leader must master multiple leadership styles and be able to switch between them as needed and extends this down to the level of the individual employee. This model means that a leader operating from the perspective of a leader-member exchange theory needs to be aware of the individual needs of each person in the organization, so that the leader may tailor his or her style to support their performance (Jones, McCormick, and Dewing 2012). Thus, under path-goal theory, a leader might realize that the staff in Department A work best under a servant leadership model in most situations, while the staff in Department B tend to respond more positively to a charismatic leadership style.

In contrast, leader-member exchange theory requires a leader to be aware of the most effective leadership style to adopt with each particular person in both departments—a much more difficult task. One issue that is often raised regarding leader-member exchange theory is that if it is not implemented skillfully, it can actually erode trust in the leader, as members of the organization begin to question whether any of the leader's styles are truly authentic or being put on for their benefit. This has been referred to as the "chameleon paradox" because the leader's ability to adapt to individual expectations about leadership styles can sometimes backfire (Lindgren 2012).

Innovation leadership takes into account this reality and other strengths and weaknesses of both theories, and takes a slightly different direction. Instead of the leader focusing on practicing the leadership styles preferred by teams or individuals, the innovation leader's goal is to arrive at the right combination of styles that will create an innovative environment within the organization. In other words, the focus of the leader shifts from the needs of individuals or groups to the needs of the organization as a whole.

Weather is a frequent metaphor used to describe innovation leadership: Many different atmospheric conditions must interact in just the right way to produce a thunderstorm, and in the same way, many different organizational factors must interact to allow innovation to coalesce (Hill 2014). Earlier thinking about innovation suggested that leaders should focus on one or two organizational factors to produce creative output; this, however, is akin to trying to produce a thunderstorm by only manipulating the humidity but ignoring other factors such as temperature and wind speed. A leader operating from this frame of reference might be adept at tuning in to the needs of individual employees but fail to understand how the employees' interactions with one another might be inhibiting innovation. Innovation leadership seeks to look at the big picture of organizational dynamics, concentrating not on individual influences but taking a more holistic approach to the organizational climate.

FURTHER INSIGHTS

Research has identified several factors that, if present in the organization's environment, tend to support or inhibit innovation. One supportive factor is the amount of encouragement individuals receive for their creative efforts. This encouragement can come from coworkers, supervisors, or the organizational culture as a whole. Before one can begin to think creatively, one must feel that doing so is an act that will be perceived in a positive, or at the very least neutral, light.

Organizations and individuals can set a tone that conveys this attitude toward innovation by concentrating not so much on the success or failure of projects but on what has been learned from them, regardless of the outcome. This strategy makes clear to everyone that the most important work of the organization is continuing to try new things, rather than playing it safe and only engaging in work with a high chance of success (Vasan and Przybylo 2013). "Safe" projects may result in fewer sleepless nights, but they also rarely result in innovation.

The Role of Resources

Other factors that influence an organization's innovations are the availability of resources and the amount of pressure placed on those within the organization. Resources can take many forms, from support staff to physical materials to overtime wages (Bouteligier 2013). There is a widespread perception that there is a direct, linear relationship between the availability of resources and an organization's ability to innovate, meaning that the more resources one has available, the greater the chances for innovative outcomes. A number of studies have shown that this situation is true but only up to a point, beyond which continuing to add resources produces a smaller and smaller beneficial effect.

To explain this leveling off of benefits, some have suggested that a certain degree of scarcity of resources can actually promote creativity, by forcing people to look for nonobvious solutions. An oft-cited example is the achievement of the first powered flight by the Wright brothers. Although others with greater wealth and scientific knowledge were trying to be the first to invent a powered flying machine that could carry a human passenger, the Wright brothers were the first to accomplish the deed (Echeverría 2012).

The Role of Pressure
A similar leveling-off phenomenon can be seen in the amount of pressure placed on an organization's members. The conventional wisdom suggests that a reasonable amount of pressure is a positive influence on those pursuing innovation, as it inspires them to draw upon their innermost resources to see problems in a new light and achieve more than they might under less demanding conditions. This type of pressure, however, often develops from internal sources rather than external ones; that is, individuals place pressure on themselves to do the best work they possibly can, in order to live up to their own expectations and earn the admiration and gratitude of their friends and family. Extrinsic pressure comes from outside such as one's boss or friends. An example is the pressure to develop a vaccine to prevent the suffering of large numbers of people.

Extrinsic pressure can also be a strong motivator, but it is frequently associated with negative outcomes for employees' mental and physical health (Hill 2014). Regardless of whether pressure to innovate arises from within or without, there comes a point at which the application of additional pressure achieves no measurable gains and may actually diminish performance. As with resource availability, it is possible to have too much of a good thing. Excessive pressure decreases creativity because the pressure itself and the concomitant fear of failure begin to dominate the consciousness of the employee. Instead of thinking about creative solutions to a challenging problem, people begin to think only of how difficult the problem is and what consequences they will face if they do not find a solution.

The Four-Level Model
One development in the literature regarding innovation leadership has been the so-called four-level model, which suggests that there are four different contexts or types of innovation that can occur in an organization: operational, transformative, market-based, and categorical (Wang 2012). Each of these types of innovation can produce value for an organization, but each has its own particular requirements and limitations. Operations-based innovation usually involves new ways of accomplishing tasks that are already known and well understood; while not as attention-grabbing as some breakthroughs, operational innovations can nevertheless profoundly change the way others experience the organization and its services.

Market-based innovation differs from operational innovation because it is more visible to those outside the organization. While operations-based innovations often do their work behind the scenes, market based innovations happen out in the open and thus attract attention from customers and others outside the organization (Kohanov 2013). This situation can both help and hurt the innovation process because while the additional attention can provide greater motivation to achieve, it can also increase the risks of failure and the fear of failure for those implementing the innovation and place them under too much pressure.

Categorical innovation is a type of market-based innovation that takes knowledge already in the public consciousness and applies it in a new way or in service of resolving a completely different type of problem. For example, the realization that magnetism, a well-understood concept from physics and chemistry, could be used to store information on magnetic media by changing the magnetic fields of particular locations on the media was a categorical innovation because it took knowledge from one field and found a new application for it in a completely different field.

Finally, transformative innovation is the most dramatic form of innovation, and typically involves a brand new realization that causes all of society to look at the world in a new way. An example of a transformative innovation is the invention of the telegraph, which almost immediately made the world seem like a much smaller place because instead of needing weeks to send a letter across the country, people on opposite sides of the nation could communicate with one another almost instantaneously. Before much time had passed, the effects of the innovation of telegraphy were felt throughout society, as rich and poor alike began to communicate over vast distances with relative ease.

Viewpoints

Innovation leadership has proven difficult to model conceptually. A number of stages have been identified as characteristic of most innovative leaders, but there is no consistent order in which the steps must be performed. Instead, the steps can essentially proceed in almost any order, creating a process that doubles back on itself, repeats, cycles through steps repeatedly, or even skips steps entirely. The major steps include idea creation, idea analysis, and idea implementation (Leonard 2013).

Once an idea is created and shared among the work group, the members of the group analyze it to assess its strengths and weaknesses and to determine whether or not it could be brought to the implementation stage. In some cases, the analysis will lead to an implementation strategy, and implementation will begin. In other cases, analysis of the idea may reveal that it is not practical for implementation. It also happens that the analysis process sometimes results in the creation of a new idea, which is then subjected to analysis in its own right. As frustrating as this nonlinear process is for theorists to describe, it is derived from the nonlinear nature of innovative thought itself, which frequently takes intuitive shortcuts to solve challenging problems (Bouteligier 2013).

An interesting question that arises in the leadership literature concerns the likely course that innovation leadership may take. Leadership theory is often criticized for its perceived susceptibility to following trends and responding to complex issues with superficial platitudes, so there are those who view innovation leadership with a gimlet eye, anticipating that after a few years its novelty may wear off and permit it to be replaced with a new theoretical perspective. The point is a valid one, and yet the course of society and the economy seems to be one that continues to place greater and greater value upon innovation, so there is also an argument to be made that innovation leadership has many years of relevancy ahead of it, as both theoreticians and practitioners continue to search for more effective ways to encourage those they lead to produce groundbreaking ideas.

BIBLIOGRAPHY

Bouteligier, Sofie. *Cities, Networks, and Global Environmental Governance: Spaces of Innovation, Places of Leadership.* New York: Routledge, 2013.

Echeverría, Lina M. *Idea Agent: Leadership That Liberates Creativity and Accelerates Innovation.* New York: American Management Association, 2012.

Hemlin, Sven, Carl M. Alwood, Ben R. Martin, and Michael D. Munford. *Creativity and Leadership in Science, Technology, and Innovation.* New York: Routledge, 2013.

Hill, Linda. *Collective Genius: The Art and Practice of Leading Innovation.* Boston: Harvard Business Review Press, 2014.

Jones, Tim, Dave McCormick, and Caroline Dewing. *Growth Champions: The Battle for Sustained Innovation Leadership: The Growth Agenda.* Hoboken, NJ: Wiley, 2012.

Kohanov, Linda. *The Power of the Herd: A Nonpredatory Approach to Social Intelligence, Leadership, and Innovation.* Novato, CA: New World Library, 2013.

Leonard, Jack. *Innovation in the Schoolhouse: Entrepreneurial Leadership in Education.* Lanham, MD: Rowman & Littlefield, 2013.

Lindgren, Mats. *21st Century Management: Leadership and Innovation in the Thought Economy.* London: Palgrave Macmillan, 2012.

Vasan, Nina, and Jennifer Przybylo. *Do Good Well: Your Guide to Leadership, Action, and Social Innovation.* San Francisco: Jossey-Bass, 2013.

Vergranti, Roberto. "The Innovative Power of Criticism." *Harvard Business Review* 94, no. 1 (2016): 88–95. Web. 21 Dec. 2016.

Wang, Chun Xie. *Technology and Its Impact on Educational Leadership: Innovation and Change.* Hershey, PA: Information Science Reference, 2012.

SUGGESTED READING

Coutere, Berte D., and David M. Horth. "Innovation Leadership." *Training Journal* (2016): 12–15. Web. 21 Dec. 2016.

Edison Stevenson, Jane. "Breating Away—A New Model for Innovation Leadership." *Employment Relations Today* 39 (2012): 17–25. Web. 22 Mar. 2015.

Hender, Jill, and Henley Management College. *Innovation Leadership: Roles and Key Imperatives.* London: Grist, 2003.

Hender, Jill, and Henley Management College. *Innovation Leadership: Creating the Landscape of Health Care.* Henley-on-Thames, UK: Henley Management College, 2004.

Porter-O'Grady, Tim, and Kathy Malloch. *Innovation Leadership: Creating the Landscape of Health Care.* Sudbury, MA: Jones and Bartlett, 2010.

Schweitzer, Jochen. "Leadership and Innovation Capability Development in Strategic Alliances." *Leadership & Organization Development Journal* 35 (2014): 442–69.

Weberg, Dan, and Kim Weberg. "Seven Behaviors to Advance Teamwork: Findings from a Study of Innovation Leadership in a Simulation Center." *Nursing Administration Quarterly* 38 (2014): 230–37.

Scott Zimmer, M.L.S., M.S., J.D.

Job Performance

ABSTRACT

All workers have assigned duties associated with their jobs. These tasks are generally specific in nature; in some cases, particularly with industrial jobs, their origins can be traced back to the work of social theorist Max Weber and the scientific management theories of Frederick Winslow Taylor that were developed in the late nineteenth and early twentieth centuries. During this period, specialized tasks were viewed as essential in the evolution of management science, allowing managers to rate employee job performance through a standardized system of measurements. Under this system, which was later expanded to include many white-collar jobs, job performance was judged by how well an employee was able to complete a set of predetermined tasks.

OVERVIEW

The Industrial Revolution required organizations to increase the efficiency of employee outputs by designing specific tasks attributable to individual employees. In a systems framework, each assigned task works in concert with a larger group of assigned tasks, all of which are required to complete one element of the system. With the introduction of labor unions and later human resources administration, employers sought to identify methods of assessing employee job performance as a way of providing feedback to employees and providing a basis for decisions about compensation and benefits.

If an employee failed to perform at a satisfactory level according to predetermined objectives, then employers had the tools to withhold compensation or remove the employee from the workplace. These behavioral facets (process) in defining job performance as well as outcome (production) aspects relating to an individual's behavior reframed employee evaluation systems in the twentieth century. The performance of an employee became closely associated with a system of metrics used to evaluate how well the job was performed during a given time period.

In order for an organization to employ effective measurements of job performance, it must establish job descriptions that provide information about what a person is expected to do and with whom they are expected to work closely. Job descriptions not only provide the foundation for employee expectations, but also they provide the foundation to make decisions about compensation, benefits, promotions, training, and task specialization. If an organization fails to adequately establish accurate criteria for job descriptions, performance expectations, and specialization, the result will be suboptimal job performance, thus reducing the efficiency of both the employee and the organization.

As external needs and market objectives change, employers assess whether tasks listed in a job description continue to describe accurately the essential functions of the position. The process of job evaluation determines if adjustments to tasks are required based on employee job performance, whether or not

An employee on the job (Photo courtesy of Jeshoots)

more employees should be added to the workforce, or whether certain classes of jobs should be eliminated from the organization. The evaluation of job performance is part of organizational strategic planning and traditionally drives the human resources function in most organizations.

Improvements in employee job performance are perceived to be based on an organization's appreciation of its human capital and the recognition that job performance is a multidimensional concept. The foundations of job performance reside in social science theory with applications and research focusing on process and outcome. As a measure of employee satisfaction in an organization's work environment, high performance usually correlates with self-efficacy, mastery, and satisfaction.

BIBLIOGRAPHY

Aziri, Brikend. "Job Satisfaction: A Literature Review." *Management Research and Practice* 3.4 (2011): 77–86. Print.

Burke, Ronald J., and Eddy Ng. "The Changing Nature of Work and Organizations: Implications for Human Resource Management." *Human Resource Management Review* 16.1 (2006): 86–94. Print.

Garg, Pooja, and Renu Rastogi. "New Model of Job Design: Motivating Employee's Performance." *Journal of Management Development* 25.6 (2006): 572–87. Print.

Herzberg, Frederick. "One More Time: How Do You Motivate Employees?" *Harvard Business Review*. Harvard Business, Jan. 2003. Web. 29 May 2015.

Odle-Dusseau, Heather N., Thomas W. Britt, and Tiffany M. Greene-Shortridge. "Organizational Work–Family Resources as Predictors of Job Performance and Attitudes: The Process of Work–Family Conflict and Enrichment." *Journal of Occupational Health Psychology* 17.1 (2012): 28. Print.

Park, Jungwee. "Work Stress and Job Performance." *Statistics Canada* 75.1 (2007): 5–17. Print.

Roth, Philip, Kristen L. Purvis, and Philip Bobko. "A Meta-Analysis of Gender Group Differences for Measures of Job Performance in Field Studies." *Journal of Management* 38.2 (2012): 719–39. Print.

Sostrin, Jesse. *Beyond the Job Description: How Managers and Employees Can Navigate the True Demands of the Job*. New York: Palgrave, 2013.

Patricia Hoffman-Miller, M.P.A., Ph.D.

JOB SATISFACTION

ABSTRACT

Job satisfaction is defined as the degree to which an employee is pleased or happily satisfied with his or her job. Management theorists and human resource professionals traditionally view job satisfaction as indicative of an employee's willingness and interest to perform at an optimum level of performance. Job satisfaction focuses on three components—cognitive, affective, and behavioral—of organizational behavior: it is also widely used to determine overall corporate happiness and contentment in human capital management.

OVERVIEW

Frederick Winslow Taylor's theory of scientific management (also called Taylorism), which was developed in the late nineteenth and early twentieth centuries, greatly influenced the concept of job satisfaction, with numerous researchers applying the principles of scientific management as a predictor of employee satisfaction. Human relations theorist George Elton Mayo's work at Hawthorne Works in Chicago, however, further highlighted the effect of job satisfaction on employee motivation in the famous Hawthorne studies of the 1920s and 1930s. The Hawthorne studies provided the evidence for the phenomenon known as the Hawthorne effect, in which human attention to worker and to working conditions were found to be correlated to worker productivity. Implications with regard to job satisfaction were not the focus of these studies, but they were examined by subsequent generations of researchers.

Under modern organizational theories, three domains—the affective, cognitive, and behavioral—directly impact the management of human

217

Frederick Winslow Taylor

capital. The affective domain considers the emotional response of workers toward their jobs, with primary emphasis on feelings and the relationship between the organization and the worker. Whether an employee feels valued by the organization determines his or her positive or negative emotional attitude toward and perceptions of the organization. The behavioral domain determines how workers act as indicators of their levels of job satisfaction. Employee behavior is closely associated with the affective dimensions of job satisfaction. The cognitive process involves individual theories, beliefs, and perceptions regarding an organization. If employees perceive an organization to be unfair, he or she will experience a high degree of cognitive dissonance resulting in a decrease in job performance. The cognitive domain receives the most attention from researchers due to its correlation with organizational efficacy. Elements of the cognitive domain directly impact an organization through employee perceptions of how well an organization manages the reward, task, authority, and social dynamics inherent in organizational health.

The field of organizational behavior includes numerous models of job satisfaction. Edwin Locke's range of affect theory was first discussed in 1976 and remains the best known. The crux of the theory is that job satisfaction is a function of the difference between what a person wants in a job and what that person experiences in a job. Subsequent theorists identified dispositional theory, discrepancy theory, and motivation hygiene theory, among others. The majority of theories utilized in researching job satisfaction seek to understand the degree to which employees are motivated and satisfied with their organization and the subsequent impact on employee performance. Dispositional theory suggests that no matter what type of job an individual has, there are unique certain dispositions affiliated with each individual. The type of organization and its relative system of rewards and benefits is inconsequential in determining job satisfaction. Irrespective of the theory employed to measure job satisfaction, however, numerous factors affect employee performance. Environmental and personal factors such as communication style, supervision, culture, personality, and educational level may impact employee job satisfaction.

BIBLIOGRAPHY

Aziri, Brikend. "Job Satisfaction: A Literature Review." *Management Research and Practice* 3.4 (2011): 77–86. Print.

Garg, Pooja, and Renu Rastogi. "New Model of Job Design: Motivating Employees' Performance." *Journal of Management Development* 25.6 (2006): 572–87. Print.

Goddard, Jules, and Tony Eccles. *Uncommon Sense, Common Nonsense: Why Some Organizations Consistently Outperform Others*. London: Profile, 2013.

Furaker, Bengt, Kristina Hakansson, and Jan Karlsson, eds. *Commitment to Work and Job Satisfaction: Studies with Work Orientations*. New York: Routledge, 2012.

Lencioni, Patrick. *The Three Signs of a Miserable Job: A Fable for Managers (and Their Employees)*. San Francisco: Jossey-Bass, 2007.

Spector, Paul E. *Job Satisfaction: Application, Assessment, Causes, and Consequences.* Thousand Oaks, CA: Sage, 2010.

Thompson, Edmund R., and Florence T. Phua. "A Brief Index of Affective Job Satisfaction." *Group and Organizational Management* 37.3 (2012): 275–307. Print.

Westover, Jonathan H. *Examining Job Satisfaction: Causes, Outcomes, and Comparative Differences.* Champaign, IL: Common Ground, 2011.

Wood, Stephen, et al. "Enriched Job Design, High Involvement Management and Organizational Performance: The Mediating Roles of Job Satisfaction and Well-Being." *Human Relations* 65.4 (2012): 419–45. Print.

Patricia Hoffman-Miller, M.P.D., Ph.D.

Johari Window

ABSTRACT

The Johari window is a process used in group dynamics to assist individuals with their interpersonal leadership skills. It was developed in 1955 by Joseph Luft and Harry Ingham to determine how team members work together in a group environment by exploring each others' personality traits as described by each member him- or herself and by the other group members. The exercise involves choosing traits from a list of key words that individuals would use to describe themselves and others. The Johari window has been shown to be effective in team-building exercises where team cohesion depends on open and honest communication.

OVERVIEW

The Johari window is graphically represented by four quadrants, each representing a dimension of a person's character. These quadrants are: known to self, not known to self, known to others, and not known to others. As a professional development and team-building tool, this technique is highly effective in ascertaining which experiences, attitudes, beliefs, and understandings an individual shares with others and which the individual does not.

In the first quadrant of the Johari window, individuals assess what is open and known to him- or herself and others. In this quadrant, participants examine their personal likes and dislikes, public work history, attitudes, and beliefs as a method of fostering communication. This quadrant is generally superficial, allowing others to view those areas of self that are chosen to be shared in a public or group context.

The second quadrant examines the hidden nature of self: those qualities, beliefs, attitudes and feelings that are known to self but not to others. Maintaining a façade in interpersonal relationships, particularly those relationships required in team building, contributes to dysfunctional teams and toxicity in organizational culture.

Quadrant three, known as the "blind spot," represents sections of self that are not known to the individual, but are known to others. For example, leaders may not recognize the extent to which peers interpret their actions as either supportive or unsupportive. A person's lack of knowledge about his or her blind spot may hinder the effectiveness and growth of professionals in an organizational context.

Quadrant four, referred to as "unknown," is indicative of those traits, beliefs, and attitudes that are not

Johari Window

	Known to self	Not known to self
Known to others	Arena	Blind Spot
Not Known to Others	Façade	Unknown

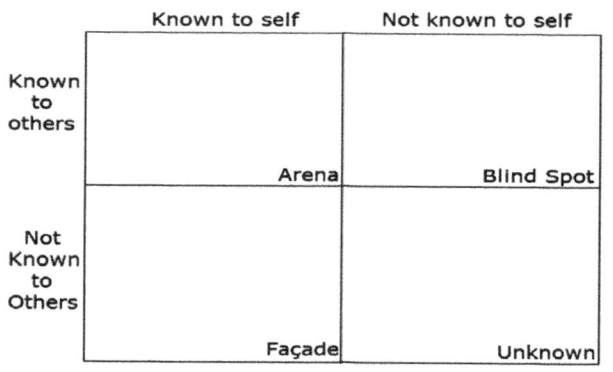

known to the individual or to others. In this quadrant individuals fail to respond to innate attributes that may either foster or hinder professional growth and success. By refusing to acknowledge those inner attributes or traits, individuals often resort to fearing the unknown and resisting change. These actions prohibit growth and detract from leadership possibilities.

CONCLUSION

When using the Johari window exercise in group training, individuals select terms from a group of adjectives to describe attitudes and beliefs in each of the four quadrants represented in the window. Participants in the exercise use this process to assess their personality as well as the personality of others in the group. As these traits are grouped into the quadrants, individuals are provided with an inner view of their personality with key input from members outside of their general locus of control. As an effective tool of assessing an individual's growth and psychosocial awareness, participants using the Johari window become more effective in interpersonal relationships as well as in developing a more accurate analysis of how they view themselves and how others view them.

BIBLIOGRAPHY

Akewukereke, Modupe A., and Ibitoye S. Olukayode. "Application of Johari Window Theory to Understanding Librarian's Changing Roles as Information Providers." *Library Philosophy and Practice.* Digital Commons, at the University of Nebraska–Lincoln, 2008. Web. 12 Aug. 2013.

Berney, Catherine. *The Enlightened Organization: Executive Tools from the World of Psychology.* London: Kogan, 2014.

Chang, Wei-Wen, et al. "Exploring the Unknown International Service and Individual Transformation." *Adult Education Quarterly* 62.3 (2012): 230–51. Print.

Fielding, Michael L., and Franzel Du Plooy-Cilliers. *Effective Business Communications in Organizations: Preparing Messages That Communicate.* Lansdowne, South Africa: Juta Academic, 2014.

Gallrein, Anne-Marie B., et al. "You Spy with Your Little Eye: People Are 'Blind' to Some of the Ways in Which They Are Consensually Seen by Others." *Journal of Research in Personality* 47 (2013): 464–71. Print.

Gibson, Margaret F. "Opening Up: Therapist Self-Disclosure in Theory, Research, and Practice." *Clinical Social Work Journal* 40.3 (2012): 287–96. Print.

Lopez, Samuel De Victoria. "The Johari Window." *Psych Central.com.* Psych Central, n.d. Web. 9 Aug. 2013.

Lowy, Alex, and Phil Hood. "Johari Window," *The Power of the 2 x 2 Matrix: Using 2 x 2 Thinking to Solve Business Problems and Make Better Decisions.* San Francisco: Jossey, 2004, 255.

Luft, Joseph, and Harry Ingham. "The Johari Window: A Graphic Model of Awareness in Interpersonal Relations." *NTL Reading Book for Human Relations Training.* Arlington, VA: NTL Inst., 1982, 32–34.

Reece, Barry L. "The Johari Window: A Model for Self-Understanding." In *Effective Human Relations: Interpersonal and Organizational Applications.* Mason, OH: South-Western, 2013, 166–69.

Shenton, Andrew K. "Viewing Information Needs through a Johari Window." *Reference Services Review* 35.3 (2007): 487–96. Print.

Wilson, Carol. *Performance Coaching: A Complete Guide to Best Practice Approaches.* London: Kogan, 2014.

Patricia Hoffman-Miller, M.P.A., Ph.D.

Leader Member Exchange

ABSTRACT

Leader-member exchange (LMX) theory is founded on the notion that leaders form, with their subordinate's relationships that fall into two broad groups: an in-group characterized by strong exchange relationships and an out-group that lacks solid leader connections. The members of the in-group are given greater responsibilities, rewards, and recognition while enjoying a larger degree of latitude in their roles compared with the out-group. They also tend to have access to the leader's inner circle of communication. Conversely, out-group members are kept outside the leader's inner circle and receive less attention, are given fewer rewards, and are subject to more formal rules and policies.

OVERVIEW

The leader member exchange theory originated in the 1970s to explain the individual relationships between a leader and each of his or her subordinates. Usually there are significant differences in the quantity and quality of each connection. Early on, the leader instigates either an in-group or an out-group exchange relationship with each member of the group.

Leader member exchange theory contends that the relationships between leaders and subordinates are formed through three progressive stages: role-taking, role-making, and routinization. Role-taking occurs when a new member first joins the team and the leader assesses his or her skills and abilities. In the role-making stage, a new team member starts to work on projects and tasks, enabling the leader to observe the member's skills and ethics and place the new member mentally into either the in-group or out-group. In the final stage, routines between the leader and the team member are established. Once an individual has been classified as a member of the in-group or out-group in the leader's mind, the classification will affect how the leader relates to that person from that point forward.

Members of the in-group are allowed to take part in decision-making processes and are given added responsibilities and access to closely held information. The leader typically invests more resources to support in-group members and gives them some latitude in their roles, establishing a connection in which the subordinate member serves as a trusted colleague. In return, the in-group member often expends more time and effort, seeks out more responsibility, and is more invested in the success of the team and organization than the out-group members. Overall, in-group members are more motivated and satisfied than their out-group counterparts.

Members of the out-group, on the other hand, are held accountable to formal employment specifications and are given much less leeway to perform beyond the parameters specifically outlined by their job contract. In these cases, the leader provides consideration and support only as mandated by duty and rarely goes beyond such limits to aid an out-group member. Essentially, the leader adheres to a contractual exchange with out-group personnel, viewing them merely as worker bees rather than substantially contributing members of the team. As a result, out-group members generally refrain from doing any more than is minimally required. With little recognition, reward, or confidence, they acquiesce to their supervisor's authority rather than his or her leadership.

In-group members are often viewed as rising stars within the team, and the leader trusts them to work and perform at a high level. They are given the most support, advice, and opportunities. Members of the out-group receive few chances to shine and have little chance to change the leader's initial opinion of them.

Bibliography

Ariani, Dorothea Wahyu. "Leader-Member Exchanges as a Mediator of the Effect of Job Satisfaction on Affective Organizational Commitment: An Empirical Test." *International Journal of Management* 29.1 (2012): 46+. Print.

Gertstner, Charlotte R., and David V. Day. "Meta-Analysis Review of Leader-Member Exchange Theory: Correlates and Construct Issues." *Journal of Applied Psychology* 82.6 (1997): 827–44. Print.

Graen, George, ed. *New Frontiers of Leadership: A Volume in LMX Leadership: The Series*. Charlotte, NC: Information Age, 2004.

Heath, Robert L., and Jennings Bryant. "Communication in Organizations." In *Human Communication Theory and Research: Concepts, Contexts, and Challenges*. 2nd ed. Mahwah, NJ: Taylor, 2000, 297–342.

Miner, John B. "Further to the Contingency Approach in Leadership Theory." In *Organizational Behavior: Foundations, Theories, and Analyses*. Oxford: Oxford University Press, 2002, 320–56.

Monahan, Kelly. "What Do Values Have to Do with It? An Exploration into the Moderating Impact of Work Values on the Relationship between Leader-Member-Exchange and Work Satisfaction." *Academy of Strategic Management Journal* 12.1 (2013): 95+. Print.

Schermerhorn, John R. "Leader-Member Exchange Describes How Leaders Treat In-Group and Out-Group Followers." In *Exploring Management*. 3rd ed. Hoboken, NJ: Wiley, 2012, 268–69.

Winkler, Ingo. "Leadership-Member Exchange Theory." In *Contemporary Leadership Theories: Enhancing the Understanding of the Complexity, Subjectivity, and Dynamic of Leadership*. Berlin: Springer, 2010, 47–54.

Shari Parsons Miller, M.A.

Leadership

Abstract

Leadership can be defined in many different ways, but in the business world it consists primarily of the ability to organize and inspire others to work together to accomplish a common goal. This definition contains a practical component—the ability to set goals or objectives, marshal resources, understand obstacles, and take steps to overcome them. It also includes an emotional and intellectual aspect because a truly effective leader must convey to his or her team members that they are part of something bigger than themselves and are engaged in important work that is worth devoting their utmost efforts to accomplish.

Overview

Much of the early thinking about leadership, which dates back to the ancient world, was an attempt to determine what causes a particular individual to excel at leading others. People wanted to understand what was different about leaders and made them able to command respect and convince others to follow them. Most felt that leadership was not something one can learn or study to acquire; rather, it was seen as an ability that a select few individuals acquired at birth. This type of belief is known as trait-based leadership because it views leadership as a characteristic that one either possesses or does not possess.

This type of thinking about leadership was common in antiquity, in part due to the widespread belief that kings, emperors, nobles, and other rulers held their positions of power because they were descended from or otherwise related to gods and other supernatural beings. This idea was known as the divine right of kings and held that rulers have been chosen by the gods to have power over their people and therefore should not be challenged or even questioned, but simply obeyed. This view of rulers inspired a similar, though more general, belief about leaders and their abilities. This belief persisted for many years, even after monarchies and other royal rulers came to be viewed as secular and fallible institutions.

Trait Theory of Leadership

The trait theory of leadership, however, did not disappear as societies secularized. Instead, it underwent a transformation and took on a different form. Leadership qualities went from being perceived as divinely distributed to being viewed as characteristics, like black hair or blue eyes, which were inherited from previous generations (Kozłowski 2016). The belief that leadership was something inborn that could not be learned remained intact; all that changed in people's minds was the source of a person's leadership qualities.

FURTHER INSIGHTS

Trait leadership theory prevailed until the late nineteenth and early twentieth centuries. At that time, there gradually developed a sense among some scholars that while many of the qualities of a leader were inherited, it did not mean that people could not be trained in such a way that their individual leadership capacities would be emphasized and nurtured. To put it another way, it began to seem that while some people are simply better natural leaders than others, it was still possible to encourage all people to be better leaders than they might otherwise be, bringing out their hidden gifts (Dunne et al. 2016).

According to the leadership style theory, people who exhibit leadership characteristics tend to have a particular leadership style with which they are most successful and they therefore tend to adopt it by default when presented with a new situation that demands leadership.

Situational Leadership

Various character-building programs were developed. These programs were designed to turn average leaders into better leaders. Eventually, the understanding that people could become better leaders through training led to the realization that some leaders were more effective in particular contexts than in others. That is, a person might be a great leader at work, but a poor leader in his or her personal life or family. This understanding became known as the situational theory of leadership, which holds that some people seem to be better leaders in particular situations than others (Garavan, Watson, Carbery, and O'Brien 2016).

According to this situational leadership theory, it is not the case that a person gifted with leadership abilities will express those abilities in every situation. Indeed, in many contexts the leader would often be unsuccessful because to a large extent, what a leader needs to do in order to be successful depends on the situation. If the situation is a battlefield in the middle of heated combat, then there may be a need for a leader to boldly charge forward and lead the troops to victory. On the other hand, if the situation is a high stakes negotiation taking place in a corporate boardroom, boldness and brashness may be the last thing one should try; it is often the case that patience and subtlety of communication are the essential qualities for a leader to possess in this context (Sinar 2016).

Another way of describing this situation, in which a person is a more effective leader in certain situations than in others, is to think not of the situation itself—describing a person as a battlefield leader, a boardroom leader, or a sports team leader—but to think of the set of leadership behaviors that each of these contexts requires. For example, a battlefield leader might need to possess bravery, decisiveness, intelligence, and cunning. This set of behaviors could then be labeled as a certain kind of style, such as aggressive. Devising leadership styles and categorizing leaders as belonging to this style or that style was the next stage in the development of how people think about leadership

Laissez-Faire Leadership

Laissez-faire is named for a phrase in French that means, "to let people do as they please." The phrase is most often heard in the context of economic policy, but when it is used to describe a leadership style, it means that the leader takes a hands-off approach and allows subordinates to exercise most of the decision-making power required. Because a leader using the laissez-faire style essentially delegates his or her authority to those who report to him or her, this style is also known as delegative leadership. Some who voice support for laissez-faire leadership do so because they feel it is a better option than having a leader constantly peering over subordinates' shoulders to monitor performance or offer criticism. Studies show, however, that worker productivity tends to decline when the laissez-faire leadership style is used because people feel neglected by their supervisors and find themselves required to monitor and motivate themselves for much of the time, and therefore do not push themselves to perform at their highest level (Witt and Stahl 2016).

Democratic Leadership

Democratic leadership represents a moderated form of laissez-faire leadership. Democratic leadership is not completely hands off but involves the leader sharing power with followers to a certain extent. Usually this model takes the form of shared decision making, with the leader developing a framework through which followers participate in setting the directions and establishing goal for a work team. Democratic leaders who include everyone in this process may develop a means of selecting certain individuals to participate. There is some variation in the types of decisions in which followers will be allowed to participate. Most often, followers are asked to decide which strategies will be used to meet a particular goal. Less frequently, followers may be consulted during the goal-development process. The idea behind democratic leadership is that followers should have a role in deciding how the team's work gets done, in the hope that this involvement will encourage them to take a more engaged approach and commit themselves to the success of the organization, instead of doing the bare minimum (Aga, Noorderhaven, and Vallejo 2016).

Authoritarian Leadership

Authoritarian leadership is a style that many employees are familiar with, but few like . A leader with an authoritarian style believes that it is the responsibility of a leader to give orders to subordinates and then monitor the subordinates to make sure that the orders are carried out correctly and on time. This style places little value on people as unique individuals with their own wants and needs, and instead views most members of the organization as little more than small parts in a large organizational machine—parts that can easily be replaced if they do not perform as expected; people do their jobs diligently to avoid being chastised or fired, but they leave for different employers as soon as they can (Murnieks et al. 2016).

Paternalistic/Maternalistic Leadership

Somewhat related to the authoritarian style is the paternalistic/maternalistic style. In this style, the relationship between the leader and the subordinates is similar to that between a parent and a child. Because this style places most of the power in the hands of a single individual (the leader), it is similar to the authoritarian style. These two styles differ is in the character of the relationship between leader and follower. Whereas authoritarian leaders keep this interaction formal and professional, paternalistic/maternalistic leaders value a strong bond of affection and respect between leaders and followers and uses this bond to motivate both parties to do their best.

Transactional Leadership

Transactional leadership is very mechanistic compared with the other leadership styles. It is somewhat similar to authoritarian leadership; however, authoritarian leaders motivate by saying "Do it because I said so," while transactional leaders motivate by offering specific rewards and punishments for specific activities or levels of performance.

Transactional leadership is based on the assumption that if people know what the expectations are and can easily measure their own performance against those benchmarks, then they will naturally seek to avoid punishment and earn praise. There is not much attention paid to employees as human beings with unique motivations because the focus is on creating and maintaining a generic system of motivations that will work for all employees, regardless of their personalities or circumstances (Brinck and Tanggaard 2016).

Transformational Leadership

Transformational leadership has arisen fairly recently and is rapidly growing in popularity. The leader who follows this style takes the time to get to know each employee as an individual and to find out that person's future plans, so that the leader can help the individual grow and develop and become what he or she wants. The transformational leader also converts the workplace or the organization into an environment that enhances the work and the teams guide and mold the employee into becoming what he or she wants to be.

Transformational leaders encourage their subordinates to examine their own strengths and goals in the context of the organization to which they belong to find out if they are on the right path, and if they are not, to make the changes that are necessary to align themselves with their true purpose.

Issues

Much has been said about different leadership styles and theories, but another aspect of the leadership literature involves the qualities leaders typically possess. There are many different views on this subject, and most tend to focus on stereotypes of leaders as so-called alpha males who are loud, opinionated, overbearing, and arrogant. Some of these characterizations may be accurate, while others appear to be motivated at least in part by jealousy on the part of the commentator who is observing the leader and who may wish to change places with that leader (Fischer et al. 2016).

Less controversial are qualities such as extroversion, meaning that leaders tend to be outgoing and comfortable speaking with other individuals and even giving speeches to groups. Much of a leader's work consists of interacting with other people to find out what they are doing, if they need help, and so on. Extroverts thrive on this type of interpersonal interaction, so it is little surprise that many leaders are extroverts. Oddly, there are sometimes situations in which a person becomes a de facto or informal leader in a group solely because he or she is an extrovert. The person may be entirely unsuited to leadership in every other respect, but their extroversion thrusts the role upon them.

It is also common for leaders to be optimists rather than pessimists. They tend to look on the bright side of life and assume that there is always a way to move forward, even if circumstances interfere from time to time and make it difficult to see the path. Pessimists, who have a negative outlook on the future and think of problems as insurmountable, often have to devote all their energy to force themselves to keep moving forward, meaning that they have little left to use in motivating others to cope with adversity. Optimists frequently find that their positive perspective is contagious. Those around them see it and are heartened by it. This can bring the optimist into a leadership role by virtue of the fact that he or she is a person others rally around and look to for guidance (Hamrin 2016).

BIBLIOGRAPHY

Aga, Deribe, Niels Noorderhaven, and Bertha Vallejo. "Transformational Leadership and Project Success: The Mediating Role of Team-Building." *International Journal of Project Management* 34, no. 5 (2016): 806–18. Web. 23 Oct. 2016.

Brinck, Lars, and Lene Tanggaard. "Embracing the unpredictable: Leadership, Learning, Changing Practice." *Human Resource Development International* 19, no. 5 (2016): 374–87. Web. 23 Oct. 2016.

Dunne, Timothy C., Joshua R. Aaron, William C. McDowell, et al. "The Impact of Leadership on Small Business Innovativeness." *Journal of Business Research* 69, no. 11 (2016): 4876–81. Web. 23 Oct. 2016.

Fischer, Michael D., Sue Dopson, Louise Fitzgerald, et al. "Knowledge Leadership: Mobilizing Management Research by Becoming the Knowledge Object." *Human Relations* 69, no. 7 (2016): 1563–85. Web. 23 Oct. 2016.

Garavan, Thomas, Sandra Watson, Ronan Carbery, and Fergal O'Brien. "The Antecedents of Leadership Development Practice in SMEs: The Influence of HRM Strategy and Practice." *International Small Business Journal* 34, no. 6 (2016): 870–90. Web. 23 Oct. 2016.

Hamrin, Solange. "Communicative Leadership and Context." *Corporate Communications: An International Journal* 21, no. 3 (2016): 371–87. Web. 23 Oct. 2016.

Kozłowski, Rafal. "Different Faces of Passion in the Context of Leadership." *Management* 20, no. 1 (2016): 71–80. Web. 23 Oct. 2016.

Murnieks, Charles Y., Melissa S. Cardon, Richard Sudek, et al. "Drawn to the Fire: The Role of Passion, Tenacity and Inspirational Leadership in Angel Investing." *Journal of Business Venturing* 31, no. 4 (2016): 468–84. Web. 23 Oct. 2016.

Sinar, Evan. "Spoiler Alert: Leadership Secrets of Best-in-Class Companies Revealed." *Employment Relations Today* (Wiley), 43, no. 1 (2016): 47–54. Web. 23 Oct. 2016.

Witt, Michael, and Gunter Stahl. "Foundations of Responsible Leadership: Asian versus Western Executive Responsibity Orientations toward Key Stakeholders." *Journal of Business Ethics* 136, no. 3 (2016): 623–38. Web. 23 Oct. 2016.

SUGGESTED READING

Fischer, Kahlib J., and Jonathan Schultz. "How Does a Covenantal Approach to Development Organizational Leadership Affect Innovation?" *Journal of Leadership Studies* 10, no. 1 (2016): 53–54. Web. 23 Oct. 2016.

McLaughlin, Lacey L., and Ian Ziskin. "A Cross-Functional Cross-Organization Model for Leadership

Development." *Employment Relations Today* (Wiley) 42, no. 4 (2016): 5–11.

Norbom, Hans M., and Patricia D. Lopez. "Leadership and Innovation: Informal Power and Its Relationship to Innovative Culture." *Journal of Leadership Studies* 10, no. 1 (2016): 18–31. Web. 23 Oct. 2016.

Rubens, Arthur, Joseph Leah, and Jerry Schoenfeld. "Using Biographies to Teach Leadership Skills: A Classroom Example." *Journal of the Academy of Business Education* 17 (2016): 116–33. Web. 23 Oct. 2016.

Scott Zimmer, J.D.

LEADERSHIP AND MOTIVATION

ABSTRACT

This article focuses on the relationship between leadership and motivation. A history of leadership theory is presented, followed by the link between leadership and motivation as it pertains to today's mainstream leadership theories. The major theories of motivation are presented in the context of leadership. This article explores how leadership theories have developed and converged and how motivation has become an integral part of the leadership construct.

OVERVIEW

Leadership is not a new concept in organizational theory. While many leadership theories have developed and converged in the last century, most business professionals and scholars consider leadership to be a critical individual skill set for employees that are committed to helping their organization succeed and to helping their own careers develop. Part of the leadership construct is the ability to motivate one's constituents, whether they are subordinates, peers, or others in an employee's work group. The best leaders know how to intrinsically motivate and inspire their employees through a variety of techniques. This article explores how leadership theories have developed and converged and how motivation has become an integral part of the leadership construct.

Evolution of Leadership Theory

In the last two centuries, many theories of leadership were developed and considered valid during their time. However, in most cases, each new theory was generally short-lived, with a new one quickly following. There is a logical progression of leadership theories through which many of them converged to create Transformational Leadership Theory, today's dominant and current mainstream leadership theory.

The Great Man Theory & Scientific Management in the 1920s

Frederick Taylor was instrumental in applying a much-needed management model, based on productivity, after the tremendous factory boom caused by the Industrial Revolution. No longer were organizations small and operating out of the home through small shop owners or agricultural farmers. Instead, the birth and fast expansion of large-scale factories changed the face of the workplace. Wren (2005) stated, "The Industrial Revolution had provided the impetus; Taylor provided the synthesis" (274). Taylor was the first to expose the importance of worker productivity through studying the motions and habits of production workers. He was the first to functionally separate the "manager" from the "worker," by essentially classifying the worker as the one who does the work, and the manager as the one who makes the decisions.

At the same time, simplistic yet formal leadership theories began to develop without scholarly research and empirical data. The predominant leadership theory that existed during the Scientific Management Era was the Great Man Theory developed by Thomas Carlyle (1841–1907). Dorfman's study (as cited in Tirmizi 2002) stated, "According to this theory, a leader was a person gifted by heredity with unique qualities that differentiated him from his followers" (270). This theory laid the foundation for several subsequent trait-based theories that evolved decades later and were often referred to as the Trait Period or Trait Theories. In the meantime, beside Carlyle's Great Man Theory, the practice of leadership was being molded by the factories and production lines

Thomas Carlyle, originator of the "Great Man Theory" (photo courtesy of Sophus Williams)

and by the work of Frederick Taylor. Taylor's work in these areas was very authoritarian and focused on control and centralization of power in the hands of managers (Rost as cited in Harrison 1999). Taylor's work clearly had influence not only on management development, but also on leadership methods.

As new leaders emerged, scholars realized that there were some inconsistencies in the Great Man Theory. Many respected land effective leaders were quite different from each other, which questioned the validity of Carlyle's assertion. In addition, Taylor's work with management theory also demonstrated some inadequacies. Viewing the employee as just a "tool" to get the work done was limiting, and the theories was not supported by any in-depth scholarly research and empirical data. This recognition led to the next era of leadership theory, which primarily centered on relationships and behavior.

Behavior Era of Leadership

Mary Parker Follet, one of the first persons to introduce elements of psychology theory into the workplace, viewed leadership from a group and organizational perspective. These views subsequently developed into the fields referred to as Organizational Behavior and Human Relations, of which leadership is a critical component. This period in time is often referred to as the Behavioral Era in leadership theory development (Van Seters and Field, 1990).

The Behavioral Era in leadership theory was the genesis of the classic nature versus nurture argument about whether leaders are born or made. Where the trait theories supported the idea that leaders are born (leadership skills are hereditary), the behavioral theories contended that leaders can be trained by modifying their behavior to emulate the behavior of past effective leaders. These two schools of thought diverged after World War II. Stogdill (1975) explained that one theory was based on the role of the leader while the other was based on the relationship between leaders and their followers, and the effectiveness of group performance. Nearing the tail end of this period, behavioral theories took over as "Carter (1953) and Startle (1956) maintained that the trait approach had reached a dead-end and suggested that the attention be directed toward the behavior of the leader" (Stogdill 1975).

The early behavioral theories began with studies at Ohio State University and the University of Michigan. The focus of these theories was on what effective leaders do, and not on what they were. For the first time in history, leadership theories now became multi-dimensional. Johns and Moser (1989) stated, "The University of Michigan leadership studies under the direction of Likert and the Ohio State leadership studies under the direction of Stogdill and Shartle were antithetical to the trait or single-continuum approach" (116). Leadership theories now included both task and relationship elements.

Behavioral theories subsequently converged with the continued development of management principles. One example is Blake and Mouton's Managerial Grid, which plotted consideration against initiating structure, and another example is McGregor's development of the Theories X and Y (Van Seters and Field 1990). From this point forward, the development of leadership theories began to emerge at a progressively rapid rate.

Where supporting research in the past had been thin to none, this era was full of scholarly research and empirical data relating to leadership. As a result, the theories became more applicable than ever, and researchers felt as if they had made tremendous progress toward finally defining leadership. In their studies, Johns and Moser (1989) stated, "Empirical research began to challenge personal trait and one dimensional views of leadership. Empirical studies suggested that leadership is a dynamic process varying from situation to situation with changes in leaders, followers, and situations" (116). Scholarly research had finally taken root in the development of leadership theories.

Situational, Contingency, & Transformational Era of Leadership
The pace of management development and the evolution of new management theories accelerated significantly from the 1960s to the present, and the knowledge and information available for continued management and leadership studies is abundant. Wren (2005) stated, "It is not possible to examine the full extent of modern management writings, for they are too diverse and too extensive for any in depth analysis" (395). During this time, the evolution of leadership theories grew at a record pace, and research findings increased rapidly as more scholars set out to finally define the concept of leadership.

Scholars continued to discover that trait and behavior theories were not enough, and something was still missing. They discovered that leaders who went beyond modeling their behavior after previous leaders by adjusting how they act to situations became more effective. This recognition led to two theories that are commonly used in organizations today: the Situation and Contingency theories. Fielder's concept of Situational Favorability was based on influencing others (Maslanka 2004). The Hersey-Blanchard Situational Model continued building on previous task relationship models and added the element of the readiness of the follower. This significant development meant that leadership might be more about the relationship between the manager and subordinate and less about the leader himself or herself, including his or her traits or behavior. The idea of leadership being a function of the relationship was expanded upon by House and Mitchell's Path-Goal Theory (Maslanka 2004).

Leadership theories have evolved from being based on the individual, to being based on the relationship between the leader and the follower. Theories now went beyond the relationship and included groups and teams. From Vroom and Yetton's Normative Model came the idea that the environment also plays a critical role for the effective leader, by placing significance on the need for acceptance and or quality within the organization. In addition, scholars began to realize that theories were starting to converge. Leadership theories during the contingency stage included elements from past theories, such as behavior, personality, influence, and situation (Van Seters and Field 1990). For example, Wren (2005) pointed out that Max Weber's Charisma Theory from the Scientific Management Era returned to leadership theory after remaining dormant for many years. The research and empirical data became sound, yet scholars still maintained that something was missing. The theories were not well-integrated and were difficult to put into practice (Van Seters and Field 1990). In other words, while the research and data was sound, the theories could not be effectively employed.

This situation led to the development of the two most recent leadership theories, Transactional and Transformational Leadership. Kinicki and Williams (2003) define Transactional Leadership as "focusing on clarifying employees' roles and task requirements and providing rewards and punishments contingent on performance" (p. 464). While effectively gaining compliance, Transactional Leadership failed to gain commitment from followers. Transformational Leadership solved this dilemma. Kinicki and Williams (2003) defined Transformational Leadership as something that "transforms employees to pursue organizational goals over self-interests" (465). Tirmizi (2002) indicated that "Transformational Leadership is defined in terms of the leader's effect on followers. They feel trust, admiration, loyalty, and respect toward the leader, and they are motivated to do more than they originally expected to do" (270). Most scholars today agree that the most effective style of leadership is one that combines elements of both Transactional and Transformational Leadership. Antonakis and House (as cited in Kinicki and Williams 2003) researched this subject and came to the conclusion that a combination of these two leadership styles, with an emphasis on the transformational portion, is the best method for leaders to motivate their employees. The implication of this insight suggests that a good leader must adapt to the necessary leadership style for different situations and objectives. These two leadership theories finally closed the loop with research and effectiveness. They have been validated through extensive research and are also effectively employed in the workplace.

Current State of Leadership Theory

The evolution of leadership theories clearly shows a convergence of ideas over more than two centuries into the mainstream theories of today. The first main convergence of ideas came in the 1970s with the contingency theories. The theories combined new ideas with elements of past theories that had been discarded as invalid or inapplicable. These theories contained elements of the Great Man and Trait theories, behavioral theories, influence-based theories and situational theories (Van Seters and Field 1990), but remained stand-alone theories. The second main convergence of theories came with the Transactional and Transformational Leadership theories. Not only did these theories contain elements from past theories but also they were well integrated and could easily be applied to today's organizations. Wren (2005) stated, "Leadership theories cycled from traits through contingency notions and back to leader styles and leader member relations in transformational, charismatic, transactional, and leader member exchange theories" (454). In addition to these points of convergence, theories have progressed from being based on the individual, to a dyad of manager and subordinate, to the group, and finally to the organization.

Today's leadership theories have become complex and specialized. Since the development of transformational leadership, other mainstream theories have emerged. Some examples include Level 5 Leadership (Collins 2001), Leadership Best Practices (Kouzes and Posner 2003), Servant Leadership (Joseph and Winston 2005), Contingent Leadership (Manning 2013), and Leadership by Creating a Learning Organization (Senge 1990). Transformative Leadership is described by Caldwell et al. (2012) as an ethical approach that seeks the benefit of all stakeholders with sustained wealth creation as a goal.

A Linkage between Motivation & Leadership

With the historical evolution of leadership in perspective, one can begin to understand the linkage between motivation and leadership. In a well-known *Harvard Business Review* article, Kotter (2001) set out to describe the differences between leadership and management, suggesting that leadership was about dealing with change, while management was about dealing with complexity. Kotter explained that leaders set directions while managers plan and budget; leaders align people while managers organize and hire staff, and leaders motivate people while managers control and problem solve. The article was based on the continued discussion on this topic introduced by Abraham Zeleznik in 1977 (Kotter 2001). In the article, Kotter referred to the argument by stating, "the theoreticians of scientific management, with their organizational diagrams and time-and-motion studies, were missing half the picture—the half filled with inspiration, vision, and the full spectrum of human drives and desires." The study of leadership hasn't been the same since. Within this perspective, motivation is clearly a significant part of the leadership construct.

Another example of how motivation and leadership are linked can be seen in how transformational leadership is defined. Bass (1999) discussed the importance of the leader-follower relationship in a transformational leadership setting. Bass stated, "Transformational leadership refers to the leader moving the follower beyond the immediate self interest through idealized influence (charisma), inspiration, intellectual stimulation, or individualized consideration. It elevates the follower's level of maturity and ideals as well as concerns for achievement, self-actualization, and the well-being of others, the organization, and society" (11). Further, Bass (1999) asserts that these four factors will result in followers wanting to identify with this leadership. In other words, a leader who embraces and practices these elements of leadership would certainly help motivate his or her employees to achieve common organizational goals.

A third linkage between leadership and motivation can be observed in the five best leadership practices presented by Kouzes and Posner (2003). Kouzes and Posner (2003) stated, "As we looked deeper into the dynamic process of leadership, through case analysis and survey questionnaires, we uncovered five practices common to personal-best leadership experiences" (73). These five practices include (1) model the way, (2) inspire a shared vision, (3) challenge the process, (4) enable others to act, and (5) encourage the heart. The authors asserted that by following these practices, employees could be intrinsically motivated to be committed to the organization's goals and objectives. These five behaviors are directly related to motivating the employee, especially in reference to inspiration, encouragement, and empowerment.

By looking at these examples of current leadership theory, one can see how motivation is linked to leadership and how motivation is a critical aspect within modern leadership theory.

APPLICATION

Organizational practitioners often concentrate on developing leaders and managers to effectively motivate their employees. Kinicki and Kreitner (2006) defined motivation as "psychological processes that caused the arousal, direction, and persistence of voluntary actions that are goal directed" (149). The employee's performance is directly related to how motivated they are to achieve their goals. Having the skills alone is often not enough for employees to achieve high performance at their job. As such, it is the leaders' jobs to motivate their employees to the extent that they can achieve high performance with their current skills and limitations. Motivation can be looked at from three perspectives: needs, process, and reinforcement (Lussier 2005). The needs theories of motivation are critical to the effectiveness of one's leadership. It is in the context of the needs theories that the leadership principles discussed in the first section can be applied. The process and reinforcement theories of motivation are better viewed from a management perspective, rather than a leadership perspective. The following sections give an overview of the most well-known needs theories of motivation.

Maslow's Hierarchy of Needs

The most widely known motivational theory preached by today's organizational practitioners is Maslow's Hierarchy of Needs Theory. Tutt (1989) noted that human behavior continues to be based on instinct and that humans desire to fulfill their institutional needs. The theory suggests that one's needs are categorized into five categories of a hierarchy—that is, one must satisfy the lowest level of needs before satisfying the higher-level needs. These levels, from lowest to highest, are physiological needs, safety needs, social needs, esteem needs, and the need for self-actualization (Lussier 2005). Many suggest that excellent leaders understand where their employee's needs fall within this hierarchy and can satisfy them accordingly.

McClelland's Needs Theory

A second widely used needs theory was developed by David McClelland (Kinicki and Kreitner 2006). McClelland suggested that individuals have three needs: a need for achievement, a need for power, and a need for affiliation. He suggested that every individual is different with regards to his or her needs, and in order to adequately motivate someone, a leader should have a clear understanding of his or her own employees' needs with regards to these three areas. For example, someone with a high needs for affiliation might be well-suited for a human resources position, while someone with a high need for achievement might be well-suited for a sales position. Understanding each employee as a unique individual can help a leader or manager determine the best position and the best job tasks for a particular employee.

Herzberg's Hygiene Theory

The third prevalent needs theory, developed by Frederick Herzberg, is often referred to as the Hygiene Theory of Job Satisfaction (Kinicki and Kreitner 2006). Herzberg suggested that organizations have aspects that can be classified as satisfiers and dissatisfiers to employees. In order to satisfy and motivate employees, a leader or manager should alleviate the things that dissatisfy employees and improve the things that satisfy employees. Dissatisfiers, or hygiene factors, include rules and regulations, salary, work environment, and supervisors. Promotion opportunities, learning opportunities, job recognition, and challenging work are satisfiers. While both are important to motivating employees, oftentimes organizations only concentrate on removing the dissatisfiers, which does not intrinsically motivate the employee, especially in the long run.

Viewpoint

Leadership and motivation are directly related to employee performance. Leadership theories have evolved since the late 1800s, and today's current leadership theories include motivation as a major part of their construct. Mainstream leadership theories such as Bass's Transformational Leadership, Collins' Level 5 Leadership, and Kouzes and Posner's Best Practices of Leadership are built on the concept that effective leaders need to know how to motivate their employees. Motivation theories can be broken down into needs, process, and behavioral reinforcement. Leadership relies heavily on understanding the needs of theories of motivation, such as Maslow's Hierarchy of Needs, McClelland's Need Theory, and Herzberg's Hygiene Theory of Job Satisfaction. A leader can be most effective by understanding the needs of his or her employees, which will result in optimizing the overall performance of the leaders' constituents as well as the organization.

BIBLIOGRAPHY

Bass, Bernard M. "Two Decades of Research and Development in Transformational Leaderships." *European Journal of Work & Organization Psychology* 8, no. 1 (1999): 9–32. Web. 14 Mar. 2007.

Berry, John. "Revolutionizing Motivation." *Training Journal* (2014, Oct.): 10–13. Web. 17 Nov. 2014.

Buble, Mario, Ana Juras, and Ivan Matic. "The Relationship between Managers' Leadership Styles and Motivation." *Management: Journal of Contemporary Management Issues* 19, no. 1 (2014): 161–93. Web. 17 Nov. 2014.

Caldwell, Cam, Rolf Dixon, Larry A. Floyd, et al. "Transformative Leadership: Achieving Unparalleled Excellence." *Journal of Business Ethics* 109, no. 2 (2012): 175–87. Web. 31 Oct. 2013.

Collins, Jim. *Good to Great.* 1st ed. New York: HarperCollins Publishing, 2001.

Harrison, R. "The Nature of Leadership: Historical Perspectives & the Future." *Journal of California Law Enforcement* 33, no. 1 (1999): 24. Print.

Johns, Horace E., and H. Ronald Moser. "From Trait to Transformation: The Evolution of Leadership Theories." *Education* 110, no. 1 (1989): 115. Web. 14 Mar. 2007.

Joseph, Errol E., and Bruce E. Winston. "A Correlation of Servant Leadership, Leader Trust, and Organization Trust." *Leadership & Organization Development Journal* 26, nos. 1-2 (2005): 6. Print.

Kinicki, Angelo, and Robert Kreitner. *Organization Behavior: Key Concepts, Skills, and Best Practices.* 2nd ed. New York: McGraw Hill, 2006.

Kinicki, Angelo, and Brian Williams. *Management: A Practical Introduction.* 2nd ed. New York: McGraw-Hill, 2003.

Kotter, John P. "What Leaders Really Do." *Harvard Business Review* 79, no. 11 (2001): 85–96. Web. 24 Mar. 2007.

Kouzes, James, and Barry Posner. *The Leadership Challenge.* 3rd ed. San Francisco: Jossey-Bass, 2003.

Lussier, Robert N. *Human Relations in Organizations.* 6th ed. New York: McGraw-Hill, 2005.

Manning, Tony. "A 'Contingent' View of Leadership: 360 Degree Assessments of Leadership Behaviours in Different Contexts." *Industrial & Commercial Training* 45, no. 6 (2013): 343–51. Web. 31 Oct. 2013.

Maslanka, Ann M. Evolution of Leadership Theories. Unpublished M.S., Grand Valley State University, United States—Michigan, 2004.

Robnagel, Christian Stamov. "Leadership and Movitation." *Leadership Today.* (2017, July 31). Print.

Senge, Peter. *The Fifth Discipline: The Art & Practice of the Learning Organization.* 1st ed. New York: Doubleday Dell Publishing, 1990.

Stogdill, Ralph M. "The Evolution of Leadership Theory." *Academy of Management Proceedings.* (1975): 4–6. Web. 14 Mar. 2007.

Tirmizi, Syed. "The 6-L Framework: A Model for Leadership Research and Development." *Leadership & Organization Development Journal* 23, no. 5–6 (2002): 269. Print.

Tutt, B. "Great Instincts: Nature vs. Nurture Questions Fire Ongoing Debate." *Houston Chronicle.* 1989. (pre-1997 Fulltext), 6.

Van Seters, David A., and Richard H.G. Field. "The Evolution of Leadership Theory." *Journal of Organizational Change Management* 3, no. 3 (1990): 29. Web. 14 Mar. 2007.

Wren, Daniel. *The History of Management Thought.* 5th ed. New York: John Wiley and Sons, 2005.

SUGGESTED READING

Humphreys, John, and Walter Einstein. "Leadership and Temperament Congruence: Extending the Expectancy Model of Work Motivation." *Journal of Leadership and Organizational Studies* 10, no. 4 (2004): 58. Web. 14 Mar. 2007.

Ilies, Remus, Timothy Judge, and David Wager. "Making Sense of Motivational Leadership: The Trail from Transformational Leaders to Motivated Followers." *Journal of Leadership and Organizational Studioes* 13, no. 1 (2006): 1. Web. 14 Mar. 2007.

Ellemers, Naomi, Dick De Gilder, and S. Alexander Haslam. "Motivational Individuals and Groups at Work: A Social Identity Perspective on Leadership and Group Performance." *Academy of Management Review* 29, no. 3 (2004): 459. Web. 14 Mar. 2007.

Rao, M.S. "Transformational Leadership: An Academic Case Study." *Industrial and Commercial Training* 46, no. 3 (2014): 150–54. Web. 17 Nov. 2014.

John D. Benson, M.B.A.

MANAGEMENT COMPETENCIES

ABSTRACT

The purpose of this article is to explore the subject of management competencies and provide a framework for contextualizing competency modeling within organizations. First, a background discussion will ensue with an examination of the origins of competency modeling, along with a definition of the term "competencies." From there, the types of competencies typically employed in the construction of competency models will be discussed followed by the various approaches for developing competency dimensions, typical organizational uses for competency models, types of competency models, and management competencies as predictors of performance. The article concludes with an example of an actual competency model and an outline of some perceived drawbacks of competency modeling.

OVERVIEW

Global interest in the utilization of management competencies as a management tool parallels the recognition of human resources as the most valuable asset within any organization. Directly in line with this recognition, management competencies are gaining widespread use in organizations. Competencies clarify work expectations, generating a common language that catalyzes and reinforces changes in individual behavior. In short, competency models develop a set of expectations within organizations that serve as benchmarks for superior performance. However, as shall be seen, there are several beneficial aspects associated with competency models.

Origins of competency-based methodology are grounded largely in the research of Harvard behavioral psychologist David McClelland in the 1970s, and management theorist Richard Boyatzis's research in the 1980s. McClelland (1973), in his article "Testing for competence rather than for intelligence," made the case for competency modeling as opposed to intelligence testing, proposing that intelligence test scores are not reliable predictors of job success. Essentially, McClelland's competency methodology focused on the identification of key behaviors in high performers versus lesser performers.

Management competency pioneer, Richard Boyatzis (1982), is noted for his work in competency modeling as a predictor of effective manager performance. Boyatzis defines competencies as "an underlying characteristic of an employee (i.e., motive, trait, skill, aspects of one's self image, social role, or a body of knowledge), which results in effective, and/or superior performance in a job" (Boyatzis 1982, 20). Likewise, Seal, Boyatzis and Bailey (2006, 193) state:

> In the purest sense, a competency is defined as a capability or ability that leads to a successful outcome. It is a set of related but distinct sets of behaviors organized around an underlying purpose or goal, called the "intent." Competencies, therefore, are the result of appropriate behaviors used effectively in the situation or time to further the underlying goal or purpose that emerges from the intent.

Additionally, LeBleu and Sobkowiak (1995) summarize competency modeling by stating: "In its crudest form, it is a yardstick for measuring how someone is performing, comparing current performance to an ideal, and suggesting actions that can be taken to improve that performance."

Types of Competencies

Competencies span three broad categories (Byham and Moyer 1996):

1. Organizational Competencies—those unique competitive attributes that form the basis upon which organizations compete—sometimes referred to as core competencies. It is an organizational strength that gives an organization a competitive advantage over competitors. For example, Dell Computer's core competence lies in superior supply chain management—namely its superior efficiency in the procurement of production parts/supplies, manufacturing processes, and the distribution system.
2. Personal Competencies—characteristics representing general standards for acceptable performance (level of achievement or output) in a given role. Consider the job of a sales manager. A sales manager is said to have personal competency if he or she can adequately perform at a level typically expected of a sales manager. Thus, personal competence is the ability to adequately perform in a given job—as opposed to superior performance.
3. Job/Role Competencies—skills and behaviors necessary to achieve superior performance in a specific job, role, function, task, duty, organizational level, or entire organization. Job/role competencies are the focus of this article. These job/role competencies exist on a number of job levels (Byham and Moyer 1996):
   - A role (leader of a meeting)
   - A job or position (a manufacturing team leader)
   - A job level (first-line leaders)
   - Several job levels (middle management)
   - A broad band of jobs (professional/technical jobs)
   - An entire organization.

It is these job/role competencies that provide the footing for this discussion. Job/role competencies measure knowledge, skills, and abilities shown to predict superior performance. As applied to managers in organizations, job/role competencies define effective management performance and are thought of as management competencies. (Throughout the remainder of this article, the terms competency and management competencies shall be used interchangeably). Job/role competencies may be broken down into a number of observable items, i.e., behavior, knowledge, and motivation (Bynam and Moyer 1996). Behavioral Competency: Behaviors a person exhibits that result in good performance—that which a person says or does that determines performance. Example: Consider the HR competency dimension of performance management. A manager would be expected to exhibit certain behaviors such as communicating clear performance standards, monitoring employees' performance, providing performance feedback and recommending corrective action when necessary.

The most widely used behavioral competencies include:

1. Team orientation
2. Communication skills
3. People management
4. Customer focus
5. Results orientation
6. Problem-solving
7. Planning and organizing (Rankin 2005)

Knowledge Competency: A person's knowledge of facts, technologies, processes, or procedures related to their job. Diplomas, licenses, certificates, as well as a person's ability to apply their knowledge, are signs of such knowledge competency.

Motivational Competency: An individual's feeling about their job, organization, or geographic location which may impact upon performance. Motivational competencies focus on the motivational aspects of proper job fit, organizational fit, or location fit. Generally motivational competencies cannot be developed.

Example: The position of sales manager requires an entrepreneurial orientation as manifested by a predisposition to seeking out opportunities, and a willingness to take calculated risks. If a sales manager is lacking these qualities, a poor job fit results and that individual would most likely lack the motivation and ability to perform at high levels.

Competency Models in Organizations

Research affirms that competency models are widely deployed, with adoption rates likely to increase in the future. A UK-based benchmarking study (Rankin 2005) of competencies in organizations found that 60% of respondents had a competency framework in

A manager's work station (Photo courtesy of Dai Lygad)

place. Of those firms lacking a competency framework, about half (48 percent) intended to introduce one in the future. Furthermore, among those organizations with competency frameworks, approximately four out of five employees (78 percent) were included in their competency model. Also, one-half (50 percent) of the firms reported having a single, common competency framework across the entire organization.

Changes in the business world have made the use of management competency models more prevalent for the following reasons (Byham and Moyer 1996):

- Rapidly changing, team-oriented, and "virtual" organizations mean that the traditional definitions of jobs are increasingly rare. Thus, management competencies fill the void by clearly defining what is expected of employees.
- Flattened organizations with fewer layers have fewer advancement opportunities that translate to a more horizontal selection process—creating less room for error due to a smaller number of promotional jobs. This phenomenon increases the need for defining and using competencies to aid in selection accuracy.
- With a more dynamic workplace and the path to advancement less clear, well-defined competencies provide better self-guidance in career planning. As individuals become increasingly responsible for their career planning, career guidance assistance is needed. Competencies provide this needed assistance.
- With increased overlap between employee and management roles, clearly defined work roles are imperative. Competencies fill the void by clarifying organizational expectations and individual responses.
- Global workforce requirements require an ability to operate effectively in cross-cultural assignments. Competencies are uniquely suited to providing benchmarks for uniform standards that can be applied worldwide (Byham and Moyer 1996).

APPLICATIONS

Approaches to Defining Competencies

There are two basic approaches to defining and developing competencies in organizations—the behavioral approach and the clinical approach (Byham and Moyer 1996). The behavioral approach concentrates on behaviors, motivations, and knowledge relevant to a particular job—i.e., job-relevant behavior. On the other hand, the clinical approach identifies underlying personal characteristics of the individual as the basis for defining competencies independent of any job connection. In essence, the clinical approach targets the personal characteristics of superior performers. Unless otherwise stated, this discussion relies on the behavioral approach—the approach most widely used in developing competencies.

Competency Model Types

The following is an overview of competency models involving U.S.-based firms (Rothwell and Lindholm 1999). Although the models are based on data specific to the United States, these models may be found across cultures to varying degrees, regardless of country origin.

Borrowed Approach—The easiest and least expensive competency modeling approach, the borrowed approach simply borrows an approach from an existing organization, without taking into consideration the uniqueness of the adopter. An obvious shortcoming lies in the possibility of the borrowed model not being appropriate for the borrowing organization.

Borrowed and Tailored Approach—A variation of the borrowed approach is the borrowed and tailored approach—which borrows a competency framework from an existing organization, yet tailors the model to the borrower's structure, culture and resources (human, technical, financial, informational, etc.).

Tailored Approach—As its name suggests, the tailored approach tailors a competency model according to the unique needs of the organization. The process-driven and outputs-driven approaches are classic tailored approaches that have been in use for some time and are more commonly utilized. Several new approaches are the invented approach, the trends-driven approach, and the work responsibilities approach.

Process-Driven Approach—Emphasizes work process (job activities, personal characteristics, behaviors) required for exemplary job performance.

Outputs-Driven Approach—Identifies key outputs of a given job that successful performers produce. Competencies are then developed based on these key outputs.

Invented Approach—A new competency model is developed without regard to an existing approach. This approach is used when exemplary performers are unavailable or the organization is about to undergo drastic changes.

Trends-Driven Approach—Focuses on what people must know or be able to do in response to managing a changing environment.

Work Responsibilities-Driven Approach—"Derives work outputs, competencies, roles, and quality requirements from work responsibilities or activities" (Rothwell and Lindholm 1999, 99).

Competency Model Uses

Early usage of competency models focused on two areas: performance management and career development. These early models typically applied primarily to senior managerial personnel (Rankin 2005). However, management competency frameworks are now being applied across the entire range of the human resource management function. For example, the various uses of competency models are:

- Executive development
- Recruitment and selection
- Compensation
- Performance appraisal
- Career development
- Job design
- Organization design
- Training and development
- Training needs analyses
- Succession Planning (LeBleu and Sobkowiak 1995; Bynam and Moyer 1996)

Also, Rankin (2005) identified (in order) the primary applications of competency models in organizations:

- Performance reviews/appraisal
- Improving employee effectiveness
- Achieving greater organizational effectiveness
- Training needs analysis
- Career management

Management Competencies & Performance

In the 1970s, the American Management Association (AMA) and McBer Company (a consulting company founded by David McClelland) studied 1,800 managers over a five-year period, with the aim of identifying the competencies of successful managers. The result of their research yielded five management competencies deemed essential in determining a manager's job success (Rothwell and Lindholm 1999):

1. Specialized knowledge
2. Intellectual maturity
3. Entrepreneurial maturity
4. Interpersonal maturity
5. On-the-job maturity

Research verifies a number of management competencies serving as accurate predictors of outstanding manager performance (Boyatzis, Stubbs, and Taylor 2002). These competencies reside within three broad categories:

- Cognitive or intellectual ability, as in the ability to make sense out of complex scenarios with any number of conflicting and sometimes obscure variables which may affect decisions;
- Intrapersonal abilities, such as personal adaptability, i.e., the ability and willingness to deal with change; Interpersonal abilities (sometimes referred to as emotional intelligence), motivating others to perform, network, communicate, etc.); and
- A person's desire to apply his or her ability in any one of the aforementioned areas. Without the requisite desire to use these abilities, competencies lose their quality for predicting outstanding performance (Boyatzis, Stubbs, and Taylor 2002).

A Competency Model
The National Institutes of Health (NIH), (the primary federal agency for conducting and supporting medical research) developed an organization-wide competency model for its entire workforce. NIH defines competencies as "the combination of knowledge, skills and abilities that contribute to individual and organizational performance." Suggested uses for the model are decisions pertaining to recruitment and selection, promotion readiness, selection and approval of training, and leadership readiness (http://hr.od.nih.gov/workingatnih/competencies/faqs.htm).

The NIH Competency Model comprises of three components: Core competencies, administrative leadership and management, and occupation-specific areas. Core competencies form the foundation of the NIH model and represent the knowledge, skills and abilities required of all NIH employees—regardless of function. Occupation-specific competencies represent the set of knowledge, skills and abilities expected within a particular functional area (e.g., Accounting, Contracting, Human Resources, Information Technology, etc.). Also, NIH managers and supervisors must display an additional set of competencies in Leadership and Management. Within each competency dimension, individuals are rated on a proficiency scale of "not applicable" to a high score of 5 which indicates Expert proficiency. (The rating NIH Proficiency Scale is as follows: N/A—Not applicable, 0—Not Demonstrated, 1—Fundamental Awareness, 2—Novice, 3—Intermediate, 4—Advanced, 5—Expert.)

I. Core competencies are split into Business Competencies and Communications/Interpersonal Competencies:

Business Competencies
- Enterprise Knowledge
- Analysis, Decision Making & Problem Solving
- Customer Service
- Driving Results
- Personal Effectiveness

Communications/Interpersonal Competencies
- Written Communication
- Oral Communication
- Interpersonal Effectiveness

II. Leadership & Management Competencies
- Visionary Leadership
- Developing & Managing Talent
- Strategic Decision Making

III. Occupation-Specific Competencies
Occupation-specific competencies vary according to occupation, i.e., an Accountant will have a different set of occupational competencies from that of an Information Technology specialist. The following list illustrates the occupation-specific competencies for NIH Information Technology Management staff (http://hr.od.nih.gov/workingatnih/competencies/occupation-specific/2210/default.htm).

1. **Information Technology (IT) Adeptness.** Possesses the ability to learn new technologies and the aptitude to understand IT concepts.
2. **Information Technology Expertise.** Able to use the technologies needed to perform in one's IT specific area and understands the technologies of importance to NIH Institutes.
3. **Information Technology Awareness.** Keeps up to date with trends and changes in the technology market relevant to one's area of professional expertise.
4. **Information Technology Legislative Requirements.** Understands and applies comprehensive knowledge of government IT laws, regulations, policies, and procedures.

5. **Federal and Departmental Acquisition Policies and Procedures Knowledge.** Understands the Federal Government industry and how it functions as a buyer of services and products.
6. **Project Management.** Creates and maintains an environment that guides a project to its successful completion.
7. **Technical Information Communication.** Communicates technical information in a manner consistent with the level of the target audience.

Key Behaviors:
- Grasps the "how and why" of information technology and its opportunities and limitations.
- Shares information learned at conferences, seminars, and training on new tools and technologies.
- Enhances knowledge and capabilities by engaging in discussions with other IT professionals.

Issues

A number of criticisms have been leveled at the concept of competency modeling over the years (Rankin 2005). Some of the major criticisms of competency frameworks are:

Competency-based models can be overly elaborate and bureaucratic, affecting their utility to varying degrees. Also, they can be expensive—costing 2 to 3 million dollars for larger organizations, and are likewise very time-consuming to implement. Furthermore, in a rapidly changing environment, a given competency model may quickly become outdated, thus consuming additional time and expense in ensuring it remains relevant and up-to-date.

Also, when placing too much emphasis on employees' inputs (competencies) instead of their actual production (outputs), there is a danger of favoring employees who are good performers in theory, but not in actual practice. In a similar vein, because some behavioral competencies are essentially personality traits a person is unable to change, it may be more prudent to judge someone on what they actually achieve.

Competency modeling runs the risk of producing clones that mimic one another, at the risk of minimizing work teams with diverse skill sets who offset and balance the strengths and weaknesses of other team members. Also, because competencies are based on models of good performers' past performance, this potentially overlooks a dynamic environment whereby new ways of addressing work issues may be needed. Also, if an organization is not very proficient in differentiating between successful and unsuccessful performers, competency modeling adds little value to the organization.

CONCLUSION

Used correctly, competency models can be powerful, unifying agents for change—changing and directing individual behavior toward organizational goals. Through the clarification of organizational expectations, competency models can be instrumental drivers of superior performance. Aside from enhancing the performance management process, competency models can be effective tools for recruiting and selecting the right person for the right job. Yet, competencies are also useful tools for designing jobs, career development, compensation planning, determining training and development needs, and making organizational design decisions. Though there are some drawbacks to the use of competency models, the positive contributions tend to outweigh any negative aspects. In light of the wide-ranging benefits of competency models and their ability to elicit superior performance, competency modeling has continued to gain traction.

BIBLIOGRAPHY

Boyatzis, Richard E. *The Competent Manager: A Model for Effective Performance.* London: Wiley, 1982.

Boyatzis, Richard, Elizabeth Stubbs, and Scott Taylor. "Learning Cognitive and Emotional Intelligence Competencies through Graduate Management Education." *Academy of Management Learning & Education* 1, no. 2 (2002): 150–62. Web. 21 May 2007.

Byham, William, and Reed P. Moyer. Using Competencies to Build a Successful Organization. Development Dimensions International. Pittsburgh, 1996.

Hsiu-Chuan, Lin, Lee Yen-Duen, and Tai Chein. "A Study on the Relationship between Human Resource Management Strategies and Core Competencies." *International Journal of Organizational Innovation* 4, no. 3 (2012): 153–73.

Kronenburg, Maria A. "Evaluating Important Healthcare Management Competency Areas and

Preparation for Healthcare Reforms." *International Journal of Business & Public Administration* 11, no. 1 (2014): 31–40. Web. 1 Dec. 2014.

Latukha, Marina O., and Andrei Y. Panibratov. "Top Management Teams' Competencies for International Operations: Do They Influence a Firm's Result?" *Journal of General Management* 40, no. 4 (2005): 45–68. Web. 4 Dec. 2015.

LeBlue, Ronald, and Roger Sobkowizk. "New Workforce Competency Models." *Information Systems Management* 12, no. 3 (1995): 7. Web. 28 May 2007.

McClelland, David C. "Testing for Competence Rather Than for Intelligence." *American Psychologist* 28, no. 1 (1973): 1–14. Print.

Mendenhall, Mark E., Audur Arnardottir, Gary R. Oddou, and Lisa A. Burke. "Development Cross-Cultural Competencies in Management Education via Cognitive-Behavior Therapy." *Academy of Management Learning & Education* 12, no. 3 (2013): 436–51. Web. 15 Nov. 2013.

Montier, Richard, David Alai, and Diana Kramer. "Competency Models Develop Top Performance." *T+D* 60, no. 7 (2006): 47–50. Web. 23 May 2007.

Mukhopadhyay, Kankana, Jaya Sil, and N.R. Banerjea. "A Competency Based Management System for Sustainable Development by Innovative Organizations: A Proposal of Method and Tool." *Vision* 15, no. 2 (2011): 153–62. Web. 15 Nov. 2013.

Parry, Scott. "Just What Is a Competency?" *Training* 35, no. 6 (1998): 58. Print.

Rankin, N. "The Competency Researcher's Toolkit." *Competency & Emotional Intelligence* 14, no. 1 (2006): 26–29. Web. 23 May 2007.

Rankin, N. "The DNA of Performance: The Twelfth Competency Benchmarking Survey." *Competency & Emotional Intelligence* 13, no. 1 (2005): 2–24. Web. 9 May 2007.

Rejas-Muslera, Ricardo, Alfonso Urquiza, and Isabel Cepeda. "Competency-Based Model through It: An Action Research Project." *Systemic Practice & Action Research* 25, no. 2 (2012): 117–35. Web. 1 Dec. 2014.

Rothwell, William, and John Lindholm. "Competency Identification, Modeling and Assessment in the USA." *International Journal of Training & Development* 3, no. 2 (1999): 90. Web. 28 May 2007.

Seal, Craig, Richard Boyatzis, and John Bailey. "Fostering Emotional and Social Intelligence in Organizations." *Organization Management Journal* 3, no. 3 (2006): 190–209. Web. 21 May 2007.

SUGGESTED READING

Boyatzis, Richard E. "Rendering unto Competence the Things That Are Competent." *American Psychologist* 49, no. 1 (1994): 64–66. Web. 31 May 2007.

Dubois, David D. *Competency-Based Performance Improvement: A Strategy for Organizational Change.* Amherst: HRD Press Inc., 1993.

Griffiths, Bruce, and Enrique Washington. *Competencies at Work: Providing a Common Language for Talent Management.* New York: Business Expert Press, 2015.

McLagan, Patricia. "Competency Models." *Training & Development Journal* 34, no. 12 (1980): 22. Web. 31 May 2007.

Spencer, Lyle M., and Signe M. Spencer. *Competence at Work: Models for Superior Performance.* New York: John Wiley & Sons, 1993.

Strobel, Kari. "Competency Proficiency Predicts Better Job Performance." *HR Magazine* 59, no. 10 (2014): 67. Web. 1 Dec. 2014.

Edwin D. Davison, M.B.A., J.D.

MANAGEMENT OF HUMAN RESOURCES

ABSTRACT

The management of human resources has undergone much transformation over the past decades, due to changes in markets, industry, technology, costs, workforce, and employer-employee relationships. The management of human resources is no longer restricted to a single department: it is now a shared responsibility across organizations. In an era of heightened competition, firms are turning to innovative human resource practices for competitive advantage, and human resource policies and practices are increasingly integrated with business strategy, both domestically and internationally.

OVERVIEW

People are the most important asset of every organization. This is especially true in the twenty-first century's challenging business environment, where human resources are seen as an indispensable input for organizational effectiveness. Since there is a strong relationship between the quality of human resources and the performance and success of an organization, organizations the world over are striving for effective management of their human resources. The management of human resources has evolved in several phases over the twentieth- and into the twenty-first century. As an occupation or a department within an organization, this area first came to light between the first and second world wars, under the term "human relations." Subsequently, as trade unions became increasingly powerful in the middle of the century, the term "industrial relations" became popular. The terms "personnel administration" and "personnel management," together with the less popular "employee relations" and "manpower management" emerged in the late 1960s and 1970s, due to the growing complexity of employment law, and ongoing concern about trade unions. At the time, the management of people in organizations was seen to be the responsibility of the personnel function.

As the personnel function grew in scope and importance, monopolizing the management of people, those in managerial and supervisory positions were left with little to do when it came to such activities as the acquisition, development and compensation of human resources; the design of work systems; and labor relations. At the same time, because personnel specialists were increasingly concerned with rules and regulations and were mainly seen as preoccupied with problem solving, they were often left out of the strategic thinking of their firms. The 1980s presented new challenges for business organizations. In an era of increasing competition, as the global playing field became far more competitive and volatile than ever before, firms had to strive to gain competitive advantage whenever and wherever possible. Business was also changing at a much faster rate which was accompanied by high uncertainty. As a result of rising costs and increasing competitive pressures on profit margins, firms also realized the need to be more cost-effective. Trade union power declined, and the "me" generation emerged, with its emphasis on individualism. There were also changes in organization structure, as firms decentralized responsibility to business units built around products and markets to get closer to their customers. Organizations became flatter, leaner, and more flexible. The technological revolution also posed great challenges for businesses, with innovations such as the introduction of information technology and computer-integrated manufacturing, which led to issues that had to be managed "across" the organization and which themselves called for a more integrated view of the organization. The accelerated pace of new product development also meant that people in different functions such as design, marketing, production, and finance had to work much more closely together than before. Rapid technological change also led to increased demands for new skills through sourcing, educating, and retraining. In addition, workforce values changed: the higher proportion of better-educated "knowledge workers" were increasingly likely to demand self-actualization, causing greater attention to be paid to such issues as communications, participation, and motivation. Firms in countries with aging populations faced the extra challenge of limited availability of labor, amid a shrinking workforce. Thus, a premium was placed on the recruitment and retention of high quality employees.

In general, the firms that survived or came on the scene after these changes, have been more complex in terms of products, location(s), technologies, business functions, customers, and markets. These changes led to a change in the image and role of the personnel function, leading to another change in name to "Human Resource Management." At the same time, the management of human resources moved from a department function, to a shared responsibility among managers and nonmanagers, personnel or human resource directors, and line managers. In the highly competitive, internationalized business structure that emerged in the twenty-first century, human resource management became essential to gaining or retaining an edge on rivals (Anca-Ioana 2013; Brauns 2013).

APPLICATIONS

With the changes in image, role and name of the human resource management function came a quest for a new kind of innovation, as firms recognized

The employees of the British Columbia Electric Railway, 1904 (photo courtesy of Wadds Brothers)

that the traditional sources and means of competitive advantage, such as capital, technology or location, had become less significant. Innovative human resource practices have now become one of the bases for competitive advantage—no longer as a matter of trend, but rather of survival.

Categories of Human Resource Practice

Agarwala (2003) has identified fourteen categories of human resource practice, highlighting examples of innovative practices for each:

1. **Employee Acquisition.** Employee acquisition refers to internal and external selection and recruitment of employees to jobs. It includes the hiring of temporary work assistance and the use of external consultants (Grønhaug and Nordhaug 1992). Pre-acquisition tasks include planning and forecasting, job analysis, job evaluation, job design, and work system design. The latter relates to how tasks and responsibilities in the firm are distributed among job incumbents and the degree to which sharp borderlines exist between jobs (Grønhaug and Nordhaug 1992). Employee acquisition tasks are best performed in the context of an organization's culture. All things being equal, selection should favor those candidates who appear to "fit in" with the prevailing organizational culture, be it a culture of empowerment, participation, equal opportunity, and/or any one of the many other facets of culture. Innovative employee acquisition strategies include (Agarwala 2003):
   - greater importance attached to the fit between person and company culture
   - emphasis on "career," not "job"
   - selling company image to attract potential employees' referral bonuses
   - sign-on bonuses for new employees
   - psychological testing
   - developing industry-academia interface

2. **Employee Retention Strategies.** Employee retention refers to the measures put in place to keep employees in an organization, thus reducing the labor turnover rate. Innovative employee retention strategies include (Agarwala 2003):
   - evolving a pleasant work environment
   - deferred compensation
   - competitive salaries
   - faster promotions
   - greater work autonomy

3. **Compensation and Incentives.** Compensation includes the whole range of rewards and incentives that are applied to employees. Intrinsic rewards are those that are internal to a person, such as job satisfaction and self-esteem; extrinsic rewards are more tangible and range from wages to employee stock ownership plans (Grønhaug and Nordhaug 1992). Compensation must be managed, along with employee attitudes towards compensation. Incentives are those offerings that have a tendency to motivate employees to act as the organization desires. Innovative compensation and incentive strategies include (Agarwala 2003):
   - increasing the component of variable pay
   - stock options
   - combining individual and team incentives
   - performance-linked incentives customization of perks to individual needs
   - offering a variety of allowances
   - conducting compensation surveys

4. **Benefits and Services.** Similar to compensation and incentives, benefits and services may

form part of an employee's remuneration package, and may include medical care, loans, travel, accommodation, catering, and so on. Many employers, for instance, offer Employee Assistance Programs, which are employee benefit programs typically offered in conjunction with a health insurance plan. Such programs aim to help employees handle personal problems so that they do not negatively impact their work ability, health, or well-being. These programs usually include assessment, short-term counseling and referral services for employees and their household members. Innovative benefits and services strategies include (Agarwala 2003):

- a focus on long-term benefits for employees through alternative insurance and health management schemes
- giving benefits directed at employees' families
- flexible employee benefits or the cafeteria approach, where employees choose from a menu of benefits
- child and elder care programs
- improvements in retirement benefits

5. **Rewards and Recognition.** Rewards and recognition are used to encourage and motivate an organization's employees, and effective reward management will promote consistency of practice in this area. Innovative rewards and recognition strategies include (Agarwala 2003):
    - performance-linked rewards
    - flexible rewards
    - cash rewards for extraordinary performance
    - rewarding team performance
    - rewarding team performance
    - public recognition of good performance at a company meeting or function
    - recognition from coworkers
    - a blend of financial and nonfinancial rewards

6. **Technical Training.** Human resource development concerns the maintenance, refinement and advancement of competencies possessed by the firm's employees (Grønhaug and Nordhaug 1992). Technical training refers to training for specific competence on the job, with regard to technology and/or business process change. Training may take place on-the-job or outside the workplace. Innovative technical training strategies include (Agarwala 2003):
    - systematic training
    - needs assessment
    - cross-functional training
    - job relevant training
    - transfer of training to actual job performance

7. **Management Development.** The effectiveness of management is recognized as one of the determinants of organizational success, and investment in management development can have a direct economic benefit to organizations, since management development helps to develop leadership, supervision and control. Innovative management development strategies include (Agarwala 2003):
    - linking management development to individual needs
    - linking management development to organizational objectives
    - using innovative management development methods, like stress management programs
    - providing adventure training
    - organizing leadership and attitudinal training
    - supporting study leave

8. **Career Planning and Development.** Career planning and development refer to the assistance given to employees to help them plan for, execute and manage their career development within an organization. Some organizations may link the career progress of their members to succession planning. Innovative career planning and development strategies include (Agarwala 2003):
    - developing career paths
    - providing fast-track career plans
    - providing mentors to employees
    - arranging cross-functional career paths
    - providing mentors to employees
    - creating career counseling

9. **Performance Appraisals.** Performance management is the process linking goal setting and rewards, coaching for performance, aspects of career development and performance evaluation and appraisal into an integrated process (Sparrow, Schuler, and Jackson 1994). Performance appraisals are a key component of performance management; they may seek to measure and motivate customer service, quality, innovation and risk-taking behavior. Innovative performance appraisal strategies include (Agarwala 2003):
    - giving weight to individual, team and organizational performance while appraising
    - using quantifiable criteria for appraisals
    - organizing participative appraisals
    - holding open appraisals to increase transparency
    - giving appraisal feedback
    - linking rewards to appraisals
    - creating sixty-degree appraisals, where feedback comes from all around the employee: from subordinates, peers and managers in the organizational hierarchy, as well as a external sources such as customers and suppliers or other interested stakeholders
    - requiring self-assessment

10. **Potential Development.** Potential development is a company-wide management development program that seeks to cultivate performance and leadership at the top of the organization, through the provision of the necessary training, support and opportunities. Innovative potential development strategies include (Agarwala 2003):
    - job rotations
    - use of assessment centers
    - coaching
    - conducting potential appraisals

11. **Succession Planning.** This is a management development program aimed at filling specific positions with one of two potential candidates. Innovative succession planning strategies include (Agarwala 2003):
    - identifying replacements
    - providing of fall-back positions in case of failure
    - preparing to assume higher responsibility

12. **Employee Relations.** As firms seek to empower and include employees in the organization, they ought to treat their employees with concern through effective internal communication; enhancement of the quality of work life; good labor relations; and health, welfare and safety programs. Innovative employee relations strategies include (Agarwala 2003):
    - information sharing
    - open and transparent communication
    - family get-togethers
    - humanizing work environment
    - respect for employees
    - fairness in management practices
    - promotion of risk-taking

13. **Employee Exit and Separation Management.** Employee exit and separation management refers to the planning, facilitation, and management of the departure of employees from an organization. Exit and separation may be initiated by employees themselves; by the state, through retirement; or by firms conducting specific "decruitment" activities such as downsizing and skills reprofiling. Innovative employee exit and separation management strategies include (Agarwala 2003):
    - benefits extended to retirees for lifetime
    - retirement planning workshops for about-to-retire employees
    - exit interviews
    - outplacement services
    - voluntary retirement schemes

14. **Corporate Responsibility.** As their corporate responsibility, firms seek to recognize and incorporate aspects of the external environment such as the general quality of the labor force, legal regulations or concerns about environmental quality, and social responsibility. They also ensure an effective flow and sharing of information outside of the organization. Innovative strategies for corporate responsibility include (Agarwala 2003):
    - adult education programs
    - community development projects
    - concern for greening and protection of the environment
    - research promotion

When well planned and implemented, the "right" combination of the above variables should lead to job satisfaction, motivation, employee commitment and participation for employees, and ultimately, competitive advantage for an organization.

Issues

As the management of human resources is seen increasingly in terms of competitive advantage, the question that arises is, what must be done to gain and maintain this advantage? The answer is: strategic business change, with human resource processes at its core. Before the 1990s, attempts to coordinate human resource management with a firm's business strategy had taken one of three limited approaches: correlating managerial style or personnel activities with strategies; predicting manpower requirements based on strategic objectives or environmental conditions, and discovering ways to assimilate human resource management into the comprehensive attempt to equalize strategy and structure (Lengnick-Hall and Lengnick-Hall 1988). Since the early 1990s, however, the management of human resources has been integrated with business strategy. Rather than existing in a vacuum, the human resource activities in a firm are now expected to directly support business strategy and the satisfaction of customer needs. The integration of the management of human resources with business strategy means that the management of human resources involves a wide variety of policies and procedures, which are strategically significant for the organization and are typically used to promote employee commitment, flexibility, good quality of work life as well as to realize overall business goals such as organizational values, structure, productivity, and production techniques (Sparrow, Schuler, and Jackson 1994).

This change has led to a concept in the management of human resources called "human resource strategy," which refers to the set of decisions or factors that shape and guide the management of human resources in an organizational context. It is also a set of strategic processes communally shared by human resources and line managers to resolve people related business issues. It is directly related to the business strategy and focuses on the formulation and alignment of human resource activities to achieve organizational competitive objectives. Through human resource strategy, human resource management aims to increase value through issue identification, assessment, and resolution. The main issues targeted are those critical to the organization's viability and success. It is a more action oriented strategy than traditional human resource planning. Strategic human resource management works through many means, including the following:

- coordinating available resources with necessary staffing levels and abilities, through recruitment, selection, assignment, and other strategic staffing processes
- aligning individuals and groups with overall business objectives through the management of performance.
- developing needed capabilities and performance through training, education, and job-related learning
- enhancing the quality of management through an emphasis on management development
- bridging the gap between the strategic and the operational through the relationship between employee and line manager.

The personnel or human resource management function advises the manager on how he/she can carry out these objectives, and line managers implement the strategic objectives of the organization through their leadership style and the way in which they manage their people. Conducting human resource planning (predicting future business and environmental costs and generating the personnel requirements determined by those future conditions) has become a key aspect of strategic planning. The resulting plans are strategic if they address significant change of direction—not merely continuity.

In the 2010s, companies such as Google and Netflix have been lauded as models of innovation in terms of human resources management. As of 2014, Google had become known not only for its more luxurious employee perks and benefits, but also for its use of data-based analytics in the hiring process and in maintaining more positive employee attitudes (Rafter 2015). At the same time, Netflix had become famous for its agile approach to managing its workforce, including a dedication to hiring only the most qualified individuals, promoting open communication about employee performance rather than formal review processes, and maintaining a philosophy of treating employees maturely (McCord 2014).

In the international arena, there has been a growing interest in international human resource management, as more markets internationalize, more nations become integrated into the international world economy, and more businesses choose to expand their operations across national borders. The increasing attention drawn to this area reflects the realization that efficient and effective human resource management internationally is a key factor in the success of a business. Evidence suggests that human resource constraints are often the limiting factor when attempting to implement international business strategies. Recently it has been argued that the fast pace of internationalization and globalization has led to a more strategic role for human resource management, and it also leads to changes in the content of human resource management (Scullion and Starkey 2000). It is important for multinational firms to know which human resource policies and practices they can consider using in their worldwide operations, to assist them in gaining competitive advantage. This awareness leads to the questions whether different parts of the world practice human resource management differently; and whether there is some uniformity that firms can pursue in their efforts to manage their worldwide workforces successfully.

International businesses are increasingly turning their attention to issues such as expatriate management, where employees are transferred by organizations to work outside their country of origin or permanent residence. Effective management in this area helps to reduce the early return of expatriates; to minimize disruption to international operations; and to prevent the situation where expatriates are not retained by the organization after completing their assignments. Since the quality of management is more critical in the international arena than in domestic operations (Tung 1984), international firms are also examining the plethora of issues stemming from cross-cultural management, along with those issues surrounding the management of diversity in multicultural domestic workforces. As the pace of internationalization has accelerated, the need for cross-cultural awareness, cross-cultural sensitivity, and understanding the daily operations of international businesses, has become more salient. Academicians too have advanced understanding in these areas through the development of the distinct subfield of International Human Resource Management, within the management discipline. Marler (2012), for example compares scholarship in the field from the United States, Germany and China, three countries with widely differing histories, economic and political systems, and business cultures.

Bibliography

Anca-Ioana, Munteanu. "New Approaches of the Concepts of Human Resources, Human Resource Management and Strategic Human Resource Management." *Annals of the University Of Oradea, Economic Science Series* 22 (2013): 1520–25. Web. 31 Oct. 2013.

Agarwala, Tanuja. "Innovative Human Resource Practices and Organizational Commitment: An Empirical Investigation." *International Journal of Human Resource Management* 14 (2003): 175–97. Web. 8 Mar. 2007.

Brauns, Melody. "Aligning Strategic Human Resource Management to Human Resources, Performance and Reward." *International Business & Economics Research Journal* 12 (2013): 1405–10. Web. 31 Oct. 2013.

Camp, R. *Managing Human Resources: Productivity, Quality of Worklife, Profits/Strategic Human Resource Management: A Guide for Effective Practice/Human Resource Management: A Practical Approach* (Book). *Personnel Psychology* 40 (1987): 128–33. Web. 8 Mar. 2007.

Craft, J. "Human resource strategy." In *Blackwell Encyclopedic Dictionary of Human Resource Management*, 2005. Web. 17 Mar. 2007.

De Cieri, Helen, Marilyn Fenwick, and Kate Hutchings. "The Challenge of International Human Resource Management: Balancing the Duality of Strategy and Practice." *International Journal of Human Resource Management* 16 (2005): 584–98. Web. 8 Mar. 2007.

Grønhaug, Kjell, and Odd Nordhaug. "International Human Resource Management: An Environmental Perspective." *International Journal of Human Resource Management* 3 (1992): 1–14. Web. 8 Mar. 2007.

Handy, Lawrence, Kevin Barham, Sara Panter, and Amelie Winhard. "Beyond the Personnel Function: The Strategic Management of Human Resources." *Journal of European Industrial Training* 13 (1989): 13–18. Web. 8 Mar. 2007.

Lenghick-Hall, Cynthia, and Mark Lengnick-Hall. "Strategic Human Resources Management: A

Review of the Literature and a Proposed Typology." *Academy of Management Review* 13 (1988): 454. Web. 8 Mar. 2007.

Marler, Janet. "Strategic Human Resource Management in Context: A Historical and Global Perspective." *Academy of Management Perspectives* 26 (2012): 6–11. Web. 31 Oct. 2013.

McCord, Patty. "How Netflix Reinvented HR." *Harvard Business Review* 92, nos.1–2 (2004): 70–76. Web. 4 Dec. 2015.

Rafter, Michelle. "Just Google Him." *Workforce* 94, no. 4 (2015): 40–49. Web. 4 Dec. 2015.

Schuler, Randall, and James Walker. "Human Resources Strategy: Focusing on Issues and Actions." *Organizational Dynamics* 19 (1990): 4–19. Web. 8 Mar. 2007.

Scullion, Hugh, and Ken Starkey. "In Search of the Changing Role of the Corporate Human Resource Function in the International Firm." *International Journal of Human Resource Management* 11 (2000): 1061–81. Web. 8 Mar. 2007.

Sparrow, Paul, Randall Schuler, and Susan Jackson. "Convergence or Divergence: Human Resource Practices and Policies for Competitive Advantage Worldwide." *International Journal of Human Resource Management* 5 (1994): 267–99. Web. 8 Mar. 2007.

Tung, Rosalie. "Strategic Management of Human Resources in the Multinational Enterprise." *Human Resource Management* 23 (1984): 129–43. Web. 8 Mar. 2007.

Walker, James. "Integrating the Human Resource Function with the Business." *Human Resource Planning* 17 (1994): 59–77. Web. 8 Mar. 2007.

Walker, James. "Strategic Human Resource Planning." In *Blackwell Encyclopedic Dictionary of Human Resource Management*. Web. 8 Mar. 2007.

Warner, Malcolm. "Review Symposium: From Human Relations to Human Resources." *International Journal of Human Resource Management* 8 (1997): 124–28. Web. 8 Mar. 2007.

SUGGESTED READING

Agarwala, Tanuga. "Innovative Human Resource Practices and Organizational Commitment: An Empirical Investigation." *International Journal of Human Resource Management* 14 (2003): 175–97. Web. 8 Mar. 2007.

Armstrong, Michael. *A Handbook of Human Resource Management Practice*. 10th ed. London: Kogan Page, 2006.

Noe, Raymond A. *Human Resources Management: Gaining a Competitive Advantage*. 9th ed. New York: McGraw-Hill Education, 2015.

Vanessa A. Tetteh, Ph.D.

MANAGERIAL LEADERSHIP

ABSTRACT

This paper provides an overview of the necessary qualities of effective management and discusses ways that adhering to core values and maintaining standards of ethical conduct are necessary to achieve managerial leadership. There are certain necessary qualities for effective management: strong organization skills, the ability to communicate, and the capacity to make decisions. These skills are essential for effective management whether one is managing a small business, a division within a company, or a group in any other work environment. However, truly successful managing requires a business owner or a manager to go beyond these basic skill sets in order to set a higher standard of quality. In order to accomplish this goal, managers need to lead. Moreover, managerial leadership requires that a manager adhere to certain core values and standards of ethical conduct.

OVERVIEW

Managerial Skills

Regardless of the type of business or work situation, a successful enterprise requires effective management. There are certain basic skill sets that managers must have in order to be effective.

- First, a manager must be highly organized; they need to manage their time efficiently, prioritize their responsibilities and assume responsibility for the workflow of the group by delegating expediently.

- In order to delegate, a manager must also be able to communicate effectively. Successful communication requires a manager to speak and write clearly as well as to listen intently. In fact, listening is probably one of the more important abilities a manager must have to communicate effectively. This skill is necessary because managers need to have a clear understanding of the group and what people can and cannot do. The best managers are those that recognize people's capabilities so that they delegate responsibilities effectively. In short, employees should be put into positions where they are most likely to fulfill their duties successfully. By having strong communication skills, a manager will be able to delegate, and to act decisively (Ramona, Emanoil, and Lucia 2012).
- Being able to make decisions, whether popular or unpopular, also lends itself to serving as a successful leader.

Essentially, having a successful business, agency or other enterprise requires having effective managers. Effective managers need to have strong organizational, communication and decision-making skills. More than these areas, successful managers must be capable of leading.

Managerial Function

In order to lead, a manager must first master the basic functions of management. In his article, Justice Walton (2005) states that there are four functions of management:

- Planning for the short and long term
- Organizing a line or staff
- Directing (taking charge of a department or organization and controlling)
- Implementing various techniques for managerial control

Managers are supposed to delegate duties, not perform those duties. Moreover, a manager usually has the responsibility of choosing the people that will be doing the work which means that the manager is in charge of hiring, firing, training, and disciplining employees. Managers are also responsible for the work that the group performs. To ensure that the group is meeting consistent standards of quality, a manager must be able to motivate people and provide

Jack Welch (photo courtesy of Hamilton 83)

them with a sense of accomplishment. Managers need to communicate the big picture to employees by linking their role to the enterprise's main function.

One factor that determines how well a manager will perform these functions is his or her personality. A person's temperament, character and personality are directly related to how he or she will not only manage, but also lead. Another important factor is a manager's emotional intelligence (Boyatzis, Good, and Massa 2012; Davis 2011). There are certain traits that allow one to be an effective leader. Leaders must be able to work with others and show employees that their role does make a difference. Managers must be positive thinkers and perform their role with energy. In so doing, they will instill energy in the team. Some of the traits that will enable a manager to lead include: integrity, pride, sincerity, curiosity, passion, and courage (Walton 2005).

APPLICATIONS

Indicators of Successful Management

There are ways to determine if a company or enterprise is being successfully managed. Success usually manifests itself in results and is normally reflected in financial outcomes, such as profit in a sales organization. Success can also be reflected by a number of outcomes in an educational setting—such as the test scores of a particular grade level or the percentage of students graduating in a school district. Such results are also referred to as quantitative results and while they are important, other qualitative results also that need to be reviewed: These results can be reflected in a business enterprise by employee satisfaction, customer satisfaction, quality control, customer retention, and employee retention. Charles Kerns contends that there are six dimensions of quality results: (1) results need to be values driven, (2) results should be grounded in ethical behavior, (3) results must be related to the overall purpose of the entity, (4) results need to be geared toward learning, (5) results must be able to be measured, and (6) results need to provide a balanced perspective—both quantitative and qualitative, in determining the success of the enterprise (Kerns 2005).

Importance of Core Values & Ethics
It is becoming more evident that the success of businesses, educational institutions, hospitals, and healthcare providers, as opposed to for profit organizations, government agencies, and any other group dynamic where people are working toward a common goal, is directly related to the entity's values. This success is reflected in both quantitative and qualitative results. A sales enterprise that is lacking a core set of values may be able to sustain itself in the short run, but at the end of the day, its long-term success will be the result of actions rooted in a set of core values. Adhering to a set of values lends itself to actions that are constructive and ethical.

Since values are directly related to the long-term success of an enterprise, these values must first be identified and then become part of the entity's basic function. There should also be a means to ensure that these values are adhered to over time. In order for a manager to achieve this, he or she must follow those values. In so doing, managers set an example for the group and thereby gain credibility.

Once a set of core values has been established, the attitudes and behaviors that arise should be grounded in ethical behavior. Ethics has become a buzzword in the wake of the financial accounting scandals that arose throughout the first decade of the 2000s (for companies like Enron in 2001 and Bernard L. Madoff Investment Securities in 2008), but ethical behavior in the long run will enable an organization to sustain qualitative and quantitative results. It is ultimately the responsibility of managerial leaders to adhere to high standards of ethical conduct. A manager can lead the way by being truthful, having integrity, extending kindness, treating staffers with fairness, taking responsibility for his or her actions, and the performance of the group, and finally treating others with respect. In the end, a leader must have integrity since his or her effectiveness and leadership will be affected by whether the staff believes in a manager's integrity.

Creating a Successful Environment
In addition to adhering to a set of values and acting ethically, a leader must be able to link the results of the enterprise and its people to the organization's purpose. According to Kerns (2005), "without a positive connection between work and organizational purpose—what we do each day becomes less meaningful."

Making Employees Matter
People need to believe that what they are doing has meaning and that their role makes a difference. In a sales organization, sales people can clearly see this link. But the operations personnel—the accountants, customer service reps, and clerical staff—often cannot see such a clear connection between their work and results. At times, people serving these basic but vital functions tend to lose sight of the big picture; after all, the sales people who are successful and receive the most commissions usually are compensated at a higher level than the operations personnel. In order to ensure that they continue to achieve quality results, an operations manager must be able to remind his or her staff how their functions are connected to the overall success of the business which can only happen if the manager has mastered one of the basic skills—the ability to communicate—mentioned earlier:

A manager can only be successful at connecting a team's work to the larger purpose of the organization if he or she can communicate clearly and thereby create an environment that people believe is a good place to work. Not only must a leader ensure that the people he or she is responsible for managing believe their role is important, but also a leader must ensure the quality of a team's performance by putting team members in situations where they can learn. There are a number of ways to accomplish this goal. First a leader must ensure that he or she has hired the right people to do the job. Once the right people are in place, the manager is responsible for ensuring that people learn the functions required to perform that role. But what happens when an employee has mastered that role? If employees stop learning they become stagnant. One way to prevent this stagnation involves cross-training his or her team members so that they perform a variety of roles.

Evaluating & Responding to Results

While it is clear that quantitative results can be measured in numbers such as profits for a sales organization or numbers of students in a graduating class, qualitative results must also be measured. This situation can be achieved by incorporating the values and ethical behaviors into the basic functions of the enterprise and into roles and responsibilities of the employees. If a manager has mastered the organizational skills that allow him or her to establish priorities, has communicated these priorities to staff members, and then ensures that these priorities are being fulfilled by providing people with consistent feedback, he or she can then make necessary decisions such as rewarding, firing or disciplining people. At the end of the day, it is the manager's job to determine annual pay raises, bonuses and promotions, which can be difficult decisions to make. Even harder than rewards, though, comes the responsibility of doling out punishment. At times, employees in a particular group or a division of a large corporation may not meet the organization's objectives and goals. At such times, the manager must make the tough decision to discipline certain individuals or even to close entire divisions. In the case of the former, the values of fairness and respect come directly into play. If an employee is treated fairly in a situation that requires disciplinary action, and if the person is also treated with respect, the decision and actions required will be handled more effectively. In a situation where an entire division of a company is closed, a leader must ensure that the decision was based on a valid reason and that the action will ensure the long term profitability of the entity. Not everyone can make these tough calls and they go beyond the basic skill sets required for effective managing; such decisions require managerial leadership.

VIEWPOINTS

Measuring Quantitative & Qualitative Results

Quantitative and qualitative results must be balanced, and they must be monitored in a number of areas such as financial (profits and other similar results), customer satisfaction (easily measured through a strong orientation to customer service) and internal business purposes (linking the role of each group and the people in each group to the entity's overall purpose and potential for learning and growth) (Kerns 2005). These measurements are ultimately the responsibility of the manager, and in order to effectively assume that responsibility, the manager must master the basic organizational, communication, and decision-making skills required of the position. Beyond this set of skills, a manager must have the ability to lead. Leadership requires that a manager have certain core values and act in an ethical manner. This pattern of behavior will encourage others to act ethically as well. By inspiring others to act ethically and in adherence to the organization's core values, a manager will have greater success linking a group's or individual's performance to the business entity's purpose which can only happen if a manger has integrity. There are other leadership traits such as courage, pride, sincerity, vision, passion, curiosity, and daring. These are not theoretical notions and many successful businesses, education, and other leaders have spoken and written extensively about such leadership traits.

Jack Welch of GE on Successful Leadership

One such leader is Jack Welch, the former chief executive officer (CEO) of General Electric Corporation. In his book, *Winning*, Welch comments that before becoming a leader, an individual's success in an organization is about self-development. Becoming a leader changes the focus from growing oneself to growing others. When one becomes a manager, one becomes responsible for other people, and because of this responsibility, a manager must go beyond basic functions of managing and become a leader. This shirt requires a manager to "resolve problems, assume responsibility, offer valid criticism, and set an example by pursuing high quality and acting with integrity" (Welch 2005).

There are a number of ways for a leader to pursue high quality and emanate positive energy, and maintain an optimistic outlook. "An upbeat manager that goes through the day with a positive outlook ends up running a team or organization filled with upbeat people" (Welch 2005).

In order to demonstrate successful managerial leadership, people in positions of authority must also have courage. This trait rises from being able to make decisions centered on ensuring that the organization is fulfilling its purpose. At times, this situation requires an organization to take risks, and ultimately someone is responsible for making those decisions. As Welch states, "Winning companies embrace risk taking and learning this requires freely admitting mistakes..." (Welch 2005).

In order to make those decisions and to get people to act in a way that will bring about that vision, a leader must also have sincerity. People need to be able to trust managers (i.e., leaders) and in order to trust them; people need to believe that leaders have integrity. The way for a leader to establish his or her integrity is to be trustworthy. In turn, the way for a leader to establish trust is by being open and honest. Being candid means that a leader communicates in a way that people know where they stand in terms of their performance. People also need to know how the business is doing. If things are going well, people need to know that their efforts contributed to the organization's success. Another way to establish trust is for a leader to credit people for their efforts.

By giving credit when appropriate, people are filled with a sense of pride, another trait necessary for managerial leadership. Not only must a manager take pride is his role, and the goal of the entity, he or she must also take pride in the success of others. One way to ensure these feelings is by having vision. It is the responsibility of the leader to determine the team's vision and bring it to fruition (Welch 2005).

To get people to share a vision, a manager must also have passion for that vision and the ability to communicate it clearly. Passion is not only necessary for attaining managerial leadership; it is essential to being successful in any endeavor. One way to get people to be passionate about their work is by linking their efforts to the overall purpose of the organization, and it is the leader's responsibility to bring forth this passion by manifesting positive energy. In the end, though, passion comes from within. Not only does managerial leadership require passion but also a great deal of curiosity. A leader's job is not to have all the answers, but rather, to have all the questions.

Not only must a leader have all the questions, the questions must engender open and honest debate. Finally a leader needs to ensure that the questions he or she raises will result in effective action. Questions must lead to results and sometimes those results may not be what were originally intended. Another trait essential to leadership is daring. A leader must be willing to face confrontations that may arise from his or her passion, curiosity and tough decisions. A leader must also be able to resolve those conflicts. In these instances, a leader will be more inclined to be successful if he or she adheres to a core set of values and establishes trust by conducting himself or herself ethically.

CONCLUSION

There are certain fundamental skills required for effective management. Included in these skills are organizational, communication and decision making skills necessary to fulfill the four basic functions of management. Other skills include planning for the short and long term, organizing a line or staff, directing (taking charge of a department or organization and controlling), and implementing various techniques for managerial control.

Whether an organization is being managed successfully will be reflected in quantitative and qualitative results. Quantitative results are normally manifested in financial outcomes. Qualitative results, on the other hand, are measured in a number of other ways including results that are values driven and grounded in ethical behavior. Ultimately, the person responsible for these results is the manager who must have basic skill sets to ensure that the basic functions of management are being fulfilled and must act as a leader.

Managerial leadership requires managers to have certain traits, such as integrity, ethical values, and trustworthiness. A leader that has integrity will ensure that the business entity's results are values driven, will conduct himself or herself ethically, and in so doing engender the trust of the people under the manager's direction. In the end, that trust will manifest itself in the purpose or goals of the enterprise.

BIBLIOGRAPHY

Boyatzis, Richard E., Darren Good, and Raymond Massa. "Emotional, Social, and Cognitive Intelligence and Personality." *Journal of Leadership & Organizational Studies* 19, no. 2 (2012): 191–201. Web. 20 Nov. 2013.

Curtiss, Russ, and John J. Sherlock. "Wearing Two Hats: Counselors Working as Managerial Leaders in Agencies and Schools." *Journal of Counseling and Development* 84, no. 1 (2006): 120–26. Web. 11 Dec. 2006.

Davis, Steven A. "Investigating the Impact of Project Managers' Emotional Intelligence on Their Interpersonal Competence." *Project Management Journal* 42, no. 4 (2011): 37–57. Web. 20 Nov. 2013.

Fast, Nathanael, Ethan R. Burris, and Caroline A. Bartel. "Managing to Stay in the Dark: Managerial Self-Efficacy, Ego Defensiveness and the Aversion to Employee Voice." *Academy of Management Journal* 57, no. 4 (2014): 1013–34. Web. 18 Nov. 2014.

Kerns, Charles D. "Are All Results Created Equal? Auditing Organizational Outcomes for Quality." *Total Quality Management* 16, no. 7 (2005): 827–40. Web. 11 Dec. 2006.

Ramona, Todericiu, Muscalu Emanoil, and Fraticiu Lucia. "Reflections on Managerial Communication." *Studies in Business & Economics* 7, no. 1 (2012): 153–59. Web. 20 Nov. 2013.

Sprier, Scott W., Mary H. Fontaine, and Ruth L. Malloy. "Leadership Run Amok." *Harvard Business Review* 84, no. 6 (2006): 72–82. Web. 11 Dec. 2006.

Vyas, Ruta. "Managing the Dimensions of Ethos, Pathos and Logos of Change through Transformational Leadership." *IUP Journal of Soft Skills* 7, no. 3 (2013): 7–22. Web. 18 Nov. 2014.

Walton, Justice. "Searching for Managerial Leadership Skills along the Yellow Brick Road." *Healthcare Purchasing News* 29, no. 8 (2005): 60. Web. 11 Dec. 2006.

Welch, Jack, and Suzy Welch. *Winning.* New York: Harper Business/An Imprint of HarperCollins, 2005.

SUGGESTED READING

Creech, Bill. "Leadership Manageship." In *The Five Pillars of TQM. How to Make Total Quality Management Work for You,* edited by Bill Creech, 294–348. New York: Truman Talley Books/Dutton, 1994.

Covey, Stephen. *The Seven Habits of Highly Effective People.* New York: Simon & Schuster, 1989.

Guliani, Rudy W. *Leadership.* New York: Miramax Books/Hyperion, 2002.

Hall, J.L. "Managing Teams with Diverse Compositions: Implications for Managers from Research on the Faultline Model." *SAM Advanced Management Journal* 78, no. 1 (2013): 4–10. Web. 18 Nov. 2014.

Mckee, Annie, Frances Johnston, and Richard Massimilian. "Mindfulness, Hope and Compassion: A Leader's Road Map to Renewal." *Ivey Business Journal* 70 (2006): 1–5. Web. 11 Dec. 2006.

Richa S. Tiwary, Ph.D., M.L.S.

MANAGING CONFLICT WITHIN ORGANIZATIONS THROUGH NEGOTIATIONS

ABSTRACT

This article will focus on negotiation. Negotiation, as a tool of conflict management and conflict resolution in modern business organizations, will be described and analyzed. The article will provide an overview of organizational conflict and conflict management. The role of conflict manager will be described. The article will include discussion and analysis of the main models, tactics, and strategies for negotiation. Integrative and distributive approaches to negotiation will be addressed.

OVERVIEW

Negotiation, which refers to the process of bargaining preceding an agreement, is part of a larger process of managing conflict within organizations. While this article focuses on business negotiations, negotiation should be understood as a central and fundamental conflict resolution and management tool used by individuals, governments, and businesses alike. Negotiation skills, used to manage interpersonal, intergroupinterorganizational, and international conflict, are crucial for participation in the modern business world. Organizational conflict and organizational change, and related negotiation mechanisms and tools for managing these processes, are characteristic of current business practices across businesses and industries. Changes in contemporary business practices are causing the role of negotiation in business to evolve from conflict resolution to conflict management. In the twenty-first century, private sector organizations are increasingly moving from traditional authoritative, hierarchical structures to cooperative, team-based structures. The new team-based model of organizations, dependent upon cooperation and functioning work relationships, requires high-level knowledge of negotiation skills, conflict management skills, and mediation tactics. This structural change is occurring in large part as a result of globalization and its related processes as well as the internet and related technologies. Businesses and industries are increasingly transnational, decentralized operations. Goods and services may be produced in one region and sold in another. Telecommuting is a common work choice made in businesses with virtual rather than brick-and-mortar headquarters and stores. The increased pace of technological development and innovation requires businesses to become learning organizations to remain competitive in the marketplace. Cooperative management and participatory problem solving, both requiring negotiation skills, are common in team-based, decentralized business organizations. Furthermore, a culture that includes conflict as creative tension but not as a destructive force is an element of successful team-based organizations (Boni and Weingart 2012). The following sections provide an overview of organizational conflict and conflict management. These sections will serve as the foundation for a discussion and analysis of negotiation, mediation, and the relationship between negotiation and conflict management.

Organizational Conflict
Organizational conflict, which refers to an interactive process manifested in incompatibility, disagreement, or dissonance within or between social entities, creates organizational change. Types of conflict include interpersonal, intergroup, interorganizational, and international conflict. Conflict is a social process. Contextual antecedents, such as individual, team, project, and organizational characteristics, influence and may exacerbate conflict (Barki and Hartwick 2001). The conflict process can be positive or negative. Functional conflict creates positive change within the organization; dysfunctional conflict creates negative change within the organization. Organizational conflict can arise from problems within work activities as well as incompatible preferences and goals. Singleton et al. (2011) suggest that definitions of conflict will differ depending on the level of volatility, or perceived volatility, in the conflict. In the least volatile realm, the word conflict implies dissension, disagreement, opposition, and lack of consensus among two or more people. In the most volatile realm, the implication is associated animosity, anger, antagonistic words and/or behavior, and increasing levels of frustration. In either case, those involved in the conflict should understand the difference between functional and dysfunctional conflict and whether, and the extent to which, conflict management and conflict resolution theories and tools are needed.

Occurrence of Organization Conflict
Organizational conflict often occurs in the following situations and scenarios (Rahim 2002):

- Parties are required to engage in an activity that is incongruent with their needs or interests.
- Parties hold behavioral preferences that are incompatible with another person's implementation of his or her preferences.
- Parties want some mutually desirable resource that is in short supply.
- Parties possess attitudes, values, skills, and goals that are appropriate for directing their behavior but contradict the attitudes, values, skills, and goals held by others within an organization.
- Two parties have contradictory preferences regarding their joint actions.

Interpersonal Conflict
"Interpersonal conflict" refers to a phenomenon that occurs between interdependent parties as they experience negative emotional reactions to perceived disagreements and interference with the attainment of their goals. Interpersonal conflict within organizations often occurs on project teams involving multiple parties with potentially conflicting agendas, goals, styles, personalities, and objectives. Symptoms of interpersonal conflict include hostility; jealousy; steamrolling;

poor communication; political maneuvering; a proliferation of technical rules, norms, regulations, and frustration; and low morale. Interpersonal conflict is characterized by interdependence, disagreement, interference, and negative emotion. Interpersonal conflict within organizations can produce positive or negative change. Examples of negative outcomes from interpersonal conflict include distrust of others, hostility, decreased group coordination and cohesiveness, reduced job satisfaction and motivation, higher absenteeism and turnover, grievances, lower performance, and lower productivity. Examples of positive outcomes from interpersonal conflict include greater self-awareness, creativity, adaptation, and learning (Barki and Hartwick 2001).

Diagnosis of Organizational Conflict

Most people, groups, and organizations have conflict thresholds that must be exceeded for conflict to occur. Managers are generally responsible for the diagnosis of organizational conflict. The diagnosis of organizational conflict generally specifies the type of conflict, parties involved, and level and type of intervention needed. A diagnosis should indicate whether there is need for an intervention and the type of intervention needed.

Goals & Objectives of Intervention

Interventions in situations of organizational crisis are designed to accomplish the following goals and objectives (Rahim 2002):

- Interventions in situations of organizational crisis are designed to attain and maintain a moderate amount of substantive conflict in nonroutine tasks at various levels.
- Interventions in situations of organizational crisis are designed to reduce affective conflict at all levels.
- Interventions in situations of organizational crisis are designed to enable the organizational members to select and use the appropriate styles of handling conflict so that various situations can be effectively addressed.

Despite the fact that conflict often serves a function within organizations, conflict management most often attempts to reduce, resolve, and minimize conflict (Rahim 2002).

Conflict Management

Across a wide range of businesses and industries, managers oversee organizational conflict to ensure successful resolution. Conflict is managed by organizational leaders often referred to as "conflict managers." "Conflict management," which refers to designing effective macro-level strategies to minimize the dysfunctions of conflict and enhance the constructive functions of conflict in order to enhance learning and effectiveness in an organization, is recognized as its own field (Rahim 2002). Examples of conflict management include negotiation, bargaining, mediation, and arbitration. There are two main categories of conflict management techniques including conflict stimulation and conflict resolution. Conflict stimulation refers to the creation of conflict within organizations to promote change. Conflict resolution includes techniques (such as problem solving, expansion of resources, avoidance, compromise, authoritative command, altering human variables, and altering structural variables) to reduce conflict within the organization.

Conflict Management Styles

Different conflict management styles have different outcomes. Conflict management styles refer to general strategies or behavioral orientations individuals adopt when dealing with conflicts. There are five different modes or styles of conflict management including asserting, accommodating, compromising, problem solving, and avoiding (Barki and Hartwick 2001):

Asserting: Conflict, within the asserting management approach, is considered a win-lose situation. This approach is also referred to as "competing," "dominating," and "forcing."

Accommodating: The accommodating approach to conflict management involves individuals obliging or yielding to others' positions or cooperating in an attempt to smooth over conflicts. This approach is also referred to as "cooperating," "obliging," "yielding," and "sacrificing."

Compromising: The compromising approach to conflict management involves give and take behaviors where each party wins some and loses some. This approach is also referred to as "sharing" and "splitting the difference."

Problem solving: The problem-solving approach to conflict management occurs when individuals in conflict try to fully satisfy the concerns of all parties. This approach is also referred to as "integrating," "cooperating," and "collaborating."

Avoiding: The avoiding approach to conflict management occurs when individuals are indifferent to the concerns of either party and refuse to act or participate in conflict. This approach is also referred to as "withdrawing," "evading," "escaping," and "apathy."

Research has shown that demographic and personality traits affect which mode or style of conflict management individuals choose to employ in the workplace. For instance, gender research suggests women tend to accommodate, compromise, or avoid conflict while men tend to assert or compete more (Sone 1981; Cardona 1995, qtd. in Prause and Mujtaba 2015). Similarly, a person's dominant values influence his or her conflict management style: those who value self-transcendence (humility, cooperation, etc.) are more accommodating; those who prize conservation (self-image, recognition, etc.) are inclined to avoid conflict; those for whom self-enhancement (authority, power, wealth, etc.) is of prime importance tend to dominate; and those with an openness to change (independence, curiosity, harmony) are likely to engage in problem solving (Anjum Karim, and Bibi 2014).

Criteria Necessary for Successful Conflict Resolution

Team-based organizations increasingly work to manage conflict rather than resolve conflict. All conflict management strategies, including asserting, accommodating, compromising, problem solving, and avoiding, must satisfy certain criteria to be effective. These criteria include organizational learning and effectiveness, needs of stakeholders, and ethics:

Organizational learning and effectiveness: Conflict management strategies, designed to enhance organizational learning, and critical and innovative thinking. Organizational members, including employees and managers, are expected to learn the process of conflict diagnosis and intervention.

Needs of stakeholders: Conflict management strategies, designed to satisfy the needs and expectations of the strategic stakeholders and to attain a balance among them, involve these parties in a problem-solving process that will lead to collective learning and organizational effectiveness. This conflict management strategy is intended to lead to stakeholder satisfaction and confidence.

Ethics: Conflict management designed to define organizational problems so that they lead to ethical actions that benefit humankind is referred to as "ethical conflict management."

Conflict management in a contemporary business organization's functions requires a supportive organizational culture. Employees in contemporary business organizations that value conflict management are encouraged by managers and leadership to engage in the process of diagnosis of and intervention in problems. An organizational culture that supports conflict management encourages task-related conflict and discourages emotional conflict; supports organizational learning; risk taking, openness; diverse viewpoints; continuous questioning and inquiry; and sharing of information and knowledge. Within a supportive organizational culture, conflict management has the potential to enhance organizational learning that involves knowledge acquisition, knowledge distribution, information interpretation, and organizational memorization (Rahim 2002).

APPLICATIONS

Negotiation In the business sector is used within and between organizations. Negotiation is used in the commercial arena of buying and selling and solving industrial relations problems (Baines 1994). Commercial or business negotiation refers to the process for resolving differences of opinion that arise in contract dealings between a buyer and seller. Commercial negotiations can involve a complex range of financial, business, and contractual issues. Planning, conducting, and analyzing the outcomes of commercial negotiations are key elements of a successful business (Ashcroft 2004). Negotiations between individuals and organizations can be adversarial, coercive, emotional, cooperative, logical, courteous, or mutually advantageous. Negotiation of all kinds requires preparation, discussion, offers, and bargaining. While these are viewed as distinct stages, they build on one another. Preparation involves clarifying basic assumptions, selecting the negotiating team, choosing the leaders, discovering information, deciding on aims for the process, and arranging the physical environment or meeting place. The negotiating session involves introductions, presentation of cases, listening, offering options, summarizing, taking breaks, not rushing, making a deal when appropriate, and formalizing the negotiated agreement by signing a document (Baines 1994).

Traditional Models of Negotiation
Traditionally, there have been three main models of negotiation: integrative, distributive, and interdependence (Donohue and Roberto 1996):

Integrative model of negotiation: The integrative model of negotiation focuses on multiple issues, engages in problem solving, offers concessions and acceptances, and focuses on mutually beneficial solutions.

Distributive model of negotiation: The distributive model of negotiation involves parties within a distributive orientation that may conceal information, exaggerate their positions, and use threats, attacks, demands, and repetitive arguments. Distributive negotiation behavior works to create a context that makes integration less acceptable.

Interdependence model of negotiation: The interdependence model of negotiation combines integrative and distributive models. Negotiators continuously and explicitly define their interdependence by offering information, strategies, and tactics that foster both cooperation and competition. The interdependence model exists along a continuum of integrative-distributive processes.

Contemporary Models of Negotiation
Changes in contemporary business practices, due to globalization, new technology, and emergence of team-based organizations, have expanded the field of negotiation strategies to include additional approaches (and models) of negotiation such as power based, interests based, needs based, dignity model, comprehensive systemic, SWOT, and stage.

Power-based model of negotiation: The power-based model of negotiation, based on distributive principles, is characterized by selfishness, aggressive behavior, and competition. Power-based disputants will work to maximize their individual self-interest (Chaterjee 2006).

Interest-based model of negotiation: The interest-based model of negotiation, also referred to as "interest-based bargaining" or "mutual gains bargaining," refers to bargaining processes that are focused on understanding and building on interests and using problem-solving tools as a way of avoiding positional conflicts and achieving better outcomes for all stakeholders. Interest-based negotiation skills and tactics include active listening, converting positions into underlying needs or interests, joint data collection, brainstorming, joint task forces, facilitation, and effective communication with constituents (Fonstad 2004). The interest-based model of negotiation, based on integrative negotiation, separates disputants from the problem, focuses on interests and not positions, generates a variety of possibilities before creating an agreement, and insists that the results be based on some objective criteria (Chaterjee 2006).

Need-based model of negotiation: The human needs approach to conflict negotiation treats disputants as sociopsychological beings with certain needs that require fulfillment not as rational actors interested in the furtherance of self-interest. The need-based approach assumes that conflict arises from a threat to fundamental needs. The need-based model of negotiation works toward win-win solutions (Chaterjee 2006).

Dignity model of negotiation: The dignity model of negotiation assumes that situations of conflict arise from inhuman physical and verbal violence that compromise individual and group dignity. The dignity model of negotiation is based on the following premises: acceptance of humanity, validation of gender, class, race identities, recognition of each party, understanding, fairness, security, inclusion, autonomy, trust, and access to relationship recovery (Chaterjee 2006).

Comprehensive systemic model of negotiation: The comprehensive systemic model of negotiation addresses conflict as mediation between structure and agency. Structure refers to the broad framework that a social system functions within, and agency refers to individual and collective action (Chaterjee, 2006).

SWOT model of negotiation: The SWOT model of negotiation is used to evaluate the company's strengths, weaknesses, opportunities, and threats. This business management tool is an effective business negotiation strategy. Looking at a firm's production and marketing goals and assessing the firm's operations and management policies and practices in light of those goals, the SWOT model is used to plan negotiating tactics and strategy. Knowledge of company's strengths, weaknesses, opportunities, and threats allows for savvy and informed negotiation (Cellich 1990).

The stage model of negotiation: The stage model of negotiation specifies a fixed number of stages that negotiators move through as they interact and move toward closure. Negotiators begin in a distributive mode, concealing information and using aggressive and contentious strategies, and then move toward an integrative mode emphasizing problem solving and supportive strategies (Donohue and Roberto 1996).

Determining the Negotiation Model to be Used

Conflict managers, and individual parties or disputants, decide which negotiation model or approach to use based on multiple factors including consistency of frame, nature of negotiator training, time allocated to negotiate, goals of disputants, and level of uncertainty (Donohue and Roberto 1996):

Consistent frame: Numerous factors emerge during negotiations that push parties into a consistently integrative or distributive frame.

Nature of negotiator training: Negotiators are usually trained to use a specific sequence of behaviors in the course of their negotiation proceedings.

Time to negotiate: The amount of time available or allocated to negotiation sessions varies by negotiator, organization, business, and industry.

Goals of disputants: The goals of disputants involved in negotiation may initially be implicit or explicit as well as reasonable or unreasonable. Negotiators describe the key points of each disputant's case, claim, or position to make goals clear to everyone involved in the negotiation session.

Level of uncertainty: When disputants enter into a negotiation session uncertain of their knowledge of the issues, their understanding of their opponent's position, or their ability to predict their opponent's goals and strategies, instability and volatility is likely to result.

Steps to Negotiation

Ultimately, despite the specific negotiation model or approach chosen by the negotiator, similar processes or subprocesses will be present in all negotiations. For example, negotiators are competitors with their counterparts in claiming scarce resources; negotiators are collaborators with their counterparts in creating value; negotiators are relationship-shapers; and negotiators are coalition managers and consensus builders within their own organization (Fonstad, McKersie, and Eaton 2004). In addition, all the negotiation models described above include the same basic steps. The standard steps of the negotiation process include preparation, the opening phase, reaching agreement, and closure (Manning and Robertson 2004).

Preparation: Preparation establishes the issues, gathers quality information, prepares the case, and prepares for the encounter.

The opening phase: The opening phase creates a positive climate in which disputants state their individual cases.

Reach agreement: Reaching agreement involves disputants challenging the opponent's case, responding to challenges, making concessions, and trading, linking, and moving to reach agreement.

Closure: Closure summarizes and records agreements as well as establishes monitoring and review procedures.

Issues & Variables That Impact Negotiation Processes

Issues and variables that impact all steps of the negotiation process described above include clarity of focus, flexibility of strategy, win-win values, and interactive skills (Manning and Robertson 2004).

Clarity of focus: Clarity of focus includes defining the issues, having a clear and simple case, using different types of information from a variety of sources, taking time before making decisions, agreeing to the outcome, monitoring, and reviewing.

Flexibility of strategy: Flexibility of strategy involves finding out about the other party and what they want, taking a long-term perspective, planning around issues rather than in a strict sequence, and using concessions, adjournments, and doing whatever is necessary to reach an agreement.

Win-win values: Win-win values involves having respect for the other party and what they want, considering a wide range of options and outcomes, ensuring both parties clearly present their case, and cooperating openly to achieve mutually acceptable outcomes.

Interactive skills: Interactive skills involve showing personal warmth, seeking information and clarification throughout, summarizing and testing understanding of what is said, and being open and nondefensive.

Negotiation has the potential to manage conflict and promote collaboration, learning, and more effective business operations. If the negotiation process is ineffective and conflict persists within the organization or between parties, then parties or disputants move toward mediation or arbitration. Mediation refers to the use of a third party in the negotiation process to facilitate a resolution through persuasion or alternative ideas. Arbitration refers to the involvement of a neutral third party in the negotiation process who has the authority to decide on an agreement. Mediation is one of a group of alternative methods to resolve business disputes including arbitration, mini-trials, expanded use of value billing, and alternative fee arrangements with counsel. Mediation of business disputes often allows disputants to avoid the filing of a lawsuit entirely (Berman 1994). Mediation is a dispute resolution tool used to settle disputes between individuals, companies, workers, and states that fosters agreement and reduces conflict. Mediators or arbitrators are disinterested, neutral third parties (Greig 2005).

CONCLUSION

Ultimately, conflict management strategies, which range from negotiating, asserting, accommodating, compromisingproblem solving, and avoiding, serve to minimize conflicts at various levels as well as work to attain and maintain a moderate amount of substantive conflict to promote healthy change and growth within business organizations. Conflict managers have the responsibility to select and use the appropriate conflict management strategy for the conflict and the disputants (Rahim 2002). General guidelines for negotiating, relevant to all the negotiation models described in this article, include taking time to break the ice, presenting the case, listening, being prepared to suggest many options, summarizing regularly, and being prepared to take a break when negotiation stalls (Baines 1994).

Negotiation outcomes tend to vary based on the perspective and orientation of disputants. Parties with integrative orientation view negotiation as a win-win endeavor. Parties with a distributive orientation view negotiation as a win-lose endeavor. Additionally, there is evidence that the perceived effectiveness and use of different conflict resolution behaviors varies across cultures (Sadri 2013). Conflict managers must assess the positional bias of each participant to ensure a successful negotiation outcome for all involved.

BIBLIOGRAPHY

Anjum, Muhammad, Jahanvash Karim, and Zainab Bibi. "Relationship of Values and Conflict Management Styles." *IBA Business Review* 9, no. 1 (2014): 92–103. Web. 10 Dec. 2015.

Ashcroft, Stephen. "Commercial Negotiation Skills." *Industrial and Commercial Training* 36, nos. 6–7 (2004): 229–33. Web. 31 May 2007.

Baines, A. "Negotiate to Win." *Work Study* 43 (1994): 25–27. Print.

Barki, Henri, and Jon Hartwick. "Interpersonal Conflict and Its Management in Information System Development." *MIS Quarterly* 25 (2001): 195–228. Web. 31 May 2007.

Bazerman, Max, and Jared Curhan. "Negotiation." *Annual Review of Psychology* 51 (2000): 279. Web. 31 May 2007.

Berman, Peter. "Revolving Business Disputes through Mediation and Arbitration." *CPA Journal* 64 (1994): 74. Web. 31 2007.

Boni, Art A., and Laurie Weingart. "Building Teams in Entrepreneurial Companies." *Journal of Commercial Biotechnology* 18 (2012): 31–37. Web. 5 Nov. 2013.

Cellich, Claude. "Skills for Business Negotiations." *International Trade Forum* 26 (1990): 8. Web. 31 May 2007.

Cheung, S., K. Yiu, and H. Suen. "Construction Negotiation Online." *Journal of Construction Engineering & Management* 130 (2004): 844–52. Web. 31 May 2007.

Fonstad, Nils, Robert McKersie, and Susan Eaton. "Interest-Based Negotiations in a Transformed Labor Management Setting." *Negotiation Journal* 20 (2004): 5–11. Web. 31 May 2007.

Greig, J. Michael. "Steping into the Fray: When Do Mediators Mediate?" *American Journal of Political Science* 49 (2005): 249–66. Web. 31 May 2007.

Manning, Tony, and Bob Robertson. "Influencing, Negotiating Skills and Conflict-Handling: Some Additional Research and Reflections." *Industrial and Commercial Training* 36, nos. 2–3 (2004): 104. Print.

Prause, Daria, and Bahaudin G. Mujtaba. "Conflict Management Practices for Diverse Workplaces." *Journal of Business Studies Quarterly* 6, no. 3 (2015): 13–22. Web. 10 Dec. 2015.

Rahim, M. Afzalur. "Toward a Theory of Managing Organizational Conflict." *International Journal of Conflict Management* 13 (1997–2002): 206. Web. 31 May 2007.

Sadri, Golnaz. "Choosing Conflict Resolution by Culture." *Industrial Management* 55 (2013): 10–15. Web. 5 Nov. 2013.

Singleton, Lisa, Leslie Toombs, Sonia Taneja, et al. "Workplace Conflict: A Strategic Leadership Imperative." *International Journal of Business & Public Administration* 8 (2011): 149–63. Web. 5 Nov. 2013.

SUGGESTED READING

Adair, Wendi, and Jeanne Brett. "The Negotiation Dance: Time, Culture, and Behavioral Sequences in Negotiation." *Organization Science* 16 (2005): 33–51. Web. 31 May 2007.

Hunt, Courtney, and Mary Kernan. "Framing Negotiations in Affective Terms: Methodological and Preliminary Theoretical Findings." *International Journal of Conflict Management* 16 (2005): 128–56. Web. 31 May 2007.

McKersie, Robert, Adrienne Eason, and Thomas Kochan. "Kaiser Permanente: Using Interest-Based Negotiations to Craft a New Collective Bargaining Agreement." *Negotiation Journal* 20 (2004, Jan.): 13–35. Web. 31 May 2007.

Rosenthal, Michael. "Mediating Conflict." *Training* 52, no. 4 (2015): 72. Web. 10 Dec. 2015.

Simone I. Flynn, Ph.D.

MANAGING IN A TURNAROUND ENVIRONMENT

ABSTRACT

Turnaround is the process of reviving and growing underperforming companies. Turnaround efforts are usually led by experienced turnaround managers, who are consultants brought into a company during its decline phase. The turnaround process has three phases: the crisis stage, stabilization stage, and recovery stage. Turnaround managers, already working under difficult conditions, face many challenges from factors both internal and external to their company.

OVERVIEW

A turnaround is a process whereby a company that has been experiencing an extended period of poor performance is led to experience substantial and sustained positive performance. As a topic in the field of business management, turnaround is attracting increasing attention from researchers, educators, investors, managers, and consultants. Developments in this area have led to the establishment of the discipline of turnaround management, the profession of turnaround managers, and the practice of turnaround investing. Turnaround managers are consultants who are hired during financial crises to save distressed companies from bankruptcy and turn around their fortunes. Turnaround managers join a company either as chief executive officer (CEO) or consultant, so that they can direct the turnaround process. This circumstance is largely preferable to the situation where a company's owners or senior mangers attempt to turn around their company themselves, since their lack of objectivity and emotional involvement often lead them to create new problems without resolving the old ones. Much depends on the turnaround manager: If he or she is not able to save a company from bankruptcy, or if the company's core business is not profitable, the company will be liquidated.

Even though turnarounds can be one of the best means by which a company can attain long-term sustainability, many of those in top positions in ailing companies find it difficult to even accept that they need a turnaround. This denial is one of the biggest obstacles to turnaround, and it is based on several factors: First, many corporate executives believe that to initiate a turnaround is tantamount to admitting failure. Second, some corporate executives believe that turnarounds lead to mass redundancies, and this attitude leads them to resist the idea of a turnaround. However, it is only those employees who do not add value in the workplace that will typically be laid off during the turnover process. Third, there is a misconception that other companies will cease to do business with a company undergoing a turnaround. On the contrary, however, firms tend to be drawn to a company in turnaround, because the very fact that it has initiated a turnaround implies that it is a responsible and serious company.

Even when CEOs accept that their company needs a turnaround, they often take a long time to arrive at such a decision. Due to such hesitation, turnarounds are often initiated by third parties such as lenders (such as banks), bankruptcy attorneys, or investors who have a stake in the company. Companies that need a turnaround most often experience underperformance in the areas of management, finances, competition, operations, and strategy. Management underperformance can usually be seen in areas such as leadership issues; skills issues; micromanagement instead of delegation; organizational structure issues; ineffective communication; misplaced compensation and incentives; and high employee turnover. Financial underperformance is usually evident in excessively low sales volume; excessively low prices; excessively high expenses; poor balance sheet management; debt; and insufficient working capital. Competitive under-performance tends to be characterized by factors such as uncompetitive products; service and support issues; obsolescence; and quality issues. These problems can lead to a loss of established business and/or a failure to get new businesses. Operational underperformance is characterized by lean manufacturing opportunities; poor capacity planning; poor scheduling; and process inefficiencies. The last area of underperformance, strategic underperformance, is characterized by market channel issues; supply chain tier issues; and scale issues.

Further Insights

A turnaround environment can be defined as the social, technological, economic, and political environment in which a turnaround company functions. The internal turnaround environment consists of stakeholders such as customers, suppliers, employees, board of directors, and creditors; the external turnaround environment consists of factors and forces beyond the control of the company, including the economic environment, technical environment, legal environment, political environment, and cultural environment. The nature of a company's internal and external turnaround environment has an effect on that company's decisions, turnaround strategies, processes, and performance. Needless to say, managing a turnaround is a challenging experience. For instance, those managing in a turnaround environment must do so under intense time pressure. Today's turnaround managers are being given less time to carry out their tasks, with some being expected to complete a turnaround in six months. Turnaround managers need special skills and competencies to effectively manage the unique planning and control processes that are required in managing and turning around a distressed and loss making company. As if these challenges were not enough, turnaround managers also have to deal with opposition from within their assigned company, for instance from senior managers who resist replacement, or from employees who fear losing their jobs.

Stages of the Turnaround Process

The turnaround process comprises three stages: crisis, stabilization, and recovery. Each stage has a different objective and requires a different type of action by the turnaround manager. The objectives and turnaround actions of each stage are depicted in the table 1 below.

Turnaround Actions	Crises Stage Objective	Stabilization Stage Objective	Recovery Stage Objective
Financial	Positive cash flow situation		
Operational		Profit	
Strategic			Growth

Table 1: Stages of the turnaround process (adapted from Fredenberger, Lipp, and Watson, 1997)

Pre-Turnaround Stage: Decline

Before the beginning of any turnaround, there is a significant phase that the company must have gone through. This stage is called "decline," and it is characterized by sustained poor performance. Management perceptions and actions during this phase will determine whether or not a company requires a turnaround, since timely intervention can reverse the decline process. Even if a company does require a turnaround, management perceptions and actions during this phase will determine whether the company actually embarks on the turnaround; and how successful the turnaround is likely to be. Decline can be caused by internal and external factors. For example, an internal factor such as the processing and analysis of company information, if ineffective, can lead to a decline. Likewise, companies that fail to keep up with changes in the external environment are also likely to decline.

Crisis Stage
The first of the three stages of a turnaround is the crises stage. At this stage, a company is close to bankruptcy or liquidation. By this stage, a company would have sustained heavy losses, and therefore, cash outflows would have exceeded cash inflows. As such, the crises stage calls for financial action to create a positive cash flow situation. The dire situation may lead to changes in the top management team (this situation tends to happen often in Western countries and in companies which have relatively high outsider control of the board of directors). A turnaround manager would typically be hired at this stage. The main reason why top managers are asked to leave companies that are embarking on a turnaround, is that the top managers find it difficult to recognize problems, since they are usually responsible—at least in part—for those same problems, and it would be difficult for them to put together the necessary creative solutions while having the same mindset that led to the problems in the first place.

Analysis
To be able to make proper evaluation and diagnoses of the situation at hand, a turnaround manager would need to conduct seven types of analyses with current—not past or future—company information. These seven analyses include: financial analyses, working capital analyses, cost analyses, expense analyses, personnel analyses, asset analyses, and market analyses. Of the seven, financial and working capital analyses tend to be considered by turnaround managers to be the most important. Financial analyses are used to first improve cash flow, and second, reschedule debt, reduce expenses, reduce costs, and scale-back operations. All seven analyses are prepared into reports and their contents are typically as follows (Fredenberger, Lipp, and Watson, 1997):

- **Financial analyses:** Balance statements & income statements.
- **Working-capital analyses:** Cash-flow statements (daily, weekly, monthly, and quarterly); accounts receivable sales/collection/aging analyses; notes receivable aging analyses; inventory turnover, on hand, sales per day, ABC analyses; accounts payable aging analyses; notes payable aging analyses; secured debt analyses; lender availability.
- **Cost analyses:** Direct and indirect labor compensation (monetary value and percentage of sales); product material cost (percentage of sales); product material cost per supplier (percentage of sales).
- **Expense analyses:** Sales/marketing other expense (percentage of sales); finance/administration other expense (percentage of sales); engineering in-house/contract product-related expense (percentage of sales); warranty expense (percentage of sales).
- **Personnel analyses:** People-related variable and fixed expense (percentage of sales); compensation expense per direct and indirect labor employee; overtime premium expense per direct and indirect labor employee; sales/marketing people-related expense (percentage of sales); finance/administration people-related expense (percentage of sales); engineering in-house/contract people-related expense (percentage of sales).
- **Asset analyses:** Plant-related variable and fixed expense (percentage of sales); sales income per plant square foot; capacity utilization as a percentage of plant, equipment and machinery.
- **Market analyses:** Product line gross margin as a percentage of profitability; product, model, catalog number gross margin percentage; cumulative margin funds by product, model, catalog number; customer gross margin funds profitability and as a percentage of profitability; cumulative gross margin funds by customer/region/channel/rep; product line margin/customer/region/channel/representative; sales dollars per employee.

Turnaround managers face the challenge of gathering a lot of information as quickly as possible. As important as it is to have the necessary information at the right time, many turnaround managers find that the information available to them is often not in a usable condition, and even when it is usable, it usually gets to the turnaround manager too late. When it comes to information, turnaround managers specifically have to deal with problems such as neglected information systems, inadequate or missing financial information, 'creative' accounting, improper information formats, reports that are not matched to problems, and so on. Information is such a key part of any turnaround, that in order to resolve these kinds of information problems, some companies go to the extent of hiring experienced turnaround chief information officers (CIOs). The lack of information faced by turnaround managers can partly be attributed to a deliberate ploy on the part of employees, to either hold back information, or to misinform the turnaround manager. These actions are often taken out of fear, and it is therefore imperative that the turnaround manager quickly gain the trust of employees to prevent fear from arising, and to facilitate access to information. This trust can be achieved through effective collaboration with the human resources department to ensure that the entire company buys into the turnaround process; that the employees are kept informed about what is happening throughout the turnaround; that the employees are constantly reminded of the strengths of the company; and that the employees are ultimately allocated jobs that make the best use of their skills and talents.

Strategy Formulation

Next during the crisis stage, a turnaround manager would need to formulate a strategy to recover from the crisis or crises. The turnaround strategy will be based on the factors which led to the corporate decline, and for this reason, it is imperative that the problem which caused the underperformance be accurately identified. For instance, if a company has had a single large financial setback such as a legal settlement, fraud or embezzlement, the solution will be mainly financial. If a company is facing efficiency problems, the solution will be mainly operational. If the problem is to do with the reconfiguration of the firm's portfolio of businesses or the positioning of units within that portfolio, the solution will be mainly strategic. In general, however, the primary cause of company nonperformance is some form of managerial incompetence, especially related to improper control of the internal elements of a company. Once a turnaround manager has discovered the core reason for the underperformance, he or she would need to develop a strategic and operating plan. This work is quite a challenging task, because the revival of a declining company often calls for the improvement of operations, but under decline conditions, a company can hardly invest in the necessary plant and equipment. This weakness affords the company the opportunity to fully utilize its creative ability through initiatives like extended targets and suggestion forums. Creative negotiations with financial institutions will also support the financial management undertaken during the crises. The strategic and operating plan may include details of the following actions:

- Retrenchment, which may involve all of some of the following:
  - Reduction of expenses;
  - Reduction of receivables;
  - Reduction of inventory levels;
  - Reduction of personnel.

- Raising the necessary capital, through means such as:
  - Lenders (e.g., banks and finance companies);
  - Equity capital from turnaround investors and strategic acquirers;
  - Asset sales;
  - Bankruptcy reorganization.

- Management of the external stakeholders, including, for example:
  - Joint cost reductions with suppliers;
  - Improved trade credit;
  - New strategic partnerships with suppliers;
  - Change in distribution channels;
  - Outsourcing of inefficient processes.

- Management of the internal climate through such means as:
  - Management of the decision processes;
  - Transformation of organizational structures;
  - Formalization of control structures;
  - Restructuring of lines of communication.

- Process improvement, which may result in quality improvement and improved productivity; as well as a reduction in expenses and inventory investment.
- Continuous improvement based on market needs.
- Strategic pricing for certain customers, where possible.

Stabilization Stage

Once the turnaround manger has decided on the best strategy to implement, he or she must take action to address the crises. At the point when cash inflows are at least equal to or greater than cash outflows, the financial crisis would have passed, and it can be said that the company has reached the stabilization stage (also known as renewal). This second stage of the turnaround process calls for operational action to bring about profits. At this stage, the turnaround manager endeavors to motivate the company and allow it to become profitable and grow. Depending on the circumstances and the turnaround manager's leadership qualities, a turnaround manager can stabilize and motivate a company by either exercising authoritarian leadership to get employees to follow a highly structured turnaround plan; or by empowering employees. Employee empowerment in a turnaround situation involves inverting the organization, practicing team-based problem solving with cross-functional teams, putting in place a simple reporting structure, supporting senior management and corporate staff, setting measurable customer-driven goals for the entire organization, and measuring results.

Recovery Stage

The third and final stage of the turnaround process is recovery, also termed the expansion stage. This stage calls for strategic action to bring about a return to normal profits and growth. A turnaround manager can achieve growth through improved performance by selling more units of a company's product; by adding more products to its range; by raising prices; and/or by reducing fixed and variable expenses.

The achievement of growth, however, should not be an end in itself—the ultimate aim of a turnaround is to strengthen the company's position so that it will not fall back into a loss situation. At this stage, a turnaround manager will typically leave for the next assignment, possibly helping the owners of the company to hire a professional manager, before departing.

Issues

Turnaround management differs from country to country because of variations in culture, institutional factors, commercial practices, and other environmental factors. The actions of individuals and organizations—including managers and employees—toward any given activity are largely determined by institutional factors such as culture. For instance, cultural differences can account for differences in the rate of recognition of company decline; differences in the speed of initiating or starting a turnaround effort; and so on. In some countries, due to the prevailing culture, it is extremely difficult to get a CEO to agree to step down for a turnaround consultant to take over. In the West, top management typically has sufficient autonomy to make the necessary changes and cutbacks during a turnaround, but in some developing countries, there may be significant constraints on managerial action, or there may be conflicting stakeholder priorities posing obstacles to a turnaround. No matter the cultural setting, for a turnaround effort to have any chance of success, it must be adapted to suit the local setting.

BIBLIOGRAPHY

Abebe, Michael A., Arifin Angriawan, and Liu Yanxin. "CEO Power and Organizational Turnaround in Declining Firms: Does Environment Play a Role?" *Journal of Leadership & Organizational Studies* (Sage Publications Inc.) 18, no. 2 (2011): 260–73. Web. 15 Nov. 2013.

Ahlstrom, David, and Garry Bruton. "Turnaround in Asia: Laying the Foundation for Understanding This Unique Domain." (Guest Editors' Introduction to Special Issues). *Asia Pacific Journal of Management* 21, no. 1 (2004): 5–24. Web. 6 Dec. 2007.

Banaszak-Holl, Jane. "Turnaround Research: Past Accomplishment and Future Challenges." (Advances in Applied Business Strategy, Vol. 5). *Administrative Science Quarterly* 45, no. 3 (2000): 633–35. Web. 6 Dec. 2007.

Barker, Vincent III, Paul Patterson, and George Mueller. "Organizational Causes and Strategic Consequences of the Extent of Top Management Team Replacement during Turnaround Attempts." *Journal of Management Studies* 38, no. 2 (2001): 235–69. Web. 6 Dec. 2007.

Bruton, Garry, David Ahlstrom, and Johnny Wan. "Turnaround Success of Large and Midsize Chinese Owned Firms: Evidence from Hong Kong and Thailand." *Journal of World Business* 36, no. 2 (2001): 146. Web. 6 Dec. 2007.

Feder, Warren. "Keeping the Doors Open: Financing Options for Troubled Companies." *Investment Guides Series: Turnaround Management II* (2003, Spring): 91–95. Web. 6 Dec. 2007.

Fredenberger, William, Astrid Lipp, and Hugh Watson. "Information Requirements of Turnaround Managers at the Beginning of Engagements." *Journal of Management Information Systems* 13, no. 4 (1997): 167. Web. 6 Dec. 2007.

Harker, Michael, and Debra Harker. "The Role of Strategic Selling in the Company Turnaround Process." *Journal of Personal Selling & Sales Management* 18, no. 2 (1998): 55–67. Web. 6 Dec. 2007.

Milite, George. "Turnaround Management: Charting a New Beginning." *HR Focus* 76, no. 11 (1999): 9. Web. 6 Dec. 2007.

Mueller, J. "Turnaround Investing in One Easy Lesson." *Secured Lender* 55, no. 2 (1999): 38. Web. 6 Dec. 2007.

Murak, G. "Turnaround with Help from Your Staff." *Restaurant Hospitality* 88, no. 7 (2004): 68–77. Web. 6 Dec. 2007.

O'Kane, Conor, and James Cunningham. "Leadership Changes and Approaches during Company Turnaround." *International Studies of Management & Organization* 42, no. 4 (2012): 52–85. Web. 3 Dec. 2014.

O'Kane, Conor, and James Cunningham. "Turnaround Leadership Core Tensions during the Company Turnaround Process." *European Management Journal* 32, no. 6 (2014): 963–80. Web. 3 Dec. 2014.

Pant, Laurie. "An Investigation of Industry and Firm Structural Characteristics in Corporate Turnarounds." *Journal of Management Studies* 28, no. 6 (1991): 623. Web. 6 Dec. 2007.

Raina, B., P. Chanda, O. Mehta, and Sunil K. Maheshwari. "Organizational Decline and Turnaround Management." *Vikalpa: The Journal for Decision Makers* 28, no. 4 (2003): 83–92. Web. 6 Dec. 2007.

Rose, Kenneth H., and Darren Dalcher. "Managing Projects in Trouble: Achieving Turnaround and Success." *Project Management Journal* 44, no. 1 (2013): 109. Web. 15 Nov. 2013.

Sutton, Gary. "Confessions of a Turnaround Guy." *Investment Guide Series: Turnaround Management II* (2003, Spring): 14–22. Web. 6 Dec. 2007.

Yandava, B. "A Capability-Driven Turnaround Strategy for the Current Economic Environment." *Journal of Business Strategies* 29, no. 2 (2012): 157–85. Web. 15 Nov. 2013.

SUGGESTED READING

Arogyaswamy, Kamala, Vincent Barker III, and Masoud Yasai-Ardekano. "Firm Turnarounds: An Integrative Two-Stage Model." *Journal of Management Studies* 32, no. 4 (1995): 493–525. Web. 6 Dec. 2007.

Bibeault, Donald B. *Corporate Turnaround: How Managers Turn Losers into Winners.* New York: McGraw-Hill, 1982.

Gadiesh, Orit, Stan Pace, and Paul Rogers. "Successful Turnarounds: Three Key Dimensions." *Strategy & Leadership* 31, no. 6 (2003): 41–43. Print.

Hofer, Charles W. "Turnaround Strategies." *Journal of Business Strategy* 1 (1980): 19–31. Pring.

Hoffman, R. "Strategies for Corporate Turnarounds: What Do We Know about Them?" *Journal of General Management* 14, no. 3 (1989): 46–66. Print.

O'Callaghan, Shaun. *Turnaround Leadership: Making Decisions, Rebuilding Trust and Delivering Results after a Crisis.* Philadelphia: Kogan Page, 2010.

Robbins, D. Keith, and John A. Pearce II. "Turnaround: Retrenchment and Recovery." *Strategic Management Journal* 13 (1992): 287–309. Print.

Scherer, P. Scott. "From Warning to Crises: A Turnaround Primer." *Management Review* 77, no. 9 (1988): 30–36. Print.

Scherer, P. Scott. "The Turnaround Consultant Steers Corporate Renewal." *Journal of Management Consulting* 5, no. 1 (1989): 17–24. Print.

Vanessa A. Tetteh, Ph.D.

MANAGING THE PROCESS OF INNOVATION

ABSTRACT

The article will provide an overview of the main types of innovation found in organizations, including incremental and breakthrough innovation, the trajectory of innovation, barriers to innovation, and the history of private and public sector innovation. A case study of Boeing's formalized innovation program will be included. The case study will provide an example of how a company can effectively manage the innovation process on an extremely large scale and the ways in which successful innovation creates a competitive advantage in the marketplace.

OVERVIEW

There is an established relationship between business strategy, innovation, and organizational performance. Innovation, which refers to the use of a new product, service, or method in business practice immediately subsequent to its discovery, influences economic success and market share in increasingly competitive global markets. In response to new technology-driven global markets, companies have increased their use of advanced technologies as well as their innovation efforts (Zahrah and Covin 1993). Innovation is associated with competitive advantage in both growing and mature markets. Innovation, unlike most other business practices, can change the competitive balance in mature markets (Brown 1992). The concept and practice of innovation became closely associated with economic gain and competitive advantage in the 1930s. In the 1930s, economist Joseph Schumpeter (1883–1950) created a theory of economic development based on five types of economic innovations: set up or discovery of a new product, a new manufacturing process, a new market, source, or new organization (Leteneyei 2001). Contemporary business theory argues that companies must compete to keep or gain market share. Innovation is considered to be the key to creating competitive advantage (Stalk 2006).

The following sections will provide an overview of the main types of innovation found in organizations, the trajectory of innovation, barriers to innovation, and the history of private and public sector innovation.

Types of Innovation

Numerous types of innovation occur in organizations. Examples include marketing innovation, technological innovation, organizational innovation, product innovation, service innovation, and process innovation.

Marketing Innovation: Marketing innovation refers to a process in which people gradually become familiar and accepting of a new idea. Marketing innovation is a social learning process that results in consumers slowly changing their attitudes and values. Market innovations are often technologically driven. When a technology is developed, the new technology is often in need of a new type of market application. Market innovation is based on the following assumptions: innovation is driven by a learning process within social groups; some individuals have a higher propensity to try innovative products than others; and the speed of adoption may vary from one business to another (Brown 1992).

Technological Innovation: Technological innovation is the process by which industry generates new and improved products, services, and production processes. Technological innovation includes activities ranging from the generation of an idea, research, development and commercialization to the diffusion throughout the economy of new and improved products, processes and services. Effective technological innovation includes either the diffusion process or the spread of the innovation commercially (Zairi 1992). Technological innovation requires and is followed by new technology exploitation. New technology exploitation (NTE) refers to the utilization of new technology or scientific developments to improve the performance of products or manufacturing processes. The failure of management to recognize and manage breakthrough technology innovation often results in organizational inefficiencies and frustration (Bigwood 2004).

Organizational Innovation: Organizational innovation can be defined as the process of changing the organization by introducing different methods of production or administration. Organizational innovation includes the adoption of ideas from outside the organization and the generation of ideas within. Organizational innovation involves planning initiation, execution, selection, and implementation (Spender & Kessler 1995).

> **Product innovation:** Product innovation involves the introduction of a good that is new or substantially improved.
>
> **Service innovation:** Service innovation involves the introduction of a service that is new or substantially improved.
>
> **Process innovation:** Process innovation involves the implementation of a new or significantly improved production or delivery method.

All of the innovation types described above have elements and trajectories in common. There are two main

Boeing's headquarters in Chicago (photo courtesy of J. Crocker)

approaches to innovation that span and characterize all innovation processes: incremental and breakthrough innovation. Incremental innovation refers to improvement of technology performance or product feature enhancement. Breakthrough innovation, also referred to as disruptive, radical, or discontinuous innovation, refers to innovation based on technologies previously new to the world. These two different types of innovation have separate development trajectories and associated management strategies (Hacklin, Raurich, and Marxt 2005).

The Trajectory of Innovation

The trajectory of innovation is most often conceived of as an S-shape pattern with three distinct levels of diffusion and adoption of the innovation. For example, the S-curve for technology innovation includes three main phases (Hacklin, Raurich, and Marxt 2005):

Pacemaker technology phase: Emerging technology is called a pacemaker technology as it is new to the world and the future potential and applications are identified. The diffusion of the innovative technology has not yet started in this phase.

Disruptive technology phase: Established technology evolves into disruptive technology when it has managed to outperform competing technologies in respective mainstream markets. The diffusion of the innovative technology is occurring at a rapid pace in this phase.

Key technology phase: The performance of the technology becomes more efficient and the technology becomes widely adopted by the customer base. The diffusion of the innovative technology is complete in this phase. The innovative technology, if successful, has saturated its market and become ubiquitous technology among its users.

Organizational Barriers to Innovation

Innovation, which requires active learning, risk-taking, insight, and vision, does not occur in every firm. Common organizational barriers to innovation include (Brown 1992):

- A heavy reliance on market research to minimize risk when drawing up and approving plans for new products.
- The use of financial techniques, such as risk minimization, to assess innovation projects that are inherently risky.
- A tendency to invest in and rely on what has served the company well in the past rather than what may serve it better in the future.
- Systems of rewards and promotion that encourage a low-risk, custodial approach to management rather than a high-risk management approach.

History of Private & Public Sector Innovation

Innovation in the twentieth century was characterized by public and private sector partnerships and relationships. The private and public sectors significantly influence one another's innovation processes. The relationship between public and private sector innovation became very close during the Cold War from the 1940s until the early 1990s. After World War II, and during the Cold War era, publicly funded science and technology research, development, and innovation grew for three main reasons: First, science and technology research was fueled by the belief in the need for strong national defense technologies. Second, science and technology research was fueled by the belief that scientific research, which had delivered nuclear weapons, antibiotics, and jet aircraft, would produce other innovations of national interest. Third, science and technology research was fueled by the belief that a large national science system was perceived by other countries as representative of national prestige and cultural achievement. Cold War era, science and technology research and innovation, motivated by concerns for national defense more than economic growth, produced many of the university research and laboratory programs, government laboratories, and other technical institutes such as the National Science Foundation (NSF) and the National Aeronautics and Space Administration (NASA). The United States, along with other countries such as Canada, Australia, Great Britain, France, and Switzerland, invested in significant national scientific infrastructures during the Cold War years (de la Mothe and Dufour 1995). Cold War-era defense-related spending resulted in the development of such high-technology industries as semiconductors, computers, and commercial aircraft. During the 1980s and 1990s, private sector science and technology development and innovation grew and defense-related, military research and innovation slowed. In contrast to the pattern of the previous five decades, technological development began to flow from civilian to military applications. In 2000, the Clinton administration reduced the role of defense-related research and design funding in U.S. technology policy. Instead, the Clinton administration focused resources and policies on commercial technology research, development, innovation, procurement, and adoption (Ham and Mowery 1995). The largest high-tech private sector innovators will remain tied to the public sector for two main reasons: First, the public sector, including the military, remains one of the main customers of high-tech innovators. Second, the public sector has the funds available for public private partnerships and cooperative research and development programs.

APPLICATIONS

Managing the Innovation Process

The success of an innovation is connected to a market forecast of customer needs and wants as well as effective management of the innovation process. Firms have numerous economic tools and approaches for successfully developing a market and customer forecasts but are only recently, in the last two decades, developing and articulating management practices for the innovation process. While firms may or may not institute a formalized innovation policy and procedure to guide employees and managers, there are a set of principles that guide the innovation process across businesses and industries:

- Innovations should meet customer needs, please shareholders, and motivate staff.
- Innovation requires vision to drive the change process.
- Innovation requires a risk-tolerant environment.
- Innovation requires a lifelong learning orientation that involves all members of the organization.
- Innovation requires creative thinking in a diverse and information-rich organizational environment.
- Innovation requires a cross-functional systems perspective for analyzing the impact of change and overseeing implementation.

Managers of the innovation process address numerous issues within the organization to ensure successful development and implementation of an innovation. The main innovation management responsibilities include reducing the sense of risk; managing the customer interface; training customers; managing staff performance; engaging frontline staff; and using information technology (Riddle 2000). Managers of the innovation process need feedback about their management performance. While market share will eventually reflect the success of management efforts, there exists another method for management review. Innovation management can be judged and evaluated through an innovation management measurement framework. The framework of the innovation management process consists of seven categories: inputs management, knowledge management, innovation strategy, organizational culture and structure, portfolio management, project management, and commercialization. Innovation management measurement is used within firms by managers and executives. The innovation management measurement framework allows managers to evaluate their own innovation activity, explore the extent to which their organization is innovative, and identify areas for improvement (Adams, Bessant, and Phelps 2006).

Issues Managing Breakthrough Innovation
The process of managing breakthrough innovation, also referred to as disruptive or discontinuous innovation, varies greatly from managing incremental changes in products and technologies. The objectives of incremental innovation, such as speed, cycle time, profit impact, and quick cash recovery, generally do not apply to the breakthrough innovation process. Innovation managers recognize that the evaluation process for new products, processes, or services differs significantly from that used for extension projects. The potential market for incremental innovations is evaluated through conventional market research methods such as written surveys, focus groups, or concept tests. Breakthrough innovation projects are generally evaluated on their long-term value, impact on the market, and magnitude. The potential market for breakthrough innovations is evaluated through three main venues:

1. Professional conferences and meetings
2. The demonstration of the product via early prototypes for reaction within the firm
3. Potential customers' evaluations of early working versions

Determining the value of the innovation within the market is a speculative process. The project life cycle for breakthrough innovations includes unpredictability, long-time horizons, starts and stops, and periods of stagnancy. Management practices that facilitate the breakthrough innovation process include:

- Mechanisms for directing the technology-market arenas in which breakthrough innovations occur
- Mechanisms for proactively stimulating discontinuous breakthrough innovation
- Mechanisms for protecting projects that operate with high risk, uncertainty, and potential for failure

Innovation managers are responsible for encouraging and facilitating the development of new businesses, product lines, and production processes based on breakthrough innovations. In addition, managers are responsible for developing and implementing management practices that reduce the high uncertainty associated with developing and commercializing breakthrough innovations. Managers, responsible for managing the breakthrough innovation process, use five types of managerial strategies to influence the process:

1. Innovation mangers set boundaries to direct and constrain discontinuous innovation activities.
2. Innovation mangers take proactive approaches to stimulating discontinuous innovation.
3. Innovation mangers stabilize a systematic approach to evaluation and screening breakthrough innovation.
4. Innovation mangers create incubating organizational arrangements.
5. Innovation mangers recognize the key role of individual initiative and capabilities in the innovation process.

Ultimately, the breakthrough innovation process is not deliberately managed so much as encouraged and facilitated. Traditional management techniques are unsuitable for breakthrough innovation projects up until the point that uncertainty is reduced. The managers' main job is to reduce uncertainty and fear of failure until the point where traditional management practices once again are appropriate. Managers of a breakthrough innovation project must be cognizant of and accept the realities of the life cycle of a discontinuous innovation project. Breakthrough innovation projects are long term, lasting ten years or longer; have highly uncertain and unpredictable outcomes; are sporadic, with many stops and starts, deaths and revivals; have changing leaders and personnel; and require extensive exploring and experimenting rather than targeting and developing. Ultimately, breakthrough innovation projects, though potentially profitable to the business, are most successful when they are separated from traditional business expectations and ongoing business activities (Rice, O'Connor, Peters, and Moroone 1998).

Case Study: Boeing's Global Enterprise Technology System (GETS)

In 2003, Boeing, a $54-billion-a-year aerospace company, developed and applied a new process for managing its enterprise-level research and development called the Global Enterprise Technology System (GETS). The Global Enterprise Technology System (GETS), which combines strategies from systems engineering, software process improvement, organizational psychology, and anthropology, provides a strategically driven and systems-engineering based approach to managing innovation. GETS is an example of applying the concepts of systems engineering to research and design. It involves collaboration between all of Boeing's business units, including Boeing Commercial Airplanes, Integrated Defense Systems, and Phantom Works. The scale of Boeing's business operations includes customers in 145 countries with products and services such as commercial airplanes, defense products such as military airplanes, rotor-craft, missiles, communications systems, and space products such as satellites and launch vehicles.

Technological innovation within Boeing's huge system and markets occurs primarily at its research organization, Boeing Phantom Works. Boeing Phantom Works is often referred to as Boeing's catalyst of innovation. The scale of Boeing's enterprise necessitated an approach to managing innovation across many areas in a manner that is focused and connected without squashing vision and creativity. Boeing developed the GETS program to satisfy the following processes and goals for its products: highly collaborative, systematic, efficient, continuous, traceable, effective, and simple. The Global Enterprise Technology System is organized into four distinct phases including Discover, Decide, Develop, and Deploy. These four phases occur continuously at various levels.

- **Discover:** The discovering process is rooted in the constant dialogue between what is desirable in the marketplace and what is possible to accomplish with technology.
- **Decide:** The deciding process draws on the outcomes of the discovering phase. Managers ask the following questions: What have we learned about the future? What new opportunities have surfaced? What assumptions have changed? What areas of emphasis are changing?
- **Develop:** The developing process, characterized by focus and efficiency, is about carrying out the work ideas. Technologists develop plans for the chosen research and design efforts and execute them within existing resource constraints.
- **Deploy:** The deployment process involves the placement and marketing of the innovative technology.

Boeing's GETS program has produced a generic model of technology and product development management that is used as a guide to establish research and development management processes for different parts of the enterprise. The GETS program facilitates process development workshops, conducts a broad-based formal inspection of the process, and promotes a continuous improvement philosophy. Boeing considers the GETS program to be successful in guiding and managing the innovation efforts of their 2,500 researchers and their managers. Boeing reports the followings benefits and gains from the GETS program (Lind 2006):

- Stronger working relationships across technology, product, and market arenas
- More strategically focused portfolio that delivers greater value to Boeing business units
- More effective long-term focus, strategic planning, and synergy
- Reduced meetings and travel associated with the portfolio planning
- More flexible technology portfolio to meet the changing needs of the business
- Reduced complexity and a stronger innovation process that is easier to apply to new areas.

The GETS program is a model of large-scale innovation management. Boeing created GETS as an institutionally approved, supported, and overseen space for creativity and breakthrough innovation.

CONCLUSION

In the final analysis, the management of the innovation processes across businesses and industries shares numerous characteristics. Patterns of disciplined innovation management include understanding the product development process, making support functions time invisible, grouping critical resources together, and maintaining management continuity (Stalk 2006). Managers of the innovation process can improve their firm's chances at successful innovation by lowering sales expectations, assessing risks and rewards, sharing the rewards, encouraging innovation, allowing for learning and failure, and promoting experimentation and the need for change (Brown 1992). Questions that managers of the innovation process should ask themselves as they develop and implement their management strategies include the following: Is innovation stated as part of your corporate objectives and business plan? Do you provide support to staff that try out new ideas, even if the ideas fail? Do you have experiments or pilots of new service concepts being conducted within your business? Does your financial reporting system reflect innovation as an investment or a cost? (Riddle 2000). Ultimately, innovation, when properly managed, gives companies competitive advantage in the marketplace.

BIBLIOGRAPHY

Adams, Richard, John Bessant, and Robert Phelps. "Innovation Management Measurement: A Review." *International Journal of Management Reviews* 8, no. 1 (2006): 21–47. Web. 6 June 2007.

Bigwood, Michael. "Managing the New Technology Exploitation Process." *Research Technology Management* 47, no. 6 (2004): 38–42. Web. 6 June 2007.

Brown, Rick. "Managing the 'S' Curves of Innovation." *Journal of Consumer Marketing* 9, no. 1 (1992): 61. Web. 6 June 2007.

Costa Souza, Jonito, and Maria de Fatima Bruno-Faria. "The Innovation Process in the Organizational Context: An Analysis of Helping and Hindering Factors." *Brazilian Business Review* (English Ed.). 10, no. 3 (2013): 108–29. Web. 15 Nov. 2013.

de la Mothe, John, and Paul Dufour. "Techno-Globalism and the Challenges to Science and Technology Policy." *Daedalus* 124, no. 3 (1995): 219–37. Print.

Eschenbaecher, Jens, and Falk Graser. "Managing and Optimizing Innovation Processes in Collaborative and Value Creating Networks." *International Journal of Innovation & Technology Management* 8, no. 3 (2011): 373–91. Web. 15 Nov. 2013.

Hacklin, Fredrik, Vicente Raurich, and Christian Marxt. "Implication of Technological Convergence or Innovation Trajectories." *International Journal of Innovation & Technology Management* 2, no. 3 (2005): 313–30. Web. 6 June 2007.

Ham, Rose Marie, and David Mowery. "Enduring Dilemmas in U.S. Technology Policy." *California Management Review* 37, no. 4 (1995): 4–107. Web. 27 Apr. 2007.

Letenyei, Laszlo. "Rural Innovation Chains." *Review of Sociology* 7, no. 1 (2001): 85–100. Print.

Lind, Jeffrey. "Boeing's Global Enterprise Technology Process." *Research Technology Management* 49, no. 5 (2006): 36–43. Print.

Morris, Langdon. "Three Dimensions of Innovation." *International Management Review* 9, no. 2 (2013): 5–10. Web. 15 Nov. 2013.

Rice, Mark, Gina O'Connor, Lois Peters, and Joseph Morone. "Managing Discontinuous Innovation." *Research Technology Management* 41, no. 3 (1998, May): 52–58. Web. 6 June 2007.

Riddle, D. "Managing Change in Your Organization." *International Trade Forum* 2 (2000): 26–27. Web. 6 June 2007.

Spender, J.C, and Eric Kessler. "Managing the Uncertainties of Innovation: Extending Thompson (1967)." *Human Relations* 48, no. 1 (1995): 35–37. Web. 6 June 2007.

Stalk, George Jr. "Hardball Innovation." *Research Technology Management* 49, no. 1 (2006): 20–28. Web. 6 June 2007.

Zahrah, Shaker, and Jeffrey Covin. "Business Strategy, Technology Policy and Firm Performance." *Strategic Management Journal* 16, no. 6 (1993): 451–78. Web. 27 Apr. 2007.

Zairi, Mohamed. "Managing User-Supplier Interactions: Management of R&D Activity." *Managerial Decision* 30, no. 8 (1992): 49–58. Print.

SUGGESTED READING

Schroeder, Roger, Andrew Van de Ven, Gary Scudder, and Douglas Polley. "Managing Innovation and Change Processes: Findings from the Minnesota

Innovation Research Program." *Agribusiness* 2, no. 4 (1986): 501–32. Web. 6 June 2007.

Tvaronaviciene, Manuela, and Renata Korsakiene. "The Role of Government in Implementation of Innovation." *Business: Theory & Practice* 8, no. 1 (2007): 9–13. Web. 6 June 2007.

Voelpel, Sven, Marius Leibold, and Christoph Streb. "The Innovation Meme: Managing Innovation Replicators for Organizational Fitness." *Journal of Change Management* 5, no. 1 (2005): 57–69. Web. 6 June 2007.

Simone I. Flynn, Ph.D.

Motivation, Productivity, and Change Management

ABSTRACT

This article will focus on the importance for a manager to understand how to motivate employees and manage change within an organization, and how productivity is affected by the nature of the information-based organization. A summary of motivation theories is presented, including the needs-based, process-based, and reinforcement motivation theories followed by an overview of mainstream change management models for creating organizational transformation. Finally, the article discusses how productivity is affected by employee motivation, and how contemporary fast-paced information-based organizations can take advantage of motivational and change management theory.

OVERVIEW

In the year 2000, the well-known management guru Peter Drucker predicted a changing organizational landscape, one that was centered around information rather than productivity, focusing on worker knowledge, information sharing, and task specialists. Looking at the state of contemporary organizations, one can conclude that Drucker was right. Contemporary organizations face the challenges resulting from exponential growth in global competition, short product life cycles and quickly changing consumer demand (Muthusamy, Wheeler, and Simmons 2005). These factors, combined with information availability and accessibility described by Drucker, have led organizations to find success through innovative and creative thinking, employee empowerment, and the sharing and management of knowledge. This situation has created a significant paradigm shift in how organizations motivate employees, how much value they place on worker productivity, where it fits, and how organizations deal with change (the foundational basis of 'innovation' and 'transformation'—popular buzzwords for contemporary organizational practitioners). This paper provides an overview of each of these topics, and ways they are interrelated with each other.

Motivation

Never before has motivation played such a critical role in the workplace. Employees, in general, have more freedom than ever in getting their jobs done. The idea of self-managed employees and a democratic workplace is no longer the organization of the future. Rather, companies are beginning to embrace these concepts in order to have a changing organization that can adapt to an unstable and increasingly changing work environment. Some suggest that a completely democratic workplace is inevitable (Collins 1997). This awareness is creating a shift in emphasis from managing to leading, and motivation plays a big role in this new reality. The best leaders understand how to motivate their employees, using a transformational leadership style that is inspiring, intellectually stimulating, and individually focused on each employee (Bass 1999). Leaders of contemporary organizations must know how to motivate each of their employees in order for them to thrive in dynamic work environments. Understanding the various motivation theories is the first step to putting them into practice.

Motivation Theories can be categorized into three areas; needs-based, process, and reinforcement (Kinicki and Williams 2003). All three categories should be considered by managers and leaders in the right situational context.

John Kotter, creator of an 8-step model for creating change (photo courtesy of Keiradog)

Needs Theories

Maslow's Hierarchy of Needs theory is probably the most widely recognized motivational theory. Maslow asserted that our needs are fulfilled in a progressively complex way—a hierarchy consisting of five levels. An individual's needs are prioritized by the position in the hierarchy, whereby certain needs cannot be achieved until the needs in the lower level of the hierarchy are fulfilled. The five levels (from bottom to top) include physiological needs, safety needs, social needs, self-esteem needs, and self-actualization. The physiological needs that one has are elements such as food shelter, clothing, and other most basic necessities. The safety needs include protection from physical and emotional harm, and the elimination of conflict. Clearly, in an industry such as construction, safety is a larger concern than it might be for computer programmers (Halepota 2005). The social needs include the need for love, friendship, affiliation, and belonging. The self-esteem needs include job status, respect, promotion, and recognition. Finally, self-actualization is a level where all of the needs are met, and one is completely satisfied with one's surrounding environment. Organizational leaders should concentrate on where their employee's needs fit within the hierarchy. For example, it would not make sense to promote an employee without first offering an adequate salary.

A second widely-used needs theory was developed by David McClelland (Kinicki and Kreitner 2006). McClelland suggested that individuals have three needs: a need for achievement, a need for power, and a need for affiliation. He suggested that every individual is different with regards to his or her needs, and in order to adequately motivate someone, a leader should have a clear understanding of the employees' needs with regards to these three areas. For example, someone with a high need for affiliation might be well-suited for a human resources position, while someone with a high need for achievement might be well-suited for a sales position. A leader can make a critical mistake by exclusively using motivational techniques that concentrate in the wrong area, such trying to fulfill affiliation needs for a group of engineers that enjoy working in solitude.

The third needs theory that is often embraced was developed by Frederick Herzberg; it is often referred to as Hygiene Theory of Job Satisfaction (Kinicki and Kreitner 2006). Herzberg suggested that organizations have elements that can be classified as satisfiers and dissatisfiers, and that in order to satisfy and motivate employees, a leader/manager should remove the elements that dissatisfy employees and improve the elements that satisfy employees. Such elements as rules and regulations, salary, work environment, and supervisors are classified as dissatisfiers, or hygiene factors. Promotion opportunities, learning opportunities, job recognition, and challenging work are classified as satisfiers. While both are important to motivating an employee, oftentimes organizations only concentrate on removing the dissatisfiers, which does not intrinsically motivate the employee, especially in the long run. Offering an employee who is not happy with his or her career progression and attempts to resign, an increase in salary is only a short-term solution that does not create the desired satisfaction.

Process Theories

There are three predominant process theories of motivation: Victor Vroom's expectancy theory, equity theory, and goal-setting theories.

The expectancy theory of motivation has three components (Kinicki and Williams 2003). First, the employee has an expectation that his or her efforts will lead to high job performance. Second, the employee understands that if he or she performs at a high level, there will be a positive outcome. Finally, the employee understands the value of the possible outcome. These components—expectancy, instrumentality, and valence—are three elements of Vroom's theory. An example to demonstrate this needs process might be a commissioned salesman who is preparing for a sales call to a potential new customer. The salesman knows that in order to get the sale, an effort must be made, rather than having the purchase order just "drop in his lap." He spends half the night preparing his presentation, knowing that he will not present well without adequate presentation (effort leading to expectancy). He knows that if the presentation goes well, he will likely get the sales order (performance leading to instrumentality). Finally, he knows that an order will lead to a sales commission, and he'll be closer to his monthly sales goal (outcome leading to value or valence). He is motivated to prepare and get the sale.

Another process needs theory is Adam's equity theory. Adam asserted that the employee/employer relationship is a two-way street where the employee has a number of inputs into the organization, and expects a number of resultant outputs that are fair and equitable. For example, an employee might bring past job experience, educational accomplishments and might work 10 hours per week more than the average. To make these inputs feel equitable, the employee is motivated by good pay, promotional opportunities, and a good working environment. When there is an imbalance between input and outputs resulting in a feeling of inequity, the employee will have a feeling of dissonance—something is not right in the relationship. As a result, he or she won't be motivated towards achieving high performance. To remedy this situation, an employer might consider the individual's inputs separately, and compensate them accordingly to satisfy the inequity. Ramlall (2004) suggested that the Equity theory also considers the comparison to others. In other words, employees are motivated by positioning themselves in relation to their fellow employees through their work inputs, and expect to be rewarded accordingly.

A third process theory is the goal setting theory. Drucker (as cited in Hoopes 2003) asserted that the manager/employee relationship was immoral due to the power imbalance between the manager and the subordinate. His solution was the process of Management-by-Objective (MBO), where the employee has control over his or her work goals and tasks, which result in varying compensation levels and gives the employee a perception of being in control of their performance. Locke and Latham (Kinicki and Williams 2003) formalized the goal-setting theory as a motivational construct, and this work led to the birth of the SMART goals acronym (Specific, Measurable, Achievable, Relevant, and Time bound) that is commonly embraced by organizations, organizational practitioners, and management scholars.

Reinforcement Theory
Reinforcement theory is based on the reasoning that actions lead to consequences, which then lead to future behaviors. In this realm, there are four ways to reinforce behavior: positive reinforcement, negative reinforcement, extinction, and punishment (Kinicki and Williams 2003). Positive reinforcement uses rewards to encourage continued behavior, such as a bonus for performing well. Negative reinforcement is the removal of consequences after a positive change in behavior has occurred, such as a sales manager who no longer calls three times a day to check up on a new salesperson. Extinction is the reinforcement process by which rewards are withheld or eliminated due to poor performance, such as the engineering manager who does not offer public recognition of an employee who does not have good performance, while publicly complimenting everyone else in the department. The last way to reinforce is through punishment, such as the manager that docks an employee's pay for coming in late to work on several occasions.

Productivity
Productivity is closely related to motivation. For employees to be effective and efficient in their job tasks, having the technical knowledge and ability is not necessarily enough. Employees also need the resources required to do the job. They need supportive management and leadership with a vision that is aligned with their own goals and objectives. Most importantly, employees need to be driven (or motivated) by some means to achieve high performance.

Employees are significantly influenced by the leadership and management styles employed by their managers and supervisors. In a time where innovation and change is expected, the transformational leadership style can be closely tied to employee performance. Much research has indicated that behavior and performance are positively influenced by transformational leadership (Caillier 2014). Inspiring employees is a major element of that leadership style.

Kouzes and Posner (2003) also discussed how motivation and inspiration could affect employee performance. They claimed that leaders who routinely engaged in their five recommended practices—model the way, inspire a shared vision, challenge the process, enable others to act, and encourage the heart—are not only more productive in their jobs, but they are viewed as better leaders and have higher job satisfaction. They clearly established a link between a motivational style of leadership and employee performance.

Another model of performance was presented by T.R. Mitchell and D. Daniels (as cited in Kinicki and Kreitner 2006). The creators of this model asserted that an employee's motivated behavior results from three things. First, the employee brings certain skills, such as job knowledge, traits, emotions, and beliefs to the workplace and the job setting. Second, the employer provides the job context, such as the environment, support, rewards, task types, and work culture. Third, the manager of the employee uses processes that motivate the employee, such as giving them attention and direction, creating arousal, or being intense or persistent. These three things (employee inputs, job context, and motivating processes) result in the motivating behavior or drives that employees have towards completing tasks or achieving goals. The resulting behavior includes employee focus, effort, strategy, and persistence in accomplishing the desired objectives or tasks. The model is based on the assertion that performance and productivity are directly related to motivated behavior, and that managers and leaders need to understand how to motivate their employees, in addition to providing the technical skills and an accommodating work environment. In all three instances, performance is directly related to how motivated employees are.

Change Management
With an emphasis on creativity, innovation, and transformation due to the new information-based organizational (Drucker 2000) and transformational leader-ship environment (Bass 1999), understanding how to manage change is critical to the organizational strategy and process. Goodstein and Burke (as cited in French, Bell, and Zawacki 2005) put it this way, "American corporations are accepting the 'New Age' view of organizations as a 'nested subset of open, living systems, dependent upon the larger environment for survival'" (388). The fast-changing business environments of the twenty-first century, especially due to globalization and increased competition, have resulted in a significant need to not only be open to organizational change, but also to understand how to manage the change process. There are several theories of change that exist, and they all have much in common. Some of the more popular change theories are Kurt Lewin's three-step change theory, appreciative inquiry, and John Kotter's eight-step model of change.

Kurt Lewin's Three-Step Change Theory
Considered the father of understanding organizational change, Kurt Lewin suggested that there are three steps one should take when undergoing organizational change: unfreezing, moving, and then refreezing. Through this process, the group undergoing change can first be destabilized—that is, allowing behaviors to move away from the status quo. The second step, moving, allows the change agents to implement the different processes or desired behaviors to the point that seems most desirable. Once this movement has been achieved, the third stage is to refreeze, which stabilizes the change, making it the norm in terms of actions and behaviors (French, Bell, and Zawacki 2005). This model is one of the more popular change models but also one that many consider outdated. However, Lewin's work should not be discounted as his theory continues to influence emerging thought, such as complexity theory (Burnes 2004).

Appreciative inquiry is a change model that is gaining in popularity and acceptance. Using this model of change, organizational change agents focus on the successes rather than the failures in order to pinpoint areas in which to change. The positive essence of the methodology makes it attractive to those who are generally concerned with employees' natural resistance to change. Johnson (Johnson and Leavitt 2001) stated, "Appreciative inquiry is an approach that is uniquely suited to organizations that seek to be collaborative, inclusive, and genuinely caring for both the people within the organization and those they serve" (129). In the field of organizational development, where major transformations take place, appreciative inquiry is the most common and most preferred method used by contemporary organizational practitioners (Rita Williams, as cited in French, Bell, and Zawacki (2005). The appreciative inquiry method not only serves as a catalyst for change but also is the most easily accepted transformation process for those that resist change. By looking at possibilities rather than problems, the appreciative inquiry process, provides a different perspective for those involved in an organizational transformation.

John Kotter, a Harvard University professor, is well known as a leader in change management theory. His most famous work was his eight-step model for creating change (Kotter 1998). The eight steps in his model were:

1. Establish a sense of urgency.
2. Form a powerful guiding coalition.
3. Create a vision.
4. Communicate a vision.
5. Empower others to act on a vision.
6. Plan and create short-term wins.
7. Consolidate improvements and produce even more change.
8. Institutionalize new approaches.

This model provided organizational change agents with a logical, action-oriented formula for implementing change, and as such has become popular on most bookshelves of modern managers and leaders. The first four steps are intended to change the status quo—perhaps building on Lewin's model. Steps three through seven allow the organization to introduce and begin implementing the change. The last step is intended to make the change permanently imbedded into the fabric of the organization.

APPLICATION

Motivating employees in a changing environment is no easy task. A leader of a twenty-first-century information-based organization is faced with a multitude of challenges (such as keeping productivity high) as information and knowledge sharing is encroaching into the space that productivity once exclusively held at the top of the organizational priority list. The leader must engage in the leadership style that is most effective for an unstable and constantly changing environment.

Antonakis and House (as cited in Kinicki and Williams 2003, 465) concluded that a combination of transformational leadership and transactional leadership styles, with an emphasis on the transformational portion, is the best method for leaders to motivate their employees. Leaders need to be aware of the individual needs of their employees, including the best way to motivate them. Every employee is different, and as such, leaders benefit by considering the different motivating theories, some based on need, some based on process, and some based on behavior and reinforcement. However, understanding how to motivate each employee should not over shadow the need for the developmental and technical skills needed to perform job tasks, as well as the requirement to provide the appropriate resources to the employees. Michaelson (2005) warns that where motivational theories are applied for the sole purpose of driving productivity, productivity will almost inevitably decline. Management that views workers paternalistically or as units to be manipulated ultimately dehumanizes its workforce, however fair and beneficial the methods. In fact, respect, justice, and fair compensation may align with a worker's own idea of proper management, but if such reasonable treatment is transparently applied as "motivational" rather than humane, the worker may not respond in a positive way.

In addition to motivating employees, being a transformational leader also means that the leader is constantly striving for change through innovation and creative thinking. As leaders push for change, in order to keep up or stay ahead of the competition, they should expect to see significant resistance, unless an effective change management strategy is employed.

The bottom line is that the concepts of motivation, change management and productivity are intertwined and linked. All three should be a major consideration for a contemporary transformational leader.

BIBLIOGRAPHY

Bass, Bernard M. "Two Decades of Research and Development in Transformational Leadership." *European Journal of Work & Organizational Psychology* 8 (1999): 9–32. Web. 14 Mar. 2007.

Boerner, Sabine, Silke Astrid Eisenbeiss, and Daniel Griesser. "Follower Behavior and Organizational Performance: The Impact of Transformational Leaders." *Journal of Leadership & Organizational Studies* 13 (2007): 15. Print.

Burnes, Bernard. "Kurt Lewin and Complexity Theories: Back to the Future?" *Journal of Change Management* 4 (2004): 309–25. Web. 31 Mar. 2007.

Callier, James G. "Toward a Better Understanding of the Relationship between Transformational Leadership, Public Service Motivation, Mission Valence, and Employee Performance: A Preliminary Study. *Public Personnel Management* 43 (2014): 218–39. Web. 5 Nov. 2014.

Collins, Denis. "The Ethical Superiority and Inevitability of Participatory Management as an Organizational System." *Organization Science* 8 (1997): 489. Web. 14 Mar. 2007.

Cranston, Susie, and Scott Keller. "Increasing the 'Meaning Quotient' of Work." *Mckinsey Quarterly* (2013, Jan.): 48–59. Web. 7 Dec. 2015.

Drucker, Peter F. *Coming of the New Organization* [Electronic Version]. Web. 14 Mar. 2006.

French, Wendell L., Cecil H. Bell, and Robert A. Zawacki. *Organization Development and Transformation: Managing Effective Change*. 6th ed. New York: McGraw-Hill Irwin, 2005.

Halepota, Hassan. "Motivational Theories and Their Application in Construction." *Cost Engineering* 47 (2005): 14–18. Web. 31 Oct. 2013.

Hoopes, James. *False Prophets*. 1st ed. Cambridge, MA: Perseus Publishing, 2003.

Jelavic, Matthew, and D. Salter. "Performance Measures and Rewards: The Alignment of Management Goals and Employee Motivation." *Canadian Manager* 39 (2014): 26–27. Web. 5 Nov. 2014.

Johnson, Gail, and William Leavitt. "Building on Success: Transforming Organizations through an Appreciative Inquiry." *Public Personnel Management* 30 (2001): 129. Web. 31 Mar. 2007.

Kinicki, Angelo, and Robert Kreitner. *Organizational Behavior: Key Concepts, Skills, and Best Practices*. 2nd ed. New York: McGraw Hill, 2006.

Kinicki, Angelo, and Brian Williams. *Management: A Practical Introduction*. 2nd ed. New York: McGraw-Hill, 2003.

Kotter, John P. "Winning at Change." *Leader to Leader* (1998): 27–33. Print.

Kouzes, James, and Barry Posner. *The Leadership Challenge*. 3rd ed. San Francisco: Jossey-Bass, 2003.

Merrell, Phil. "Effective Change Management: The Simple Truth." *Management Services* 56 (2012): 20–23. Web. 31 Oct. 2013.

Michaelson, Christopher. "Meaningful Motivation for Work Motivation Theory." *Academy of Management Review* 30 (2005): 235–38. Web. 31 Oct. 2013.

Muthusamy, Senthil K., Jane V. Wheeler, and Bret L. Simmons. "Self-Managing Work Teams: Enhancing Organizational Innovativeness." *Organization Development Journal* 23 (2005): 53. Web. 31 Mar. 2007.

Ramlall, Sunil. "A Review of Employee Motivation Theories and Their Implications for Employee Retention within Organizations." *Journal of American Academy of Business, Cambridge* 5, nos. 1–2 (2004): 52. Web. 31 Mar. 2007.

Silvera, Ian. "Motivation Schemes Can Build Long-Term Engagement." *Employee Benefits* (2013, June 4): 7. Web. 7 Dec. 2015.

SUGGESTED READING

Ashkenas, Ron. "Change Management Needs to Change: Interaction." *Harvard Business Review* 91 (2013): 18–19. Web. 31 Oct. 2013.

Berry John. "Revolutionising Motivation." *Training Journal* (2014): 10–13. Web. 5 Nov. 2014.

Clegg, Chris, and Susan Walsh. "Change Management: Time for a Change!" *European Journal of Work and Organizational Psychology* (2004, June): 2. Web. 5 Apr. 2007.

Houkes, Inge, Peter Janssen, Jane de Jonge, and Arnold Baker. "Specific Determinants of Intrinsic Work Motivation, Emotional Exhaustion, and Turnover Intention: A Multisample Longitudinal Study." *Journal of Occupational & Organizational Psychology* 76 (2003): 427. Web. 5 Apr. 2007.

Mautz, Scott. *Make It Matter: How Managers Can Motivate by Creating Meaning*. New York City: AMACOM, 2015.

Schwinn, Carol, and David Schwinn. "Lessons for Organizational Transformation." *Journal for Quality & Participation* 19 (1996): 6. Web. 5 Apr. 2007.

Strickler, Jane. "What Really Motivates People?" *Journal for Quality & Participation* 29 (2006): 26. Web. 5 Apr. 2007.

John D. Benson, M.B.A.

NEGOTIATIONS

ABSTRACT

Wherever people work together, there is a potential for conflict, particularly in organizations where the needs and focus of the different stakeholders are often in opposition. Conflict can negatively impact an organization's performance and effectiveness. Negotiation is a process used to help conflicting parties reach a mutually acceptable agreement. There are two primary factors that can affect the effectiveness of negotiations: the conflict management skills of the negotiator and various situational variables. To be successful in negotiations, good preparation is essential. There are a number of tactics that a negotiator can use to help become better prepared for the negotiating table including gathering information about the strengths, weaknesses, and assumptions of the opponent. In addition, it is important for the negotiator to be mentally prepared for the negotiating table through understanding his or her own strengths, weaknesses, and assumptions as well.

OVERVIEW

In many ways, globalization has revolutionized the way that many organizations do business. The practice of off shoring enables organizations to relocate part of their operations to another country with lower costs or to outsource functions or activities to other companies with lower rates both around the country and around the world. Typically, domestic employees previously performed this work. However, these practices are often necessary to combat another result of globalization: the increased competition from other organizations at home that are able to charge less because of work outsources around the world. Although organizations potentially have a greater, global marketplace in which to market their products or services, this marketplace is also populated by more competitors than ever before.

Stakeholder Interest & Conflict

Most organizations have multiple stakeholders—persons or groups that can affect or be affected by a decision or action. These stakeholders may include the organization's employees, suppliers, distributors, and stockholders. Often the interests of the different stakeholders are in conflict. For example, most stockholders will be primarily concerned with earning a high return on their investment. In the abstract, keeping labor prices down or raising the sales price of widgets in the marketplace are equally possible strategies. Workers, of course, have a different view of the situation. They want an income that not only represents a living wage but also a fair one as well. Therefore, keeping down the organization's costs by keeping employee wages low (particularly vis à vis comparable wages within the industry) is likely to harm rather than help the organization's bottom line in the long run as workers leave for organizations with better compensation packages.

Another group with a stake in organizational operations is management. This group is often more likely to take the long view of organizational effectiveness, realizing that holding down wages will lead to worker unrest and dissatisfaction and have a negative impact on the viability of the organization. However, they typically also realize the need to stay competitive in the global marketplace with its increased competition and potentially cheaper labor rates.

The needs and focus of the different constituencies within the organization often lead to conflict—the situation where one or more parties believes that its interests are negatively affected by another party. For example, conflict can arise between labor and management over a wage increase. One of the goals of management is to keep costs down, and wages are one of the costs of doing business. Employees, on the other hand, are more concerned about their own costs and taking care of their families, so they seek higher wages. There are two ways that such a situation can be viewed. In the win-lose orientation, one or more of the parties in the conflict look at the situation as a fixed pool of resources that can be divided among the parties. In this view of conflict, the more one side receives, the less the other side receives. So, for example, labor might balk at the implementation of a new research and development department because they view it as increasing the number of employees that needs to be paid from a limited source of funds for wages. Management, similarly, might view this situation as win-lose because the more that they have to pay the current workers, the less money they will have available to support the proposed research function that theoretically can develop new products to gain more income for the company with which they may be able to give workers higher compensation in the long term.

However, in many conflict situations, it is not necessary for a winner and a loser. In the win-win orientation, one or more of the parties to the conflict believe that it is possible to arrive at a mutually beneficial solution for all parties involved. In the example of a conflict over wages, a win-win orientation might mean that both sides are cognizant of the fact that having a nominal cost of living raise in the short term so that more monies can be devoted to research and development efforts may mean an overall higher wage in the long term after the success of the research and development efforts.

Resolving Organizational Conflict
One of the ways that conflict between groups within an organization is often resolved is through negotiation. This interactive process between two or more conflicting parties involves attempts by both parties to reach a mutually acceptable agreement about an issue or issues of mutual interest. In negotiation, the conflict is redefined in terms of interdependence of the parties. For example, in the illustration above, although the employees could push for the highest raise possible, if that action would cause the organization to go out of business, neither side would win. Similarly, if the organization refused to listen to the employees' arguments for a raise and only paid minimum wage, it might soon lose not only the current employees but also the possibility of hiring new employees. The employees, similarly, would lose the security of their current job and have to look for new work. Both sides lose because both sides are dependent on each other. Because of this fact, negotiation between the two parties in the wage dispute discussed would have as one of its goals to move both parties from a win-lose orientation to a win-win orientation. So, the employees might settle for a cost-of-living increase for the next year with a promise of a greater increase after the new research and development effort increased the organization's cash flow or some other agreement in which both sides win.

Approaches to Effective Negotiation
Competition, accommodation, or other win-lose strategies are not typically effective in negotiations. Although some theorists posit that collaboration is the best negotiating approach, others believe that other win-win orientations can also be effective. One must be careful of adopting a collaborative approach until mutual trust can be established between the parties. In addition, collaboration requires the sharing of information between the parties in the conflict. However, complete transparency in negotiations can be ill advised. Information is power, and if one side in the negotiation has too much power, the situation can quickly become win-lose rather than win-win. Most skilled negotiations tend to share information slowly, particularly at the beginning of the negotiation. This strategy allows trust to be built slowly. In addition, although a win-win approach is typically preferable, if it becomes apparent that such an approach will not work, it may be necessary to switch to a win-lose approach.

As shown in figure 1, negotiation is a process in which the goal is to move the position of the parties involved to a point where a mutually acceptable agreement can be reached. This area of potential agreement is called the "bargaining zone." In negotiation, each party begins by describing its initial offer for each point on the agenda. This strategy may be what each believes to be the best that it can achieve out of the negotiation, or it may be a best-of-all-possible-worlds scenario. For example, representatives of the employees may start with asking for a cost-of-living increase (i.e., a best achievable approach) or a 25-percent increase (i.e., an ideal-world approach), and representatives of management may start with refusing to give any raise (i.e., an ideal-world approach). However, this initial offer is typically recognized by all involved to be only a starting point for discussions and that both sides will make concessions (i.e., move closer to the bargaining zone). The target point for each party is what it believes to be a realistic expectation for the outcome of the negotiation. The resistance point is the point beyond which each party is willing to continue negotiations because it will be giving away too much to the other party (i.e., the situation becomes too win-lose).

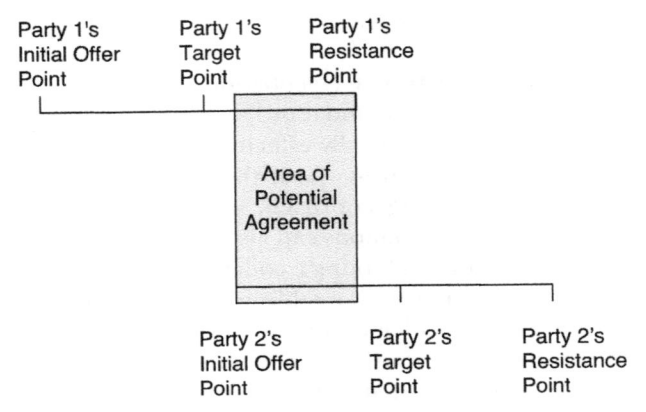

Figure 1: Bargaining zone model of negotiations (adapted from McShane and von Glinow, 403)

For example, the employees in the illustration above may start with what they believe to be a good outcome of a cost-of-living increase plus an additional 8 percent as their initial offer. Given the circumstance of the company, however, they may reasonably expect to get a cost-of-living increase plus 2 percent as a target point. Further, they may also have determined that they cannot afford to receive less than a cost-of-living increase with a promise of renegotiations in a year once the research and development effort is finished.

If the negotiation is being conducted with a win-lose orientation, the parties do not reveal their target or resistance points so as not to give an advantage to the other side. In a win-win negotiation situation, however, sharing information often can help to reach a mutually acceptable solution. If, for example, a supplier needs to postpone delivery dates and the buyer does not care as long as the dates are before a certain date, an agreement can be reached. In this scenario, the supplier would probably concede something to the buyer, such as a lower price, financing, or a willingness to deliver more items.

Factors Affecting the Success of Negotiations

The primary factors that can affect the effectiveness of negotiations are the skill of the negotiator in conflict management skills and various situational variables. Research shows that negotiators who plan and set goals are more likely to facilitate a satisfactory agreement for all parties involved. A negotiator needs to carefully consider all known information in order to develop the best possible initial offer, target point, and resistance point. This work includes articulating and checking what assumptions are being made in the situation, what the values of his or her party are, and what the goals are for the situation. In addition, a good negotiator will go through the same thought processes for the other party's position in order to better understand how to reach a mutually acceptable agreement. To aid in this process, the negotiator needs to be skillful at gathering information. Part of this task means engaging in active listening—an approach to improved communication in which the receiver of the message attempts to better understand the message being transmitted—formulates a response based on this understanding, and responds in a way that clarifies the message. Information gathering also involves asking the other party for details about its position in order to better understand what is desired. This process can often be helped by using a team of negotiators rather than a single individual. In this way, more information can be gathered and additional insights applied to help achieve an optimal solution for all parties involved.

Necessary Negotiator Skills

A good negotiator needs not only to be a good listener, but also a good communicator. Part of this task means working to make sure that the emotional or interpersonal conflict is kept to a minimum and that the situation is viewed as objectively as possible. Good negotiators are also persuasive, excelling in the art of convincing the other party to take a particular course of action or hold a particular point of view by using argument, reasoning, or entreaty. In other words, a good negotiator is not only able to clearly articulate the position of his or her side so that the other party can understand it, he or she is also able to get the other party to accept the goals of his or her side.

Particularly in win-win situations, however, negotiation is not just about getting one's way, but also about making concessions in order to reach the optimal solution for all parties involved. When both sides are willing to make concessions, they are able to move closer to the bargaining zone, where they can potentially reach an agreement. Concessions also signal to the other party that one is negotiating in good faith and is truly trying to reach a mutually agreeable solution to the conflict. However, concessions also show the other party what one considers to be important in the negotiating situation. It is often unwise to give away too much information at least until mutual trust has been established. Therefore, most negotiators offer just enough concessions to keep the lines of communication open without giving away too much. Otherwise, concessions might be perceived as a sign of weakness by the other party and encourage power and resistance in the negotiation rather than working toward a mutually acceptable solution.

Situational Factors Affecting the Success of Negotiations
In addition to the skills of the negotiator, the success of negotiations can be affected by various situational factors. One of these is the location of the negotiation. People often try to keep the negotiations in their own environment so that they can keep to their normal routines, not have to cope with travel-related stress, or depend on others for the various resources they might need during the negotiation. For this reason, many negotiations are held in a neutral environment. Although twenty-first-century telecommunications technologies mean that negotiations can potentially be held at a distance so that both parties can be on home ground, most negotiators find that in-person negotiations are preferable. This situation is true in part because it is easier to read body language and other nonverbal communication in a face-to-face situation and it is possible to hold additional sidebar discussions outside the negotiating room. In addition, the physical layout of the negotiating room can influence the outcome of the process. For example, people who sit on opposite sides of the table in negotiations are more likely to take a win-lose orientation than those who are interspersed around the table or all facing a whiteboard that symbolizes their common problem.

Another factor that can affect the negotiation process is time, including the length of the process and the associated deadlines. The longer the process, the more invested the parties will be in resolving the situation. However, this reality can also mean that the parties are more likely to make unwarranted concessions just to ensure that the negotiation will not fail. Similarly, deadlines may help negotiations stay on track so that a timely agreement is reached. On the other hand, deadlines may also make the parties more willing to make unwarranted concessions, not allow sufficient time for a collaborative approach to succeed, or not give the parties sufficient time to gather the information they need for successful negotiations.

Finally, negotiations do not occur in a vacuum. They are closely watched by various stakeholders and even the general public. When negotiations are closely watched, the negotiators tend to be more competitive and less willing to make concessions. In addition, when they are being watched, negotiators are often more concerned about saving face than they are about reaching an optimal solution.

APPLICATIONS

Preparation—both information gathering and mental preparation—is one of the keys to successful negotiations. One of the pitfalls in negotiations is overconfidence that one's perceptions of the situation are truly reality. Research has found that negotiator's predictions of their behavior at the negotiating table are frequently incorrect, partially due to a tendency to take an optimistic view of the future and to hope for the best. In addition, people often do not fully understand the impact of their motivations and emotions on their behavior, including the desire to reach an agreement even at the cost of giving away more than they should. These factors lead to a situation of overconfidence that is not warranted by the actual negotiating situation.

To better predict one's behavior in a negotiation, it is important to recognize that the assumptions and predictions about what will happen will not necessarily be shown to be true in the actual situation and to develop ways to cope with the unexpected. Negotiations can be very emotionally charged situations. Although one might assume that one will remain calm under pressure, this behavior will not necessarily occur or last. To help one cope with the possibility of reacting in an emotional way during a negotiating situation, it is important—in advance—to determine coping mechanisms that can be employed.

For example, when negotiating on an emotionally charged issue, it could be helpful to visualize how one would react in such a situation and what tactics could be taken to defuse the situation or keep it from escalating. In addition, one should have a best alternative to a negotiated agreement (BATNA) in mind before negotiations. This alternative action that will be taken if a mutually satisfactory negotiated agreement cannot be reached (e.g., if the employees in the earlier example cannot reach a satisfactory agreement, they are willing to strike) can make the negotiations more successful. Having a BATNA enables the negotiator to have a back-up position to keep from making too many concessions in order to reach an agreement.

To help keep from being overconfident in a negotiation situation, there are several things that one can do. First, it is important to collect as much information about the other party, including their strengths, weaknesses, and motivations. Information is power, and the more one knows about one's opponent, their strengths and weaknesses, their motivations, and the parameters within which they must work, the better one will be able to negotiate. Second, it is important to consider that one's own assumptions may not be accurate and that the opposite might occur. In such a situation, it is helpful to have previously thought through the ramifications of potentially unexpected actions on the part of one's opponent and ways one can handle them. Third, it can be helpful to work with a colleague or other trusted person who can play devil's advocate. This person can help the negotiator think through his or her own assumptions and motivations and be better prepared for the actual negotiation.

BIBLIOGRAPHY

Crump, Larry. "Negotiation Process and Negotiation Context." *International Negotiation* 16, no. 2 (2011): 197–227. Web. 29 Nov. 2013.

Diekman, Kristina A., and Adam Galinsky. "Overconfident, Under-prepared: Why You May Not Be Ready to Negotiate." *Negotiation* (2006, Oct.): 6–9. Web. 19 June 2007.

Kuang, Xi, and Donald Moser. "Wage Negotiation, Employee Effort, and Firm Profit under Output-Based versus Fixed-wage Incentive Contracts." *Contemporary Accounting Research* 28, no. 2 (2011): 616–42. Web. 19 Nov. 2013.

McShane, Steven L., and Mary Ann Von Glinow. *Organization Behavior: Emerging Realities for the Workplace Revolution*. 2nd ed. Boston: McGraw-Hill/ Irwin.

Miles, Edward W. "Development Strategies for Asking Questions in Negotiation." *Negotiation Journal* 29, no. 4 (2013): 383–412. Web. 19 Nov. 2013.

Moore, Don. "Are You an Overconfident Negotiator?" *Negotiation* (2007, June): 7–9. Web. 19 June 2007.

Sokolova, Marina, and Guy Lapalme. "How Much Do We Say? Using Informativeness of Negotiation Text Records for Early Prediction of Negotiation Outcomes." *Group Decision & Negotiation* 21, no. 3 (2012): 363–79. Web. 19 Nov. 2013.

SUGGESTED READING

Bacon, Nicolas, and Paul Blyton. "Conflict for Mutual Gains?" *Journal of Management Studies* 44, no. 5 (2007): 814–34. Web. 19 June 2007.

Bordone, Robert C. "Divide the Pie—Without Antagonizing the Other Side." *Negotiation* (2006, Nov.): 4–6. Web. 19 June 2007.

Hackley, Susan. "Focus Your Negotiations on What Really Matters." *Negotiation* (2006, Sept.): 9–11. Web. 19 June 2007.

Kolb, Deborah M., and Peter J. Carnevale. "When Dividing the Pie, Smart Negotiators Get Creative." *Negotiation* (2007, Jan.): 9–11. Web. 19 June 2007.

Liljenquist, Katie A., and Adam D. Galinsky. "How to Diffuse Threats at the Bargaining Table." *Negotiation* (2006, Sept.): 1–4. Web. 19 June 2007.

Malhotra, Deepak. "Dealing with Distrust? Negotiate the Process." *Negotiation* (2006, Nov.): 7–9. Web. 19 June 2007.

Menkel-Meadow, Carrie. "Know When to Show Your Hand." *Negotiation* (2007, June): 1–4. Web. 19 June 2007.

Movius, Hal. "When Individual Bargaining Skills Aren't Enough." *Negotiation* (2007, Mar.): 4–6. Web. 19 June 2007.

Nadler, Janice. "Build Rapport—and a Better Deal." *Negotiation* (2007, Mar.): 9–11. Web. 19 June 2007.

Overbeck, Jennifer R., Margaret Neale, and Elizabeth A. Mannix. *Negotiation and Groups*. Bingley, England: Emerald, 2011. Web. 19 Nov. 2013.

Schweitzer, Maurice E. "Aim High, Improve Negotiation Results." *Negotiation* (2006, Aug.): 4–6. Web. 19 June 2007.

Susskind, Lawrence. "Find the Sweet Spot in Your Next Deal." *Negotiation* (2007, May): 7–9. Web. 19 June 2007.

Swaab, Roderick I., and Adam D. Galinsky. "How to Negotiate When You're (Literally) Far Apart." *Negotiation* (2007, Feb.): 7–9. Web. 19 June 2007.

Woolcock, Stephen, and Nicholas Bayne. *The New Economic Diplomacy: Decision-Making and Negotiation in International Economic Relations.* Farnham, UK: Ashgate Publishing, 2011. Web. 19 Nov. 2013.

Ruth A. Wienclaw, Ph.D.

Nonprofit Leadership and Management

ABSTRACT

Nonprofit leadership and management is an important area of concern because of the impact of nonprofit organizations on society. The mission statements of most nonprofits are geared towards helping people or addressing a need that is not met through government or private sources. For a long time, nonprofit leadership and management were not considered a priority because the organizations were doing good work. However, as nonprofits grew and became more complex and as funding sources demanded tighter accountability for the use of funds nonprofits have found themselves in a position of having to act more like for-profit businesses in structure, strategy, and accountability. Accountability in any organization starts with top management and the leadership team. Without these individuals directing and leading the organization in the proper direction, it is unlikely that nonprofits will grow and expand. There is more emphasis on formal training for nonprofit executives and board members to increase their knowledge of their responsibilities and their abilities to support organizational sustainability.

OVERVIEW

Nonprofit organizations are legal entities that are formed with a mission to do work in the interest of specific constituencies. For example, a nonprofit organization could be formed to support educational interests, advance community development, address health or housing issues, and make improvements in other needed areas. Nonprofits often do work that no one else will do. Many nonprofits do not sell a product or service like a for-profit business although nonprofits may do so. Instead, many nonprofits receive the bulk of their funding through fundraising for personal donations or through government and private grants.

Nonprofits, like for-profit businesses, are growing rapidly. Dolan (2002) noted that in a ten-year period, the number of nonprofits grew from 1.2 million to 1.6 million. Dolan (2002) also indicated that nonprofits constitute 7 percent of the workforce, employing more people than federal and state governments combined to the tune of over 11 million workers. Nonprofit organizations, like small businesses, are often located in the community, giving people an opportunity to work where they live. Nonprofits also give employees an opportunity to do something that matters, and employees often receive intrinsic value from the knowledge that the work they do helps others.

While for-profit companies have always had a focus and emphasis on leadership, management and continuous improvement in all areas of business, nonprofits have been more concerned that the result of nonprofit operations resulted in good work. But as nonprofits expand and grow, many may have budgets that rival for-profit companies, and they are run and managed like a business. In addition, private donors as well as government agencies and foundations are requiring nonprofits to be more professional and formal in the way they document the activities and use of funds and the way they manage the organization.

ORGANIZATION OF A NONPROFIT

Executive Director

Nonprofit organizations are governed by a board of directors who serve in a fundraising and advisory capacity providing oversight for a nonprofit. The top employee at most nonprofit organizations has the

The headquarters of National Public Radio, a non-profit company, in Washington D.C. (photo courtesy of Aude)

title of executive director, chief executive officer, or president. This individual is responsible for day-to-day leadership of the organization and supervision of staff; he or she also serves as the primary spokesperson, advocate and face of the organization. The executive director works closely with the board of directors who have the responsibility of hiring and evaluating the executive director. Small nonprofits may only have an executive director and fulfill their mission with the work of volunteers. Other large nonprofit organizations rival for-profit businesses with fairly large staffs. Large nonprofit organizations typically have a development officer who is responsible for organizing and raising funds. The development officer has contact with personal donors and may write grant proposals to seek money from government and private foundations. A program officer is the nonprofit employee in charge of developing, managing, and monitoring the programs the nonprofit offers to its constituents. A communications officer manages the public relations and marketing for a nonprofit organization.

The executive director wears many hats, one of which is hiring staff and supervising staff members. The executive director must have a sound team of employees to keep things running effectively. Hiring and selecting the right people can be a determining factor in the growth and success of a nonprofit organization. Studies have shown that employees in nonprofit organizations somehow identify with the mission and that the mission factors into job satisfaction and on some level it is as important as compensation (Brown and Yoshioka 2003).

Volunteers

All nonprofits need volunteers to fulfill their missions. Volunteers are unpaid workers who either give their time, financial support or talents to for the organization. Volunteers may also advocate for the organization and recruit others to become involved. Volunteers are often people who are passionate about the work a nonprofit engages in and enjoy spending time serving the mission of the organization. Larger and more organized nonprofits often provide orientation and training for their volunteers. Some organizations that serve sensitive populations such as children may also require volunteers to undergo training and even background checks to avoid the possibility of liability on the part of the nonprofit as a result of the actions of a volunteer. While volunteers are useful, they can be difficult to organize and control since they give their time freely. Some nonprofits specify what is required of volunteers and provide guidelines for volunteer behavior and minimal amounts of time that a volunteer must give to remain in good standing. In this way, people who are not truly dedicated do not volunteer.

Mission Statement

Individuals who decide to become involved with a nonprofit organization as an employee are often people who are dedicated to the mission of the organization. Brown and Yoshioka (2003) described a nonprofit's mission as "a strong management tool that can motivate employees and keep them focused." Nonprofit organizations typically promote the value of being involved in an organization that supports communities or fights social ills to balance the fact that many nonprofits do not always have budgets to pay salaries comparable to for-profit organizations. Competition for good nonprofit employees can be fierce. However, says Stephen C. Rafe, "Most volunteers who are truly service-oriented need little recognition. For them, the satisfaction comes from helping, from contributing to a job that needs to be done, and from the feeling that they're appreciated and are making a difference" (Rafe 2013).

Both for-profit and nonprofit organizations have missions that drive the activity of the organization.

A mission statement is a statement of the values of an organization and is useful in defining the organization and its activities. For-profit leaders push the quality of the products and services their company produces as an embodiment of the corporate mission. For-profit leaders attract buyers, investors and employees through their mission. Nonprofit leaders are a visible embodiment of the organization's mission and the mission is used to attract donors, volunteers, funders, and employees.

Capacity Building
As nonprofits grow and expand, they become increasingly interested in capacity building, improving the value of internal processes and resources to be able to expand the work that is done. Expansion can mean being able to serve more people of a different population or it can mean serving more people of the same population. It can also mean being able to offer additional services. Internal capacity also means better skills among employees, better management of technology and processes, and better ability to raise and manage funds.

Interorganizational networks may bring together two or more nonprofits and are "becoming the new shape of governance as they bring more opportunities to increase the capacities of communities" (Kapucu and Demiroz 2013). Large scope services such as health care delivery, disaster preparedness and response, or disease control often exceed the capacity of single organizations and require community capacity for collective action, thus improving communities' capacity to achieve service delivery goals and increasing their well-being. Fostering involvement of community stakeholders, especially nonprofit organizations, and other actors for service provision distributes the overall burden of individual organizations.

Resource Acquisition
Resources usually are the biggest obstacle for nonprofits. Cargo (2005, 552) noted "the nonprofit sector is characterized in large part by its struggle to match resources with oversized missions." Nonprofits with lofty missions must realize that there is only operational capacity to operate a limited number of programs or provide services to a finite number of constituents. Nonprofits usually struggle with the amount of money needed operationally versus the amount of money spent on programs. Some infrastructure is needed to provide services but donors and grant makers are most interested in minimizing administrative costs and maximizing direct service costs. Some nonprofits also engage in selling products and services to provide value to constituents and to create a revenue stream for the organization. Some nonprofits are connected to for-profit companies where the for-profit company provides funds for the nonprofit. In other cases, a for-profit wants to engage in a social mission and needs a nonprofit structure to do it.

As funding sources require more professionalism in operations and reporting from nonprofit organizations, more nonprofits have been seeking help in capacity building and organizational development. For years, for-profit companies have seen the benefit of investing in leadership to provide value to companies. Now, many nonprofits are doing similar things to bolster nonprofit leadership. At times, this training can be at the executive director or board level; at other times, it includes senior staff. Other leadership programs emphasize leadership with staff assuming that many new leaders of nonprofits may be sourced from within the organization. Dolan (2002) noted the decrease in the provision of certain services by government means that nonprofits may have to step up to the plate to fill the gaps. Increased demand for nonprofits to provide services has increased the demand for skilled people to do the jobs of leading and managing nonprofit organizations.

The Executive Director's Job
As the top leaders of nonprofit organizations, executive directors need many skills to be effective in their jobs. Executive directors must be good communicators since much of the executive director's job involves serving as an advocate for the organization and its mission and as a persuasive voice to potential donors. Executive directors are typically the most visible person within the organization. The same leadership and management skills that are required of other types of organizational leaders (chief executive officer [CEO], chief operating officer [COO], president) are required of an executive director.

Many experts feel that the mission statement of a nonprofit organization should be used as a management tool and serve as the source of performance improvement in nonprofits (Brown and Yoshioka 2003). "Mission statements are formal declarations of organizational values" (Brown and Yoshioka 2003, 6). Many nonprofits are started by people who are very passionate about a cause and who decide to create a nonprofit organization to fulfill that passion. Although passion about the mission is important, executive directors also need to be organized. They have supervisory responsibility over employees and have to organize and direct the nonprofit's activities. The director has to execute the organization's strategic plan, monitor daily operations, engage in fundraising and have contact with constituents. Since there is a great deal of competition for philanthropic dollars, the executive director must be good at networking with key individuals in business, government, the nonprofit community, and the community at large. An executive director must be an expert at developing relationships at all levels.

Finances

Executive directors need to have some financial knowledge since they participate in the documentation of financial activities and explaining them to the board, constituents, and funding sources. Nonprofits usually have external accountants and auditors to audit financials in addition to an internal financial person. However, the executive director is responsible for any issues related to finances and can benefit from having an understanding of financial reporting obligations. Executive directors have difficult and demanding jobs without the high level of support that they might find in a corporate setting which is where external training and development is often useful. Executive directors who attend external nonprofit training programs can network with other nonprofit leaders as they learn. These individuals can also identify strategies that other organizations are using and may be able to identify partners with whom they can jointly develop funding and marketing campaigns or jointly apply for funds.

Leadership Skills

Leadership skills are important for the executive director as they are the most visible and important leader of a nonprofit organization. Leadership skills must be used by the executive director and modeled for other employees. Denhardt and Campbell (2006) suggest that transformational leadership is important because leaders with transformational leadership skills are better at leading organizations through change. Nonprofit organizations are often the creators of change in the communities they serve and transformational leadership skills can make the adjustment to change easier. Nonprofits can benefit from transformational leadership because there is also a moral component to it. There are two parts to the process of transformational leadership (Denhardt and Campbell 2006): the self-discovery of values and the reflection on these values within a social context.

Executive directors must continuously reflect on the activities of the organization to ensure that they are moral in context, beneficial to constituents and society, and true to the organizational mission. If these components are in place, the job of leading a nonprofit organization can remain exciting and satisfying for the executive leader.

The Board

The board is a very important entity within a nonprofit organization. The board has governance responsibilities, meaning that the board is responsible for planning and influencing the nonprofit's activities. "To measure its effectiveness, a nonprofit must ask itself, 'Are we really delivering on our mission, not just meeting budget, and are we getting maximum impact from our expenditures?'" (Epstein and McFarlan 2011). Board members can lend support by providing advice and resources to the executive director. Board members select the executive director and evaluate the director's performance. Nonprofit board members are usually unpaid and are selected based on their ability to raise funds, make personal donations, and exert personal influence in the community. Typically, board members are people who feel passionate about the cause and understand its ramifications.

Board Member Recruitment

One of the challenges of the nonprofit board is picking board members who are committed, have good skills, and are available. The problem is that nonprofit board members are typically unpaid, and the types of board members nonprofits want—those who are well connected and can personally donate–are typically among the busiest people around. Highly qualified people who are willing to give of their time often have many interests and concerns vying for their attention.

Sometimes, nonprofit boards end up being made up of people who are available and not the most skilled. Nonprofits then may choose to engage in board development so that people who are enthusiastic can learn their role as board members and be in a position to contribute. Board development also shows board members how they should conduct strategic planning, create a vision, and develop plans for the organization several years into the future. The board should give operational guidance to staff, but not supervise staff (although the board does evaluate the performance of the executive director).

Assistance to Board Members

There are many sources of assistance to nonprofit board members, volunteers and employees who want to learn more about involvement in a nonprofit organization. Cargo (2005) noted over 2,000 books available on nonprofit management and over 300 research papers. In addition, many universities offer certificate and degree programs in nonprofit management. Dolan (2002) observed training programs for board and nonprofit leadership are often patterned after traditional business leader training while other training was developed based on information from practitioners and other experts. Some training is created based on what nonprofit leaders feel they need to be successful on the job. Surveys (Dolan 2002, 281) of nonprofit leaders listed the following areas as most important to completing the task of managing and leading a nonprofit organization:

- Fundraising
- Grant writing
- Volunteer administration
- Planning
- Cooperative ventures
- Communication
- Computer skills
- Program evaluation
- Nonprofit accounting

Nonprofit organizations often seek board members with specific skills that needed in governance, operations, and legal issues. Bankers, attorneys, accountants, and other professionals are usually sought after because they have intimate knowledge of the issues that nonprofits face. Board members are charged with selecting new board members when the terms of current members expire as well as with selecting a diverse group of members. Board members may have an attachment to the power, control and title associated with board service and may resist efforts to expand or include others on the board. These actions can often slow or stop nonprofit growth and expansion.

Board Capital

Brown (2005) noted that if a board is well organized and performs well, it will lead a high-performing nonprofit organization due to what Brown (2005, 322) calls board capital. It is a combination of "expertise, experience and reputation." These key components are then available to the nonprofit for its use. Direct expertise and experience can save the nonprofit the cost of acquiring the expertise over time or hiring it externally. Solid reputations of board members can attract donors, volunteers, and additional board members while also providing a nonprofit with credibility. The task of the board is to guide the strategic planning and long-term agenda for the organization, a task best done by those who have specific capabilities and expertise.

VIEWPOINT

For-Profit vs. Nonprofit Leadership Challenges

Leaders of all kinds have complex tasks and duties. For-profit leaders often must oversee complex structures, large budgets and many employees. Nonprofits can also have similar demands, depending on size. Large nonprofits must compete with for-profit companies for employees and must create a structure with systems and processes that support the organizational mission. Nonprofit leaders must be accountable for results just as for-profit leaders are. However, the stakeholders in the accountability system for nonprofit leaders may be board members, donors, grant-makers, employees, and constituents. Meanwhile, for-profit companies may be concerned about stockholders, customers, suppliers, and employees.

Smaller nonprofit organizations struggle for resources and funding in a way that is very similar to the struggle faced by small businesses. With fewer resources, these organizations force those who lead and manage the organizations to carry many responsibilities. Since nonprofit institutions usually do not have a product or service being sold for a profit, production and sales numbers are not metrics usually being measured. Nonprofit institutions instead may measure the number of constituents served, number of donors, and total donor dollars.

Economic Challenges

For-profit organizations approach the task of adapting to falling sales or economic challenges by reducing expenses which can result in raising prices, reducing the number of employees or selling off assets. Nonprofit leaders may not have assets to sell and can't force donors to contribute more. Nonprofit organizations will not be able to serve as many constituents with fewer dollars.

For-profit leaders are most vulnerable to massive changes in buyer behavior and supplier behavior. If buyers decide not to buy, the for-profit institution cannot sell. If suppliers raise their prices it costs the for-profit institution more to produce the same products or services. If a for-profit business is successful, it becomes profitable and has money to reinvest into the business. If a nonprofit organization is successful, it may have enough money to cover operating costs and serve a larger number of people.

If the nonprofit experiences massive changes in donor and funding streams or massive changes in constituent behavior, the result will be a financial impact. If donors decide to contribute less, nonprofit leaders will have to decide how to increase funds in other ways. The decision could involve the makeup of donors or increasing the number of donors to fill the gap. If the nonprofit finds that the number of constituents requesting help grows considerably, the nonprofit may have to turn away some or may provide fewer services to constituents in order to serve more persons. A nonprofit organization is not able to raise prices. Even if it charges a reduced fee for services to constituents, vulnerable constituents most often cannot afford to pay. For-profits are driven by the bottom line–whether money is made and whether the company is profitable at the end of the day. Nonprofits are driven by the mission and allow it to be the bottom line, driving all activity (Brown and Yoshioka 2003).

CONCLUSION

Both nonprofit and for-profit leaders must understand financial budgeting and understand where the money originates. Both types of leaders have to engage in careful planning to make sure resources are utilized properly and to avoid future problems. For-profit and nonprofit leaders are similar in that they must possess a high level of management skill and both must be cognizant of expenses and operational issues. For-profit and nonprofit organizations differ in the missions they have but both use the mission as the driving force behind all activity and have missions based on organizational values. The mission is the force that shapes what the organizations will become.

BIBLIOGRAPHY

Brown, William A. "Exploring the Association between Board and Organizational Performance in Nonprofit Organizations." *Nonprofit Management & Leadership* 15 (2005): 317–39. Web. 21 Nov. 2007.

Brown, William A., and Carlton F. Yoshioka. "Mission Attachment and Satisfaction as Factors in Employee Retention." *Nonprofit Management & Leadership* 14 (2003): 5–18. Web. 21 Nov. 2007.

Butler, Linda G. "Top Tips for Improved Leadership." *Nonprofit World* 32 (2014): 26–28. Web. 17 Nov. 2014.

Cargo, R. "Book Review: *The Jossey-Bass Handbook of Nonprofit Leadership and Management* (2nd ed.)." *Nonprofit & Voluntary Sector Quarterly* 34 (2005): 550–52. Web. 21 Nov. 2007.

Denhardt, Janet V., and Kelly B. Campbell. "The Role of Democratic Values in Transformational Leadership." *Administration & Society* 38 (2006): 556–72. Web. 21 Nov. 2007.

Dolan, Drew A. "Training Needs of Administrators in the Nonprofit Sector." *Nonprofit Management & Leadership* 12 (2002): 277. Web. 21 Nov. 2007.

Epstein, Marc J., and F. Warren McFarlan. "Measuring the Efficiency and Effectiveness of a Nonprofit's

Performance." *Strategic Finance* 93 (2011): 27–34. Web. 16 Nov. 2013.

Kapacu, Naim, and Fatih Demiroz. "Collaborative Capacity Building for Community-Based Smal Nonprofit Organizations." *Journal of Economic & Social Studies* 3 (2013): 83–117. Web. 16 Nov. 2013.

McGovern, Gail. "Lead from the Heart." *Harvard Business Review* 92 (2014): 38. Web. 17 Nov. 2014.

Rafe, Stephen. "Motivating Volunteers to Perform." *Nonprofit World* 31 (2013): 18–19. Web. 16 Nov. 2013.

Suggested Reading

Dolan, Drew A., and Jim Landers. "Gambling on an Alternative Revenue Source: The Impact of Riverboat Gambling on the Charitable Gambling Component of Nonprofit Finances." *Nonprofit Management & Leadership* 17 (2006): 5–24. Web. 21 Nov. 2007.

Eisenberg, Pablo. "Solving the Nonprofit Leadership Crisis Will Take Much Work." *Chronicle of Philanthropy* 17 (2004): 44. Web. 21 Nov. 2007.

Fader, Betsy. "When CEO Precedes Ph.D. (or MBA, or J.D....)." *National Civic Review* 86 (1997): 261–65. Web. 21 Nov. 2007.

Fram, Eugene. "What's in a Name? Benefits of the President/CEO Title." *Nonprofit World* 32 (2014): 8–9. Web. 17 Nov. 2014.

Glasrud, Bruce. "Nonprofits Can Be Cool." *Nonprofit World* 21 (2003): 29–30. Web. 21 Nov. 2007.

Harrison, B.J. "For-Profit or for Purpose?" *Associations Now* 2 (2006): 59–65. Web. 21 Nov. 2007.

Marlanda English, Ph.D.

ORGANIZATION DESIGN

ABSTRACT

Organization design is the process of structuring an organization in a way that facilitates employee productivity and supports the organization in reaching its goals. The basic building blocks of organizational structure are division of labor, centralization of authority, and formalization. The organization can also be departmentalized functionally or divisionally. However, the requirements of today's electronically enabled organizations have resulted in changes in the way that some organizations are structured. Matrix, network, and even virtual approaches are becoming more common. Organization design is an iterative process, however. As the organization grows and changes, the design may need to be reconsidered in order to keep the organization competitive.

OVERVIEW

Not every organization is created equally. Universities have formal organizational structures at the top of the hierarchy, but individual professors are given the authority to evaluate students and assign grades. Banks are run by strict rules and the individual tellers must follow strict procedures for fund disbursement, record keeping, and other tasks. Engineering firms are often run as teams that direct their own activities, with each person reporting both to a functional or departmental manager (e.g., programming department) and to a project manager (e.g., widget development project). Depending on what they are trying to accomplish—e.g., encourage creativity, mass produce products, provide services——different types of organizations need to be structured differently. These structures include how labor is divided among employees, how communication flows both down and up the organizational hierarchy, and how formal power is consolidated or distributed. The design of the organization is the structure through which it is organized to conduct its business.

Organization design sets limits on how work can be accomplished. An appropriate organization design can support employees in meeting organizational goals by giving them the freedom or the structure necessary to perform their tasks. For example, a team-based structure often works well for creative tasks where employees working together can experience the synergy that results in an outcome that is greater than they could have developed as individuals. An inappropriate organization design, on the other hand, can hinder the employees in their tasks and keep the organization from reaching its goals. For example, giving employees too much freedom in a bank could lead to bad or inconsistent decisions about lending, poor record-keeping, and a lack of profits for shareholders.

The design of an organization involves consideration of several things, including the division of labor and concomitant patterns of coordination of work activities, centralization and the structure of power relationships, and the degree of formalization of the organization. Division of labor is the way that work in the organization is divided into separate jobs. The more that work is subdivided, the greater the degree of specialization the individual employee needs to have to be able to do the job well. The development of a simulator to teach aircraft mechanics how to maintain and repair a fighter jet, for example, would require the inputs of numerous types of employees, including the subject matter experts who know what activities are involved in these tasks, the training specialists who determine the best way to teach these tasks to students, the engineers who know how to turn the trainers' requirements into a piece of equipment that can be used to teach these tasks, the computer programmers who write the programs that run the simulator and present the information to students, and the production workers who actually put together the equipment for delivery to the customer. In addition to the workers performing the tasks, there are usually supervisors for each type of job. These individuals understand the nature of the work to be done, can support the employees in their tasks, and make sure that the needs of the organization are met. When jobs are divided in this way, they also need to be coordinated so that the work done by the individual employees or groups will fit together to create the work product needed by the organization.

There are several general ways to coordinate work. Every organization uses informal communication when employees share information about tasks they are working on or when they form mutual ways to coordinate their work activities. Although informal communication can be quick and easy, it tends to work best when the organization is small and there are few barriers to communication. The mom-and-pop grocery store on the corner, for example, is more likely to use informal communication to coordinate the activities of workers than they are to have a formal set of procedures that cover every possible task. No matter the size of the organization, however, informal communication can occur directly (e.g., Harvey tells Chuck that he needs him to close out the cash register for the day) or through liaison or integrator roles (e.g., the project leader of the simulator development team encourages the various work groups to communicate with each other and coordinate their activities). Coordination can also be done through a formal hierarchy, where formal organizational power is given to an individual who directs work and allocates resources. This communication often is accomplished through direct supervision (e.g., George's boss tells him to finish the report by the end of the day) or through the corporate structure (e.g., the head of the Zenda operation of the organization coordinates the work for the organization in that country). Coordination can also be accomplished through standardization of skills, processes, or outputs. In this approach to coordination, the organization sets policies and procedures for dealing with various common activities. This pattern is helpful in routine situations (e.g., the receiver in each of the organization's stores enters information into the computer in the same format) but is not so helpful in unusual circumstances.

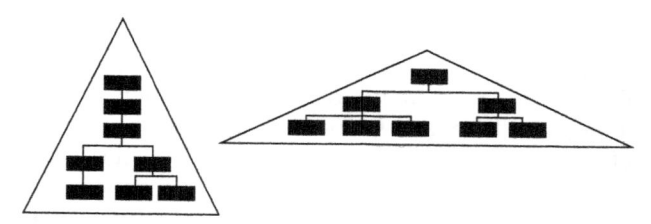

Figure 1: Tall (narrow span of control) vs. flat (wide span of control) organizational structures

The power structure within the organization is determined by its span of control and degree of centralization (see figure 1). Span of control is the number of employees that report directly to a supervisor in the next level up in the organization. At one time it was thought that a narrow span of control of 20 employees or less was the best approach to structuring an organization. Research has found, however, that in today's environment, the average span of control in effective organizations is 31. The most appropriate span of control will depend on what the organization is trying to accomplish and what types of people it employs. Larger spans of control are harder to supervise. However, when the employees self-manage (either as professionals or as self-managing work teams), this task becomes easier. Another characteristic of an organization's structure is the degree to which formal decision-making power is centralized or carried out by a small group of people. In a centralized organization, a very limited number of individuals—usually at the top of the organizational hierarchy—have the power to make decisions. This situation is particularly true in smaller or emerging organizations where the founder or chief executive officer (CEO) tends to make most, if not all, of the decisions. However, as an organization grows, one person (or even a small group of people) is no longer able to make all the decisions, so the authority is distributed throughout the organization. For example, in a multinational firm, it is logical to have some of the decisions made at a local level. Similarly, decisions about various activities can be made at a departmental or operational level.

Finally, organizations differ on the degree to which they formalize behavior through the imposition of rules, policies, practices, procedures, or formal training. Formalization can help employees know how to do their jobs. It can also help customers know that they are getting the same product no matter which of the organization's stores they patronize.

A franchise coffee shop, for example, may specify the temperature to which the coffee is kept heated, how frequently the coffee is brewed, how much milk is added to a latte, and so forth. Formalization is more effective in organizations where employees' tasks are routine. So, for example, it is easier to formalize an organization such as a fast food franchise than it is to formalize a think tank. Although formalization can make an organization's processes more efficient, it can have the opposite effect when an unusual situation arises and a variance from the normal procedure is needed. Although very small or emerging companies can function effectively with a simple structure, as the organization expands and grows, it is useful to group employees together to perform common tasks. This arrangement facilitates supervision of employees and coordination of their work, helps in resource allocation, and provides common goals and measures of performance.

There are several traditional ways to organize employees. The functional structure organizes employees around their knowledge or skills (e.g., the engineering department, the production department). This approach to structuring an organization makes supervision easier and can help foster professional identity. However, the functional approach to organizational structure can also result in a situation where the goals of the unit are given priority over the goals of the organization. The very intra-unit cohesiveness fostered by functional structuring can also lead to increased conflict and communication difficulties with other departments. Another way to structure an organization is through the creation of divisions based on geographic location (e.g., the US division vs. the Zenda division), clients (e.g., the hospital division vs. the consumer division), or products (e.g., the widget division vs. the gizmo division). Like functional structures, divisional structures can encourage a feeling of camaraderie and belongingness within the group. In addition, such divisional structures support growth and increased complexity better than do functional structures. However, this approach to organizational structure also creates the requirement for duplicate knowledge (e.g., each division needs a human resources function). As with functional structures, the divisional structure also results in more communication problems across groups. Another type of organization that is used in many complex organizations—particularly those that work on time-limited contracts—is the matrix structure (see figure 2). This approach to organizational structure combines the features of the functional organization and the divisional organization. In a matrix structure, employees typically are hired for a functional department (e.g., programming, engineering, production). They are brought together on a temporary basis, however, as functional teams (e.g., the widget contract) or as part of a division. This arrangement means that each employee actually reports to two bosses: the functional boss (e.g., the programming department head) and the divisional boss (e.g., the widget project manager). Matrix structures have the advantage of efficient deployment of talent throughout the organization. This approach to organization design also can help the organization to be more flexible and efficient. However, this approach requires more coordination than the simpler approaches of functional or divisional structures. The dual-reporting relationship can be difficult to manage and the very fluidity of the design that is attractive to the organization can be stressful to the employee.

APPLICATIONS

Organization design for the 21st Century

Globalization, e-commerce, the ability to telecommute, and the high tech nature of many jobs have changed the way that many organizations do business. This fact, in turn, impacts the way that the organizations need to be structured in order to best support the high performance of the employees and the success of the organization. The strict military model of command and control that was often used in the past does not work as well for today's organizations comprised of highly creative or highly educated employees. As a result, new paradigms for organizational structure are emerging. Team-based structures (also called lateral, cluster, or circle structures) are departmentalized with a flat span of control and little formalization. The work in these organizations is performed by self-directed work teams—cross-functional groups that work without typical management supervision. When teams work well, they can achieve synergy, producing products or ideas that are greater than those that could have been accomplished by the individuals alone. An increasing number of organizations are finding the team-based structure to be a flexible way to respond to the needs of the organization and to reduce the levels in the managerial hierarchy and their concomitant costs. Since self-directed work teams have more independence and self-determination than other types of groups in an organization, they can respond more quickly to the needs of the organization or process and make better informed decisions. However, team-based structures also require increased interpersonal communication skills and training. In addition, teams cannot merely be created by fiat; it takes time to develop a team that works well together. Further, the very flexible nature of team-based structures can also lead to role ambiguity, increased conflict, and more stress for the team members.

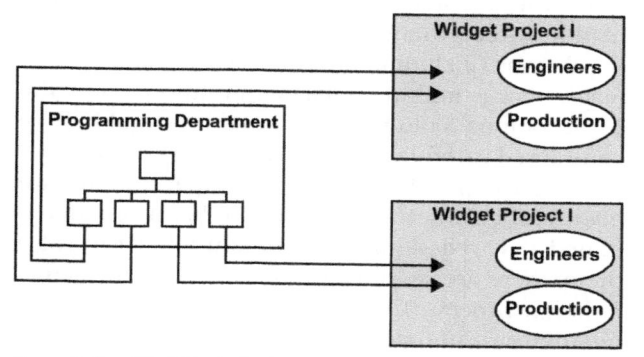

Figure 2: Simplified Matrix Design

Organizations can also be structured around a network of affiliates that together create a product or serve a client base. For example, a network structure (also called a modular or lattice structure) may be a useful form for an accounting firm, marketing firm, product development firm, and manufacturing firm that all work together. In the network structure, the emphasis is on creating value for the organization, focusing on customer-centered activities that enhance the value of processes and products rather than on management induced activities that do not. The various units in the network organization form alliances or partnerships to meet organizational needs. Communication in the network organization flows not only vertically along the lines of command, but horizontally between the work units. This approach to organizational structure is particularly appropriate in multinational companies that do a significant amount of communication electronically.

Another contemporary approach to organization design in the twenty-first century is the virtual organization. The virtual organization is actually an association of multiple organizations that are allied for the purpose of product development or serving a client. For example, large government contracts such as ship design and development are often bid by such alliances, since it is difficult for any one organization to have all the skills necessary to develop a complex weapons system from cradle to grave. By joining together to form a product team, however, normally separate engineering, shipbuilding, and training companies (among others) can create a temporary organization that will meet all the customer's needs. Virtual organizations usually consist of a prime contractor that performs most of the work and leads the team, and a number of subcontractors that may change as the needs of the project demand.

Redesigning the Organization
A running joke in many organizations is that when managers do not know how to solve its problems, they reorganize. Sometimes reorganization is merely the business equivalent of rearranging the deckchairs on the *Titanic*: a way to look like one is doing something while ignoring the bigger, harder problem. However, reorganization also can be a legitimate effort. The goals and operations of organizations change as does the marketplace in which they operate. In order to stay competitive, there are occasions when the organization needs to reinvent and reorganize itself in order to be more competitive in the marketplace. For example, when adding operations in a different country, a very hierarchical, centralized structure more than likely will need to be changed. In such situations, managers on the ground need the empowerment to make decisions appropriate to the new location without first asking permission from a corporate headquarters located in a country with a different culture and legal and economic systems. However, reorganization is not something to be taken lightly. It is a costly undertaking not only in terms of the time it takes to design and implement the new structure, but in terms of the impact on employees and their ability to perform and contribute to the success of the organization. In most reorganizations, there are losers: those whose jobs were downsized, from whom power was

taken, or who are now forced to form a new work team. This new reality can result not only in a situation where the employees must learn a new way of doing something or where they need to bond into a new work team, but also can result in employee dissatisfaction or a nonsupportive work environment. The pros and cons of any contemplated reorganization must be carefully considered and weighed to determine whether or not a reorganization is appropriate.

Before embarking on the process of reorganization, the management team should consider several things. First, reorganization should be done as part of the organization's ongoing strategic planning process. Reorganization should not be attempted unless it would significantly improve the organization's competitive edge. However, different market segments such as separate product lines or operations in different countries frequently benefit from being structured so that they receive sufficient management attention and do not compete with each other. For example, a company manufacturing two products might want to organize itself around the two product lines rather than having each in the same reporting structure. Similarly, it may be strategically advantageous to have different reporting structures for operations that are located in different countries (see figure 3). Organizational redesign should be structured so that the corporate headquarters supports the various operations of the organization rather than makes their tasks more difficult by imposing unreasonable reporting structures or not giving them sufficient management attention to support their success in the marketplace.

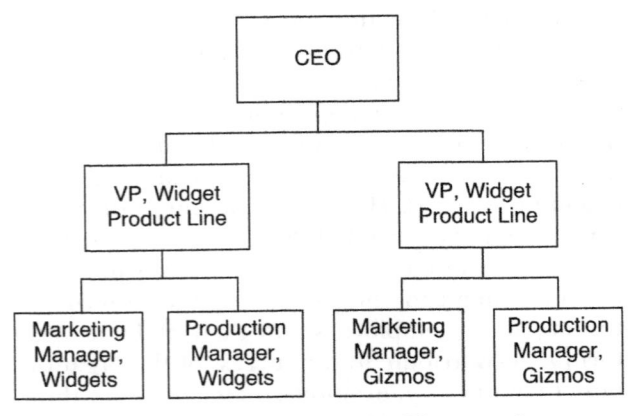

Figure 3: Simplified organizational chart showing different reporting structure

The design of an organization should exploit the strengths of its human capital. For example, an organization that employs a significant number of professional workers involved in a creative process (e.g., engineers) should take care not to impose too many strictures on their ability to do their jobs. Such employees need to be able to make decisions on the local level rather than going through a complex chain of command. On the other hand, it is also important that each function within the organization is manageable. If one cannot find competent managers for a given function in a proposed reorganization scheme, the system probably needs to be redesigned. Other constraints that may affect the feasibility of an organizational redesign include the interests of the organization's stakeholders, the ability of the information systems to support the structure, government regulations (including international regulations that may affect a multinational organization), and the organizational culture. Such variables should all be considered carefully before a redesign is attempted.

Once the problems facing the organization have been sufficiently analyzed and it has been determined that redesigning the organization will solve them, there are several considerations for the actual redesign process. One consideration is whether or not there are any groups within the organization with special cultures that need to be separated from the other groups. For example, although marketing functions can fall within product lines, they often are a separate function because of their different tasks and attitudes. Similarly, a new product development laboratory might need to be put in as a separate function so that it is not influenced by the way current products are designed. A related consideration concerns the ease of coordination between groups within the organization. For example, if coordinating the functions of a given product line that has operations in two separate countries is too difficult, it might make more sense to separate them organizationally and not just geographically.

Another consideration that needs to be taken into account, particularly in decentralized organizations, is whether there is sufficient accountability built into the organization design. In particular, it is important to look at the proposed organizational structure to determine if multiple groups have shared responsibilities. In such instances, it is easy for problems to arise when one group assumes that the other will accomplish the task or blames the other group for its own failure. In addition, it is important to determine how groups whose performance is difficult to measure will be held accountable. For example, it is not necessarily reasonable to expect a new product development group to create 20 viable new product ideas a quarter. On the other hand, it is important to ensure that the group is doing its best to produce new ideas. Finally, the organization design should be flexible enough to accommodate the organization's needs in the future. An organizational structure that cannot do so is not going to be useful for supporting organizational effectiveness and success in the long run. However, molding the structure of an organization can be a continuing process as the needs of the organization and the marketplace change. For the organization to continue to meet the challenges of the future, it is important that the structure be adapted to support those needs as necessary.

Bibliography

Csaszar, Felipe A. "An Efficient Frontier in Organization Design: Organizational Structure as a Determinant of Exploration and Exploitation." *Organization Science* 24, no. 4 (2013): 1083–1101. Web. 31 Oct. 2013.

Friesen, G. B. "Organization Design for the 21st Century." *Consulting to Management* 16, no. 3 (2005): 32–51. Web. 3 Apr. 2007.

Goold, Michael, and Andrew Campbell. "Do You Have a Well-Designed Organization?" *Harvard Business Review* 80, no. 3 (2002): 117–34. Web. 3 Apr. 2007.

Hearn, Sung-Nyun, and Injun Choi. "Creating a Process and Organization Fit Index: An Approach toward Optimal Process and Organization Design." *Knowledge & Process Management* 20, no. 1 (2013): 21–29. Web. 31 Oct. 2013.

McShane, Steven L., and Mary Ann Von Glinow. *Organizational Behavior: Emerging Realities for the Workplace Revolution.* 2nd ed. Boston: McGraw-Hill/Irwin, 2003.

Miozzo, Marcela, Mark Lehrer, Robert DeFillippi, et al. "Economies of Scope through Multi-unit Skill Systems: The Organization of Large Design Firms." *British Journal of Management* 23, no. 2 (2012): 145–64. Web. 31 Oct. 2013.

Worren, Nicolay. "Hitting the Sweet Spot between Separation and Integration in Organization Design." *People & Strategy* 34, no. 2 (2011): 24–30. Web. 31 Oct. 2013.

Suggested Reading

Brusoni, Stefano, and Andrea Prencipe. "Making Design Rules: A Multidomain Perspective." *Organization Science* 17, no. 2 (2006): 179–89. Web. 3 Apr. 2007.

Child, John, and Rita McGrath. "Organizations Unfettered: Organization Form in an Information-Intensive Economy." *Academy of Management Journal* 44, no. 6 (2001): 1135–48. Web. 3 Apr. 2007.

Dunbar, Roger L. M., and William H. Starbuck. "Learning to Design Organizations and Learning from Designing Them." *Organization Science* 17, no. 2 (2006): 171–78. Web. 3 Apr. 2007.

Harris, Milton, and Artur Raviv. "Organization Design." *Management Science* 48, no. 7 (2002): 852–65. Web. 3 Apr. 2007.

Muchinsky, Paul M. *Psychology Applied to Work: An Introduction to Industrial and Organizational Psychology.* 7th ed. Belmont, CA: Thomson/Wadsworth, 2003.

Ruth A. Wienclaw, Ph.D.

Organization Development

Abstract

Organization development is a long-range effort to improve an organization's problem-solving and renewal processes. Organization development involves the application of behavior science knowledge to the problems of the workplace. Organization development consultants tend to look at the organization as a symptom and diagnose not only obvious symptoms, but deeper, more systemic problems. The organization development process comprises multiple steps, tends to be long term, and often includes multiple iterations of the diagnosis, planning, action, and stabilization/evaluation steps. Organization development interventions are typically more successful if carried out by an external consultant as change agent.

OVERVIEW

Each generation brings with it new technologies and new challenges. From a business perspective, organizations need to adapt and change to meet the changing needs and demands of the marketplace, or fail. Organization development is a long-range effort to improve the organization's problem-solving and renewal processes. Organization development involves the application of behavioral science knowledge to the problems of the workplace. Sometimes the changes that need to be made in an organization are relatively simple, even obvious. For example, most modern businesses need to have a presence on the web in order to be taken seriously by potential customers. Other changes are less simple to implement. For example, although it may be obvious to most observers that an organization needs to computerize its inventory, the ramifications of this change may be widespread and complex. The organization will have to hire someone to design the system, install it, and input the inventory data into the new system. The human resources department will need to develop or contract training for the people using the new inventory system. Old procedures will need to be updated to take into account the new procedures and their requirements. These challenges illustrate the nature of the organization as a system: changes in one part of the system result in changes in the other parts of the system as well.

Organizational Culture: The Informal Organization

Although the installation of a new inventory database system can be a complex task involving most (if not all) of the organization, other changes can be even more complex, such as those that attempt to change the organization's culture or norms. French and Bell (1973) use the metaphor of an iceberg to describe the nature of an organization (see figure 1). According to this theory, an organization comprises both a formal organization and an informal organization. When a symptom arises in an organization, it may be due to problems in the formal organization, the informal organization, or both. Like an iceberg, the formal organization—that part of the organization that is easily observable (and more easily fixable)—represents only a small portion of the organization as a whole. The formal organization comprises the goals of the organization, the structure of the organization (i.e., the design of an organization including its division of labor, delegation of authority, and span of control), the skills of its employees, the technology it employs, and the resources it has to accomplish its tasks. The example of the need to install a computerized inventory system is an example of an intervention within the formal organization.

However, as illustrated in figure 1, like an iceberg, the majority of the organization is harder to see and diagnose. The informal organization comprises such things as attitudes, values, feelings, interactions, and group norms that are more difficult to deal with than the aspects of the formal organization. Often, problems that appear to be part of the formal organization may in fact be related to the informal organization or may be a combination of problems in both the formal and the informal organization. Therefore, it is important for the organization's organization development practitioner to separate the symptoms the organization is experiencing from the underlying problems. Although some organizational problems (such as the example of the need to implement a new inventory database) are obvious and relatively straightforward to fix, others are more systemic and thus more difficult to diagnose. There are many symptoms for which an organization requires an organization development intervention. For example, communication or intra- or interteam conflict is frequently cited as a problem in many organizations. Similarly, managerial strategies are often found to be ineffective or onerous by those who must live under them. Other obvious symptoms of organizational problems include:

- Lack of motivation on the part of the worker,
- Lack of clear or functional structure or roles within the organization,
- Problems with the organizational climate, or
- Problems stemming from cultural norms.

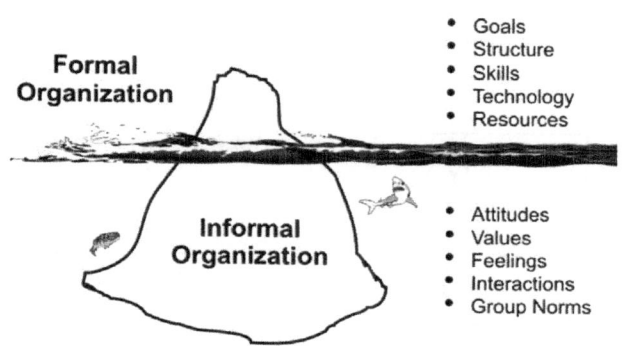

Figure 1: The formal and informal organization (adapted from French and Bell 1973)

- Goals
- Structure
- Skills
- Technology
- Resources

- Attitudes
- Values
- Feelings
- Interactions
- Group Norms

Formal Organization

Informal Organization

There are some situations where organization development interventions should be considered, such as the need to perform strategic planning or cope with a merger. However, for the most part, these are only symptoms. The problems underlying these symptoms are often not the same. Communication problems, for example, might occur because the organization has set two or more groups in competition with each other, and they need to compete for scarce resources. Apparent lack of motivation may be the result of inadequate control, lack of training, or unfair or inadequate rewards. Part of the job of the organization development consultant is to determine what underlying problems are responsible for the symptoms being experienced by the organization.

FURTHER INSIGHTS

The Organization Development Consultant/Change Agent

Although for the most part, organizations employ their own organization development staff, for organization development to be effective requires an outside change agent. This person, who is external to the organization, guides an organization through a change effort. To be effective, change agents need to have knowledge of how to conduct a change effort, an understanding of the organization, and sufficient power to be able to implement the change. There are a number of reasons why an external change agent is more likely than an internal change agent with the same credentials to accomplish change successfully within an organization. External consultants typically have a more clear-cut role than do internal consultants. When an external consultant is hired to do organization development for an organization, it is typically with the understanding that his or her purview comprises the activities associated with organization development and not with other organizational tasks or objectives. If the external change agent is properly introduced into the organization, everyone will know what purpose this individual serves. An internal consultant, on the other hand, typically has more difficulty articulating his or her role within the organization. Although organization development may be part of the internal consultant's role, she or he will often be called upon to perform other human resources activities as well. These demands make it more difficult for the organization to see an internal consultant as an expert. It also makes it less likely that the affected employees will be as open with an internal consultant as with an external one, because they will tend to see him or her as part of the organizational hierarchy with loyalties to management rather than to the employees.

External consultants are more likely to be effective as organization development change agents because they are less affected by organizational norms than internal consultants. Whereas internal consultants are more ready to accept the organizational system as given, external consultants are more likely to be able to look at the organization objectively and see problems in areas that an internal consultant might take for granted. An external consultant is also freer to look at the organization from a larger, systems view while an internal consultant is more likely to focus on a micro view of the organization. It is essential that an organization development consultant consider the problems in both the formal and the informal organization and recognize that changing the organization in one area is likely to have a direct or indirect effect on other areas. An internal consultant, however, often is either (a) unable to have that degree of objectivity because she or he is part of the system or (b) is only tasked with very circumscribed activities because she or he is a direct employee of the organization. For example, if the organization is experiencing difficulties in communication, an internal consultant might be tasked with developing and conducting a training course in communication skills. An external consultant, given the same set of symptoms, would more than likely look at the system as a whole and might find out that the communication problem was only a symptom of a deeper underlying problem such as conflict over scarce resources or differing norms between groups. The internal consultant is unlikely to be able to successfully address this problem because she or he has only been tasked with giving a training course. Finally, external consultants typically have easier access to upper-level management in the organization. Since the support of upper-level management is essential for the success of organization development interventions, this makes external consultants more likely to be successful. Internal consultants, on the other hand, are part of the system that they are trying to change. Since they are unlikely to have the same access to upper-level management as an external consultant, they are less likely to have the support necessary to ensure the success of their interventions. As a result, internal consultants typically spend little effort toward organizational renewal, whereas external consultants are free to do so.

ORGANIZATION DEVELOPMENT PROCESSES

Scouting

Organization development is a multistage process (see figure 2). The first step for both the consultant and the organization is scouting, a mutual exploration between the two parties to determine whether or not they can work together. Sometimes, for example, the organization development consultant may not have experience or interest in the type of intervention needed by the organization. In other cases, the organization may be unable or unwilling to guarantee the support and resources necessary to ensure that change will occur. In order for the organization development intervention to be successful, the organization must be willing to implement the changes suggested by the organization development consultant based on the research. Key management within the organization (especially at top organizational levels) must be involved in the change process. Further, those persons who will be affected by the change must be brought on board as soon as possible, and any persons involved must be informed about the change, the reasons for it, and rationale to implement it. If the organization cannot make these assurances, it is unlikely that the intervention will be successful.

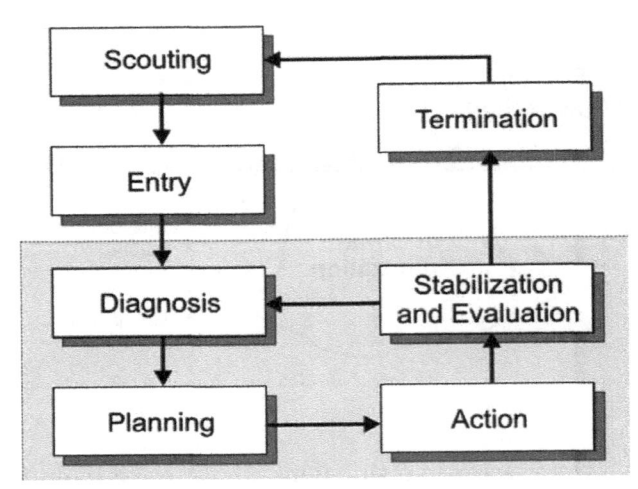

Figure 2: Stages in an Organization Development Intervention

Entry

If the organization and the consultant mutually decide that working together would be beneficial, they move into the entry stage. During this time, the two parties set roles for the desired change, share expectations for the results of the organization development intervention, establish a commitment (typically through contractual arrangement), and establish an effective power base to help ensure that the intervention will be effective.

Diagnosis

The next stage is diagnosis. During this stage, the organization development consultant looks at the problems as perceived by the client. Although these are typically symptoms rather than underlying problems, this place is usually the most reasonable starting point for an intervention. In addition, the change agent at this point will look at the goals of the client and determine how best to meet them. This determination will take into consideration both the resources and commitment of the client to the organization development intervention and change process as well as the resources of the consultant.

There are a number of methods that are applied by organization development consultants to aid in the diagnostic process. One of the most frequently used is the questionnaire, used in the context of the survey research feedback methodology (see figure 3). This type of research collects data about the opinions, attitudes, or reactions of the members of a sample using a survey instrument. The phases of survey research are goal setting, planning, implementation, evaluation, and feedback. As opposed to experimental research, survey research does not allow for the manipulation of an independent variable. The questionnaire or survey used in this technique comprises a data collection instrument designed to acquire information on the opinions, attitudes, or reactions of people. The consultant may choose to survey all employees using this instrument or may select a sample of workers who are asked questions concerning their opinions, attitudes, or reactions, which are gathered using a survey instrument or questionnaire for purposes of scientific analysis.

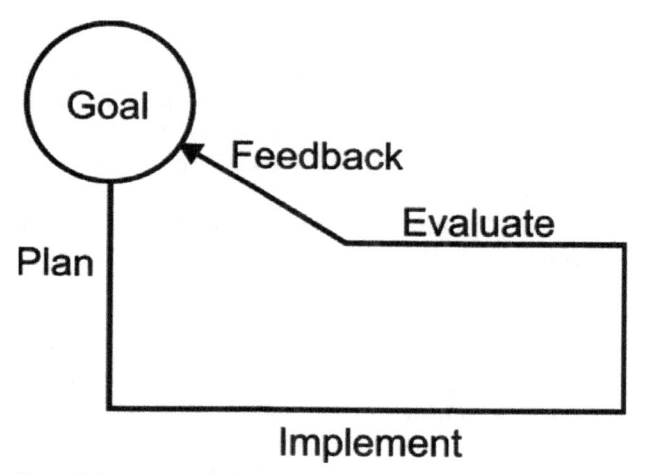

Figure 3: Survey research feedback methodology

In addition to surveys, the organization development consultant may conduct interviews with key individuals across the organization. For example, there are typically individuals who better understand the causes of various symptoms and problems, who can better articulate these, or who are informal leaders within the organization. The organization development consultant often includes his or her personal observations of the organization. Fruitful sources of such observations come from staff meetings, interdepartmental memos, and other records of communication.

Another source of data that is useful in making a diagnosis of problems is objective data which can include such statistics as absenteeism, turnover, antiorganizational behavior, production rates, reject rates, or union activity. Similarly, outside opinions of the organization from customers, clients, and competitors can also be useful in determining underlying problems. Another useful tool for diagnosing problems within the organization is the confrontation meeting. The purpose of confrontation meetings is to tap management resources within the organization and to apply these to solving the organization's problems. To conduct a confrontation meeting, the change agent starts by establishing the proper climate for the meeting by articulating the goals, philosophy, and other ground rules for conduct of the meeting. She or he then describes the task that the group is to undertake. At this point, the consultant emphasizes the need for problem solving and brainstorming skills. The meeting then breaks into working subgroups that are usually composed of members from different levels and sections within the organization. These subgroups then identify the major problems facing the organization and come back together to discuss and categorize the problems that were identified. These problems may then be assigned to various subgroups for further study and analysis.

Planning, Action & Stabilization

Once the problem has been diagnosed, the next step in the organization development process is to plan the intervention. At this point, the decision needs to be made as to whether the intervention should be systemwide or only implemented at certain levels. Once the nature and scope of the intervention has been determined, the next step in the organization development process is to implement it. The consultant next works with the organization to stabilize the change so that it becomes internalized. Once this change has happened and the change state becomes the status quo, the consultant then evaluates the effectiveness of the change in solving the problem of the organization. At this point, if it is determined that further action it is necessary, the organization development process then continues with further diagnosis, planning, action, and stabilization. Eventually, when it is determined that the underlying problem has been adequately addressed and that the change process has been internalized within the organization, the consultant and the organization dissolve their relationship.

CONCLUSION

Organization development is more than management consulting. It is the application of behavioral science knowledge to the problems of the workplace. Organization development is a long-range effort to improve the organization's problem solving and renewal processes and often takes more than one iteration before the underlying problem is properly diagnosed and adequately addressed. Although some organizations have internal organization development consultants on staff, in general, an external change agent is more likely to accomplish the long-term change desired by the organization. Properly applied, the organization development process can be very effective in diagnosing and fixing deep or systemic problems in the organization.

Bibliography

Anderson, Donald L. "Organization Development Interventions and Four Targets of Post-Acquisition Integration." *Organization Development Practitioner* 44, no. 3 (2012): 19–24. Web. 27 Nov. 2013.

French, Wendell. "Organization Development, Objectives, Assumptions and Strategies." *California Management Review* 12, no. 2 (1969): 23–34. Web. 27 Apr. 2010.

French, Wendell L. and Bell, Cecil H., Jr. *Organization Development: Behavioral Science Interventions for Organization Improvement*. Englewood Cliffs, NJ: Prentice-Hall, 1973.

Nicholas, John M. "The Comparative Impact of Organization Development Interventions on Hard Criteria Measures." *Academy of Management Review* 7, no. 4 (1982): 531–42. Web. 27 Apr. 2010.

Rao, T.V., and S.S. Ramnarayan. *Organization Development: Accelerating Learning and Transformation*. New Delhi, India: SAGE/Response Business Books, 2011.

Yaeger, Therese F. Peter F. Sorensen, and Homer H. Johnson. *Critical Issues in Organization Development: Case Studies for Analysis and Discussion*. Charlotte, NC: Information Age Pub., Inc., 2013.

Suggested Reading

Akdere, Mesut, and B.A. Altman. "An Organization Development Framework in Decision Making: Implications for Practice." *Organization Development Journal* 27, no. 4 (2009): 47–56. Web. 27 Apr. 2010.

Bate, Paul, Raza Khan, and Annie J. Pyle. "Culturally Sensitive Structuring: An Action Research-Based Approach to Organization Development and Design." *Public Administration Quarterly* 23, no. 4 (2000): 445–70. Web. 27 Apr. 2010.

Burke, W. Warner, and Allan H. Church. "Managing Change, Leadership Style, and Intolerance to Ambiguity: A Survey of Organization Development Practitioners." *Human Resource Management* 31, no. 4 (1992): 301–18. Web. 27 Apr. 2010.

Chattopadhyay, Samnath, and Udai Pareek. "Organization Development in a Voluntary Organization." *International Studies of Management and Organization* 14, nos. 2–3 (1984): 46–85. Web. 27 Apr. 2010.

Cobb, Anthony T., and Newton Margulies. "Organization Development: A Political Perspective." *Academy of Management Review* 6, no. 1 (1981): 49–59. Web. 27 Apr. 2010.

Dahl, J.G., and A.M. Glassman. "Public Sector Contracting: The Next 'Growth Industry' for Organization Development?" *Public Administration Quarterly* 14, no. 4 (1991): 483–97. Web. 27 Apr. 2010.

Deaner, C.M. Dick, and Kathryn Miller. "Our Practice of Organization Development: A Work in Progress." *Public Administration Quarterly* 23, no. 2 (1999): 139–51. Web. 27 Apr. 2010.

Gabris, Gerald T., and Jack King. "Making Management Training More Effective and Credible through Organization Development: Results in One City." *Public Administration Quarterly* 13, no. 2 (1989): 215–31. Web. 27 Apr. 2010.

Huse, Edgar H. "Organization Development." *Personnel and Guidance Journal* 56, no. 7 (1978): 403–6. Web. 27 Apr. 2010.

Jaeger, Alfred M. "Organization Development and National Culture: Where's the Fit?" *Academy of Management Review* 11, no. 1 (1986, Jan.): 178–90. Web. 27 Apr. 2010.

Lau, Chung-Ming, and Hang-Yue Ngo. "Organization Development and Firm Performance: A Comparison of Multinational and Local Firms." *Journal of International Business Studies* 32, no. 1 (2001): 95–114. Web. 27 Apr. 2010.

Marshak, Robert J., and David Grant. "Organizational Discourse and New Organization Development Practices." *British Journal of Management* 1, no. 19 (2008): S7–S19. Web. 27 Apr. 2010.

McDonagh, Joe, and David Coghlan. "Information Technology and the Lure of Integrated Change: A Neglected Role for Organization Development?" *Public Administration Quarterly* 30, nos. 1–2 (2006): 22–55.

Miranda, Shaila, and Carol Saunders. "Group Support Systems: An Organization Development Intervention to Combat Groupthink." *Public Administration Quarterly* 19, no. 2 (1995): 193–216. Web. 27 Apr. 2010.

Porras, Jerry I., and P.O. Berg. "The Impact of Organization Development." *Academy of Management Review* 3, no. 2 (1978): 249–66. Web. 27 Apr. 2010.

Sanchez, Marisa. "Maturing toward Enterprise Organization Development Capability." *Organization Development Practitioner* 45, no. 4 (2013): 49–54. Web. 27 Nov. 2013.

Sinzgiri, Jyotsna, and Jonathan Z. Gottlieb. "Philosophic and Pragmatic Influences on the Practice of Organization Development, 1950-2000." *Organizational Dynamics* 21, no. 2 (1992): 57–69. Web. 27 Apr. 2010.

Terpstra, David E. "The Organization Development Evaluation Process: Some Problems and Proposals." *Human Resource Management* 20, no. 1 (1981): 24–29. Web. 27 Apr. 2010.

Umstot, Denis D. "Organization Development Technology and the Military: A Surprising Merger?" *Academy of Management Review* 5, no. 2 (1980): 189–202. Web. 27 Apr. 2010.

White, B. Joseph, and V.J. Ramsey. "Some Unintended Consequence of 'Top Down' Organization Development." *Human Resource Management* 17, no. 2 (1978): 7–14. Web. 27 Apr. 2010.

White, J.D. "Phenomenology and Organization Development." *Public Administration Quarterly* 14, no. 1 (1990): 76–85. Web. 27 Apr. 2010.

Ruth A. Wienclaw, Ph.D.

Organizational Behavior

ABSTRACT

Organizational behavior is the study of the functioning and performance of individuals, groups, and teams within organizations as well as of organizations as a whole. Based on scientific research and empirical data, organizational behavioral theorists attempt to understand, predict, and influence behavior at all levels within the organization. There are many practical applications of organizational behavior theory for managers. For example, at the individual level, organizational behavior theory can help managers learn to be better leaders and communicate with and motivate their workers. At a team level, organizational behavior theory helps managers understand how teams are formed and function, and how to best support them so that synergy occurs. At the organizational level, organizational behavior theory can help managers better understand how the organization works and how each subsystem within it works together to make up the organization as a whole.

OVERVIEW

Organizational behavior is the systematic study and application of how individuals and groups think and act within organizations and how these activities affect the effectiveness of the organization as a whole. Organizational behavior theorists take a systems approach, looking not only at individuals or groups as isolated entities, but also as part of an interactive social system in which the actions of one part influence the functioning of another. Rather than merely focusing on the profitability of the organization in isolation, the discipline of organizational behavior attempts to improve organizational effectiveness at all levels within the organization. To accomplish this goal, organizational behavior theorists attempt to understand, predict, and influence events on the individual, group, and organizational levels.

The field of organizational behavior is based on several principles. First, organizational behavior theory and practice does not operate in isolation, but is multidisciplinary, drawing on the insights arising not only from its own research but also the research and insights of other disciplines. For example, psychology has contributed to organizational behavior theory by helping explain issues relating to individual and interpersonal behavior, as well as the dynamics of groups and teams. Sociology has contributed to the knowledge of organizational behavior by increasing the understanding of how groups and teams act and interact, working together to contribute to

Businessmen mingle (Image courtesy of Guiga7777)

the functioning of the organization as a social system. Anthropology contributes understanding of culture and rituals, while political science helps us understand conflict between groups as well as organizational environments, power, and decision making. Newer disciplines, such as information systems theory, help organizational behavior theorists understand the dynamics of teams, how organizations manage knowledge, and how decisions are made.

Just as the disciplines from which it gathers insights are based on empirical evidence, organizational behavior applies the scientific method in an attempt to systematically study the actions and interactions of individuals and teams within an organization. The scientific method involves observing behavior within organizations, formulating a theory based on the observations to explain why the behavior occurs, experimenting and collecting data to determine the truth of a hypothesis, and validating or modifying the hypothesis as appropriate. This process differs from some early management theorists who often took lessons learned in isolated situations (such as the success of one large manufacturing company) and turned them into a list of simple steps to follow for success in all businesses. Currently, organizational behavior theory takes a contingency approach which assumes that an action does not necessarily always have the same consequences, and may result in a different reaction in different situations. What this approach means practically is that one solution is not universally the best and behavior cannot be distilled into simple lists of steps that ensure success. In general, it has been found that seemingly absolute or universal rules need to be tempered by too many exceptions. For example, in the study of leadership, researchers and practitioners alike have found that there is no one best way to lead, but that the "ideal" management style is contingent on the needs, abilities, and personalities of both the employees performing the tasks and of their leader or manager. Because of real world experiences, organizational behavior theorists tend to temper their theories by trying to better understand when and why a principle works and by not stating absolutes. One of the reasons that it is necessary to take a contingency approach when trying to understand behavior in organizations is that organizations are systems comprised of numerous subsystems. The functioning of each subsystem impacts the functioning of the other subsystems.

In addition to the contingency approach, organizational behavior theory is founded on systems theory. In this approach, the organization is viewed as a system made up of interdependent subsystems, each of which affects the effectiveness of the other as well as the effectiveness of the organization as a whole. For example, a strike by one segment of workers in an organization negatively impacts the ability of the organization as a whole to meet its objectives whether to efficiently collect garbage, transport passengers, or produce auto parts. However, systems theory affects organizations in less obvious ways. For example, when writing a proposal for a new contract, if one work group fails to meet its deadline for writing the technical response, a budget cannot be developed to submit to the prospective client and the production of a professional proposal cannot be done in a timely manner. If enough of these small actions with negative impacts occur, the organization will not win the contract. This situation, in turn, could affect the profitability and even the viability of the organization and, along with it, the jobs and lives of the individuals and teams in the company. Each subsystem (technical work group, accounting or costing group, and proposal production group) affects the ability of the other groups—as well as of the organization in general—to do their jobs. Although such insights are interesting in the abstract, organizational behavior is a practical discipline that not only attempts to understand and predict behavior but also to influence it. To this end, organizational behavior theorists have made significant contributions to management theory and practice.

APPLICATIONS

The field of organizational behavior is concerned with all three levels of functioning within the organization: individual, groups and teams, and the organization as a whole. At the individual level, organizational theorists study the characteristics, thought processes, and behaviors of employees. This subset of organizational behavior includes analyzing employees' personality, motivation, roles, and cultural differences and ways these elements affect their behavior and interactions within the organization. Understanding these processes prepares the manager to better motivate individuals and help them reach their full potential within the organization. At the team level, organizational behavior theorists look at such concepts as what distinguishes a team from a group, what processes are involved in the formation of a team, how leadership arises within a team, and the best way to manage teams. At the organizational level, theorists examine how the actions of individuals and teams affect the organization and its effectiveness, as well as how the organization interacts with the greater culture and society.

Individual Behavior
When setting up a new organization, there are many considerations that impact how it will be structured. For example, a computer software development firm will need programmers through necessity. The number and type of employees needed will depend on what products the firm is trying to deliver and what level of work is sustainable. If these employees could work completely on their own, they would each be able to do their jobs however they wish. For example, Harvey may like to start at noon and work through the evening or keep his work area in a constant state of controlled chaos while Chuck may be a morning person who keeps everything in its place. If they could work alone, these differences would not be a problem. In reality, however, people typically do not work in isolation and individual differences in work style, ability to communicate, and desire to be in charge can bring about clashes. Harvey and Chuck may need to share an office and reach an accommodation about how best to work together. Or, the programmer must depend on input from the designer and must also coordinate with other programmers working on other parts of the project. She or he may also be called on to demonstrate the new software to potential customers or work with marketing personnel to support efforts to maintain and increase the company's market share. One of the roles of the manager in an organization is to help minimize such differences, utilizing the abilities of the workers to meet the needs of the organization and supporting the needs of the workers with the resources of the organization. Organizational behavior theorists examine many aspects of human behavior in order to help understand, predict, and control how people act and interact in the workplace.

One practical application of the knowledge of individual differences is situational leadership theory. In this approach to leadership, theorists state that effective leaders change the style of their leadership depending on the ability and even the personality of the people they are trying to lead. For example, in cases where the workers do not have sufficient knowledge of how to do the job, the leader typically must be more directive than in situations where the workers are highly skilled and experienced. Similarly, the contingency leadership model suggests that effective leadership depends on whether the leader's style is appropriate to the situation. For example, a leader who prefers to tell people what to do will not be successful in a situation where a team works best through synergy; piggybacking ideas off each other and developing a product or idea may be greater than what they could have done alone.

Another area, in which organizational behavioral theorists are interested, regarding the effects of individual differences and their impact on management effectiveness, is employee motivation. Motivation is the study of the needs and thought processes that determine a person's behavior. Understanding what motivates a person can help a manager better reward that person for behavior that contributes to achieving the objectives of the organization. For example, if a worker is motivated by money, a manager can use the possibility of raises or bonuses to motivate the desired behavior. On the other hand, if the worker is motivated by status or power, a promotion or corner office may offer a greater incentive for desired behavior.

There are two general approaches to motivation considered by organizational theorists. Content theories of motivation examine the dynamics of people's needs, and use these to explain why the same person may be motivated differently at different times. Process theories of motivation, on the other hand, examine the processes by which needs are translated into behavior. These theories help both organizational theorists and managers better understand, predict, and influence the performance of employees. In addition to idiosyncratic differences between people based on individual personality types and preferences, organizational behavior theorists and managers alike are concerned with individual differences between people based on their cultures. Certainly, it is important not to offend others in the course of getting a task done, but this issue goes deeper. Different cultures have different ways of doing things, and unless these differences are understood and accommodated, motivating the worker and meeting organizational objectives will be more difficult than necessary. For example, when communicating, most women prefer to make eye contact with the person to whom they are speaking and tend to devote their full attention to the conversation. Many men, on the other hand, do not expect these things in a conversation and often multitask while talking. This difference can lead to miscommunication and conflict when variations in communication styles result in situations where people believe that they are not being listened to or not being taken seriously. In another example, in the Japanese culture one must be able to not only understand what the other person is saying, but to also correctly understand the nonverbal cues that accompany the verbal part of the communication. For example, in order to be polite, Japanese businesspersons may say what they think the other person wants to hear—such as saying that they will give serious consideration to a proposal—while giving nonverbal cues that say that they have already rejected the other person's idea. Each culture has its own subtleties of communication. Such differences must be understood in order to facilitate effective communication so that organizational goals can be met.

Team Behavior & Processes
An increasing amount of contemporary work is performed by teams rather than by groups or individuals. Although some tasks are better performed by the single individual working alone, organizations are finding that many tasks are better accomplished through teamwork. There are several differences between a team and a group of individuals working together. Whereas the group may have a common goal (e.g., complete 100 new widgets before the close of business), work teams tend to develop their own mission and their members become vested in accomplishing it. Therefore, although both groups and teams may be accountable to a manager, team members are also accountable to each other for getting their part of the work done. Therefore, in work groups, leadership is typically held by a single person, whereas in a team, all members tend to share leadership. Another major difference between groups and teams is that groups do not have a stable culture; as a result, conflict frequently arises. True teams, on the other hand, have a collaborative culture in which the team members trust each other. As a result, work groups may or may not accomplish their goals whereas true teams tend to achieve synergy, producing products or ideas that are greater than those that could have been accomplished by the individuals alone.

Not all teams are created equally, however. Organizational behavior theorists have observed four different types of teams: manager-led work teams, self-managing work teams, self-designed work teams, and self-governing work teams. In the manager-led work team, the manger is responsible for the design of the organizational context of the team's activities as well as the design of the team performing the work. Although the team itself is responsible for performing the work, the manager is responsible for monitoring and managing the performance of the team. In the self-managing work team, although the manager designs the organizational context of the team and the structure of the group, the team itself not only performs the task to be done but monitors and manages its performance. In the self-designing work team, the manager sets the organizational context within which the work must be performed, but the team organizes itself and specifies how it will perform this work. Finally, the self-governing work team performs all these tasks as well as designing the organizational context in which they occur. When the manager understands such underlying dynamics of team behavior, he or she can be better able to support the team and promote the synergy that is possible through team efforts.

Whether work is being performed in a work group or in a team setting, eventually conflicts will arise. Organizational behavior theorists study these aspects of the organization also, and help managers understand how best to minimize the negative impact of such situations. The key to conflict resolution often lies in understanding when it is best to be assertive and when it is best to be cooperative. The scientific observation of organizational behavior has led to several theories about what situations are best suited for various conflict resolution styles. For example, when each side knows that it has to work with the other and that the interests of both parties are important, collaboration (when both parties try to find a mutually beneficial solution to a shared problem) or compromise (when both parties give a little and get a little in return) are frequently the best approaches to conflict resolution. However, when one of the parties views the conflict as a win/lose situation, it is often necessary to compete. In other situations it may be best to accommodate the other person's desires in the short term in order to win a more important battle later on. Even avoidance—walking away from the problem—can be an effective way to manage conflict in the shortterm if it allows tempers to cool down and the parties to come back later and resolve the conflict.

Organizational Processes
In addition to the assumptions, values, and beliefs of the individual workers and the shared assumptions, values, and beliefs of work teams, it is important to understand the assumptions, values, and beliefs of the organization as an entity. Although one can learn about an organization from observing formal aspects like its goals, structure, and other resources, such data only gives part of the picture. To truly understand the organization, one also needs to understand the informal aspects of the organization—those things understood by the employees but that are not written down or formalized. These elements include attitudes, values, feelings, interactions, and norms. The differentiation between the aspects of the formal organization and the informal organization is often described as an iceberg, with the formal structures being equivalent to the ten percent of the iceberg that is observable above the waterline, but the real nature of the organization remains hidden beneath—not readily observable to the casual observer but requiring careful study and analysis. Organizational behavioral theorists and practitioners need to understand not only the easily observable aspects of the organization but also the organizational culture in order to truly understand the behaviors and processes that make the organization run. Although organizations can experience problems stemming from their formal structures and aspects, more often it is the aspects of its informal culture that can create problems. To be truly effective, a manager must understand not only the requirements set out in the formal organization but also those implied as part of the informal organization. Understanding the values of one's workers or team members, for example, will help the manager know better how to motivate them. Understanding their values and feelings will help the manager avoid destructive conflict or defuse conflict situations when they occur. Understanding how employees interact with each other and the informal norms of work teams will help the manager be better able to support their efforts and facilitate their synergy and contributions to organizational effectiveness.

BIBLIOGRAPHY
Daniela, Pipas M. "The Interdependence between Management, Communication, Organizational Behavior and Performance." *Annals of the University of Oradea*, Economic Science Series 22 no. 1 (2013): 1554–62. Web. 20 Nov. 2013.

De Ven, Andrew, and Arik Lifschitz. "Rational and Reasonable Microfoundations of Markets and Institutions." *Academy of Management Perspectives* 27, no. 2 (2013): 156–72. Web. 20 Nov. 2013.

McShane, Steven L., and Mary Ann Von Glinow. *Organizational Behavior: Emerging Realities for the Workplace Revolution*. 2nd ed. Boston: McGraw-Hill/Irwin, 2003.

Nahavandi, Afsaneh. "What Is a Team?" In *The Art and Science of Leadership*, edited by Afsaneh, Nahavandi. 2nd ed. Upper Saddle River, NJ: Prentice Hall, 2000.

Thompson, Leigh L. "What Kinds of Teams Are There?" In *Making the Team: A Guide for Managers*, edited by Leigh L. Thompson. Upper Saddle River, NJ: Prentice Hall, 2000.

Yuki, Gary. "Effective Leadership Behavior: What We Know and What Questions Need More Attention." *Academy of Management Perspectives* 26, no. 4 (2012): 66–85. Web. 20 Nov. 2013.

SUGGESTED READING
Eubanks, James L., C. Merle Johnson, William K. Redmon, and Thomas C. Mawhinney. "Chapter 14: Organizational Behavior Management and Organization Development: Potential Paths to Reciproaction." In *Handbook of Organizational Performance: Behavior Analysis and Management*. (2001): 367–90. Web. 23 Mar. 2007.

Johnson, C. Merle, Thomas C. Mawhinney, and William K. Redmon. "Chapter 1: Introduction to Organizational Performance: Behavior Analysis and Management." In *Handbook of Organizational Performance: Behavior Analysis and Management* (2001): 3–22. Web. 23 Mar. 2007.

Johnson, C. Merle, Thomas C. Mawhinney, and William K. Redmon. "Epilogue." In *Handbook of Organizational Performance: Behavior Analysis & Management*. (2001): 457–59. Web. 23 Mar. 2007.

O'Hara, Kirk, C. Merle Johnson, and Terry A. Beehr. "Organizational Behavior Management in the Private Sector: A Review of Empirical Research and Recommendations for Further Investigation." *Academy of Management Review* 10, no. 4 (1985): 848–64. Web. 23 Mar. 2007.

Raver, Jana L., Mark G. Ehrhart, and Ingrid C. Chadwick. "The Emergence of Team Helping Norms: Foundations within Members' Attributes and Behavior." *Journal of Organization Behavior* 33, no. 5 (2012): 616–37. Web. 20 Nov. 2013.

Wageman, Ruth. "Critical Success Factors for Creating Superb Self-Managing Teams." *Organizational Dynamics* 26, no. 1 (1997, Summer): 49–61. Web. 23 Mar. 2007.

Ruth A. Wienclaw, Ph.D.

Organizational Consulting

ABSTRACT

This article focuses on how organizational consultants use the concept of human performance technology to improve performance in an organization. In order to effectively make changes to the processes and structures, a change agent would need to have the ability to interpret various situations occurring within the organization. One field of study that evaluates how to effectively make change in people and systems is human performance technology. The goal of the human performance technology field is to use systems approaches to ensure that individuals have the knowledge, skills, motivation, and environmental support to do their jobs effectively and efficiently. Human performance technology (HPT) is important to the world's economic future because practitioners, such as organizational consultants, strive to provide organizations with solutions to their performance problems. An effective human performance technologist will use a systematic approach to improve the productivity and competence of the workforce so that organizations are able to compete in a global economy.

OVERVIEW

Organizations can be very complex. There will be times when the management team may decide the organization needs assistance with making changes throughout the different units in the company. As a result, individuals may be assigned to facilitate the change process. In order to effectively make changes to the processes and structures, a change agent would need to have the ability to interpret various situations occurring within the organization. "Reading" an organization requires one to be able to understand situations as they occur and know how to handle any problems that may occur. Skilled leaders and managers learn how to reading situations with various scenarios in mind in order to create appropriate actions based on their knowledge (Morgan 1995). One field of study that evaluates how to effectively make changes in people and systems is human performance technology. According to the International Society of Performance and Instruction (ISPI), human performance technology (HPT) can be described as "the systematic and systemic identification and removal of barriers to individual and organizational performance." The meaning of the concept can be broken down by each word in the phrase. "Human" refers to the individuals that make up the organization, and "Performance" implies that the activities of the employees can be assessed by measurable outcomes. "Technology" assumes that a systematic and systemic approach can be developed to resolve problems within the organization.

Human performance technology (HPT) draws from many academic disciplines such as psychology, instructional systems design, organizational development and human resources. The focus of the interdisciplinary field requires the practitioner to be able to (1) assess and analyze the performance gap between where the organization is and where it wants to go, (2) identify the causes for the performance gap, (3) make recommendations on how to close the gap and improve performance, (4) facilitate the change management process, and (5) evaluate the results to make sure that the desired change has occurred. The human performance technology field aims to ensure that the knowledge, skills, motivation and environmental support necessary for employees to complete their work successfully is available through a systems approach. According to Jacobs (1987), the conceptual domain of human performance technology can be defined by three key aspects:

1. Management functions—guides, controls and facilitates the development of human performance systems
2. Development functions—examines all aspects of a problem, relates results from a set of decisions to other decisions, and uses resources to develop performance systems
3. Systems functions—provides the conceptual means for viewing people, materials, events, and resources required to achieve goals

Performance tends to be measured in terms of quality, productivity, and cost. As a result, human performance is tied to the bottom line—organizational success. Both individual and organizational goals must be considered when implementing processes and policies that will improve performance. "Use of systems approaches to develop human performance systems is one of the most significant aspects of the field. The end result of using a systems approach is a combination of materials, events, peoples and strategies called a performance system. A performance system is the structure, within the work setting, in which people use resources and tools to perform their work. Human performance systems have five main components: (1) a job or context; (2) individual abilities, motivations, actions, decisions, and behavior; (3) responses required for performance; (4) consequences of the response; and (5) feedback on the consequences" (Jacobs 1987)

In summary, organizations may require the services of human performance technologists to facilitate changes, such as process improvement, within the company. These individuals will act as consultants to the organization as it charts a new course and direction. Armed with the concept of performance technology and performance systems, organizational consultants will be tasked with improving the bottom line of the company's initiatives so that it remains competitive.

APPLICATIONS

Human Performance Technologists as Organizational Consultants

Human performance technology is important to the world's economic future because practitioners such as organizational consultants strive to provide organizations with solutions to their performance problems. Human performance technology uses instructional technologies to improve individual performance so that organizational goals can be achieved. Being a good organizational consultant requires an individual to navigate the company through innovations, changes, and processes. An effective human performance technologist will use a systematic approach to improve the productivity and competence of the workforce so that organizations are able to compete in a global economy. According to Morgan (1995), these individuals must (1) have the capacity to remain open and flexible, (2) reserve judgment until all facts are known, and (3) gain new insight by viewing situations from different angles. These skills are required of both the internal and external organizational consultants.

Guiding Principles

In order to differentiate the concept from other disciplines, ISPI has developed a set of principles for human performance technologists to follow when assisting organizations in managing change. The principles are:

1. Human performance technology focuses on outcomes. If an organization focuses on outcomes, the consultant may use tools that support obtaining data to determine whether or not a process is effective and whether the employees share the same vision and goals. In addition, outcomes can measure whether or not the performance gap has been closed.

2. Human performance technology takes a systems view. There is a need to implement an approach that analyzes the performance of the employees in order to determine if the organization is on track with fulfilling its vision, goals and objectives. A system implies that the divisions and people of an organization are interconnected. The people must support the process. It is important to take a systems approach because the complexity within an organization has the power to affect the performance of its employees. The success of a single unit itself and the success of the entire organization at large are deeply dependent on one another. A systems approach considers the entire organizational environment including inputs as well as pressures, expectations, constraints, and consequences.

3. Human performance technology adds value. At the end of the process intervention, clients should leave with a set of tools which will assist them with making choices, establishing measurable goals, identifying barriers and tradeoffs, and taking control of the destiny of the organization. Although the actual human performance technology techniques address issues such as improving quality, customer retention and cost reduction, there should be a link to how the efforts impact business goals and outcomes such as sales, profits, and market share.

4. Human performance technology establishes partnerships. Human performance technology is built on collaboration among all of the stakeholders in an effort to improve the overall performance of the organization. Everyone should be involved in the decision-making process, and the advice and experience of subject matter experts (SMEs) should be taken into consideration. Working collaboratively includes sharing decisions about goals, determining the next steps to take in the process, and viewing implementation strategies as shared responsibilities. Partnerships are created from listening closely, trusting and respecting each other's knowledge and expertise.

5. Human performance technology is systematic in the assessment of the need or opportunity. The needs assessment occurs in the beginning of the project. The consultant should analyze and evaluate the effectiveness of different aspects of the organization in order to identify the external and internal pressures affecting it. This process will determine the deficiencies or performance gaps that need to be corrected.

6. Human performance technologists are systematic in the analysis of the work and workplace. They need to identify the causes or factors that limit performance. Cause analysis is about determining why a gap in performance or expectations exists. This step in the systematic process will determine what should be addressed to improve performance.

7. Human performance technology is systematic in the design of the solution or specification of the requirements of the solution. Design is about identifying the key attributes of a solution. The output is a communication that describes the features, attributes, and elements of a solution and the resources required to implement the solution.

8. Human performance technology is systematic in the development of all or some of the solution and its elements. Development is about the creation of some or all of the elements of the solution. It can be done by an individual or a team. The output is a product, process, system, or technology. Examples include training, performance support tools, a new or reengineered process, the redesign of a workspace, or a change in compensation or benefits.

9. Human performance technology is systematic in the implementation of the solution. Implementation is about deploying the solution and managing the change required to sustain it. This standard is about helping clients adopt new behaviors or use new or different tools.

10. Human performance technologists are systematic in the evaluation of the process and the results. Evaluation is about measuring the efficiency and effectiveness of what was done, how it was done, and whether the solution produced the desired results so that the cost incurred and the benefits gained can be compared. This standard is about identifying and acting on opportunities throughout the systematic process to identify measures and record the data that will help identify needs, adoption, and results.

ISSUES

Choosing the Best Organizational Consultant
External versus Internal Consulting

Many organizations will assign someone to complete the task of assessing the organization. When selecting this individual, the organization must evaluate the environment to determine whether or not it is best to use someone within the organization or outside of the organization. Facilitators, or consultants, are requested as a result of their expertise in a given area as well as their ability to collaborate with others in order to accomplish a given task. Human performance technologists can facilitate the process if an organization is attempting to make a change with the workforce and systems that are currently in place. Human performance technologists work in various industries such as academia, financial services, manufacturing, government, and pharmaceuticals. In addition, their expertise covers many functions such as human resources, training and development, and line management. Given the vast number of sources for finding these individuals, organizations will have to decide what works best.

Although most references on organizational consulting discuss the role of the external consultant, the role of internal consulting is becoming popular. External consultants are viewed as neutral because they do not have a history with the organization, and they tend to work on a project for a specific period of time. In other words, there is a beginning and an end. They are from outside the company, work for the duration of the contract, and may leave (Kleiner 1992). In some cases, part of the external consulting contract is to transition the outcomes into a "Train the Trainer" workshop for a select group of employees. Once they have completed their mission, they may train employees to maintain the changes once they are gone. These employees can become the internal organizational consultants. However, depending on the organization's culture, the management team may elect to use external consultants on a continual basis in order to maintain a sense of trust and objectivity. Internal consultants are organizational development professionals who work exclusively for one organization and are direct reports to a designated level of management (Lacey 1995). These individuals may work alone or as part of a team. In addition, there may be others such as specialists in organizational development, human resources, training, or communications who report to the internal consultant in an effort to complete the assigned tasks. Both external and internal organizational consultants are challenged with developing a systematic approach to managing change in an organization. As they go through each phase of the consulting process, they will be faced with obstacles that they must overcome. There are advantages and disadvantages for using internal and external consultants to evaluate an organization. Cummings and Worley (1993) created a process consisting of five phases in the consulting process. These phases are entering, contracting, diagnosing, intervening, and evaluating.

1. **Entering**
   a. **External Consultant**—This stage tends to be the most difficult stage for the external consultant because the individual needs to market himself or herself and build a client base. Once clients have been identified, the external consultant must build relationships and become familiar with the organization.
      - Advantages: Select projects based on their criteria
      - Disadvantages: Need to learn company
   b. **Internal Consultant**—Little time is spent on entry for the internal consultant since he or she is considered an insider of the organization.
      - Advantages: Ready access to clients
      - Disadvantages: Obligated to work with everyone

2. **Contracting**
   a. **External Consultant**—The consultant must work with the client to develop a mutual understanding of what the expected outcomes and deliverables will be. At this stage, the consultant and client communicate expectations and create a legal contract that both will be bound by. The purpose of the contract is to clarify goals, roles, use of resources, and ground rules (Block 1981).
      - Advantages: Can terminate project at anytime; maintain "outsider" role
      - Disadvantages: May incur "out of pocket" expenses, especially if unexpected events occur
   b. **Internal Consultant**—The internal consultant works under a contract as well. However, most are verbal versus written. The internal consultant has internal clients that require services. However, one of the disadvantages is that the internal consultant must be sensitive to the personalities and politics of the organization. An external consultant can be more vocal with his or her opinions because the individual will eventually leave. However, the internal consultant has to

remain within the organization and be sensitive to backlash and retaliation.
- Advantages: Information can be open or confidential
- Disadvantages: Must complete projects assigned; may experience client retaliation and loss of job

3. **Diagnosing**
   a. **External Consultant**—During this stage the external consultant will start collecting data such as employee surveys, meeting with focus groups to get follow-up information and feedback, and conducting individual meetings in order to develop an analysis and make recommendations for change. The consultant may also evaluate leadership styles of key players (Darling and Heller 2012). Once the plan has been developed, the consultant will schedule a meeting to provide the client, and special guests, with feedback on what needs to occur in order to implement the plan.
      - Advantages: Prestige from being external
      - Disadvantages: Confidential data can increase political sensitivities
   b. **Internal Consultant**—This phase is the same for both the internal and external consultant.
      - Advantages: Has relationships with many organization members
      - Disadvantages: Openly sharing data can reduce political intrigue

4. **Intervening**
   a. **External Consultant**—The design of what issues need to be addressed are the focus of this stage. It's important that the external consultant can get the participants to buy-in to the process because authentic information is required at this point. There has to be commitment on the part of the participants, and the external consultant may include this request at the beginning when the contract is being written. The external consultant needs to be assured that there will be individuals taking ownership of the outcomes and the process will be implemented and maintained once he or she has left.
      - Advantages: Can insist on receiving authentic data and internal commitment
      - Disadvantages: Must confine activities within boundaries of client organization
   b. **Internal Consultant**—Although this phase is the same for both the external and internal consultant, there is one exception for the internal consultant. Buy-in is key for the external consultant. However, the internal consultant considers it a luxury. Many employees do not have the opportunity to be authentic and recognize the political ramifications if they are completely honest. The internal consultant recognizes this dilemma. "Although most change projects begin with testing the waters of opportunity, hoping to build critical mass that will sweep in all members and result in commitment to change, all projects are not successful in generating enthusiasm for change" (Lacey 1995).
      - Advantages: May run interference for client across organizational lines to align support
      - Disadvantages: Cannot require information and internal commitment is a luxury

5. **Evaluating**
   a. **External Consultant**—During this phase, the external consultant is constantly assessing the process and results while making revisions to the plan. The external consultant may make some assumptions and solicit feedback from the client to see what level of customer satisfaction is present.
      - Advantages: Can use project success as a means of gaining repeat business and customer referrals
      - Disadvantages: Seldom see long term results
   b. **Internal Consultant**—This phase is similar for both types of consultants. The client will require more measurable results as the amount of money spent on the project intervention increases. In addition, there are potential personal rewards for the internal consultant. If the project is successful, there are opportunities for an increase in salary as well as promotions. However, there is a down side. Being an internal consultant can

be lonely because many people within the organization may not understand the job. There will be questions regarding what the consultant actually does and whether or not the work adds value to the bottom line.
- Advantages: Can see change become institutionalized
- Disadvantages: Little recognition for a job well done

Both external and internal consultants perform many of the same functions throughout the consulting process as each attempt to create a plan of improvement for the organization However, each will face unique sets of challenges and obstacles as he attempts to obtain his goals.

CONCLUSION

If one has a desire to lead change in an organization, he or she must have the ability to see the organization from the big picture perspective. Understanding the mission and vision will assist consultants in determining the best course of action for the organization at any given time. "Effective managers and professionals in all walks of life have to become skilled in the art of reading the situations they are attempting to organize or manage" (Morgan 1995). Human performance technology is a technique that both external and internal organizational consultants may use in order to assist companies with achieving the bottom line, implementing process improvement, and navigating change throughout the organization. Jacobs (1987) provided eleven propositions that emerged as a result of his research on HPT.

1. Human performance and human behavior are different, and knowledge of the difference is important for achieving the goals of the field.
2. Any statement about human performance must also include organizational performance.
3. Costs of improving performance should be regarded as investments in human capital, yielding returns in terms of increased performance potential.
4. Both organizational and individual goals must be considered in order to determine the desired performance.
5. Human performance technology consists of management functions, development functions, and systems functions.
6. Knowing how to engineer human performance and the conditions that affect it is as important as explaining why the behavior occurred.
7. In order to diagnose problems in an organization, the consultant must analyze the present system first, then examine the differences between the present and ideal system.
8. Exemplary performance provides the most logical referent for determining job performance standards.
9. Human performance problems can have different root causes, and these causes are generally classified as either originating from the person, from the person's environment, or from both.
10. Performance of one subsystem affects the performance of other subsystems in predictable ways, which will require problem causes to be analyzed at more than one level of an organization.
11. Many different solutions may be used to improve human performance. Selection of any one solution is dependent upon the cause and nature of the performance problem, and the criteria used to evaluate a solution must include its potential to make a measurable difference in the performance system.

BIBLIOGRAPHY

Battenfield, Ann E., and Jeanne Schehl. "Practice Analysis for Human Performance Technologists." *Performance Improvement* 52, no. 8 (2013): 15–20. Web. 31 Oct. 2013.

Block, Peter. *Flawless Consulting*. Austin, TX: Learning Concepts, 1981.

Cummings, Thomas, and Christopher Worley. *Organization Development and Change*. 8th ed. New York: South Western College Publishing, 1993.

Darling, John, and Victor Heller. "Effective Organizational Consulting across Cultural Boundaries: A Case Focusing on Leadership Styles and Team-Building." *Organization Development Journal* 30, no. 4 (2012): 54–72. Web. 31 Oct. 2013.

Free Management Library. *Human Performance Technology*. Web. 20 Apr. 2007.

Handbook of Human Performance Technology. *HR Magazine* 51, no. 8 (2006): 134. Web. 20 Apr. 2007.

Jacobs, Ronald L. *Human Performance Technology: A Systems-Based Field for the Training and Development Profession.* (SERIES NO. 326). Columbus: ERIC Clearinghouse on Adult, Career, and Vocational Education, The National Center for Research in Vocational Education, The Ohio State University, 1987. (ERIC Document Reproduction Service No. ED 290 936). Print.

Kleiner, Art. "The Gurus of Corporate Change." *Business and Science Review* 18 (1992): 39–42. Web. 20 Apr. 2007.

Lacey, Miriam Y. "Internal Consulting: Perspectives on the Process of Planned Change." *Journal of Organizational Change Management* 8, no. 3 (1995): 75–84. Web. 20 Apr. 2007.

Morgan, Gareth. *Images of Organization.* Thousand Oaks, CA: Sage, 1995.

Rush, Ann J. "Client Partnership throughout the Performance Improvement/Human Performance Technology Model." *Performance Improvement* 51, no. 9 (2012): 29–37. Web. 31 Oct. 2013.What Is Human Performance Technology? International Society of Performance and Instruction. (n.d.). Web. 20 Apr. 2007.

SUGGESTED READING

Dervitisiotis, Kostas. "Building Trust for Excellence in Performance and Adaptation to Change." *Total Quality Management & Business Excellence* 17, no. 7 (2006): 795–810. Web. 20 Apr. 2007.

Hsu, I-Chieh, Carol Yeh-Yun Lin, John Lawler, and Se-Hwa Wiu. "Toward a Model of Organizational Human Capital Development: Preliminary Evidence from Taiwan." *Asia Pacific Business Review* 13, no. 2 (2007): 251–75. Web. 20 Apr. 2007.

Old, Dianna. "Consulting for Real Transformation, Sustainability, and Organic Form." *Journal of Organizational Change Management* 8, no. 3 (1995): 6. Web. 20 Apr. 2007.

Prajogo, Daniel, and Prevaiz Ahmed. "Relationships between Innovation Stimulus, Innovation Capacity, and Innovation Performance." *R&D Management* 36, no. 5 (2006): 499–515. Web. 20 Apr. 2007.

Talaq, Jaleel, and Pervaiz Ahmed. "Why HPT, Not TQM? An Examination of the HPT Concept." *Journal of Management Development* 23, no. 3 (2004): 202–18. Web. 20 Apr. 2007.

Marie Gould, Ph.D.

ORGANIZATIONAL CULTURE

ABSTRACT

Organizational culture refers to the formal environment and norms that characterize a specific organization, as well as its informal behavioral and the social phenomena that occur among individuals in an organization. The study of organizational culture usually includes exploring intangible characteristics, such as shared understandings, beliefs, and values, and the many ways in which culture influences human behavior. More tangible characteristics such as codified norms—for example, in the form of employee handbooks and company hierarchy—are also elements of an organizational culture. Theories of organizational culture seek to understand and define these elements to gain a better understanding of the internal culture of organizations and the performance of their members. A solid understanding of the phenomenon of organizational culture helps organizations strengthen the work environment within and outside of the company.

Brief History

The idea that organizations may have specific cultures is not recent. Around the world, the spread of civilizations required the development of management and organization. Ancient cultures developed systems of organization and transmitted them to others. The most influential theories of modern organizational culture, however, were developed from more recent historical events.

The Industrial Revolution began with the creation of large factories, steamships, and railroads in the late eighteenth and early nineteenth centuries. These businesses created an array of new management problems, such as the logistics of transporting

Factory workers in a Taylorized workplace (Photo courtesy of Fortepan)

and managing vast numbers of people, products, and equipment. Among new organizational models arose the system of scientific management, also known as Taylorism, created by Frederic W. Taylor. Taylor's system was based on the interchangeable parts of industrial machinery and viewed an organization's members as an engineer views passive and exchangeable machine parts. (Taylor's system did suggest that human fatigue, the need for breaks, and worker safety be taken into consideration.) In this system, tasks were divided minutely and efficiently among workers, increasing productivity and reducing human idiosyncrasy and error. This work led to the creation of new organizational fields such as quality control, industrial engineering, and human resources. Other scholars, such as Emile Durkheim and Max Weber, produced an important body of work that looked at the ways organizations formalized and managed their practices and workers.

In time, rationality, codified rules, and bureaucracy replaced openness to human variability which, in turn, created widespread dissatisfaction among workers who felt dehumanized. Although the model of scientific management has since been greatly reformed and its tenets modified, its basic characteristics remain popular today. Concerns about job tedium and workers' feelings of depression, however, led labor activists to demand reform and researchers to investigate the discrepancy between how workers were expected to perform and how they actually behaved. This research led to the psychology-based human relations movement, which fostered a greater focus on groups and well-being rather than solely on individual performance and productivity, and gave way to a more trusting and humanitarian environment.

FURTHER INSIGHTS

It is difficult to develop theories of organizational culture because many organizational cultures are unique. From the American models of Fordism and post-Fordism to the Japanese model of Kaizen, organizational cultures are created within the organization and, in turn, are also influenced by members of the organization in which they grow. Social, geographic, and historical elements also determine how organizational cultures evolve. For example, during the Industrial Age in the nineteenth century, a great many firms were manufacturing companies. Organizational culture has changed greatly since then with most firms focused on thriving in a postmodern environment of vast, rapidly circulating information.

Experts widely consider that organizational culture is the most important determinant of behavior in organizations. It is also understood as one of the factors that can be managed in order to improve performance and efficiency. When problems arise in an organization, managers often look to the culture as the possible source for both conflict and solutions. Some approaches look to the culture as a cohesive unit built around common values and ethics. These models, their supporters argue, offer a sense of uniformity that makes for a strong cultural model. Other theoretical models hold that there is significantly more correlation among an organization's practices than among the individual attitudes or beliefs of its members. People in an organization often recruit like-minded people, and an organization therefore tends to create a cohesive culture. The culture may change, if perhaps merely incrementally, only when older managers are replaced with new ones.

Other models look at organizational culture as a set of constantly shifting subcultures and coalitions and suggest that the permeability of subcultures is the point from which an organization's culture should be studied. This model also considers diversity a better platform for productive performance. However, focusing solely on subcultures, critics argue, is problematic; because every culture is unique, theoretical generalizations are difficult to make. Whichever model is used, there is an understanding that organizational culture is complex. Researchers must analyze the individuals in the organization, as well as their behavior, actions, rituals, and stories. There are also other elements that affect the cultural dynamics of an organization. These include structure, marketing, finance, consumers, the varied interests of different departments, and others.

CONCLUSION

Cultures in modern organizations are increasingly rich and diverse. Many managers today understand that it is possible to manage cultural change as a flexible and continuous process, rather than merely as damage control when problems arise. Many organizational culture theories function on the premise that, because an organization must constantly develop and adapt, long-term stability is unlikely. Another difficulty in creating generalized theories of organizational culture and fostering a shared understanding of the topic derives from the significant differences between organizations in the private and public sectors, as well as between the for-profit and nonprofit sectors. Economic, legal, and political barriers increasingly overlap in today's environment, and cultural diversity emerges as a core challenge to organizational success. In today's world, then, it is important for organizational managers, scholars, and experts to understand the cultural underpinnings of organizational culture and its dynamics.

BIBLIOGRAPHY

Adler, Nancy J., and Allison Gunderson. *International Dimensions of Organizational Behavior.* Boston: Cengage, 2007.

Alvesson, Mats. *Understanding Organizational Culture.* Thousand Oaks, CA: Sage, 2012.

Bhagat, Rabi S., and Richard M. Steers, eds. *Cambridge Handbook of Culture, Organizations and Work.* New York: Cambridge University Press, 2011.

Ericksson-Zetterquist, Ulla, Thomas Mullern, and Alexander Styhre. *Organization Theory: A Practice-Based Approach.* Oxford: Oxford University Press, 2012.

Hatch, Mary Jo, and Ann L. Cunliffe. *Organization Theory: Modern, Symbolic, and Postmodern Perspectives.* Oxford: Oxford University Press, 2012.

Kinicki, Angelo. *Organizational Behavior: Key Concepts, Skills and Best Practices.* New York: McGraw-Hill/Irwin, 2011.

Maitland, Alison, and Peter Thomson. *Future Work: Understanding Organizational Culture for the New World of Work.* Basingstok, UK: Palgrave McMillan, 2014.

Martin, Joanne. *Organizational Culture: Mapping the Terrain.* Thousand Oaks, CA: Sage, 2001.

Robbins, Stephen P., and Timothy A. Judge. *Organizational Behavior.* Upper Saddle River, NJ: Prentice Hall, 2012.

Schafritz, Jay M., J. Steven Ott, and Yong Suk Jang. *Classics of Organization Theory.* Boston: Cengage, 2010.

Schein, Edgar H. *Organizational Culture and Leadership.* San Francisco: Jossey-Bass, 2010.

Trudy Mercadal, Ph.D.

ORGANIZATIONAL EFFECTIVENESS

ABSTRACT

Organizational effectiveness is a measure of how effectively an organization performs its mission. An organization is a group of individuals who join together to achieve a mutual goal. Effectiveness is how well a group achieves its goals. Effectiveness is typically measured via minimal costs and maximum gain. When discussing effectiveness, costs and gains can include a wide range of variables, including time, money, personnel, or other resources. The history of organizational effectiveness is closely tied to the history and sociology of groups and businesses.

Background

The background and history of organizational effectiveness derives from the study of the development of groups. The origins can be found in the ancient Greek and ancient Roman militaries. The next major milestone in organizational effectiveness was seen with the development of the production and assembly line, used by the Italians. The Industrial Revolution, beginning in the eighteenth century, saw the next advancement with its focus on factory work and carefully defined roles played by employees and managers. The incorporation of organizational effectiveness into business coincides with the birth of sociology and the study of business as an academic discipline in the middle of the nineteenth century.

The origins of organizational effectiveness are found in the militaries of Rome and Greece. The armies modified typical tactics as they changed opponents. Realizing that the same maneuvers did not work against all enemies, these two armies changed their tactics to suit their foes, managing to consistently win. This methodology exemplifies the notion that effectiveness changes as the challenge changes.

The Italians of Venice were renowned as shipbuilders. The construction of the Venetian Arsenal began in 1104. The Venetians used the assembly line and production line process in order to speed up production, increasing both efficiency and effectiveness; it was the primary reason the Venetian Arsenal was able to produce the quality and quantity of ships it did. At its peak, the Venetian Arsenal was producing a completed ship on a daily basis. The total organization of the production and assembly line would be seen at a later point in time in conjunction with the production of the Model T Ford in the early 20th century. It is unknown why other cultures and organizations did not adopt the use of the production line and assembly line, The Industrial Revolution was the next major milestone for organizational effectiveness. Starting in the mid-eighteenth century, the Industrial Revolution saw the introduction and increasing use of machines to mass produce goods and materials that individual workers had previously crafted by hand. In this case, organizational effectiveness was not allocated to or the result of any one group or individual but a collective effort on behalf of all aspects of industry and commerce in order to reduce costs and improve profits.

The movement of organizational effectiveness in the business and academic realms started near the end of the Industrial Revolution, and became mainstream activities by the turn of the twentieth century. Academics began experiments and studies in order to analyze, improve, and increase organizational effectiveness, primarily in commercial and industrial ventures. It also applied, to a lesser degree, to academia and the service oriented sector as well.

Organizational Effectiveness Today
In the twenty-first century, organizational effectiveness has been divided between two realms: the academic and the practical. The academic version of organizational effectiveness is driven by experiments and studies, with the goal of determining a more cohesive and well-defined theory of how to improve an organization's effectiveness. The practical version of organizational effectiveness is driven by increasing a venture's profits, while at the same time reducing costs in both time and money.

Theoretical applications of organizational effectiveness focus on adaption, inertia, selection, and constraints, as well as cost and profit. Adaption entails that an organization will adapt to its limitations in order to overcome them. Effective organizations are able to adapt and thrive within these limitations, while the less effective groups cannot. The result is that groups that cannot adapt to the limitations imposed upon them will not succeed, and they often fail to realize a profit. Inertia entails the willingness of a group to adapt. A group with strong, immobile, unchanging traditions will be less effective than a group that is malleable and willing to change its environment.

Another factor within the inertia realm is the knowledge base of the group members. If the members are not willing to learn new procedures and techniques, or if they are not willing to learn new technologies, the growth in productivity of the group will slow, leading to an ineffective group. Selection entails that the group that is best able to adapt to its limitations will be best suited for effective work. To maximize the potential for selection, a group must allow for and promote traits that permit the group the freedom to adapt and overcome challenges and limitations. Legal, moral, or capability-based constraints are the limitations that a group faces, and they force the group to forgo options that may be viewed as acceptable to the group.

The last elements that the academic and theoretical models consider are cost and profit. Costs and profits can be monetary, time based, or both. The overall goal is to minimize costs, while at the same time increasing profits. The groups that are effective manage to meet both milestones.

The practical version of organizational effectiveness is much less detailed than the academic model. The practical version is concerned with what works in the real world, not in the academic world. Many of the Forbes 100 and Fortune 500 companies have found techniques that maximize organizational effectiveness. The primary way this goal is accomplished involves the proper selection of employees, those who are highly qualified, so that they can adapt to the challenges, and are empowered by their employer to do so. Without the ability to effect any change, there can be no improvement to the organization.

BIBLIOGRAPHY

Bass, Bernard, and Avolio, Bruce, eds. *Improving Organizational Effectiveness through Transformational Leadership*. Thousand Oaks, CA: SAGE Publishing, 1993.

Cherrington, David. *Organizational Effectiveness*. Salt Lake City: Brigham Young University Press, 2003.

Chidambaranathan, Kumaresan, and BS Swaroop Rani. "Knowledge Management as a Predictor of Organizational Effectiveness: The Role of Demographic and Employment Factors." *Journal of Academic Librarianship* 41.6 (2015): 758–63. *Education Research Complete*. Web. 10 Jan. 2016.

Doshi, Neel, and Lindsay McGregor. *Primed to Perform*. San Francisco: Harper Business, 2015.

Galford, Robert M., Bob Frisch, and Cary Greene. *Simple Sabotage: A Modern Field Manual for Detecting and Rooting Out Everyday Behaviors that Undermine Your Workplace*. San Francisco: Harper One, 2015.

Goffee, Rob, and Gareth Jones. *Why Should Anyone Work Here? What it Takes to Create an Authentic Organization*. Boston: Harvard Business Review Press, 2015.

Lawler, Edward W., and Chris Worley. *Built to Change: How to Achieve Sustained Organizational Effectiveness*. Hoboken, NJ: Wiley, 2006.

Levenson, Alec. *Strategic Analytics: Advancing Strategy Execution and Organizational Effectiveness*. San Francisco: Berrett-Koehler, 2015.

Martin, Karen, and Mike Osterling. *Value Stream Mapping: How to Visualize Work and Align Leadership for Organizational Transformation*. New York: McGraw, 2013.

Petro, Yacoub, and Paul Gardiner. "An Investigation of the Influence of Organizational Design on Project Portfolio Success, Effectiveness and Business Efficiency for Project-Based Organizations." *International Journal of Project Management* 33.8 (2015): 1717–29. *Business Source Complete*. Web. 10 Jan. 2016.

Douglas R. Jordan

ORGANIZATIONAL LEARNING

ABSTRACT

Organizational knowledge is a concept that represents the sum total of all of the knowledge and experience that members of the organization both possess and bring to the table as they engage in the work of the organization. Organizational learning is the process developed by an organization with the goal of increasing the overall amount of organizational knowledge available, and of making sure that this organizational knowledge is applied in the most timely and effective ways possible.

OVERVIEW

Organizational learning can be thought of as an aggregation of the process of individual learning by members of a larger group—the organization. As individuals acquire experience at various tasks, the accumulation of this experience eventually produces knowledge. When many individuals are working together in an organization, their acquisition of individual experience and the subsequent production of knowledge at the level of the individual also benefits the organization, because the organization acquires experience and knowledge at the same time as the individuals who compose it do. Seen in this way, organizational learning can seem as an almost natural process that occurs without the need for intentional drive to motivate it, almost like sediment accumulating on the ocean floor. Yet there is also a deliberate aspect to organizational learning, because organizations can choose to focus their knowledge of management efforts in ways designed specifically to improve their own learning capacity. An organization might recognize that one of its weaknesses involves retrieving and analyzing sales data for transactions using foreign currency. The organization could either continue to operate as is, in this area, or it could implement changes in its practices to make such information easier to get a hold of and to analyze (Wellman 2013). This type of thinking about the ways in which one thinks, whether at the level of an individual or of an organization, is known as metacognition, or thinking about thinking.

APPLICATIONS

Organizations operate within an environment characterized by constant change, whether due to the weather, the economy, social and political developments, or some combination of these factors. Because the environment is perpetually in flux, organizations cannot afford to approach the environment with the same ideas and thought processes used years or even decades ago. Instead, organizations must continue to build their knowledge by using information acquired through experience operating in the ever-changing world. An organization that continues to learn by acquiring experience and analyzing it to produce knowledge will be better equipped to deal with changing circumstances (Gino and Staats 2015). Another major motivation for organizations to optimize their learning is to help them stay ahead of their competitors. Many types of organizational knowledge pertain to ways in which the organization can operate more efficiently and more effectively (Argyris 2012). For example, a company that operates a chain of coffee stores might focus entirely on constant expansion into new markets, while its competitor, who possesses many more years of experience in the coffee business, may have learned to take a slower approach and conduct a thorough market analysis of every region it considers moving into, before committing to the move. This methodically analytical, go slow approach could help the more established company avoid rushing into economically unstable regions just for the sake of short-term expansion. In this way, the older company's ability to put its own knowledge to more effective use helps the company to outperform its competition in the long run, by avoiding the unnecessary expense of opening stores in areas where there will not be enough business to sustain them at a profitable level (Cameron and Spreitzer 2012).

Knowledge management is an umbrella term used to describe all of the different ways that an organization manipulates knowledge, from acquiring it and organizing it to distributing and storing it. Generally speaking, the more adept an organization is at knowledge management, the greater will be that organization's aptitude for organizational learning. The experience curve describes a theoretical model that explains the tendency for overall production costs to decrease as the volume of production increases. In other words, the experience curve shows how an organization learns how to operate more efficiently and more effectively, the more it engages in a particular type of production. Often, it may not be immediately clear how the savings are being achieved, but the reality of the savings is beyond question.

Viewpoints

The fundamental mechanism of organizational learning is change. This reality does not refer to any kind of gradual evolution that occurs randomly and without direction. The change at the heart of organizational learning is caused by the process of the individuals who make up the organization acquiring experience, on the organization's behalf, through the course of their regular work, and sharing that experience with others in the organization (Anderson 2010). As this experience accumulates, it is also analyzed by various sectors within the organization (e.g., the finance department, the marketing department, and the research and development department) and the product of this analysis is knowledge. An example of such knowledge in the scenario discussed above might be the realization that coffee stores do not do well when they are located in zip codes that have experienced more than seven percent unemployment within the last three years. This piece of information is no doubt interesting, but it does not really mean much unless it is put to use by the organization to make a change in its behavior. This type of using information for change is central to organizational learning. Perhaps the more experienced coffee chain, after realizing the importance of the seven percent unemployment metric for predicting the success of its location, would decide to change its business practices to exclude from consideration any potential location that has experienced greater than seven percent unemployment in the last three years. This change would be the result of organizational learning—that is, observing information in the real world, analyzing that information and making predictions about it, and then adjusting company behavior based on those predictions (Boonstra 2013).

Single- and Double-Loop Organizations
Because organizational learning is a field that lends itself to multiple layers of abstraction, there have been several theories developed to try to explain the different mechanisms used by organizations to acquire, store, process, and transfer knowledge. Some of these are the single- and double-loop theories, which analyze the ways in which organizations respond to failure. Single-loop organizations that experience a failure in their efforts respond by adjusting the methods used in those efforts and trying again to see if the change produces a success. An example of this situation might be a company that tries to increase sales of its products by advertising on the radio, only to find this method ineffective. The company might decide to try again by using television advertising instead of radio. Conversely, a double-loop organization in this situation would be unlikely to try a different advertising medium, and more likely to reconsider whether the product being marketed was actually viable in the marketplace. This difference derives from the fact that double loop organizations, upon experiencing failure, tend to reconsider the overall goal of their efforts rather than question the methods used. While these two different types of organizational learning may seem very different, they actually exist at different times and at different levels of most organizations, and can even be employed side by side under some circumstances (Godwyn and Gittell 2012).

Learning Curves
A learning curve in the context of organizational knowledge management is a graph that represents how an organization's performance of a task improves over time, as the organization gains experience at performing the task. Often this improvement is due to the organization discovering ways that it can perform the task more efficiently, though other factors may also play a role. The factors that play the most significant role in an organization improving its performance typically fall into one of three categories: individual, structural, and technological. Individual changes are also fairly straightforward, as these include the experience acquired by individual members of the organization while they perform their duties. The more complex concept is that of structural change which refers to adaptations the organization makes in response to information it receives, because these changes affect the structure of the organization's operations and processes (Eddy 2014). Technological changes are enabled by advances in technology (Iyengar, Sweeney, and Montealegre 2015). The classic example is of a sales force, in the days before the internet, receiving personal digital assistants that enable them to collect and share their sales data much more quickly and easily. Each of these factors is at play in every organization as it interacts with its environment, but the particular nature of an organization influences the degree to which it responds to information. This reality explains why different organizations exhibit faster or slower responses to the information they receive, and why some organizational responses are more effective than others.

Different theorists have tried to explain variations in organizational performance using a variety of models. The models that have garnered the most attention are those developed by John F. Muth, Bernardo A. Huberman, and Christina Fang. Muth's main area of focus was adaptations that increase an organization's cost effectiveness. Huberman continued this general approach but sought to simplify the number of steps used in the analysis conducted by the organization. Fang's model explored the propagation of credit throughout the organization as part of the analytical process, making it possible for the organization to identify information more accurately to help improve institutional processes (Lewis 2015).

Explicit and Tacit Knowledge
Not all types of information and knowledge that are used in organizational learning are equally accessible. Many researchers acknowledge the distinction between knowledge that is explicit within the organization and that which is tacit. Explicit knowledge

consists of information that the organization "knows that it knows." The organization is aware of this information and deliberately tries to put it to good use, whether it is sales data, transcripts of focus groups discussing the relative merits of potential products in development, or responses to an annual employee satisfaction survey. The foremost quality that makes explicit information easier to deal with is that the organization knows it exists and has a place to keep it so that it can be put to good use. This situation is not the case with tacit knowledge. Tacit knowledge is the organization's set of unwritten rules; those who need to know a particular rule are aware of it, but these rules are not written down anywhere, and might even be at odds with the company's official statements. An example of tacit knowledge might be the fact that every scientist working for company X's research and development department knows that the only way to get a research proposal approved is to have someone from marketing included as a co-author of the proposal (Burke 2014). This inclusion may not be the company's official policy, and the company might prefer not to have this information about its internal workings made public knowledge, but it remains a fact of life known to all of the company's employees that are affected by it. Companies that wish to take full advantage of their learning opportunities must make every effort to pay as much attention to tacit organizational knowledge as they do to explicit knowledge. Tacit knowledge is often possessed by those members of the organization with the longest tenure or the deepest insight into the hidden machinations of the institution. As such, it tends to be some of the most precious information that the organization possesses, and it is vital to try to capture it before it disappears, either through the departure from the organization of those who possess it or through its tendency to fade away as more pressing matters confront the organization and demand its collective attention (Argote 2013).

Bibliography

Anderson, Donald L. *Organization Development: The Process of Leading Organizational Change.* Los Angeles: Sage, 2010.

Argote, Linda. *Organizational Learning: Creating, Retaining, and Transferring Knowledge.* New York: Springer, 2013.

Argyris, Chris. *Organizational Traps: Leadership, Culture, Organizational Design.* Oxford, UK: Oxford University Press, 2012.

Boonstra, Jaep J. *Cultural Change and Leadership in Organizations: A Practical Guide to Successful Organizational Change.* Chichester, UK: John Wiley & Sons, 2013.

Burke, Warner W. *Organization Change: Theory and Practice.* Los Angeles: Sage, 2014.

Cameron, Kim S., and Gretchen Spreitzer. *The Oxford Handbook of Positive Organizational Scholarship.* New York, UK: Oxford University Press, 2012.

Desei, Vinit. "Learning through the Distribution of Failures within an Organization: Evidence fom Heart Bypass Surgery Performance." *Academy of Management Journal* 58, no. 4 (2015): 1032–50. Web. 3 Jan. 2016.

Eddy, Pamela L. *Connecting Learning Across the Institution.* San Francisco: Jossey-Bass. 2014.

Gino, Francesco, and Bradley Staats. "Why Organizations Don't Learn." *Harvard Business Review* 93, no. 11 (2015): 110–18. Web. 3 Jan. 2016. Web. 3 Jan. 2016.

Godwyn, Jody, and Judy H. *Sociology of Organizations: Structures and Relationships.* Thousand Oaks, CA: Pine Forge Press, 2012.

Iyengar, Kishen, Jeffrey R. Sweeney, and Ramiro Montealegre. "Information Technology Use as a Learning Mechanism: The Impace of Its Use on Knowledge Transfer Effectiveness, Absorptive Capacity, and Franchisee Performance." *MIS Quarterly* 39, no. 3 (2015): 615–A5. Web. 3 Jan. 2016.

Lewis, Harold, ed. *Organizational Learning: Individual Differences, Technologies and Impact of Teaching.* Hauppauge, NY: Nova Science, 2015.

Wellman, Jerry L. *Organizational Learning: How Companies and Institutions Manage and Apply Knowledge.* Houndmils, UK: Palgrave Macmillan, 2013.

Suggested Reading

Döös, Marianne, Peter Johansson, and Lena Wilhelmson. "Organizational Learning as an Analogy to Individual Learning? A Case of Augmented Interaction Intensity." *Vocations and Learning* 8, no. 1 (2015): 55–73. Print.

Evans, Scotney, and Natalie Kivell. "The Transformation Team: An Enabling Structure for Organizational Learning in Action." *Journal of Community Psychology* 43, no. 6 (2015): 760–77. Print.

Jain, Ajay K., and Ana Moreno. "Organizational Learning, Knowledge Management Practices and Firm's Performance: An Empirical Study of a Heavy Engineering Firm in India." *Learning Organization* 22, no. 1 (2015): 14–39. Print.

Mena, Jeanette A., and Brian Chabowski. "The Role of Organizational Learning in Stakeholder Marketing." *Journal of the Academy of Marketing Science* 43, no. 4 (2015): 429–52. Print.

Schilling, Melissa A., and Christina Fang. "When Hubs Forget, Lie and Play Favorites: Interpersonal Network Structure, Information Distortion, and Organizational Learning." *Strategic Management Journal* 35, no. 7 (2014): 974–94. Web. 3 Jan. 2016.

Scott Zimmer, J.D.

ORGANIZATIONAL LIFE CYCLE

ABSTRACT

Organizational life-cycle theory acknowledges that, just like living organisms, organizations go through identifiable stages from the time they are established until their eventual dissolution. The hope is that by studying how organizations grow and develop, people within an organization will be better able to recognize the stage they are at and take appropriate steps to guide it toward the most favorable outcomes available to it. This goal applies to the end-of-life stage for organizations just as much as to the earlier stages because an orderly dissolution is vastly preferable to a sudden collapse.

OVERVIEW

Several models have been proposed to help describe the stages of an organization. The most widely used model breaks the life cycle down into the five stages of creation, survival, maturity, renewal, and decline. These stages, not coincidentally, correspond to the traditional stages of the human life cycle: birth, youth, adulthood, middle age, and old age. Each of these stages is characterized by certain types of activities that the organization undertakes during that phase. This model does not preclude these activities from occurring during other phases; it simply means that some activities predominate at certain times.

During the creation phase of the life cycle, an organization is first established. When the organization is a business entity, the creation phase is sometimes called the entrepreneurial stage (Beuren, Rengel, and Rodrigues 2015). Typically, one or more people engage in business activities on an informal, freelance basis for some time as they discover whether there is a demand for a set of services or products that they are able to provide. This exploration may proceed for a period of weeks, months, or even years before the decision is made to formalize the business or organizational structure and create the organization as its own distinct entity. For the remainder of this creation stage, the organization usually expands as more and more people become aware of it and the resources it has to offer. An example of this growth might be a corner market that opens in a neighborhood that has long been without a grocery store. After the opening, more people each day will come across the store or hear about it from friends, expanding the market's base of current and potential customers (Primc and Cater 2016). During the creation phase, the primary transition requires that one move from the realization that there may be a large enough number of customers to support an ongoing business, to actually locating those customers and connecting with them in a way that makes it possible for the business to survive.

After the creation phase, the next stage for an organization is survival. This phase is perhaps the most critical in the organizational life cycle, because what happens during this period, as well as how the organization responds, defines the difference between those organizations that will continue and those that fold almost as soon as they begin. This period of great energy and activity in the organization includes various projects and initiatives drawing upon the organization's resources and pulling its attention in numerous directions. There is an urgently felt need for the organization to get on track and establish its own internal structure and processes, but, at the same time, there is a constant drive for more growth in order to stay afloat and to begin building up reserves that can be drawn upon for new projects or to respond to unforeseen emergencies. If these competing demands can be kept in balance and the environment in which the organization operates does not experience any sudden upheavals, then it is likely that the organization will survive. If there are unexpected shifts in the landscape or if the leaders of the organization miscalculate as they balance growth with security, then the organization may very well cease to exist (Elsayed and Wahba 2016).

The third phase of organizational life is maturity, also referred to in some circles as consolidation. During the rapid growth of the survival phase, it often happens that the organization reaches a plateau in terms of growth. Efforts to grow beyond this point begin to fail because of the organization's lack of the internal systems and structures needed to be able to both serve existing clients and acquire new clients. When this plateau is reached, the organization has a choice to make between two different pathways: pull back on the growth initiatives while establishing and solidifying internal infrastructure, or continue expansion efforts and hope that internal systems develop either on their own or with minimal supervision. As one might expect, the latter option is rarely if ever successful, as there are simply too many factors at work in the contemporary business environment for matters to have a significant chance of working out on their own. The better option at this stage is for the organization to perform a thorough and honest self-assessment to identify strengths, weaknesses, opportunities, and threats—a SWOT analysis of strengths, weaknesses, opportunities, and threats (Souza, Guerreiro, and Oliveira 2015).

The purpose of this self-analysis is to give the organization a realistic view of itself and what it needs to do. If this step is not taken, then it is all too easy for an organization to follow the whims and predilections of its leaders, rather than developing a strategy appropriate to the circumstances. In most situations, the analysis reveals that the organization needs to devote additional resources to developing its internal structure. The reason is that during the previous phases, growth and expansion are the priorities. Little time is given to make sure that consistent processes and procedures are in place; therefore, many functions of the organization are accomplished somewhat haphazardly. For example, the manager in charge of payroll might be so busy that she does not have time to process paychecks until the night before they are due, instead of doing so well in advance and in an orderly fashion, with meticulous attention to detail to ensure that no mistakes are made. The maturity phase is the time for organizations to correct shortcomings like these, hiring additional staff as needed and following best practices wherever possible. The danger to be avoided during this phase is making the organization needlessly complex. As with so many other aspects of life, the maturity phase teaches the lesson that balance is needed—the organization must create for itself a structure that is elaborate enough to sustain its operations in prosperous times and in less favorable ones, but not so labyrinthine that it becomes challenging to navigate (Deokro, Soyoung, and Sung-Hyun 2014). For example, before the organization decides whether to establish a field office in a new state, there needs to be a process of gathering data and evaluating it to make sure that the new office is warranted and will have enough activity to support its operations. At the same time, if the data collection and evaluation process is too onerous and time-consuming, it may ultimately act as a disincentive for the organization to expand, even at a healthy pace and when expansion makes sense.

Finding the middle ground between these extremes is an inexact science, and even when it is achieved, it rarely lasts for a long time. The maturity phase of the organizational life cycle is characterized by a continuing process of refinement and adjustment to try to find and maintain this balance (Rahimi and Fallah 2015).

The fourth stage of an organization's existence, the renewal stage, actually exemplifies this ongoing balancing act. During the maturity phase, which ideally will last many years, it is almost inevitable that at some point the organization will stray from its original purpose in some fashion. This change can take the form of distractions such as pursuing growth over quality or neglecting the organizational mission in favor of short-term gains. When this shift happens, the most positive outcome is for the organization to reinvent or rediscover itself, thus initiating the renewal phase. Usually reinvention happens as a result of conscious effort that is undertaken once the organization realizes that it has lost its way. This series of events is frequently played out in the media for all to see; a company or similar institution makes a major misstep with a product launch or an offensive advertising campaign and determines that it needs to get back on track in some way. Sometimes this situation involves an organization-wide training initiative and/or a rearrangement of senior management. At the conclusion of this corrective action, the organization is renewed in the sense that its members collectively have recalled what their true purpose is and have regained their passion for it. This renewal allows the organization to continue its operations in a manner similar to that seen in the maturity phase, at least until the organization once again loses its way at some point in the (hopefully distant) future (Carson and Cumber 2013).

The fifth and final stage of the organizational life cycle is decline. An organization may begin this stage and then return to the renewal stage, which sometimes occurs multiple times before the final decline. During this stage, the organization loses track of its mission and focuses on short-term gains and internal politics. Instead of the organization's members working together toward a common goal, internal stakeholders pursue personal agendas, sometimes maneuvering to get ahead of each other and constantly looking for any means to gain an advantage that they can leverage into financial or political gain. This loss of collective direction is more damaging to an organization than most outside threats that might arise, and once the process of decline gains momentum, it is extremely difficult to reverse. While this situation can be distressing for those who rely on the organization and its services as well as the organization's employees, ultimately it is for the best in many cases because the dissolution of the organization frees up resources that were being underused or misused and makes them available for more productive application elsewhere (Md. Auzair 2015).

Issues

During each phase of the organizational life cycle, some degree of growth is desirable, though not always feasible. Researchers have distinguished several different types of expansion, each one bearing some similarity to one or more phases of the life cycle. The creative form of growth tends to occur early in the organization's life, as the organization first comes into being and decisions are made about its character and purpose; eventually this creativity is brought back to earth by the need for organization and direction. This change ushers in directional growth, which seeks to channel the creative growth into a particular direction so that the organization can make progress toward a goal rather than pursuing growth in all directions. Directional growth can produce friction in the organization as not everyone is likely to agree on a single direction, at least at the outset. This friction can lead to the development of various factions within the organization, each with its own hierarchy and agenda. As directional growth continues and the organization becomes more successful, it also becomes more complex which makes possible delegation-based growth, in which an organization's senior members learn to delegate some of their functions to their subordinates, making it possible for the organization to operate more efficiently.

Eventually, some organizations move beyond the delegation form of growth to exhibit growth based on cooperation or collaboration, much more productive forms of interaction in which members of the organization work together to accomplish shared objectives rather than individual goals (Gray and Farminer 2014). It is important to keep in mind that as laudable a pursuit as expansion is, it is not possible under every circumstance, and it should not override all other considerations. This reason is why the significance of growth as an organizational motivator goes up and down from one phase of the life cycle to the next. In some situations, such as the maturity stage, it is more important for an organization to consolidate its gains and use them to make itself stronger, instead of pushing for more growth and potentially running the risk of overextending itself and risking huge losses. Some in the business world are fond of saying that one of the golden rules of corporations is that "If you are not growing, you are dying" (Cunha, Klann, and Lavarda 2013). Such a dramatic statement should hardly be taken at face value. Not every organization is driven solely by profits and the desires of shareholders. For many organizations, reputation, integrity, and dedication are more important than income.

BIBLIOGRAPHY

Beuren, Isla M., Silene Rengel, and Moacir M. Rodrigues. "Relation of Management Accounting Attributes and the Organization Life Cycle Stages." *Revista Innovar* 57 (2013): 63. Print.

Carson, Charles M., and Carol J. Cumber. "Carson's Department Store: When to Stay and When to Go." *Journal of the International Academy for Case Studies* 19, no. 4 (2013): 61. Web. 23 Oct. 2016.

Cunha, Paulo Robert Da, Klann, Roberto Carlos, and Carlos Eduardo Facin Lavarda. "Organizational Life Cycle and Management Control: An Analysis of Articles." Revista De Gestão, Finanças E Contabilidade. *International Journal of Accounting* 3 (2013): 170. Print.

Deokro, Lee, Kim Soyoung, and Cha Sung-Hyun. "Evaluating the Effectiveness of Research Centers and Institututes in Universities: Disciplines and Life Cycle Stages." *KEDI Journal of Educational Policy* 11, no. 1 (2014): 119. Print.

Elsayed, Khaled, and Hayam Wahba. "Reexamining the Relationship between Inventory Management and Firm Performance: An Organizational Life Cycle Perspective." *Future Business Journal* 2 (2016): 65–80. Print.

Gray, Brendan, and Andrea Farminer. "An No Birds Sing—Reviving the Romance with International Entrepreneurship." *Journal of International Entrepreneurship* 12, no. 2 (2014): 115. Web. 23 Oct. 2016.

Lo-Iacono-Ferreira, Vanessa G. et al. "Organizational Life Cycle Assessment: Suitability for Higher Education Institutions with Environmental management Systems." *The International Journal of Life Cycle Assessment* (2017, July 13). Print.

Md. Auzair, Sofiah. "A Configuration Approach to Management Control Systems Design in Service Organizations." *Journal of Accounting & Organizational Change* 11, no. 1 (2015): 47. Web. 23 Oct. 2016.

Primc, Kaja, and Tomaz Cater. "The Influence of Organization Life Cycle on Environmental Proactivity and Competitive Advantage." *Organization & Environment* 29, no. 2 (2016): 212–30. Web. 23 Oct. 2016.

Rahimi, Farideh, and Saeed Fallah. "Study of Organizational Life Cycle and Its Impact on Strategy Formation." *Procedia—Social and Behavioral Sciences* 207 (11th International Strategic Management Conference), 50–58. Print.

Souza, Paiva, Reinaldo Guerreiro, and Marcos V. Oliveria. "Relationship between the Maturity of Supply Chair Process Management and the Organisational Life Cycle." *Business Process Management Journal* 21, no. 3 (2015): 466–81. Web. 23 Oct. 2016.

SUGGESTED READING

Albuquerque, Alexandre F., Edmundo Filho, Marcelo Nagano, and Luiz A. Philippsen Jr. "A Change in the Importance of Mortality Factors throughout Life Cycle Stages of Small Businesses." *Journal of Global Entrepreneurship Research* 6, no. 1 (2016): 1. Web. 23 Oct. 2016.

Baldassarri, Catia, Fabrice Mathieux, Fulvio Ardente, et al. "Integration of Environmental Aspects in to R&D Interorganizational Projects Management: Application of a Life Cycle-Based Method to the Development of Innovative Windows." *Journal of Cleaner Production* 112 (2016): 3388–3401. Web. 23 Oct. 2016.

Campos, Hector M., Francesc S. Parellada, Gerardo H. Atondo, and Madet R. Quintero. "Strategic Decision Making Entrepreneurial Orientation and Performance: An Organizational Life Cycle Approach." Revista De Administração. *FACES Journal* 14, no. 2 (2015): 9–24. Web. 23 Oct. 2016.

Fang, S.R., Enchi Chang, Chueh-Chu Ou, and Chia-Hui Chou. "Internal Market Orientation, Market Capabilities and Learning Orientation." *European Journal of Marketing* 48, nos. 1-2 (2014): 170–92. Web. 23 Oct. 2016.

Phan, Thanh, Kevin Baird, and Bill Blair. "The Use and Success of Activity-Based Management Practices at Different Organisational Life Cycle Stages." *International Journal of Production Research* 52, no. 3 (2014): 787–803. Web. 23 Oct. 2016.

Voznenko, Natayla, and Teodora Roman. "Building Industry Enterprises Logistic System according to Their Lifecycle and Organizational Adaptation." *Journal of Economics & Business Research* 22, no. 1 (2016): 7–18. Web. 23 Oct. 2016.

Scott Zimmer, J.D.

Participative Leadership

ABSTRACT

Participative (or democratic) leadership is a style of management that relies on the input of the group as a whole. When compared to authoritarian and laissez-faire leadership, democratic leadership lies in the middle of a spectrum, with authoritarianism on one end and laissez-faire on the other. Participative leadership relies on understanding the behavioral patterns of those who are being led. Democratic leadership is increasingly becoming the governance model of choice in the twenty-first century.

Brief History

For much of early human history, civilizations have been ruled by authoritarian forms of government. The primary leaders of some of the earliest civilizations were kings, queens, and emperors. Many of these rulers were also believed to be representatives of the gods or deities themselves. Authoritarian regimes were established as a means to unify divided and often warring subgroups. Decisions that came from a single, all-powerful leader simplified governance in a complex political environment.

In the sixth century BCE, however, a new form of governing emerged in the city-state of Athens. The leader of that civilization, Cleisthenes, introduced a set of reforms called *demokratia*, which means rule by the people, and included a council of Athenian representatives and a judiciary aided by a jury of the public. This fledgling democracy created a more unified populace and largely eliminated the divisions between the ruling elite.

The Athenian democratic model did not last, however, with the Roman Empire quickly returning to the authoritarian style. This trend continued in a broad sense (although local feudal systems experienced a limited degree of autonomy despite remaining dedicated to a monarch) over the centuries. However, during the sixteenth and seventeenth centuries, the Protestant Reformation fostered a pursuit of religious freedom, a principle that brought a large group of colonists to North America where the most significant advance in the notion of democracy, culminated in the American Revolution.

Participative Leadership in the Modern Era

A participative, or democratic, government features a well-established government institution that resembles aspects of the Athenian model. Typically, this system is composed of an executive charged with the overall administration of government (including foreign affairs, security, and the bureaucracy), a judiciary to uphold the rights of the people, and a legislative body representing each established region of the area being served. In such a system, the executive members and the legislature are elected by the constituency.

In the twenty-first century, developing nations are increasingly adopting democratic regimes, usually following civil unrest. There are a number of factors that contribute to the success of a participative or democratic government. In a recent study of fifty-five countries (Rossberger, 2015), the economic and innovative success of participative leadership was shown to be driven in large part by the average level of education of the constituents. Another study, which involves a semiautonomous region of Pakistan, validated these findings. The survey showed that educating and sharing knowledge with constituents strengthened the political leadership.

One of the most pivotal characteristics of a successful participative government is the connections between the constituents and the leader. This concept includes the notion that all constituents have the ability to influence government. In the United States and in Europe, every participative/democratic government offers universal suffrage, which gives every constituent the opportunity to participate in government. Additionally, the

USAID workers strategize (Photo courtesy of USAID Pakistan)

governments of the United States and Germany, among other participative governments, are bound to the tenets of their respective constitutions, which clearly establish the rights and liberties of their populations. While these governments have executive level leadership in place, these leaders must act with consideration of the rights and interests of the people who elected them.

In a democratic system, the participants are just as important as the leaders who serve them. Choi points out (2007) that ideal democratic leadership encourages individual and group participation and does so in a friendly and helpful way, and as Brian Wampler for the *Washington Post* reports, the lives of citizens are improved if community leadership makes use of participatory programs (Wampler, 2014). Brazil, for example, is one of the largest democracies in the world. Between 1990 and 2008 over 120 Brazilian cities incorporated a program called Participatory Budgeting, whereby citizens decided where public money would be allocated throughout the community. As Wampler explains, the cities that took advantage of participatory budgeting spent more on sanitation and education and witnessed a reduction in infant mortality as compared to cities that did not utilize the program, which indicated that communities and programs "flourish when elected officials are committed to implementing participatory institutions" (Wampler, 2014).

Not all democracies are fully participatory. For example, Pop-Eleches's 2014 study of four post-Soviet era democracies—Kyrgyzstan, Georgia, Ukraine, and Serbia—revealed that all four governments were pursuing democratic change in the form of freedom of speech, elimination of corruption, and inclusive political institutions. Kyrgyzstan showed rapid and intensive democratization of its institutions, but executive leadership was predominantly held by members of the president's family, each of whom reportedly used their position for personal gain. Ukraine also showed an inclusive, participatory government, but that nation's democratic system has been weighed down by an ongoing civil war in the Crimean Peninsula and eastern Ukraine (Pop-Eleches, 2014). Georgia and Serbia emerged from brutal civil wars in the 1990s and have since moved rapidly toward a participatory government. The political divisions that were evident in these countries in the 1990s undermined participatory leadership, however.

Ethnic and class divisions can also be a hindrance for participative governments. Prior to 2010 democratic institutions had been established in nations like Libya, Tunisia, and Egypt. However, a lack of jobs, widespread corruption, and broad gulfs between the citizens and their respective governments generated overwhelming political dissent and undermined democratic institutions. This situation resulted in a wave of antigovernment protests and demonstrations that began in Tunisia in December 2010 and spread throughout the Middle East region for several years. One of several reasons for this violence was an absence of participatory leadership and government in this region (Ogbonnaya, 2013).

CONCLUSION

Although participate leadership is increasing in many countries, there are many obstacles to its success. Participative leadership is reliant on the input of the constituency, and when that input is either inconsistent or nonexistent, the leadership must be wholly reliant on its own devices, which is contrary to the principles of a democratic government.

BIBLIOGRAPHY

Choi, Sanghan. "Democratic Leadership: The Lessons of Exemplary Models for Democratic Governance." *International Journal of Leadership Studies* 2.3 (2007): 243–62. Print.

"Democracy." ICPD. International Center for Peace and Development, n.d. Web. 1 May 2015.

Ferraris, Victor A. "'Lead from the Front': Participative Leadership." *Journal of Thoracic and Cardiovascular Surgery* 150.6 (2015): 1413–15. Print.

Harrison, Thomas. *The Great Empires of the Ancient World*. Los Angeles: J. Paul Getty Museum, 2009.

Hendriks, Frank, and Niels Karsten. "Theory of Democratic Leadership." In *The Oxford Handbook of Political Leadership*, edited by R. A. W. Rhodes and Paul T. Hart. New York: Oxford University Press, 2014, 41–56.

Hilmer, Jeffrey D. "The State of *Participatory* Democratic Theory." Annual Meeting of the Midwest Political Science Association. Chicago, IL. Apr. 2008. Conference Presentation.

Lam, Catherine K., Xu Huang, and Simon C. H. Chan. "The Threshold Effect of Participative Leadership and the Role of Leader Information Sharing." *Academy of Management Journal* 58.3 (2015): 836–55. Print.

Newman, Alexander, Philip S. Rose, and Stephen T. T. Teo. "The Role of Participative Leadership and Trust-Based Mechanisms in Eliciting Intern Performance: Evidence from China." *Human Resource Management* 55.1 (2016): 53–67. Print.

Ogbonnaya, Ufiem Maurice. "Arab Spring in Tunisia, Egypt, and Libya: A Comparison Analysis of Causes and Determinants." *Alternatives: Turkish Jour. of International Relations* 12.3 (2013): 4–16. Print.

Pop-Eleches, Grigore, and Graeme Robertson. "After the Revolution: Long-Term Effects of Electoral Revolutions." *Problems of Post-Communism* 61.4 (2014): 3–22. Print.

Rossberger, Robert J., and Diana E. Krause. "Participative and Team-Oriented Leadership Styles, Countries' Education Level, and National Innovation: The Mediating Role of Economic Factors and National Cultural Practices." *Cross-Cultural Research* 49.1 (2015): 20–56. Print.

Wampler, Brian, and Mike Touchton. "Brazil Let Its Citizens Make Decisions About City Budgets: Here's What Happened." *Washington Post*. Washington Post, 22 Jan. 2014. Web. 12 May 2015.

Michael Auerbach, M.A.

PEOPLE SKILLS

ABSTRACT

People skills are the tools used during effective interactions, whether verbal or nonverbal, with other individuals (peers, colleagues, superiors, etc.) in school, work, and community settings. These skills include the ability to respond appropriately to stressful, new, and conflict-based situations. Because these adaptations are dependent on cultural and environmental settings, individuals with the best people skills are often also adept at changing their mannerisms and speech to match the expectations of new audiences and the parameters of new communities. While some scholars believe that people skills can only be acquired at a young age, others believe that individuals can improve their people skills at any time in their lives; in general, experts agree that the ability to interact well with others can play a significant role in a wide variety of settings and situations.

Background

The study of people skills emerges from psychology and the desire to understand how individuals work and communicate in small and large groups. In the workplace, special attention initially turned to interpersonal skills. Books such as Dale Carnegie's *How to Win Friends and Influence People* (1936) were written to guide individuals who wanted to improve their social standing in both their personal and professional lives through better behavior and expressions. These books focused on individuals entering new social situations, communities, and cultures. However, because these guidebooks were designed for a mass market, their authors seldom interacted with academic researchers.

Scholars also focused on emotional intelligence, which is the observation and regulation of one's own emotions as well as the emotions of others. This concept was introduced by scholars such as Peter Salovey and John D. Mayer, who in 1990 separated emotional

A delivery man presents an invoice

intelligence into three parts: observing the expression of emotion, regulating emotion, and utilizing emotion. While early scholars claimed that these skills were fixed either at birth or in early childhood, academics are now investigating if, and how, individuals might improve their emotional intelligence throughout their lives.

The fields of interpersonal skills, emotional intelligence, and organizational psychology have produced a number of advice columns, books, and coaches aiming to inspire and instill people skills. All of these materials and professionals strive to make an individual better liked, more successful, and a more productive communicator in the workplace and other environments involving human interaction. At the same time, there is no set number or list of people skills, and these skills typically vary between cultures—what might be an acceptable display of trust or approval in one community could be considered offensive in another. Regardless, at the center of these skills is the ability to show that an individual cares about and trusts their peers or coworkers. Being able to relate to colleagues by sharing similar stories, experiences, or simply acknowledging the validity of another person's opinions, are a critical element of strong people skills. Patience is also considered a valuable people skill as it is critical for establishing respect, training new employees, moving into new teams, and overcoming delays as well as conflicts. Being persuasive without frustrating or antagonizing the person that you are trying to convince is also a critical people skill.

While the immediate effect of strong people skills—such as a calm resolution to a problem—are readily noticed, some scholars are working to prove that people skills also have long term effects. For example, scholars are attempting to demonstrate that high emotional intelligence and strong people skills in childhood can be used to predict future academic success. Other scholars believe that high emotional intelligence can result in better health, less stress, and more productive workplaces.

OVERVIEW

A large number of self-help books have been published for employees, students, and community members who wish to improve their people skills. Among children, the phrase "plays well with others" is often used to identify a child with strong people skills. These skills are often established in school, religious and/or community activities, and family settings. Children are coached in how to greet their elders and peers, and through demonstration and mimicry they learn which phrases, body language, and behaviors to use. Similar lessons are given for essential skills such as sharing, taking turns, demonstrating table manners, and negotiating conflicts. Each of these lessons is culturally coded, meaning that the child is learning how to interact in a specific cultural, class, religious, and political setting. Those lessons might not transfer to other cultures and might make it difficult for a student to move up or down the class ladder. However, despite this limitation, these lessons are an important part of a child's acculturation.

Some scholars worry, however, that the contemporary use of electronic screens, such as tablets and cellular phones, will have an adverse effect on a child's development of people skills. The problem is that children learn by observing the ways that adults interact. For example, children might learn how to interact with people on the subway by watching their parents' interactions. However, if the children are playing games on their tablets throughout the entire subway ride, they are missing these critical moments of observation. For adults, a general concern exists that increased dependence upon and captivation with advanced electronic devices, particularly cell phones and computers, means that people do not interact with one another as often in person, since they devote more time to these devices or choose to communicate using formats—such as email or texts—that lack the more personal touch. In a more digital world, people skills remain important, but these abilities may prove more challenging and less refined than in the past.

CONCLUSION

Psychologists, academics, and self-help book authors have continued to stress that strong people skills are critical to success in the workplace and community. Some corporations have heavily invested in developing their employees' emotional intelligences, with the understanding that doing so will make for smoother interactions between customers and employees. However, psychologists have also warned that some people may negatively take advantage of such abilities, as those with exceptionally good people skills might be tempted to manipulate other employees or customers. According to these psychologists, individuals with exceptional people skills might use their talents to gather information from colleagues or peers and then use that information to generate gossip, rumors, or even blackmail, creating problems in the workplace and community.

BIBLIOGRAPHY

Armstrong, Michael. *Armstrong's Handbook of Management and Leadership: Developing Effective People Skills for Better Leadership and Management*. 3rd ed. Philadelphia: Kogan Page, 2012.

Berman, Evan M., and Dira Berman. *People Skills at Work*. Boca Raton, FL: CRC, 2012.

Harms, Louise. *Working with People: Communication Skills for Reflective Practice*. 2nd ed. South Melbourne, Australia: Oxford University Press, 2015.

Jain, Samta, and Afreen S. Syed Anjuman. "Facilitating the Acquisition of Soft Skills through Training." *IUP Journal of Soft Skills* 7.2 (2013): 32–39. Print.

Kerpen, Dave. *The Art of People: 11 Simple Skills That Will Get You Everything You Want*. New York: Crown Business, 2016.

Malone, Samuel A. *People Skills for Managers*. Dublin, Ireland: Liffey, 2008.

Smith, Jacquelyn. "The 20 People Skills You Need to Succeed at Work." *Forbes*. Forbes Media, 15 Nov. 2013. Web. 16 Sept. 2016.

Thompson, Neil. *People Skills*. 4th ed. New York: Palgrave, 2015.

Allison Hahn, Ph.D. and Elena Popan, M.A.

PERFORMANCE APPRAISAL

ABSTRACT

Performance appraisal is the process of evaluating an employee's performance and providing feedback. Appraisals are necessary not only for employees to understand and improve their performance on the job and for employers to adequately evaluate and select their employees for rewards (e.g., money, prestige, promotion), but they are also important for the organization to determine the degree to which its employees are contributing toward meeting strategic goals and objectives. There are many ways to judge an employee's performance on the job ranging from objective performance data to global rating scales to more detailed rating scales that represent each of the important aspects of the job. No matter the method used, however, it is vital that the rating scales be anchored to objective, well-defined criteria of job success. This action will help ensure that the performance appraisal system is not only accurate but also fair.

OVERVIEW

There is an old saying that advises, "If you do not know where you are going, you will never get there." Certainly, nowhere is this truer than in a business or organizational setting. From an employee's perspective, knowing where one wants to go may mean wanting to do the things on the job that will help ensure a pay raise or promotion. From the organization's perspective, knowing where one is going may mean wanting to do the things that will improve its effectiveness and efficiency and, in general, help it become a high-performing organization. However, neither the employee nor the organization can meet these goals

PERFORMANCE APPRAISAL

Employee Name : _____

Job Function : _____

Date of Review : _____

Reviewer Name : _____

Quality of Work

Work is performed accurately and neatly. Work is consistent, though and complete	Comments
Outstanding Exceeds Expectations Meets Expectations Improvements Needed Unacceptable Not Applicable	

Quantity of Work

Amount of work performed on a daily basis appropriate for job function	Comments
Outstanding Exceeds Expectations Meets Expectations Improvements Needed Unacceptable Not Applicable	

Job knowledge

Understands the job requirements and has specific content knowledge where appropriate	Comments
Outstanding Exceeds Expectations Meets Expectations Improvements Needed Unacceptable Not Applicable	

A sample performance appraisal form (image courtesy of Rahulkepapa)

unless they know how they are currently performing and can determine what changes must be made in order to improve overall performance. For the individual, this information usually comes in the form of feedback from a performance appraisal or review.

Performance appraisal is the process of evaluating an employee's work performance and providing feedback on how well he or she is doing, typically against some standard of performance for that job. Performance appraisal can also provide the organization with some of the information that it needs in order to make strategic decisions to help it succeed in the marketplace.

Uses for Performance Appraisal Information

Performance appraisal is one of the key functions of an organization's human resources department. Organizations use the data collected in performance appraisal systems for several purposes. Perhaps the most well known of these is to establish standards and an evaluation system that can be used to form the basis of judgments as to whether to reward employees for good performance or punish them for poor performance. For example, management might set an individual productivity target of manufacturing two hundred widgets per day. Those who meet this standard might be given a pay raise or bonus and those who do not might not receive a monetary reward or may be put on probation. Performance appraisal data are also used to provide the criterion information that is used to select new candidates for a job. For example, the results of a job analysis might tell management what tasks a production worker needs to perform on the job. This information is used in conjunction with performance appraisal data that provide information regarding performance standards in order to develop criteria to be used in hiring new employees for the job.

Another use for performance appraisal data is to provide objectives for organizational training programs. For example, if a department wide performance appraisal finds that widget makers do not have the necessary skills to meet the organization's goal of two hundred widgets per employee per day, the human resources department might design or contract for a training program that would teach line workers the skills necessary to be better able to meet this goal. Finally, performance appraisal data can provide management with information needed to provide feedback to employees and to better control their behavior on the job. In most cases, both the employees and management would like to see improved performance on the job. From the employees' perspective, improved performance can be the key to raises, bonuses, perks, and promotions. Such things can help them better meet their needs on the job or in other areas of their lives. Similarly, management would like to see improved performance because it helps to improve the effectiveness and efficiency of the organization, improves the return on investment for hiring and training, and helps the organization reach its strategic goals and become a high-performing organization.

Job Analyses

Before an objective performance appraisal system can be developed, one must first perform a job analysis to determine what tasks are actually performed on the job, the standards to which these tasks need to be performed, and the knowledge, skills, abilities,

327

and other characteristics necessary in order to adequately perform these tasks. Job analysis is the systematic, empirical process of determining the exact nature of a job, including the tasks and duties to be done; the knowledge, skills, and abilities necessary to adequately perform these tasks and duties; and the criteria that distinguish between acceptable and unacceptable performance. The results of a job analysis are typically used in writing job descriptions, selecting new employees for hire, and setting standards for performance appraisals.

Performance appraisals need to be based on the tasks that are actually required to be performed on the job rather than on some general impression of the performance of the employee. These tasks and the standards to which they must be performed are usually based on a solid job description based on an objective, thorough job analysis. Good job descriptions and the performance appraisals that are based on them are competency based, describing the job in terms of measurable, observable, behavioral competencies that the employee must demonstrate in order to perform the job well. For example, rather than saying that a salesperson needs to have good customer rapport, the employee would be required to do such things as greet the customer within thirty seconds of entering the store, immediately drop any tasks not directly related to helping customers in the store if a customer needs help, or any other requirement found to be important to good work performance as determined by the job analysis. The performance standards developed as a product of a thorough job analysis are then used not only to frame the performance appraisal criteria but also to communicate to employees what kind of behavior will be rewarded (or not rewarded) by the organization. Performance appraisal data are then used to give employees feedback on how well they are meeting the standards in order to encourage high performance.

FURTHER INSIGHTS

Methods of Data Collection

There are many sources of data that can be used in developing a performance appraisal system. For some jobs, empirical, quantitative data are available to objectively judge the quality of an employee's work. For example, for production workers, one might use a combination of quantitative data such as the average number of widgets produced per hour, the amount of waste material produced as a byproduct of manufacturing that number of widgets, and the number of widgets produced that are within specifications.

In addition to objective production data, in some situations there are personnel data that are available that need to be taken into account when judging an employee's performance. For example, one might want to consider the number of days the employee was late to work, excessive days taken off, or other hard data that might be found in the employee's personnel file that address the employee's level of performance on the job. Although sometimes personnel data can be useful adjuncts when judging performance, they are typically not a substitute for data more directly related to performance.

Of course, not every job can be neatly reduced to quantifiable data. Although one can judge the performance of manufacturing workers, for example, based on the number of widgets they produce per hour, such objective data are not available for every position. In the twenty-first century, an increasing number of employees are knowledge workers and deal in the realm of information and expertise rather than in the realm of tangible products. For example, although it is possible to collect data on the number of calls a technical support employee takes on a help line, this data does not provide information on how difficult the problem was, how well it was solved, how polite the employee was to the customer, or how satisfied the customer was with the service. As those who use technical support lines know, these pieces of information are important and are not captured in the easily collectible "number of calls per hour" statistic. To help management make better informed decisions regarding an employee's performance, it is often necessary to collect subjective, judgmental data regarding performance. An example of this kind of data collection instrument is the "short survey" that often pops up after an online interaction with a sales or support employee.

Rating Scales

There are many approaches to designing a rating scale to be used in performance appraisal. The simplest of these is the global rating scale in which each employee is given a single score that rates his or her overall performance. However, global ratings do not give the employee sufficient data for how to improve his or her performance. In addition, such scales are prone to various kinds of rating error (see below). Therefore, many organizations develop rating scales based on job-related data and standards. One can use a job description, for example, to break out the major aspects of the job and then rate employees on each of these elements. However, without well-defined standards for poor, acceptable, and outstanding performance, such rating scales can also be highly subjective in nature and prone to rating errors. Behaviorally anchored rating scales and mixed standards rating scales are two techniques that can be used to increase the objectivity of rating scales and link them to tangible, job-related criteria. Both these methods are based on the collection of critical incidents to discern between good and poor performance on the job. These critical incidents are used to anchor the rating scales and judge current employees against these criteria of success or failure on the job. Rating scales and other instruments that are used to collect subjective data can be easily affected by various rating errors. The most common of these are halo error, leniency error, and central tendency error.

The halo error (sometimes referred to as the halo/horn error depending on which direction the error is made) occurs when a manager or other rater judges a person in all aspects of job performance based on a single aspect of the job or, on whether he or she likes the individual. For example, if someone is seen as an excellent worker (or nice person) in general, the rater may overlook performance problems in the individual's work and rate him or her highly on all aspects of the job.

The leniency error (sometimes referred to as the leniency/severity error) occurs when a rater tends to rate employees in general higher (or lower) than they would be if the rater had been more objective. For example, some supervisors tend to be lenient in the ratings because they want to be kind to their employees and, as a result, rate them higher than they deserve. Similarly, some supervisors believe that everyone can always improve and, therefore, tend to rate their employees more severely than they objectively deserve.

The central tendency error occurs when a supervisor tends to give ratings toward the middle of the scale, believing that although the employees have room for improvement, they also do not deserve to be punished for their performance.

Management by Objectives (MBO)

It is important to evaluate an employee's performance by measuring it against a predetermined standard or set of specific goals to be achieved during the appraisal period. Rating scales are one way to accomplish this goal; another popular way is through a method called Management by Objectives (MBO). In management by objectives, managers or the manager and employee together set objectives for the employee to meet during the upcoming appraisal period. Employees are evaluated in terms of how well they have met these goals in the intervening period. Management by objectives can be used not only to evaluate the performance of an individual employee but also that of a work group, department, or the organization as a whole. Under this approach, organization-wide goals and objectives based on its strategic plan (e.g., increase company profits from the widget product line by $500,000 over the next year) are first set. Using this information, each department or workgroup then sets its own goals and objectives to support the organization's goals (e.g., increase sales of widgets in the Eastern Region by 10 percent over the next year). Managers and individual employees then discuss these goals and possible contributions that can be made by each individual and set specific, short-term goals (e.g., obtain ten more customers per quarter; call on five more potential customers per week; include two more cities in the region), and individual objectives are set.

Like rating scales, however, management by objectives is not without its drawbacks. One of the most frequent is the development of objectives that are either unclear or unmeasurable. For example, in the example of "good customer rapport," if there is no operational definition of the concept, then the objective is as open to rating error as a poorly written rating item. Similarly, some objectives are unreasonable, such as the objective for a research scientist to develop a cure for cancer within the next year. Another difficulty with using management by objectives is that supervisors tend to set objectives that are too difficult to meet while employees tend to set objectives that are too easy to meet.

360-Degree Feedback

To help ensure fair evaluations under a performance appraisal system, human resource policies or procedures are developed and implemented to help increase the objectiveness of the appraisal feedback or give the employee feedback from multiple sources. A technique called 360-degree feedback (because the feedback comes from people who work all around the employee, not just from one person working above him or her) gives employees feedback on their job performance from representatives of the major groups with whom they interact on the job both inside and outside the organization. Under 360-degree feedback, for example, employees may receive feedback not only from their supervisors but also from their subordinates, coworkers, customers, and other groups with whom they work. By using this method, an employee receives more feedback than he or she would receive under the traditional supervisor only appraisal system. This approach to feedback can also help neutralize biased opinions of one person by giving the employee and the supervisor a range of reactions to look at so that they can look at the preponderance of evidence rather than reactions from just one person and, in general, give the employee a better idea of how he or she can improve performance.

Issues

Pay-for-performance appraisal tools and systems are not ends in and of themselves. Among the major purposes of performance appraisal are the ability to provide employees with measurable criteria of success on the job and to provide feedback on how they can improve their performance in order to better meet their performance goals and objectives and move ahead with their careers. One of the ways in which performance appraisal data are frequently used involves linking pay to performance. Under this paradigm, an employee is rewarded financially for high performance and contributing to the organization's goals. Pay-for-performance systems can be used at all levels of the organization, including "C-level" personnel (e.g., chief executive officer, chief operating officer).

The U.S. Government Accountability Office (GAO) has investigated the viability of pay-for-performance systems and has found a number of factors that make them successful. First, it is important to use objective competencies to assess the quality of the employee's performance. This requirement means that performance objectives need to be based on the empirical data developed through a thorough job analysis and be written in such a way that employees can achieve them. Second, employee performance ratings need to be directly tied to pay increases or rewards so that employees can see a direct, positive consequence of their actions. In this way, employees are more likely to continue to perform at a level that will bring rewards. Third, fair pay-for-performance systems need to consider both the employee's current salary and his or her contribution to the organization so that rewards for similar contributions are equitable. Finally, pay-for-performance systems need to be clear and well published so that employees know the basis on which decisions are made and what kind of awards are made across the organization.

CONCLUSION

Performance appraisal is one of the key elements of the human resources function within an organization. This process of evaluating an employee's performance and providing feedback is necessary not only for the individual to improve his or her performance on the job so that he or she can earn the rewards for which he or she is working, such as a promotion or raise, but it is also important so that the organization can determine the degree to which its employees are contributing to meeting its strategic goals and objectives. Performance appraisal data can also be used for other purposes as well, including as data to design training programs or to develop criteria on which to hire new employees. There are many ways to judge an employee's performance on the job ranging from objective performance data to global rating scales to more detailed rating scales that represent each of the important aspects of the job. However, whenever a subjective rating method is used, it is vital that the rating scales be anchored to objective, well-defined criteria of job success. This action will help ensure that the performance appraisal system is not only accurate but fair.

BIBLIOGRAPHY

Ayers, Rebecca S. "Aligning Individual and Organizational Performance: Goal Alignment in Federal Government Agency Performance Appraisal Programs." *Public Personnel Management* 44, no. 2 (2015): 161–91. Print.

Boachie-Mensah, Francis O., and Peter Seidu. "Employees' Perception of Performance Appraisal

System: A Case Study." *International Journal of Business & Management* 7 (2012): 73–88. Print.

Cascio. Wayne F. *Applied Psychology in Human Resource Management*. 5th ed. Upper Saddle River, NJ: Prentice Hall, 1998.

Dessler, Gary. *Human Resource Management*. 10th ed. Upper Saddle River, NJ: Pearson Education/Prentice Hall, 2005.

Farndale, Elaine, and Clare Kelliher. "Implementing Performance Appraisal: Exploring the Employee Experience." *Human Resource Management* 52 (2013): 879–97. Print.

Harrington, James R., and Ji H. Lee. "What Drives Perceived Fairness of Performance Appraisal? Exploring the Effects of Psychological Contract Fulfilllment on Employees' Perceived Fairness of Performance Appraisal in U.S. Federal Agencies." *Public Personnel Management* 44, no. 2 (2015): 214–38. Print.

Landy, Frank J., and Jeffrey M. Conte. *Work in the 21st Century: An Introduction to Industrial and Organizational Psychology*. Boston: McGraw Hill, 2004.

Muchinsky, Paul. *Psychology Applied to Work*. 7th ed. Belmont, CA: Wadsworth/Thomson Learning, 2003.

Pichler, Shaun. "The Social Context of Performance Appraisal and Appraisal Reactions: A Meta-Analysis." *Human Resource Management* 51 (2012): 709–32. Print.

US General Accounting Office. Human capital: Implementing Pay for Performance at Selected Personnel Demonstration Projects. (2004). GAO Reports (GAO-04-83). Print.

Suggested Reading

Ahn, Tae S., I. Hwang, and M.-I. Kim. "The Impact of Performance Measure Discriminability of Rate Incentives." *Accounting Review* 85 (2010): 389–417. Print.

Chan, Hon S., and Jie Gao. "Putting the Cart before the Horse: Accountability or Performance?" *Australian Journal of Public Administration* 68 (2009): S51–S61. Print.

Cichello, Michael S., C. Edward Fee, Charles J. Hadlock, and Ramona Sonti. "Promotions, Turnover, and Performance Evaluation: Evidence from the Careers of Division Managers." *Accounting Review* 84 (2009): 1119–43. Print.

Ellis, Shmuel, Rachel Mendel, and Merav Aloni-Zohar. "The Effect of Accuracy of Performance Evaluation on Learning from Experience: The Moderating Role of After-Event Reviews." *Journal of Applied Social Psychology* 39 (2009): 541–63. Print.

Goffin, Richard D., R. Blake Jelley, Deborah M. Powell, and Norman G. Johnston. "Taking Advantage of Social Comparisons in Performance Appraisal: The Relative Percentile Method." *Human Resource Management* 48 (2009): 251–68. Print.

Iqbal, Muhammad, Saeed Akbar, and Pawan Budhwar. "Effectiveness of Performance Appraisal: An Integrated Framework." *International Journal of Management Review* 17, no. 4 (2015): 510–33. Print.

Kaplan, Steven E., and Priscilla S. Wisner. "The Judgmental Effects of Management Communications in a Fifth Balanced Scorecard Category on Performance Evaluation." *Behavioral Research in Accounting* 21 (2009): 37–56. Print.

Kumar, Jagadesh. "Evaluating Scientists: Citations, Impact Factor, H-Index, Online Page Hits and What Else?" *IETE Technical Review* 26 (2009): 165–68. Print.

Lau, Chong M., Kuan M. Wong, and Ian R.C. Eggleton. "Fairness of Performance Evaluation Procedures and Job Satisfaction: The Role of Outcome-Based and Non-Outcome-Based Effects." *Accounting and Business Research* 38 (2008): 121–35. Print.

Narcisse, Sharon, and Mark Harcourt. "Employee Fairness Perceptions of Performance Appraisal: A Saint Lucian Case Study." *International Journal of Human Resource Management* 19 (2008): 1152–69. Print.

Sholinhin, Mahfud, and Richard Pike. "Fairness in Performance Evaluation and Its Behavioural Consequences." *Accounting and Business Research* 39 (2009): 397–413. Print.

Tan, Hun-Tan, and Premila G. Shankar. "Audit Reviewers' Evaluation of Subordinates' Work Quality." *Auditing* 29 (2010): 251–66. Print.

Varma, Arup, and Shaun Pichler. "Interpersonal Affect: Does It Really Bias Performance Appraisals?" *Journal of Labor Research* 28 (2007): 387–412. Print.

Williams, Sheryl L., and Mary Lee Hummert. "Evaluating Performance Appraisal Instrument Dimensions Using Construct Analysis." *Journal of Business Communication* 27 (1990): 117–35. Print.

Wren, Brent M. "Examining Gender Differences in Performance Evaluations, Rewards and Punishments." *Journal of Management Research* 6 (2006): 114–124. Print.

Ruth A. Wienclaw, Ph.D.

PROFESSIONAL ETHICS

ABSTRACT

Professional ethics include the personal, organizational, and corporate standards of behavior expected of professionals. To ensure that employees properly represent themselves and the companies for which they work, most institutions have a set of ethics to which all employees must adhere—this situation is especially true for university employees, medical workers, police, other public service officers, military personnel, and corporate employees. Many professional societies also have ethical declarations or codes of conduct. Because organizational credibility is based on reputation, penalties for violating an ethics code are often steep and can include demotion, suspension, firing, and at times, imprisonment.

Brief History

Among the oldest standards for professional ethics is the Hippocratic Oath. Beginning in the fifth century BCE, Greek doctors swore to help the sick and to avoid doing harm. This solemn oath was taken in the name of Greek gods and goddesses. While modern doctors do not take the oath in the name of Greek gods and goddesses, many still pledge to follow an ethical code based on serving and not doing harm to the best of their abilities. Additionally, doctors pledge to pay primary attention to the human whom they are treating, rather than to focus on physical symptoms solely.

Professional ethics also have long traditions in military organizations where officers are bound by specific expectations of how to interact with colleagues, how to treat those who rank above and below them, and how to engage the enemy. Historically, these ethical standards were different among various militaries. However, modern international agreements, such as the Geneva Convention of 1949 govern the ways that militaries interact with civilians, religious authorities, and medical personnel, and how weapons are used on civilian populations. For example, it is a violation of the Geneva Convention to kill either an enemy who has surrendered or civilians who are not engaged in a conflict. While this code of ethics does not always prevent conflicts, it does provide a framework for punishing those who have acted unethically. For example, after the 1994 Rwandan genocide, the United Nations established an International Criminal Tribunal to prosecute those who had violated military professional ethics.

Modern organizations build upon historical examples of professional ethical codes to adapt to modern situations. These adaptations account for the rapid pace of scientific advancement, questions about personal privacy, and cultural struggles over topics such as racism and sexism. As professional ethics change, so do the ways that professionals interact with one another, with the public, and with the media. Professionals are typically trained and retrained to ensure that they have kept up with the most current professional ethical standards.

Professional Ethics Today

Professional ethics govern many different workplaces and careers. One of the strictest set of professional ethics is used for scientists and has been designed to ensure that human and animal subjects are not abused during scientific research. In the United States, research occurring within a university is overseen by an institutional review board (IRB). Before beginning a new project, each researcher must request approval for the research by submitting paperwork outlining what research will occur, why that work is necessary, what risks it will pose to test subjects, and what actions will be taken to mitigate or resolve those risks. When subjects are put at risk

Hippocrates, originator of the Hippocratic Oath

because of a study, such as trying out a new drug, they must be made aware of the risks and often must be compensated for their time and potential harm.

Research occurring outside a university, such as at a private biomedical lab, does not undergo IRB approval. However, employees of private laboratories are still subject to professional ethical codes, as well as to governmental ethical codes if they are funded by government grants. These codes are continually redefined to match the advancement of science. For example, when scientists began to conduct research on human stem cells, their professional organizations began to debate how they should respond to and regulate such research.

Professionals in other fields—such as lawyers, clerks, and judges—are also guided by professional ethical codes that regulate such issues as who is able to speak during a court case and how long a judge can serve in a specific post. Because clients might wish to share sensitive information with a lawyer, lawyers are bound by their own professional ethics that determine what information they must share with the court and what information they can keep secret.

Religious workers are another group regulated by professional ethics. Religious leaders often hold positions of power and prestige in their communities; therefore, they are also guided by a strict set of ethics regarding their work with both members of their religion and of the larger community. While these ethics may differ for each religion, the way that the US government respects those ethics is the same. Information shared with religious figures is often seen as private and protected from government interference. However, the subject of public statements by religious figures is contentious. Scholars and members of religious communities have often debated how religious tenets interact with professional ethics—for example, whether or not religious views should affect the ways that a congressperson makes political decisions.

Teachers are bound by a special set of professional ethics known as "in loco parentis," which is Latin for "in place of the parent." This phrase means that teachers are expected to act as a moral authority and guardian for children in their care. On a daily basis, teachers should set good examples for their students. Teachers are also allowed to enforce dress codes, codes of conduct, and school rules; in crisis situations, teachers make decisions regarding a child's welfare. The concept of in loco parentis has been the subject of many Supreme Court cases. For example, such cases have asked if school officials have the right to silence a student's speech (therefore taking away the student's right to free speech) and if schools can force children to say the pledge of allegiance.

Many other careers are also guided by professional ethics. Accountants, nurses, and athletes each have different professional ethical codes. These professional ethics are continually reviewed and revised to respond to contemporary issues, emergent technology, and societal expectations.

BIBLIOGRAPHY

Corey, Gerald, Marianne Scheider Corey, and Patrick Callanan. *Issues and Ethics in Helping Professions*. Belmont, CA: Thomson, 2007.

Davies, Richard J. "Codes, Complacency and Confidence: Are Professional Standards or Ethics Enough to Produce Good Results in the Public Interest?" *Education Today* 64.3 (2014): 14–17. Print.

Flite, Cathy A., and Laurinda B. Harman. "Code of Ethics: Principles for Ethical Leadership." *Perspectives in Health Information Management* (2013): 1–11. Print.

Heubel, Friedrich. "The "Soul of Professionalism" in the Hippocratic Oath and Today." *Medicine, Health Care, and Philosophy* 18.2 (2015): 185–94. Print.

Johnson, Bonnie J. "Codes of Ethics, Public Values, and What Public Servants Offer the Bureaucratic Compact." *International Journal of Organization Theory and Behavior* 17.4 (2014): 459–96. Print.

Sadowski, Jathan. "Leaning on the Ethical Crutch: A Critique of Codes of Ethics." *IEEE Technology & Society Magazine* 33.4 (2014): 44–72. Print.

Schwandt, Thomas A. "Reconstructing Professional Ethics and Responsibility: Implications of Critical Systems Thinking." *Evaluation: The International Journal of Theory, Research and Practice* 21.4 (2015): 462–66. Print.

Allison Hahn, Ph.D.
Elena Popan, M.A.

Project Management

ABSTRACT

Project management is the process of planning, monitoring, and controlling a unique set of tasks that have a discrete beginning, end, and outcome. The project management process is performed within the three constraints of time, costs, and scope. The goal of project management is to produce a technically acceptable product that is both on-time and within budget. To do this work, project management attempts to reduce the risks associated with the project and maximize the benefits, including profit and marketability. A number of tools and techniques are available to help the project manager monitor and control projects.

OVERVIEW

A project is a unique, discrete set of tasks with a defined beginning, end, and outcome. It may be as simple as completing a paper for class or as complex as designing, developing, and testing a new destroyer for the Navy. No project is accomplished in a vacuum, however. Each task must be accomplished under the three constraints of time (e.g., the paper is due on Friday; the first destroyer must be operational and in the fleet ten years from the start of the contract), cost (e.g., research for the paper must be done in the local library rather than paying to download articles from professional sites; the destroyer must be built within the budget set by Congress), and scope (e.g., the paper can only be 5,000 words long, so it needs to be limited to a narrow topic even though the background information is very interesting; the destroyer needs to be built to the specifications set at the beginning of the project even though the customer or the project team think that additional features would make it better). Project management is a process that helps the project team accomplish its goals within the three constraints of time, cost, and scope. Using the principles and tools of project management, one can plan, organize, and manage the tasks to be done within the given constraints in order to accomplish the goal of the project.

Unfortunately, not every project is run using sound project management principles. Instead, many companies manage projects by doing the organizational equivalent of putting out brush fires, paying attention to whichever problem is most pressing at the time, while letting other problems grow only to be dealt with later at the expense of other project tasks. In a well-run project, on the other hand, the project manager—the project authority for planning, coordinating, and managing the project—needs to be proactive rather than reactive, keeping a constant eye on all aspects of the project so that no one area is allowed to develop problems that could sabotage the overall project in order to accomplish the project goals.

Project management is essentially the art of project control, with the continuing goal of keeping the project on time and within budget. This interactive process involves keeping the project within technical scope (i.e., not adding work to the project outside that which was originally planned), within the budget negotiated for accomplishment of the project tasks, moving along according to the predetermined schedule, and balancing the risks associated with changes in any of these areas and how they affect the accomplishment of the overall goal of the project. To do these things, project management activities focus on three things: the project and its goals, the processes of how these goals are met, and the performance of individuals and organizations to accomplish these goals. If a project is managed well, its goals can be accomplished on-time and within budget, not only giving the organization a profit in the short term, but enhancing its reputation for good work at a reasonable cost; thereby enhancing its ability to continue to make a profit in the future.

APPLICATION

There are a number of tools available to help project managers manage their projects efficiently and effectively. Several project management software packages are available that help project managers crunch the required numbers associated with risk management and other project management activities. However, project management is not a task that can be completely automated; human experience and judgments are necessary.

To successfully manage a project, one must first understand the scope of the project (what needs to be done, what the end result should be and the limits placed on these elements by the schedule and budget). In many cases, technical specifications will have been provided by the customer. For the example of the research paper, they may be simple: The paper needs to be 4,900–5,100 words long, follow a specific broad outline, focus on a given topic, and use at least three professional references cited in APA format. For the example of the destroyer, however, the task is more complicated. Although the customer undoubtedly will provide technical specifications for what they want the new ship to be able to do, such specifications are long and complex, and need to be distilled and synthesized so that they can be tracked for project management purposes. One way to do this distilling is through the use of a work breakdown structure (WBS). A good WBS provides a solid foundation for performing the tasks of project management on a complex project. By developing a thorough WBS, project management can be better prepared to control the project proactively, rather than constantly react in emergency mode to unforeseen problems.

At its most basic, a WBS is a list of all the tasks that need to be done to complete the project. It is written as a hierarchy, starting with general tasks and then breaking these general tasks into more specific steps that need to be taken. For the project of writing a paper, the general outline of the project might be to define the topic, collect data, write the paper, edit the paper, proofread the paper, and submit the paper. The initial step of defining the topic could further be broken down into substeps such as scanning the textbook and materials provided by the professor to narrow the topic into areas of interest, bounding the problem by doing preliminary research in the library or on the internet to see what the components of the topic are, and developing an outline defining the sections of the paper that will be used both for data collection and for writing the paper itself. An example of a portion of a WBS for writing a paper is shown in figure 1.

WBS Number	Task Description
1.0	Project initiation
1.1	Define topic
1.1.1	Scan textbook and other materials
1.1.2	Preliminary library research
1.1.3	Develop preliminary outline
1.2	Perform research
1.2.1	Gather library books on topic
1.2.2	Search professional database for articles

Figure 1: Work Breakdown Structure (WBS)

In addition to developing a WBS, for more complex projects it is often helpful to determine the critical path that defines which activities are critical to accomplishing the project in a timely manner. Critical path management (CPM) is a tool that helps project managers analyze the activities that need to be performed to accomplish the project and when each needs to be accomplished so that the rest of the project can proceed in a timely manner. This work includes determining the order in which the tasks need to be accomplished, what tasks feed into them, and how long each task will take to accomplish. In the example of writing a paper, the critical path might include a target date for finishing the library research that allows sufficient time to synthesize the material before actually writing the paper. For example, a target date for finishing the first draft of the paper should be in place to leave sufficient time to do quality control on the paper, checking it for coherence and flow, grammar and spelling errors, and inclusion of all needed data. In the more complicated example of ship design and development, the development of the critical path would allow the project manager to determine that the training component could not be started until it was determined what tasks needed to be performed both in normal operations and in battle. An example of a portion of a critical-path diagram for writing a paper is given in figure 2. Note that there are two tasks that cannot be performed until the previous task is accomplished.

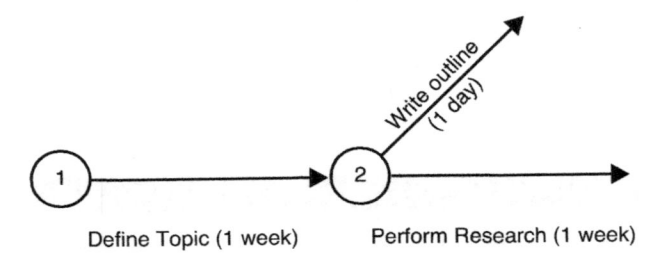

Figure 2: Critical Path Diagram

Another technique that may be of help in project management is resource loading, the process of examining the project to determine which resources are most critical to the success of the project, and proportioning them among the various activities. In the example of the paper, most students find that their most critical resource is time. Resource allocation for writing the paper might include determining how much time can be devoted to the paper from start to finish while still getting other necessary activities accomplished (e.g., eating, sleeping, doing homework for other classes), then allocating that limited time appropriately within the project to each of the activities. For the development of the ship, of course, resources are not limited to time, but also to personnel available to work on the project, materials necessary to perform the activities associated with the project (e.g., computer workstations, software licenses; steel, fiberglass, and other building materials), and the money to acquire both. So, for example, if the budget only allows for the hiring of ten programmers, it must be determined which programming tasks are the most critical and how much of the programmers' time should be allocated to each to best keep the project on time and within budget.

Another widely used project management tool is the program evaluation review technique (PERT). PERT is a variation on the critical-path method, and estimates not only the expected length of time to complete each activity in the project, but also the shortest and longest times that each activity could take. This gives project managers a window for each activity and helps them better predict future impact on the project if schedule estimates are not met. This system also helps project managers determine the exact status of the project and predict any potential trouble areas that might negatively impact either the schedule or budget of the project. To accomplish this goal, PERT divides the project into separate, detailed tasks on a schedule. These tasks are then put together as part of an integrated network that shows how each task impacts the others as well as the overall critical path for the system. Each task is also associated with the appropriate resources—including time, manpower, and capital—that it have been allocated. After the system has been put into place, PERT implements a reporting system so that project managers can compare actual performance and planned progress, and can continually check the status of the project.

Another popular scheduling tool for projects is the Gantt Chart. On the vertical axis, the Gantt chart lists all the tasks to be accomplished for the project. On the horizontal axis, the chart lists the time for the accomplishment of these tasks, usually broken down into some predefined unit such as days, weeks, or months. Within the body of the chart, the various tasks to be performed are placed on the time line with an indication of the projected start and end dates for each activity. An example of a simplified Gantt chart for part of the paper writing task is shown in figure 3.

Tasks	Week 1
	S M T W Th F S
1.0 Define the topic	△──▽
1.1 Scan available material	△─▽
1.2 Perform library research	△──▽
1.3 Outline paper	△────▽

Figure 3: Simplified Gantt Chart

When managing a project, cost and schedule often interact, affecting project performance. For example, budget constraints that prevent the organization from hiring additional programmers mean that there is less programming work that can be done on the project. Alternative solutions could include asking programmers to work overtime, hiring temporary or part-time workers for the short term, or using only the current programmers and letting them finish their tasks as they can. Each alternative, however, has risks associated with it. The overtime option might require additional money or reduce the effectiveness of overworked human beings, impacting both budget and schedule. The temporary employee option would also require additional funds for personnel and for training them, but would minimize these by using the additional personnel on an as-needed status. The option of working only with the current employees without overtime could run the risk of missed deadlines while still requiring additional funds as the programmers work not longer hours in the day, but more hours in the project. Risk management is a generic term applied to considering such alternatives and balancing the impacts on the cost, schedule, and design in order to determine which alternative has the least impact on the overall performance of the contract.

The risks associated with not meeting the schedule or budget of a project can affect not only the organization in the short term, but also its long-term viability as well as the career of the project manager. Business risks are the risks that could damage the organization in either the short term or long term if the project fails. Short-term risks might include such things as incurring unexpected expenses on a fixed price contract or not earning an expected incentive if a delivery schedule is not met. In addition, not meeting deadlines or technical requirements could have long-term impact on the organization's reputation and ability to obtain future business. For the project manager, there are also the personal and career risks incurred if the project fails. For all involved, therefore, it is important that risks be honestly recognized beforehand and plans put into place so that their negative impact can be minimized if a task or activity runs into trouble.

Some of the risks associated with a contract depend in part on the type of contract for the project. The two basic types of contracts are the fixed price contract and the cost-reimbursable contract. In the fixed price contract, all project costs are built into the contract and the contractor must pay for any costs incurred over and above the contract amount. This type of contract is generally used where the contract requirements are well-defined in advance and the associated costs can be predetermined. The cost reimbursable contract, on the other hand, is typically used in situations where the costs associated with the project cannot be adequately and accurately estimated beforehand. In this type of contract, the contractor is reimbursed for costs allowable under the terms of the contract and, therefore, the contractor incurs less risk. Contract type is actually a continuum from contracts where the risk is incurred by the contractor (e.g., firm fixed price contracts, fixed price with redetermination contracts, and fixed price incentive contracts in decreasing order of risk) or on the customer (e.g., cost plus fixed fee, cost plus incentive fee, and time and material, in order of increased risk for the customer). Contracts with high risk for the contractor require better risk management.

There are two aspects to risk management. Risk analysis is a planning activity to determine the possibility of risk and ways to reduce its impact. As part of this process, the project manager and key personnel determine three things: (1) what factors could cause the project to fail, (2) what the consequences of such failure might be, and (3) how likely failure is to occur. Various formulas are available to then determine the comparative severity and importance of each risk. For example, an activity that is likely to go wrong but that has little impact on the overall completion of the project is probably less important than an activity that has a smaller chance of failing but that would prevent successful completion of the project. After such determinations are made, a plan can be developed and implemented to handle the possibility of failure at any one of these points.

It is not enough to know what to do if a task or activity on a project fails. Good risk management also requires risk control. This project management responsibility includes such activities as monitoring the project risks so that they can be caught earlier rather than later in the process so that the contingency plan can be put into effect as soon as possible. Maximizing the effectiveness of the risk monitoring process, particularly on larger projects, also requires having a risk reporting structure in place so that those working closely on the at-risk activities can report problems to management in a timely manner.

There are a number of tools and techniques available for project risk management including software programs and risk calculation formulas. Computer simulations alone, however, are not adequate to predicting the impact of risk or for preventing it. Large projects typically build in periodic formal reviews held between both the contractor and the customer to jointly determine the status of the project and whether or not mid-course corrections are needed. Two major reviews that are often built into the schedule are the preliminary design review (PDR) and the critical-design review (CDR). The PDR is conducted after the preliminary design is complete but before the detail design is begun. During the PDR, the contract describes any changes made to the original design along with the rationale for these changes. At PDR, the contractor may also provide a hands-on demonstration or proof-of-concept for the product. The CDR is conducted before the design is released for manufacturing. Progressive or incremental CDRs may occur for subsystems of the project, followed by a system-level CDR to determine the completeness and feasibility of the design as a whole.

BIBLIOGRAPHY

Hajek, Victor G. *Management of Engineering Projects*. 3rd ed. New York: McGraw-Hill Book Company, 1984.

Human, W.J., and Herman Steyn. "Establishing Project Management Guidelines for Successfully Managing Resettlement Projects." *South African Journal of Business Management* 44, no. 3 (2013): 1–14. Web. 25 Nov. 2013.

Kumar, P.P. "Effective Use of Gantt Chart for Managing Large Scale Projects." *Cost Engineering* 47, no. 7 (2005, July): 14–21. Web. 19 Mar. 2007.

LaBrosse, M. "Project Management in the Real World." *Plant Engineering* 58, no. 11 (2004): 29–32. Web. 19 Mar. 2007.

Lehman, Bill. "Project Risk Management." *Mortgage Banking* 67, no. 5 (2007): 99–100. Web. 19 Mar. 2007.

Linton, Jonathan. "Managing the Project." *Circuits Assembly* 17, no. 6 (2006): 12–14. Web. 19 Mar. 2007.

Parker, David, Joshua Charlton, Ana Ribeiro, and Rashuvar D. Pathak." Integration of Project-Based Management and Change Management Intervention Methodology." *International Journal of Productivity & Performance Management* 62, no. 5 (2013): 534–44. Web. 25 Nov. 2013.

Ward, John, and Elizabeth M. Daniel. "The Role of Project Management Offices (PMOs) in IS Project Success and Management Satisfaction." *Journal of Enterprise Information Management* 26, no. 3 (2013): 316–36. Web. 25 Nov. 2013.

SUGGESTED READING

Besner, Claude, and Brian Hobbs. "An Empirical Identification of Project Management Toolsets and a Comparision among Project Types." *Project Management Journal* 43, no. 5 (2012): 24–46. Web. 25 Nov. 2013.

Grant, Kevin P., William M. Cashman, and David S. Christensen. "Delivering Projects on Time." *Research Technology Management* 49, no. 6 (2006): 52–58. Web. 19 Mar. 2007.

Griffith, Andrew F. "Scheduling Practices and Project Success." *Cost Engineering* 48, no. 9 (2006): 24–30. Web. 19 Mar. 2007.

Krane, Hans P., Nils E. Olsson, and Aslgørn Rolstadås. "How Project Manager-Project Owner Interaction Can Work within and Influence Project Risk Management." *Project Management Journal* 43, no. 2 (2012): 54–67. Web. 25 Nov. 2013.

Madlin, Nancy. "Streamlining the PERT Chart." *Management Review* 75, no. 9 (1986): 67–68. Web. 19 Mar. 2007.

Spencer, Gary R., and Rose M. Lewis. "Schedule Analysis Indices." *AACE International Transactions* (2006): 4.1–4.5. Web. 19 Mar. 2007.

Uppal, Kul B. "Project Management Process and Action Plans." *AACE International Transactions* (2004): 3.1–3.10. Web. 19 Mar. 2007.

Ruth A. Wienclaw, Ph.D.

Public Relations

ABSTRACT

Public relations is the part of the marketing mix designed to build or maintain a positive organizational image among an organization's stakeholders. Public relations is a slow process that gradually changes the impressions, attitudes, and opinions of the various publics over time. Although public relations sometimes can be used to "spin" negative information into a more favorable light, it cannot build a positive reputation for an organization when it is not deserved. Similarly, public relations cannot smother deserved criticisms or malpractice. There are a number of tools for promulgating the organization's message through public relations. In addition to media relations, public relations activities may include face to face techniques, research, the use of the internet, various in house publications, and the design and protection of the corporate logo and other branding.

OVERVIEW

According to conventional wisdom, if one does "build a better mousetrap, the world will beat a path to your door." The reality, however, is more complex. Whether or not one's "mousetrap" is truly better will depend on a number of factors, including what kind of mousetrap customers want or need and how good the competition's mousetraps are. Pricing, too, will come into play. The potential customer must decide how much "better" is worth. If the benefit achieved from using the better mousetrap is not worth the price, most customers will not purchase it.

However, even if the mousetrap is truly better, needed by the customer, unparalleled by the competition, and gives value for its price, customers still will not purchase the new mousetrap if they do not know about it. For this reason, businesses carry out various marketing activities ranging from word of mouth to elaborate marketing campaigns. The marketing function creates, communicates, and delivers value to customers and manages customer relationships in ways that benefit the organization and its stakeholders.

When thinking about marketing, many people consider first the various techniques that directly advertise the organization's goods and services. These activities include advertising media such as print, television, and radio, billboards and other advertising signage, internet advertisements, sales promotions, and direct marketing. In addition, another vital part of the marketing effort includes public relations, the process of creating and managing a public image or reputation with outside agencies and groups. In business, the public relations function is responsible for developing positive messages about the organization and reducing the impact of negative events and information on the organization's reputation. The public relations function focuses efforts on various internal and external stakeholders, including stockholders, employees, the government, public interest groups, and society as a whole. It is the function of public relations to monitor its various constituencies and provide positive information to reinforce its Integrated Marketing Communications (IMC) strategy and advertising direction as well as to react quickly to counteract a shift in the desired position of any of its publics.

The Marketing Mix

As shown in figure 1, each of the various elements in the marketing mix is designed to move prospective customers closer to a sale. At first, these activities are targeted toward making the customer aware of the organization and its products or services. Publicity and advertising in particular are effective in achieving this goal. Once the prospective customer is made aware of the organization and what it has to offer, marketing efforts focus on generating interest in the customer for purchasing the organization's goods or services. Publicity and advertising tend to be particularly successful in generating interest. However, as shown in figure 1, personal selling efforts tend to become increasingly successful as the customer acquires more information about the organization and what it has to offer. These activities also help prospective customers understand the nature and value of the organization's products or services and can help promote the conviction that the product or service being offered is something appropriate for the customer. Once this connection has been accomplished, marketing efforts attempt to turn this conviction that the product or service is appropriate or needed into a desire to purchase it. At this point, sales promotions can also be effectively used in making a prospective customer a current customer.

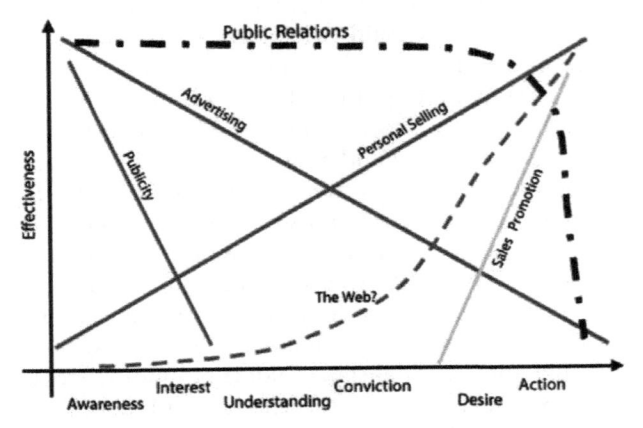

Figure 1

In addition to the more direct elements of the marketing effort—publicity, advertising, personal selling, and sales promotion—there is also the public relations function. As shown in the figure, public relations efforts can be effective throughout the process of turning prospective customers into current customers by helping them better understand the organization (or at least the image that the organization wishes to portray).

The marketing mix is the combination of product, price, place, and promotion used to get a product into the hands of the consumer. One of the primary tasks of marketing is to optimize the mix to best position the product for success in the marketplace. The public relations function of the organization can positively contribute throughout the entire marketing program. During new product development, public relations can contribute by monitoring competitor activity and helping to determine the nature of the marketing opportunity. The public relations function can also determine the public relations objectives and strategy. For example, the type of development (whether or not it is an innovation, a reintroduction of a previous product, an extension of the organization's current line, a reappraisal or revitalization of a current product, or a managed decline or withdrawal of a product) will influence whether stakeholders need to be educated about the product, service, or brand, or reassured (e.g., if a product is going off the market); public relations actions need to be taken to support the sales strategy; or if the strategy requires a reassessment. Marketing research can also be used to formulate reports or news stories that can be used in public relations efforts.

In addition to activities directly related to marketing a product or service, public relations has many functions that can help the organization in meeting its goals and objectives. Primarily, public relations is used to build or maintain a positive image among the various stakeholders. For example, public relations can be used to help employees feel good about the organization that they are working for or be used as a selling point to attract and acquire high quality new employees. Public relations can also be used to raise the awareness of various stakeholders or publics about the organization or its products or services, and educate them in an attempt to build a positive and attractive image. It can also help maintain investor confidence or attract new investors and raise financing. In addition, public relations can help launch new products or services. Public relations efforts can also be used to manage issues that might otherwise negatively affect the organization or its reputation and help defuse potential damaging impact of crisis situations on the organization.

However, public relations is not a magic wand that can immediately gain and maintain customer loyalty. As opposed to other marketing channels, public relations is a slow process that gradually changes the impressions, attitudes, and opinions of the various publics over time. Although public relations sometimes can be used to "spin" negative information into a more favorable light, it cannot build a positive reputation for an organization when it is not deserved. Similarly, public relations cannot smother deserved criticisms or malpractice.

Further, although public relations can help raise the awareness of the organization in the eyes of its various publics or stakeholders, it does not substitute for other elements of the marketing mix (e.g., advertising, publicity, promotion, and personal sales) needed to market the organization's products or services. In addition, although good public relations practices can help increase the chances of getting media coverage, it cannot guarantee it. Similarly, although good public relations can increase the likelihood of increased sales, it cannot guarantee them.

APPLICATIONS

Face-to-Face Public Relations

Public relations techniques encompass more than media relations. There are also face-to-face techniques that allow organizations to spread their message and widen their recognition. Venues for face-to-face techniques used in public relations include seminars, meetings, conferences and conventions, and exhibitions. For example, the public relations department of an organization can set up an exhibit of its products, do demonstrations, or pass out literature at one or more conferences or conventions that are held each year. These opportunities allow the organization to choose one or more specific target audiences to whom it wishes to market and focus its message to best communicate with that market. Face-to-face approaches are the most direct of the public relations tools and may be one of the most powerful methods to reach stakeholders. These techniques also allow the organization to focus the public relations effort so that it can be presented in more detail. If the organization is in charge of the event (e.g., a seminar put on by an investment business that teaches people about retirement planning), it has control over what information is presented and how the seminar is conducted. If the event is being put on by a larger organization (e.g., exhibiting at a convention), the organization may enjoy a larger audience than if putting on the event independently and have the added benefit of being associated with the reputation of the larger organizer. Face to face events, however, are not without their drawbacks. The cost of such events is typically higher than for other public relations techniques. In addition, if working through a third party, one must also work within the parameters set by that party.

Public Relations Research

Another tool of public relations is research. Publishing research on a topic in which the organization has an interest or a proposed solution can not only generate greater interest in the topic but also in the organization's solution. In some cases, the link between the research and the organization's interests may be obvious or overused. However, there are situations where the publication of research findings may be particularly successful. In particular, the publication of research findings is likely to help the organization when it is truly newsworthy or has an interesting angle, is parallel to a strong educational campaign, or includes good case histories. Research can do more than generate media coverage, however. It can also provide a point of departure for discussions with stakeholders or serve as a basis for a conference or other face to face method. In addition, research can be used to reinforce the message of an advertising or a direct marketing campaign. However, if an organization decides to use research as a public relations tool, it must be very careful that the research is impeccable; otherwise, it will harm the organization's reputation rather than enhance it.

Mediums for Public Relations Outreach

With advances in electronic communications technology, one of the first choices for many public relations communications is the organization's website. Increasingly, stakeholders turn to this medium for information and updates about the organization and to compare the offerings of one organization to another. The organization's public relations function should regularly review the organization's website, make recommendations on how to keep it up to date, and use it proactively to manage the organization's reputation. The organization's website can be used as a virtual press office and can include press releases, summaries of research, and information about products or services, as well as advertising and contact information. A website can also be used to collect data and report the results of analysis, publicize events, or announce outstanding employee achievement.

Electronic communications need not be limited to the internet, however. Intranets also offer an important medium for public relations efforts with employees. In addition, email newsletters can be sent to employees or other stakeholders. Electronic communications methods have both advantages and disadvantages. Websites can potentially deliver the organization's message to virtually any place in the modern world not only quickly, but cost-effectively. In addition, electronic communications methods allow two-way communication between the organization and its stakeholders. The information on websites can be quickly and easily updated, a feature essential for getting out information in a timely manner. This feature also means that public relations can issue rebuttals or deal with adverse comments in a timely fashion. However, to be useful from a public relations standpoint, a website needs to be monitored and frequently updated. This work requires web-savvy personnel who understand how to update websites. In addition, it must be remembered that public relations information tends require a more subtle presentation than overt advertising. A light hand is required when developing public relations materials for one's website. Otherwise, the material may have the opposite effect than intended.

The internet is not the only modern technology that is useful for public relations activities. Other technologies such as video and audio recordings can be used to promulgate the organization's message to stakeholders. Multimedia efforts can be used for sending out the organization's message in the form of such things as company reports, internal communications, education, recruitment, documentaries, business development, demonstrations, welcome materials for visitors, and issues management. To determine which medium is most appropriate, several considerations need to be taken into account. First, the organization needs to determine what message it is trying to communicate to the stakeholders. Some messages are more appropriate to certain media than are others. For example, if the organization is trying to communicate that it is on the cutting edge of technology, dispersing this message via audio cassette tape may be considered oxymoronic. Another question to be answered is to whom the message is being delivered. Stakeholders who are facile with modern media will appreciate being communicated with in that manner and will interpret the organization's use of such media as a demonstration that their needs are understood. In addition, it must be determined what the purpose of the message is. Just because a medium is available does not mean that it is appropriate to use it. Similarly, just because the message does not utilize all the storage space on the medium does not mean that the message should be longer. In many cases, shorter is better.

Another way that the organization can get out its message to stakeholders is through in-house publications, such as company bulletins, newsletters, newspapers, or magazines. Potential targets of these publications might include internal employees (e.g., workers, management, sales personnel), distributors (e.g., retailers, wholesalers), current or prospective customers, supporters (e.g., donors, guests, passengers), and opinion leaders (e.g., business leaders, academics, politicians).

Similarly, the organization's message can be promulgated through various printed materials—in particular, educational literature, corporate reports, and research or other special reports. For example, a manufacturer of a new drug might provide several different types of information to stakeholders. They might develop a simple leaflet for patients that discusses the disease, the actions of the drugs, and patients' frequently asked questions. A more detailed document could be developed for healthcare professionals that summarizes scientific research on the drug and explains the actions of the drug on the human body. Package inserts might also be prepared for the patient. All this material might also be posted on the organization's website.

Public Relations & Branding

Last but not least, the public relations department should be involved in the design and safeguarding of the corporate logo and other branding. These things are closely related to the corporate identity and public relations needs to make certain that they are appropriate to the image that the organization is trying to portray. Careful research needs to be done before changing these things to determine how they will be perceived by the public. Similarly, public relations needs to be watchful that the corporate logo or branding is not infringed by others. For example, several major snack manufacturers filed suit against a person who modified their branding to package drug laced candy and soda. Organizations need to be vigilant so that their logo and branding only bring up positive associations in the minds of their stakeholders.

BIBLIOGRAPHY

Black, Caroline. *PR Practitioner's Desktop Guide*. London: Thorogood, 2001.

Clow, Kenneth E., and Donald Baack. "Public Relations." In *Concise Encyclopedia of Advertising*, edited by Kenneth E. Clow and Donald Baack, 133. Binghamton, NY: Haworth, 2005. Web. 10 July 2007.

Dach, Leslie. "Don't Spin a Better Story: Best a Better Company." *Harvard Business Review* 91, no. 10 (2013): 42. Web. 19 Nov. 2013.

Horn, Sabrina. "Social Media's Online Advantage: The Evolution of Public Relations to Digital Communications." *Public Relations Tactics* 20, no. 1 (2013): 16. Web. 19 Nov. 2013.

"The PR Professional of 2015: Analyzing the Future of Public Relations." *Public Relations Tactics* 19, no. 3 (2015): 14–15. Web. 19 Nov. 2013.

Ruskin-Brown, Ian. "Promoting a Service." In *Marketing Your Service Business*, edited by Ian Ruskin-Brown, 199–221. London: Thorogood, 2005. Web. 10 July 2007.

SUGGESTED READING

Carayol, Valerie, and Alex Frame. *Communication and PR from a Cross-Cultural Standpoint: Practical and Methodological Issues*. Brussels: Peter Lang, 2012. Web. 19 Nov. 2013.

Dunn, Jim. "Crisis Public Relations: How to Handle Emergencies." In *Public Relations Techniques That Work Pocketbook*, edited by Jim Dunn, 121–37. London: Thorogood, 2001a. Web. 10 July 2007.

Dunn, Jim. "The Nature of Public Relations." In *Public Relations Techniques That Work Pocketbook*, edited by Jim Dunn, 3–12. London: Thorogood, 2001b. Web. 10 July 2007.

Gottschalk, Petter. *Corporate Social Responsbility, Governance and Corporate Reputation*. Hackensack, NJ: World Scientific, 2011. Web. 19 Nov. 2013.

Ikonen, Pasi. "Transparency for Sponsored Content: Analyzing Codes of Ethics in Public Relations, Advertising and Journalism." *International Journal of Strategic Communication* 11, no. 2 (2016). Web. 29 June 2017.

Knights, Kieran. "Getting Out What You Put In." In *Strategic Planning in Public Relations*, edited by Kieran Knights, 16–23. London: Thorogood. Web. 10 July 2007.

"What Is Strategic Planning and Why Do We Need It?" In *Strategic Planning in Public Relations*, edited by Kieran Knights, 1–6. London: Thorogood. Web. 10 July 2007.

Moloney, Kevin. "The PR Industry from Top to Bottom." In *Rethinking Public Relations*, edited by Kevin Moloney, 17–30. New York: Routledge, 2000. Web. 10 July 2007.

Ruth A. Wienclaw, Ph.D.

Quality Management

ABSTRACT

Quality management is a process by which an organization creates and maintains high quality in its plans, projects, products, and relationships with customers. Although definitions of quality in business vary somewhat, they generally relate to processes and products that meet requirements and satisfy customers. The main components of quality management, which extend across the entire project lifecycle, are quality planning, quality assurance, quality control, and quality improvement. By addressing these components, businesses can greatly increase customer satisfaction, which will in turn benefit the business.

OVERVIEW

The word *quality* may be applied in many contexts. In its general usage, it may simply be a way of describing whether something is good or bad or denoting something that is excellent. In business contexts, however, the meaning of the word takes on more dimensions and complexity. The basic business definition of quality is the degree to which something (usually a product or process) fulfills particular requirements set by the businesspeople or their customers or stakeholders.

Quality has been a vital feature of businesses and other organizations for hundreds of years, ever since economies began. Even the earliest merchants and service providers had to be concerned with providing quality work for fear of losing their customers and being driven out of business. In the industrial era, the range of products and services ballooned, as did competition between businesses and demands from consumers.

As business grew, analysts and consultants looked for ways to improve sales. In the last half of the 1900s, one of the focal points was on quality. Consultant W. Edwards Deming was among the first proponents of examining quality as a way to improve businesses worldwide. His work expanded on the idea of quality, changing it from a mere measure of good or bad into a multifaceted process based around satisfying the ever-changing requirements of customers.

Consultant Joseph M. Juran created his own definition of quality. He acknowledged that, in organizations, the word had two meanings: the simplest meaning pertained to good products that were free of defects and the second meaning referred to a wider range of product features and business activities intended to meet customer needs.

In modern organizations, all versions of quality are important to success. Business leaders and consultants have found that quality is just as important as more easily measured factors such as time, cost, and scope. In fact, quality is in some ways more important than those factors because it should never be altered or reduced; it should be required in all products and processes.

Quality management is essential to organizations and requires constant work and maintenance. Organization members have to plan and manage their actions carefully to keep quality at its peak. Ultimately, a commitment to quality will benefit the business by satisfying customers and increasing sales.

Components of Quality Management

Quality has many definitions and involves all aspects of an organization's work. Despite this variety, managing quality generally involves similar key components. The primary components shared by most quality management initiatives include quality planning, quality assurance, quality control, and quality improvement.

Quality planning is the first step, which takes place in the development stage before the main tasks begin. Managers, engineers, and other designers need to find ways to plan for the highest quality product made with the highest quality processes. Designers may consult lists of organizational or industry

W. Edwards Deming (Photo courtesy of the FDA)

practices, or they might determine their own standards for quality. They may also conduct various tests to find the best routes to product and project quality. Once planning is complete, the work task may begin. The crucial stages of quality assurance and quality control now come into play.

In **quality assurance**, managers must oversee the creation of the product or supervise the main tasks being undertaken. The managers need to make sure that their plans for quality are being put into practice. To accomplish this goal, managers may conduct tests such as checking benchmarks, comparisons with other quality products, or performing audits, in-depth reviews of various stages of the task to ensure the best possible quality.

Quality control occurs toward the end of the main tasks. During this stage, managers examine the output of their projects and determine whether the product has lived up to expectations of quality. Some factors in quality control include process adjustments, or revisions in the way the project is being conducted, and rework, fixes to products that do not meet quality requirements.

The final step, **quality improvement,** often takes place after the other stages but may occur during them as well. In quality improvement, managers work to review their processes and products with the goal of constantly making them better. During this stage, managers and other organization members may examine goals for reworking products or address customer feedback to ensure customers are satisfied. Quality improvement is especially important in the healthcare industry.

CONCLUSION

Quality management has become an essential part of many organizations. Managers feel it is essential for creating excellent work and maintaining success in competitive markets. For that reason, many organizations put significant effort into researching quality, sometimes internally and sometimes by employing outside groups and standards. One of the most widespread sets of quality standards is the ISO 9000, an internationally accepted quality management plan. The benefits of achieving and maintaining quality are many. Quality projects generally lead to quality products, which will satisfy customers. Satisfied customers will buy the products and return to the company for future offerings. These customers will also refer the company to their friends, which will further increase the company's revenue. At the same time, quality processes usually involve higher efficiency and lower waste, which can save companies money. All of these factors contribute to an organization's increased stability, competitiveness, and prosperity.

BIBLIOGRAPHY

Kennelly, Pat. "The History, Tools, and Techniques of Quality Management." *Geospatial Technology Project Management.* John A. Dutton E-Education Institute, College of Earth and Mineral Sciences at the Pennsylvania State University, 2014. Web. 6 Feb. 2015.

Kennelly, Pat. "Quality Planning, Assurance, and Control." *Geospatial Technology Project Management.* John A. Dutton E-Education Institute, College of Earth and Mineral Sciences at the Pennsylvania State University, 2014. Web. 6 Feb. 2015. l

Kim, Daniel. "Systemic Quality Management: Improving the Quality of Doing and Thinking." *The Systems Thinker,* 8 Apr. 2016. Web. 1 Nov. 2016.

Office of Government Commerce, UK. "Quality Management Strategy." *The Project Management Hut.* PM Hut, 2009. Web. 6 Feb. 2015.

"Quality Management." *Investopedia,* 20 June 2016. Web. 1 Nov. 2016.

Rose, Kenneth H. *Project Quality Management: Why, What, and How.* Boca Raton, FL: J. Ross Publishing, Inc., 2005, 5–12.

Mark Dziak

RACE, ETHNICITY, AND PUBLIC POLICY

ABSTRACT

This article will focus on the relationship between race, ethnicity, and public policy and will provide an overview of the ways in which the federal government conceptualizes and measures race and ethnicity. This discussion of race-based statistics will serve as a foundation for the subsequent discussion of public policies targeted at racial and ethnic groups. Examples of race-based public policies such as affirmative action will be introduced. Discussions of race-based statistics and race-based public policies will be situated within the context of the modern debates over race-based public policy responses to social problems.

OVERVIEW

The U.S. government creates public policy for its citizens in order to meet a perceived social need or solve a perceived social problem. Public policy, which refers to the basic policy or set of policies that serve as the foundation for public laws, is often characterized as a social goal that enables objective or social solution. Public policy is often requested explicitly and implicitly by society and enacted by government and unites and mediates the relationship between society and government. Public policy, which encompasses and regulates nearly all areas of human and social behavior, is created within a specific historical context, sociocultural context, and political system.

The categories of race and ethnicity have influenced American public policy decisions since the founding of the modern federal government. The federal government has collected and based policy upon race- based statistics since the first population census in 1790. In the first census (conducted in 1790), African-American slaves were counted as three-fifths of a person and American Indians were not counted. During the eighteenth century, race was believed to influence character, moral, intellect, and ultimately rights and was viewed as relevant and important for analysis of social, political, and economic variables. Since 1900, twenty-six different racial terms have been used by the U.S. Census Bureau to identify populations.

Race and ethnicity influenced voting, housing, education, and civil rights policy in the United States throughout the twentieth century. In the 1950s and 1960s, the Civil Rights movement raised public consciousness about discrimination encountered by minority groups in public and private institutions. The Affirmative Action program and public policies were created in the 1960s to remedy the economic and social discrimination faced by racial and ethnic minorities in America. These policies have undergone scrutiny, debate, and change since their inception five decades ago. Society's many stakeholders debate the proper and desirable relationship between race, ethnicity, and public policy.

In the twenty-first century, race remains significant in relation to government census taking and policy making (Chiswick and Chiswick 1984). Race-based public policies (such as the Civil Rights Act and affirmative action) were developed during the twentieth-century to address and remediate the problem of racial discrimination. The federal government developed race-based affirmative action policies and programs to create equal opportunity for people of all races and ethnicities. Affirmative action, as a contested strategy and policy within American society, encompasses and raises the moral, political, and social issues of values, diversity, equality, and discrimination. The modern federal government supports and promotes affirmative action policies and programs that create compensatory education, training, and job counseling, and intensive recruitment for racial populations that have historically experienced discrimination and repression.

This article focuses on the evolving relationship between race, ethnicity, and public policy. The following section provides an overview of the way in which the federal government conceptualizes and measures race and ethnicity. This discussion of race-based statistics will serve as a foundation for the subsequent discussion of affirmative action public policies. Discussions of race-based statistics and race-based public policies will be situated within the context of the modern controversies over race-based public policy responses to social problems in America.

Race-Based Statistics & Public Policy

The U.S. government collects and uses statistics about society to direct and shape public policy. Examples of important and influential statistics include:

- Social indicator statistics: social statistics gathered to assess the impact of social policy as well as continued or emerging social needs.
- Poverty threshold statistics: poverty statistics measured annually by the U.S. Census Bureau to determine eligibility criteria for social welfare programs and public assistance.
- Standards for the Classification of Federal Data on Race and Ethnicity: standards intended to provide consistent and comparable data on race and ethnicity throughout the federal government for an array of statistical and administrative programs.

The use of race-based statistics and of racial and ethnic classifications by the federal government raises numerous ethical and policy issues. The federal government's Office of Management and Budget (OMB) is responsible for establishing the standards and categories used to measure and assess race and ethnicity in America. The Office of Management and Budget defines the category of race as a self-identified data item in which residents choose the race or races with which they most closely identify. Ethnicity refers to the identification with population groups characterized by common ancestry, language, and custom. In 1977, the Office of Management and Budget developed Statistical Policy Directive No. 15, entitled Race and Ethnic Standards for Federal Statistics and Administrative Reporting and then revised it in 1997. The federal race and ethnicity data standards and categories were developed initially in 1977 for multiple reasons:

- The data standards are intended to serve as a common language to promote uniformity and comparability for data on race and ethnicity.
- The data standards are intended to provide consistent data on race and ethnicity throughout the federal government.
- The data standards are intended to aid the government in efforts to enforce civil rights laws in areas such as equal access in housing, education, and employment for populations that historically had experienced discrimination and differential treatment because of their race or ethnicity.
- The data standards are intended for use in the decennial census, household surveys, administrative forms such as school registration and mortgage lending applications, and in medical research.

The Office of Management and Budget's Statistical Policy Directive No. 15 includes five race and two ethnicity categories. The categories, which are used for federal statistics, program administration, and civil rights enforcement, include the following:

Race

American Indian or Alaska Native refers to a person having origins in any of the original peoples of North and South America (including Central America) and who maintains tribal affiliation or community attachment.

Asian refers to a person having origins in any of the original peoples of the Far East, Southeast Asia, or the Indian subcontinent including, for example, Cambodia, China, India, Japan, Korea, Malaysia, Pakistan, the Philippine Islands, Thailand, and Vietnam.

Black or African American refers to a person having origins in any of the black racial groups of Africa. Terms such as "Haitian" or "Negro" can be used in addition to "Black or African American.

Native Hawaiian or Other Pacific Islander refers to a person having origins in any of the original peoples of Hawaii, Guam, Samoa, or other Pacific Islands.

White refers to a person having origins in any of the original peoples of Europe, the Middle East, or North Africa.

Ethnicity

Hispanic or Latino refers to a person of Cuban, Mexican, Puerto Rican, South or Central American, or other Spanish culture or origin, regardless of race.

The term, "Spanish origin," can be used in addition to "Hispanic or Latino."

Not Hispanic or Latino refers to a person with no Cuban, Mexican, Puerto Rican, South or Central American, or other Spanish culture or origin.

The standards, as described above, are the product of the 1997 revisions that made the following changes. First, the Asian or Pacific Islander category was separated into two the categories of "Asian" and "Native Hawaiian or Other Pacific Islander." Second, the term "Hispanic" was changed to "Hispanic or Latino." The 1997 revisions were undertaken in an effort to represent the demographic diversity created by the growth in immigration and in interracial marriages. As a result of the 1997 revisions, respondents on federal forms have the option of selecting one or more racial designations. The newly revised standards acknowledge interracial and multiracial identities.

The Office of Management and Budget maintains that the current standards, as revised in 1997, are intended for reporting purposes rather than policy-making purposes. The OMB describes the purpose and purported parameters of the updated race and ethnicity categories:

- The data standards provide a minimum set of categories for data on race and ethnicity.
- The data standards permit the collection of more detailed information on population groups provided that any additional categories can be aggregated into the minimum standard set of categories.
- The data standards underscore that self-identification is the preferred means of obtaining information about an individual's race and ethnicity except in instances where observer identification is more practical.
- The data standards do not identify or designate certain population groups as "minority groups."
- The data standards continue the policy that the categories are not to be used for determining the eligibility of population groups for participation in any federal programs.
- The data standards do not establish criteria or qualifications that are to be used in determining an individual's racial or ethnic classification.
- The data standards do not attempt to inform an individual of who he or she is or to specify how an individual should classify himself or herself.

The Office of Management and Budget standards have been criticized for two main reasons. First, the standards have had far wider influence than intended or explicitly allowed. While the Office of Management and Budget asserts that the data standards will not be used to determine policy or eligibility, the data standards have far reaching influence on and implications for public policy. The data standards were developed to support and enable the civil rights legislations of the 1960s that were designed to combat the legacy of racial and ethnic discrimination. The Office of Management and Budget classification system influences federal funding allocations as well as congressional districts and enforcement of equal access provisions. In addition, the Office of Management and Budget classification system influences public health research and practice (Bennett 1997).

Second, the continued use of the word *race* as a classification tool is questioned because it is an evolving and self-identified label. Racial analyses, understood to be a socially constructed category, is a somewhat illusory and shifting category. Multiracial heritage or identity is a growing reality and experience for many in American society but is a challenge to a census-taking process that requires fixed categories. Racial and ethnic categories are chosen to correspond to previous incarnations of the census, to reduce chances for racial tensions and fragmentation, and to reduce the creation of overly small and specialized samples. There is no reporting option for all racial combinations nor is there a multiracial category. The reporting categories are limited and fixed while the experience of race is expansive and fluid. While the Office of Management and Budget recognizes that, "The categories represent a sociopolitical construct designed for collecting data on the race and ethnicity of broad population groups in this country, and are not anthropologically or scientifically based," fixed race-based categories continue to characterize U.S. census data.

The continued use of race and ethnicity classification by the federal government has been challenged by social scientists. In 1997, for example, the American Anthropological Association (AAA) challenged and opposed the racial and ethnic classifications used in U.S. statistics. In their Response to OMB Directive No. 15, the association recommended that *race* and *ethnicity* be combined in both Directive 15 and in the 2000 census to form "race/ethnicity," and by the 2010 census that the term *race* be eliminated altogether, arguing that more specific social categories such as "ethnicity" or "ethnic group" were better suited for scientific purposes and have fewer negative connotations than does "race."

In 2010, in the U.S. Census Bureau mailed experimental questionnaires to over 488,000 households and conducted over 60 focus groups in order to test the combined questions on race and Hispanic origin. The majority of U.S. households received a census form with separate questions about race and Hispanic origin. The experimental group, however, received a form that combined race and Hispanic origin. The goal was to determine whether different census questions would improve the reporting rates in the race and ethnic categories, would decrease participant nonresponse in those categories, and would increase the reliability of the results. The results found that a greater percentage responded to the combined question of race and Hispanic origin than to separate questions. Fewer people also left the combined question blank than did people who left the separate questions blank.

APPLICATIONS

Affirmative Action

Following World War II, American society was characterized by deindustrialization, suburbanization, political and racial tensions, and governmental restructuring of urban jobs and housing. Race and ethnicity were the focus of American society and American public policy from the 1950s through the 1970s. The Civil Rights movement inspired and necessitated new anti-discriminatory civil rights policies and laws. Examples of race-based laws and policies include the Civil Rights Act of 1964 and the Voting Rights Act of 1965. The Civil Rights Act of 1964 (Title VII of the United States Code) prohibits discrimination based on race, color, religion, or national origin and provides the federal government with the power to enforce desegregation. The Voting Rights Act of 1965 outlaws literacy tests, poll taxes, and other requirements that were previously used to restrict black voting (Trotter 1998).

Affirmative action policies were first developed in the early 1960s to support, reinforce, and implement the requirements of Title VII. In 1961, the Kennedy administration introduced the idea of affirmative action as a means to implement Title VII goals. Kennedy passed Executive Order 10925, which empowered the Committee on Equal Employment Opportunity to take affirmative action to ensure that hiring and employment practices were free of racial bias. In 1965, the Johnson administration proclaimed that the Civil Rights law was an insufficient remedy to discrimination and passed Executive Order 11246 to enact affirmative action into law. The new policy required government contractors to take affirmative action toward prospective minority employees in all aspects of hiring and employment (Brunner 2006). In addition, the Office of Management and Budget's Directive No. 15 was developed in response to the Civil Rights legislation of the 1960s. Explicit and implicit race-based public policies of the last four decades have been influenced and defined by the Civil Rights Act, affirmative action, and Office of Management and Budget's Directive No. 15.

The years since Kennedy and Johnson introduced affirmative action have been characterized by both increased opportunities in all facets of society for racial minority groups and by problems with reverse discrimination, which have been characterized by lawsuits challenging the legality and ethicality of affirmative action. Several states, including California and Washington, have passed legislation prohibiting state or local agencies from granting preferential treatment of individuals based on race, sex, ethnicity, or national origin. Affirmative action was viewed as a temporary measure when it was developed, but it has become deeply enmeshed in educational and employment public policymaking process.

Up until the mid-1990s, state governments were divided over the proper role race could or should play in government. Prior to the Supreme Court's decisions in *Grutter v. Bollinger*, federal courts were split over the proper role race could play in government affirmative action plans, policies, and programs. The Supreme Court resolved the issue of how and when governments may consider race in their decisions in the 2003 *Grutter v. Bollinger* lawsuit. While the lawsuit concerned academic admission issues, the Court's ruling about the scope of race-based decisions applies generally to private and public sector actors. The Supreme Court (5–4) upheld the University of Michigan Law School's policy of using race as an admission factor or variable and ruled that race can be one of many factors considered by admissions departments because consideration of race has the potential for creating educational benefits such as a diverse student body (Brennen 2003).

ISSUES

Implementation of Affirmative Action

Public policy is created within or through a policy cycle involving agenda setting, policy formation, implementation, and evaluation. The policy cycle process involves both politics and administration. There are numerous people involved in each stage of the policy cycle, and there is little agreement on the essences of these roles. The major players in the policy process are referred to as policy entrepreneurs, social entrepreneurs, issue initiators, policy brokers, strategists, fixers, brokers, or caretakers. While public policy is created by politicians and legislative representatives, public administrators are responsible for policy implementation. In policy implementation, administrators are granted varying degrees of discretion in details, range, and scope of the policy. Public policy administrators are allowed to fill in the details of legislation, define appropriate levels of program performance, and exercise other kinds of program judgment as needed.

Examples of discretionary choices made by public policy administrators include rule making, adjudication, law enforcement, and program operations. In addition to the influence provided by implementation discretion, policy administrators may provide advice and counsel to political officials through reports, testimony, recommendations, monthly economic indices, and legislative proposals. Public administrators in some instances work in collaboration with judges and interest groups to force politicians to strengthen or create new public policies and services. Policy implementation and public administrative actions in general are watched over by the legislature, the chief executive's staff, and agency political appointees (Skok 1995).

The implementation and interpretation of the affirmative action policy transformed the meaning and scope of the policy. The implementation process changed the implicit range and scope of the 1960s affirmative action from a policy that was intended to encourage hiring on the basis of ability and qualifications (not race or religion) to a policy interpreted in the 1990s as a tool to facilitate the incorporation of race and gender in governmental decision making.

This transformative process that occurs during policy implementation is known as the phenomenon of co-optation of policy. Administrative implementation of public policy changes public policy during the time from the statement of legislative intent to the implementation of the policy. Administrators implement policy as they understand and interpret it. The large number of policy administrators and implementers create ample room and time for co-optation of affirmative action policy. For example, the following list of agencies comprises the many government actors who have had the responsibility for implementation of non discrimination employment policies

- The U.S. Civil Service Commission (CSC) establishes employment policies and maintains merit principles within the federal work force.
- The Equal Employment Opportunity Commission (EEOC) applies non discrimination policies to both government and private employment.
- The Office of Federal Contract Compliance (OFCC), within the Department of Labor, monitors compliance among companies doing business with the federal government.
- The U.S. Commission on Civil Rights (USCCR) serves as an overall advisor and watchdog.
- The Civil Rights Division of the Department of Justice (DOJ) enforces federal nondiscrimination statutes.

The agencies listed above while all having very different agendas, rights, and responsibilities have implemented non discrimination policies to separate segments of the U.S. economy. The implementation of non discrimination employment policies by different agencies has created numerous disputes, new precedents, and an evolving set of anti-discrimination policy standards (Lee 1999).

CONCLUSION

In the final analysis, American public policies of the twentieth and twenty-first centuries have been deeply influenced by racial and ethnic categories, goals, and parameters provided in the Civil Rights Act, affirmative action initiatives, and Statistical Policy Directive No. 15. Ultimately, race, as the basis for and variable within much of the public policy created today may simultaneously provide opportunity for racial groups historically oppressed by economic and social discrimination and perpetuate the idea of fundamental social differences based on race (Chiswick and Chiswick 1984).

BIBLIOGRAPHY

American Anthropological Association. (1997). Response to OMB Directive 15. Web. 21 Nov. 2013.

Bennett, Trude. "'Racial' and Ethinic Classification: Two Steps Forward and One Step Back?" *Public Health Reports* 112 (1997): 477–81.

Brennen, David. "Race-Conscious Affirmative Action by Tax-Exempt 501(C) Corporations after Grutter and Gratz." *St. John's Law Review* 88 (2003): 711–33. Web. 12 Apr. 2007.

Brown, Hana E. "Race, Legality, and the Social Policy Consequences of Anti-Immigration Mobilization." *American Sociological Review* 78 (2013): 290–314. Web. 21 Nov. 2014.

Brunner, Borgna. "Timeline of Affirmative Action Milestones." *Infoplease Database* (2006). Web. 10 Apr. 2007.

Chiswick, Barry, and Carmel Chiswick. "Race and Public Policy: The Statistical Connection." *Challenge* 27 (1984): 51. Web. 10 Apr. 2007.

Clark, Ronald C. Jr., Holona Ochs, and Michael Frazier. "Representative Bureaucracy: The Politics of Access to Policy-Making Positions in the Federal Executive Service." *Public Personnel Management* 42 (2013): 75–89. Web. 21 Nov. 2013.

Craig, Gary. "Invisibilizing 'Race' in Public Policy." *Critical Social Policy* 33 (2013): 712–20. Web. 21 Nov. 2013.

Lee, R. "The Evolution of Affirmative Action." *Public Personnel Management* 28 (1999): 393. Web. 10 Apr. 2007.

Manville, Michael. "). People, Race and Place: American Support for Person- and Place-Based Urban Policy, 1973–2008." *Urban Studies* (Sage Publications, Ltd.). 49 (2012): 3101–19. Web. 21 Nov. 2013.

Ortiz, Selena E., and Frederick J. Zimmerman. "Race/Ethnicity and the Relationship between Homeownership and Health." *American Journal of Public Health* 103 (2013): E122–E129. Web. 21 Nov. 2014.

Response to OMB Directive 15: Race and Ethnic Standards for Federal Statistics and Administrative Reporting. (1997). American Anthropological Association. Web. 10 Apr. 2017.

Revisions to the Standards for the Classification of Federal Data on Race and Ethnicity. (1997). Executive Office of the President, Office of Management and Budget (OMB), Office of Information and Regulatory Affairs. Skok, James. "Policy Issue Networks and the Public Policy Cycle: A Structural-Functional Framework for Public Administration." *Public Administration Review* 55 (1995): 325-33. Web. 10 Apr. 2007.

Trotter, Joe. "Race, Public Policy, and History: The Question of Priorities." *Labor History* 39 (1998): 57-60. Web. 10 Apr. 2007.

Weiner, Ronald. *Lake Effects: A History of Urban Policy Making in Cleveland, 1825-1929*. Columbus: Ohio State University Press, 2005.

SUGGESTED READING

Chrisman, Robert. "Affirmative Action: Extend It." 43, no. 3 (2013): 71–72. Web. 21 Nov. 2014.

Feltovich, Nick, Lata Gangadharan, and Michael P. Kidd. "Implementation and Removal of an Affirmative-Action Quota: The Impact on Task Assignment and Workers' Skill Acquisition." *Canadian Public Policy* 39 (2013): S123-S140. Web. 21 Nov. 2013.

Kennedy, Randall. "Conservatives' Selective Use of Race in the Law." *Harvard Journal of Law & Public Polic*, 19 (1996): 719-21. Web. 10 Apr. 2007.

Patterson, James. "Race Relations and the 'Underclass' in Modern America: Some Historical Observations." *Qualitative Sociology* 18 (1995): 237-62. Web. 10 Apr. 2007.

Payne, Angela R., and Bharat S. Thakkar. "The Hypocrisy of Affirmative Action: Race and the Labor Market." *International Journal of Innovations in Business* 1 (2012): 274–92. Web. 21 Nov. 2013.

Zambrana, Ruth E. "Income and Wealth Gaps, Inequitable Public Policies, and the Tentacles of Racism." *American Journal of Public Health* 107, no. 10 (2017): 1531-32. Web. 21 Mar. 2018.

Zieger, Robert. "Recent Historical Scholarship on Public Policy in Relation to Race and Labor in the Post-Title-VII Period." *Labor History* 46 (2005): 3-14. Web. 10 Apr. 2007.

Simone I. Flynn, Ph.D.

Religious Accommodation in the Workplace

ABSTRACT

The subject of religious accommodation in the workplace concerns the extent to which employers, both public and private, can be required by law to permit employees to be exempt from workplace requirements that they would otherwise be subject to, on the grounds that those requirements conflict with the employee's religious beliefs and practices. In some cases the employer will be forced to permit the employee to follow her religion rather than workplace policy, while in other cases the employee will have to either abide by workplace policy or seek employment elsewhere.

OVERVIEW

Religious accommodation in the workplace has been a subject of controversy in the United States since the nation was founded. One of the most fundamental principles enshrined in the Declaration of Independence and the Constitution is that of the need for separation of church and state; that is, the United States has no official state religion. The nation protects the right of its citizens to hold whatever religious beliefs they wish—or none at all—but the nation does not give any kind of preference to any religion. From time to time, these two imperatives come into conflict such as when a person's need to exercise his or her religion has the potential to interfere with the government's commitment not to favor any particular religion. Lawsuits based on claims of religious discrimination in the workplace have been on the rise, led by charges of denial of reasonable accommodation (Mihelich 2014).

The Civil Rights Act of 1964 made it illegal to discriminate against people because of their race, religion, national origin, or sex. The Religious Freedom Restoration Act was enacted in 1993 in an effort to protect what was seen as the potential for governmental power to impinge upon individuals' free exercise of their religious beliefs. It was later found unconstitutional as applied to the states, but it continues to be applied to the federal government. The law regarding religious accommodation in the workplace in the United States provides that if an employee, who holds a sincerely held religious belief that is interfered with by the nature of the work or workplace of the employee, is entitled to an accommodation by the employer unless providing the accommodation would cause the employer to experience an undue hardship (Cañas and Sondak 2011). In essence, what this regulation means is that if an employee's religion requires him or her to behave in a way not ordinarily permitted at his or her workplace, the employer must find a way to permit this behavior unless doing so would be too expensive, too disruptive, or too dangerous.

APPLICATIONS

In 2015, Kim Davis, who was employed as county clerk for Rowan County, Kentucky, refused to issue marriage licenses to gay couples after the U.S. Supreme Court effectively legalized marriage for same-sex couples. Davis argued that doing so would violate her Christian beliefs. Her action initiated a standoff between advocates of religious freedom insisting that Ms. Davis should be permitted to follow her conscience rather than have her employer force her to violate her religious beliefs, and proponents of the principle that it is not the government's place to endorse a specific religion (here, Christianity) by allowing the personal beliefs of a government employee to trump the legal rights of other citizens (the couples seeking marriage licenses). While Davis was briefly jailed for contempt of court after refusing to comply with a court order to issue the marriage licenses, eventually she returned to work and permitted her deputy clerks to issue the licenses even though she, personally, would not (Rao 2013).

Prayer breaks are a classic example of a religious accommodation that is not likely to impose an undue hardship on the employer. For example, if employees are permitted two ten-minute breaks and one thirty-minute lunch period per day, but a Muslim employee has a religious mandate to pray five times per day, then the employee would need an accommodation from the employer in order to be able to take five prayer breaks. One option would be for the employer to adjust the employee's hours so that he or she would have a slightly longer workday to make up for the extra breaks, so that other employees could not complain that he or she was receiving favorable treatment by being allowed to work less than everyone else. It is extremely unlikely that this type of accommodation request would be considered to cause an undue hardship. Usually, for an accommodation to be considered an undue hardship, it must either cost an amount of money in excess of minor costs (paying overtime periodically would usually not be considered undue hardship, for example) or it must cause the employer significant inconvenience, as might occur in the case of an accommodation that would have a serious, negative effect on the morale of other employees (Lefebvre and Beaman 2014).

Some of the most common requests for accommodations include requests for particular days off in order to respect religious holidays or holy days; requests for alterations to the employer's dress code to allow the employee to wear garments with religious significance, such as head scarves or the yarmulke worn by some Jews; and requests for being excused for certain duties (Alidadi, Foblets, and Vrielink 2012). The latter type of request can take several forms. One example is that of a flight attendant whose religious beliefs do not permit him to drink or serve alcohol; most of the time this situation would not be an issue, but on occasions when a passenger does order an alcoholic beverage, a problem could arise. When this situation has arisen in the real world, the situation has not usually risen to the level of the employee needing to request an accommodation. Instead, the employee has explained the situation to his or her coworkers, and they have been able to work together to make sure that employees without religious objections to serving alcohol can assist the employee with the task so that he or she does not need to do so.

Another type of request involving a change in duty occurs when an employee objects to working on a particular project, as when an employee at a manufacturing plant that ordinarily makes farm equipment objects to being asked to work on a project building weapons for a Department of Defense contract (Lindemann, Kadue, and Lindemann 2012).

Viewpoints
Employers must be cautious when responding to employee requests for accommodation because the nature of the response can cause long-term consequences for the entire workplace, without regard to the request. If the employer denies the request for accommodation in a way that is unreasonable or demonstrates excessive rigidity, then there may be resentment from not only the employee whose request was rejected, but also other members of the workforce who may be concerned that their requests will also be denied in an offhand manner, or who may be angry that their supervisor does not appear to be interested in helping subordinates.

On the other hand, if the request for accommodation is approved, this action also can provoke hard feelings. Other employees may feel that the person receiving the accommodation is receiving an unfair benefit, causing them to be angry at the employee and at the employer (Giacalone and Jurkiewicz 2010). In some cases, these employees may begin treating the employee receiving the accommodation in a hostile manner (Lund Dean, Safranski, and Lee 2014), or may even act out against the employer. It is also possible that employees who see others receive accommodations may attempt to receive similar accommodations themselves, by feigning religious beliefs that would require special adjustments. In order to avoid situations like these, the best course of action employers can take when receiving a request for accommodation is to take time to respectfully consider the request. A quick denial will send the employee the message that the employer did not really listen to the request or think it worth giving thoughtful consideration to. A quick approval is likely to upset other employees, making them more likely to feel that either the employer is a pushover or that the employee whose accommodation request was approved is benefitting from some type of favoritism. Either way, morale is likely to suffer.

When considering a request for accommodation, employers need to do their best to give the request fair consideration and use their creativity to find a way in which the request can be accommodated, rather than just half-heartedly mulling over the request for long enough to make it seem to the employee that the request was honestly considered. The most important quality an employer can bring to the decision about whether or not to comply with an accommodation request is sincerity. The employer needs to act without regard to the potential consequences of granting the request, determining whether the request is truly a reasonable one or if there is simply no way to comply with it without causing significant injury to the organization (Friedman 2014).

Several factors have arisen which have tended to increase the number of situations in which employees request religious accommodations. One of these is that the workforce is becoming increasingly diverse, not only in terms of ethnicity, gender, sexual orientation, and similar qualities, but also in terms of religious affiliation. With more and more employees possessing a wider array of religious beliefs, there are more opportunities for these religious beliefs to come into conflict with employer expectations. This increased religious diversity in the workforce has been driven in part by the influence of globalization, which has seen the workplace transform completely into a decentralized, remotely accessible and geographically dispersed network of offices that are able to interact virtually using the Internet (Bureau of National Affairs 2011).

At the same time, the nature of work has changed. In the past, a person's working life and personal life could be kept far more distinct because when a person left the office, there was usually no way to continue working at home. In the modern world, ubiquitous internet connectivity has made it possible for people to work from almost any physical location, at almost any time of the day or night. Because this situation is now possible, there are inevitably employers who wish to have their employees take advantage of these new opportunities. This increased flexibility of the working world also creates new opportunities for potential conflicts between workplace requirements and religious beliefs, which make it more important for employers to treat accommodation requests with respect and decorum.

CONCLUSION

Some feel that religious accommodation requests are somehow less deserving of consideration than accommodations for disabilities, because religious beliefs (the thinking goes) are a matter of "choice" while disabilities are not. It is important that this type of value judgment about the relative merits of the different types of accommodation requests not enter into the employer's decision-making process, because under the law the determinative factor should not be what type of accommodation is being requested, but simply whether or not the accommodation is a reasonable one that the employer can make without compromising its own interests (Gregory 2011; Flake 2015).

BIBLIOGRAPHY

Alidadi, Katayoun, Marie-Claire Vrielink, and Jogchum Vrielink. *A Test of Faith? Religious Diversity and Accommodation in the European Workplace*. Farnham, UK: Ashgate, 2012.

Bureau of National Affairs. *Muslim Employees: Accommodation and Integration in the Post-9/11 Workplace*. Arlington, VA: BNA, 2011.

Cañas, Kathryn A., and Harris Sondak. *Opportunities and Challenges of Workplace Diversity: Theory, Cases, and Exercises*. Upper Saddle River, NJ: Prentice Hall, 2011.

Flake, Dallan. "Image Is Everything: Corporate Branding and Religious Accommodation in the Workplace." *University of Pennsylvania Law Review* 163, no. 3 (2015): 699–754. Web. 3 Jan. 2016.

Friedman, Ron. *The Best Place to Work: The Art and Science of Creating an Extraordinary Workplace*. New York: Perigee Book, 2014.

Giacalone, Robert A., and Carole L. Jurkiewicz. *Handbook of Workplace Spirituality and Organizational Performance*. Armonk, NY: M.E. Sharpe, 2010.

Gregory, Raymond F. *Encountering Religion in the Workplace: The Legal Rights and Responsibilities of Workers and Employers*. Ithaca, NY: ILR Press, 2011.

Lefebvre, Solange, and Lori G. Beaman. *Religion in the Public Sphere: Canadian Case Studies*. Toronto, ON, Canada: University of Toronto Press, 2014.

Lindemann, Barbara, David D. Kadue, and B. Lindemann. *Workplace Harassment Law*. Arlington, VA: BNA Books, 2012.

Lund Dean, Kathy, Scott Safranski, and E. Scott Lee. "Religious Accommodation in the Workplace: Understanding Religious Identity Threat and Workplace Behaviors in Legal Disputes." *Employee Responsibilities & Rights Journal* 26, no. 2 (2014): 75–94. Web. 3 Jan. 2016.

Mihelich, Max. "Sacred Grounds—for Lawsuits." *Workforce* 93, no. 4 (2014): 18–19. Web. 3 Jan. 2016.

Rao, Pramila. *Taking Sides: Clashing Views in Human Resource Management*. New York: McGraw-Hill, 2013.

Suggested Reading

Fowler-Hermes, Jennifer, and Luisette Gierbolini. "Religious Accommodation in the Workplace: The Devil is in the Detail." *Florida Bar Journal* 88, no. 5 (2014): 34–38.

Lund Dean, Kathy, Scott Safranski, and E. Scott Lee. "Beyond Accommodation: Avoiding Religious Expression Disputes in the Workplace." *Academy of Management Annual Meeting Proceedings* (2012): 1.

Robinson, Robert K., Geralyn M. Franklin, and Robert F. Wayland. *Employment Regulation in the Workplace: Basic Compliance for Managers.* Armonk, NY: M.E. Sharpe, 2010.

Scott Zimmer, J.D.

SERVANT LEADERSHIP

ABSTRACT

Servant leadership is essentially the idea that a true leader is not one who seeks power or authority over others, but one whose primary goal is to be of service to others, helping them to grow and develop as individuals in addition to simply accomplishing objectively identifiable goals. The mantle of leadership is taken up by such an individual only as a means to achieving the end of improving the community's quality of life.

OVERVIEW

The concept of servant leadership is a relatively simple one that has been around in various forms for thousands of years. It features in the philosophical and religious traditions of several cultures, such as the Christian story of Jesus washing the feet of his disciples, and the writings of the Chinese sage Lao-Tzu, who describes the ideal leader as one of whom the people being led are barely aware—they think that the leader's achievements are actually their own, so supportive and self-effacing is he or she.

More recently, this concept has appeared in management literature, beginning with the work of Robert Greenleaf in the 1970s, who coined the phrase "servant leadership." Greenleaf was born in 1904 in Terre Haute, Indiana. He worked for AT&T and spent much of his life studying management literature and theory. He ultimately came to believe that the most effective form of leadership, as well as the most spiritually rewarding, is servant leadership. Greenleaf's descriptions of servant leadership tend to straddle the line between organizational theory and religious inspiration. Greenleaf identified 10 principles or aptitudes as being particularly important for the servant leader to possess: listening, empathy, healing, awareness, persuasion, conceptualization, foresight, stewardship, commitment to others' growth, and community building.

Servant leadership, as noted above, features indirectly in a number of religious contexts because most religions focus on examining the ways that people should behave toward one another, and servant leadership, in its own way, has the same purpose. While religions teach conduct that bring their adherents into alignment with the purported expectations of a divine realm, servant leadership also describes the types of behaviors that lead to the best outcomes for the greatest number of people in a group. Both schools of thought draw upon many years of experience and observation of human behavior to conclude that by helping others rather than by pursuing self-interest, people are most likely to attain congenial ends.

Contemporary scholars tend to define three broad categories of leadership styles. The first, laissez-faire ("let them alone"), is rarely practiced and thus receives scant attention in literature. Its infrequent use is likely attributable to the unpredictable results it produces; because it permits those being supervised to develop their own procedures without interference from superiors, the quality of work created by organizations using the laissez-faire approach depends largely upon the personalities of the organization's members at a particular time. Businesses and many other organizations try to avoid risk by selecting courses of action for which future performance is highly predictable, which is not the case under a laissez-faire model.

A second type of leadership approach is known as the authoritarian or autocratic style. This leadership strategy depends heavily on the existence of a hierarchy of power. Those near the top of the hierarchy make the decisions and issue orders to be followed by those whose position is lower in the hierarchy. The assumption is often that those at the lower end of the hierarchy are incapable of making the necessary decisions without specific instructions from their superiors and continuous monitoring and supervision are necessary to ensure that the instructions are being followed. This type of leadership does not leave much room for creativity or innovation; it instead relies more on obedience and tradition.

The third major style of leadership is known as participative leadership, meaning that decisions are made with input from more than just the people in charge—those who will be responsible for implementing the decisions are encouraged to participate in the decision-making process. Participative leadership also tends to result in a greater proportion of work being delegated to other employees rather than being jealously guarded by supervisors because there is greater trust among employees and supervisors. In addition, it relies on the assumption everyone is willing to work together to accomplish the goals of the organization. Servant leadership fits squarely within the domain of participative leadership styles, and there is a great deal of overlap between the two concepts.

APPLICATIONS

An interesting feature of the skills listed as comprising the toolkit of the servant leader is that many of them pertain not to outward demonstrations of ability or attention, but to methods of developing internal awareness of one's own emotional reactions and processes. These strategies include the competencies of awareness, conceptualization, foresight, and—to some extent—healing. More than one-third of the servant leader's key performance indicators pertain to the regulation of his or her own behavior and thinking. This situation is surprising to many who are accustomed to thinking of the role of leader as primarily consisting of the regulation of the behaviors of others.

Greenleaf and others, however, picked up on one of the key concepts underlying the servant leadership model: before one can be of service to others, one must thoroughly understand one's self, including motivations, fears, and the types of situations most likely to cause negative reactions. For example, an office manager who had practiced servant leadership for a number of years might be aware that one of her least favorite things to do is to refill the copy machines with toner. She only has to do it occasionally, but it still bothers her every time. One night as she is leaving the office, she notices that one other staff member is still at work, preparing to complete his final task—refilling the copiers with toner—before leaving. The manager in this situation is confronted by a choice—stay a few minutes extra doing something she detests in order to help out a coworker, or rely on her seniority to avoid the dreaded task. A person accustomed to one of the more traditional leadership approaches, or a person with relatively little self-awareness, might not even notice the choice inherent in the moment and would simply follow her own preference. One who has embraced the concept of the servant leader, however, will be aware of her own preference but will weigh this factor against the potential benefits to be gained from staying and helping. She will consider that the work will get done quicker, allowing her staff member to leave a little earlier; her staff member will also learn something about his manager, seeing that not only does she emphasize the importance of cooperation when she speaks at staff meetings, but she also lives up to those words by backing them up with action, even when it may be inconvenient for her. This kind of consistency between theory and practice is one of the hallmarks of servant leadership.

Servant leadership is experiencing a resurgence of interest in recent years, particularly in the corporate world. One explanation that has been proposed for this trend is the character of young people entering the workforce. The conventional wisdom indicates that members of generation X (those born somewhere between the early 1960s and the early 1980s) and millennials (those who reached the age of adulthood within a few years of 2000) are less disposed to work well in an environment that is characterized by a rigid, hierarchical system of organization. Generation X and the millennials find this type of setting to be oppressive in its oversight of people's behavior and frequently object to the stifling effect it has on creativity and collaboration. Instead, these generations prefer environments that offer support instead of competition.

Evidence suggests that these types of environment can actually operate more effectively than those not making use of a servant leadership model. Among startup companies, data shows that leaders who are perceived as most effective and most desirable to work for are those who exemplify the traits of the servant leader. One trait that is raised time and again in descriptions of these leaders is that they have learned to view the staff who report to them as another type of customer. In many companies and service organizations, an "us against them" mentality exists in which employees feel that they are engaged in a struggle with their customers. This attitude tends to happen when employees feel that they do not have enough resources, or the right kind of resources, to adequately cope with customer demands. A skilled manager can help avoid or minimize this mentality by training employees to view their relationship to the customer differently and by reallocating resources so that employees are more able to respond to customers effectively. Some leaders adopt this approach because they know that it produces superior results to simply leaving their staff to their own devices, an approach often referred to as sink or swim. Other leaders, those who understand the power of servant leadership, engage in this behavior for more than pragmatic reasons; they do it because they believe it is the right way to treat people. Just as a business performs better when employees strive to make their customers happy, employees perform better when their leader strives to make them happy.

VIEWPOINTS

Critics of the servant leadership model advance a number of different reasons for their opposition. One of the foremost objections is that most people do not have the capacity to lead because they are not decisive enough and lack the ability to develop a vision for the future and then take the practical steps to make that vision a reality. This way of thinking is based upon the idea that some people possess special qualities that make them unusually adept at leading others. This attitude has been around for much of human history and is similar to old notions of the divine right of kings, which held that kings and other members of the nobility had been specially selected by the gods in order to represent the gods on Earth. Because they had been granted this "divine right," others had to obey them and could not question their authority. Similarly, modern critics of servant leadership often feel that managing others, whether through a position of leadership in the government or a private company, requires exceptional talents that are either inborn or developed through rigorous education at elite institutions of higher learning. Servant leaders take a contrary approach, believing that the only quality that is absolutely essential for a servant leader to possess is the desire to help others reach their full potential. This perspective reflects the fact that many of the qualities of the servant leader, as Greenleaf defined them, pertain to the ability to focus one's attention on others. The modern stereotype of a leader is someone who has a large ego and tends to think about his or her own desires before considering the needs of others; the servant leader does just the opposite.

One of the weaknesses of traditional ideas of leadership, particularly authoritarian leadership, is that leaders who follow authoritarian models are much more vulnerable to being replaced than servant leaders because their power is derived solely from the fear of the organization—fear of being fired from the company, of being put in prison, or of some other negative consequence. The authoritarian leader has control over some resource—employment, money, or some other necessary commodity—and the leader uses this control and the fear it inspires to force others to do as they are told. However, there eventually comes a time when people lose their fear, either by outgrowing it or consciously rejecting it, and at that point they no longer have any reason to follow the leader.

For the servant leader, on the other hand, the culmination of his or her tenure in office is rarely a rebellion of this sort because the servant leader's authority rests not on fear, which can evaporate, but on loyalty and human connection, built up over time by connecting with those in the organization on a one-to-one basis. The servant leader establishes a personal connection to those he or she works with, and it is easier for people to reject a leader they are afraid of than a leader they respect and value as a colleague. The servant leadership values of community building, stewardship, and commitment to others' growth are particularly effective at creating and strengthening loyalty in others because they are behaviors through which the servant leader demonstrates respect for the needs of others in the group.

It is worth noting that servant leadership is based upon some fairly powerful assumptions about human nature. In the past, when scientific management theories prevailed, many people believed that a fundamental part of human nature as expressed in the workplace is that people tend to be lazy and corrupt. Therefore, unless they have a boss looking over their shoulder constantly, they will take every opportunity to do as little as possible and take every advantage for themselves that they can. More recently, studies have contradicted this mindset, showing that on average people want to do their best at their work and make a positive contribution to the goals of the community to which they belong. To the extent people deviate from these tendencies, the reason for the deviation can usually be traced back to inhumane treatment by their superiors.

The employee-centric focus demanded by servant leadership can only work if the employee is cooperative and willing to make a connection with the leader. Ultimately, the servant leader understands that leadership and followership are two sides of the same coin and must both be in place if each is to function optimally. When this situation occurs, then the organization becomes capable of new levels of synergistic functionality as leaders and followers bring out the best in one another, challenging each other to reach new heights of accomplishment. This powerful experience produces long-lasting effects, even after the leadership/followership relationship has concluded, providing a positive example to its participants that helps them to recreate the relationship in other areas of their lives.

BIBLIOGRAPHY

Baron, Tony. *The Art of Servant Leadership: Designing Your Organization for the Sake of Others.* Tucson, AZ: Wheatmark, 2010.

Ferch, Shann R. *Forgiveness and Power in the Age of Atrocity: Servant Leadership as a Way of Life.* Lanham, MD: Lexington Books, 2012.

Greenleaf, Robert K., Don M. Frick, and Larry C. Spears. *On Becoming a Servant-Leader.* San Francisco: Jossey-Bass, 1996.

Hunter, James C. *The Servant: A Simple Story about the True Essence of Leadership.* New York: Crown Business, 2012.

Prosser, Stephen. *Servant Leadership: More Philosophy, Less Theory.* Westfield, IN: Greenleaf Center for Servant Leadership, 2010.

Sarros, James C. "Servant Leadership Influence on Trust and Equality Relationship in Organizational Settings." *International Leadership Journal* (2016). Web. 31 July 2017.

Selladurai, Raj, and Shawn Carraher. *Servant Leadership: Research and Practice.* Hershey, PA: Business Science Reference, 2014.

Trompenaars, Fons, and Ed Voerman. *Servant Leadership across Cultures: Harnessing the Strength of the World's Most Powerful Philosophy.* New York: McGraw-Hill, 2010.

van Dierendonck, Dirk, and Kathleen Patterson. *Servant Leadership: Developments in Theory and Research.* Hampshire, UK: Palgrave Macmillan, 2010.

Wallace, Rocky. *Servant Leadership: Leaving a Legacy.* Lanham, MD: Rowman & Littlefield Education, 2012.

Wheeler, Daniel W. *Servant Leadership for Higher Education: Principles and Practices*. San Francisco: Jossey-Bass, 2012.

SUGGESTED READING

Baldner, Gerald. *Successful Servant Leadership: Insights from Servant Leaders in Education, Business, Healthcare, Politics, Athletics, & Religion.* La Crosse, WI: D.B. Reinhart Institute for Ethics in Leadership at Viterbo University, 2012.

Day, David V. *The Oxford Handbook of Leadership and Organizations.* New York: Oxford University Press, 2014.

Greenleaf, Robert K. "The Servant as Leader." (1970). Web. 1 Apr. 2015.

Keith, Kent M. *The Case for Servant Leadership.* Honolulu: Terrace Press, 2012.

Liden, Robert C., Sandy J. Wayne, and Jeremy D. Meuser. "Servant Leadership and Service Culture: Influence on Individual and Unit Performance." *Academy of Management Journal* 57, no. 5 (2014): 1434–52. Web. 22 Mar. 2005.

Ngunjiri, Faith W. *Women's Spiritual Leadership in Africa: Tempered Radicals and Critical Servant Leaders.* Albany: State University of New York Press, 2010.

van Dierendonck, Dirk, and Kathleen Patterson. "Compassionate Love as a Cornerstone of Servant Leadership: An Integration of Previous Theorizing and Research." *Journal of Business Ethics* 128, no. 1 (2015): 119–31. Web. 22 Mar. 2015.

Zhijun, Chen, Zhu Jinb, and Zhou Mingjian. "How Does a Servant Leader Fuel the Service Fire? A Multilevel Model of Servant Leadership, Individual Self Identity, Group Competition Climate, and Cusomter Service Performance." *Journal of Applied Psychology* 100, no. 2 (2015): 511–21. Web. 22 Mar. 2015.

Scott Zimmer, M.L.S., M.S., J.D.

SERVICE OPERATIONS MANAGEMENT

ABSTRACT

An increasing number of businesses are offering services rather than tangible goods. Although customers' opinions of service quality are directly related to a company's profitability, many organizations fail to control and improve their customer service processes. These processes tend to be difficult and costly to control because of their intangibility, heterogeneity, and inseparability. However, operations management principles can be applied to service industries in an effort to improve quality. One must first understand what the customer wants from the customer service process and then identify fail points in the process where it is likely to go wrong. No matter how well the customer service process is designed and implemented, problems are unavoidable. Customer dissatisfaction as a result of errors, however, is not. There are a number of ways to recover from customer service problems and maintain customer loyalty.

OVERVIEW

As the state-of-the-art twenty-first century technology continues to expand and high tech solutions proliferate, more and more businesses offer services instead of, or in addition to, tangible products. In fact, the service industry is the largest and fastest growing business sector in the United States. Despite the opportunities offered by this growing sector, however, businesses are faced with the problem of determining how to manage operations where the products are intangible. As a result, research has found that most consumers are dissatisfied with the customer service they receive from these businesses. This fact, combined with the increasing service competition that arises out of the growing trend toward globalization, means that increased emphasis needs to be placed on operations management in service organizations just as it is in manufacturing organizations.

Operations Management & the Service Sector
Operations management comprises those areas of management that are concerned with productivity, quality, and cost in the operations function (i.e., those activities necessary to transform inputs such as business transactions and information into outputs such as completed transactions) as well as strategic planning for the organization. The service sector has been described in many ways. In its essence, the service sector includes those industries and businesses that provide services rather than tangible products for individual consumers, businesses, or a combination of the two. These can include physical, mental, or aesthetic activities (e.g., legal services, entertainment, auto repair) or the transformation of something through such an activity (e.g., hair cutting, education, management consulting). Like defining the service sector itself, defining operations management for the service sector is more problematic than defining operations management for other sectors (i.e., transportation, communications, and utilities; wholesale or retail trade; finance, insurance, and real estate; public administration). It is relatively easy to determine when a widget does not meet acceptable quality standards. The manufacturer will have a manufacturing specification that describes what the tolerances are for the product and quality control will accept or reject the product based on whether or not it is within the specifications. Similarly, a manufacturing process can be evaluated to see where there is waste in the process or where efficiencies

Service sector managers talk shop (Photo courtesy of PvdS)

can be introduced. However, it is not so obvious where to improve quality or cost-effectiveness for service industries. For example, how does one specify the quality of a new hairstyle? Although in some cases a bad haircut can be obvious to all, a new hairstyle may be a matter of aesthetics; what looked good in the magazine on the 20-year-old model may not look so good on the middle-aged customer with a different bone structure. Similarly, how does one evaluate the cost of creating a new work of art or the training of a hotel employee? Yet, the quality of customer service must be operationally defined in order for the organization to be consistently effective.

Quality Improvement & Control

Despite the fact that research has shown that customers' opinions of service quality are directly related to company profitability, many service organizations do not try to control and improve quality due in part to the fact that service quality is often difficult and costly to control and improve. It is also due to the differences between the activities and products of the service industry and those of the manufacturing industry. In manufacturing, results are tangible and can be quantified. This fact makes it easier to control quality than in the service industry where the "product" is intangible. Further, in manufacturing, statistical quality control methods can be built into the process so that quality is monitored and corrected at several key points in the process. In most manufacturing processes, there are typically several points at which the product can be quality tested so that substandard parts or products can be rejected or the process can be rectified as necessary before the products reach the consumer. This approach, however, is not possible in the service industry; one cannot do a quality control check on services before they reach the customer.

Three Reasons for Control Difficulties

There are three reasons that services are difficult to control: intangibility, heterogeneity, and inseparability. The quality of customer service is not based on a product that one can touch. Characteristics of good customer service more often have to do with speed of delivery of the service, the competence with which the service is delivered and the courtesy with which it is offered. Such factors are difficult to quantify for a number of reasons, not the least of which is the perceptions and expectations of the customer. It can be difficult to operationally define good customer service. For example, does walking the customer through a troubleshooting procedure step-by-step in an attempt to be thorough constitute good customer service, or does listening to the customer in an attempt to find out what she or he has already tried constitute good customer service? The former situation is apt to antagonize someone who is knowledgeable about the process while the latter approach is likely to miss important steps with a customer who only thinks she or he is knowledgeable. In some situations, there are, of course, some aspects of customer service that are tangible (e.g., receiving starter checks when opening a new bank account). However, these tend to be much poorer predictors of customer satisfaction than are the intangible factors.

Factors that Affect Quality of Service

In addition to being intangible, services tend to be heterogeneous in nature, and not consistently performed. Quality of service depends on a number of factors, including the personalities and expectations of each of the parties involved. For example, when a technophobe calls a technical support help line to troubleshoot what is wrong with his computer, he expects and needs to be treated with a step-by-step, hand-holding approach that will allow him to trust the person on the other end to walk him through the steps. If an experienced computer programmer calls the technical help line, however, the same step-by-step approach based on the assumption that the customer is clueless is more apt to be irritating than helpful. Similarly, the retail assistant who greets the customer at the door and follows him or her throughout the shopping experience may be perceived as helpful by some customers and intrusive by other customers. Human nature makes customer service a complicated process. What works with a given customer today (e.g., when the customer wants help) may not work with the same customer tomorrow (e.g., when the customer is in a hurry and does not want to linger over the process). A third characteristic of customer service is inseparability. Customer service is performed in the presence of the customer and becomes inseparable in the customer's mind from the organization as a whole. So, for example, if a software manufacturing company provides poor

Firm Framework of Time	Fault-Freeness	Flexibility	Style	Steering	Soft Safety
■ Availability of service (i.e., hours/day)	■ Physical items of the service	■ To customize the service	■ Appropriateness of attitudes	■ Perceived importance	■ Trust
■ Availability of all aspects of the service		■ To cope with mistakes	■ Accessibility (to people and location)	■ Feelings of being in control	■ Confidence
■ Responsiveness (i.e., how long to react to customer)	■ Correctness of information/advice	■ To introduce new services (to complete a service package)	■ Perceived value	■ Clarity of service (e.g., where to go, what to do, whom to see)	■ Honesty of advice/information
■ Queue time			■ Ambience (e.g., decoration, lighting, temperature, cleanliness, dress)	■ Consistency	■ Security
■ Process time				■ Psychological timing (how long the service seems to take)	
■ Dependability/repeatability of service time					

Table 1: Dimensions of Customer Service (adapted from Armistead 1989, 249)

customer service to someone logging on to the support database or calling the technical help line, in the customer's mind, the service will be inseparable from the product. Most customers do not differentiate between the quality of the product and the quality of the service. An overview of the dimensions of customer service is given in table 1.

Steps to Improving Customer Service

Despite the more nebulous nature of service versus manufacturing, operations management principles can be applied to service industries in an effort to improve quality. The first step in improving customer service is to ascertain whether or not one is offering the service that the customer wants. For example, no matter how good an automated troubleshooting system is, if the customer wants the personalized service of talking to a live person, the automated system will never be sufficient. Another action taken to improve customer service is to improve the service system itself. Various program management techniques including PERT (program evaluation and review technique) charts and Six Sigma programs can be used in an attempt to regularly assess and ensure quality. However, when dealing with the service industry, these tools tend to miss one of the major components of the system: The customer's interaction with the service.

The Blueprint Method

Once the service for which the customer is looking has been determined, one can next determine how to better provide that service for the customer. One of the ways to overcome this omission is through the "blueprint" method. The various steps part of this method includes:

Flowcharting

The first step in the blueprint method is to specify the complete service process in a flow chart. This schematic should distinguish between those operations or activities that are seen by the customer and those that are not. Even though part of the process is not seen by the customer, it still can affect overall customer satisfaction with the service. For example, the computer software used by a credit card company will probably never be seen by the customer. However, if the software prints out credit card statements in a format that the customer finds difficult to decipher, the software will negatively impact customer satisfaction. Similarly, many grocery stores use software to help design the store layout in order to give customers easier access to certain items or to give designated stock a place of prominence for promotional purposes. Although the customer will probably never see that software, either, if she or he has to search for the Nutty Crunchy cereal for the third time in two months, she or he is not likely to be satisfied with the store's customer service.

Determining Fail Points

Once the service process has been flow charted, the next step in the blueprint method is to analyze it to determine where there are fail points—the critical points in the process where the provider has the opportunity to make a serious mistake that can negatively impact the customer's satisfaction with the process or his/her perception of quality. This analysis allows the provider the opportunity to design fail-safe subprocesses that can be integrated into the overall service process so that potential missteps are caught before they affect the customer's perceptions of the service or the process. The determination and elimination of fail points is one of the most difficult steps in the blueprint process. One of the reasons is that it is important to determine the time frame of the fail points since time is an important factor in service cost. However, the more complex the service process, the more difficult it is to pinpoint time frames.

Determining Time Frame

To do this part of the analysis, it can be helpful to first determine how long it takes to perform the process when all aspects of the situation are normal. From a customer's point of view, satisfaction with the process or service decreases in direct relations to the degree to which the process or service takes longer than expected. Once this "ideal" time frame is developed, time frames can be developed for various foreseeable deviations from the normal case. For example, a grocery store could determine the amount of time it should take a checkout clerk to ring up an order with a given number of items. From there, it could be determined how long it would take if one of the items were not marked with the price or the SKU had not been entered into the system. This process could be performed for other deviations from the ideal checkout situation such as the use of coupons, the customer not having picked up sufficient items to qualify for a sale price, and so forth.

Profitability Check

Once the ideal and deviation time frames have been determined, the blueprint should next be checked for profitability. This activity involves quantifying the cost of various deviations on profitability. For example, the situation where an item is not entered into the computer means that the transaction needs to be stopped while someone is sent to look for the correct price on the shelves or in the sales flyer. This person needs to return to the checkout line or call the checker with the correct price. This deviation not only affects the time frame for service of the person's order with the undocumented item, but also affects the time frame for service for the people standing in line behind that person.

Use of Technology

In some instances, there are ways to speed up processes or increase efficiency through the use of technology. For example, to help get the customer through to the correct person on a telephone help line, many businesses use an automated telephone answering system. From the organization's point of view, the use of this technology can get customers help in a more timely manner while reducing the number of employees that the organization needs to hire to answer the phones. The automated system can even offer the customer answers to frequently asked questions while they are waiting on hold. However, if from the customer's point of view the answering system is too impersonal or cumbersome, then customer satisfaction decreases and counteracts the efficiencies gained by implementing the system. When dealing with customer service issues, the object of the exercise is not only to increase the efficiency of the process, but to do so while not decreasing the customer's perception of quality.

APPLICATIONS

No matter how well the customer service process is designed and implemented, errors and problems are unavoidable. Customer dissatisfaction as a result of these things, however, is not. It may be tempting to consider the one complaining customer as an outlier who does not represent customers in general or whose opinion does not reflect badly on the organization's service process. However, such customers should not be dismissed since they typically represent a silent number of other customers who did not bother to complain. In addition, according to industry experts, it costs five times more to replace a customer than to retain one. Therefore, customer satisfaction is important to the success of the business. At virtually every fail point, there is a concomitant opportunity for recovery. To take advantage of these opportunities, however, appropriate mechanisms need to be in place. The best way to recover from problems with customer service is to empower front-line employees to handle them as they arise. Being told that the problem is not the fault of the employee and that she or he can do nothing about it is not going to soothe the customer. The customer sees the front line employee as a representative of the organization at large; if the front-line employee is powerless or incompetent, the customer is more likely to take the same view of the business in general.

Therefore, although it is important to manage service operations well, it is equally important to be able to manage service recovery well for those inevitable situations where problems arise. There are several ways to ensure quality service recovery. First, management needs to understand the costs associated with mismanaged customer service as well as the costs to recover from the situation. For example, at Club Med, a satisfied customer typically visits the resort chain four more times after the initial visit whereas a dissatisfied customer does not. On average, for every customer who does not return, Club Med loses $2,400 in income. This loss is in addition to the expenses of marketing to find replacement customers. Another way to improve customer service is to listen closely to what the customer has to say. One way, of course, is to listen to customer complaints and take them seriously since they provide opportunities to learn how to improve the service process. However, although some customers freely complain to the organization about poor service, most do not, and just slip quietly away. To help overcome this problem, the business should make it easy for customers to complain. Asking customers how the service was is one way, as are toll-free 24-hour complaint hot lines. However, no matter the medium, it is important to really listen to the customer so that the complaint and the underlying problem are well understood and appropriate action can be taken. It is also important that this action be taken quickly before the customer's negative reaction to the business becomes solidified. Although management is sometimes required to intervene in order to solve a customer service problem, the best way to handle problems quickly and to minimize negative impact is to train employees to identify problems and empower them to respond to them. Training can help employees know where the fail points in the process are and help them learn to detect when a problem occurs. In addition, employees who deal with customers need to be given both the authority and responsibility to react to customer service problems and rectify the situation appropriately. To further encourage trained, empowered employees to give excellent service, it is helpful to put incentives in place to encourage good customer service and to recognize those who rectify problems quickly, quietly, and well. Through this combination of actions, the impact of inevitable customer service problems can be minimized and the business can keep and expand its customer base.

BIBLIOGRAPHY

Armistead, Colin G. "Customer Service Operations Management in Service Businesses." *Service Industries Journal* 9, no. 2 (1989): 247–60. Web. 29 May 2007.

Hart, Christopher W. L., James L. Heskett, and W. Earl Sasser Jr. "The Profitable Art of Service Recovery." *Harvard Business Review* 68, no. 4 (1990): 148–56. Web. 29 May 2007.

Idris, Fazli. "Achieving Flexibility in Service Operations Using the Rigid Flexibility Framework: An Exploratory Study." *International Journal of Business & Society* 13, no. 3 (2012): 279–82. Web. 15 Nov. 2013.

Liu, X., and Kelley Donalds. "Stimulating Reflective Learning in Teaching a Service Operations Management Course." Proceedings for the Northeast Region Decision Sciences Institute (NEDSI), 792–97. Web. 15 Nov. 2013.

Montoya, Mitzi M., Anne P. Massey, and Vijay Khatri. "Connecting IT Services Operations to Services Marketing Practices." *Journal of Management Information Systems* 26, no. 4 (2010): 65–85. Web. 15 Nov. 2013.

Tinkham, Mary A., and Brian H. Kleiner. "New Developments in Service Operations Management." *Industrial Management* 34, no. 6 (1992): 20–22. Web. 29 May 2007.

Suggested Reading

Craighead, Christopher W., Kirk R. Karwan, and Janis L. Miller. "The Effects of Severity of Failure and Customer Loyalty on Service Recovery Strategies." *Production & Operations Management* 13, no. 4 (2004): 307–21. Web. 29 May 2007.

Harvey, Jean. "Designing Efficient and Manageable Public Professional Service Processes." *International Journal of Operations & Production Management* 9, no. 1 (1989): 35–44. Web. 29 May 2007.

Johnston, Robert. "Service Operations Management: Return to Roots." *International Journal of Operations & Production Management* 19, no. 2 (1999). Web. 29 May 2007.

Killeya, John C., and Colin G. Armistead. "The Transfer of Concepts and Techniques between manufacturing and Service Systems." *International Journal of Operations & Production Management* 3, no. 3 (1983): 22–28. Web. 29 May 2007.

Morris, Barbara, and Robert Johnston. "Dealing with Inherent Variability: The Difference between Manufacturing and Service?" *International Journal of Operations & Production Management* 7, no. 4 (1987): 13–22. Web. 29 May 2007.

Ruth A. Wienclaw, Ph.D.

Sexual Harassment

Abstract

Noted legal scholar and feminist Catherine MacKinnon defined sexual harassment as "the unwanted imposition of sexual requirement in the context of a relationship of unequal power" (MacKinnon 1979). Sexual harassment generally falls under two categories: quid pro quo harassment and hostile environment. The majority of victims reporting instances of sexual harassment are women, and the vast majority of reported aggressors are men. Title VII of the Civil Rights Act of 1964 and the Equal Employment Opportunity Commission provide legal recourse for victims of sexual harassment.

Some sociologists associate the full integration of women into the modern workforce with an increase in instances of sexual harassment. Social scientists are somewhat critical of common approaches to dealing with sexual harassment, particularly in the workforce. Many organizations have made concerted efforts to heighten awareness of issues related to sexual harassment, though social scientist recommend shifting the focus from identifying instances of sexual harassment to pinpointing factors that contribute to instances of sexual harassment with the ultimate aim of lessening future occurrences.

Overview

Sexual harassment remains a common occurrence in society. According to the US Equal Employment Opportunity Commission, 6,862 sexual harassment charges were filed in 2014, and a 2015 *Cosmopolitan* survey found that as many as 33 percent of women aged 18 to 34 having experienced sexual harassment in the workplace and, in 70 percent of cases of verbal harassment, did not report it. However, the challenge of defining exactly what constitutes sexual harassment remains. According to Kingsley Browne (2006) of Wayne State University Law School,

Catharine MacKinnon

Courts have declared that all of the following kinds of conduct may constitute sexual harassment: forcible rape; extorting sex for job benefits; sexual or romantic overtures; sexual jokes; sexually suggestive pictures or cartoons; sexist comments; vulgar language; harassing actions of a non-sexual form; and even 'well intended compliments.' (145)

Sexual harassment is defined as a form of sex discrimination under Title VII Federal Law Civil Rights Act of 1964, which prohibits employment discrimination based on race, color, religion, sex, or national origin (U.S. Equal Opportunity Commission 2002).

Feminist attorney Catherine MacKinnon argued for the legal recognition of sexual harassment as sex discrimination in her 1979 book *Sexual Harassment of Working Women*. In the book, MacKinnon states that because of the traditional gender roles of our society, women disproportionately occupy inferior positions in the workplace. One psychologist writing on the subject concurred with MacKinnon, seeing sexual harassment, "as a form of sex discrimination that keeps the sexes separate and unequal at work" (Berdahl 2007, 435).

MacKinnon (1979) argued that "intimate violations" of women by men were "sufficiently pervasive" as to make the practice nearly invisible (1). She also found that internalized power structures within the workplace kept anyone from discussing sexual harassment, making it "inaudible" (1). In her words, the abuse was both acceptable for men to perpetuate and a taboo that women could not confront either publicly or privately. MacKinnon stated that the "social failure" to address these pervasive intimate violations hurt women in terms of the economic status, opportunity, mental health, and self-esteem (1). Many believe that sexual harassment is about the abuse of power, others believe it is about access to sexual favors, and still others believe that sexual harassment is about access to power and sex. In legal terms, sexual harassment is divided into two main categories.

Quid Pro Quo
Quid pro quo harassment occurs when an employee is made to submit to some form of sexual advance in order to obtain a benefit (e.g., a promotion) or to avoid a burden (e.g., being fired). In such cases, sexual harassment is considered sex discrimination because presumably the demand would not have been made if the employee were of the same sex (Browne 2006). Initially, researchers and courts believed that this type of harassment was motivated by sexual desire, but research has subsequently suggested that it is instead meant to assert dominance over or derogate the target (Berdahl 2007).

Hostile Environment
Hostile environment harassment occurs when a work environment is "permeated with sexuality" or "discriminatory intimidation, ridicule, and insult" (Smith, Craver, and Turner 2011). Within this type of harassment, the victim does not claim specific harassment, but rather that the general work environment is discriminatory. Generally, it is believed that this type of harassment seeks to undermine and humiliate its target and is likely to be motivated by sexual hostility rather than sexual desire (Berdahl 2007).

Men & Women in the Workplace

As women gain greater equity in the workplace, it might be assumed that the instances of sexual harassment in the workplace would diminish. However, the causes of sexual harassment are complex and hard to identify, and sexual harassment remains prevalent in modern society. Women's increasing presence in the workforce has meant that men and women work together more closely in the twenty-first century than at any other time in history. In fact, there are fewer and fewer male only professions as women become much more fully integrated into all corners of the workforce. According to one researcher, "one effect of the breakdown of the sexual division of labor is the expansion of opportunities for sexual conflict in the workplace" (Browne 2006, 145). One outgrowth of this conflict may be sexual harassment. Wayne State University law professor Kingsley Brown (2006) analyzed data from numerous studies to argue that sexual harassment is rooted in sociocultural causes, as well as biological and psychological causes. Sociocultural theories of sexual harassment, he says, hold that harassment is a means for the harasser to gain power over his target. Biological and psychological theories, on the other hand, hold that men are biologically and psychologically predisposed to be sexually aggressive and that sexual harassment is an outgrowth of these predispositions (Browne 2006).

Further, Browne (2006) argues that men tend to interpret female interest as sexual, while women are more likely to interpret male attention as mere friendliness. According to Browne, these differing perspectives may often lead to miscommunication and unintentional harassment. In other words a man, perceiving a woman's friendliness to indicate sexual interest, may escalate his attention to a level that the woman sees as threatening (Browne 2006).

Token Resistance to Sexual Harassment

Token resistance is a concept that originated in date rape literature and describes the belief that women may ostensibly discourage sexual attention when in fact they wish it to continue (Osman 2004). In other words, a woman may say "no" when what she really means is "yes."

Research suggests that a sexual aggression continuum exists with nonviolent sexual aggression at one end and rape at the other (see figure 1). Researchers believe that sexual harassment could fall at the less extreme end, a belief that, if correct, could offer insight into the perceptions of aggressors who partake in similar behaviors (Begany and Milburn 2002). The implications for studying token resistance and sexual harassment could be promising: men who have a strong belief in token resistance on one end of the spectrum may hold similar beliefs at the less extreme end. Research suggests that men who have a strong belief in token resistance have difficulty determining when their advances are unwanted. They may need stronger signals (verbal resistance, physical resistance, or both) to convince them that their actions are being rejected.

Continuum of Sexually Aggressive Behaviors	
Non-physically violent Sexual aggression (sexual harassment)	Extreme physical violence Rape

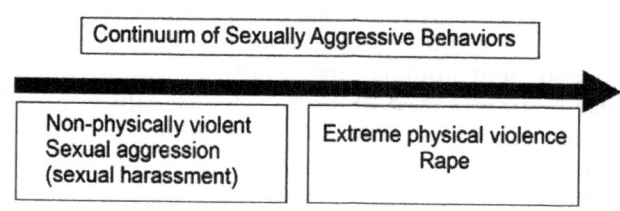

Figure 1: Continuum of Sexually Aggressive Behaviors.

The study of token resistance and sexual harassment may reveal not only why men may see attention as harmless, but also why women may see it as threatening. As one researcher found, women are more likely than men to identify less severe instances of harassment as harassment. However, this difference tends to disappear as harassment becomes more severe and the target's resistance becomes stronger (Osman 2007). Osman also points out that most women do not offer direct resistance to unwanted sexual attention, which may fail to dissuade men who have a strong belief in token resistance. Although verbal resistance may be enough to alert most men that their attentions are not wanted, Osman argues that women should also know that in some cases simultaneous verbal and physical resistance is needed to get their message across.

What Motivates Sexual Harassment?

Much contemporary research focuses on the indirect evidence that illuminates the causes of sexual harassment. This investigation includes determining the targets of sexual harassment as well as the motives of the harasser (Berdahl 2007). Psychologists Joseph J. Begany and Michael A. Milburn examined the personality characteristic of authoritarianism to see if there was a correlation between it and sexual harassment. According to Adorno, Frenekl-Brunswik, Levinson, and Sanford (1950), an authoritarian personality can develop as "a result of harsh, punitive child rearing and the consequential displacement of negative emotions into the public realm" (Begany and Milburn 2002, 119). These theorists suggested that authoritarian personalities displace the anger they experienced during childhood onto those who are weaker than themselves and unlikely to retaliate. Additionally, highly authoritarian personalities are likely to "exhibit signs of underlying resentful disrespect for women generally" (Adorno et al. 1950, 107, as quoted in Begany and Milburn 2002, 119).

These people may exhibit "fear of a dangerous world, self righteous attitudes and vindictive envy" (Begany and Milburn 2002, 119) and, as a result, may be predisposed to sexually harass others. Men with authoritarian traits may also exhibit a tendency toward hypermasculinity and adhere strictly to traditional cultural norms. Authoritarianism has been found to be predictive of sexual and physical aggression as well as battering (Begany and Milburn 2002).

Begany and Milburn identified two types of sexism that are mediating factors in between authoritarianism and sexual harassment: hostile and benevolent sexism, both of which serve to rationalize men's dominance over women. Men who exhibit benevolent sexism see themselves as protectors of women and have favorable attitudes toward women in traditional gender roles, such as those of a wife, mother, or homemaker. Hostile sexism espouses that men are superior to women and ought to sexually dominate them. The authors found that "authoritarianism … predicts the likelihood that a man will report a greater likelihood of engaging in sexual harassment" (Begany and Milburn 2002, 126). Men with sexist attitudes tend to endorse gender role distinctions that in turn may serve to enhance their own sense of male identity (Berdahl 2007).

Begany and Milburn's findings support those of psychologist Jennifer Berdahl (2007), who found that women who violate gender ideals are likely to be subjected to sexual harassment. Men who exhibit either benevolent or hostile sexism are likely to view women who possess masculine personality traits as a threat, which can increase the likelihood that they will harass them. According to Berdahl (2007), while sexual harassment of women who exhibit feminine ideals may be more common in the quid pro quo scenario, women who violate feminine gender ideals are much more likely to be subjected to hostile environments. As Berdahl put it, "sexual harassment is driven not out of desire for women who meet feminine ideals but out of a desire to punish those who violate them" (2007, 434). As a result, having masculine traits may not help women fit into male-dominated fields and may even hurt them.

APPLICATIONS

Gender Ideals in the Workplace

One should not assume that women who conform to archetypal feminine ideals fare better than those who exhibit personality traits traditionally considered masculine. In many cases for women in the workforce, a double bind exists: women who exhibit traditional feminine traits are dismissed and disrespected, while those who have more masculine traits are scorned and disliked (Berdahl 2007).

Research on the topic of sexual harassment proposes many theories as to why sexual harassment occurs. Harassment that is motivated by sexual desire may or may not be contingent upon a condition (quid pro quo), but at least some harassment does appear to be directed toward women with archetypal feminine traits. Harassment that targets gender-role deviants (those who violate feminine ideals) is more likely to fall into the category of hostile environment (Berdahl 2007).

Sexual Harassment as Hazing

There appear to be many factors that contribute to sexual harassment, and social scientists and others continue to question how often sex is a motive. If sexual harassment is not really about sex, but power, then the term is a bit of a misnomer. Kingsley Browne (2006) asked whether "abuse that takes a sexual form … is necessarily directed at the target 'because of the sex?'" (147).

Browne suggests that sexual harassment may be just another form of hazing—which occurs between men as well as between men and women. Hazing was common in the workplace long before women entered the workforce. Browne's theory is that people who wish to offend deliver messages to which their targets will be especially sensitive. Men might use one message to harass other men (possibly sexual in nature) and a different message to harass women (very often sexual). In the majority of cases, Browne argued, harassment against women will contain sexual overtones because it is a type of harassment to which they are especially sensitive. However, the harassment may not be specifically about sex (Browne 2006). If some sexual harassment is indeed a form of hazing—particularly in the workplace—it is possible to conclude that some harassment is about demonstrating power over others.

CONCLUSION

Perceptions of harassment vary widely. There is often ambiguity in the line between what constitutes harassment and what is just harmless attention (Osborne 2007). The goal of sexual harassment training is to increase employee awareness and sensitivity. However, some sociologists argue that awareness is not enough; employees need to be taught to avoid the miscommunications and attitudes that can contribute to harassment.

Sexual harassment training tends to focus on teaching employees to identify what harassment is and not very much on the underlying attitudes that contribute to harassment. It is extremely common for sexual harassment training programs to be judged upon an employee's ability to recognize sexual harassment as opposed to recognizing the actions and emotions that lead to it (Browne 2006). In other words, employees are given many examples of what behaviors might be construed as sexual harassment, but far less information about why harassment occurs (Berdahl 2007).

Sociologists understand that there are many theories about why sexual harassment occurs; research continues to examine the psychological and social factors that contribute to the phenomenon. Much of the literature about sexual harassment focuses on the perspective of the target rather than the harasser; however, some sociologists argue that research needs to be conducted on harassers in order to understand how to address their behavior (Browne 2006).

BIBLIOGRAPHY

Begany, Joseph, and Michael Milburn. "Psychological Predictors of Sexual Harassment: Authoritarianism, Hostile Sexism, and Rape Myths." University of Massachusetts. 3, no. 2 (2002): 119–26. 23 May 2008.

Berdahl, Jennifer. "The Sexual Harassment of Uppity Woman." *Journal of Applied Psychology* 92 (2007): 425–27. Web. 23 May 2008.

Browne, Kingsley. "Sex, Power and Dominance, the Evolutionary Psychology of Sexual Harassment." *Managerial and Decision Economics* 27 (2006): 145–58. Web. 23 May 2008.

Buckner, Grant, Hugh Hindman, Timothy Huelsman, and Jacqueline Bergman. "Managing Workplace Sexual Harassment: The Role of Manager Training." *Employee Responsibilities & Rights Journal* 26, no. 4 (2014): 257–78. Web. 25 Jan. 2016.

Galdi, Silvia, Anne Maass, and Mara Cadinu. "Objectifying Media: Their Effort on Gender Role Norms and Sexual Harassment of Women." *Psychology of Women Quarterly* 38 (2014): 398–413. Web. 12 Jan. 2015.

Holland, Kathryn J., and Lilia M. Cortina. "When Sexism and Feminism Collide: The Sexual Harassment of Feminist Working Women." *Psychology of Women Quarterly* 37 (2013): 192–208. Web. 6 Nov. 2013.

Leskinen, Emily, Lilia Cortina, and Dana Kabat. "Gender Harassment: Broadening Our Understanding of Sex-Based Harassment at Work." *Law & Human Behavior* 35 (2011): 25–39. Web. 6 Nov. 2013.

MacKinnon, Catherine A. *Sexual Harassment of Working Women: A Case of Sex Discrimination.* New Haven, CT: Yale University Press, 1979. Web. 28 May 2008.

McLaughlin, Heather, Christopher Uggen, and Amy Blackstone. "Sexual Harassment, Workplace Authority, and the Paradox of Power." *American Sociological Review* 77 (2012): 625–47. Web. 6 Nov. 2013.

Nye, Christopher D., Bradley J. Brummel, and Fritz Drasgow. "Understanding Sexual Harassment Using Aggregate Construct Models." *Journal of Applied Psychology* 99 (2014): 1204–21. Web. 12 Jan. 2015.

Osman, Suzanne. "Victim Resistance: Theory and Data on Understanding Perceptions of Sexual Harassment." *Sex Roles: A Journal of Research* 50, nos. 3–4 (2004): 265–75. Print.

Osman, Suzanne. "Predicting Perceptions of Sexual Harassment Based on Type of Resistance and Belief in Token Resistance." *Journal of Sex Research* 44 (2007): 340–46. Web. 19 Web. 2008.

Smith, Arthur B., Charles B. Craver, and Ronald Turner. *Employment Discrimination Law: Cases and Materials.* 7th ed. New Providence, NJ: Lexis Nexis, 2011.

U.S. Equal Opportunity Commission. (2002). Federal Laws Prohibiting Job Discrimination: Questions and Answers. Web. 19 May 2008.

SUGGESTED READING

Buchanan, NiCole T., Isis H. Settles, Angela T. Hall, and Rachel C. O'Connor. "A Review of Organizational Strategies for Reducing Sexual Harassment: Insights from the U.S. Military." *Journal of Social Issues* 70, no. 4 (2014): 687–702. Web. 25 Jan. 2016.

Bursik, Krisanne, and Julia Gefter. "Still Stable after All These Years: Perceptions of Sexual Harassment in Academic Contexts." *Journal of Social Psychology* 151 (2011): 331–49. Web. 6 Nov. 2013.

Key, Colin W., and Robert D. Ridge. "Guys Like Us: The Link between Sexual Harassment Policy and Blame." *Journal of Social & Personal Relationships* 28 (2011): 1093–1103. Web. 6 Nov. 2013.

Nelson, J. "Out of Bounds." *Essence* 38 (2008): 160–63. Web. 19 May 2008.

"Prevention of Sexual Harassment in the Workplace and Education Setting." *American Academy of Pediatrics* (2000). Web. 23 May 2008

"Sexual Harassment in the Workplace." *Sexual Violence Justice Institute.* (2004). Web. 23 May 2008.

Carolyn Sprague, M.L.S.

SHARED LEADERSHIP

ABSTRACT

Shared leadership refers to a team of people leading each other rather than following one appointed leader. Collective leadership, horizontal leadership, and distributed leadership are similar concepts. The traditional leadership model is called vertical or hierarchical leadership, in which there is one leader for each group and one group leads another group. In contrast, shared leadership involves the broad distribution of leadership across a team or organization, in which individuals pool their expertise for the benefit of the entire group.

OVERVIEW

A shared leadership model maximizes the human resources of an organization by giving multiple individuals the opportunity to lead in their areas of expertise. This opportunity empowers individuals and in turn makes them more likely to work hard toward goals for which they are personally responsible.

The concept of shared leadership emerged in business and psychology literature in the late twentieth and early twenty-first centuries, even though its existence can be traced back to the ancient Roman Republic, when a system of co-leadership lasted for several centuries. Most scholarly studies of leadership have focused on the hierarchical model in which a single leader inspires, commands, and controls followers. Scholarly work on shared leadership, in contrast, notes that leadership may be collective, with two or more individuals involved in leadership roles.

Teamwork has become increasingly important in the workplace, and leaders of these teams are credited with the effectiveness or ineffectiveness of their teams. This emphasis on teamwork, along with an understanding of the importance of team leaders, has led to an increase in shared leadership among teams of many organizations.

The modern business world consists of organizations that are expanding globally, merging with other organizations, and restructuring both within the organization and throughout the industry. Given the challenging nature of these changes—particularly for a single leader who is unlikely to have all of the expertise necessary—a number of organizations have turned to shared leadership to help ease the transitions and grow. Shared leadership combines the best of each leader's abilities so that a broad base of knowledge may be drawn from to help an organization take the right steps. Susan Misra, Michael Allison, and Elissa Perry for the *Nonprofit Quarterly* highlight four prerequisites for shared leadership: a commitment to change on the part of senior leadership; an investment in education and planning; existing management practices already in place; and accountability and engagement.

BIBLIOGRAPHY

Barnett, Kerry, and John McCormick. "Leadership and Team Dynamics in Senior Executive Leadership Teams." *Educational Management Administration and Leadership* 40.6 (2012): 653–71. Print.

Bergman, Jacqueline Z., et al. "The Shared Leadership Process in Decision-Making Teams." *Journal of Social Psychology* 152.1 (2012): 17–42. Print.

Goldsmith, Marshall. "Sharing Leadership to Maximize Talent." *Harvard Business Review.* Harvard Business School, 26 May 2010. Web. 17 Oct. 2013.

Hoch, Julia. "Shared Leadership and Innovation: The Role of Vertical Leadership and Employee Integrity." *Journal of Business and Psychology* 28.2 (2013): 159–74. Print.

Kocolowski, Michael D. "Shared Leadership: Is It Time for a Change?" *Emerging Leadership Journeys* 3.1 (2010): 22–32. Print.

Lindsay, Douglas R., David V. Day, and Stanley M. Halpin. "Shared Leadership in the Military: Reality, Possibility, or Pipedream?" *Military Psychology* 23.5 (2011): 528–49. Print.

McIntyre, Heather H., and Roseanne J. Foti. "The Impact of Shared Leadership on Teamwork Mental Models and Performance in Self-Directed Teams." *Group Processes and Intergroup Relations* 16.1 (2013): 46–57. Print.

Misra, Susan, Michael Allison, and Elissa Perry. "Doing More with More: Putting Shared Leadership into Practice." *Nonprofit Quarterly.* Nonprofit Quarterly, 21 Apr. 2014. Web. 8 July 2015.

Pearce, Craig L., and Jay A. Conger, eds. *Shared Leadership: Reframing the Hows and Whys of Leadership.* Thousand Oaks, CA: Sage, 2003.

Shuffler, Marissa L., et al. "Leading One Another across Time and Space: Exploring Shared Leadership Functions in Virtual Teams." *Revista de psicologia del trabajo y de las organizaciones* 26.1 (2010): 3–17. Print.

Julia Gilstein

STRATEGIC THINKING

ABSTRACT

Strategic thinking is a method frequently used by leaders in business settings to evaluate factors, create plans, and make decisions. Compared to more conventional styles of thinking, strategic thinking involves fresh perspectives, unique innovations, and imaginative approaches to challenges. Although strategic thinking often leads to greater possibility for risk, many business experts feel it is an important component in business success. In fact, it may be more important than ever, due to the rapid changes in global business in the past decades.

Conventional and Strategic Thinking

Business owners and other people in leadership roles can practice several thinking methods. Many people practice conventional thinking, which is considered the most used and straightforward way of making decisions, evaluating options, and approaching problems. However, business experts generally feel that conventional thinking, while useful for many everyday tasks, is not the best option for leaders who wish to make their organizations grow and thrive.

Conventional thinkers usually focus on their immediate surroundings and circumstances. They may dedicate most of their mental energy to daily duties and other short-term goals, such as meeting upcoming deadlines—which, while important, may serve to inhibit their ability to consider long-term decisions. Often due to excessive caution, conventional thinkers are more likely to react to outside factors than they are to take the initiative and make changes. They may also exhibit self-satisfaction with their current level of performance as well as an unwillingness to improve their abilities or deviate from their usual decisions even when new approaches might yield better results.

Because of the shortcomings of conventional thinking in business, experts usually recommend that leaders employ more strategic methods of thinking. The term strategic thinking can be interpreted in various ways. In general, though, strategic thinking involves thinking and planning in diverse and imaginative ways to find or invent new opportunities for success.

A businessman plots his strategy while taking a train ride (Photo courtesy of Hell9)

Strategic thinkers usually look beyond the short term into the future and try to anticipate new trends, obstacles, and opportunities that may arise. One aspect of this focus on the future is a willingness to make decisions that may be risky in the present but bring greater rewards in coming months or years. Strategic thinkers often go out of their way to research changes and trends in their organization and industry as well as the world beyond them. This broader perspective allows them to think of new and creative ideas to motivate their organization. Creative thinkers acknowledge that their plans may not always work as hoped. They are open to adjusting and changing their plans and are dedicated to continually gathering new knowledge and learning new skills.

The Process of Strategic Thinking
Some business analysts consider strategic thinking to be a complex process with several steps and facets. This process encompasses two phases, a research phase and a strategy phase. The research phase involves learning about the desires and demands of customers. It also requires business leaders to motivate and engage their employees and to set benchmarks, or standards and expectations, for the upcoming activities of the organization.

In the strategy phase, leaders combine three methods of thinking and planning: innovation, strategic planning, and operational planning. Innovation involves looking ahead to the future and creating unique approaches to goals. Leaders try to find creative new ways of approaching problems and improving the goods and services offered to customers. During strategic planning, leaders address the basic questions of how and when various actions should take place. Deciding the specific details of how the strategic plans will be implemented is part of the operational planning stage.

Put together, the research and strategy phases create the process of strategic thinking, which provides answers to questions such as what an organization should be doing and why that is the best option. To ensure that strategic thinking is performed effectively and ethically, leaders often engage in follow-up steps such as assessing values and principles and measuring results. In assessing values and principles, leaders ensure that their thoughts and decisions align with an organization's beliefs. They must also be sure that employees accept the strategies and incorporate strategic ideals into their daily work. By measuring the results of decisions, leaders can determine the concrete effects of their choices and evaluate whether a choice is sound or whether it needs to be adjusted or replaced.

Some business analysts believe that strategic thinking, while always an important tool for leaders, has become increasingly important in recent decades. With business technology, global trade and communication, international competition, and means of reaching customers ever increasing, leaders need even more creative planning, critical thinking skills, and adaptability to forge courses toward likely future success.

Analysts stress that few people are born as strategic leaders, and many of the skills required in strategic thinking must be learned and then practiced regularly. Leaders aiming to improve their strategic thinking should question themselves and their preexisting ideas. Some old ideas may be valuable, but others may be inaccurate, presenting more obstacles than opportunities. Leaders can expand their thinking by meeting with a diverse range of experts, employees, and fellow leaders. Many leading strategies have been created by interactions between people of different departments or fields of study. Finally, although strategic thinking typically affects business decisions, some of the best strategic insights come from outside the office. Experts suggest that leaders regularly take some time away from work to reflect and consider new thoughts and plans.

BIBLIOGRAPHY

Hill, Brian. "Why Is Strategic Thinking Important to the Success of Business?" *Houston Chronicle.* Hearst Newspapers, n.d. Web. 7 Mar. 2016.

Schoemaker, Paul. "6 Habits of True Strategic Thinkers." *Inc.* Mansueto Ventures, 20 Mar. 2012. Web. 7 Mar. 2016.

Stanleigh, Michael. "The Role of Strategic Thinking in Business Planning." *Business Improvement Architects.* Business Improvement Architects. Web. 7 Mar. 2016.

Walsh, Peter. "Are You a Strategic Thinker? Test Yourself." *Harvard Business.* Harvard Business School, 20 May 2014. Web. 7 Mar. 2016.

Mark Dziak

Talent Management

ABSTRACT

Talent management describes an organization's commitment to finding, hiring, managing, and retaining quality employees. Talent refers to staff members. While some organizations depend on human resources professionals to manage staff, talent management focuses on the role of managers in employee relations. This business strategy may encompass all employees or focus on particular high-value recruits or staff members exclusively.

OVERVIEW

Talent management works best when it is developed out of an organization's goals, mission, values, and vision and is embraced at all levels of management. Organizations can more fully invest in growth by integrating human resources and strategic planning. When the people who recruit staff know the goals of the organization, they can more capably target individuals who will help the organization perform at its best. When employees know the path of an organization, they are best able to determine their place and plot their growth within it.

The strategy begins with job descriptions that clearly explain the experience and skills needed. Job candidates are evaluated for these qualities as well as their likelihood of fitting into the culture of the organization. The organization establishes development opportunities that benefit the organization and the workers. It also provides clearly defined compensation systems that reward accomplishments.

Employees receive encouragement through coaching and feedback as well as regular discussions of performance development. In some cases, talent may be engaged in mentoring programs. A clear sense of purpose not only motivates individuals to be highly productive and dedicated members of organizations, but it also helps organizations attract the best talent.

Succession planning and career path developments encourage workers to pursue their interests and actively seek challenges within the organization. For example, Facebook has allowed employees who finish a project to choose another team to spend a month working with on a new project. At the end of the month, employees may choose to stay with the team or try another project. This freedom to focus on what most excites an individual leads to engagement in the work and greater employee satisfaction. It also attracts passionate talent to an organization.

Talent management's emphasis on worker development encourages movement within an organization, and employees are often aided in planning a career path. Department heads and key players may be informed of the advancement of quality talent. In turn, as positions become available or as an employee gains further experience, management in other departments may choose to approach some individuals with information about openings and opportunities. The focus is on keeping highquality talent and benefiting the organization by placing employees where they are most needed.

Organizations are increasingly seeing the value of talent mapping, anticipating areas in which growth will be needed in the future and ensuring that the organization has talent in place and ready for the challenge. Talent mapping requires strategic planning and shrewd recruitment as well as intentional in house career development activities and encouragement.

Employees who are deemed high potential talent may be groomed in several ways, including mentoring programs, rotational assignments, and coaching. Mentoring programs pair talent with experienced executives who offer guidance. Rotational assignments allow individuals to work in different aspects of an organization's functions and gain insight into how operations work together. Coaching involves hiring an outside coach to help the individual grow and increase his or her range of abilities.

A meritocracy, or organization that rewards individuals for their abilities and accomplishments, is an attractive workplace for driven employees. Organizations committed to talent management often draw the best people simply because high quality workers recognize the value of an organization that will help them advance.

Retention Efforts

Retention efforts may involve regular assessments of highvalue staff members' satisfaction with the work, compensation, life/work balance, and other factors. The goal is to quickly identify and address issues that arise and could affect workers' decisions to remain with the organization or to leave. Retention efforts should be directed toward creating and maintaining a welcoming work environment in which all employees feel valued. Career pathing, or helping individuals maximize their potential within the organization by helping them advance, is another useful strategy to retain workers.

Metrics, or standards of measurement, benefit an organization by quantifying progress toward goals. Metrics also benefit workers by clearly spelling out what is expected, enabling employees to know what constitutes success and how it is evaluated. Such knowledge may help organizations retain valued talent. For an organization to thrive, managers and employees should also be evaluated for upholding the standards of the organization, and failure at any level to sustain the supportive culture should be corrected.

Organizations that are focused on future growth are cautious about cutting staff, even in hard times. They recognize the investment they have made in finding and developing talent and are reluctant to lose it. Commitment to the future is attractive to individuals being recruited, who see the benefit of employment with such an organization. Should a valuable worker leave, information from an exit interview should be evaluated to determine if the organization should make changes to prevent further defections.

CONCLUSION

The ultimate goal of talent management is to maximize the potential of the organization. Managers who recognize that staff members are corporate assets are more likely to treat them as important, and this emphasis is likely to be reflected in the bottom line when quality individuals choose to remain with the organization.

BIBLIOGRAPHY

Heathfield, Susan M. "Best Talent Management Practices." *About Money*, About.com. Web. 27 Mar. 2015.
Heathfield, Susan M. "What Is Talent Management—Really?" *About Money*, About.com. Web. 27 Mar. 2015.
Millar, Bill. "Essential Tools of Talent Management." *Forbes*, 24 Apr. 2013. Web. 27 Mar. 2015.
Ready, Douglas A., Linda Hill, and Robert J. Thomas. "Building a Game-Changing Talent Strategy." *Harvard Business Review*, Jan. 2014. Web. 30 Mar. 2015.
Sullivan, John. "A Case Study of Facebook's Simply Amazing Talent Management Practices, Part 1 of 2." *Ere.net*, Ere Media, 9 Sept. 2013. Web. 30 Mar. 2015.
"Talent Management." *Johns Hopkins University Human Resources*, Johns Hopkins University. Web. 27 Mar. 2015.

Josephine Campbell

TEAM MANAGEMENT

ABSTRACT

This article focuses on the complexities of managing teams in today's contemporary organizations. With organizations shifting from tall hierarchical functional structures to flat team and network structures, managers are faced with some new challenges. These challenges include how to manage team types, team stages, communication strategies, and team leadership strategies and styles. The manager is faced with juggling between advocating change and controlling/evaluating team performance. It appears that the new

A manager meets with her team (Photo courtesy of Tim Gouw)

manager should emphasize transformation rather than transaction when managing a team environment.

OVERVIEW

Role of Teams in Contemporary Organizations

Many environmental forces, such as information, technology, and new decision-making strategies, have caused organizations to move towards integrating employee work teams into their structural makeup. One such environmental force has been the shift from the industrial worker to the knowledge worker as a result of the information boom (Drucker, as cited in LaRue, Childs, and Larson 2004). With the speed, availability, and accessibility of information, a need to share knowledge within organizations has been a prime driving force for creating an atmosphere of teamwork. Technology advancements make it possible for social capital to be as strategically important to organizations as intellectual capital. Never in history has the technological infrastructure made it so easy to implement collaborative strategies such as cross-functional teams, self-managed teams, committees, and virtual work groups. The way decisions are made has transformed them from a top management activity to a responsibility of all employees (LaRue et al. 2004). These forces, among others, have created a need for employees to work together, formally or informally, in order to share information and employ interdependency as a means for accomplishing organizational objectives. The use of teams, groups, committees, and other collaborative work structures are gaining in use as organizations attempt to adjust to these environmental changes. Consequently, leaders and managers must consider their approach to teams (their style, behaviors, strategies, role, and their disposition towards the team structure) as part of their leadership and management framework.

Team Formation Decision Factors for Managers

The decision to implement a team within the confines of an organization should not be taken lightly. Creating work teams is an investment in people, time, energy, resources, and workspace. As such, the conditions that favor the creation of organizational teams should be carefully considered before making the risky leap into team implementation. Steps should be taken to ensure that the conditions are right; the decision to implement a team structure is often considered a crucial strategic decision.

Several conditions should exist before creating a team. First, a clear and concise team vision and mission should be defined and closely aligned with the overall organizational strategy (Caplan et al. 1992). Second, the business needs goals and objectives that are complex and require high quality decisions (Pitman 1994). Third, the benefits of pooling knowledge must outweigh the efficiency lost because of group engagement (MacNeil 2003). Fourth, those recruited to the team must be mutually committed to the tasks involved (Pitman 1994). Fifth, the organization must have a trusting environment that allows for mutually effective collaboration between team members (Politis 2003). Finally, the team needs to have the full support from the management and leaders of the organization (Jones and Schilling 2000). Organizational managers and leaders need to engage in a research phase to ensure that these conditions exist. Otherwise, the organization may simply be setting up teams for subsequent and unanticipated failure.

Management & Leadership in Teams

In a team environment, an organizational manager/leader should consider two things; (1) the type of team, and (2) the stage of development in which the team resides.

Team Type

Different team types include cross-functional teams, self-managed teams, virtual teams, task forces, committees, ad hoc groups, quality circles, and process improvement teams, among others. Managers should consider team type as part of their management style. For example, the management required for a cross-functional product development team, for example, would likely be more directive than the leadership and management required for a virtual self-managed team, where the leadership roles are shared between the members. Using the wrong leadership or management behavior while interacting in a particular team type can be catastrophic—such as the manager recruited to participate in a self managed team who behaves in a directive and authoritarian manner.

Team Stage

Understanding the team stage is also important. Beck and Yeager (1996) described four team stages: team orientation, clarifying roles and responsibilities, doing the actual work or project, and solving problems. Depending on the stage that the team is in, the leader should be directing, delegating, empowering, or developing, or some combination thereof. In addition to leadership/management behaviors and style, a manager's communication strategy should also be based on team stage. The most widely recognized model for organizational team stages was developed by Tuckman (Kinicki and Williams 2003), and consisted of five stages; (1) forming, (2) storming, (3) norming, (4) performing, and (5) adjourning. The forming stage is the initial break-in stage of the team members. Members try to determine where they fit in, what the team focus is, and what their individual role will be. In the storming stage, the power within the group is ironed out, and individuals start to understand what their roles and influences on the team will be. In the norming stage, teams begin to come together as a cohesive group. Cooperative group discussions replace bids for power. In the performing stage, the group has matured and is operating in a tight-knit committed group that holds each other mutually accountable. The project goal becomes the main task at hand, rather than relationships and leadership concerns. Once complete, the team adjourns, where an evaluation and postmortem analysis can often lead to the dismantling of the team.

Ranney and Deck (1995) developed a useful matrix for a communication strategy when leading teams—a strategy that is dependent on the team stage. Their examples included (1) being a coach and promoter in the forming stage, (2) being a coach, giving frequent feedback, reinforcing vision, and reviewing boundaries in the storming stage, (3) managing team membership and coaching in the performing stage, (4) being encouraging, recognizing achievement, and being supportive in the high performance stage, and (5) expressing appreciation in the completing stage. Successful management and leadership approaches often emphasize the importance of being conscious of team type and process stage in order to apply the most effective leadership/management methodology.

Leadership Strengths & Weaknesses

A manager's strengths and weaknesses should also be considered when managing teams. For example, a manager's strengths might be his or her ability to be rational, pragmatic, logical, practical, and emotionally stabile. His or her weaknesses might be a need for perfection, micromanaging, and lack of delegation. Strengths and weaknesses such as these take on an entirely new meaning when evaluating management and leadership from a team perspective. As such, there are additional considerations that should be modified and included in any plan to form teams.

Team Member Perspective

A manager who is pragmatic and focused on logic can easily conflict with a fellow team member's style on a self-managed team. A team member, who is creative, works at a quick pace and is outgoing, may have difficulty with the manager's behavior. The manager's need for perfection might be an excellent style to use in a quality circle, but is likely very ineffective in a new product think tank. A manager should create a process in which he or she is always conscious of the team type, team stage, and his or her own leadership strengths and weaknesses and the ways they match with the team needs.

Team Leader Perspective

Conger (1999) presented nine leadership styles that portray a convergence of three main leadership theories. The leadership dimensions were: creating vision, providing inspiration, role modeling, intellectual stimulation, meaning making, appealing to higher-order needs, empowering, setting high expectations, and fostering collective identity. These particular dimensions of leadership seem even more appropriate for the team environment. In particular, creating vision and fostering collective identity will be extremely beneficial to a team leader. In creating and implementing an organizational team, a clear and concise team vision and mission should be defined and closely aligned with the overall organizational strategy (Caplan et al. 1992). High performance teams require mutual commitment and accountability (Pitman 1994). These elements will help produce the desired collective identity. In addition, the other dimensions will also help lead a team, especially when creating change or transformation. The nine dimensions identified by Conger help team managers and leaders determine their approach and style.

Leading Change within a Team

Using the wrong leadership style at the wrong time can be a roadblock to team success. Some research suggests that team leadership is one of the major reasons why teams fail within organizations (Katzenbach, as cited in Sivasubramaniam, Murry, Avolio, and Jung 2002). Some researchers suggest that leaders use a style that was less transactional and more transformational (Kinicki and Williams 2003), based on the leader-follower relationship. In the team context, especially when driving change through a team effort, the leadership style and behaviors should emphasize the transformational leadership style as much as possible. Another word for change is to transform, the essence of transformational leadership—to drive continuous change through the organization. In a team environment, once the team members have become familiar with their roles and mission, an effective team leader will focus on transformational behavior, and only use transactional behavior when an adjustment to the team is required, or when the results are not acceptable. Yukl found that transformational leaders "formulate a vision, develop a commitment to it among internal and external stakeholders, implement strategies to accomplish the mission, and imbed the new values and assumptions in the culture of the organization" (as cited in Strang 2005, 76). Formulating the vision is the first and likely the most important step in driving change through the implementation of teams. Nanus (2003) described what vision is and what vision is not. He defined vision as a perspective that is appropriate for the organization, clarifies purpose and direction, sets standards of excellence, inspires enthusiasm and commitment, is easily articulated and understood, is different, and ambitious. He indicated that vision was not a prophecy, not a mission, not factual, not true or false, not static and not a constraint. Kouzes and Posner (2003) discussed finding the leader's voice as a key leadership behavior in creating vision, inspiring a team, and motivating others. Other research suggests that employing a transformational leadership style will result in a team that trusts leader judgment, comprehends its mission, supports team values, and has strong emotional ties (Avolio, Waldman, and Einstein 1988). This formula certainly appears to be successful in driving organizational change through teams, and provides a framework for managers and leaders to embrace in creating an effective vision for leading change within a team.

Evaluation & Control

Performance evaluation is often considered a management function, rather than a leadership function. However, one of the major differences between management and leadership in Kotter's (2001) model is that managers control and problem solve while leaders motivate and inspire. Evaluating performance and making adjustments to improve performance would seem to fall under the management function of controlling. Popular management textbooks continue to emphasize controlling as a managerial function. However, part of the leadership construct in the team environment is to do exactly that—evaluate and control performance.

The element that links evaluation and control to leadership is trust. Bennis (1991) suggested that developing trust is one of the key ingredients for achieving personal growth in others. The team evaluation process builds this trust. Jones and Schilling (2000) stated, "The team-performance measurement process shows management the results of team performance, so management can trust that teams are doing the right things" (2). Even in self managed teams, evaluating performance is critical for maintaining the support of the management team, which is an important component to team success. Mintzberg indicated that the leadership and management components of one's job cannot be separated from a behavioral standpoint. The model suggested that leadership is simply a component of the management framework. In this context, there is little difference between team management and team leadership.

Managing Performance in Self-Managed Virtual Teams

There are three main areas that relate to leadership performance in a self-managed virtual team. The first area relates to the type of leadership that the team uses within the virtual team environment. The second area relates to shared accountability for individual contributions and overall team results. The last area relates to the decision-making methods employed by the team to complete work assignments.

Management and leadership in a self-managed, self-directed, virtual learning team are quite different from the traditional management/leadership role in workplace teams. Traditional teams in the workplace had one leader/manager who would act as the director, facilitator, coach, guide, and conduit to the rest of the organization. Self-managed, self-directed, virtual learning teams are a different animal. In general, leadership is a shared responsibility in a self-managed team. In a shared leadership environment, the first priority of team leadership is the task itself (Bell and Kozlowski, as cited in Carte, Chidambaram, and Becker 2006). Carte, et al. (2006) posited that there are two primary modes of leadership in a self-managed team environment: expertise leadership, where team members tend to adopt leadership roles in their areas of expertise, and collective participatory management, where team members work together to help the team accomplish its goals.

Mutual Accountability

Part of the shared leadership in a self-managed virtual team derives from mutual accountability. Team members have the task of holding each other accountable for their roles and expected deliverables, and members are expected to manage any resulting conflict effectively within the team. In academia, for example, Hackman (1990) asserted that academic teams have the challenge of managing differing work styles and work pace. This team phenomenon leads to the team having to "fit an indeterminate amount of work into a fixed amount of time" (Hackman 1990, 110). One effective way to manage this challenge in a virtual self-managed team is to hold each other accountable for individual tasks and expected content, timely submission of individual contributions, and involvement in the integration of individual ideas into a team product. High expectations of accountability in this team environment lead to each member trying to go above and beyond expectations in order to please and support their fellow team members.

Decision Making

One of the major challenges that a self-managed team faces is the desire by team members to have an environment of conformity, consensus, and cohesiveness. Often, self-managed teams find themselves engaged in the phenomenon of groupthink (Kinicki and Williams 2003), where team members make decisions that they do not believe in, simply to be agreeable and pleasing to others on the team. The team might also engage in making satisficing decisions, where team members agree to decisions that satisfy a problem need without evaluating all the alternatives from which the best solution or decision may evolve and without trying to make an excellent decision. Part of the shared leadership in a self-managed virtual team is to ensure that the team consciously engages in constructive decision-making methods.

Creating an environment for effective decision making is essential for the success of self-managed virtual teams. Manz and Neck (1995) created a decision-making model that can prevent groupthink and satisfy decision making called Teamthink. The model contains eight steps in the decision-making process: "encouragement of divergent views, open expression of concerns/ideas, awareness of limitations/threats, recognition of each member's unique value, recognition of views outside of the group, discussion of collective doubts, adoption/utilization of non-stereotypical views, and recognition of ethical and moral consequences of decisions" (Manz and Neck 1995, 7). An effective self-managed team will adopt these behaviors and expectations. During the brainstorming, each team member should be encouraged to provide critical input regarding approach, content, and project interpretation. All team members should accept constructive criticism gracefully and should be open to new ideas that conflict with their own beliefs and assumptions. One area that can proactively improve the process is to actually formalize these steps. Such an approach might make sense if the team were to remain together for a long time and not just a few weeks.

CONCLUSION

The discussion concerning team management and leadership revolved around four areas. First, an acute understanding of team type and team stage has a direct impact on the leadership style, behaviors, and communication strategies that one should employ in a team environment, both as a team manager/leader and as a team participant. Second, the manager should consider development areas that relate to his or her strengths and weaknesses and how these fit within an organizational team. Third, the mix of transformational and transactional leadership behaviors needs to emphasize transformational leadership in a team environment, more so than in a traditional leader/constituent relationship. Finally, a new paradigm emerges; one in which the leadership falls under the management umbrella, rather than a separate entity. This paradigm shift was the result of analysis regarding how evaluation and control of team performance is critical to team success and critical to developing organizational trust.

As organizations have moved from employing a traditional mechanistic form into a more modern and contemporary form, formal organizational hierarchies and centralized decision-making structures have been replaced by hybrid, matrix and network forms that include the incorporation of high performance work teams. Modern-day managers and leaders need to be prepared to understand the nature of teams, including when to implement teams, how to set teams up for success, and how to make teams integrated as an organizational cultural norm. This paper presented ideas to facilitate the understanding of managing teams, including organizational context, framework, and processes. Team creation and implementation within an organization is complex, since there are social, behavioral and process dynamics. Understanding these complex issues makes the decision to implement a team less risky.

BIBLIOGRAPHY

Avolio, Bruce, David Waldman, and Walter Einstein. "Transformational Leadership in a Management Game Simulation." *Group & Organization Studies* 13, no. 1 (1988): 59–80. Web. 14 Mar. 2007.

Beck, John D. W., and Neil M. Yeager. "How to Prevent Teams from Falling." *Quality Progress* 29, no. 3 (1996): 27. Print.

Bennis, Warren. "Leading Followers, Following Leaders." *Executive Excellence* 8, no. 6 (1991): 5. Print.

Caplan, D.W., D. Givens, G. Luff, et al. "A Practical Roadmap for High Performing Natural Teams." The *Journal for Quality and Participation* 15, no. 3 (1992): 60. Print.

Carte, Traci A., Laku Chidambaram, and Aaron Becker. "Emergenct Leadership in Self-Managed Virtual Teams." *Group Decision and Negotiation* 15, no. 4 (2006): 323–43. Web. 1 May 2007.

Conger, Jay A. "Charismatic and transformational Leadership in Organizations: An Insider's Perspective on These Developing Streams of Research." *Leadership Quarterly* 10, no. 2 (1999): 145, Web. 1 May 2007.

Hackman, R. Richard. *Groups That Work (and Those That Don't)*. 1st ed. San Francisco: Jossey-Bass, 1990.

Hall, James L. "Managing Teams with Diverse Compositions: Implications for Managers from Research on the Faultline Model." *SAM Advanced Management Journal* 78, no. 1 (2013): 4–10. Web. 19 Nov. 2014.

Hoch, Julia E., and Steve Kozlowski. "Leading Virtual Teams: Hierarchical Leadership, Structural Supports, and Shared Team Leadership." *Journal of Applied Psychology* 99, no. 3 (2014): 390–403. Web. 19 Nov. 2014.

Hodes, Bruce. "Stupid Games." *Sales & Service Excellence* 14, no. 9 (2013): 21. Web. 15 Nov. 2013.

Jones, Steven D., and Don J. Schilling. *Measuring Team Performance: A Step-by-Step Customizable Approach for Managers, Facilitators, and Team Leaders*. 1st ed. San Francisco: Jossey Bass, 2000.

Kinicki, Angela, and Brian Williams. *Management: A Practical Introduction*. 2nd ed. New York: McGraw-Hill, 2003.

Kotter, John P. "What Leaders Really Do." *Harvard Business Review* 79, no. 11 (2001): 85–96. Web. 14 Mar. 2007.

Kouzes, James, and Barry Posner. *The Leadership Challenge*. 3rd ed. San Francisco: Jossey-Bass, 2003.

LaRue, Bruce, Paul Childs, and Kerry Larson. *Leading Organizations from the Inside Out: Unleashing the Collaborative Genius of Action-Learning Teams*. 2nd ed. New York: John Wiley and Sons, 2004.

Lorinkova, Natalia M., Matthew J. Pearsall, and Henry P. Sims Jr. "Examining the Differential Longitudinal Performance of Directive versus Empowering

Leadership in Teams." *Academy of Management Journal* 56, no. 2 (2013): 573–96.

MacNeil, Christine. "Line Managers: Facilitators of Knowledge Sharing in Teams." *Employee Relations* 25, no. 3 (2003): 294–307. Web. 1 May 2007.

Manz, Charles C., and Christopher P. Neck. "Teamthink: Beyond the Groupthink Syndrome in Self-Managing Work Teams." *Journal of Managerial Psychology* 10, no. 1 (1995): 7–15. Web. 1 May 2007.Mintzberg, Henry, Joseph Lampel, James B. Quinn, and Sumantra Ghoshal. *The Strategy Process*. 4th ed. Saddle River, NJ: Prentice Hall, 2003.

Nanus, Burt, ed. *Business Leadership*. 1st ed. San Francisco: Jossey-Bass, 2003.

Nielsen, Bo, and Sabina Nielsen. "Top Management Team Nationality Diversity and Firm Performance: A Multilevel Study." *Strategic Management Journal* 34, no. 3 (2013): 373–82. Web. 15 Nov. 2013.

Politis, John D. "The Connection between Trust and Knowledge Management: What Are Its Implications for Team Performance." *Journal of Knowledge Management* 7, no. 5 (2003): 55. Print.

Pitman, B. "Get a G.R.I.P.—On Building High Performance Teams." *Journal of Systems Management* 45, no. 8 (1994): 26. Print.

Ranney, J., and K. Deck. "Making Teams Work: Lessons from the Leaders in New Product Development." *Planning Review* 23, no. 4 (1995): 6–13. Web. 1 May 2007.

Sivasubramaniam, Nagaraj., William Murry, Bruce J. Avolio, and Dong I. Jung. "A Longitudinal Model of the Effects of Team Leadership and Group Potency on Group Performance." *Group & Organization Management* 27, no. 1 (2002): 66–96. Web. 1 May 2007.

Strang, Kenneth D. "Examining Effective and Ineffective Transformational Project Leadership." *Team Performance Management* 11, nos. 3–4 (2005): 68. Print.

SUGGESTED READING

Gibson, Cristina, and Freck Vermulen. "A Health Divide: Subgroups as a Stimulus for Team Learning Behavior." *Administrative Science Quarterly* 48, no. 2 (2003): 202–39. Web. 1 May 2007.

McLean, John. "Prepare for the Future: It's Happening Fast!" *British Journal of Administrative Management* 58 (2007): 17. Web. 1 May 2007.

Rosen, Benson, Stacie Furst, and Richard Blackburn. "Training for Virtual Teams: An Investigation of Current Practices and Future Needs." *Human Resource Management* 45, no. 2 (2006): 229–47. Web. 1 May 2007.

Yang, Inju. "What Team Members Meets in a New Team: An Exploration of Team Development." *Human Systems Management* 32, no. 3 (2013): 181–97. Web. 19 Nov. 2014.

John D. Benson, M.B.A.

TEAMS & TEAM BUILDING

ABSTRACT

Increasingly, teams are the foundation of the twenty-first century workplace. The philosophy behind this widespread use of teams is that their use can create an environment in which synergy is achieved and the final outcome is greater than that which would have been achieved by individuals alone. Team development comprises several stages. However, this process is not always linear, and teams may experience multiple stages simultaneously or revert to previous stages. Team-building efforts conducted by an outside party can help teams to acquire the knowledge, skills, and abilities necessary for functional teamwork and achieving synergy and to avoid pitfalls of team situations such as group-think. Team-building efforts usually focus on defining the roles of team members, setting team goals, problem solving, and interpersonal processes.

OVERVIEW

Groups vs. Teams

At one time or another, most people in the twenty-first century workplace will find themselves working as part of a team. Teams in an organizational setting can be as simple as two people working together to write a white paper or technical document or as complex as multiple businesses working together to bid a proposal or build the next-generation destroyer for

Employees of a Dutch company perform a team building exercise (photo courtesy of Antoon Versteegde)

the navy. However, not every group of people who work together can be considered a team. In general, groups in the workplace comprise two or more individuals who are interdependent and who interact over time. So, for example, the sales staff of a retail store might be considered a group. They interact with each other, ask each other for help (e.g., ring up a customer, find an item in stock or inventory), and support each other in accomplishing the tasks necessary for running a successful retail store. Groups work toward a common goal, are accountable to a manager, and may (ideally) accomplish their goals. Leadership of a group is held by a single individual. However, groups do not have a clear, stable culture, so conflict may be frequent.

Teams, on the other hand, are a special type of group. In a team, there is a differentiation of skills where one individual does a specific part of the task and other individuals do other specific parts of the task. Another way teams are different from groups is that the members of a team perform their work in the context of a common fate. For example, although the members of the retail staff may help each other in the context of doing their jobs, they also all tend to do the same job. For the most part, dealing with one salesperson in a retail store should be the same as dealing with another person in the retail store. Further, members of a sales group typically do not share a common fate. For example, if Harvey does not do his job adequately, it will be Harvey—and not the rest of the sales staff—who will be reprimanded or fired.

On the other hand, some sales and marketing staffs are truly teams where there is differentiation of skill among the team members. For example, when trying to sell a learning management system for a computer-based training system, one member of the marketing team may specialize in comparing the business's system with that of the competition, while another team member might specialize in answering technical questions regarding the programmability of the system. If the remuneration of the team members is based in part on commission for making the sale, then the fate of the individual members of the team depends on the fate of the team as a whole (i.e., whether or not they sell the system). Leadership of a team is shared, and members are mutually accountable to each other. Because of these team characteristics, team members are committed to the goal and mission of the team, trust each other, and have a more collaborative and interdependent culture than groups in general. As a result, teamwork often leads to a situation of synergy (Nahavandi 2000).

Types of Teams

In general, four types of teams can be found in the workplace:

- Manager-led teams
- Self-managing teams
- Self-designing teams
- Self-governing teams (Hackman 1987)

In manager-led teams, the design of the organizational context, the design of the team as a performing unit, and the monitoring and managing of the performance processes of the team is all a responsibility of the team manager. In self-managing teams, the design of the organizational context in which the team works as well as the design of the group as a performing unit are both done by management. However, the self-managing team not only executes the task, but also monitors and manages the performance processes used in the performance of the task. In a self-designing team, the organizational context in which the team operates is designed by management. However, all other aspects of the team functioning (i.e., design of the group as a performing unit, monitoring and managing of performance processes, and executing the task) are the responsibility of the team. In self-governing teams, all aspects of the team—including its design within the context of the organization—are the responsibility of the team.

Further Insights Team Development
Although organizations sometimes act as though teams can be created by fiat, team development is in fact a multistage process (Robbins 1996). As illustrated in figure 1, before a team is formed, it is a collection of individual entities. The persons may be part of a group (e.g., a sales staff), or they may not even know each other (e.g., individuals from two or more business who will write a proposal together). Once it is decided that a team will be formed (Stage 1), the team members still have a great deal of uncertainty concerning the nature of the team such as its mission and purpose, the capabilities of the other team members, what processes will best result in synergy, and the leadership of the team. During the forming stage of team development, members of the team try to determine the answers to these and other questions. Members learn to know each other better, determine each other's areas of expertise and experience, and try to determine what types of behavior is acceptable within the group. The forming stage is completed once the members no longer consider themselves to be a random collection of individuals but as part of a team.

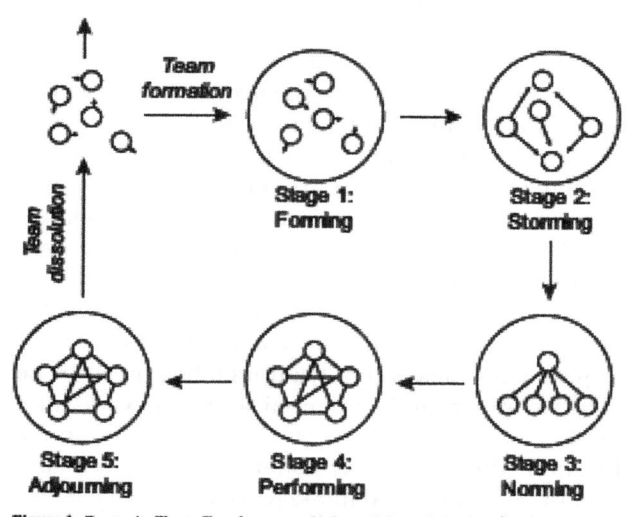

Figure 1: Stages in Team Development (Adapted from Robbins, 1996)

According to this theory, the second stage in team development is storming. This stage of conflict within the team involves members struggling with the constraints placed on them as individuals. For example, every semester, a teacher requires her students to do a team research project. Within these broad parameters, they are allowed to divide the tasks of the group in any way they want, are able to establish individual or team leadership, and, in general, perform the tasks of the team in whatever way they determine will best allow them to develop a project that will earn them a good grade. Every semester, at least one of these teams rebels and announces unequivocally that it is unfair to require them to depend on each other for a grade on the project. However, since satisfactory completion of the project is necessary to pass the course, these teams must use their conflict management skills in order to come to some level of mutual understanding about the leadership hierarchy within the group. This situation mimics that of the real work places in which team members must learn to relinquish some of their individuality in favor of the potential that can be gained through teamwork and establish an acceptable leadership hierarchy in order to accomplish its tasks.

During the norming stage, the team develops norms—rules, standard, or patterns of behavior that are accepted as normal within the team—so that the team can accomplish its tasks. During this stage of team development, the team members bond with each other within the context of the team and its tasks and become cohesive. Another characteristic of this stage of team development is the development and assimilation of a set of common assumptions and expectations about what defines acceptable behavior within the group. For example, a project team in one class might decide that all members are expected to complete and submit their portion of the project on time according to a mutually agreed upon schedule and that each of the members is responsible for writing a specific part of the final report. In the workplace, a team may make similar arrangements for the development of a technical document or proposal.

The fourth stage of team development is performing. By this phase, the members of a functional team will have learned to know each other (forming), worked through the initial conflicts (storming), and determined how the team will operate (norming). It is time for the team to actually do the work for which it was brought together: conduct the research project, write the proposal, build a working model, etc. In some cases, teams are set up on a permanent basis to perform a certain kind of task. For example, an engineering team might be established to develop prototypes of new products. After the completion of one prototype, the team is then assigned to develop the prototype for another product. For such permanent teams, team development ends at this point.

However, a great many teams are established on a temporary basis. Once the project (or the class) is over, members (or students) are unlikely to continue to work together on other projects. Similarly, in the workplace, there are temporary teams such as Red Teams, task forces, and temporary committees. When the work of such teams has been accomplished, they move into the final stage of team development: adjourning. The team no longer needs to focus on accomplishing its task and, instead, focuses on the tasks necessary to wrap up the project, disband the group (e.g., final reports, distribution of products), and complete whatever evaluation is expected. As the work of the team winds down, the bonds between the members dissolve as the team disbands and members go back to other activities that do not involve the entire team. At this point, the team members once again become unassociated individuals.

Team Building
Although there is always the potential for teams to be dysfunctional and produce a lower-quality outcome than an individual, the concept of synergy resulting from teamwork is an attractive one, and many organizations use teams in order to foster this synergy and produce superior outcomes. Similarly, it is virtually impossible for many single organizations to be successful in meeting the needs of large contracts (e.g., development of a new destroyer), so the establishment of functional teams is essential. The question, then, becomes how to best help a team to work together harmoniously while reducing the likelihood of group-think and increasing the likelihood of synergy. Team building is the process of turning a group of individuals who work together from a collection of individuals doing related tasks to a cohesive unit where the efforts of the team members act synergistically to yield results that could not have been done by the individuals alone. Typically, team-building efforts focus on defining the roles of team members, setting goals for the team, solving problems, and coordinating interpersonal processes (McShane and Von Glinow 2003). Team building often comprises activities such as physical exercises that force team members to depend on each other in order to achieve a desired goal, communication exercises to teach team members to be better communicators, and small group sessions in which team members get to know each other in a nonthreatening situation.

Knowledge, Skills & Abilities
Team-building efforts can take the form of many different types of activities targeted toward helping team members to manage conflict, avoid group-think, and become synergistic. Although the methods used may differ, in general there are certain interpersonal and self-management knowledge, skills, and abilities that need to be present in a team—or taught through team building—that can help achieve these goals. According to Stevens and Campion (1994), from an interpersonal perspective, team members need to have strong conflict management knowledge and skills, collaborative problem-solving knowledge and skills, and communication knowledge and skills. For conflict management, team members need to be able to identify and use positive conflict, discourage and stifle undesirable team conflict, and analyze sources of conflict so they can be addressed or resolved. Finally, team members need to be able to "employ an integrative (win-win) negotiation strategy rather than the traditional distributive (win-lose) strategy" (Stevens and Campion 1994, 505).

In addition to conflict management knowledge and skills, team members also need to collaboratively solve problems in order for the team to be functional. Specifically, team members need to be able to identify situations requiring "participative group problem solving and to utilize the proper degree and type of participation" (505) and recognize the obstacles to collaborative group problem solving and implement appropriate corrective actions.

Further, team members need the knowledge and skills necessary for clear communication. This requirement means that team members need to be able to understand communication networks and utilize decentralized networks to enhance communication where possible; communicate openly and supportively (i.e., send messages that are behavior- or event-oriented, congruent, validating, conjunctive, and owned); listen nonjudgmentally and use appropriate active listening techniques; maximize consonance between nonverbal and verbal messages; recognize and interpret the nonverbal messages of others; and engage in ritual greetings and small talk, with a recognition of their importance (Stevens and Campion 1994, 505).

High functioning teams need to not only possess the interpersonal appropriately knowledge and skills discussed above, but must also have the appropriate knowledge and skills for self-management of the team. Specifically, team members need to be able to set goals and manage performance within the team. Knowledge and skills necessary for this aspect of team functionality include helping establish specific, challenging, and accepted team goals and monitoring, evaluating, and providing feedback on both overall team performance and individual team member performance. In addition, team members need to be able to plan and coordinate the tasks of the team. These skills include the abilities to "synchronize activities, information, and task interdependencies between team members and to help establish task and role expectations of individual team members, and to ensure proper balancing of workload in the team" (Stevens and Campion 1994)

Viewpoints

Tuchman's five-stage model of team development described by Robbins has been popular since the 1960s. However, although it does describe the general progression of team development, it does so simplistically. For example, it is unlikely that all conflict will be permanently resolved at the conclusion of the storming stage. In fact, many experts believe that conflict is necessary to accomplish the synergy desired from teamwork. Otherwise, a situation of group-think can arise in which group members tend to have the same opinion as each other in order avoid conflict, reduce interpersonal pressure, or maintain an illusion of unity or cohesiveness without thoroughly thinking through the problem. This condition works against the process of good decision making and can result in a poorer product from a group effort rather than the synergy desired from teamwork. Similarly, the five-stage model presents team development as a linear process, proceeding neatly from one stage to another. In actuality, many teams return to previous stages or even exist in multiple stages at the same time (e.g., storming and performing simultaneously).

Most teams are a reality of the twenty-first century workplace. The goal of teams is to develop a physical, written, or conceptual product that is better than that which any one individual could have developed alone. However, the development of a functional team takes work, and each team must go through several stages before it becomes optimally functional. External team-building efforts can help teams become more functional, avoid potential pitfalls such as group-think, and work together synergistically to produce a better product. Research continues into the dynamics and performance of teams and other groups, with companies and other organizations continually looking for ways to improve teamwork and therefore overall efficiency, productivity, and satisfaction. For example, psychological tests may be used to evaluate employees or contractors in an effort to identify the best members for an ideal team.

BIBLIOGRAPHY

Hackman, J. Richard. "The Design of Work Teams." In *Handbook of Organizational Behavior*, edited by Jay W. Lorch. Upper Saddle River, NJ: Prentice Hall, 1987.

Hillier, Janet, and Linda M. Dunn-Jensen. "Groups Meet … Teams Improve: Building Teams That Learn." *Journal of Management Education* 37, no. 5 (2013): 704–33. Web. 27 Nov. 2013.

McShane, Steven L., and Mary Ann Von Glinow. *Organizational Behavior: Emerging Realities for the Workplace Revolution.* 2nd ed. Boston: McGraw-Hill/Irwin, 2003.

Nahavandi, Afsaneh. *The Art and Science of Leadership.* 2nd ed. Upper Saddle River, NJ: Prentice Hall, 2000.

Pentland, Alex. "The New Science of Building Great Teams." *Harvard Business Review* 90, no. 4 (2012): 60–70. Web. 27 Nov. 2013.

Radomes, Amando. "The Whole Can Be Worse Than the Sum of Its Parts: Counterintuitive Consequences of Group Facilitation." *Harvard Business Review* 90, no. 4 (2013): 60–70. Web. 27 Nov. 2013.

Rahman, M. Motiar, and Mohan M. Kumaraswamy. "Multicountry Perspectives of Relational Contracting and Integrated Project Teams." *Journal of*

Construction Engineering & Management 138, no. 4 (2012): 469–80. Web. 27 Nov. 2013.

Rentsch, Joan R., Lisa A. Delise, Abby L. Mello, and Melissa Staniewicz. "The Integrative Team Knowledge Building Training Strategy in Distributed Problem-Solving Teams." *Small Group Research* 45, no. 5 (2014): 568–91. Print.

Robbins, Stephen P. *Organizational Behavior: Concepts, Controversies, and Applications*. Upper Saddle River, NJ: Prentice Hall, 1996.

Stevens, Michael J., and Michael A. Campion. "The Knowledge, Skill, and Ability Requirements for Teamwork: Implications for Human Resource Management." *Journal of Management* 20, no. 2 (1994): 503. Web. 28 Apr. 2010.

Wilsher, Simon. "Behavior Profiling: Implications for Recruitment and Team Building." *Strategic Direction* 31, no. 9 (2015): 1–5. Web. 4 Dec. 2015.

SUGGESTED READING

Aldag, Ray J., and Loren W. Kuzuhara. *Creating High Performance Teams: Applied Strategies and Tools for Managers and Team Members*. New York: Routledge, 2015.

Aritzeta, Altor, Stephen Swailes, and Barbara Senior. "Belbin's Team Role Model: Development, Validity and Applications for Team Building." *Journal of Management Studies* 44, no. 1 (2007): 96–118. Web. 28 Apr. 2010.

Boss, R. Wayne. "Is the Leader Really Necessary? The Longitudinal Results of Leader Absence in Team Building." *Public Administration Quarterly* 23, no. 4 (2000): 471–86. Web. 28 Apr. 2010.

Bottom, William P., and N. Baloff. "A Diagnostic Model for Team Building with an Illustrative Application." *Human Resource Development Quarterly* 5, no. 4 (1994): 317–36. Web. 28 Apr. 2010.

Buller, Paul F., and Cecil H. Bell Jr. "Effects of Team Building and Goal Setting on Productivity: A Field Experiment." *Academy of Management Journal* 29, no. 2 (1986): 305–28. Web. 28 Apr. 2010.

Chen, Yin-Che, Yun-Chi Che, and Ya-Lun Tsao. "Multiple Dimensions to the Application for the Effectiveness of Team Building in ROTC." *Education* 129, no. 4 (2009): 742–54. Web. 28 Apr. 2010.

Darling, John. "Team Building in the Small Business Firm." *Journal of Small Business Management* 28, no. 3 (1990): 86–91. Web. 28 Apr. 2010.

Horak, Bernard J., Karen Hicks, Susan Pellicciotti, and Anne Duncan. "Create Cultural Change and Team Building." *Nursing Management* 37, no. 12 (2006): 12–14. Web. 28 Apr. 2010.

Jones, Mary C. "Large Scale Project Team Building: Beyond the Basics." *Communications of the ACM* 51, no. 10 (2008): 113–16. Web. 28 Apr. 2010.

McCune, William B. "Internal Communications and Participatory Management: An Experiment in Team Building." *Public Relations Quarterly* 34, no. 3 (1989): 14–18. Web. 28 Apr. 2010.

McSherry, Mark, and Paul Taylor. "Supervisory Support for the Transfer of Team-Building Training." *International Journal of Human Resource Management* 5, no. 1 (1994): 107–19. Web. 28 Apr. 2010.

Page, Diana, and Joseph G. Donelan. "Team-Building Tools for Students." *Journal of Education for Business* 78, no. 3 (2003): 125–28. Web. 28 Apr. 2010.

Scarfino, Deborah, and Carol Roever. "Team-Building Success: It's in the Cards." *Business Communication Quarterly* 72, no. 1 (2009): 90–95. Web. 28 Apr. 2010.

Staggers, Julie, Susan Garcia, and Ed Nagelhout. "Teamwork through Team Building: Face-To-Face to Online." *Business Communication Quarterly* 71, no. 4 (2008): 472–87. Web. 28 Apr. 2010.

Svyantek, Daniel J., and Scott A. Goodman, Lori L. Benz, and Julia A. Gard. "The Relationship between Organizational Characteristics and Team Building Success." *Journal of Business and Psychology* 14, no. 2 (1999): 265–83. Web. 28 Apr. 2010.

Thomas, Michael, Paul H. Jacques, John R. Adams, and Julie Kihneman-Wooten. "Developing an Effective Project: Planning and Team Building Combined." *Project Management Journal* 39, no. 4 (2008): 105–13. Web. 28 Apr. 2010.

Turaga, Revathi. "Building Trust in Teams: A Leader's Role." *IUP Journal of Soft Skills* 7, no. 2 (2013): 13–31. Web. 27 Nov. 2013.

Wigtil, James V., and Richard C. Kelsey. "Team Building as a Consulting Intervention for Influencing Learning Environments." *Personnel and Guidance Journal* 56, no. 7 (1978): 412–16. Web. 28 Apr. 2010.

Ruth A. Wienclaw, Ph.D.

Time Management

ABSTRACT

The key to time management lies in understanding how the brain perceives the construct of time. Several theories abound, trying to explain the science to managing time and increasing awareness of how to effectively accomplish tasks within an allotted time frame. Understanding the science of time management and its antonym, procrastination, have proven to be very effective in using time appropriately and effectively with physical and mental benefits.

OVERVIEW

Scientists have trouble finding an exact definition for the term "time management," but the most widely agreed upon understanding of it is the planning and execution of activities within a specific period or on a schedule. It is therefore a twofold concept—it involves both the preparation and the actual doing of the idea. Although it may appear counterintuitive, an important task involves dedicating some time to the organization of ideas and the completion of the tasks. Oddly enough, time spent planning is essential to proper time management; without it, a person would be blindly acting out assignments. A plethora of literary sources agree that with proper time assessment, a person can feel more in control of their time, more content with academic or professional careers, and most of all less stressed. Additionally, individuals who exercise time management report high productivity and numerous benefits from extra free time. Many researchers and theorists have explored what happens to a person psychologically and biologically when planning a course of action. Moreover, for many to fully comprehend time organization, it is easier to compare it with its complete opposite—procrastination, the act of delaying tasks and "putting off" assignments to very lastminute.

The Science of Managing Time

Many people see the perception of time as the key to understanding time management. One major theory in this field of study is the Planning Fallacy. Pioneered by researchers Roger Buehler, Dale Griffin, and Michael Ross, it is the concept that a person underestimates how long a task will require, particularly if he or she spends a large amount of planning time foreseeing a pleasant outcome without accounting for possible obstacles. Hofstadter's law states that no matter how much planning goes into an activity, every task takes longer than anticipated. Alternatively, other studies turn to past experiences with similar circumstances rather than looking to the future; they found that previous experience provides both a realistic result as well as a fairly accurate gauge for how long the activity will take. The University of Belgium conducted a study in which they found that the more details imagined on a future project, the more imminent and critical it feels.

Perhaps the reason time management may be so difficult to achieve for some is because of the nature of the brain. According to Timothy A. Pychyl, the limbic system (the portion of the brain primarily concerned with instinct and emotion) uses its reflexes to avoid activities that cause distress. In other words, it is an unconscious coping mechanism to evade tasks considered unpleasant. In the same study, Pychyl found that the prefrontal cortex may be both a newer and weaker portion of the brain. Because this portion of the brain is where the responses to problems originate, it requires active thought and energy to generate a solution. However, particularly if the problem at hand is unpleasant, the limbic system creates a drive to ignore the task. But when an individual carves out the proper time to plan before acting, a surge of dopamine is released in the brain, producing a euphoric feeling of accomplishment.

A workstation shows signs of poor time management (Photo courtesy of AlainV)

Understanding Time Management and Procrastination

The key to understanding how to properly manage time is to understand what happens when time is improperly managed through procrastination. A coping mechanism for avoiding displeasing tasks, it leads to higher stress levels than if the task was completed sooner. Again, the limbic system's response to unpleasant situations tends to push people to not accomplish the assignment, leaving less time to accomplish it as well as a variety of physical symptoms associated with heightened anxiety—nausea, headache, weakness of limbs, etc. The two main types of procrastination are linked to behavior and decisions respectively. In one form of procrastination, a person self-sabotages to avoid action; in the other, a person avoids conflict and decisions. Both involve a multitude of psychological factors, including negative self-image, anxiety, high stress, and more.

A study from Carleton University found that nearly half of procrastinators found that their habit has been detrimental to their happiness. Joseph Ferrari from DePaul University in Chicago found that procrastination could be an unconscious method of rebellion, particularly for those with very strict parents. Clary Lay from York University published the General Procrastination Scale, which takes into consideration dreams and obligations. He also found that chronic procrastinators have a genetic makeup that makes them actually neurologically disorganized thinkers, and they cannot help but procrastinate.

Having proper time management does just the opposite—it boosts productivity, reduces stress, and the release of neurotransmitters such as dopamine creates a happy feeling that further boosts productivity. The process of collecting oneself and allotting time to finish a job is surprisingly more effective than going into a plan without the proper planning it requires, even leading to successes both short term (such as good test grades or commendation on work presentations) and long term (such as graduating with honors or receiving a promotion).

Strategies to Accomplish Proper Time Management

Mastering effective time management skills may seem daunting, but with a few basic skills, it can prove to be quite easy. Some of the common strategies include:

- *Maintaining a routine using a planner or daily "to-do" list.* Use of one of these notebooks makes managing time easier, helping to establish continued, long-term success.
- *Making a habit of organizing time, factoring in distractions, and recognizing the Planning Fallacy.* These strategies can help a person prioritize his or her time and learn to value it.
- *Ignoring and even turning off electronic devices, apps, and social media.* In this modern age of technology, directing all focus to the task at hand helps.
- *Sleeping.* An exhausted brain cannot think as quickly or with as much clarity as a well-rested brain can. Proper rest is also physiologically important; with sleep being such a vital life process disrupting it could lead to health complications as well.
- *Taking shorter and longer breaks.* Shorter breaks refocus energy on the matter at hand, and longer weekend breaks and vacations improve long term productivity. Proper nourishment is just as important for keeping the mind alert and attentive.

CONCLUSION

Having knowledge and insight into the concept of time management, through the concepts of time itself and procrastination, have proven to be quite beneficial. With an understanding of the various theories associated with the construct of time as well as comprehension of its polar opposite procrastination, one can use several strategies to manage time more effectively and accomplish more work.

BIBLIOGRAPHY

Booth, Francis. "30 Time Management Tips for a Work-Life Balance." *Forbes*. Web. 28 Aug. 2014.

Herbert, Liu. "How Your Brain Perceives Time (and How to Use It To Your Advantage." *Lifehacker*. Web. 13 June 2013.

Letham, Susan. "The Procrastination Problem." *Success Consciousness*. Web. (n.d.).

Spencer, Amy. "The Science Behind Procrastination." *Real Simple*. Web. (n.d.).

Courtney Brogle

Toxic Leadership

ABSTRACT

Toxic leadership is characterized by a leader whose actions toward subordinates are abusive and generally self-centered or narcissistic. A toxic leader's dictatorial management style creates an unhealthy organizational climate. Although such leaders may be regarded as effective and hardworking by their superiors, their behavior toward subordinates is far different. While toxic leadership is a concern in any organization, it has drawn particular attention in the US military.

OVERVIEW

Toxic leaders may not be poisonous in all situations or with all subordinates. However, by definition, they inflict harm on individuals or groups, such as employees, communities, and organizations. Like school-age bullies, toxic leaders often feel inadequate and attempt to boost themselves by exerting power over others. Toxic leaders blame others for failures and demoralize workers. They take credit for workers' accomplishments and dismiss subordinates' ideas. High turnover in a department is often an indicator of toxic leadership. When a business or organization bleeds competent workers, it may become weakened, particularly if good workers defect to the competition.

A *Journal of Nursing* report on toxic nurse managers identified a number of characteristics of toxic leaders, including self-centeredness, exploitation of others, controlling behavior, disrespect for others, suppression of employees' innovation and creativity, and inadequate emotional intelligence (Zangaro et al., 2009). According to the authors, toxic leadership threatens the well-being of healthcare organizations. They regard this concern as particularly troubling in light of how difficult it is for such organizations to attract and retain skilled registered nurses. The authors also found that countering toxic leadership is extremely difficult when it is accepted and ignored by employers. When toxic leadership is entrenched in an organization, workers often become demoralized and resigned to the situation.

Toxic Leadership in the Military

Toxic leadership can go unchallenged and flourish within the military culture because individuals do not wish to be labeled as troublemakers. In military cultures, withstanding such abuse is regarded as a sign of strength. Some soldiers have reported being singled out by superior officers. They were shunned and repeatedly given the lowest duties, such as taking out the trash. Some likened it to being bullied at school. Many attempted to commit suicide, prompting military leadership to investigate the reasons for these attempts. As part of its review, the US Army began soliciting anonymous performance evaluations of commanders. As a result, some high-ranking officers whose subordinates reported frequent abuse were removed. A similar situation in the US Navy prompted the removal of some commanders as well.

One difficulty in weeding out toxic leaders, particularly in the military, is that many qualities that make good leaders become hindrances when taken to the extreme. For example, narcissism in a leader can be beneficial: narcissistic leaders may be willing to take risks that are likely to succeed and narcissistic leaders often have phenomenal interpersonal communication skills. However, narcissists create a toxic work environment when they are unable to recognize the feelings of others, cannot take criticism, are focused on power, or fly into a rage when questioned.

In 2012, the US Army revised the leadership manual *Army Doctrine Publication 6-22* to define toxic leadership and its negative effects on subordinates, mission performance, and the organization as a whole.

Why Toxic Leaders Often Thrive

Humankind is psychologically driven to find authority figures. This need may be related to a wide variety of interests, ranging from basic concerns about security, shelter, and sustenance to a drive to find greater purpose in life. Practical needs, such as earning a paycheck to pay the bills, may take precedence over a desire to escape a toxic leader. For others, a desire to have a meaningful life leads them to accept toxic leadership as long as the toxic leader promises to fulfill this existential need.

Jean Lipman-Blumen, author of *The Allure of Toxic Leaders: Why We Follow Destructive Bosses and Corrupt Politicians—and How We Can Survive Them* (2005), cites politicians, religious leaders, and heads of hate groups as examples of toxic leaders who garner huge followings of devotees. Such leaders offer grand illusions to their followers. Uncertainty, such as the anxiety created by the terrorist attacks of September 11, 2001, helped feed many individuals' need for orderliness, which may be promised by toxic leaders who appear to be sure of their actions and purpose.

Some individuals need to experience success vicariously through others. This need, often evident in cults or gangs, may inspire followers to orbit seemingly powerful people, no matter the cost. Such organizations often foster an us versus them philosophy, in which the leader is seen to be protecting the group from an enemy and reassuring followers of the group's superiority.

Followers often remain under the control of toxic leaders because they rationalize their situation. Workers may believe they will not be able to find other jobs or fear that they will lose status if they defy the leader. However, according to Lipman-Blumen, followers do have options. A worker might document a leader's toxic behavior over time and use this record to bring attention to the problem with senior leaders of the company or organization. Some people might find solidarity with other victims of a toxic leader's wrath and attempt to change the environment together as a group.

BIBLIOGRAPHY

Doty, Joe, and Jeff Fenlason. "Narcissism and Toxic Leaders." *Military Review*, Jan.–Feb. 2013, 55–60. Web. 31 Oct. 2016.

Lipman-Blumen, Jean. "The Allure of Toxic Leaders: Why Followers Rarely Escape Their Clutches." *Ivey Business Journal*, Jan.–Feb. 2005. *Business Source Complete*. Web. 31 Oct. 2016.

Mourdoukoutas, Panos. "How Toxic Leaders Prompt the Most Talented Employees to Jump Ship." *Forbes*, 4 Nov. 2014. Web. 31 Oct. 2016.

Ulmer, Walter F., Jr. "Toxic Leadership: What Are We Talking About?" *Army*, June 2012, 47–52. *Academic Search Complete*. Web. 31 Oct. 2016.

Zangaro, George A., et al. "Recognizing and Overcoming Toxic Leadership." *Journal of Nursing*, RN-Journal.com/Times Publishing, 2009. Web. 31 Oct. 2016.

Zwerdling, Daniel. "Army Takes On Its Own Toxic Leaders." *NPR*, 6 Jan. 2014. Web. 31 Oct. 2016.

Josephine Campbell

TRAINING ANALYSIS

ABSTRACT

Training analysis refers to a company's decision to evaluate its employee performance against the company's desired performance outcomes and to concentrate specifically on improving its training program (and by definition its incoming employees) as a way to align the company's day-to-day operations with overall company goals. By clarifying its needs through careful and methodical evaluation and by focusing on training programs, a company can not only improve its overall performance operation but also ensure that new employees start with a clear understanding of what the company expects.

OVERVIEW

No employee starts at a company without needing some level of training. Although the interview process is designed to vet those candidates least qualified for a position, any hired employee brings to the company at best a background of field experience and or a relevant educational experience. He or she does not know the company itself. Whether involved in producing goods or providing services, a company conducts its operations in a way specific to that company. Of course, any new hire comes into a company with a broad learning curve—whether a lower echelon employee or a management/supervisor—to learn the culture, operational processes, polices, and vision of the company and to begin to contribute effectively to those same business operations.

According to conventional thought, companies do not need to spend a great deal of time creating an orientation session or refining a training program. Those sessions were often little more than an impersonal day or two spent shadowing those current employees engaged in that job or reading through procedural binders or viewing training videos. New employees would be given broad ideas about how the company functions, specifics about necessary paperwork to process the new hire, and then a walkthrough of the facility or the office to meet the staff.

Because these presentations were full of stock information, they could not reflect current operations nor were they expected to. Conventional thought considered the best training to be what followed these orientation sessions—that is, on the job training itself. New employees would simply learn by shadowing or by doing. Whatever training would be offered in these orientation stages would largely be considered preliminary. The new employee would learn best by actually doing the job. The trainee designation would indicate to coworkers and supervisors that special consideration might need to be extended, but new hires were largely on their own to learn the business operations. Whether assuming secretarial duties, performing customer sales, assuming a place within an industrial product assembly line, or working in any business operation, the hire would learn by watching, by doing, and by asking questions.

What is lost in this structure is organization performance, whatever the business, whatever the service provided or the goods produced. Offices and factories must operate at peak efficiency, but staffing is always changing. Turnover, terminations, and retirements impact companies. Even promotions leave gaps in operations that need to be filled by hires that, in turn, need to be trained. Hires can also learn ineffective practices from employees who have been at the company for a long time since they develop behaviors, attitudes, and ways to do their job that sometimes do not directly contribute to or help overall company performance.

New Hires
The conventional system thus places enormous stress on the new hire. Most often, new hires were put on some sort of probation, often three months, as a way to assess their performance (rather than the company performance)—and even then the entire process gave management no clear idea of how successful that orientation process actually had been. Ineffective performance—that is, employees who were ironically creating the very conditions management wanted to ameliorate—led inevitably to ineffective hires—and nothing in the operations could be reasonably expected to change.

Training needs analysis posits a radically different model. New hires, the argument goes, become part of a company staff, and if the company monitors its own job performance and notices problems in critical areas, then expectations and deficiencies can be best addressed through rigorous attention to the training programs provided. The definition, then, of what are termed training needs follows a kind of simple arithmetical formulation: A company takes its desired outcome, subtracts its current state of performance and operations, and what is left becomes in essence, a training need.

The principal areas any company monitors are, thus, directly related to its training program. Those areas include customer service and overall interaction with those customers whether face to face or through electronic communications; time management—that is, how carefully and efficiently employees use the workday; morale and attitude; and the efficiency of the complete operation model—that is, how the different parts or departments or personnel of a company communicate, work together, understand each other in an effort to optimize business operations and in turn revenues and profit. By measuring these desired outcomes (setting specific goals for each) and then comparing those desired outcomes with actual operations through a range of evaluative processes, a company can ultimately define its specific training needs. Thorough and careful training will lead necessarily to correct operations and in turn to operations far more in line with company expectations.

A company focuses, then, not so much on the needs and deficiencies of incoming hires but rather on the company needs and the deficiencies in its current operations. Training analysis directly links those desired optimum outcomes to current staff behaviors and current staff procedures; incoming employees are viewed as critical elements in raising the general character and efficiency of the company workforce.

Under this protocol, the new hires are critical in the company's broad evolution. New hires are no longer viewed as maintaining the status quo—instead, a company views its every hire as a new opportunity to improve its operations. Training analysis is a way then to close the gap between operations and desired operations. Businesses can actually use training itself as a way to improve its overall operations and to better meet its targeted expectations and objectives.

APPLICATIONS

Training analysis begins with what companies often find to be the most challenging area: the critical self-evaluation of its current operations and its current staff. Without that ongoing assessment training needs can never be fully and helpfully defined. First, a company must define what it expects in those critical areas—customer service, time management, morale, and efficiency—and what metrics it can use to determine what levels would be deemed optimum.

Setting Goals
Before undertaking training needs analysis, a company has to distinguish what particular skills, behaviors, and attitudes cannot be taught even in the best designed, carefully delivered and meticulous training sessions. After all, a training program is no place to introduce aptitudes that education and/or previous work experience should have provided. In addition, a new employee must bring certain characteristics with them—a training program cannot teach a positive attitude, a sense of efficiency, logical thinking, organization, or a range of social skills. If such areas are critical to a position or to a company, the company needs to rely on the human resources representatives to find the best hires initially.

A company must undertake a rigorous self-examination (Murphy 2015). Most often, before setting up a training needs analysis, a company hires an external agent to oversee the ongoing process. Sources of reliable data are few. Companies can use online customer survey responses and in-store customer evaluation forms. Personnel can themselves be surveyed or even interviewed (although that is time consuming and raises thorny questions about protecting confidentiality as a way to access honest responses). Managers and upper echelon management can be interviewed or even asked to provide detailed and particular assessments of their division or of the personnel directly under their watch, and they can be asked to provide self-assessments about how they are doing their job in an effort to target specific areas for improvement (Reed and Vakola 2006). Focus groups made up of selected customers and/or clients can be impaneled to provide feedback, and employees who are departing the company either through job relocation or retirement or even termination can be given exit interviews as a way to better monitor business operations.

The best way to evaluate company operations is for the particular supervisor and/or senior management personnel to actually engage the operations first hand and observe the operations regularly (Stanley 2013). Spot inspections often yield uneven results. Whatever the process, the interrogation of operations centers on basic questions: What would you change? Where is the company at risk? Where might the company do a better job? What operation elements are redundant? This information is critical for a company to define its performance gaps.

Because such information assessments can generate quite a list of operation deficiencies, a company inevitably prioritizes these deficiencies before it begins to revisit its training processes. Some are critical, some less so. Some can be addressed in training programs. Because training analysis is designed for long term effectiveness, a company can use this data to build an operational profile. Once the priorities are set, the management considers options for actually putting those objectives into specific training programs.

The options are as varied and customizable. Programs can be designed to fit a company budget or to accommodate a business's computer services. The extent of training may depend on how much staff time can be allocated for the training program, but a company should be able to offset the program's cost with long-term gains in productivity. It is essential to be able to evaluate the program's success and the extent to which the company's training program has met its broader needs.

Program Design
At the center of these protocol questions is how a company's expectations can best be delivered. Often the preferred method involves person to person contact.

Assigned facilitators can meet with small groups of new hires, or new hires can be assigned a mentor. With such protocols, hires feel more comfortable asking questions, clarifying procedures, and addressing their concerns. In addition, the hire(s) can meet others in the organization and become better acclimated socially. Alternatively, the company can sponsor off hour events—socials or weekend retreats—as a way to help hires learn the company operations and in turn understand what the company expects and how best to move the company toward those operational desires.

Less efficient but often used, web-based information presentations can often raise questions with new hires, and they involve technology that may or may not respond appropriately, thus distracting the employees from the discussions of a training session. If a company can afford it and has the facility resources, hires can be directed to nearby universities where, in cooperation with specialized faculty advisors, they can be walked through both the practical and theoretical paradigms that the company wants to actualize. If a company maintains other facilities, a hire can be sent to those facilities in an effort to demonstrate the reach of the company and the expectations of uniform productivity and operations. In any event, companies most often provide copious reading material to supplement the training process as a way to reinforce the information, which can be overwhelming.

Because the template of training analysis assumes it will be ongoing, companies follow up the training sessions. Evaluation of the training analysis process is vital (HR Space 2009). New hires are asked within the traditional 90-day probationary period to provide helpful feedback on the success of the sessions. Supervisors can observe whether operations, as defined by the company's own need assessments, are being better met (Carman 2013).

CONCLUSION

Critics of training analysis as a commitment of company resources point out that critical areas of company performance cannot actually be traced to worker performance. Problems with outdated equipment (e.g., poor performing computer software), soft marketing, and down sales all contribute to problems of productivity and efficiency (Shipley and Golden 2013). The larger issue raised by training needs analysis, however, is far more simple; a company cannot train attitudes, and attitude is largely indicated by research to be the most critical factor in job performance and, consequently, in overall company performance. If a company elects to invest its time, its staff hours, and its monies into a more elaborate training protocol, hard quantitative data indicating the actual impact of the program is virtually impossible to secure. After all, being trained appropriately does not guarantee performing appropriately.

However, a training analysis does provide a company with a clear imperative to maintain constant overview of its own performance, logic for reviewing its operational goals, and a compelling reason to monitor closely the performance, behaviors, skills, and attitudes of their own workforce. A commitment to analyzing the training process is a commitment to the future of the company itself, and the process provides continual opportunity for refreshing skills and improving known weaknesses (Hegarty, 2016). Human resource management research indicates that analyzing the training process can create a more unified community like workplace. Training analysis argues that addressing company problems begins with company employees. Effective monitored training sets clear expectations and better clear ways to meet those expectations.

BIBLIOGRAPHY

Carman, Michael. "Hitting the Mark: Using Training Needs Analysis to Improve Customer Satisfaction." *Training & Development* 40, no. 1 (2013): 10–11. Web. 23 Oct. 2016.

Hegarty, T. "All Aboard the Training Needs Analysis." *Money Marketing* 43 (2016). Web. 23 Oct. 2016.

HR Space. "Training & Coaching Today." (2009): 16. Web. 23 Oct. 2016.

Murphy, Nigel. "Reliable TNA in Seven Steps." *Training Journal* (2015): 29–32. Web. 23 Oct. 2016.

Reed, Jacqueline, and Maria Vakola. "What Roles Can a Training Needs Analysis Play in Organizational Change?" *Journal of Organizational Change Management* 19, no. 3 (2006): 393–407. Web. 23 Oct. 2016.

Shipley, Fina, and Pat Golden. "How to Analyze and Address Your Organization's Learning Needs." *T + D* 67, no. 3 (2013): 29–31. Web. 23 Oct. 2016.

Stanley, T. "Good Training Programs Don't Just Happen." *Supervision* 74, no. 2 (2013): 8–11. Web. 23 Oct. 2016.

SUGGESTED READING

Court, Charles M., Gregory B. Prothero, and Roy L. Wood. "The Value of Training: Analysis of DAU's Requirements Management Training Results." *Defense Acquisition Research Journal: A Publication of the Defense Acquisition University* 22, no. 2 (2015): 154–73. Web. 23 Oct. 2016.

da Silva Viana, F., and Gustavo Q. Souki. "Proposal for an Interactive Analysis Model of Training and Management of Strategic Alliances." *Business Management Dynamics* 4, no. 7 (2015): 12–23. Web. 23 Oct. 2016.

Ghosh, P. "Training Needs Analysis: A Comparative Study of Private Sector vs. Public Sector Hotels in Chandigarh." *CLEAR International Journal of Research in Commerce & Management* 6, no. 6 (2015): 68–79. Web. 23 Oct. 2016.

Handsaw, Dick. *Training That Delivers Results: Instructional Design That Aligns with Business Goals.* New York: AMACOM, 2014.

McGoldrick, Beth, and Deborah Tobey.). *Needs Assessment Basics.* 2nd ed. Alexandria, VA: Assessments for Training Development Press, 2016.

Joseph Dewey, Ph.D.

TRAIT LEADERSHIP

ABSTRACT

Trait leadership, a concept that began to develop in earnest in the nineteenth century, was the first attempt to theorize the factors considered essential to efficient leadership. There are many branches of trait leadership, across a wide variety of organizational and academic fields. However, critics warn that the widespread prevalence of trait beliefs contributes to the development of stereotypes. Most contemporary personality trait theories take into account, to different degrees, the influence of sociocultural phenomena such as physiology, psychology, culture, socioeconomic status, and globalization.

OVERVIEW

Since the ancient Greeks, individuals have sought to identify and understand what makes some people become leaders while most others do not. They have also examined if there are special characteristics that make for an effective leader and the extent to which leadership is related to the achievements of a leader's followers. The nineteenth century saw the rise of the "Great Man Theory," which synthesized ideas about great leaders being born to their position. In other words, some men—for leaders were usually male—were born with genetic or inheritable characteristics called "traits" that marked them as natural leaders. These traits were varied and invariably identified as masculine. Followers or people considered inferior were believed not to possess such traits. Trait theories, then, stemmed from the idea that people were born with an inherent set of innate talents, abilities and skills, referred to as traits, which flourished into leadership, and these traits could not be acquired in any other way.

The Great Man theory was first proposed by a Scottish historian and essayist named Thomas Carlyle (1795–1881). In Carlyle's view, history and great leaders were inextricably linked, because great leaders were the movers and shakers of great historic events. Carlyle believed that men such as Alexander the Great, Julius Caesar, or Abraham Lincoln were born with extraordinary natural traits, which at the time included martial virtues—the ability to lead men in battle and strategize successfully. This theory became very influential, for it provided an easily comprehensible explanation for many complex sociological phenomena.

Trait theory did not shed light, however, on the ways in which privilege and political mythmaking, for example, make some leaders appear more effective at their job than they were in reality. Carlyle's view seems quaint in the twenty-first century, as decades of research has shown that the behavior of people

Raymond Cattell (photo courtesy of the Cattell family)

is largely situational and contextual, and human beings are born with characteristics that develop and express differently throughout their lives. Moreover, the status of leaders often colors the perception of their followers, who may ascribe to them traits they do not have. Nevertheless, Carlyle's ideas inspired early empirical research on leadership. In fact, it is still considered the first theory of leadership of the modern era.

Trait theories and those related to them focus on different personality traits that are usually expected to remain constant across a wide variety of situations. Some of the influence of Carlyle is clear in theories that examine how certain traits produce specific behaviors and how behavioral traits may be consistent or change across different situations. Moreover, experts in some fields continue to believe that people are born with traits that help them become successful leaders (Cherry 2014). Early trait theories, then, used successful leaders as their case studies, seldom questioning the conditions that bolstered their leadership, such as the social class they were born into. However, individuals with similar traits who were born into less privileged status seldom achieved extraordinary levels of leadership.

Other individuals of that period, such as scientist Herbert Spencer (1820–1903), disagreed with Carlyle's view and proposed that it was the impact of their environment that which made individuals who they were. Nevertheless, the idea that prominent leaders have the right traits or personality for their position—and that these traits are inherent—continues to be a popular idea. The traits considered imperative for successful leadership vary, with the most common across the board being intelligence, self-confidence, determination, integrity, and sociability (Shriberg and Shriberg 2010).

In fact, studies show that there are very few traits that can be identified that distinguish between leaders and followers. One of these is extroversion, which leaders seem to express more, but the differences tend to be minimal. In time, then, trait theories began to run into problems, such as the fact that some obviously strong leaders did not possess the leadership traits supposed to identify great men. Theories that focused on traits became more nuanced and empirical, so that these were modified to take into account other variables, such as gender, social class, the ways in which people interpret the elements of success, and others (Cherr, 2014). Other research results suggest that people with some specific traits may be effective leaders in one specific context, while much less so in others. In other words, leadership is contingent and contextual. Moreover, there is no definite list of traits that guarantees leadership success in all circumstances (Lussier and Achua 2012).

By the mid-twentieth century, studies performed by Ralph M. Stodgill (1904–1978), a leading expert in leadership research, suggested that successful leadership resulted from the interaction between an individual and his or her social environment, rather than from inborn traits. Stodgill added more variables to his studies, including age, appearance, knowledge, responsibility, emotional control, social skills, self-confidence, and integrity. By 1974, a study conducted by leadership researchers Barry Posner and Jim Kouzes interviewing over 1,500 managers, determined that there are four main traits associated with leadership: honesty, forward looking, the ability to inspire, and competence. In 1989, another study found that some traits can be associated with good leadership across situations: task competence, intelligence, people skills, the ability to motivate others, self-confidence, assertiveness, flexibility, courage, credibility, empathy, and decisiveness (Cherry 2014). Leadership and personality theories tend to incorporate some trait research, because it is an invaluable asset for leaders and organizations to understand how personality affects performance.

Trait theories have raised concerns among some scholars. For instance, they claim that the lists of traits linked to strong leadership are usually perceived as being "male" traits, according to several surveys worldwide, or neglect to take into account gender and cultural differences. Others argue that traits in general are often ineffectual predictors of behavior. Many trait theories do not explain why individual differences emerge nor why some individuals score high when measured on some traits but do not always behave the same way in similar situations (Cherry 2014).

Further Insights
Trait theories are mainly concerned with measuring individual personality traits or dispositions. Not all of them, however, argue that traits are the most powerful factors that determine how an individual behaves in different contexts or scenarios. Most contemporary trait theories take into account different social, cultural, environmental, and psychological variables, as opposed to early trait theory, which simply argued that leaders had different—and better—traits than most other people (Unsar and Karalar 2013).

Social scientists who focus on trait theories, generally believe that there are general and specific traits linked to leadership, some of which are inheritable and others are acquired or developed. In fact, most traits are acquired or developed, and many characteristics long believed to be unchangeable traits, have been shown to change with the passage of time, experience, or specific sets of circumstances. Among the most influential contemporary theories are the works of Gordon Allport, Raymond Catell, Hans Eysenck, and Geert Hofstede.

In the mid-1930s, Gordon Allport created a list of 4,000 words from the English language that described different personality traits, and organized them into three kinds of traits: (1) cardinal traits; (2) central traits; and (3) secondary traits. Cardinal traits are the dominant and outstanding characteristics of a specific individual. In fact, these characteristics may be so salient among extraordinary leaders that they become known for that individual's name and become part of the vocabulary: Christ-like, Machiavellian, the "Napoleon complex," and so on. Cardinal traits, however, are found solely among a few unique individuals and are not common to the general population. On the other hand, everybody has central traits, that is, those characteristics that prove foundational to each personality. These are not salient to the extent that cardinal traits are, but are prevalent enough that they are used by others to describe the person who possesses them. For instance, a person may be described by most who know him or her as honest, intelligent, energetic, shy, and so on. These characteristics are coherent with cardinal traits, when an individual possesses both. Finally, secondary traits are related to tastes, preferences or attitudes; that is, they are contextual or expressed only under some circumstances. For instance, a person may become anxious only when he or she has to speak in public—also known as stage fright—or become impatient when he or she has to wait in traffic. What is unique to each person, according to Allport, is his or her specific pattern of traits (Cherry 2014; Unsar and Karalar 2013).

Raymond Cattell followed up on Allport's research by reducing the number of main personality traits from Allport's list of 4,000 to 171, and surveyed a large sample of individuals along these traits, eventually reducing the number to 16 key personality traits, from which he created one of the most important personality measures, known as the Cattell's Sixteen Factor Questionnaire or 16PF (Cherry 2014).

British psychologist Hans Eysenck developed a model of personality based upon three universal traits: (1) introversion/extraversion; (2) neuroticism/emotional stability; (3) psychoticism. Introversion/extraversion and neuroticism/emotional stability measure the extent to which people are inner or outer directed. After studying people affected by mental disease, Eysenck added the dimension of psychoticism. Individuals who rate high on this trait have difficulties dealing with people, and may lack empathy or have problems dealing with reality (Cherry 2014).

The work of Cattell and Eysenck form the basis for considerable contemporary research and personality test instruments, much of which builds upon these theories to identify strong leadership. One of these is the "Big Five" theory, which proposes 5 core personality traits that interact with each other in every human being. These are commonly known as (1) extraversion, (2) agreeableness, (3) conscientiousness, (4) neuroticism, and (5) openness.

The twenty-first century saw a surge in interest in the personality attributes of effective leaders, in part due to the resurgence of theoretical and empirical work on charismatic and transformational leadership approaches. Charismatic and transformational leaders are those able to change the status quo by inspiring and energizing their followers, capable of moving them to respond quickly and efficiently to a call for action. These studies, then, focus on personality attributes as a way to predict future leadership performance and effectiveness. Other studies suggest that individual leadership styles exist, and much of the current theories focus on "trait activation," the idea that traits require specific situations to be activated or expressed. Therefore, individuals who possess specific traits will behave in trait-like ways only in situations that actually prompt or cause those traits to spring into action.

On the other hand, because of globalization and the growing diversity in the workplace, much of business training is based on building up emotional intelligence, communication and interpersonal skills, mentorship and coaching, and other skills based on development activities rather than purely activating traits. Some of these theories, however, are based on Hofstede's findings on cultural studies who found that different cultures have different attributes or characteristics that are so prevalent as to be practically inherent. These characteristics include: (1) power distance, (2) uncertainty avoidance, (3) humane orientation, (4) collectivism, (5) assertiveness, (6) gender-egalitarianism, (7) future orientation, and (8) performance orientation. Based on this theory, then, although a culture may have trait-like characteristics that are crucial to understand in a globalized world, perceptions of desirable leadership traits are societal; that is, they are embedded in a society's culture and beliefs, and thus may differ across cultures (Pressentin 2015).

On the other hand, some studies have identified a few leadership traits across cultures. Research shows some correlations in traits such as extroversion, conscientiousness, and openness across graduate-level (MBA) business students in different cultures. Globalization and the internationalization of business schools have had an impact on how new generations are educated for leadership. The links between personality traits and leadership continues to be a popular subject in the leadership research in many fields, including education and the military (Unsar and Karalar 2013).

Viewpoints

Research on traits and personality attributes has become more sophisticated, reflecting increasingly complex societal dynamics and the diverse interests of leaders and organizations. Some of these include the expansion of businesses across borders into other countries and others, growing awareness of diverse workplaces.

Not only are different sets of leadership traits viewed as desirable across cultures, there may be different perceptions of desirable leadership traits with specific cultures and age groups. Authoritarian and paternalistic leadership traits may be preferred among organizational leaders from an older generation while a younger generation may connect better with transformational leadership. Very hierarchical environments may also promote traits that are better expressed in a vertical power structure whereas organizations based on transformational leadership, based on consensus and motivation, are suited to different leadership traits (Pressentin 2015). Situations such as these are increasingly common as businesses continue to grow and internationalize.

Other issues uncovered by trait-based studies, include the extent to which the perception of desirable traits is cultural and gender-based. For example, researchers question the extent to which a recognized leader truly possesses leadership traits, and the extent to which such traits are in the eye of the beholder. Studies have shown, for example, that once a person has been identified as a leader, it is common for others to assign to the leader attributes considered crucial for good leadership. Such traits include intelligence, ability, empathy, support, creativity, consistency, and power. Traits negatively related to perceived leadership are suspiciousness, self-centeredness, radical tendencies, and hypocrisy. A 1960s study found that leadership stereotypes were prevalent and that these perceptions and stereotypes affected the rating behavior of those assessing the leaders (Frye 1965).

Twenty-first century studies suggest that stereotypes continue to affect the ways in which people perceive and rate leaders according to traits. For example, a study conducted across Australia, Germany, and India found that managers were perceived as possessing traits that are stereotypically male. People surveyed in all three countries assessed traits for male and female executives, as well as individuals identified solely as an executive. Both men and women rated women executives as more interested in people. In fact, men were consistently rated as more proactive ("agentic") than women, and women more communally oriented than men, reflecting age old stereotypes of women as caretakers and nurturers, and men as breadwinners and active. In fact, the results supported the contention that many visualize a male when they think about a manager. These trait-based gender stereotypes can be observed in studies performed in other advanced countries as well (Sczesny, Bosak, Neff, & Schyns, 2004). Moreover, male participants were likelier to describe female executives as having negative traits such as nervousness, passivity, and uncertainty, and male executives as competent, ambitious, and objective. Therefore, when women reach leadership roles, they may be rated and evaluated according to biased perceptions and stereotyped trait attributions (Sczesny, Bosak, Neff, and Schyns 2004).

CONCLUSION

Despite these concerns, some experts advocate for studying and taking into account the impact of personality traits, albeit within certain parameters. Admittedly, abundant research supports the argument that psychological factors such as temperament, emotions and biases affect decision making. Traits may be important in some contexts but, even in the presence of traits, emotions and beliefs affect the rational processes and contribute significantly to decisions and behavior (Rzeszutek, Szyzska, and Czerwonka 2015).

BIBLIOGRAPHY

Cervone, Daniel, Lawrence A. Pervin. *Personality: Theory and Research.* 12th ed. New York: Wiley, 2013.

Cherry, Kendra. "What Is the Trait of Leadership?" *About Health.* (2014, Sept. 18). Web. 28 Dec. 2015.

Frye, R.L. "Relationship between Rated Leaders and the Traits Assigned to These Leaders." *Journal of Social Psychology* 66, no. 1 (1965): 95–99. Web. 28 Dec. 2015.

Lussier, Robert, and Christopher Achua. *Leadership: Theory, Application, and Skill Development.* Mason, OH: Cengage Learning, 2012.

Pressentin, Maria. "Universal Leadership Approaches and Cultural Dimensions: The Expression of Asian Leadership Traits." *Amity Global Business Review* 10 (2015): 19–38. Web. 28 Dec. 2015.

Rzeszutek, Marcin, Adam Szyzska, and Monika Czerwonka. "Investors' Expertise, Personality Traits, and Susceptibility to Behavioral Biases in the Decision Making Process." *Contemporary Economics* 9, no. 3 (2015): 337–51. Web. 28 Dec. 2015.

Sczesny, Sabine, Janine Bosak, Daniel Neff, and Birgit Schyns. "Gender Stereotypes and the Attribution of Leadership: A Cross-Cultural Comparison." *Sex Roles* 51, nos. 11-12 (2004): 631–45. Web. 28 Dec. 2015.

Shriberg, Arthur, and David Shriberg. *Practicing Leadership Principles and Applications.* 4th ed. New York: Wiley, 2010.

Unsar, Agah, and Serol Karalar. "The Effect of Personality Traits on Leadership Behaviors: A Research on the Students of Business Administration Department." *Journal of Economics and Business* 11, no. 2 (2013): 45–56. Web. 28 Dec. 2015.

SUGGESTED READING

DuBois, Melissa, Jodi Koch, John Hanlon, et al. "Leadership Styles of Effective Project Managers: Techniques and Traits to Lead High Performance Teams." *Journal of Economic Development, Management, IT, Finance & Marketing* 7, no. 1 (2015): 30–46. Web. 28 Dec. 2015.

Mallia, Karen L., Kasey Windels, and Sheri J. Broyles. "An Examination of Successful Leadership Traits for the Advertising-Agency Creative Director." *Journal of Advertising Research* 53, no. 3 (2013): 339–53.

Northouse, Peter G. *Leadership: Theory and Practice.* 7th ed. Thousand Oaks, CA: Sage Publications, 2015.

Trudy Mercadal, Ph.D.

Transactional Leadership

ABSTRACT

Transactional leadership is a style of management based on the distribution of rewards and punishments. Transactional leaders are primarily concerned with maintaining order in daily operations. They rely on authority instead of personal charisma and tend to disregard the feelings of their employees. Transactional leadership is often contrasted with transformational leadership.

Early Theorists
Political theorist James MacGregor Burns proposed both transactional leadership theory and transformational leadership theory. Burns used his research of leadership types to categorize major political figures (Burns, 1978). Researcher Bernard M. Bass blended Burns' politically oriented leadership theories with psychology. Bass asserted that leaders' transformational and transactional qualities could be quantified and measured primarily by examining their influence on their subordinates. Bass also developed the Multifactor Leadership Questionnaire, a detailed survey used for quantifying a leader's characteristics (Bass, 2015).

Transactional Leadership
Transactional leaders rely on authority to motivate subordinates. Managers believe their job is to delegate tasks and supervise and that employees should do as they are told. These leaders assume that most subordinates are only working out of self-interest and threatening punishment is the best way to motivate subordinates to work harder. Transactional leaders do not tolerate any challenges to authority nor do they allow subordinates to question their decisions. These types of managers set goals and then use their authority to punish any employee who fails to meet these goals. They believe that doing high quality work at the pace dictated by the leader is part of the work contract and thus only praise truly exemplary work. In employment situations, the constant threat of punishment and lack of praise often causes low job satisfaction and low employee retention rates.

Because transactional leaders focus on punishments for breaking rules or submitting substandard work, transactional leadership tends to work best in an organization that already has clearly defined rules and goals. This method enforces the status quo and does not challenge it. For this reason, transactional leaders are a poor choice for any organization that needs a new direction. Instead, transactional leaders are best at keeping an already successful organization on track.

Transformational Leadership
Transformational managers do not utilize a system of rewards and punishments to motivate employees. Instead, they motivate their employees by setting a goal that is greater than their employees' self-interests. Transformational leaders earn respect by leading through example, acting as a role model for their subordinates, and demonstrating their care for members of the organization. They use a clear vision for the future of their organization to motivate their subordinates. They intellectually stimulate employees, challenge the status quo, and answer questions. They may even individually coach and mentor employees.

Transformational leadership is best used when an organization needs to be revitalized or redirected. Unlike transactional leaders, transformational leaders are not afraid to take risks and completely change an organization's goals. They earn loyalty and respect of their subordinates in a way that transactional leaders cannot.

However, transformational leadership does have downsides. Excessive risks are dangerous to an organization. For example, a few bad gambles can ruin a company. Additionally, because transformational managers act as role models for the rest of the company, their negative traits or bad habits may be emulated by their employees. These managers may also focus the organization on a single goal to the detriment of other objectives.

Which Theory Works Best?
Researchers disagree about which leadership theory works best, or if a leader can blend the two techniques for better results. Burns asserted that transactional leadership and transformational leadership were mutually exclusive techniques. However, Bass and many of his contemporaries believed

that the best leaders display both transactional and transformational qualities. The late Apple Inc. founder and chief executive officer Steve Jobs is a commonly cited example of a leader who successfully blended both leadership theories. Jobs was extremely harsh on employees who failed to meet his expectations, sometimes even insulting them in front of other coworkers. However, he highly praised those who impressed him. Jobs also took risks, trusted his personal vision above everything else, and inspired followers and admirers.

Studies show that the best technique to use depends on the specific situation. When researchers studied the leadership tactics of several sports coaches, they discovered that teams being coached by a transactional leader usually performed better than teams coached by a transformational leader. Additionally, researchers studied military exercises where officers used transactional or transformational leadership techniques. They found that teams with a transactional commanding officer usually scored higher than teams with a transformational commanding officer.

On the other hand, most leadership studies involving businesses show that companies with a transformational leader tend to have happier employees with higher levels of productivity than businesses with a transactional leader. Strict regulation and fear of punishment seem to motivate employees less. Employees who have respect and admiration for their superiors typically are more motivated, and the motivation lasts for a long time. For this reason, some experts suggest that low-level managers act in a transactional manner to ensure structured employee productivity, while high-level executives act in a transformational manner to guide the company and inspire employees.

BIBLIOGRAPHY

Benjamin, Tia. "Transactional Leadership Limitations." *Houston Chronicle*. Web. 6 Apr. 2015.

Burns, James MacGregor. *Transformational Leadership*. New York: HarperCollins, 1978.

"Bernard M. Bass." *Society for Industrial and Organizational Psychology*. Web. 6 Apr. 2015.

Celse, Kimberly Marie. "A Critique of the Leadership Style of Steve Jobs." *Academia.edu*, 2 Feb. 2014. Web. 6 Apr. 2015.

Doherty, Alison J. "The Effect of Leader Characteristics on the Perceived Transformational/Transactional Leadership and Impact of Interuniversity Athletic Administrators." *Journal of Sport Management* 11: 275–85. Web. 6 Apr. 2015.

Duggan, Tara. "Negatives of Transformational Leadership." *Houston Chronicle*. Web. 6 Apr. 2015.

McCleskey, Jim Allen. "Situational, Transformational, and Transactional Leadership and Leadership Development." *Journal of Business Studies Quarterly*-5, No. 4 (2014). Web. 1 Nov. 2016.

Stone, A. Gregory, and Kathleen Patterson. "The History of Leadership Focus." *School of Leadership Studies*. Web. 6 Apr. 2015.

"Transactional Leadership Theory." *Management Study Guide*. Web. 6 Apr. 2015.

"Transformational Leadership." *Langston University*. Web. 6 Apr. 2015.

Tyler Biscontini

TRANSFORMATIONAL CHANGE

ABSTRACT

Transformational change is the process by which a company alters the fundamental elements of its business model. It often involves changing everything from structure and leadership styles to company culture, norms, and values. Transformational change often happens more rapidly than other forms of change or improvement. Although transformational change requires a company to make internal modifications, both internal and external forces may drive the need for change. Experts have identified several keys to successful achievement of transformational change and a number of barriers that can hinder progress.

Companywide Change

Companies are constantly changing. They may fine-tune a system here or make an adjustment to simplify a process there. Companies regularly implement these minor modifications—called continuous improvement—to enhance performance or output. Such changes may be applied at the local level without much impact on companywide structures or functions.

In contrast, transformational change affects the entire company. It involves simultaneous and overlapping changes in employee behavior, management style, reward systems, technology, marketing, production, and so on. Changes occur at all levels and in all sectors at once. Changes made at the local level must align to changes made at other levels in the company's hierarchy. Without this alignment, transformational change cannot succeed. The purpose of transformational change is not just to modify how a company does what it does but to fundamentally alter what a company is at its core. Lawrence M. Miller, who wrote *Getting to Lean: Transformational Change Management*, has described transformational change more simply as "revolution rather than evolution" (Miller, 2013).

Driving Forces
The driving forces behind transformational change are varied and many. Some stem from external sources beyond a company's control. For example, the establishment of new regulatory laws or the emergence of new competition may force a company to change. Fluctuations in the economy or the introduction of new technologies can also drive the need for transformational change. Suppliers, distributors, customers, natural resources, politics, social trends—are just some of the many external forces that drive transformational change within companies.

Not all driving forces are external, however. Transformational change may be driven internally. For example, company shareholders may demand increased output while decreasing available resources, thus creating the need to optimize performance. Employees may develop innovations to replace old, outdated processes. Managers may bring about transformational change by developing a plan to move the company toward future success and motivating employees to work to achieve this goal.

The driving forces of transformational change, whether internal or external, all have one thing in common; they push a company to achieve significant, systemic change.

Keys to Success
Changing the foundation upon which a company has been built and the culture to which employees and managers have become accustomed is not easy. By taking the right steps, however, a company can succeed in its transformation.

A company should build a team to establish a clear purpose and vision for change. The members of this team should include managers and other leaders in the company. They should present a united front and create a shared voice to communicate ideas to the company employees. At every level, but especially at the local level, members of this team should demonstrate ownership of and accountability for the revised purpose and vision to bolster employees' confidence in future outcomes. These actions will help to minimize disruptions to people, processes, and systems as changes begin to occur.

To enact transformational change, a company should engage and empower employees. Employees who have become accustomed to a particular culture may show resistance to change. When leaders engage employees in the change process, however, employees feel motivated and empowered. Leaders can engage and empower employees in several ways. For example, they may encourage employees to develop innovations; provide education or training to expand employees' skills; or reward employees who actively implement changes and show commitment to their success.

A company attempting to undergo transformational change should identify several small, short-term goals. Achieving each goal becomes another step on the road to success. When employees see newly implemented changes leading to continuous achievement, they will begin to feel more comfortable and may even start to recognize opportunities to play a more significant role in the change process.

Finally, change leaders from all levels of the company hierarchy should regularly observe and assess implementation and achievement. In particular, they should notice the reactions of those most affected by changes and find ways to reduce or eliminate negative experiences. By doing this work, change leaders can keep the company moving in the right direction. Only then can the company achieve transformational change.

Barriers to Success
Barriers to transformational change are essentially the reverse of the keys to success. They include failure to communicate a purpose or vision, which can leave

employees feeling vulnerable and uncertain about the company's future; failure to create a team of leaders with a shared voice, which can lead to confusion and disruption among employees; failure of change leaders to show ownership of and take responsibility for the purpose or vision, which can cause employees to lose faith in the change process; failure to engage and empower employees, which can result in resistance to change; failure to identify short-term goals, which can lead to lost momentum in the change process; and failure to observe and assess implementation at regular intervals, which can halt progress and cause some to withdraw support for the change.

BIBLIOGRAPHY

Thompson, John, and Frank Martin, eds. "15.4 Transformational Change and Strategic Regeneration." *Strategic Management: Awareness & Change.* 6th ed. Mason, OH: South-Western, 2010. 688–93.

Magloff, Lisa. "Examples of Transformational Change." *Houston Chronicle.* Hearst Newspapers, n.d. Web. 3 Mar. 2016.

Miller, David. "Delivering Transformational Change." *European Business Review.* European Business Review, 23 Mar. 2012. Web. 3 Mar. 2016.

Miller, Lawrence M. *Getting to Lean: Transformational Change Management.* New Iberia, LA: Miller Management Press, LLC, 2013.

Miller, Lawrence M. "Transformational Change vs. Continuous Improvement." *IndustryWeek.* Penton, 14 May 2013. Web. 3 Mar. 2016.

Scheele, Paul R. "Processes of Transformational Change and Transformative Learning." *Scheele Learning Systems.* Scheele Learning Systems, n.d. Web. 3 Mar. 2016.

Lindsay Rohland

TRANSFORMATIONAL LEADERSHIP

ABSTRACT

Transformational leadership is a style of leadership that emphasizes the ability of the leader to inspire and motivate others. With other leadership styles, workers usually have very straightforward reasons for following a superior's directions—for example, they want to get paid. Transformational leadership, on the other hand, relies on followers having confidence in their leader to such an extent that they may be willing to work on that leader's behalf for less money than they could make elsewhere, or even no money at all, as happens with many political campaigns' employment of interns.

OVERVIEW

Many different styles of leadership have been identified and described over the years, including transactional leadership, participative leadership, autocratic leadership, and laissez-faire leadership. Each of these styles has advantages and disadvantages, and each one tends to be more successful in some situations than in others; for example, an autocratic leadership style is much more appropriate within a military organization than it would be in an educational institution. Each style is rooted in pragmatism; they differ in their view of what behaviors are most effective at motivating people. An autocratic leader believes that people need a strong and decisive person in charge, while a participative leader feels that allowing everyone to have a voice will encourage cooperation. All essentially agree that if a leader gives followers enough of something (autocratic orders, participation) then the followers will follow. The differences between these styles are differences of degree but not of kind. Transformational leadership is the only style that takes an altogether different approach to leading (Kim, Liden, Kim, and Lee 2015).

Traits of Transformational Leadership

The reason for the distinctiveness of transformational leadership is that it takes as its purpose not the accomplishment of some task or the acquisition of some new resource, but the personal development of both leaders and followers in conjunction with one another. The transformational leader seeks to discover what followers are passionate about and then help them pursue those activities in ways that help them develop into more accomplished human beings by inspiring them to greatness.

Transformational leadership earns its name because it seeks to encourage people to become more than they are, perhaps more than they ever thought they could be, by working together and validating each other. When a transformational leader is present, people begin to stop thinking of work as "work" and instead see it almost as a mission. People are often willing to work long hours for little or no pay simply to be part of the movement that the transformational leader is bringing into being.

Many political leaders use the transformational style of leadership, which is why they are able to inspire people to not only vote for them but also to work on their campaigns as volunteers for months at a time. Followers believe in their candidate's ability to change the world for the better. This statement does not mean that transformational leadership is a style that one can pick up and use like a tool when the situation calls for it. Other leadership styles are more amenable to this situation, but transformational leadership often seems to be a trait that one either possesses or does not possess—that is, it is difficult to learn how to be a transformational leader by study or practice because transformational leadership is based on optimism about the future, faith in one's associates to accomplish great things when they give their all, and an enthusiastic commitment to helping others. One may be born with these qualities or one may acquire them later in life through a juxtaposition of circumstances, but they are rarely the result of deliberate efforts to attain them (Richter, et al. 2016).

Four I's

Because transformational leadership appeals to people on an emotional or even spiritual level, its mechanisms of operation can be difficult to define. One approach has been to identify what are known as the "four I's" of transformational leadership: individualized consideration, intellectual stimulation, idealized influence, and inspirational motivation. While these four qualities are not a complete description of what transformational leadership entails, they do capture its essence.

Individualized consideration refers to the fact that transformational leaders attempt to connect personally with those who follow them, even when the number of followers is quite large. They get to know each person on the team so that they may better understand what that person is interested in and what he or she wishes to accomplish. The transformational leader can then use this information to provide tailored support to individual followers to help them make progress toward achieving their vision for themselves (Henker, Sonnentag, and Unger 2015). For example, it is not unusual for a transformational leader to schedule informal, periodic meetings with each follower to sit down over coffee and discuss the follower's career options for the future. Once the leader is aware of the follower' interests, the leader will then keep them in mind and as opportunities arise for activities related to that follower's interest area, the leader will make the follower aware of those opportunities and help him or her take advantage of them, whether this involves attending a conference, participating in a research project, or some similar activity.

Related to these pursuits is the second "I," intellectual stimulation. While other leadership styles generally do not concern themselves with whether or not a person finds his or her assigned work interesting, unless there is a performance issue that must be addressed, transformational leaders see this important factor as impacting how engaged the person is and how satisfied the person is with his or her overall place in the group or organization. Transformational leaders want to provide their followers with frequent opportunities to practice their creativity and apply their imaginations to interesting problems because this is how one can learn to expand one's horizons and see issues in new ways (Deschamps, Rinfret, Lagacé, and Privé 2016). This focus strengthens the follower's bond with the leader on at least three different levels: first, the follower is appreciative that the leader is interested enough in each person's growth to intervene; second, the follower is thankful for the benefit of being able to pursue more intellectually challenging work; and third, the follower feels that the leader respects his or her intellect and values it.

Idealized influence is the part of transformational leadership that causes followers to view the leader as a role model to be emulated wherever possible, which can happen for various reasons. In some cases, followers identify so strongly with the vision articulated by the leader that they wish to be as effective as the leader by becoming more similar to him or her. In other situations, the personal qualities of the leader may be so compelling that followers are captivated by the leader's personality or wish to imitate it in order to inspire others. This situation can combine with the leader's inspirational motivation (the fourth "I") to create a highly dedicated group of followers.

Further Insights

One reason that transformational leadership appears to exist in a category of its own is that its ultimate purpose is to create positive change which can happen on a large scale, on a systemic level, or at the level of the individual. This reality explains why so many examples of transformational leadership are drawn from the world of politics. Many of those who possess the qualities necessary to an effective, transformational style are drawn to the political arena, having found that creating transformative change is not a practice universally appreciated in the business world or similar large organizational settings. Risk aversive corporate environments generally prefer to maintain the status quo and a clear hierarchy rather than introduce what might turn into chaos or upheaval.

Another sphere where one tends to encounter transformational leaders is that of religion and spirituality. While doctrines and their interpretations differ from person to person and from faith to faith, one factor that remains consistent among many religious leaders is their ability to inspire people. As with politics, religion carries the message that people can do more together than they can as solitary individuals, and both politics and religion seek to motivate their adherents to realize a particular vision of a better world.

Issues

While there are few outright critics of transformational leadership, there are those who have highlighted a number of potential drawbacks.. The main disadvantage to transformational leadership can be described as a collective overdependence on the leader¾. This situation happens when a leader is so charismatic and effective at motivating others that the leader becomes the lifeblood of the organization, movement, or other group of followers. Because followers can become dependent on the leader's presence, to lean on and expertise to draw from, a leadership vacuum may be created when the leader is absent for any length of time.

Transformational leadership has the potential of becoming a personality cult if careful attention is not paid to developing followers' own leadership capacity. The organization must possess the internal resources needed to carry on with its duties during the leader's absence or departure. This type of excessive focus on the personality of the leader can also distract followers from doing their own personal development work, so that they devote more of their time to trying to become like the leader instead of working on their own growth. The purpose of transformational leadership is not to produce followers who are clones of the leader, but to inspire followers to do good work while expanding their own awareness and scope (Cheng, Bartram, Karimi, and Leggat 2016).

Another potential drawback to transformational leadership is the inappropriate imposition of a collaborative work style on some or all of the leader's followers. A central focus of transformational leadership is to inspire people to come together and combine their efforts in order to accomplish more, but in some situations there are people for whom this shift may not be possible or desirable. Some people have a strong preference for working independently and are uncomfortable when they must collaborate too extensively with others. Those who feel this way may see their productivity decline when required to follow a transformational leadership style, and they may even decide that they no longer wish to be part of the organization.

In other cases, particularly in the business world, some positions may not allow extensive collaboration for legal reasons or because of company policy. In a human resources department, for example, much of a person's daily work must be kept confidential from other staff, making it difficult to work closely with others outside the department. Transformational leadership requires that one remain aware of subtleties such as these situations in order to prevent potential conflicts from arising (Geier 2016).

Fortunately, if the priorities of transformational leadership are followed, the leader will develop an understanding of those individuals who might be placed in an uncomfortable position by excessive collaboration and will help them to avoid problems before they even develop. It is easy to see why so many people are proponents of transformational leadership because when properly performed, it has such positive results that it even is able to self-correct potential issues and keep itself on course.

BIBLIOGRAPHY

Avolio, Bruce J., et al. "How Follower Attributes Affect Ratings of Ethical and Transformation Leadership." *Academy of Management* (2016). Web. 31 July 2016.

Cheng, Cindy, Timothy Bartram, Leila Karimi, and Sandra Leggat. "Transformation Leadership and Social Identity as Predictors of Team Climate, Perceived Quality of Care, Burnout and Turnover Intention among Nurses." *Personnel Review* 45, no. 6 (2016): 1200–16. Web. 23 Oct. 2016.

Cole, Michael S., and Arthur Bedeian. "Leadership Consensus as a Cross-Level Contextual Moderator of the Emotional Exhaustion-Work Commitment Relationship." *Leadership Quarterly* 18, no. 5 (2007): 447–62. Web. 23 Oct. 2016.

Deschamps, C., N. Rinfret, M. C. Lagacé, and C. Privé. "Transformational Leadership and Change: How Leaders Influence Their Followers Motivation through Organizational Justice." *Journal of Health Care Management* 61, no. 3 (2016): 194–212. Web. 23 Oct. 2016.

Geier, Michael T. "Leadership in Extreme Contexts: Transformational Leadership, Performance Beyond Expectations?" *Journal of Leadership & Organizational Studies* 23, no. 3 (2016): 234–47. Web. 23 Oct. 2016.

Henker, Nils, Sabine Sonnentag, and Dana Unger. "Transformational Leadership and Employee Creativity: The Mediating Role of Promotion Focus and Creative Process Engagement." *Journal of Business and Psychology* 30, no. 2 (2014): 235. Web. 23 Oct. 2016.

Kim, Tae-Yeol, Robert C. Linen, Sang-Pyo Kim, and D. Lee. "The Interplay between Follower Core Self-Evaluation and Transformation Leadership: Effects on Employee Outcomes." *Journal of Business and Psychology* 30 (2015): 345. Web. 23 Oct. 2016.

Moon, Kuk-Kyoong. "The Effects of Diversity and Transformational Leadership: Climate on Organizational Citizenship Behavior in the U.S. Federal Government: An Organizational Level Longitudinal Study." *Public Performance & Management Review* 40, no. 2 (2017): 361–38. Web. 23 Oct. 2016.

Richter, Anne, Ulrica von Theile Schwarz, C. Lornudd, et al. "iLead—a Transformational Leadership Intervention to Train Health Care Managers' Implementation Leadership." *Implementation Science* 11 (2016): 11–13.

SUGGESTED READING

Bedi, Akanksha, Can. M. Alpaslan, and Sandy Green. "An Analytic Review of Ethical Leadership Outcomes and Moderators." *Journal of Business Ethics* 139, no. 3 (2016): 517–36. Web. 23 Oct. 2016.

Fernet, Claude, Sarah-Genevieve Trépanier, S. Austin, et al. "Transformational Leadership and Optimal Functioning at Work: On the Mediating Role of Employees Perceived Job Characteristics and Motivation." *Work & Stress* 29, no. 1 (2015): 11–31. Web. 23 Oct. 2016.

Iqbal, Qaisar. "Organizational Politics, Transformation Leadership and Neglect in Banking Section." *International Journal of Management, Accounting & Economics* 3, no. 10 (2016): 609–22. Web. 23 Oct. 2016.

Pongpearchan, P. "Efffect of Transformational Leadership and High Performance Work System on Job Motivation and Task Performance: Empirical Evidence from Business Schools of Thailand Universities." *Journal of Business & Retail Management Research* 10, no. 3 (2016): 93–105. Web. 23 Oct. 2016.

Shin, Jiseon, Myeong0Gu Seo, Debra L. Shapiro, and M. Susan Taylor. "Maintaining Employees' Commitment to Organizational Change." *Journal of Applied Behavior Science* 51, no. 4 (2015): 501–28. Web. 23 Oct. 2016.

Scott Zimmer, M.L.S., M.S., J.D.

Types of Business Organizations

ABSTRACT

This article focuses on different forms of business. There are a number of ways to structure a business— these include sole proprietorships, different types of partnerships, limited liability companies, and corporations. Each form of business organization has advantages and disadvantages, and they are largely influenced by the purpose of the enterprise as well as a number of other factors. Each type of organization poses different legal ramifications and income tax considerations. This article provides an analysis of the different types of business organizations as well as a brief discussion of the advantages and disadvantages of each structure.

OVERVIEW

There are a number of ways to structure a business, and the factors involved in choosing the appropriate legal structure include: the purpose of the organization; the size of the entity; the costs involved in starting the entity; state, federal, and local laws and rules governing the business; and tax considerations. Essentially, there are four types of legal structures for business:

1. Sole Proprietorship
2. Partnership
3. Limited Liability Company
4. Corporation

There are advantages and disadvantages to each type of business organization and these are driven by a number of factors. The following is an analysis of the four legal structures.

Sole Proprietorship

A sole proprietorship, the most basic business form, is frequently utilized by a single person owning or running a business on his or her own. Such business enterprises are often run from the person's home. Owners pay taxes on the business profits which are reflected on individual tax returns (Form 1040 and Schedules C and E). In some states, the costs of a business that is being operated from an individual's home may be deducted from income taxes. However, at the same time, certain counties and states may require a sole proprietor to pay property taxes on the value of any office equipment used for the business. In addition to tax liabilities, sole proprietors are also responsible for the debts of the business (Butow 2004).

Partnership

A partnership is the legal structure for a business enterprise when two or more people start a business. There are different types of partnerships, including general partnerships, limited partnerships, and limited liability partnerships. In order to set forth how the business will operate, the partners enter into a partnership agreement. The partnership agreement specifies who the partners are, what their roles and responsibilities are, and most importantly how the profits will be divided between or among the partners. A general partnership is a business structure where each partner is liable beyond what he or she has invested in the enterprise. Also, each partner can take actions that may bind the entire partnership. A general partnership is not a taxable entity because the income and losses pass to each partner who, in turn, reports the profit and loss on individual tax returns. Because the income and losses pass to each partner, these entities are also referred to as "pass-through" enterprises. In a general partnership, the profits and losses are normally distributed equally between or among the partners. At the same time, each partner is jointly and severally liable for all the obligations of the partnership. That means a person suing the partnership can choose to collect from any partner and does not have to collect an equal amount from each partner. (Rianda 2011).

On the other hand, a limited partnership (LP) is one where two or more partners agree to operate a business jointly. In this structure, each partner is liable only to the extent of the amount each has invested in the business. This entity is also a pass-through enterprise. A limited partnership can also include both general and limited partners. In these cases, the general partners usually are responsible for running the operations of the business while the limited partners are essentially investors. Further, each partner shares the profits and losses according to the partnership agreement (Butow 2004).

A 21st century office (Photo courtesy of Korulczyk)

Another type of partnership is a limited liability partnership (LLP). These structures are normally used by professional organizations such as law firms and accounting companies. An LLP has similar features to a partnership, but the partnership as a business entity is responsible for any debts and the individual partners are shielded from these liabilities. Some US states also recognize limited liability limited partnerships (LLLPs), which mix features of limited partnerships and limited liability partnerships.

Limited Liability Companies (LLC)

A limited liability company is a cross between a corporation and a partnership. This type of business organization offers more protection from creditors' claims than a partnership. In this way, it is similar to a corporation, but it is also a pass-through entity so it shares the features of a partnership. However, limited liability companies (LLCs) have distinct features and requirements. In a limited liability company, the owners are called members. Members, in turn, can be individuals or corporations. However, unlike a partnership where profits and losses are evenly distributed according to the partnership agreement, there is greater flexibility in this regard for a limited liability company. Further, in order to establish a limited liability company, it is necessary to file articles of organization with the secretary of state. Another way that limited liability companies are similar to partnerships is that a limited liability company is required to have an operating agreement. The operating agreement specifies who the members are, what the role and responsibility of each member will be, and how profits will be shared between or among the members.

The operating agreement also contains information about changes in ownership if other members are invited to join the enterprise or if an existing member decides to sell his or her interest. Finally, because a limited liability company is also a pass-through structure, members report income and losses on personal income tax returns. Some states require that certain types of professionals that provide special types of services, such as doctors, lawyers, or architects, do not form normal limited liability companies to ensure that the liability for their services is not limited in way that could potentially harm consumers. Instead, these professionals may register as a professional limited liability company (PLLC), which restricts the limitations on liability to business matters.

Corporations

A corporation is essentially an entity that exists separate and apart from its owners. Corporations are required to have at least one owner, and owners are called shareholders or stockholders; ownership interests are referred to as stock. Because a corporation exists separate and apart from the owners, the owners are protected from debts and liabilities. The corporation itself assumes liability for the debts and obligations of the business, putting aside the issue of personal guarantees (Rianda 2011). A corporation is established when articles of incorporation are filed with the secretary of state. This document establishes the reason for the enterprise, and in some states it is referred to as a certificate of incorporation or a company's charter. The articles state the business purpose, but at the same time that description allows the business flexibility to grow and evolve. The basic information stated in the articles includes the business' name and address, the name of the incorporators, the intended duration of the business entity (either perpetual or of limited duration), and the purpose of the business (Arend 1999). An incorporator is the individual responsible for filing the articles with the secretary of state. In many states, the incorporator cannot be an owner, officer or director of the business entity. A legal agent is a third party who is not affiliated with the business entity who will be responsible for accepting any legal process papers filed against the business. A legal agent can be a law firm, but there are also professional organizations that perform these duties.

Corporations are also required to have written bylaws, the governing document of the business, which establishes the operating procedures for the entity. bylaws describe the management structure and the roles and responsibilities of the officers and directors. Generally, directors are senior executives or managers who are responsible for the day-to-day operations of the business while officers are the individuals appointed to implement the policies and procedures established by the directors. Officers report to the directors who are ultimately accountable to the owners, that is, the shareholders. Bylaws also specify the voting procedures, notice requirements, proxy, and the minimum number of people who must be present for a vote to be effective—the quorum. Corporations are required to have an annual meeting, but meetings can also be held once every quarter, once a month, or at any time an action is taken that affects the operations of the business. Such action includes mergers, establishing new business ventures and promoting or terminating officers and directors. Minutes, or a written record of meetings, must be prepared and the actions taken during these meetings are often memorialized in written resolutions. Resolutions, minutes, and notices are required to be maintained with the company's books and records along with the articles of incorporation and bylaws.

There are two types of corporations: "C" corporations and "S" corporations. The former refers to a business that meets the minimum requirements for the definition of a corporation established by the Internal Revenue Service tax code while the latter is a designation for a business that is established pursuant to subchapter "S" of the code. A subchapter "S" designation allows a business to be taxed like a partnership where the profits and losses are passed through to the shareholders. At the same time, owners are provided with protection from debt liability. Finally to qualify as an "S" corporation there must be one or more, but fewer than seventy-five owners. On the other hand, a "C" corporation does not have a limit to the number of owners; however, these businesses are not pass-through entities and the corporation's profits are taxed. Because of this fact, "C" corporations are subject to what has been termed "double taxation." In addition to the profits being taxed, shareholders are taxed on the dividends that are paid on the stock that they own. Further, shareholders are also taxed on any profits they receive on shares of stock that they sell, a capital gains tax.

Corporations are required to pay salaries to the directors, officers and employees, who are also required to pay taxes on that income (Barney 1997). Finally, unlike pass-through entities, C corporations do not separately state income or loss items. These items are combined to arrive at total taxable income, with the same tax rates applying to ordinary income and capital gains. Since income does not retain its original character in a corporation, many of the benefits available at the individual level are unavailable when the corporate form is chosen (Wong and Zambrano 2012). Corporations may also be subdivided, combined, and controlled in various ways. Holding companies are often formed as the owner of a corporation's stock in order to reduce ownership risk. Corporations may merge into one larger entity, sometimes requiring government approval due to antitrust measures. Corporations may also be considered conglomerates, in that they own and run many smaller, often seemingly unrelated businesses.

APPLICATIONS

The type of legal structure that is appropriate for individuals starting a business depends on a number of factors. The following is a comparative analysis of the advantages and disadvantages of each form of business organization. The most basic form of business, the sole proprietorship, is the best option for a single owner of a business. These entities are relatively easy to establish since they do not require extensive documents to be filed. At the same time, some states require certain business enterprises to be licensed. This category includes, but is not limited to, electricians, plumbers, home-improvement contractors, real estate brokers, mortgage brokers, financial planners, and even hairdressers. Some of the advantages of a sole proprietorship are that individuals can start these businesses without significant initial costs. Further, taxes are not paid by the business, but rather by the owner, and any profits are reported on individual tax returns. Therefore there is no need for extensive financial statements. The main disadvantage to this form of business organization is that the individual is responsible for any debts incurred by the business as well as other legal claims that can be initiated in the courts. This issue is especially relevant if the sole proprietor is a homeowner or owns other residential property. If the individual running the business does not pay debts or if a lawsuit is commenced against the business, a judgment can subsequently attach these debts to the person's dwelling. In short, a sole proprietor exposes their real property and other assets to debt and legal liabilities.

Another form of business organization that has been discussed is the partnership. This legal structure is frequently used by family businesses. Other than the possible licensing requirements, there is no need for extensive documentation and filings. Moreover, the profits of the business are not taxed since these are passed through to the individual partners. One disadvantage to this type of legal structure is that each partner is subject to a certain amount of liability for debts. Further, unless the partnership agreement states what should occur in the event of the death of a partner, partnerships do not provide for continuity of life. So if one of the partners dies, the partnership agreement may need to be renegotiated, and the surviving partner can find himself or herself doing business with people who were not originally part of the business. A hybrid of partnerships and corporations is commonly known as a limited liability company; this type of business draws on the advantages of partnerships and corporations. The main advantage is that the operating agreement can establish a flexible means for the members to share the profits and losses. Some of the factors in making this determination include the financial investment of each member as well as his or her role and responsibilities. Like a corporation, members of limited liability companies are protected from debts. Thus members can protect their assets from claims arising from creditors or lawsuits. However, this legal structure does not provide the flexibility that is available to a corporation with respect to arranging for financing the business operations.

Finally, there are a number of advantages for establishing a corporation. An "S" corporation is probably the best option for a business with one owner or where few people are involved in the business. The main benefit is that the profits are not subject to double taxation. More importantly, an "S" corporation enables owners to protect their private property and other assets. This designation is well suited for a small business and is only available to business entities that have seventy-five or fewer owners. A "C" corporation has a great deal of flexibility to finance its operations. Corporations can sell more stock, issue debt, and obtain lines of credit from a variety of financial institutions. Another benefit of such corporations is that they provide continuity of life which means that the business entity will continue in the event of the death of an owner or if an owner decides to sell his or her ownership interest (Barney 1997). However, the main disadvantage of a corporate structure is that the entity is subject to double taxation. At the same time, corporations have a number of means at their disposal to mitigate tax consequences. Many of the expenses associated with running the business can be deducted from income taxes, and an array of financial and accounting mechanisms enable corporations to minimize tax liabilities.

Further, many states offer corporations tax relief in order to attract these entities to do business in the state. If a corporation is large, generates sufficient revenue, and offers employment opportunities to a number of people, such incentives ultimately benefit a state's economy. Oklahoma, for example, offers a tax incentive that exempts horizontally drilled oil and gas wells from the state's 7 percent production tax for a limited period of time (Watts 2013). Another way for a corporation to mitigate its tax liability is to incorporate in a state in which it is not actually located. For instance, many Fortune 500 companies incorporate in the state of Delaware because this state has procedures in place that enable business entities to establish themselves quickly. Further, Delaware does not tax the profits of the corporation if business is not actually conducted in the state (Vinzant 1999). Such states, or even other countries, with favorable tax laws that attract many businesses are often referred to as corporate havens. Some regulators see these and other tax loopholes as unfair, however, and some jurisdictions have penalties for businesses that seek to exploit them.

CONCLUSION

In the final analysis, the type of legal structure business people choose depends on a number of variables. There are numerous legal and tax implications to consider, as well as federal, state, and local laws that may apply to a particular business. They are important point because some types of business are subject to a great deal of oversight. Moreover, for corporations that are also publicly traded entities, that is, a company whose shares of stock are bought and sold on one of the stock exchanges or other trading outlet, there are substantial financial and reporting requirements that stem from the Sarbanes-Oxley Act of 2002. Further if deficiencies are discovered in a corporation's financial statements, the business and the responsible individuals (chief executives and the like) are subject to felony prosecution.

Another matter to consider is the potential for lawsuits. Sole proprietors who fail to fulfill their obligations in a business transaction expose themselves to legal actions and if the person suing them prevails, the businessperson's real property and other assets will not be protected. In this regard, business enterprises can also be exposed to product liability lawsuits. A partnership or small business that makes toys for children, for example, can be sued if those toys cause harm or injury to a consumer. While the owners of corporations can protect their real property and assets from such legal claims, large corporations that generate a lot of profit are invariably the targets of class action lawsuits—and whether or not these lawsuits have merit, such legal actions can be costly.

Ultimately, the appropriate form of business organization depends on the purpose of the business, the number of people who will have an ownership interest, the amount of profit or revenue that will be generated, and finally the number of people that the business will employ. At the end of the day, the final factor that needs to be considered is that any type of business consists of people and the success of the enterprise will be significantly affected by the roles and responsibilities of these individuals, and the relationships that they create. In short, business people should carefully consider all of these variables and, moreover, rely on the advice of financial advisers and legal counsel. In this regard, the matters discussed in this article are for informational purposes only and should not be construed as financial or legal advice.

Bibliography

Aghina, Wouter, Aaron De Smet, and Suzanne Heywood. "The Past and Future of Global Organizations." *Mckinsey Quarterly* 3 (2014): 97–106. Web. 4 Dec. 2015.

Anderson, B.L. "Benefit Issues Regarding Partnerships, S Corporations, and Sole Proprietorships." *Journal of Pension Benefits* 11 (2004): 26–31. Web. 2 Jan. 2007.

Arend, T.E., and J.A. Jacobs. "Drafting Proper Governance Documents." *Association Management* 51 (1999): 111–13. Web. 2 Jan. 2007.

Barney, D.K. "Understanding the Appropriate Business Form." *National Public Accountant* 42 (1997): 9–16. Web. 2 Jan. 2007.

Butow, Eric E. "Starting Your Own Business: Costs, Structures, and Pitfalls." *Intercom* 51 (2004): 20–23. Web. 2 Jan. 2007.

Bacq, Sophie, and Jill Kickul. "Hybrid Organizations: Origins, Strategies, Impacts, and Implications." *California Management Review* 57, no. 3 (2015): 5–12. Web. 4 Dec. 2015.

Rianda, P.A. "Those letters at the End of Company Name Say a Lot." *ISO & Agent* 7 (2011): 17. Web. 3 Nov. 2013. Web. 3 Nov. 2013.

Vinzant, Carol. "Why Do Corporations Love Delaware So Much?" *Fortune* 139 (1999): 32. Web. 2 Jan. 2007.

Watts, J. "Oklahoma: Tax Reform Cuts Both Ways." *Bond Buyer* 385 (2013): 9. Web. 3 Nov. 2013.

Wong, Alan, and Jose Zambrano. "How Changes in Corporate Tax Rate Can Affect Choice of C vs. S Corp." *Tax Adviser* 43 (2012): 646–47. Web. 3 Nov. 2013.

Suggested Reading

Hillman, Robert W., and Mark J. Loewenstein. *Research Handbook on Partnerships, LLCs and Alternative Forms of Business Organizations.* Cheltenham, UK: Edward Elgar Publishing, 2015.

McCahery, Joseph A. "Comparative Perspectives on the Evolution of the Unincorporated Firm: An Introduction." *Journal of Corporation Law* 26 (2001): 803–18. Web. 2 Jan. 2007.

Olson, Eric E. "Strategically Managing Risk in the Information Age: A Holistic Approach." *Journal of Business Strategy* 26 (2005): 45–54. Web. 2 Jan. 2007.

Slemrod, Joel L. "What Corporations Say They Do and What They Really Do: Implications for Tax Policy And Tax Research." *Journal of American Taxation Association* 27 (2005): 91–99. Web. 2 Jan. 2007.

Yu, Xiaoyun. "Securities Fraud and Corporate Finance: Recent Developments". *Managerial & Decision Economics* 34, nos. 7–8 (2013): 439–50. Web. 3 Nov. 2013.

Richa S. Tiwary, Ph.D., M.L.S.

Virtual and Traditional Teams

ABSTRACT

In work settings, team members traditionally work on projects in close physical proximity. The development of new technology in modern organizations, however, has made it increasingly convenient for individuals to work together while physically distant. This situation has created places of employment with a mix of those who work in the office and those who work in other settings.

Traditional Teams

Though individuals may work in different departments or buildings, members of traditional or co-located teams generally meet regularly to discuss progress. Such face-to-face meetings are often supplemented with email, instant messaging, and other forms of communication. Subgroups work together and report back to the larger body or consult with other members.

Frequent personal contact encourages so-called water cooler meetings, which can generate spontaneous ideas. Such contact can also foster camaraderie, whether workers share a passion for a local sports team, bond over lunch, or discuss the morning commute. This contact helps team members understand how their contributions fit into the big picture of a project and how their work benefits the organization overall.

Leaders should work to develop strong relationships with each member of a team to ensure everyone feels included. To keep workers motivated, the leader should also be sure that members are aware of how their work contributes to the project.

Virtual Teams

While some studies have found that virtual or dispersed teams outperform traditional teams, virtual teams present a unique management challenge and must be led carefully to thrive. Members may be separated by space and time zone and come from different cultures. Teams may be configured unevenly—some members may work in one place, while others work from home or far-flung locations.

The strength of these teams lies in their flexibility. They are not limited to tapping expertise in the same geographic region; instead they can draw from the knowledge of individuals with different work experiences, such as those who are familiar with an international market. Using virtual teams can allow employers to avoid the expense of buying and maintaining large office buildings or other facilities, and they can also save time and money that would otherwise be used for travel. These savings can be reinvested in the company, even potentially into benefits for the virtual team members, such as better computer equipment or other communications technology.

To ensure virtual teams work smoothly, leaders should take charge at the start by establishing clear duties, procedures, and standards of measurement. Members should emphasize quality in communication over quantity. Conflicts may benefit a team but should focus on work, not interpersonal matters. As with traditional teams, leaders should develop relationships with each member, though this work might require more planning or increased use of various types of technology.

Though virtual team meetings may be impractical if members are working in multiple time zones, this obstacle can be overcome. One solution is to have team members pass along work from time zone to time zone. As workers in one office are ending the business day, the team leaves updates for the next group, which is preparing to open for business as the day dawns in another part of the world. For example, four o'clock in the afternoon in London is nine o'clock in the morning in Los Angeles, so a team in England could hand off a project at the end of the day to a team in California, where the work day is still young. Thus, work on the project follows the sun around the globe and can continue around the clock.

Differences and Challenges

Working together from different locations presents challenges, but personal contact can help teams tremendously. Leaders may have to address issues such as trust, communication, team spirit, and workflow in creative ways when team members are far apart from one another. In forming a team, leaders should consider each member's functional skills; some individuals may perform well in traditional teams, but they may be less adept and comfortable when using technological and communication tools. Such factors can affect the effectiveness of a team.

Shared leadership has been found to be very effective for virtual teams because many individuals are working independently or in very small groups and may need to make decisions quickly. This democratic approach may be less successful in traditional teams in which the leader has more control over day-to-day efforts. A leader of a virtual team must be careful to clearly define job descriptions and duties to ensure work is not duplicated.

One drawback of virtual teamwork is the lack of everyday casual contact. Informal virtual gatherings and similar social practices establish teamwork and should be supported to encourage cooperation and prevent feelings of isolation that may arise, especially in unevenly configured groups in which several team members have face-to-face contact while others do not. While quality of communication is vital, frequent contact between members of small groups builds camaraderie. Leaders of virtual teams may find it helpful to create small teams to work closely together on small components of a project. Leaders can also encourage team spirit by sharing success stories with the entire team.

Trust is an essential component of any team effort and can be developed through an awareness of who is doing what and how it benefits the team. These feelings are more easily achieved with traditional teams, but leaders of virtual teams can help members develop trust as well. Workers who know that their colleagues are skilled and are making progress are less likely to feel that unseen teammates are not contributing equally. Such impressions are particularly likely to occur when some members work from home.

Cultural diversity in a traditional team is more likely to be understood by individuals who see each other often. The nature of virtual teams makes it increasingly likely that members come from different and possibly unfamiliar social and/or cultural backgrounds.

Members of a team communicate remotely (Photo courtesy of Narek75)

Decision making may vary in different countries, and leaders should clearly define how decisions will be made—whether informally by consensus or by other means. Individuals in some cultures may be offended by brief email messages, which can seem curt, while others may feel impatient waiting for a reply. Even a video conference could cause conflict if individuals are unaware of body language differences around the world. Team leaders may need to establish ground rules such as mandating time limits for email responses. Sharing profiles help individuals who have never met get to know one another, which encourages trust.

Bibliography

Bailey, Sebastian. "How to Beat the Five Killers of Virtual Working." *Forbes*. Forbes.com LLC, 5 Mar. 2013. Web. 26 Mar. 2015.

Ferrazzi, Keith. "Virtual Teams Can Outperform Traditional Teams." *Harvard Business Review*. Harvard Business School Publishing, 20 Mar. 2012. Web. 26 Mar. 2015.

Harkiolakis, Nicholas. *Leadership Explained: Leading Diverse, Virtual, and Distributed Teams in the 21st Century*. New York: Routledge, 2016.

Meyer, Erin. "The Four Keys to Success with Virtual Teams." *Forbes*. Forbes.com LLC, 19 Aug. 2010. Web. 27 Mar. 2015.

"Virtual Teams vs. Traditional Teams." *Management Study Guide*. Management Study Guide. Web. 27 Mar. 2015.

Wheelan, Susan A. *Creating Effective Teams: A Guide for Members and Leaders*. Thousand Oaks, CA: Sage, 2016.

Josephine Campbell

WOMEN IN THE WORKFORCE

ABSTRACT

Women's lives have changed substantially since the mid-twentieth century. Most US women worked outside the home as of 2013, regardless of whether or not they had children. Women have long worked as teachers, administrative assistants, nurses, childcare providers, hairdressers, retail workers, and domestic workers. However, in recent decades more have joined professions such as medicine, law, engineering, finance, factory work, and so forth that were previously dominated by men. Some of this change is due to initiatives by governments and nongovernmental organizations to improve access to education for women. Some of the change is due to changing social mores in which women are now both expected and desire to be self-sufficient. While these initiatives have helped propel women into rewarding careers in all professions, improving their quality of life by advancing their economic power, debate over traditional gender roles and pay equality remain critical issues in the United States and in many countries around the world.

OVERVIEW

In the decades following World War II, the number of women in the workforce in the United States and many other Western countries increased. This increase can be attributed to a number of factors, including increased employment opportunities open to women, access to education, a breakdown of traditional gender roles, affordable healthcare and childcare, federal protection of workers' rights, antidiscrimination laws, and a decrease in women's economic dependency on men. Overall, the increased presence of women in the workforce is considered to have had a dramatic impact on the economic stability of many nations and contributed to the success of many international efforts aimed at the protection of women's rights and family health.

Additionally, international organizations such as the United Nations and the World Bank reported increases in women entering the workforce of many developing nations due in part to expanded educational opportunities for girls and women, improved healthcare, and increased international focus on women's rights, including pressure on legal systems to prosecute violence against women. In fact, the *No Ceilings* report issued by the Full Participation Project in early 2015 found that by 2010 there was near-parity in primary education enrollment in all global regions except sub-Saharan Africa.

In early 2010, the US government reported that women represented the majority of the professional workforce for the first time in history. Statistical data also revealed that more women were enrolled in university and professional educational programs, with a graduation rate double that of their male counterparts. Despite this trend, women typically earn less than men for the same jobs, and a 2013 federal report showed that families headed by

Two businesswomen consult with each other (Photo courtesy of Christina Morillo)

females earned far less than two-person households headed by men. A 2013 *Pew Social and Demographic Trends* report showed that as of 2012, young women began their careers earning 93 cents on the dollar as compared to their male peers, yet during the preceding three decades, young women's earnings had tended to fall off over time relative to men's. Despite recent increases, women are also reported to represent a lower percentage of workers in the science, technology, mathematics, and engineering (STEM) professions.

Many researchers recognize that sex discrimination and cultural values remain serious hindrances to women's full participation in the paid workforce. The *No Ceilings* report found that the number of women participating in the formal global workplace was stuck at 55 percent, with much lower percentages in socially conservative countries, such as Saudi Arabia, Yemen, and even Japan. Researchers believed unfavorable maternity leave policies and social pressure to remain in the home, as well as a gender gap in internet access among citizens of developing nations, to be contributing factors to this stagnation. Others point to drops in workplace participation among women in developed nations, such as the United States, due in part to the global recession of the late 2000s and ensuing budget cuts to fields traditionally dominated by women, such as education.

CONCLUSION

Women's rights groups and international organizations continue to push to for pay equality and new opportunities for women in the workforce. For example, the national push for gender equality in the workforce helped prompt the US military to open restricted combat work roles to qualifying women in 2013, with integration to be completed by 2016. Despite the debate, research suggests that women in the workforce have had a positive impact on the health of the global economy and the improved health and well-being of families across the world.

BIBLIOGRAPHY

Cobble, Dorothy Sue. *The Other Women's Movement: Workplace Justice and Social Rights in Modern America.* Princeton, NJ: Princeton University Press, 2003.

Eagly, Alice H., and Linda L. Carli. *Through the Labyrinth: The Truth about How Women Become Leaders.* Cambridge, MA: Center for Public Leadership, Harvard Business School, 2007.

Easton, Nina. "Why Aren't There More Women in the Workforce?" *Fortune.* Time, 5 Mar. 2015. Web. 21 July 2015.

Hamrick, Mark. "Workforce Mystery: Why Are Women Dropping Out?" *Bankrate.com.* Bankrate, 1 Oct. 2014. Web. 21 July 2015.

Jacobs, Pearl, and Linda Schain. "Professional Women: The Continuing Struggle for Acceptance and Equality." *Journal of Academic and Business Ethics* 1 (2009): 98–111. Print.

Patten, Eileen, and Kim Parker. "A Gender Reversal on Career Aspirations: Young Women Now Top Young Men in Valuing a High-Paying Career." *Pew Social & Demographic Trends.* Pew Research Center, 19 Apr. 2012. Web. 25 July 2013.

Rosin, Hanna. "The End of Men." *Atlantic.* Atlantic Monthly Group, 8 June 2010. Web. 25 July 2013.

Roush, Elizabeth. "(Re) Entering the Workforce: An Historical Perspective on Family Responsibilities Discrimination and the Shortcomings of Law to Remedy It." *Journal of Law and Policy* 31.221 (2009): 221–55. Print.

Taylor, Paul, et al. *On Pay Gap, Millennial Women Near Parity—For Now: Despite Gains, Many See Roadblocks Ahead.* Washington, DC: Pew Research Center, 11 Dec. 2013. PDF file.

US General Accounting Office. "Women's Pay: Gender Pay Gap in the Federal Workforce Narrows as Differences in Occupation, Education and Experience Diminish." *GAO.* GAO, 17 Mar. 2009. PDF file.

Walston, Sandra Ford. "Women Integrating Workday Courage." *Women in Business* 54.2 (2002): 28–29. Print.

Laura L. Lundin, M.A.

Workplace Harassment

ABSTRACT

Workplace harassment may involve behaviors such as verbal assaults, physical assaults, bullying, mobbing, humiliation, intimidation, rape, or sexual harassment and assault. Harassment may target individuals or groups of people such as women, minorities, or LGBTQ (lesbian, gay, bisexual, transgender, and queer) people. Depending on extent and levels of intensity, impacts of workplace harassment may lead to threats to employee health and/or financial status, high employee turnover, low productivity, employer recruitment difficulties, high job dissatisfaction, anxiety, posttraumatic stress disorder, and suicide. Workplace harassment may also have implications far beyond the individual and her or his workplace, leading to job shortages in critical fields.

OVERVIEW

Federal law and the laws of all states ban workplace harassment and discrimination on the basis of race, color, national origin, gender, religion, pregnancy age, and disability. Some states also prohibit harassment and discrimination based on sexual orientation. The courts have upheld the argument that workplace harassment is a form of workplace discrimination. In 2014, there were nearly 89,000 harassment cases filed with the Equal Employment Opportunity Commission (EEOC). In 2014, employer costs for payments and settlements of federal cases were reported to be $296 million. Experts have identified three common types of workplace discrimination that may constitute harassment through the creation of hostile working environments: (1) treating people differently based on characteristics that have nothing to do with job performance, (2) creating classes that have a disparate impact on certain classes, and (3) failing to accommodate employees.

A disparate impact case might involve an employer requiring all employees to have a high school diploma, even though the job requires physical strength rather than academic ability. The impact of that requirement would be disproportionately felt by African Americans who have a lower high-school completion rate than other races. The failure to accommodate may include such actions as not meeting the access needs of a disabled employed, not providing a prayer room for a Muslim employee, or not furnishing a place for nursing mothers to express and store breast milk. Compensation for employees who win federal harassment suits is capped at $50,000 to $300,000, but some states have no caps on compensation. Employers who have a reputation of tolerating harassment may have trouble hiring and retaining employees, and they may experience low employee morale and job satisfaction.

Jagdish Khubchandani and James Price (2015) examined the impact of workplace harassment on employees using data from the 2010 National Health Interview Survey. Their sample included 17,524 adults, and males and females were evenly represented. The study revealed that victims of workplace harassment were likely to be obese, have sleep problems, smoke more than coworkers, exhibit more psychosocial distress, experience more pain disorders, work less, have days when they did not get out of bed, and face worsening health issues.

The most common forms of workplace harassment are sexual harassment and harassment based on race, color, and national origin. Females make up just over half the total population, and they comprise around 47 percent of the workplace. Yet, women continue to face harassment in disproportionate numbers. Females of color are particularly vulnerable to workplace harassment. In 2015, harassment cases filed with the EEOC originated in both the public and private sector. Sexual harassment was more likely to occur in the private sector (45 percent) than the public sector (7 percent). However, racial harassment occurred more often in the public sector (36 to 34 percent, respectively), as did disability harassment (34 to 19 percent), age harassment (26 to 15 percent), and religious harassment (9 to 5 percent). There was little difference in national origin harassment in either sector (O'Malley 2017).

Scholars and legal experts accept two types of sexual harassing behaviors. The first focuses on the traditional (quid pro quo) definition of sexual harassment as demanding sexual favors as payment

William Rehnquist, who wrote the decision in *Meritor Savings Bank v. Vinson*

for hiring, keeping a job, or receiving promotions, bonuses, or benefits. The second is a legal concept of sexual harassment that defines a hostile work environment as a form of discrimination under Title VII of the Civil Rights Act of 1964. *Meritor Savings Bank v. Vinson* (1986) established the precedent, and it was this form of harassment that Supreme Court nominee Clarence Thomas was charged with in 1991 during his confirmation hearing. Anita Hill, a University of Oklahoma law professor, accused Thomas, her former boss, of sexual harassment, and the furor exposed divisions in how people viewed workplace behavior. The legal definition of a hostile work environment encompasses such behaviors as making sexual remarks, displaying sexually implicit materials, or favoring an employee who is granting sexual favors over others. In 1991, the year that Anita Hill appeared on national television to accuse Clarence Thomas of sexually harassing her, there were fewer than 7,000 sexual harassment claims filed with the EEOC. Afterwards, the number of claims jumped to more than 15,000 a year. On an ironic note, the hostile work environment Hill described was the EEOC itself, where Hill and Thomas worked together only a few years previous to *Meritor*.

Numerous studies have revealed that females and males have different attitudes on sexual harassment that begin in adolescence. While most females perceive sexual harassment as degrading and threatening, many males see it as properly flattering to females and as proof of their own masculinity. Rates of sexual harassment have changed little since 1976. Sharon O'Malley (2017) analyzed 2016 sexual harassment claims and found: sexual remarks or teasing (64 percent); leering or ogling (51 percent); touching, brushing, or pinching (34 percent); dating requests (9 percent); sexual propositions (7 percent); sexual relations (5 percent); and other forms (26 percent).

Like sexual harassment, racial harassment has been ubiquitous in the American workplace. Though the Civil Rights Act of 1964 banned employment-based discrimination, bullying behaviors have continued to occur, involving such actions as intimidation, insults, excessive monitoring, verbal and physical assaults, and exclusions from work and social situations. Even before the term hostile working environment became commonplace, the Supreme Court dealt with racial hostility in the workplace. In 1911 in *Rogers v. EEOC*, the Court equated hostility and discrimination. The case was based on the discovery by an employee that two optometrists were segregating their patients by coding patient files by color, using red for black patients and blue for all others. The court acknowledged that such an environment could negatively affect the financial and emotional well-being of employees.

In the post-Civil Rights era, a number of scholars have addressed the issue of aversive racism, which has become more common than overt racism. Aversive racism is indirect and might involve such behaviors as refusing to sit beside a person of color or the acceptance of racial stereotypes. On the job, aversive racism might be responsible for excluding an African American employee from a social gathering or accepting the racist stereotype that an Asian female is always subservient to males.

APPLICATIONS

As established by *Meritor*, a hostile working environment encompasses such behaviors as placing calendars of nude or nearly nude images on walls, in emails, or on computer screens; telling sexually explicit jokes; asking questions about an individual's sex life; inappropriately touching coworkers; making inappropriate remarks about body parts; or demanding sex. *Meritor* differentiated between explicit (quid pro quo) and implicit harassment. Explicit behaviors involve demands and threats, stating that an employee will not be hired, may lose a job, or be denied opportunities for higher incomes and better benefits if she or he does not have sexual relations with the authority figure. In the field of education, sexual harassment may involve the granting of a grade, a recommendation, or not having to turn in an assignment in return for having sex. Implicit harassment occurs as retaliation for refusing to give in to demands for sex. Perpetrators of sexual harassment may also be coworkers, fellow students, customers, vendors, or clients.

Subsequent court cases have expanded on the components of the hostile working environment. In *Harris v. Forklift Systems* (1993), the Court attempted to more clearly define the concept, stating that it was defined according to what a reasonable person would define as either abusive or hostile. In *Oncale v. Sundowner Offshores Services* (1998), the Supreme Court held that workplace harassment could be considered hostile even when it was not sexual in nature.

Employees facing harassment may also be protected under other laws. Disabled and older Americans, for instance, are protected under the Disabilities Act and the Age Discrimination in Employment Act, respectively. In 1988, the Supreme Court expanded understanding of employer responsibility in *Burlington Industries, Inc. v. Ellerth* and *Faragher v. City of Boca Raton*. Employers might not be held responsible for harassing behaviors if they could prove that they had taken definitive action to prevent hostile behaviors or if the employee had not pursued internal opportunities for dealing with the issue.

Harassing behaviors occur because perpetrators perceive their subjects to be powerless and or physically weak. They often occur as the result of males attempting to assert their superiority over females. Thus, the females most vulnerable to harassment are those who work in jobs heavily dominated by males. Such jobs range from blue collar work in construction or factories to white collar jobs like professional offices and research labs. Both sexual harassment and gender bias against females in science, technology, engineering, and mathematics (STEM) have been well documented, and that harassment contributes to the low participation of women in science, technology, engineering, and mathematics fields. In 2018, females made up 30 percent of all college graduates in science, technology, engineering, and mathematics, but only one in four of those women actually took a science, technology, engineering, and mathematics-related job. The fact that women are rejecting science, technology, engineering, and mathematics jobs is significant because it is predicted that by 2030, there will be a shortage of 962,000 positions in science, technology, engineering, and mathematics fields. Rather than continue to face harassment, women generally leave the old boys' club to their harassers. A number of lawsuits have been filed by women in science, technology, engineering, and mathematics who state that they experienced pay discrimination, were promoted at slower rates, and received lower funding for their laboratory projects (Ornes 2018).

College campuses are another fertile avenue for workplace harassment, and the prevalence of sexual harassment has been well documented in such books as Billie Wright Dziech's *The Lecherous Professor: Sexual Harassment on Campus* (1984). Sexual harassment in schools was specifically prohibited by Title X of the Education Amendments of 1972. In some cases, the harassment on college campuses may be physical as well as sexual. Following field trips to Antarctica, noted geologist David Marchant of Boston University was the subject of complaints filed by three former female graduate students who accused him of throwing rocks at them, pushing them, calling them such names as "whore" and "slut," making negative comments about their bodies, degrading them, and insisting that he would make sure that they never received research grants to conduct their own work. Charges were upheld in 2017, and Marchant was fired.

In a 2010 study of sexual harassment in the workplace, 40 to 75 percent of females and 12 to 31 percent of males reported that they had experienced at least one instance of unwanted advances while on the job. The twenty-first century definition of harassment in the workplace has been expanded due to the prevalence of electronic devices such as computers, tablets, and smartphones which have given rise to harassing behaviors such as using texting and email to send sexually explicit or derogatory images or links to web pages with offensive content. Experts, beginning with Catherine MacKinnon in 1979 in *Sexual Harassment of Working Women: A Case of Sex Discrimination*, argue that sexual harassment has become widely accepted because of trivialization, which reinforces the perception of working women as invisible.

Issues

Pat Chew and Robert Kelley (2006) found that between 1980 and 1999, more than 56,000 cases of racial harassment were filed, and 735 judicial opinions were handed down. Males filed claims in 58.5 percent of cases, and females filed in 41.5 percent. Most cases were filed by African Americans (81.6 percent). Racial harassment occurred in all fields, but the largest number of complaints came from office and administrative workers (21.5 percent), managers (10.7 percent), and salespersons (10.7 percent). In each case, harassment had been occurring for an average of 8.6 years. Males (66.6 percent) were more likely than females (33.3 percent) to be harassers, and whites (74.1 percent) were more likely than African Americans (20 percent) or Asian Americans (5.9 percent) to be charged with workplace harassment. Verbal harassment (81.2 percent) was the most common type of harassment as compared with the use of physical objects such as Confederate flags or swastikas (22.7 percent) or physical attacks (15 percent). Chew and Kelley also found that only one in four plaintiffs won their suits; African Americans and Asian Americans were least likely to win suits; and males were more successful than females.

Following the terrorist attacks on the United States on September 11, 2001, workplace harassment against Arabs and Muslims increased significantly. Two months after the attacks, the EEOC, the Department of Justice, and the Labor Department launched a joint effort to prevent harassment of Muslims, Arabs, Afghanis, Middle Easterners, and South Asians, but that effort was unable to stem attacks. Between 1997 and 2000, 8,600 claims of harassment based on religion, ethnicity, national origin, and citizenship or immigration status had been filed with federal agencies. Between 2001 and 2006, the number of incidents climbed to 11,000, making up 15 percent of all discrimination charges filed.

In 2007, 44 percent of suits filed under Title VII of the Civil Rights Act of 1964 involved national origin and another 3.5 percent involved religion (Malos 2010). Examples of workplace harassment behaviors based on national origin, ethnicity, religion, and citizenship or immigration status include an employee being harassed for wearing non-Western clothing, and verbal assaults involving the use of such derogatory terms as "the ayatollah," "terrorist," "camel jockey," and "raghead." Such behaviors have been shown to negatively affect job performance. Based on standards established in *Meritor*, employees bringing suit for being exposed to hostile environments are required to show that the verbal or physical conduct was severe and pervasive.

CONCLUSION

Employees who believe that they are victims of workplace harassment should keep careful notes of such behaviors, documenting such details as dates, times, places, persons present, and what was said, done, or worn. The next step is to file a grievance with a supervisor and follow company policy. If the employer does not satisfactorily deal with the problem, the employee may then file a complaint with the EEOC. Depending on the circumstances, the employee may also file criminal charges or bring a civil suit against the perpetrator(s). The EEOC has strict guidelines that must be followed, including filing a complaint within a designated time period and requiring the employee to show evidence of having attempted to deal with the situation with his/her employer.

BIBLIOGRAPHY

Chew, Pat K., and Robert E. Kelley. "Unwrapping Racial Harassment Law." *Berkeley Journal of Employment and Labor Law* 27, no. 1 (2006). Web. 20 Sept. 2018.

England, Deborah C. *The Essential Guide to Workplace Harassment and Discrimination*. 3rd ed. Berkeley, CA: Nolo 2015.

Gupta, Richa, and Art Bakhshi. "Workplace Bullying and Employee Well-Being: A Moderated Mediation Model of Resilience and Perceived Victimization." *Journal of Workplace Behavioral Health* 33, no. 2 (2018): 96–115. Web. 1 Jan. 2019.

Khubchandani, Jagdish, and James Price. "Workplace Harassment and Morbidity among US Adults: Results from the National Health Interview

Survey." *Journal of Community Health* 40, no. 3 (2015): 555–63. Print.

Kmec, Julia A., C. Elizabeth Hirsh, and Sheryl Skaggs. "Workplace Regulation of Sexual Harassment and Federal and State-Level Legal Environments." *Research in the Sociology of Work* 29 (2016): 215–40. Web. 1 Jan. 2009.

Malos, Stan. "Post-9/11 Backlash in the Workplace: Employer Liability for Discrimination against Arab- and Muslin-Americans Based on Religion or National Origin." *Employee Responsibilities and Rights Journal* 22, no. 4 (2010): 297–310. Web. 20 Sept. 2018.

McCord, Mallory A., Lindsay Y. Dhanani, Dana L. Joseph, and Jeremy M. Beus. "A Meta-Analysis of Sex and Race Differences in Perceived Workplace Mistreatment." *Journal of Applied Psychology* 103, no. 2 (2018): 137–63. Web. 1 Jan. 2019.

Neall, Annabelle M., and Michelle R. Tuckey. "A Methodological Review of Research on the Antecedents and Consequences of Workplace Harassment." *Journal of Occupational and Organizational Psychology* 87, no. 2 (2014): 225–57. Print.

O'Malley, Sharon." Workplace Sexual Harassment: Will the Latest Changes Lead to a Shift in Corporate Culture?" *CQ Researcher* 27, no. 38 (2017): 893–917. Print.

Ornes, Stephen. "The STEM Gender Gap." *CQ Researcher* 28, no. 31 (2018): 729–52. Print.

SUGGESTED READING

Avendaño, Ana. "Sexual Harassment in the Workplace: Where Were the Unions? "*Labor Studies Journal* 43, no. 4 (2018): 245–62. Web. 1 Jan. 2019.

Cockey, Robin R., and Laura E. Hay. "Crossing Jordan: How a Bartending Crisis Revolutionized the Law of Workplace Harassment." *University of Maryland Law Journal of Race, Religion, Gender & Class* 17, no. 2 (2017): 212–46. Web. 1 Jan. 2019.

Jaffe, Sarah. "The Collective Power of #MeToo." *Dissent* (00123846) 65, no. 2 (2018): 80–87. Web. 1 Jan. 2019.

Nadler, Joel T., and Margaret S. Stockdale. "Workplace Gender Bias: Not Just between Strangers." *North American Journal of Psychology* 14, no. 2 (2012): 281–91. Web. 19 Sept. 2018.

Parra, Gabriela. "Immigration Policy for Workplace Violence and Undocumented Women: State-Based Solutions for Wisconsin." *Wisconsin Journal of Law, Gender & Society* 30, no. 1 (2015): 99–129. Web. 1 Jan. 2019.

Tofler, I. R. "Bullying, Hazing, and Workplace Harassment: The Nexus in Professional Sports as Exemplified by the First NFL Wells Report." *International Review of Psychiatry* 28, no. 6 (2016): 623–28. Print.

Towns, D.M., and M.S. Johnson. "Sexual Harassment in the Twenty-First Century—E-Harassment in the Workplace." *Employee Relations Law Journal* 29, no. 1 (2003): 7–25. Web. 20 Sept. 2018.

Vaquez, C., S. Rueda, L. Mondragón, et al. "Sexual Harassment in the Workplace: An Examination of Undocumented Mexican Female Factory Workers in Chicago." Conference Papers—American Sociological Association (2015): 1–19.

Elizabeth R. Purdy, Ph.D.

Z

Zero Sum Game

ABSTRACT

Zero sum is a concept derived from game theory, a social theory based on the disciplines of mathematics and economics, which seeks to anticipate the rational decisions of people to a specific set of choices. Zero sum includes all social processes that may be modeled as a game or a set of probabilities, in which the gain of any actor or group can only be acquired at the expense of the opposing party. The simplest version is modeled on two players, one of which wins all because the other party losses all. Created during the postwar years, game theory gained prevalence during the Cold War and continues to be influential.

OVERVIEW

The concept of zero sum was first described in Oskar Morgenstern and John von Neumann's seminal book, *The Theory of Games and Economic Behavior* (1944). Game theory is concerned with the behavior of individuals and groups faced with win-lose situations. The basic premise of game theory is utilitarian and rational. When people must make a decision in the face of several possible outcomes, they are expected to choose the one that provides the maximum satisfaction. Zero sum refers to the idea that there is a limited or finite amount of resources—such as land, food, money, status, power, and even game points—for which individuals or groups are in constant competition. The success of one side, in this view, depends on the loss of the other. At the end of the game, when all gains and losses are added up, the total sum should give a final balance of zero; hence its name. Zero sum beliefs, then, drive individuals not only to work toward the success of their own group, or in group, but also to undermine or debilitate the ability of the rival party or out group to succeed. In zero sum theory, the gains won by one side are matched by corresponding losses to the other. Zero sum is part of a spectrum of theories known collectively as game theory, regularly used to understand and manage competition, conflict, risk, and/or market situations.

As an ideology, zero sum theory resembles Social Darwinism, the theory proposed by followers of Herbert Spencer (1820–1903), who extrapolated his social theory from Charles Darwin's description of natural selection. Herbert and his followers believed that the competitive market, as viewed in classical economics, is akin to a natural law, that is, inevitable and immutable. Furthermore, wealth and success came to those who were better able, by nature, to adapt and survive in a competitive society. In modern terms, because life is a zero sum game, the owners of wealth rightfully manage game elements so that it favors their group against the out group.

One of the most influential thinkers of zero sum theory, prior to the modern inception of the Neumann-Morgenstern theories, was Thomas Robert Malthus (1766–1834). Malthus gained fame with the publication of *An Essay on the Principle of Population* (1798), which argued that in times of abundance of resources, the population increases. However, the population multiplies geometrically, while food production increases arithmetically, so that population grows faster than food production. In other words, for Malthus, the number of workers would grow more rapidly than the availability of food; this reality, in turn, leads to a fall in earnings and, thus, in access to food, so that the poor become poorer and their poverty leads to illness, famine, and overall catastrophe.

Many thinkers who espouse zero sum views of society consider well-being and wealth to be finite; society, therefore, in all aspects, works by some individuals taking away from others. This paradigm of individuals and groups of people in endless struggle sees all society as a zero sum game; progress for some always comes at a cost to others. These views are foundational to some early political economic models, such as feudalism and absolutism.

The Enlightenment brought seismic changes in political philosophy, and eventually developed democratic social models unimaginable to many Malthusians. Enlightenment ideas highlighted an ethical view of individual liberty and rights, with market dynamics based on processes of voluntary exchanges rather than antagonistic extraction. Enlightenment principles of "Liberty, Equality and Fraternity" viewed all out groups as integral parts of society—as citizens rather than aliens or subservient classes. The idea of citizenship for all as normative for a democratic society helped erode ideas of inherently and inevitably antagonistic societies, generating—at least as an ideal—respect for multiple identities in a noncompeting world.

On the other hand, the world can fall into zero sum scenarios, which may run the gamut from international conflicts to competitive games. In fact, some societies may be more prone to relying on zero sum beliefs than others. Relations in a society—as well as within its institutions and organizations—work according to mainstream beliefs about the nature of the world. These beliefs are culturally socialized and become part of the matrix of social relations.

A generalized view of life as a zero sum game would, theoretically, lead to more antagonistic social relations, as a society would be permeated by the conviction that the gains of one person—material or symbolic—must come at the expense or failure of another. The world, according to this view, is populated by rivals—a social condition that is highly incompatible with trust or social harmony. Holders of this view often point to war theaters, as well as to societies in civil strife or to postconflict societies, as examples.

Interestingly, however, zero sum beliefs usually do not necessarily isolate or shield groups from each other. They merely ensure more antagonist relationships. For instance, it is the premise of zero sum games that each move will result in a win or loss for the players, depending on the move and who makes it. In a way, then, players on one side are involved in a relationship of dependency with the others.

Related to zero sum beliefs is a social phenomenon known as zero sum bias that refers to believing a situation to be zero sum when it is not a zero sum situation, or, as it is known in game theory, a non zero sum. A non zero sum can refer to a wide variety of situations, such as one in which both parties gain—known as a win-win situation—or when both parties lose. Even in situations of unlimited resources, for example, the belief may exist that the gains of some inevitably imply the loss of another; in other words, people may be prone to a zero sum bias even in scenarios in which these beliefs are unwarranted. Studies show that conclusions of risk and unfairness may remain unchanged even when evidence is clear that there are enough resources for everyone.

APPLICATIONS

There are many fields which use zero sum theories; they are used to explore scenarios of regional cooperation, international and maritime borders, economic zones, agreements of resource extraction, business negotiations, lawsuits, sports, and so on. During the Cold War, for example, many countries shaped their international policies in accordance with zero sum principles, often at the expense of other nations. Foreign relations were managed, then, according to a worldview of distrust, rival claims, and competing interests; it was a commonplace perception that international peace was fragile and volatile, and that the world was closer to conflagration than to international agreements and integration.

In general, there are many applications to game theory overall, of which zero sum is but a part. A great deal of it is highly complex and mathematics based, since it depends on probabilities. As such, it is quite useful in a wide variety of settings, such as that of gaming. In a sphere in which one player seeks to maximize his or her advantage at the expense of the other, it is useful to be able to calculate the sets of probabilities for either side, its reasonable outcomes, and its best solutions.

Another field in which these strategic principles are applied is in organizational management. Contemporary organizations understand the value of teambuilding, communication, and, in general, social integration in the workplace. For these conditions to happen, workplace relations, even when vertical—top-down and hierarchical—must be based on trust, transparency, and availability of information. When people believe the environment is a zero sum place, that is, one in which any gain for one worker comes at the expense of another, it is hard to develop the relationships necessary for an organization to function efficiently. To foster engagement

John von Neumann (Photo courtesy of LANL)

and cooperation, organizations often employ game theory strategies in management, seeking to reduce any zero sum scenarios and increase nonzero sum feelings, ideally that of a win-win scenario. In fact, as many studies show, increasing employee trust and satisfaction results in reduced turnover and improved productivity and profits.

Zero sum theory is often used in scientific endeavors, such as biology, forestry, and meteorology. For example, globalization has brought an increase in trade of exotic species around the world, causing problems of invasive species. With climate change, many of these species—having grown better able to adapt and survive in alien environments—are expected to thrive and to range in wider and higher latitudes. These species often thrive at the expense of native species, so that scientists study the ways in which the gains of some determine the cost of others.

Finally, zero sum views are studied in social sciences, to understand such social phenomena as inequality, race relations, discrimination, and migration. One of the core reasons for the persistence of inequality, according to many experts, is that people embrace ideologies that justify inequality. Studies show that high status individuals in a society tend to blame low status groups for their own lower status in the hierarchy, finding their claims of being discriminated against as without merit.

For example, low status groups are frequently accused by high status individuals of clinging to their low status, arguing that discontented people could change their situation if they worked harder. The difficulties faced by members of out groups are disregarded by members of advantaged groups; for example, men tend to downplay the extent to which women face discrimination. Moreover, well-resourced groups tend to see the world as zero sum, that is, believing that any gains by lower status groups comes at the expense of higher status groups. Nevertheless, zero sum is not an accurate representation of real social dynamics. People in societies integrate to different degrees in social, economic, and cultural spheres, and may be successful in some aspects while failing in others. Even unequal societies, in general, engage in negotiations, accommodations, and tradeoffs rather than winner-take-all dynamics.

Issues

Individuals may develop zero sum views based on the aggregate of personal experiences, both at the social level as well as with other individuals. On the other hand, culture shapes general beliefs and develops what some expert call "social axioms," that is, beliefs that constitute foundational premises that people support and use as a roadmap in a variety of situations, without bothering to test or challenge their validity. These axiomatic beliefs are the result of shared experiences in a culture and society; people get socialized into them, and fully internalize them so that they become unquestioned tenets taken for granted. The belief that life is a zero sum game is a common social axiom.

While zero sum as a concept can work as a cognitive mechanism in very specific situations, applied overall as a world view, it fosters the idea that most life experiences are intractable conflicts. According to a multinational study (Adamska et al. 2015), these ideas foster attitudes that affect individuals at three levels: cognitive, emotional, and behavioral.

At the cognitive level, zero sum buttresses antagonistic perceptions, a belief in the unlikelihood of shared aspirations and interests, a negative vision of the world, dependence on others, pessimism, an external center of control, and distrust of social systems. At the emotional level, it makes people prone to anxiety, rumination, sadness, fear or feelings of being a loser, and a low level of personal satisfaction. At the behavioral level, people with a zero sum outlook may withdraw from social interactions, avoid cooperation and exchange, and engage in many interpersonal conflicts. Other studies have compounded the findings that a zero sum outlook leads to conflictive behavior, as opposed to positive outlooks leading to better and more stable social relations. The conviction that life is a zero sum game leads to negative evaluations of people and organizations.

Other studies have shown that a zero sum outlook may result in inappropriate reactions to some scenarios, such as encountering the judicial system. One common belief holds that criminal investigations and court interactions are two-sided competitive endeavors in which the judge must maintain a balance on both sides. The judicial process, then, is considered as a zero sum game, with the law on one side and wrongdoers on the other. In reality, however, the relationship between the law and defendants is more complicated. The justice system is not an arena for competition, because the law deals with fundamental and inalienable rights of the people involved, including law enforcement, victims, witnesses, and defendants. Rights are not very amenable to considerations of cost-benefit. This reality does not mean that considerations of game theory are not applicable to some cases such as tort law, but the law is often meant to deal with the balance of rights and meting out justice, and zero sum principles prove inadequate for such analyses.

BIBLIOGRAPHY

Adamska, Krystyna, Pawel Jurek, and Różycka-Tran, Joanna. "The Mediational Role of Relational Psychological Contract in Belief in a Zero-Sum Game and Work Input Attitude Dependency." *Polish Psychological Bulletin* 46, no. 4 (2015): 579–86. Print.

Garrett, Amanda. "Is Integration a Zero-Sum Game? Negotiating Space for Ethnic Minorities in Europe." *French Politics, Culture & Society* 33, no. 3 (2015): 116–30. Print.

Jackson, John E., Bogdan W. Mach, and Jennifer L. Miller-Gonzalez. "Attitudes about EU Expansion and Zero-Sum Thinking." *Economics of Transition* 24, no. 3 (2016): 481–505. Web. 1 Jan. 2018.

Martin, Keir, and Alex Flynn. "Anthropological Theory and Engagement: A Zero-Sum Game?" *Anthropology Today* 31, no. 1 (2015): 12–14.

Simmons, Ric. "Ending the Zero-Sum Game: How to Increase the Productivity of the Fourth Amendment." *Harvard Journal of Law & Public Policy* 36, no. 2 (2013): 549–604. Web. 1 Jan. 2018.

Stephens, Andrea E., Lloyd D. Stringer, and D. Maxwell Suckling. "Advance, Retreat, Resettle? Climate Change Could Product a Zero-Sum Game for Invasive Species." *Austral Entomology* 55, no. 2 (2016): 177–84.

Stone, John. "Under-Labourer or Über-Labourer—A Zero Sum Game?" *Ethnic & Racial Studies* 38, no. 8 (2015): 1413–16.

Wellman, Joseph D., Xi Liu, and Clara L. Wilkins. "Priming Status-Legitimizing Beliefs: Examining the Impact on Perceived anti-White Bias, Zero-Sum Beliefs, and Support for Affirmative Action among White People." *British Journal of Psychology* 55, no. 3 (2016): 426–37.

SUGGESTED READING

Boitano, Aldo, Raúl Lagomarsino, and Eric Schockman. *Breaking the Zero-Sum Game: Transforming Societies through Inclusive Leadership.* Bingley, UK: Emerald Publishing, 2017.

Cheng, Eugenia. "Fruits, Veggies and How to Depict the Universe." *Wall Street Journal* (Nov. 18, 2017): 1. Web. 1 Jan. 2018.

Lidbetter, Thomas. "On the Approximation Ratio of the Random Chinese Postman Tour for Network Search." *European Journal of Operational Research* 263, no. 3 (2017): 782–88. Web. 1 Jan. 2018.

Neyman, Abraham. "The Value of Two-Person Zero-Sum Repeated Games with Incomplete Information and Uncertain Duration." *International Journal of Game Theory* 41, no. 1 (2012): 195–207. Web. 1 Jan. 2018.

Ruthig, J., Kehn, A., Gambin, B., Vanderzanden, K., Jones, K., (2017). When women's gains equal men's losses: Predicting a zero-sum perspective of gender status. *Sex Roles,* 76(1/2), 17–26.

Ruthig, Joelle, Andre Kehn, Bradlee Gambin, et al. "When Women's Gains Equal Men's Losses: Predicting a Zero-Sum Perspective of Gender Status." *Sex Roles* 76, nos. 1-2 (2017): 17–26.

Trudy M. Mercadal, Ph.D.

Glossary

Absenteeism – Being absent from the workplace or school, usually without a valid reason.

Affirmative Action – the notion that employers should recognize demographic factors and diversity in recruiting, hiring, training, and promoting employees. It is a mean of achieving equal employment opportunity.

Anarchy – a state of voluntary relationships and interactions that does not recognize any authority. In a company or other organization, anarchy typically leads to disorder and ineffective performance.

Arbitration – the process of using a neutral third party to resolve conflicts between management and unions over interpretations of the contract or practice. Typically, the decision of an arbitrator is legally binding and cannot be appealed.

Authentic Leadership – a leadership style in which the leader understands his or her own values, beliefs, and priorities and acts consistently with them. Authentic leaders inspire their followers.

Authoritarian Leadership – a style of managing employees by enforcing obedience to an individual or an established system at the expense of personal freedom. Authoritarian leaders tend to favor highly structured organizations, orderly processes, and a slow rate of change.

Autonomy Supportive Communication – a way of speaking to others that involves acknowledging their perspective, helping them to see the purpose in what they are doing, and avoiding controlling language.

Benevolent Sexism – a form of sexism that casts women in traditional gender roles, such as wife, mother, or homemaker, with men as their protectors.

Brand Alignment – actions taken by a company to make sure that all the resources of the organization contribute to making it successful and reinforce the brand image of the company.

Breakthrough Innovation – big change, also referred to as disruptive, radical, or discontinuous innovation, based on new technologies.

Bullying – Using superior power or strength or attitude – to intimidate another person by picking on them, teaching them, or mocking them in some fashion.

Burnout – the phenomenon of exhaustion, which leads to poor quality work. It often happens when employees have been overtaxed with long hours, lack of resources, and extended demands for meeting unrealistic deadlines.

Business Intelligence – information about the market, products and services, competition, customers, potential customers, and completion that is used by organizations to make decisions and to improve productivity, effectiveness, and profitability.

Business Succession Planning – the creation of a strategy or system to turn over control and ownership of a family business to family members or other outsiders.

Centralization – the focus on decision making dictated by a few people who work at the core or center of a company or organization.

Charismatic Leadership – a style of leadership in which the individual inspires followers to act in ways the leader suggests. Charismatic leaders engage employees to act enthusiastically and unquestioningly.

Collective Bargaining – the process of negotiation a labor contract or other agreement between employers and union representatives.

Consensus – a group agreement accomplished after discussion and careful deliberation. It does not mean unanimous agreement; it means enough common agreement to move forward.

Civil Rights Act of 1964 – the law that abolished discrimination in employment, transportation, public locations, and places of public accommodation.

Title VII of the act identified protected classes that had a long history of being discriminated against.

Compensation – the money, benefits (health insurance, vision insurance, dental insurance, wellness programs, professional development funds, and retirement) and other perquisites given to employees. Executive compensation refers to the range and types of pay and other rewards provided to executives who often are paid in relationship to the success of the company.

Conflict Management – the knowledge and skills of managing perceived and real difficulties between various parties or priorities. The several models of handling these challenges include: accommodation, avoiding, compromising, competing, and collaborating.

Constraint – a limitation placed on a work situation, an individual, or an organization by outside forces or by budgetary and personnel limits. Overcoming constraints is often part of a leader's job.

Crisis Management – the challenge of handling emergencies and other unforeseen events. Typically, crisis management involves implementing a well-developed system created to handle such difficulties.

Cross-Cultural – actions and activities that honor and make connections between ethnicities, religious groups, and other subgroups within a society.

Data Diddling – the process of intentionally changing data before they are entered into a system in order to damage the database and the company's ability to use the data effectively.

Delegation – the act of assigning tasks to other individuals, typically lower in the hierarchy of the organization. Good delegation requires careful planning, consideration of the skills of the person to whom the tasks are being delegated, and the power and authority to accomplish the work.

Delegator – the person to whom a task is delegated.

Diversity – differences, similarities, and related tensions among people in the workplace based on visible dimensions, secondary influences, and work diversities.

Diversity Audit – the process of examining diversity levels and issues within a company or other organization. It is also often called a cultural assessment.

Diversity Consultant – a person with expertise in managing diversity who can help a company or organization learn to value diversity within the organization's culture and circumstances.

Diversity Management – the process of making good quality decisions that recognize the value and importance of honoring diversity among employees.

Diversity Scorecard – a mechanism to evaluate the value and impact of diversity on the performance of a company or other organization.

Diversity Training – workshops, speeches, and other activities aimed to encourage honoring diversity among employees and helping individuals learn ways to improve their cross cultural communication and team building skills.

Eavesdropping – the use of electronic surveillance devices to either listen to or capture the content of electronic transmissions. It is similar to wiretapping but involves more software or computer systems.

Emotional Intelligence – the ability to recognize and monitor one's feelings and attitudes and use that knowledge to inform actions and behavior as well as the ability to identify and respond to emotions in other people.

Employee-centric – the description of a company or organization that emphasizes employee satisfaction.

Employer Branding – actions and activities undertaken by a company or other organization to represent itself in a positive manner in order to recruit new employees and encourage current employees to remain.

Equal Employment Opportunity – the regulation that each person should have an equal chance at employment regardless of race, gender, religion, or any other characteristic. Emphasis is placed on avoiding discrimination and unfairness, and on increasing the proportion of minority groups in the workplace.

Equal Employment Opportunity Commission – a Federal Agency responsible for investigating workplace discrimination, hearing cases about discrimination, and otherwise enforcing civil rights in the workplace and investigating workplace discrimination.

Ethics – the values and principles used by persons and organizations that lead to decisions that reflect the best solution for the most people or that honor values more important than simple profit.

Ethnicity – the identity of a group characterized by common ancestry, language, and custom.

Expectancy Theory – a conceptual framework that explains what people expect and their reactions when they are disappointed or wowed by the actual experiences. Expectancy can explain reactions of customers as well as employees.

Executive Leadership – the focus of persons in management positions on mission accomplishment, resource acquisition, and external affairs. Executive leadership involves matching one's leadership style with organizational culture and situation.

Firewall – computer hardware or software developed to protect a system from unauthorized access to an individual computer, a system, or a private network.

Flow – the description of a state of productivity in a work situation when there is no anxiety and a sense of real connection to the work. Flow describes that state of excitement and involvement when time seems to disappear.

Followership – the practice of taking cues from a leader and working as an effective employee who values the company goals and culture.

Gender – situation of being male or female or gender fluid; gender identity makes a difference in how an individual is treated in business; it should not be that way, but it is.

Gender Harassment – a form of hostile environment harassment aimed at individuals on the basis of their gender.

Gender Ideals – characteristics often associated with "model" male or female identities. Often, male gender ideals include independence or assertiveness, while female gender ideals might include compassion or beauty.

Globalization – current trend in which companies and other organizations increase business across the entire world. Globalization refers to using vendors and selling to customers in countries different from where the company or organization is located.

Glass Ceiling – the limit beyond which most women cannot progress in business because of assumptions about their performance or appropriateness for certain jobs. The concept is often used to explain why so few women occupy C-suite positions in businesses and other organizations. It is often more powerful in large profit making organizations and less prevalent in nonprofit organizations.

Hacker – an individual who illegally breaks into, or tries to break into, a computer system in order to harm the system.

Harassment – any unwelcome or uninvited behavior that causes feelings of discomfort, alarm, or distress.

Hierarchy – a system or structure for an organization in which there is a clear separation among layers of authority and decision-making.

Holacracy – an organizational structure in which decision-making happens in a democratic manner through self-constituted teams within a company or other organization.

Hostile Environment – a form of harassment in which an atmosphere or environment intimidates, belittles, or discriminates against an individual or individuals on the basis of their gender, race, religion, national origin, age, or disability.

Hostile Sexism – A type of sexism that, when directed against women, casts women in inferior roles to men.

It is practiced by men who need to control women through intimidation, threats, or violence.

Human Resource Management – the department or office that administers policies and procedures that benefit the employees. Human Resource Management offices often administer payroll, benefits programs, health insurance programs, and continuing education programs.

Incentives – rewards for excellent performance at work. Employees sometime respond to external incentives but more often from internal incentives such as the pride and feeling of success when completing a task or project with excellence, under budget, or before the deadline.

Inclusive Leadership – a style of leading individuals in such a manner that they feel part of the community of employees or members of an organization. Inclusive leaders want to know about their followers or employees and celebrate individual differences.

Incremental Innovation – improvement of products or services or technology through small steps and discrete changes.

Information Technology – the use of knowledge, computers, and information systems to create, store, and distribute data in an organization in order to improve the work of the company or organization.

Innovation – a new idea, policy or procedure that improves the functioning of a company or other organization.

Internal vs. External Experience – the idea that there is a difference between the image a company or other organization presents to its employees (internal) versus to its customers (external). The challenge for companies involves aligning the two images.

Intrinsic Motivation – the commitment to work effectively because an individual enjoys it, sees it as purposeful, or finds that it otherwise meets core psychological needs.

Johari Window – a model of communication with four sections based on known to the person and known to others. The sections include public, private, and undiscovered.

Learning Curve – the concept that individuals need a certain amount of time and experience to understand job expectations, work processes, or new policies and procedures.

Microaggression – activities and actions, such as hair touching or personal remarks, that express often unintentional prejudice.

Mission of an Organization – a short statement that describes the reason for the organization and the values under which it operates. It often explains who are the customers, why they are important, and what the company does for its customers and its employees. Mission Statements are often posted all over offices, warehouses, and factory floors so that employees see them often and are reminded about what the organization sees as important.

Mobbing – a term used to describe patterns of destructive workplace harassment performed over a significant period of time.

National Labor Relations Act (NLRA) – a law providing protection to workers and allowing them to unionize and enter into labor contracts.

National Labor Relations Board (NLRB) – The United States agency with responsibility to oversee laws, regulations, and procedures for collective bargaining and unionization.

Network – a collection of computers that are linked together electrically or electronically.

Organizational Commitment – a leader's or other employee's dedication and commitment to the company or other organization where they work.

Organizational Innovation – the process of improving the effectiveness of an organization by using new methods of production or administration.

Organizational innovation often includes adopting or adapting ideas from inside and outside the company or organization.

Orientation – the process of teaching new employees or volunteers the mission, values, vision, polices, and procedures of the company or organization.

Pay Philosophy – the approach of a company or organization toward compensating employees. It includes monetary and other rewards.

People Deal – the total package of benefits and rewards available to members of the organization. Organizations seek to use their people deal to attract the most talented employees while still remaining profitable.

Performance Appraisal (also known as Performance Evaluation) – the assessment of a person's skills, activities, and qualities as measured against a job description or performance program (set of goals for a period of time, most typically a year). Performance appraisals are completed by a person's supervisor and conducted on an annual basis. Good practices include a self-evaluation aspect as well.

Performance Gap – the difference between how a person or a company expects to operate an actually operates. Examining performance gaps can provide useful insights about what needs to change.

Personality – the collection of an individual's qualities, traits, likes, dislikes and patterns of thinking that make up the distinctive identity of that person.

Persuasion – the work of convincing other people through argument, encouragement, data, and deliberation to agree or to act in some way.

Piggybacking – a form of computer crime which uses codes or passwords of a system member or user to gain illegal access to a system or unauthorized use of a system connected terminal.

Presenteeism – the notion that an employee is physically present but not engaged in the work. Often, the colloquial phrase indicates a person has retired on the job.

Probation – an initial period of employment during which new employees get oriented, receive feedback, and learn the job. During this period, employees can be fired without cause.

Process Innovation – the introduction of a new or changed operating procedure, delivery method, or other activity to improve company efficiency and increase revenue and profitability.

Product Innovation – the introduction of new or changed products to increase revenue and profitability of a company.

Quid Pro Quo – one of two doctrines that define situations of sexual harassment. It means giving one thing, such as sexual favors or actions, in return for receiving another, often a favor, new assignment, raise, or promotion.

Reasonable Accommodation – the provision of support services that employers need to offer employees with disabilities but who can perform the core requirements of a job. Reasonable accommodation means that the accommodation must not place an undue burden or hardship on the employer.

Recruitment – the activities involved in finding potential new employees for a company or other organization.

Retention – the activities involved in keeping employees working in a company or other organization. There are many ways to retain employees.

Scavenging – the action of searching through physical trash cans in a computer center or the electronic trash cans in a computer to find discarded data or other information about the system's programs or processes.

Security – the systematic activities involved in protecting data, hardware, software, and information technology used by a company or other organization.

Self-determination Theory – the concept that workers want and need autonomy, relatedness, and a sense of competence.

Servant Leadership – a model of leadership focused on providing for the followers or employees and caring about their lives and their situation as well as customers. Servant leaders work on empowering employees so that they can grow and develop as well as contribute more effectively to the company or organization.

Service Innovation – the introduction of a new or improved service from a company or organization in order to expand customers or bring more quality service to current customers.

Sexual Aggression – actions that coerce or force another person into engaging in sexual behavior. Sexually aggressive behavior includes nonviolent actions, such as verbal pressure, or extremely violent actions, such as rape.

Situational Leadership – a model of leadership in which the leader shifts his or her style and focus depending on the maturity and skill level of the followers. For the past thirty years, has been a useful and powerful model for corporate and nonprofit leaders.

Smart Goals – the elements of useful goals; the letters refer to specific, measurable, achievable, results oriented, and time bounded.

Stereotypes – erroneous and simplified perception of individuals or groups. Often stereotypes block careful thinking and effective decision-making.

Strategy (or Business Strategy) – an approach by a business to accomplish its goals; often strategies include low costs, excellent service, custom products, customer relationships, or other special qualities that distinguish the business from other similar businesses

Symbiosis – the close interaction and interdependence between two companies or other organizations to the benefit of both parties.

Team Building – the range of techniques and activities used to create functional and effective working groups in business settings.

Training – the method a person uses to learn a new task and the workshops and activities provided by a business or organization to educate employees in new products, technology, or services.

Transactional Leadership – a leadership style where employees are seen as lacking internal motivation, and require rewards and consequences to produce work. Transactional leaders are often skilled in creating clear expectations and roles.

Transformative Leadership – a leadership style that empowers employees to become more effective and efficient as well as reach their own potential. Transformative leadership emphasizes partnering with employees rather than making them feel bossed around.

Turnover – the reality of employees leaving a company or other organization.

Turnover intention – an employee's intent to leave a company or organization. Recognizing an employee's turnover intention enables managers to help change that plan and retain the employee.

Vertical Organization – a structure for a company or other organization in which decisions are made at the top and information is communicated downward to other mangers and employees.

Vesting – the process of receiving full ownership over a stock, pension plan, or other benefit after completion of a specific and specified number of years as an employee.

Vetting – the process of evaluating potential employees while considering them for employment.

Virtual Teams – work groups that operate as teams but do not meet or work in the same location or office space.

Virus – a piece of code planted in a computer or a system to change the ways in which the computer or system will operate or to completely disable the computer or system. Viruses are typically installed without the user's knowledge and against the user's wishes.

Volunteer – a person that works for an organization and does not receive a salary for services rendered.

Zapping – the actions involved in damaging or erasing data and information. Zapping typically occurs as a result of the criminal bypassing the enterprise's security systems. It is a form of computer crime that raises security issues.

Zero-Sum – the concept in game theory that whatever is won by one player is lost by another.

INDEX

3M, 97
360-degree feedback, 197, 329–330

A

accessibility, inclusive leadership, 207–208
accommodating approach, conflict, 253
accommodation, conflict management, 60
accountability, corporate social responsibility, 67–68
accounts receivable, 149
active listening, 46, 255, 278
advertising, external business communications, 166
affective domain, 218
affective organizational commitment, 209
affirmative action, 119, 346, 349–350
African cultures, 55
Age Discrimination in Employment Act (ADEA), 118, 200
Allport, Gordon, 396
ambiguity, conflict management, 59
American Apparel Manufacturers Association (AAMA), 68
Americans with Disabilities Act (ADA), 200
appreciative inquiry, 273–274
arbitration, 40, 257
Arena, Johari window, 219
asserting management approach, conflict, 253
asset analyses, turnaround, 260
Athenian democratic model, 322
authentic leadership, 1–4
authoritarian leadership, 224
authoritarianism, 368
automotive industry, 73
autonomy supportive leadership, 134
availability, inclusive leadership, 207
avoiding approach, conflict, 254

B

backward vertical integration, 72, 75
Barnard, Chester, 158, 159
Bass, Bernard M., 399
battlefield leader, 223
Bayes' Decision Rule, 108
BCG matrix, 76
Becker, Gary, 189
behavioral competency, 234
behavioral domain, 218
Behavioral Era, 227–228

behavioral theories, 227
behavior-based job analysis, 201
Berdahl, Jennifer, 368
best alternative to a negotiated agreement (BATNA), 280
best practices, 5–6
Big Five theory, 397
blind spot, 219
blueprint method, 363
board capital, 285
board member recruitment
    board capital, 285
    nonprofit leadership, 284–285
Boeing Phantom Works, 268
borrowed approach, competencies, 235
brainstorming, 80
branding, public relations and, 342
breakthrough innovation, 267–268
Browne, Kingsley, 368–369
bureaucracy, 186
Burlington Industries, Inc. v. Ellerth, 132, 417
burnout, 127–128
Burns, James MacGregor, 399
business competencies, 237
business cycles, 105
business ethics, 146, 147
    compliance procedures, 148
    corporate ethics and social responsibility, 147–148
    ethical culture and compliance, enforcing an, 148
    financial reporting and Sarbanes-Oxley Act, 149
    hostile work environments, 149–150
    mission statement, 148–149
    regulations and legal action, 147
    social responsibility, 151
business intelligence, 102
business model, 148
business organizations
    applications, 408–409
    corporation, 407–408
    LLC, 407
    partnership, 406–407
    sole proprietorship, 406
business risks, 337
business strategy, 19–23, 71–72

business succession planning
    application, 27
    business' continued success, 26
    buy-sell agreement, 26
    family members, transferring interest to, 25–26
    separating ownership from control, 24–25
buy-sell agreement, 26

C

"C" corporations, 408
career planning, human resources management, 242
Carlyle, Thomas, 394, 395
Castro, Fidel, 33
categorical innovation, 213
Cattell, Raymond, 396–397
central tendency error, 329
chameleon paradox, 212
change management, 273, 274
channel stuffing, 149
charismatic authority
    Castros and Cuba, 33
    Iran and Islamic Revolution, 32–33
    legitimate authority, three types of, 31–32
    Max Weber and Charisma, 30–31
Chew, Pat, 418
chief executive officers (CEOs), 82, 103, 122, 155, 176, 184, 258, 259
Chinese culture, 55
City of Ontario, California v. Quon, 132
Civil Rights Act, 118, 200, 349, 352, 416
Civil Rights Division of the Department of Justice, 350
Civil Rights movement, 206
Civil Service Commission (CSC), 350
civil society engagement, 65
coaching
    external *versus* internal, 36
    models of, 35–36
cognitive domain, 218
cognitive/intellectual ability, 237
collective bargaining
    arbitration, 40
    art of negotiation, 39
    history of, 37–38
    partnership approach, 39–40
    strikes, 40
    traditional, 39
    unions and legislation, 40
communication, 42–48
    competencies, 237
    conflict management, 59
    corporate, 63
    cross-cultural and gender, 45
    decision making, 103
    employee engagement, 129
    external business, 164–167
    improvement, 45–47
    information and, 47
    networks, 48
    process, 43–44
company wide change, 400–401
comparative management, 53–57
    cross-cultural comparisons, 55–56
    practical concerns for expatriates, 56–57
compassion, 174
compensation, human resources management, 241
competition, conflict management, 60
competitive intelligence, 102
competitive under-performance, 259
compliance, business ethics, 148
comprehensive systemic model of negotiation, 255
compromise, conflict management, 60–61
compromising approach, conflict, 253
computer crimes, 49, 50
concentration strategies, 72–73
concentric diversification, 75
conflict management, 253–254
    accommodation, 60
    avoidance, 60
    collaboration, 60
    competition, 60
    compromise, 60–61
    goal incompatibility and differentiation, 58–59
    interdependence, 59
    issue, 61
    resolving, 59–60
    scarce resources, ambiguity, communication, 59
conglomerate diversification, 75
constructive controversy, 129
contemporary organizations, 270, 376
content coaching, 36
content theories of motivation, 301
conventional thinking, 371–372
Cooper, Cynthia, 16
corporate communication, 63
corporate crisis, 83
corporate culture, 148
corporate ethics, 147–148
corporate governance, executive leadership, 158

corporate social responsibility (CSR), 142, 143
   accountability, 67–68
   and civil society engagement, 65
   fail, 67
   human resources management, 243–244
   NGOs, 68
   opponents to, 67
   shareholders
      targets, 66
      types of, 66
   shareholder-sponsored resolution, 66
   tasks, 64
   via stockholder action, 65–66
   WRAP, 68
corporate strategy
   backward integration, 75
   business strategy, 71–72
   concentration strategies, 72–73
   concentric diversification, 75
   conglomerate diversification, 75
   defensive strategies, 74
   diversification strategies, 73–74
   divestiture, 75
   factors, 74
   forward integration, 75
   growth strategy, 72
   horizontal integration, 75
   joint venture, 75
   liquidation, 75
   retrenchment, 75
corporate structure, 25
corporation, business organizations, 407–408
cost analyses, turnaround, 260
cost-reimbursable contract, 337
creativity, 77
   brainstorming, 80
   innovative thinking, devoting resources for, 78
   issues, 79–80
   in managing technology, 92–93
   motivation and reward, 80
   strategies, 78–79
   success, determinants for, 80–81
crisis management, 82
   application, 83
   corporate crisis, 83
   government agencies
      CPSC, 83
      FDA, 83
      issue, 85
      NHTSA, 84
      Peanut Corporation of America Salmonella Scare, 84–85
      plan making, 85
      product recalls and business crisis management, 84
      risk analysis, 85–86
      team making, 85
   identifying and predicting crisis situations, 82
   strategy creation and execution, 82
critical path management (CPM), 335
critical thinking, 88
   managing technology, creativity in, 92–93
   technology problem solving, 89–90
critical-design review (CDR), 338
cross-cultural communications, 45
cross-cultural comparisons, 55–56
cross-cultural relations
   benefits of, 98
   building economic relationships, 97
   chaotic environments, bringing security to, 96–97
   culture and state, 94–95
   political accord, laying groundwork for, 95–96
cross-purchase agreement, 26
Cuba, 33
cultural assessment, 120
cultural differences, 54
culture, 97
customer service, 361

D

data diddling, 49
data leakage, 49
Davis, Kim, 352
decision making, 89
   business intelligence, importance of, 102
   communication, 103
   consultants, use of, 103–104
   debate and open exchange of ideas, 101–102
   information gathering, 102
   leadership and, 100
   manager instinct, 102
   operational decisions, 101
   strategic decisions, 100
   tactical decisions, 100–101
   team management, 379–380
   technological advancements and, 103
   technology use, 102–103

decision making (*continued*)
    under uncertainty
        Bayes' Decision Rule, 108
        categories, 106
        compromises, 108–109
        conflicting interests in, 106
        decision theory, 107
        forecasting, 109
        gaming, 108
        judgment, 109
        Markov processes, 108
        multiple criteria decision making, 106–107
        stochastic variables, 106
        trends, business cycles and seasonal fluctuations, 105–106
decision theory, 107
decision tree, 103
defensive strategies, 74
delegation, 110–111
    authority and responsibility, 112
    complications, 113
    issues, 112
    workgroups, 112–113
democratic leadership, 224
demokratia, 322
detection/interception programs, 51
diffusion curve, 210
dignity model of negotiation, 255
directional growth, 320
discriminatory behavior, 143
dispositional theory, 218
disruptive technology phase, 265
disruptive/discontinuous innovation, 267
distributive model of negotiation, 255
diversification strategies, 72–74
diversity
    advantages of, 121–122
    changing labor force, 120–121
    definition, 118
    equal employment opportunity and affirmative action, 119
    human resources, 122
    legislation, 118
    management, 119–120
    success with, 122
    training, 121
divestiture, 75
double-loop organizations, 316
driving forces of transformational change, 401

E

East Asia, 55
eavesdropping, 50
Emotional Competence Inventory (ECI), 125
emotional intelligence, 125–126, 324–325
employee acquisition, 241
employee behavior, 218
employee engagement
    burnout, 127–128
    communication, 129
    incentives and motivation, 128–129
    work flow, 128
employee exit and separation management, 243
Employee Free Choice Act, 40
employee monitoring, 131–132
employee relations, human resources management, 243
employee retention, 241
    leadership style, 133, 134
    personal employee considerations, 134–135
employee value proposition (EVP), 138–141
employee work engagement, 207
employer-centric organizations, 139
encryption technology, 51
engagement, 127
engineering organization, 54
equal employment opportunity (EEO), 119
Equal Employment Opportunity Commission (EEOC), 350, 415
Equal Pay Act, 201
Equity theory, 272
ethnicity, 347–349
European Union, 95
executive compensation, 152–155
    benefits, 153
    issues, 155–156
    long-term incentives, 154
    perquisites, 153–154
    short-term incentives, 154
executive director, nonprofit leadership, 281–284
executive leadership, 157, 160
    corporate governance, 158
    efficiency and effectiveness, 158–159
    leadership foundations and perspectives, 158
    leadership, three forms of, 159
    values, mission and vision, 159
expectancy theory, 163–164
expense analyses, turnaround, 260
explicit knowledge, 316–317

external business communications, 164–165
    advertising, 166
    financial reports, 166
    lobbying, 166–167
    press kits, 165–166
    websites, 166
external coaches, 36
external communication, 63
external consultant, 295–296, 307
    contracting, 307
    diagnosing, 308
    entering, 307
    evaluation, 308
    intervening, 308
extrinsic motivation, 133
extrinsic pressure, 213
Eysenck, Hans, 396–397

F

façade, 219
Facebook, 374
face-to-face public relations, 341
False Claims Act, 14, 15
family friendly workplace, gender
    benefits, 179
    issues, 178–179
family-limited partnership, 25
Faragher v. City of Boca Raton, 132, 417
federal law, 415
feedback, 46
feedback coaching, 35
finances, nonprofit leadership, 283–284
financial analyses, turnaround, 260
financial reporting, business ethics, 149
Financial Services Agency of Japan, 147
financial strategy, 71
financial underperformance, 259
firewalls, 51
firm-specific human capital, 191–192
five-stage model of team development, 385
fixed price contract, 337
flat organizational structure, 169–172
flattened organizations, 235
flow, 128
flowcharting, service operations management, 363
followership, 173–174
    good follower, qualities of, 173–174
    and leaders, 174
    significance, 173
    types of, 173
Food and Drug Administration (FDA), 83
Ford Motor Company, 83
for-profit leadership, 285–286
forward integration, 75
forward vertical integration strategy, 72
four I's, 403–404
four-level model, 213–214
Friedman, Milton, 67, 150
Frost, David, 30
full integration, 73

G

game theory, 420–423
gaming, 108
Gantt chart, 336
Gardner, Howard E., 125
Gateway, 72
gender, 175
    communications, 45
    family friendly workplace
        benefits, 179
        issues, 178–179
    female advancement, overcoming obstacles to, 176–177
    management, women in, 175–176
    programs, advancement, 177
    worker's unions and women, 179
    workforce participation of women, 177–178
General Electric (GE), 73–74
general human assets, 10
Geneva Convention, 332
Gen-X women, 177
Ghosn, Carlos, 74
glass ceiling
    impact, 182–183
    organizational strategies, 182
    women, workplace issues for, 181–182
Global Enterprise Technology System (GETS), 268
globalization, 23
goal incompatibility, 58–59
Goffman, Erving, 204, 205
Goleman's mixed model, 125
good communication skills, 42, 43
Government Accountability Office (GAO), 330
Great Depression, 38, 39
Great Man theory, 226–228, 394

Greenleaf, Robert K., 160, 356–358
gross national product (GNP), 24
groups, 381–382
growth strategy, 72
Grutter v. Bollinger, 349

H
hacker, 51
halo error, 329
harassment, 143
hard assets, 6
Harris v. Forklift Systems, 417
Hawthorne effect, 217
Hersey-Blanchard Situational Model, 228
Herzberg, Frederick, 271
hierarchical organizational structure, 184–187
high functioning teams, 385
high-performing organizations, 193, 200
    definition and assessing success, 195–197
    GAO, 195
    human resource practices and procedures, 194
    linking performance, 197–198
high-speed communication technologies, 48
Hispanic/Latino, 347–348
Hofstadter's law, 387
holacracy, 171, 187
honesty, 174
hope, 1, 2
horizontal integration, 73, 75
hostile environment, 366
human asset, 6
    accounting, 7
    combination uncertainty, 10
    companies, 6
    competitive advantage source, 9
    costs uncertainty, 10
    determining value, methods for, 7
    employee nature, 11
    firm specific employees, 9–10
    general human assets, 10
    human resource accounting, 7
    market changes, 10
    options, 11
    return uncertainty, 10
    risk and risk reduction, 10
    shared ownership, levels of, 8
    through compensation management, 8
    through investments, 8
    through minds and hearts of employees, 8–9
    uncertainty, 10
    volume uncertainty, 11
human capital theory, 6, 189–191
human performance systems, 305
human performance technology (HPT), 304–306
human relations, 240
human resource(s)
    accounting, 7
    diversity, 122
    economics
        firm-specific human capital, 191–192
        human capital, 189–191
        resource-based view, 189–191
        theory of production, amendment to, 189
        valuation problem, 190
    for emerging firm, 198–203
    management, 132, 240
        human resource practice, categories of, 241–244
        issues, 244–245
    strategy, 71, 244
human resource practice, categories of, 241–244
human resources information system (HRIS), 203
hybrid plan, 26
hygiene theory, 230

I
IBM/Lenovo, 74, 119
impression management, 204–205
in loco parentis, 333
incentives, human resources management, 241
inclusive leadership, 206–207
    accessibility, 207–208
    availability, 207
    openness, 208–209
incorporator, 407
in-depth coaching, 35
individual behavior, organizational behavior, 301–302
Industrial Revolution, 37, 54, 216, 310, 313
informal organization, 294–295
Information Age, 48
information gathering, 102
information technology (IT), 93
Information Technology Management Competency Model, 237–238
in-group members, 221
innovation, 78, 79, 210, 372
    GETS, 268
    issues, 267–268

leadership, 211, 212
    four-level model, 213–214
    pressure, role of, 213
    resources, role of, 212–213
  organizational barriers to, 265
  private and public sector, 266
  process, management, 266–267
  trajectory of, 265
  types of, 264–265
inspirational motivation, 160
institutional review board (IRB), 332
integrative model of negotiation, 255
intellectual stimulation, 160
interactive skills, 256
interdependence, 59
interdependence model of negotiation, 255
interest-based model of negotiation, 255
internal coaches, 36
internal communication, 165
internal consultant, 295–296
  contracting, 307–308
  diagnosing, 308
  entering, 307
  evaluation, 308–309
  intervening, 308
internal ticketing systems, 47
international businesses, 245
International Finance Corporation (IFC), 65
international organizations, 413
International Standards Organization (ISO), 64, 65
interpersonal conflict, 252–253
interpersonal skills, 43
intrapersonal abilities, 237
intrinsic motivation, 134
invented approach, competencies, 236
Iran, 32–33
Iron Chancellor, 30
Islamic Revolution, 32–33

J
Japanese management style, 56
job analyses, 201, 327–328
job description, 195
job performance, 216–217
job satisfaction, 8, 217–218
job/role competencies, 234
Johari window, 219–220
joint ventures, 74, 75
judgment, 109
Juran, Joseph M., 344

K
Kaiser Wilhelm II, 30–31
Kelley, Robert, 418
Kennedy, John F., 95, 97, 98
Kent's model, 115–116
key technology phase, 265
Khameini, Ayatollah Ali, 32
Khomeini, Ayatollah Ruhollah, 32
knowledge competency, 234
knowledge management, 315
Kotter, John P., 229

L
Laissez-faire leadership, 223
language training, 56
leader-member exchange (LMX) theory, 212, 221
leadership
  authoritarian, 224
  Behavior Era of, 227–228
  contingency and transformational era, 228–229
  and decision making, 100
  democratic, 224
  executive, 159
  foundations, executive leadership, 158
  inclusive, 206–209
  innovation, 211–214
  issues, 224–225
  Laissez-faire, 223
  and management competencies, 237
  and motivation, 226–231
  nonprofit, 281–286
  participative, 322–323
  paternalistic/maternalistic, 224
  situational, 223, 228–229
  trait theory of, 222–223
  transactional, 224
  transformational, 224
leadership theories, 53
learning curve, 316
legitimate authority, three types of, 31–32
leniency error, 329
Lewin, Kurt, 273–274
limited liability companies (LLC), 407
limited liability partnership (LLP), 407
limited partnership (LP), 406
liquidation, 74, 75
Lloyd-La Follette Act, 15–16
lobbying, external business communications, 166–167
logic bombs, 50
long-term incentives, executive compensation, 154

M

MacKinnon, Catherine, 366
mainstream leadership theories, 231
Malthus, Thomas Robert, 420
management by exception (MBE), 159
management by objectives (MBO), 196, 272, 329
management competencies
    business competencies and communications/interpersonal competencies, 237
    issues, 238
    leadership and, 237
    model types, 235–236
    model uses, 236
    occupation-specific competencies, 237–238
    organizations, models in, 234–235
    and performance, 236–237
    types of, 233–234
managerial leadership
    core values and ethics, 248
    evaluating and responding, 249
    function, 247
    General Electric, 249–250
    indicators, 247–248
    making employees matter, 248–249
    quantitative and qualitative, 249
    skills, 246–247
Mandela, Nelson Rolihlahla, 30
Mao Zedong, 33
market analyses, turnaround, 260
market-based innovation, 213
marketing innovation, 264
marketing mix, 339–340
marketing strategy, 71
Markov processes, 108
Maslow's hierarchy of needs theory, 230, 271
Max Weber and Charisma, 30–31
Mayer-Salovey-Caruso Emotional Intelligence Test (MSCEIT), 125
McClelland's needs theory, 230
Mediation, 257
meritocracy, 375
Meritor Savings Bank v. Vinson, 416
micromanaging, 111
Minnesota-based diversified technology corporation, 97
mission statement
    business ethics, 148–149
    nonprofit leadership, 282–283
Moore, Geoffrey, 210

motivation, 80, 270, 301
motivational competency, 234
motivational forces (MF), 163
Multifactor Leadership Questionnaire, 399
multiobjective mathematical programming approach, 107
multiple criteria decision making, 106–107
mutual accountability, 379

N

National Highway Traffic Safety Administration (NHTSA), 84
National Labor Relations Act (NLRA), 38
National Labor Relations Board (NLRB), 39
need-based model of negotiation, 255
needs theories, 271
negative reinforcement, 272
negotiation, 251–252
    applications, 279–280
    conflict management, 253–254
    conflict resolution, 254
    contemporary models of, 255–256
    determination, 256
    effective negotiation, approaches to, 277–278
    interpersonal conflict, 252–253
    issues and variables, 256–257
    necessary negotiator skills, 278–279
    organizational conflict, 252, 253
    outcomes, 257
    resolving organizational conflict, 277
    situational factors, 279
    stakeholder interest and conflict, 276–277
    steps to, 256
    traditional models of, 255
networks, 48, 49
new technology exploitation (NTE), 264
nongovernmental organizations (NGOs), 65, 67, 68
non-integration, 73
nonprofit leadership, 281
    board, 284
    board member recruitment, 284–285
    board members, assistance to, 285
    capacity building, 283
    economic challenges, 286
    executive director, 281–284
    finances, 283–284
    for-profit *vs.*, 285–286
    mission statement, 282–283
    resource acquisition, 283

skills, 284
volunteers, 282
Norris-La Guardia Act, 38
Northern star, 61
Notification and Federal Employee Antidiscrimination and Retaliation (No-FEAR) Act, 16

O

occupation-specific competencies, 237–238
O'Connor v. Ortega, 132
Office of Federal Contract Compliance (OFCC), 350
Office of Management and Budget (OMB), 347, 348
Oncale v. Sundowner Offshores Services, 417
online communications, 47
on-the-job training, 8
openness, 208–209
operational decisions, 101
operational underperformance, 259
operations strategy, 71
operations-based innovation, 213
optimism, 1, 2
organization(s), 21–22, 92
    design, 288–293
    development
        consultant/change agent, 295–296
        diagnosis, 296–297
        entry, 296
        organizational culture, 294–295
        planning, action and stabilization, 297
        scouting, 296
organizational behavior, 218, 299–300
    processes, 302–303
    team behavior, 302–303
organizational commitment, 134
organizational competencies, 234
organizational conflict, 252, 253, 277
organizational consultants, 304–305
    external *vs.* internal consulting, 306–307
    HPT as, 305
    phases, 307–309
    principles, 305–306
organizational context, 186
organizational culture, 79, 294–295, 310–312
organizational effectiveness, 312–314
organizational innovation, 264
organizational justice, 16–17
organizational learning, 314–317
organizational life-cycle theory, 318–320
organizational strategies, glass ceiling, 182

outputs-driven approach, competencies, 236
ownership and control, 24–25

P

pacemaker technology phase, 265
Pahlavi, Shah Reza, 32
paid expenses/perks, 153–154
participative leadership, 322–323, 357
Participatory Budgeting, 323
partnership approach
    business organizations, 406–407
    collective bargaining, 39–40
passive followers, 173
paternalistic/maternalistic leadership, 224
path-goal theory, 211
pay-for-performance appraisal tools, 330
Peace Corps, 95, 96, 98
Peanut Corporation of America (PCA), 84–85
People for the Ethical Treatment of Animals (PETA), 65
people skills, 324–326
performance appraisal, 243, 326–327
    data collection methods, 328
    issues, 330
    job analyses, 327–328
    MBO, 329
    rating scales, 328–329
    360-degree feedback, 329–330
    uses for, 327
performance system, 305
perquisites, executive compensation, 153–154
personal competencies, 234
personnel analyses, turnaround, 260
physical/tangible assets, 6
policies, 19–23
pooled interdependence, 59
positive reinforcement, 272
potential development, 243
poverty threshold statistics, 347
power-based model of negotiation, 255
predatory lending practices, 147
preliminary design review (PDR), 338
presenteeism, 127
press kits, external business communications, 165–166
pressure, innovation leadership, 213
pretty good privacy (PGP) program, 51
problem-solving approach, conflict, 253–254
process innovation, 264

process theories, 271–272
process-driven approach, competencies, 236
procrastination, 388
product innovation, 264
productivity, 272–273
Professional Air Traffic Controllers (PATCO), 40
professional ethics, 332–333
professional limited liability company (PLLC), 407
program evaluation review technique (PERT), 336
programmed thinking, 89
project management, 334–338
proof-of-concept (POC), 44
proxy server, 51
public duty, 15
public key, 51
public policy, 347, 350
public relations
    and branding, 342
    face-to-face public relations, 341
    marketing mix, 339–340
    outreach, mediums for, 341–342
    research, 341
Pychyl, Timothy A., 387

Q

quality assurance, 345
quality control, 345
quality improvement, 345
quality management, 344–345
quality planning, 344–345
quasi-integration, 73
quid pro quo harassment, 366

R

race, 346, 347
race-based statistics, 347
racial harassment, 418
rating scales, performance appraisal, 328–329
rational-legal system, 31, 33–34
Reagan's bluff, 40
reciprocal interdependence, 59
reflection, 91
reinforcement theory, 272
religious accommodation, 352–354
religious workers, 333
reorganization, organizations, 291–292
research and design strategy, 71
resiliency, 2
resource acquisition, nonprofit leadership, 283

retention efforts, 375
retrenchment strategy, 74, 75
reward, creativity, 80
risk analysis, 337
risk management, 337
Rogers v. EEOC, 416
Rogers, Everett, 210
role-taking, 221
Roosevelt, Franklin Delano, 38

S

"S" corporations, 408, 409
S curve, 210
Salmonella, 84–85
Sarbanes-Oxley Act, 15, 147, 149
scanning programs, 51
scarce resources, conflict management, 59
scavenging, 49
Schultz, Theodore, 189
science, technology, engineering, and mathematics (STEM), 417
scientific management theory, 217
seasonal fluctuations, 106
Securities and Exchange Commission (SEC) Rule, 66
self-awareness, 3
self-determination theory, 129
self-esteem needs, 271
self-managed virtual teams, managing performance in, 379
sequential interdependence, 59
servant leadership, 134, 160–161, 356–359
service innovation, 264
service operations management
    applications, 364
    blueprint method, 363
    control difficulties, three reasons for, 361
    customer service, 362
    determining fail points, 363
    factors, 361–362
    flowcharting, 363
    operations management and service sector, 360–361
    profitability check, 363
    quality improvement and control, 361
    technology, 363–364
    time frame, 363
sexual harassment, 365–366
    as hazing, 368–369

hostile environment, 366
motivation, 367–368
quid pro quo harassment, 366
token resistance to, 367
workplace, gender ideals in, 368
workplace, men and women in, 367
shared governance, 10
shared leadership, 370, 412
shared ownership, 8
shareholder(s)
   activism, 66
   targets, 66
   types of, 66
shareholder-sponsored resolution, 66
Shetach, Ana, 61
short-term incentives, 154
single-loop organizations, 316
situational leadership, 223
Six Sigma process, 23
Sixteen Factor Questionnaire or 16PF, 396
social indicator statistics, 347
social responsibility, 147–148, 151
social science theory, 217
social well-being, 145
sociocultural theories of sexual harassment, 367
socio-economic approach, 54
sociology, 299
soft assets, 6
software packages, 202–203
sole proprietorship, 406
Spencer, Herbert, 395, 420
stage model of negotiation, 256
stochastic variables, 106
stock redemption plan, 26
Stodgill, Ralph M., 395
strategic decisions, decision making, 100
strategic management process, 71
strategic planning, 20, 21
strategic thinking
   conventional and, 371–372
   process of, 372–373
strategy formulation process, 71
strikes, 40
subject matter experts (SMEs), 306
sub-Saharan African organizations, 55
succession planning, 243, 374
SWOT model of negotiation, 255
system dynamics, 102–103

T

tacit knowledge, 316–317
tactical decisions, 100–101
tailored approach, competencies, 236
talent management, 374–375
task motivation, 92
Taylor, Frederick Winslow, 217, 226–228, 311
Taylorism, 217
team(s)
   building, 384
   development, 383–384
   groups *vs.*, 381–382
   knowledge, skills and abilities, 384–385
   types of, 382–383
team management
   contemporary organizations, teams role, 376
   decision making, 379–380
   evaluation and control, 378
   leadership strengths and weaknesses, 377
   leading change, 378
   management and leadership, 376
   mutual accountability, 379
   self-managed virtual teams, managing performance in, 379
   team formation decision factors, 376
   team leader perspective, 377–378
   team member perspective, 377
   team stage, 377
   team type, 376–377
team-based delegation, 113
technological innovation, 264
Technological Revolution, 53
technology
   decision making, 102–103
   management, critical thinking in, 88–93
Tennebaum, 14
Thomas, Clarence, 416
three-step change theory, 273–274
time management, 387–388
Total Quality Management (TQM), 22, 23
toxic leadership, 389–390
traditional bargaining, 39
traditional rule, 32
traditional teams, 411
training analysis, 390–391
   new hires, 391–392
   program design, 392–393
   setting goals, 392
trait activation, 397

trait leadership, 394–398
trait theory, of leadership, 222–223
transactional leadership, 159–160, 224, 399
transformational change, 400–402
transformational leadership, 134, 160, 224, 399
    four I's, 403–404
    issues, 404–405
    traits of, 402–403
transformative innovation, 213
transparency, 3
trends, 105
trends-driven approach, competencies, 238
turnaround environment, 258–259
    analysis, 260–261
    crisis stage, 260
    decline, 259–260
    issues, 262
    process, stages of, 259
    recovery stage, 262
    stabilization stage, 262
    strategy formulation, 261
turnover intention, 134
two-way communication, 9

U

UN Global Compact, 65
unionization, 40
United States, 94, 95
UNIX-based tools, 93
unknown, Johari window, 219
U.S. Commission on Civil Rights (USCCR), 350
US Consumer Product Safety Commission (CPSC), 83
U.S. Equal Employment Opportunity Commission, 143
U.S. General Accounting Office (GAO), 195

V

vertical integration strategies, 72
Vesting, 154
virtual organization, 291
virtual teams, 411
virtual teamwork, drawback of, 412
virus(es), 49
virus protection software, 51
volunteer management system, 113
    layered approach, 115–116
    management perspective, 116–117
    preparing, 114–115
    recognition, 115
    recruiting, 115
von Bismarck, Otto, 30–31
Voting Rights Act, 349
Vroom's theory, 164

W

Wagner Act, 38
Wagner, Robert F., 37
Waley, Jacob, 38
water cooler meetings, 411
Weber, Max, 30–32, 186
websites, external business communications, 166
well-being, 142–145
whistle-blower, 16
win-win values, 256
wireless transmissions, 50
wiretapping, 50
work breakdown structure (WBS), 335
work responsibilities-driven approach, competencies, 238
workforce, women in, 177–178, 413–414
working-capital analyses, turnaround, 260
workplace harassment, 415–418
workplace health promotion, 144
Worldcom, 16
Worldwide Responsible Apparel Production (WRAP), 68

Z

zapping, 49, 50
zero sum game, 420–423